JOHN WILLIS

SCREEN WORLD

VOLUME 52

2001

ASSOCIATE EDITOR
BARRY MONUSH

APPLAUSE
THEATRE & CINEMA BOOKS

Screenworld
Volume 52
2001

Library of Congress Card No. 50-3023

ISBN: 1-55783-478-4 (cloth)
ISBN: 1-55783-479-2 (paper)

Applause Theatre & Cinema Books
151 W. 46th Street
New York, NY 10036

Phone: 212-575-9265
Fax: 646-562-5852
email: info@applausepub.com

Sales and Distribution

NORTH AMERICA:
Hal Leonard Corporation
7777 West Bluemound Road
P.O. Box 13819
Milwaukee, WI 53213
Phone: 414-774-3630
Fax: 414-774-3259
email: halinfo@halleonard.com
internet: www.halleonard.com

UK:
Combined Book Services Ltd.
Units 1/K, Paddock Wood Distribution
Paddock Wood, Tonbridge, Kent TN12 6UU
Phone: (44) 01892 837171
Fax: (44) 01892 837272

To
Hugo Uys
with gratitude for your friendship.

Julia Roberts in *Erin Brockovich*
Academy Award Winner for Best Actress of 2000
© Universal Studios

CONTENTS

EDITOR: JOHN WILLIS

ASSOCIATE EDITOR: BARRY MONUSH

Staff: Marco Starr Boyajian, William Camp, Jim Hollifield,

Tom Lynch, John Sala

Acknowledgements: Anthology Film Archives, Artistic License, Castle Hill, Castle Rock Entertainment, City Cinemas, Cline & White, Richard D'Attile, Samantha Dean, DreamWorks, Brian Durnin, Nicole Farrell, The Film Forum, First Look, First Run Features, Fox Searchlight, Gramercy Pictures, Kino International, Leisure Time Features, Mike Maggiore, Miramax Films, New Line Cinema/Fine Line Features, New Yorker Films, October Films, Paramount Pictures, Phaedra Cinema, PolyGram, Paul Reinsch, Kristen Schilo, 7th Art Releasing, Sony Pictures Entertainment, Sheldon Stone, Strand Releasing, Paul Sugarman, Twentieth Century Fox, Universal Pictures, Walt Disney Pictures, Robert Ward, Glenn Young, Zeitgeist Films.

1. Tom Cruise

2. Julia Roberts

3. George Clooney

4. Eddie Murphy

5. Russell Crowe

6. Mel Gibson

7. Martin Lawrence

8. Tom Hanks

9. Jim Carrey

10. Harrison Ford

TOP BOX OFFICE STARS OF 2000

2000 RELEASES
January Through December 31, 2000

Rhapsody in Blue

The Steadfast Tin Soldier

Carnival of the Animals

FANTASIA 2000

(WALT DISNEY PICTURES) Executive Producer, Roy Edward Disney; Producer, Donald W. Ernst; Host Sequences Director, Don Hahn; Supervising Animation Director, Hendel Butoy; Associate Producer, Lisa C. Cook; Conductor, James Levine; Music Performed by The Chicago Symphony Orchestra; *The Sorcerer's Apprentice* Conducted by Leopold Stokowski; Artistic Supervisors: Artistic Coordinator/Visual Effects, David A. Bossert; Layout, Mitchell Guintu Bernal; Backgrounds, Dean Gordon; Clean-Up, Alex Topete; Computer Generated Imagery, Steve Goldberg, Shyh-Chyuan Huang, Susan Thayer, Mary Jane "M.J." Turner; Production Manager, Angelique N. Yen; Co-Associate Producer, David Lovegren; Editors, Jessica Ambinder Rojas, Lois Freeman-Fox; Host Sequences Writers, Don Hahn, Irene Mecchi, David Reynolds; Host Sequence Designer, Pixote Hunt; Visual Effects Supervisor, Richard Hollander; Distributed by Buena Vista Distribution; Dolby; IMAX; CFI color; Rated G; 75 minutes; Release date: January 1, 2000.

Symphony No. 5

Composer, Ludwig Van Beethoven; Director and Art Director, Pixote Hunt.

Pines of Rome

Composer, Ottorino Respighi; Director, Hendel Butoy; Art Directors, Dean Gordon, William Perkins; Sequence Introduced by Steve Martin, Itzhak Perlman.

Rhapsody in Blue

Composer, George Gershwin; Conductor and Supervisor, Bruce Broughton; Piano, Ralph Grierson; Direction and Story, Eric Goldberg; Art Director, Susan McKinsey Goldberg; Artistic Consultant, Al Hirschfeld; Co-Producer, Patricia Hicks; Layout, Rasoul Azadani; Backgrounds, Natalie Franscioni-Karp. Sequence Introduced by Quincy Jones.

Piano Concerto No. 2, Allegro, Opus 102 (The Steadfast Tin Soldier)

Composer, Dmitri Shostakovich; Piano, Yefim Bronfman; Director, Hendel Butoy; Art Director, Michael Humphries; Ballet Choreographer, Kendra McCool; Based on the story *The Steadfast Tin Soldier* by Hans Christian Andersen. Sequence Introduced by Bette Midler.

Carnival of the Animals (Le Carnaval des Animaux), Finale

Composer, Camille Saint-Saëns; Direction, Animation and Story, Eric Goldberg; Art Director, Susan McKinsey Goldberg; Original Concept, Joe Grant; Sequence Introduced by James Earl Jones.

The Sorcerer's Apprentice

(Originally featured in the 1940 RKO release Fantasia) Composer, Paul Dukas; Director, James Algar; Art Directors, Tom Codrick, Charles Philippi, Zack Schwartz; Story Development, Perce Pearce, Carl Fallberg; Animation Supervision, Fred Moore, Vladimir Tytla; Production Supervision, Ben Sharpsteen; Sequence Introduced by Penn & Teller.

Pomp and Circumstance—Marches 1, 2, 3, and 4

Composer, Sir Edward Elgar; Director, Francis Glebas; Art Director, Daniel Cooper; Choral Performance, The Chicago Symphony Chorus; Feature Soprano, Kathleen Battle; Sequence Introduced by James Levine; Character Animator for Mickey Mouse, Andreas Dejá; Voices: Wayne Allwine (Mickey Mouse), Tony Anselmo (Donald Duck), Russi Taylor (Minnie Mouse).

Firebird Suite—1919 Version

Composer, Igor Stravinsky; Direction, Design and Story, Gaëtan Brizzi, Paul Brizzi; Art Director, Carl Jones; Introduced by Angela Lansbury.

Animated interpretations of eight pieces of classical music. A sequel to/continuation of the Disney production Fantasia which was released by RKO in 1940. The Sorcerer's Apprentice sequence is from that film.

© Disney Enterprises, Inc.

Donald Duck, Daisy Duck in *Pomp and Circumstance*

Firebird Suite

Pines of Rome

Symphony No. 5

Mickey Mouse in *The Sorcerer's Apprentice*

NEXT FRIDAY

(NEW LINE CINEMA) Producer/Screenplay, Ice Cube; Based on characters created by Ice Cube, DJ Pooh; Director, Steve Carr; Executive Producers, Michael Gruber, Claire Rudnick Polstein; Co-Producers, Douglas Curtis, Matt Alvarez; Photography, Christopher J. Baffa; Designer, Dina Lipton; Editor, Elena Maganini; Music, Terence Blanchard; Music Supervisor, Spring Aspers; Costumes, Jacki Roach; Casting, Kimberly R. Hardin; a Cubevision production; Dolby; FotoKem color; Rated R; 92 minutes; Release date: January 12, 2000

CAST

Craig Jones	Ice Cube
Day-Day	Mike Epps
Roach	Justin Pierce
Mr. Jones	John Witherspoon
Uncle Elroy	Don "D.C." Curry
Joker	Jacob Vargas
Lil Joker	Lobo Sebastian
Baby Joker	Rolando Molina
Karla	Lisa Rodriguez
Debo	Tommy "Tiny" Lister, Jr.
Suga	Kym E. Whitley
Miss Ho-Kym	Amy Hill
D'Wana	Tamala Jones
Baby D'	Robin Allen

and Carmen Serano, Maria Arce, Vanessa White (Girls), Clifton Powell (Pinky), Michael Blackson (Customer #1), Ronn Riser-Muhammad (Stanley/Mystery Guest), David Waterman (Sheriff #3), Cheridah Best (Sheriff Lady), Sticky Fingaz (Tyrone), Shane Conrad (Real Estate Man), Keebo (Pinky Chauffeur)

Hearing that the local bully, whom his son Craig had beaten years earlier, has escaped from jail, Craig's father sends his son to live with his eccentric relatives in the suburbs. Sequel to the 1995 New Line Cinema film Friday *with Ice Cube, Tiny Lister Jr., John Witherspoon, and Ronn Riser-Muhammad repeating their roles.*

© New Line Cinema Inc.

Ice Cube, Mike Epps

Don "D.C." Curry, Ice Cube

THE LIFE AND TIMES OF HANK GREENBERG

(COWBOY BOOKING) Producer/Director/Screenplay, Aviva Kempner; Photography, Jerry Feldman, Kevin Hewitt, Tom Hurwitz, Tom Kaufman, Christopher Li, Scott Mumford; Editor, Marian Sears Hunter; a Ciesla Foundation presentation; Color; Not rated; 95 minutes; Release date: Jan. 12, 2000. Documentary on Detroit Tigers' Hank Greenberg who became the first Jewish star in baseball; featuring Hank Greenberg, Ira Berkow, Bob Feller, Dick Schaap, Alan Dershowitz, Walter Matthau.

© Greenberg Family Collection

Hank Greenberg

Frankie Muniz, Enzo/Moose

Frankie Muniz, Enzo/Moose, Cody Linley

MY DOG SKIP

(WARNER BROS.) Producers, Mark Johnson, John Lee Hancock, Broderick Johnson, Andrew A. Kosove; Executive Producers, Jay Russell, Marty Ewing; Director, Jay Russell; Screenplay, Gail Gilchriest; Based upon the book by Willie Morris; Photography, James L. Carter; Designer, David J. Bomba; Editors, Harvey Rosenstock, Gary Winter; Music, William Ross; Costumes, Edi Giguere; Animal Trainers, Mathilde De Cagny, William S. Grisco; Casting, Mindy Marin, Marshall Peck; an Alcon Entertainment presentation of a Mark Johnson/John Lee Hancock production; Dolby; Deluxe color; Rated PG; 96 minutes; Release date: January 12, 2000

Frankie Muniz, Enzo/Moose

CAST

Willie Morris ....Frankie Muniz
Ellen Morris ....Diane Lane
Dink Jenkins ....Luke Wilson
Jack Morris ....Kevin Bacon
Big Boy Wilkinson ....Bradley Coryell
Henjie Henick ....Daylan Honeycutt
Spit McGee ....Cody Linley
Rivers Applewhite..Caitlin Wachs
Junior Smalls...Peter Crombie
Millard ....Clint Howard
Army Buddy ....Mark Beach
Mrs. Jenkins ....Susan Carol Davis
Mr. Jenkins ....David Pickens
Aunt Maggie ....Lucile Doan Ewing
and Polly Craig (Grandmother Mamie), John Stiritz (Grandfather Percy), Enzo, Moose (Skip), Harry Connick, Jr. (Narrator), Elizabeth Rice (Rivers' Friend), Nate Bynum (Man on Street), Stacie Doublin (Woman on Street), Bill Butler (Barney), Winston Groom (Mr. Goodloe), Katherine Shoulders (Mrs. Applewhite), Nathaniel Lee (Sammy), Joann Blankenship (Miss Abbott), Hunter Hays (Accordion Boy), Cannon Smith (Bible Boy), Courtney Brown (Snake Girl), Brian Witt (Armpit Boy), Jerome Jerald (Waldo Grace), Jordan Williams (Lt. Hartman), John Sullivan, Stuart Greenwell (Hunters), Harry Hood (Baseball Coach), Gordon Swaim (Umpire), Owen Boutwell, Chaon Cross (Spectators), Jim Fraiser (Veterinarian), Graham Gordy (Pump Jockey), Michael Berkshire (Older Willie), Wayne Wimberly (Older Spit), John Yates (Older Henjie), James Thweat (Older Big Boy)

Willie, a shy youngster growing up during World War II in Yazoo, Mississippi, finds a friend and a sense of freedom when he receives a Jack Russell terrier for his birthday.

© MDS Productions LLC

Diane Lane, Frankie Muniz, Kevin Bacon

SUPERNOVA

(MGM) Producers, Ash R. Shah, Daniel Chuba, Jamie Dixon; Executive Producer, Ralph S. Singleton; Director, Thomas Lee (Walter Hill); Screenplay, David Campbell Wilson; Story, William Malone, Daniel Chuba; Photography, Lloyd Ahern II; Designer, Marek Dobrowolski; Editors, Michael Schweitzer, Melissa Kent; Costumes, Bob Ringwood; Special Visual Effects and Digital Animation, Digital Domain; Visual Effects Supervisor, Mark Stetson; Special Make-up Effects Designer, Patrick Tatopoulos; Music, David Williams; Stunts/2nd Unit Director, Allan Graf; Casting, Mary Jo Slater; a Screenland Pictures/Hammerhead production; Dolby; Super 35 Widescreen; Deluxe Color; Rated PG-13; 90 minutes; Release date: January 14, 2000

CAST

Nick Vanzant	James Spader
Kaela Evers	Angela Bassett
Capt. A.J. Marley	Robert Forster
Yerzy Penalosa	Lou Diamond Phillips
Karl Larson	Peter Facinelli
Danika Lund	Robin Tunney
Benj Sotomejor	Wilson Cruz
Flyboy	Eddy Rice, Jr.
Troy Larson	Knox Grantham White
Voice of Troy Larson	Kerrigan Mahan
Sweetie	Vanessa Marshall

In the 22nd century, a medical vessel responds to a distress signal and ends up caught in the gravitational pull of a giant star about to implode.

© Metro-Goldwyn-Mayer Pictures Inc.

Freddie Prinze, Jr. Julia Stiles

DOWN TO YOU

(MIRAMAX) Producers, Jason Kliot, Joana Vicente; Executive Producer, Bobby Cohen, Bob Weinstein, Harvey Weinstein, Jeremy Kramer; Director/Screenplay, Kris Isacsson; Co-Producer, Trish Hofmann; Photography, Robert Yeoman; Designer, Kevin Thompson; Music, Edmund Choi; Music Supervisor, Tracy McKnight; Editor, Stephen A. Rotter; Costumes, Michael Clancy; Casting, Douglas Aibel; an Open City Films production; Dolby; Color; Rated PG-13; 91 minutes; Release date: January 21, 2000

CAST

Al Connelly	Freddie Prinze, Jr.
Imogen	Julia Stiles
Cyrus	Selma Blair
Eddie Hicks	Shawn Hatosy
Monk Jablonski	Zak Orth
Jim Morrison	Ashton Kutcher
Lana	Rosario Dawson
Chef Ray	Henry Winkler
Judy Connelly	Lucie Arnaz

and Lauren German (Lovestruck Woman), Zay Harding (Lovestruck Man), Amanda Barfield (Faith Keenan), Chloe Hunter (Megan Brodski), Granger Green (Haley Heller), Jed Rhein (Gabe Stiano), Joseff Stevenson (Ted McGurran), Elizabeth Levin (Carbs Girl), Lola Glaudini (Parolee), Robin Nance (Daddy's Girl), Mary Wigmore (Pearly Whites), Caroline Ambrose (Kissing Babe—Woman), Adam Carolla, Jimmy Kimmel ("The Man Show" Hosts), Jason Bailey (Angry Audience Member), Jennifer Albano (Emma), Chris Desmond (Man with Emma), Susan J. Blommaert (Psychologist), Julian Caiazzo (Young Al—5 years), Jerry Carreccio (Young Al—12 Years), Chloe Beardman (Young Imogen—11 Years), Frank Wood (Doctor), Joanna P. Adler (Piercing Woman), Mimi Langeland (Leather Woman), Elizabeth Page (Stage Manager), Mark Blum (The Interviewer), David Logan (Suburban Husband), Joanna Myers (Suburban Wife), Richard Galella, Michael J. Conti (Swat Team)

Al Connelly, a college student hoping to become a professional chef, begins a romance with Imogen, a union that is hindered when a porn starlet sets her sights on Al.

© Miramax Films

James Spader, Angela Bassett

THE BIG TEASE

(WARNER BROS.) Producer, Philip Rose; Executive Producers, Sacha Gervasi, Craig Ferguson, Kevin Allen; Director, Kevin Allen; Screenplay, Sacha Gervasi, Craig Ferguson; Photography, Seamus McGarvey; Designer, Joseph Hodges; Editor, Chris Peppe; Music, Mark Thomas; Costumes, Julie Miller-Bennett; Casting, Kris Nicolau; a Crawford P. Inc. production in association with I Should Coco Films; Dolby; Deluxe color; Rated R; 83 minutes; Release date: January 28, 2000.

CAST

Crawford Mackenzie ....Craig Ferguson
Candy Harper...Frances Fisher
Monique Geingold...Mary McCormack
Stig Ludwiggssen...David Rasche
Martin ....Chris Langham
Eamonn..Donal Logue
Mrs. Beasie Mackenzie ....Isabella Aitken
and Kevin Allen (Gareth Trundle), Angela McCluskey (Senga Magoogan), Francine York (Elegant Woman), Nina Siemaszko (Betty Fuego), Melissa Rosenberg (Dianne Abbott), David Hasselhoff, Drew Carey, Cathy Lee Crosby, Bruce Jenner, Veronica Webb, Jose Eber (Themselves), Norm Compton (Cop Driver), Loren Lazerine (Bear Suit Person), Robert Fisher (Bunny Suit Person), Steven Porter (Chicken Suit Person), Evie Peck (Reindeer Suit Person), Michael Paul Chan (Clarence), Robert Sherman (Constance), Charles Napier (Senator Warren Crockett), Lawrence Young (Dave London), Justin Pierce (Skateboard Kid), Marcia Wright (Monique's Receptionist), Koji Toyoda (Dick Miyake), Larry Miller (Dunston Cactus), Ted McGinley (Johnny Darjerling), Kyle Kraska (Bob Flaps), Richard Callen (Frank Wad), Sara Gilbert (Gretle Dickens), William Fisher (TV Reporter), Vicki Liddelle (Margaret Sim), Padam Singh (Mr. Patel), Robert Maffia (Police Officer), Evelyn Iocolano (Hotel Receptionist), Sam Rubin (TV Anchor), John Paul Dejoria (John Paul Mitchell), Elois Dejoria, Giuseppe Franco, Sascha Ferguson, Millie Gervasi (Judges), Kylie Bax (Stig's Hair Model), Kimora Lee (Dick Miyake's Hair Model), Contrelle Pinkney (Dave London's Hair Model), Emily Proctor (Young Valhenna Woman), Bobbie Bluebell (Angry Hedge Man), Sergio Brie (Ronnie the "Beefeater")

Scottish hairdresser Crawford Mackenzie arrives in Los Angeles for the World Freestyle Hairdressing Championship, mistakenly believing he has been asked to participate in the event.

© Warner Bros.

Craig Ferguson, Veronica Webb

Adrien Brody, Catherine Kellner

RESTAURANT

(PALISADES PICTURES) Producers, H.M. Coakley, Shana Stein, Eric Bross; Executive Producers, Mark D. Severini, Gary J. Palermo, Galt Niederhoffer, Michael Brysch; Director, Eric Bross; Screenplay, Tom C. Cudworth; Photography, Horacio Marquinez; Designer, Steven McCabe; Editor, Keith Reamer; Music, Theodore Shapiro; Music Supervisor, Jullianne Kelly; Costumes, Elizabeth Shelton; Associate Producer, Julie E. Chaiken; Casting, Joseph Middleton; a Chaiken Films production, presented in association with Giv'en Films; Dolby; Technicolor; Rated R; 107 minutes; Release date: January 28, 2000

CAST

Chris Calloway...Adrien Brody
Jeanine ....Elise Neal
Reggae ....David Moscow
Kenny ....Simon Baker-Denny
Nancy ....Catherine Kellner
Steven...Malcolm Jamal Warner
John English ....John Carroll Lynch
Quincy ....Jesse L. Martin
Lenore ....Sybil Temchen
Marcus...Vonte Sweet
Ethan..Michael Stoyanov
and Elon Gold (Kurt), Lori Heuring (Donna), Lauryn Hill (Leslie), Avery Waddell (Al-Tarique), Siena Goines (Carol, Actress), Gillian Bross (Jan), Meredith Scott Lynn (Karaoke Girl), Tai Bennett (Anthony), Nick Giordano (Frank), Shana Stein (Margaret), Mark Ethan (Robert), Jennifer Coolidge, Gwendolyn Bessette, Rachel Zients (Women at McClure's), Gary Palermo, Jennifer Giles (Couple at McClure's), Mwalimu (M.C. at Club), Mayor Anthony Russo (Mayor), Robert Castle (Priest), Lord Grayson (Drug Dealer), Jennifer Skinner, Alexandra Dellapenna, Cara Jedell (Karaoke Singer), Robert Capelli (Investor), Mary Jasperson, John Friemann (Anniversary Couple), Lauren Nadler (Casting Director), Sonya Wells (Prostitute)

Chris, an aspiring playwright tending bar at a Hoboken restaurant, begins a relationship with a waitress, Jeanine, despite the fact that he has not gotten over his last girlfriend.

© Palisades Pictures

Nathan Lane, Stockard Channing

ISN'T SHE GREAT

(UNIVERSAL) Producer, Mike Lobell; Executive Producers, Ted Kurdyla, Gary Levinsohn, Mark Gordon; Director, Andrew Bergman; Screenplay, Paul Rudnick; Based on the New Yorker article "Wasn't She Great" by Michael Korda; Photography, Karl Walter Lindenlaub; Designer, Stuart Wurtzel; Costumes, Julie Weiss; Editor, Barry Malkin; Music, Burt Bacharach; Music Supervisor, Gary Jones; a Mutual Film Company presentation of a Lobell/Bergman production; Dolby; Color; Rated R; 93 minutes; Release date: January 28, 2000

Bette Midler, Nathan Lane

CAST

Jacqueline Susann	Bette Midler
Irving Mansfield	Nathan Lane
Florence Maybelle	Stockard Channing
Michael Hastings	David Hyde Pierce
Henry Marcus	John Cleese
Maury Manning	John Larroquette
Debbie	Amanda Peet
Radio Actor	Terrence Ross
Shecky	Jeffrey Ross
Brad Bradburn	Christopher MacDonald
Professor Brainiac	Paul Benedict
Bambi Madison	Dina Spybey
Leslie Barnett	Pauline Little
Passerby	William Hill
Mort	Mal Z. Lawrence
Howie	Adam Heller
Sylvia	Ellen David
Guy's Doctor	Daniel Ziskie
Receptionist	Anna Lobell
Junior Editor	David Costabile

and Brett Gillen (Man with Bicycle), Olga Merediz (Mrs. Ramirez), Jacklin Webb (Nurse), Clebert Ford (Claude), Dick Henley (Doorman), Sonia Benezra (Manicurist), Richard Litt (Buddy), Maurice Carlton, Carl Alacchi (Orderlies), Edward B. Goldstein (Eddie in Lindy's), Larry Block (Herbie), Jack Eagle (Waiter), Le Clanché du Rand (Lissy Hastings), Elizabeth Lawrence (Mimsy Hastings), Helen Stenborg (Aunt Abigail), John Cunningham (Nelson Hastings), Charles Doucet (Teamster), John Moore (News Anchor), Richard McConomy (Harry Gladrey), Lisa Bronwyn Moore (Irma Gladrey), Steven McCarthy (Book Nook Clerk), James Villemaire (Jim Morrison), Karyn Quackenbush (TV Cook), Sam Street (Truman Capote), Peter Blaikie (David), Sheena Larkin (Saleswoman), Frank Vincent (Aristotle Onassis), David Lawrence (Steve Lawrence), Debbie Gravitte (Eydie Gorme), Mickey Toft (Guy at 6), Ricky Mabe (Guy at 14), Robin Andrew Wilcock (Stage Murderer), Jude Benay (Skeptical Housewife), Jean-Guy Bouchard (Wolf Whistle Teamster).

David Hyde Pierce, John Cleese

The true story of how fringe show business personality Jacqueline Susann became one of the most famous names of the 1960s when she authored the salacious but enormously popular best seller Valley of the Dolls.

© Universal Studios

Nathan Lane, Amanda Peet, Bette Midler

GUN SHY

(HOLLYWOOD PICTURES) Producer, Sandra Bullock; Co-Producer, Marc S. Fischer; Director/Screenplay, Eric Blakeney; Photography, Tom Richmond; Designer, Maher Ahmad; Editor, Pamela Martin; Music, Rolfe Kent; Costumes, Mary Claire Hannan; Casting, Laurel Smith; a Fortis Films production; Dolby; Technicolor; Rated R; 102 minutes; Release date: February 5, 2000.

CAST

Charlie	Liam Neeson
Fulvio Nesstra	Oliver Platt
Fidel Vaillar	Jose Zuniga
Estuvio	Michael Delorenzo
Jason Cane	Andy Lauer
Elliott	Richard Schiff
Howard	Paul Ben-Victor
Jonathan	Gregg Daniel
Mark	Ben Weber
Judy Tipp	Sandra Bullock
Gloria Nesstra	Mary McCormack
Dr. Bleckner	Michael Mantell

and Mitch Pileggi (Dexter Helvenshaw), Louis Giambalvo (Lonny Ward), Rick Peters (Bennett), Dusty Kay (Kapstein), Jerry Stahl (Lucien), Michael Weatherly (Dave Juniper), Hank Stratton (Josh), Frank Vincent (Carmine Minnetti), Frankie Ray (Joey), Taylor Negron (Cheemo Partelle), Joe Maruzzo (Warren Ganza), Aaron Lustig (Fulvio's Neighbor), Tracy Zahoryin (Jason's Girlfriend), Michelle Joyner (Elliott's Wife), Manny Perry (Cheemo's Bodyguard), David Carpenter (SEC Agent Cohler), Tommy Morgan, Jr. (SEC Agent Harris), Roy Buffington (FBI Agent Clemmens), Myndy Crist (Myrna), Ramona Case (First Class Stewardess), Derek Sitter (Waiter at Night Club), Ron Reaves (Manager at Bistro), Tracy Phillips, Natalie Webb, Jennifer Garrett, Lisette Boren, Edgar Godineaux, Danté Henderson (Dancers at Cheemo's House)

Charlie, an undercover agent, whose dangerous job is wrecking his nerves and health, seeks therapy and the aide of a nurse, while trying to escape the wrath of Mafia leader Fulvio Nesstra.

Oliver Platt

SCREAM 3

(DIMENSION) Producer, Cathy Konrad, Kevin Williamson, Marianne Maddalena; Executive Producers, Bob Weinstein, Harvey Weinstein, Cary Granat, Andrew Rona; Co-Executive Producer, Stuart M. Besser; Director, Wes Craven; Screenplay, Ehren Kruger; Based on characters created by Kevin Williamson; Co-Producers, Dixie J. Capp, Julie Plec; Photography, Peter Deming; Designer, Bruce Alan Miller; Editor, Patrick Lussier; Music, Marco Beltrami; Music Supervisor, Ed Gerrard; Costumes, Abigail Murray; Casting, Lisa Beach; a Konrad Pictures production in association with Craven/Maddalena Films; Distributed by Miramax Films; Dolby; Panavision; Deluxe color; Rated R; 116 minutes; Release date: February 5, 2000

CAST

Sidney Prescott	Neve Campbell
Gale Weathers	Courteney Cox Arquette
Deputy Dewey Riley	David Arquette
Jennifer Jolie	Parker Posey
Sarah Darling	Jenny McCarthy
Detective Mark Kincaid	Patrick Dempsey
Roman Bridger	Scott Foley
Tom Prinze	Matt Keeslar
Tyson Fox	Deon Richmond
Angelina Tyler	Emily Mortimer
John Milton	Lance Henriksen
Wallace	Josh Pais
Martha Meeks	Heather Matarazzo
Cotton Weary	Liev Schreiber
Caller	Beth Toussaint

and Roger L. Jackson ("The Voice"), Kelly Rutherford (Christine), Julie Janney (Moderator), Richmond Arquette (Student), Lynn McRee (Maureen Prescott), Nancy O'Dell, Ken Taylor (Reporters), Roger Corman (Studio Executive), Patrick Warburton (Steven Stone), John Embry (Stage Security Guard), Lawrence Hecht (Mr. Prescott), Lisa Beach (Studio Tour Guide), Kevin Smith (Silent Bob), Jason Mewes (Jay), Erik Erath (Stan), D.K. Arredondo (Office Security Guard), Lisa Gordon (Waitress), Jamie Kennedy (Randy Meeks), Carrie Fisher (Bianca), C.W. Morgan (Mr. Loomis)

Sidney Prescott's torment over the past murders in her small town is reactivated when terror errupts on the set of Stab 3, a horror movie based on the killings. Third film in the Dimension/Miramax series following Scream (1996) and Scream 2 (1997), with Campbell, Cox Arquette, David Arquette, Schreiber, and Kennedy repeating their roles.

Jenny McCarthy

Virginie Ledoyen, Leonardo DiCaprio, Guillaume Canet

Robert Carlyle, Leonardo Di Caprio

Leonardo DiCaprio

Leonardo DiCaprio

THE BEACH

(20TH CENTURY FOX) Producer, Andrew MacDonald; Director, Danny Boyle; Screenplay, John Hodge; Based on the book by Alex Garland; Photography, Darius Khondji; Designer, Andrew McAlpine; Editor, Masahiro Hirakubo; Costumes, Rachael Fleming; Music, Angelo Badalamenti; Co-Producer, Callum McDougall; Casting, Gail Stevens, Kate Dowd (Paris); a Figment Film; Dolby; Super 35 Widescreen; Deluxe color; Rated R; 120 minutes; Release date: February 11, 2000

CAST

Richard	Leonardo DiCaprio
Sal	Tilda Swinton
Francoise	Virginie Ledoyen
Etienne	Guillaume Canet
Daffy	Robert Carlyle
Keaty	Paterson Joseph
Bugs	Lars Arentz Hansen
Zeph	Peter Youngblood Hills
Sammy	Jerry Swindall
Sonja	Zelda Tinska
Weathergirl	Victoria Smurfit
Unhygenix	Daniel Caltagirone
Gregorio	Peter Gevisser
Mirjana	Lidija Zovkic
Guitarman	Samuel Gough
Christo	Staffan Kihlbom
Karl	Jukka Hiltunen
Sten	Magnus Lindgren
Hustler	Daniel York
Hotel Receptionist	Patcharawan Patarakijjanon
Cleaning Woman	Somboon Phutaroth
Detective	Weeratham (Norman) Wichairaksakul
Travel Agent	Jak Boon
Woman with Key	Krongthong Thampradith
Senior Farmer	Abhijati (Muek) Jusakul

and Sanya "Gai" Cheunjit, Kanueng "Nueng" Kenla, Somchai Santitarangkul, Kawee "Seng" Sirikanerat, Somkuan "Kuan" Siroon (Farmers), Myriam Acharki, Andrew Carmichael, Josh Cole, Helene De Fougerolles, Bindu De Stoppani, Stacy Hart, Nina Jacques, Sheriden Jones, Gunilla Karlson, Sian Martin, Isabella Seibert, Elizabeth Thomas, Michael Thorpe, Timothy Webster, Ramon Woolfe (Beach Community Members), Saskia Mulder (Hilda), Simone Huber (Eva), Raweeporn "Non" Srimonju (Sumet)

Richard, a young man on vacation in Thailand searching for an unusual adventure, receives a map to a mysterious island and convinces a couple to join him in journeying to the isolated spot.

© Twentieth Century Fox

THE TIGGER MOVIE

(WALT DISNEY PICTURES) Producer, Cheryl Abood; Director/Screenplay, Jun Falkenstein; Story, Eddie Guzelian; Based on characters by A.A. Milne; Executive in Charge of Production, Sharon Morrill Robinov; Music, Harry Gregson-Williams; Songs, Richard M. Sherman, Robert B. Sherman; Art Director, Toby Bluth; Director of Walt Disney Animation Japan, Takamitsu Kawamura; Supervising Animation Director, Kenichi Tsuchiya; Supervising Film Editor, Robert Fisher, Jr.; Associate Producer, Jennifer Blohm; Distributed by Buena Vista Pictures; Dolby; Technicolor; Rated G; 77 minutes; Release date: February 11, 2000

VOICE CAST

Tigger/Winnie the Pooh..Jim Cummings
Kanga...Kath Soucie
Roo...Nikita Hopkins
Owl...Andre Stojka
Eeyore..Peter Cullen
Piglet..John Fiedler
Rabbit...Ken Sansom
Christopher Robin..Tom Attenborough
Narrator...John Hurt
and Bobbi Page, Randy Crenshaw, Michael Geiger, Geoff Koch, Rick Logan, Lauren Wood (Chorus)

Tigger, wondering if there are any others in the world like himself, sets off on a journey through the Hundred Acre Wood in search of his family tree.

© Disney Enterprises

Kanga, Piglet, Rabbit, Winnie the Pooh, Owl, Tigger, Eeyore, Roo

Tigger

Roo, Tigger

Winnie the Pooh, Roo, Piglet

Josh Peck, Chris Elliott

Josh Peck, Zena Grey, Jade Yorker

SNOW DAY

(PARAMOUNT) Producer, Albie Hecht, Julia Pistor; Executive Producer, Raymond Wagner; Director, Chris Koch; Screenplay, Will McRobb, Chris Viscardi; Photography, Robbie Greenberg; Designer, Leslie McDonald; Editor, David Finfer; Costumes, Wendy Partridge; Music, Steve Bartek; Co-Producers, Grace Gilroy, Will McRobb, Chris Viscardi; Casting, Mary Gail Artz, Barbara Cohen; a Nickelodeon Movies presentation; Dolby; Panavision; Deluxe color; Rated PG; 89 minutes; Release date: February 11, 2000

CAST

Snowplowman	Chris Elliott
Hal Brandston	Mark Webber
Laura Brandston	Jean Smart
Lane Leonard	Schuyler Fisk
Mr. Zellweger	Iggy Pop
Tina	Pam Grier
Chad Symmonz	John Schneider
Tom Brandston	Chevy Chase
Natalie Brandston	Zena Grey
Wayne Alworth	Josh Peck
Chet Felker	Jade Yorker
Principal Weaver	Damian Young
Randy Brandston	Connor Matheus
Bill Korn	J. Adam Brown
Claire Bonner	Emmanuelle Chriqui
Chuck Wheeler	David Paetkau
Mona	"Chilli"
Mailman	Tim Paleniuk
Ben's Son	Josh Sealy
Ben	Orest Kinasewich
TV Newscaster Phyllis	Andrea Engel
Marla	Katharine Isabelle
Fawn	Carly Pope
Paula	Kea Wong
Patty	Desiree Lindsay

and Lorena Gale (Radio Mother), Jeff Watson (Kid), Daniel Cuthbertson (Snowplowboy), Alex Hudson (Braces Kid), Renee Christianson (Make Up Person), Frank Takacs (Technician), Dan Wilmott (Crossing Guard), Shaye Ganam (Sportscaster), Gepert Myers (Dad), Bob Chomyn (Editor), Rick Ash (Producer), Terry King (Diner Dan), Stevie Mitchell (Scout #1), Leon Frierson (Odd Ball Kid), Chad Cosgrave (Steve), Colt Cosgrave (Greg)

Chevy Chase

Members of the Brandston family see a chance to fulfill some dreams and right some wrongs when a massive storm results in a snow day from school.

J. Adam Brown, Schuyler Fisk, Mark Webber,
Emmanuelle Chriqui, David Paetkau

THE WHOLE NINE YARDS

(WARNER BROS.) Producers, David Willis, Allan Kaufman; Executive Producers, Elie Samaha, Andrew Stevens; Director, Jonathan Lynn; Screenplay, Mitchell Kapner; Photography, David Franco; Designer, David L. Snyder; Editor, Tom Lewis; Co-Producers, Don Carmody, James Holt, Tracee Stanley; Line Producer, Mike Drake; Music, Randy Edelman; Music Supervisor, Spring Aspers; Costumes, Edi Giguere; Song: *They All Laughed* by Ira Gershwin, George Gershwin/performed by The Charlie Biddle Trio, featuring Stephanie Biddle; a Morgan Creek Productions, Inc. and Franchise Pictures presentation of a Rational Packaging production in association with Lansdown Films; Dolby; Deluxe color; Rated R; 101 minutes; Release date: February 18, 2000

Matthew Perry, Bruce Willis, Amanda Peet

CAST

Jimmy "The Tulip" Tudeski	Bruce Willis
Nicholas "Oz" Oseransky	Matthew Perry
Sophie	Rosanna Arquette
Franklin "Frankie Figs" Figueroa	Michael Clarke Duncan
Cynthia	Natasha Henstridge
Jill	Amanda Peet
Janni Gogolak	Kevin Pollak
Agent Hanson	Harland Williams
Sophie's Mom	Carmen Ferlan
Mr. Boulez	Serge Christiaenssens
Waitress	Renee Madelaine Le Guerrier
Mover	Jean-Guy Bouchard
Dave Martin	Howard Bilerman
Hungarian Hood	Johnny Goar
Polish Pug	Deano Clavet
Jazz Singer	Stephanie Biddle
Bass Player	Charles Biddle
Pianist	Geoff Lapp
Drummer	Gary Gold
Mr. Tourette	Robert Burns
Mrs. Boulez	France Arbour
Sgt. Buchanan	Sean Devine
Agent Morrissey	Richard Jutras
Interrogators	Mark Camacho, Joanna Noyes
Bank Manager	John Moore

Oz Oseransky, a mild-mannered dentist, is shocked to discover that his new next door neighbor is Jimmy "The Tulip" Tudesky, a contract killer who is hiding out from a dangerous Chicago crime family.

Matthew Perry, Natasha Henstridge

Bruce Willis, Matthew Perry

Michael Clarke Duncan, Matthew Perry

HANGING UP

(COLUMBIA) Producers, Laurence Mark, Nora Ephron; Executive Producers, Delia Ephron, Bill Robinson; Director, Diane Keaton; Screenplay, Delia Ephron, Nora Ephron; Based on the novel by Delia Ephron; Photography, Howard Atherton; Designer, Waldemar Kalinowski; Editor, Julie Monroe; Music, David Hirschfelder; Co-Producer, Diaan Pokorny; Costumes, Bobbie Read; Casting, Lisa Beach; a Nora Ephron and Laurence Mark Production; Dolby; Deluxe color; Rated PG-13; 93 minutes; Release date: February 18, 2000

CAST

Eve Marks	Meg Ryan
Georgia	Diane Keaton
Maddy	Lisa Kudrow
Lou Mozell	Walter Matthau
Joe	Adam Arkin
Omar Kunundar	Duke Moosekian
Ogmed Kunundar	Ann Bortolotti
Pat	Cloris Leachman
Angie	Maree Cheatham
Dr. Kelly	Myndy Crist

and Libby Hudson (Georgia's Assistant), Jesse James (Jesse), Edie McClurg (Esther), Tracee Ellis Ross (Kim), Celia Weston (Madge Turner), Bob Kirsh (Nixon Library Representative), Stephanie Ittleson (Victoria), Venessia Valentino (Nurse at Mesh Window), R.A. Buck, Phil Levesque (Gay Men), Paige Wolfe (Six Year Old Eve), Charles Matthau (Young Lou), Ethan Dampf (Four Year Old Jesse), Mary Beth Pape (Mother at Party), Catherine Paolone (Doctor), Carol Mansell (Woman Who Recognizes Maddy), Katie Stratton (Twelve Year Old Georgia), Talia-Lynn Prairie (Four Year Old Maddy), Kristina Dorn (Young Pat), Lucky Vanous (Montana Dude), Bill Robinson (Doctor on Soap)

Three sisters, whose recent contact has been from afar, come together when their father is admitted to a Los Angeles hospital. This was the final film appearance of Walter Matthau who died on July 1, 2000.

Diane Keaton, Meg Ryan, Lisa Kudrow

PITCH BLACK

(USA FILMS) Producers, Tom Engelman; Executive Producers, Ted Field, Scott Kroopf, Anthony Winley; Director, David Twohy; Screenplay, Jim Wheat, Ken Wheat, David Twohy; Story, Jim Wheat, Ken Wheat; Photography, David Eggby; Designer, Graham "Grace" Walker; Editor, Rick Shaine; Costumes, Anna Borghesi; Visual Effects Supervisor, Peter Chiang; Creatures Designer and Supervisor, Patrick Tatopoulos; Music, Graeme Revell; Stunts, Chris Anderson; a Gramercy Pictures presentation of an Interscope Communications production; Dolby; Super 35 Widescreen; Atlab QLD color; Rated R; 107 minutes; Release date: February 18, 2000

CAST

Riddick	Vin Diesel
Fry	Radha Mitchell
Johns	Cole Hauser
Imam	Keith David
Paris	Lewis Fitz-Gerald
Shazza	Claudia Black
Jack/Jackie	Rhiana Griffith
Zeke	John Moore
Owens	Simon Burke

and Les Chantery (Suleiman), Sam Sari (Hassan), Firass Dirani (Ali), Ric Anderson (Total Stranger), Vic Wilson (Captain), Angela Makin (Dead Crew Member)

A spacecraft makes a forced crash-landing on a mysterious planet where creatures emerge from the dark to hunt for the survivors.

© Universal Studios

Vin Diesel

Ben Affleck, Giovanni Ribisi

Vin Diesel

Giovanni Ribisi, Ron Rifkin

Giovanni Ribisi, Nia Long

BOILER ROOM

(NEW LINE CINEMA) Producers, Suzanne Todd, Jennifer Todd; Executive Producers, Claire Rudnick Polstein, Richard Brener; Director/Screenplay, Ben Younger; Photography, Enrique Chediak; Designer, Anne Stuhler; Co-Producer, E. Bennett Walsh; Editor, Chris Peppe; Music, The Angel; Costumes, Julia Caston; Music Supervisor, Dana Sano; Casting, John Papsidera; a Team Todd production; Dolby; Deluxe color; Rated R; 117 minutes; Release date: February 18, 2000

CAST

Seth Davis	Giovanni Ribisi
Chris	Vin Diesel
Abby Halperin	Nia Long
Greg	Nicky Katt
Richie	Scott Caan
Marty Davis	Ron Rifkin
Adam	Jamie Kennedy
Harry Reynard	Taylor Nichols
Agent Drew	Bill Sage
Michael	Tom Everett Scott
Jim Young	Ben Affleck
Concierge	John Griesemer
Marc	David Younger
Seth's Mother	Donna Mitchell
Neil	André Vippolis
Jeff	Jon Abrahams

and Will McCormack (Mike the Casino Patron), Jared Ryan (Casino Steve), Carlo Vogel (Rude Kid), Matthew Saldivar (Series Seven Kid), Serge Skliarenko (Croatian Broker), Lisa Gerstein (Sheryl), Ross Ryman (Isaac), Marjorie Johnson (Abby's Mother), Peter Maloney (Dr. Jacobs), Russell Harper, Mark Webber, Christopher Fitzgerald (Kids), Anson Mount, Kirk Acevedo, Seth Ullian, Eddie Malavarca (Brokers), Peter Rini, Raymond Pirkle, Joe Pretlow (JP Brokers), Lori Yoffe (Secretary), Alex Webb (FBI Director), Gillian Sacco (Waitress at Mickey's), Don J. Hewitt (Local), Mark Moshe Bellows (John Fineman), Daniel Serafini-Sauli (Broker Steve), Lucinda Faraldo (Trendy Hostess), Neal Lerner (Gay Man), Taylor Patterson (Sara Reynard), Michael McCarthy (Max Reynard), Marsha Dietlein (Susan Reynard), Joseph Tudisco (Janitor), Judy Del Guidice (Office Woman), Siobhan Fallon (Harry's Supervisor)

Hoping to prove to his father that he can make a buck honestly, Seth Davis joins a brokerage firm that offers a quick road to financial success, only to discover that the business is not as legit and honest as he had initially assumed.

Tobey Maguire, Michael Douglas

Katie Holmes, Michael Douglas

Michael Douglas, Frances McDormand

Rip Torn, Robert Downey, Jr., Katie Holmes,
Tobey Maguire, Michael Douglas

Tobey Maguire

WONDER BOYS

(PARAMOUNT) Producers, Scott Rudin, Curtis Hanson; Executive Producers, Adam Schroeder, Ned Dowd; Director, Curtis Hanson; Screenplay, Steve Kloves; Based upon the novel by Michael Chabon; Photography, Dante Spinotti; Designer, Jeannine Oppewall; Editor, Dede Allen; Costumes, Beatrix Aruna Pasztor; Music, Christopher Young; Music Supervisor, Carol Fenelon; Song: *Things Have Changed* written and performed by Bob Dylan; Casting, Mali Finn; a Mutual Film Company presentation of a Scott Rudin/Curtis Hanson production; Dolby; Panavision; Deluxe color; Rated R; 112 minutes; Release date: February 23, 2000

Frances McDormand, Michael Douglas

CAST

Grady Tripp	Michael Douglas
James Leer	Tobey Maguire
Sara Gaskell	Frances McDormand
Terry Crabtree	Robert Downey, Jr.
Hannah Green	Katie Holmes
Q	Rip Torn
Vernon Hardapple	Richard Knox
Oola	Jane Adams
Miss Sloviak	Michael Cavadias
Walter Gaskell	Richard Thomas
Traxler	Alan Tudyk
Emily's Father	Philip Bosco
Fred Leer	George Grizzard
Amanda Leer	Kelly Bishop
Officer Pupcik	Bill Velin
Carrie	Charis Michelsen
Howard	Yusuf Gatewood
Emily's Mother	June Hildreth
Emily (photo)	Elisabeth Granli
Hi-Hat Bouncer	Richard Hidlebird
Poe	Screamer

and Bingo O'Malley, Patricia Cray, Marita Golden, Victor Quinaz, James Ellroy, Lenora Nemetz, Tracey D. Turner, James Kisicki (Wordfest Party Guests), Rob McElhenney, Anika Bobb, Katherine Sweeney (Students)

Grady Tripp, a college professor struggling to finish his new novel, spends an eye-opening weekend during which his mistress announces she is pregnant and a suicidal student reveals himself to be a brilliant writer.

2000 Academy Award-winner for Best Original Song ("Things Have Changed"). This film received additional Oscar nominations for screenplay adaptation and editing.

Michael Douglas

Michael Douglas, Michael Cavadias, Robert Downey, Jr.

Robert Downey, Jr., Michael Douglas

Ben Affleck

Ben Affleck, Charlize Theron

REINDEER GAMES

(DIMENSION) Producers, Marty Katz, Bob Weinstein, Chris Moore; Executive Producers, Harvey Weinstein, Cary Granat, Andrew Rona; Director, John Frankenheimer; Screenplay Ehren Kruger; Co-Producers, B. Casey Grant, Mark Indig; Photography, Alan Caso; Designer, Barbara Dunphy; Editors, Tony Gibbs, Michael Kahn; Music, Alan Silvestri; Costumes, May Routh; Casting, Mali Finn; a Marty Katz production; Distributed by Miramax Films; Dolby; Super 35 Widescreen; Alpha-Cine Color; Rated R; 105 minutes; Release date: February 25, 2000

CAST

Rudy Duncan	Ben Affleck
Ashley	Charlize Theron
Gabriel	Gary Sinise
Merlin	Clarence Williams III
Jack Bangs	Dennis Farina
Nick	James Frain
Pug	Donal Logue
Jumpy	Danny Trejo
Zook	Isaac Hayes
The Alamo	Dana Stubblefield
Mean Guard	Mark Acheson
Ugly Staffer	Tom Heaton
Distant Inmates	Michael Sunczyk, Douglas H. Arthurs
Guards	Dean Wray, Ron Sauve
Prisoner #1	Ron Hyatt
Exit Guard	Hrothgar Mathews
Old Governor	Gordon Tootoosis
Young Governor	Lee Jay Bamberry
Security Boss	Frank Jones
Bartender	Jimmy Herman
Fat Guy	John Destry
College Kid	Ashton Kutcher
Portuguese Woman	Ana Paul Piedade

and Enuka Okuma, Eva De Viveiros (Cocktail Waitresses), Joanna Piros (TV Newscaster), Robyn Driscoll (Desk Clerk), Lonny Chapman (Old Timer), Alonso Oyarzun (Casino Dealer), Rod Wolfe, Marcus Hondro (Cashiers), Sam Bob (Video Guard), Jacop Rupp, David Jacox (Park Rangers), Anna Hagan (Mother), Ken Camroux (Father), Terry O'Sullivan (Aunt Mary), Michael Puttonen (Bill), Paula Shaw (Aunt Lisbeth), Don S. Williams (Uncle Ray), Jenafor Ryane (Jill), James Hutson (Mike), Wendy Noel (Stacey), Blair Slater (Sam)

Newly released from prison, Rudy Duncan hooks up with the pen pal of a deceased inmate, only to have her crazed brother mistake him for the dead con and rope him into a heist at a casino.

© Dimension Films

Charlize Theron, Donal Logue

Clarence Williams III, Gary Sinise

JUDY BERLIN

(THE SHOOTING GALLERY) Producer, Rocco Caruso; Director/Screenplay/Editor, Eric Mendelsohn; Photography, Jeffrey Seckendorf; Designer, Charlie Kulsziski; Costumes, Sue Gandy; Music, Michael Nicholas; Line Producer, Lisa Kolaska; Casting, Laura Rosenthal, Ali Farrell; a Caruso/Mendelsohn production; Dolby; Black and white; Not rated; 96 minutes; Release date: February 25, 2000

CAST

Sue Berlin	Barbara Barrie
Arthur Gold	Bob Dishy
Judy Berlin	Edie Falco
Maddie	Carlin Glynn
David Gold	Aaron Harnick
Dolores Engler	Bette Henritze
Alice Gold	Madeline Kahn
Marie	Julie Kavner
Bea	Anne Meara
Carol	Novella Nelson

and Peter Appel (Mr. V), Marcia DeBonis (Lisa), Glenn Fitzgerald (Tour Guide), Marcus Giamatti (Eddie Dillon), Judy Graubart (Ceil), Arthur Anderson (Dr. Stern), Margaret Mendelson (Cathy), Keith Mulvihill, Bob DeMarco (Gas Station Attendants), Jeffrey Howard (Spirio), Sylvia Kauders (Woman on Bench), Diane Tyler (Neighbor in Window), Louise Millmann (Denise), Julie Kessler (Alice's Neighbor), Ellen Baer (Nurse), Louisa Shafia (Chatting Nurse), Dennis Roach (Gus), Renee Guest (P.A. Announcer), Vic Caroli (TV Announcer), Stephanie Goldberg (Stephanie), Adam Blondrage, Pamela Bossdorf, Juliana Cardella, Sandra Fleming, Jamie Giannino, Nicole Goldberg, Victoria Kaplan, Brett Lustig, Victoria Pick, Kaitlyn Rajzewski, Erica Tamburro, Gregory Tamburro, Lalenur Tastan, Suzan Tastan (Children in Class)

David Gold, having failed to make it as a filmmaker in Los Angeles, returns to his Long Island town where he meets up with his one-time crush, Judy Berlin, who is dreaming of becoming a movie actress. This was the final film of Madeline Kahn who died on Dec. 3, 1999.

© Shooting Gallery

Barbara Barrie, Bob Dishy

Bette Midler, Danny DeVito

DROWNING MONA

(DESTINATION) Producers, Al Corley, Bart Rosenblatt, Eugene Musso; Executive Producers, Danny DeVito, Michael Shamberg, Stacey Sher, Jonathan Weisgal; Director, Nick Gomez; Screenplay, Peter Steinfeld; Photography, Bruce Douglas Johnson; Designer, Richard Toyon; Editor, Richard Pearson; Costumes, Terry Dresbach; Music, Michael Tavera; Music Supervisor, Gwen Bethel; Casting, Monika Mikkelsen; a Neverland Films/Jersey Shore production; Dolby; Technicolor; Rated PG-13; 95 minutes; Release date: March 3, 2000

CAST

Chief Wyatt Rash	Danny DeVito
Mona Dearly	Bette Midler
Ellen Rash	Neve Campbell
Rona	Jamie Lee Curtis
Bobby Calzone	Casey Affleck
Phil Dearly	William Fichtner
Jeff Dearly	Marcus Thomas
Feege	Peter Dobson
Lucinda	Kathleen Wilhoite
Clarence	Tracey Walter
Tony Carlucci	Paul Ben-Victor
Jimmy D	Paul Schulze
Murph	Mark Pellegrino
Father Tom	Raymond O'Connor
Cubby	Will Ferrell

and Lisa Rieffel (Valerie), Robert Arce (Doctor Schwartz), Brittany Peterson (Maria Lasala), Philip Perlman (Motel Cashier), Yul Vazquez (French Instructor), Melissa McCarthy (Shirley), Jason Monkarsh (Benny), Brian Doyle-Murray (Co-Worker), Bonnie (Peaches)

After Verplanck's most hated citizen, Mona Dearly, dies when her car plunges into the Hudson river, police chief Wyatt Rash tries to find out who among the many suspects might have been responsible.

© Destination Film Distribution

THE NEXT BEST THING

(PARAMOUNT) Producers, Tom Rosenberg, Leslie Dixon, Linne Radmin; Executive Producers, Gary Lucchesi, Ted Tannebaum, Lewis Manilow; Director, John Schlesinger; Screenplay, Thomas Ropelewski; Photography, Elliot Davis; Designer, Howard Cummings; Editor, Peter Honess; Costumes, Ruth Myers; Music, Gabriel Yared; Music Supervisors, Happy Walters, Gary Jones; Co-Producers, Marcus Viscidi, Richard S. Wright; Casting, Mali Finn; a Lakeshore Entertainment presentation of a Lakeshore Entertainment production; Dolby; Super 35 Widescreen; Deluxe color; Rated PG-13; 108 minutes; Release date: March 3, 2000

Madonna, Rupert Everett

CAST

Abbie	Madonna
Robert Whittaker	Rupert Everett
Ben	Benjamin Bratt
Caroline Ryder	Illeana Douglas
Kevin	Michael Vartan
Richard Whittaker	Josef Sommer
Sam	Malcolm Stumpf
Helen Whittaker	Lynn Redgrave
David	Neil Patrick Harris
Cardiologist	Mark Valley
Annabel	Suzanne Krull
Finn	Stacy Edwards
Abbie's Lawyer	John Carroll Lynch
Judge	Fran Bennett
Angel	Ricki Lopez
Flavio	Ramiro Fabian
Young Mother	Tiffany Paulsen
Bel Air Matron	Joan Axelrod
Bel Air Man	George Axelrod

and Jack Betts (Vernon), William Mesnik (Ashby), Irene Roseen (Lena), Gavin Lambert (Ricky), "Gangsta" Terrell Anderson, "Kmac" Kelly Garmon, "Browski" James Reese, "Dutch" Amoa Chester (Rappers), Thomas Bankowski (Omar), Glenn Sakazian (Glen), Terrance Sweeney (Priest at Funeral), Anna Garduno (Coffee Shop Waitress), Frank James (Dad at Airport), Linda Larkin (Kelly), Tom Burke (Tom, Annabel's Husband), Benjamin Koldyke (Kelly's Boyfriend), Marie Chambers, Lee Lucas, Glenn Tannous (Party Guests), Caitlin Wachs (Rachel), Maxx Tepper (Kyle), Jessica Sara, Katelin Petersen (Kids), Holly Houston (Yoga Student), Kimberly Davies (Hostess), Alvin H. Einbender (Diner), Laurent Schwaar (Restaurant Manager), Patrick Price (Maitre'd), Michael Arnon/Misha Sacnoff (Waiter), Jay Karnes (Kevin's Lawyer)

Malcolm Stumpf, Rupert Everett

After a drunken night of self-pity, Abbie winds up pregnant by her gay friend Robert. Together they raise the child until another man enters Abbie's life, resulting in an ugly custody battle.

© Lakeshore Entertainment Corp./Paramount Pictures

Madonna, Benjamin Bratt

Madonna, Neil Patrick Harris, Rupert Everett

WHAT PLANET ARE YOU FROM?

(COLUMBIA) Producers, Mike Nichols, Garry Shandling, Neil Machlis; Executive Producers, Brad Grey, Bernie Brillstein; Director, Mike Nichols; Screenplay, Garry Shandling, Michael Leeson, Ed Solomon, Peter Tolan; Story, Garry Shandling, Michael Leeson; Photography, Michael Ballhaus; Designer, Bo Welch; Costumes, Ann Roth; Editor, Richard Marks; Co-Producer, Michele Imperato-Stabile; Music, Carter Burwell; Casting, Ellen Lewis; a Brad Grey/Bernie Brillstein production; Dolby; Deluxe color; Rated R; 104 minutes; Release date: March 3, 2000

CAST

Harold Anderson	Garry Shandling
Susan Hart	Annette Bening
Roland Jones	John Goodman
Perry Gordon	Greg Kinnear
Graydon	Ben Kingsley
Helen Gordon	Linda Fiorentino
Rebecca	Judy Greer
Randy	Danny Zorn
Rita	Harmony Smith
Don Fisk	Richard Jenkins
Nadine Jones	Caroline Aaron
Madeline	Nora Dunn
Janice	Cricky Long
Alison	Camryn Manheim
Liz	Anne Cusack

and Jane Lynch (Doreen), Richard Minchenberg (Dr. Weitzman), Drinda La Lumia (Drunken Lady), J.C. MacKenzie (John), Willie Garson (Brett), Marjorie Lovett (Neighbor Woman), Bil Dwyer (Husband), Cathy Ladman (Wife), Alexander Lyras (Male AA), Anastasia Sakelaris (Cheryl), Jane Morris (Charity Woman), Michael Dempsey (Baggage Handler), Stacey Travis (Woman), Walter Addison (Pilot), Brian Markinson (Co-Pilot), Octavia L. Spencer (Baby Nurse), Ana Mercedes (Older Nurse), Samantha Smith (Flight Attendant), Tom Dahlgren (Minister), Tammy Tavares (Hologram Woman), Wade Andrew Williams (Planet Man), Phill Lewis (Other MD), Minerva Garcia (Nurse), Jack Sydow (Minister), Rick Hoffman (Doctor), Tom Dorfmeister (Heavy Man), Neil Machlis (Dr. Tom), Mitchell Greenberg (Robotic Voice), Jerry Punch, Mike Gottfried (Football Announcers), Janeane Garofalo (Woman on Plane)

An alien from a distant solar system populated entirely by males is sent to Earth to find a woman and impregnate her, a task that results in greater challenges than he expected.

© Columbia Pictures

Garry Shandling, Annette Bening, John Goodman

Ben Kingsley

Linda Fiorentino, Greg Kinnear

Janeane Garofalo, Garry Shandling

GHOST DOG: THE WAY OF THE SAMURAI

(ARTISAN) Producers, Richard Guay, Jim Jarmusch; Director/Screenplay, Jim Jarmusch; Photography, Robby Müller; Designer, Ted Bernier; Costumes, John Dunn; Co-Producer, Diana Schmidt; Editor, Jay Rabinowitz; Music, The RZA; Casting, Ellen Lewis, Laura Rosenthal; a JVC, Le Studio Canal+ and BAC Films presentation in association with Pandora Film and ARD/Degeto Film of a Plywood production; U.S.-French; Dolby; Deluxe color; Rated R; 116 minutes; Release date: March 3, 2000.

CAST

Ghost Dog	Forest Whitaker
Louie Bonacelli	John Tormey
Raymond	Isaach de Bankolé
Ray Vargo	Henry Silva
Sonny Valerio	Cliff Gorman
Vinny	Victor Argo
Louise Vargo	Tricia Vessey
Pearline	Camille Winbush
Old Consigliere	Gene Ruffini
Handsome Frank	Richard Portnow
Big Angie	Frank Minucci
Valerio's Bodyguard	Frank Adonis
Young Ghost Dog	Damon Whitaker
Johnny Morini	Vince Viverito

and Yan Ming Shi (Chinese Kung-Fu Master), Vinnie Vella (Sammy the Snake), Joe Rigano (Joe Rags), Gary Farmer (Nobody), Clebert Ford (Pigeonkeeper), Kenny Guay (Boy in Window), Gano Grills, Touché Cornel, Jamie Hector (Gangstas in Red), Chuck Jeffreys (Mugger), Roberto López, Salvatore Alagna, Jerry Todisco (Punks in Alley), Dreddy Kurger, Timbo King, Clay Da Raider, Dead and Stinking, Deflon Sallahr (Rappers in Blue), José Rabelo (Rooftop Boatbuilder), Jerry Sturiano (Lefty), Tony Rigo (Tony), Luz Valentin (Girl in Silver), Rene Bluestone, Jordan Peck (Club Couple), Angel Caban (Social Club Landlord), Jonathan Cook, Tracy Howe (Bear Hunters), Harry Shearer (Voice of Scratchy), Vanessa Hollingshead (Deputy Sheriff), Sharon Angela (Blonde Woman with Jaguar), The RZA (Samurai in Camouflage)

Ghost Dog, a contract killer and devotee of martial arts, is ordered to exterminate the lover of the daughter of a powerful Mafia boss, only to find out that once the task is done he himself is to be eliminated.

© Plywood Productions Inc.

Forest Whitaker

Timothy Hutton, Ryan Cutrona, Kevin Pollak,
Joe McCrackin, Sheryl Lee Ralph

DETERRENCE

(PARAMOUNT CLASSICS) Producers, Marc Frydman, James Spies; Executive Producers, Maurice Leblond, Steve Loglisci; Director/Screenplay, Rod Lurie; Photography, Frank Perl; Designer, W. Brook Wheeler; Music, Lawrence Nash Groupé; Editor, Alan Roberts; a TF1 International presentation of a Battleplan production; Dolby; FotoKem Color; Rated R; 101 minutes; Release date: March 10, 2000.

CAST

President Walter Emerson	Kevin Pollak
Marshall Thompson	Timothy Hutton
Gayle Redford	Sheryl Lee Ralph
Katie	Clotilde Courau
Harvey	Badja Djola
Ralphie	Sean Astin
Irvin	Mark Thompson
Taylor Woods	Michael Mantell
Lizzie Woods	Kathryn Morris
Agent Dexter	Ryan Cutrona

and Joe McCracken (Agent Williams), Scoot Powell (Noah), J. Scott Shonka (Capt. Nick Coddington), Rigg Kennedy (Howard), James Curly (Adm. Miller), James Handy (Lancaster/President Buchanan), Graham Galloway (George Carvelli/Jeter), John Cirigliano (Martin Keller), Amit Mehta (Abu Hussein), Steve Loglisci (Nick Macario), Kristen Shaw (Alexandra Emerson), Robert Harvey (Agent Hunter), June Lockhart (Secretary of State Clift), Sayed Badreya (Omari), Roger Steffens (Daniel Golan), Leslie Harter (Sylvia Charles), Rod Lurie (John Desimio), Marc Frydman (Gestaing), E.J. Gage (Riley), Jack Angel (Secretary of Defense), Rosemary Lord (Translator), Buckley Norris (Isaacson), Fred Ornstein (Rubenstein), James Spies (Mark Stone), Uzi Gal (Iraqi Ambassador)

The President of the United States, trapped at a snowbound Colorado diner, is suddenly faced with a Mideast crisis, having to make the decision whether or not to engage in nuclear war.

© Paramount Classics

MISSION TO MARS

(TOUCHSTONE) Producer, Tom Jacobson; Director, Brian De Palma; Screenplay, Jim Thomas, John Thomas, Graham Yost; Story, Lowell Cannon, Jim Thomas, John Thomas; Executive Producer, Sam Mercer; Photography, Stephen H. Burum; Designer, Ed Verreaux; Costumes, Sanja Milkovic Hays; Editor, Paul Hirsch; Co-Producers, David Goyer, Justis Greene, Jim Wedaa; Music, Ennio Morricone; Associate Producer, Ted Tally; Visual Effects Supervisors, Hoyt Yeatman, John Knoll; Visual Effects and Animation, Industrial Light & Magic, Dream Quest Images; Casting, Denise Chamian; a Jacobson Company production; Dolby; Panavision; Technicolor; Rated PG; 113 minutes; Release date: March 10, 2000

Don Cheadle, Gary Sinise, Connie Nielsen

CAST

Jim McConnell	Gary Sinise
Woody Blake	Tim Robbins
Luke Graham	Don Cheadle
Terri Fisher	Connie Nielsen
Phil Ohlmyer	Jerry O'Connell
Sergei Kirov	Peter Outerbridge
Nicholas Willis	Kavan Smith
Reneé Coté	Jill Teed
Debra Graham	Elise Neal
Maggie McConnell	Kim Delaney
Ramier Beck	Armin Mueller-Stahl
Bobby Graham	Robert Bailey, Jr.

and Marilyn Norry, Freda Perry, Lynda Boyd, Patricia Harras (NASA Wives), Chaynade Knowles, Jeff Ballard, Anson Woods, Britt McKillop, Jillian Hubert (Children at Party), Jody Thompson, Lucia Walters, Pamela Diaz (Pretty Girls), Sugith Varughese, Story Musgrave (Capcoms), Mina E. Mina, Carlo Rota (Ambassadors), Dmitry Chepovetsky (Technician), Tracy Waterhouse (Sobbing Technician), McCanna Anthony Sinise (Young Jim McConnell), Chantal Conlin (Young Maggie), Jukka Joensuu (Priest), Bill Timoney (Computer Voice)

In the year 2020 a team of astronauts successfully lands on Mars only to be decimated by a mysterious force, prompting a rescue mission to save the one surviving crew member and to investigate the tragedy.

© Touchstone Pictures

Gary Sinise, Connie Nielsen, Jerry O'Connell

Gary Sinise

Tim Robbins, Gary Sinise

ERIN BROCKOVICH

(UNIVERSAL/COLUMBIA) Producers, Danny DeVito, Michael Shamberg, Stacey Sher; Executive Producers, John Hardy, Carla Santos Shamberg; Director, Steven Soderbergh; Screenplay, Susannah Grant; Co-Producer, Gail Lyon; Photography, Ed Lachman; Designer, Philip Messina; Editor, Anne V. Coates; Costumes, Jeffrey Kurland; Music, Thomas Newman; Music Supervisor, Amanda Scheer-Demme; Casting, Margery Simkin; a Jersey Films production; Dolby; Color; Rated R; 131 minutes; Release date: March 17, 2000

CAST

Erin Brockovich	Julia Roberts
Ed Masry	Albert Finney
George	Aaron Eckhart
Donna Jensen	Marg Helgenberger
Pamela Duncan	Cherry Jones
Kurt Potter	Peter Coyote
Matthew	Scotty Leavenworth
Katie	Gemmenne De La Peña
Dr. Jaffe	David Brisbin
Rosalind	Dawn Didawick
Donald	Valente Rodriguez
Brenda	Conchata Ferrell
Los Angeles Judge	George Rocky Sullivan
Defending Lawyer	Pat Skipper
Defendant	Jack Gill
Mrs. Morales	Irene Olga López
Beth (8 months)	Emily Marks, Julie Marks
Waitress (Julia)	Erin Brockovich-Ellis
Anna	Adilah Barnes
Babysitter	Irina V. Passmoore
Biker Friends	Ron Altomare, Charles John Bukey
Brian Frankel	Randy Lowell
Scott	Jamie Harrold
Ashley Jensen	Sarah Ashley
Shanna Jensen	Scarlett Pomers
David Foil	T.J. Thyne
Tom Robinson	Joe Chrest
Mandy Robinson	Meredith Zinner
Pete Jensen	Michael Harney
Bob Linwood	William Lucking
Laura Ambrosino	Mimi Kennedy
Mike Ambrosino	Scott Sowers
Annabelle Daniels	Kristina Malota
Ted Daniels	Wade Andrew Williams
Rita Daniels	Cordelia Richards
Beth—18th Months	Ashley Pimental, Brittany Pimental
Charles Embry	Tracey Walter
Nelson Perez	Larry Martinez

and Judge LeRoy A. Simmons (Himself), Don Snell, Michael Shamberg (PG&E Lawyers), Gina Gallego (Ms. Sanchez), Ronald E. Hairston (Car Messenger), Veanne Cox (Theresa Dallavale), Scott Allen (Town Meeting Plaintiff), Sheila Shaw (Ruth Linwood), Matthew Kimbrough (Bartender), Jason Cervantes (Check Messenger)

Erin Brockovich, a struggling single mother, lands a job at a law firm where she stumbles upon a series of medical records, exposing a cover-up involving contaminated water that has resulted in multiple illnesses within the community.

2000 Academy Award for Best Actress (Julia Roberts). This film received additional Oscar nominations for picture, supporting actor (Albert Finney), director, and original screenplay.

![Albert Finney, Julia Roberts]
Albert Finney, Julia Roberts

Ashley/Brittany Pimental, Julia Roberts

Julia Roberts, Aaron Eckhart

Scotty Leavenworth, Emily/Julie Marks,
Julia Roberts, Gemmenne De La Peña

Julia Roberts

Conchata Ferrell, Julia Roberts, Albert Finney

Aaron Eckhart, Julia Roberts

Julia Roberts

Julia Roberts

Devon Sawa, Amanda Detmer, Kerr Smith

Seann William Scott

FINAL DESTINATION

(NEW LINE CINEMA) Producers, Warren Zide, Craig Perry, Glen Morgan; Executive Producers, Brian Witten, Richard Brener; Director, James Wong; Screenplay, Glen Morgan, James Wong, Jeffrey Reddick; Story, Jeffrey Reddick; Co-Producer, Art Schaeffer; Photography, Robert McLachlan; Designer, John Willett; Editor, James Coblentz; Music, Shirley Walker; Visual Effects Supervisor/Producer, Ariel Velasco Shaw; Casting, John Papsidera; a Zide/Perry production; Dolby; Deluxe color; Rated R; 97 minutes; Release date: March 17, 2000

CAST

Alex Browning	Devon Sawa
Clear Rivers	Ali Larter
Carter Horton	Kerr Smith
Valerie Lewton	Kristen Cloke
Agent Weine	Daniel Roebuck
Agent Schreck	Roger Guenveur Smith
Tod Waggner	Chad E. Donella
Billy Hitchcock	Seann William Scott
Bludworth	Tony Todd
Terry Chaney	Amanda Detmer
George Waggner	Brenden Fehr
Larry Murnau	Forbes Angus
Christa Marsh	Lisa Marie Caruk
Blake Dreyer	Christine Chatelain

and Barbara Tyson (Barbara Browning), Robert Wisden (Ken Browning), P. Lynn Johnson (Mrs. Waggner), Larry Gilman (Mr. Waggner), Guy Fauchon (Hare Krishna), Randy Stone (Flight Attendant), Mark Holden (Co-Pilot), Marrett Green (TV News Anchor), Fred Keating (Howard Seigel), John Hainsworth (Minister), Pete Atherton (Student Singer), Nicole Robert (Ticket Clerk), Kristina Matisic (Reporter)

Alex Browning, certain that the plane he is on will explode, disembarks along with six other passengers, and is proven correct in his premonition. The survivors, initially convinced that they have cheated death, begin to meet untimely ends, causing Alex to see if he can somehow outwit the inevitable.

Chad E. Donella, Kristen Cloke

Ali Larter, Devon Sawa, Kerr Smith

Jet Li, Aaliyah

Jet Li

ROMEO MUST DIE

(WARNER BROS.) Producers, Joel Silver, Jim Van Wyck; Executive Producer, Dan Cracchiolo; Director, Andrzej Bartkowiak; Screenplay, Eric Bernt, John Jarrell; Story, Mitchell Kapner; Photography, Glen MacPherson; Designer, Michael Bolton; Editor, Derek G. Brechin; Co-Producer, Warren Carr; Associate Producers, Ilyse Reutlinger, Mitchell Kapner; Music, Stanley Clarke, Timbaland; Music Supervisors, Barry Hankerson, Jomo Hankerson; Martial Arts Supervision, Corey Yuen; Casting, Lora Kennedy; a Silver Pictures production; Dolby; Super 35 Widescreen; Technicolor; Rated R; 115 minutes; Release date: March 22, 2000

CAST

Han Sing	Jet Li
Trish O'Day	Aaliyah
Mac	Isaiah Washington
Kai	Russell Wong
Silk	DMX
Isaak O'Day	Delroy Lindo
Colin	DB Woodside
Ch'u Sing	Henry O
Po Sing	Jon Kit Lee
Vincent Roth	Edoardo Ballerini
Maurice	Anthony Anderson
Dave	Matthew Harrison
Kung	Terry Chen
Chinese Messenger	Derek Lowe
New Prisoner	Ronin Wong
Head Guard	Byron Lawson

and Kendall Saunders (Colin's Girlfriend), Benz Antoine (Crabman), Keith Dallas (Bouncer), Taayla Markell (Po's Girlfriend), Chang Tseng (Victor Ho), Tong Lung, Richard Yee, Colin Foo (Overlords), Lance Gibson (Doorman), Grace Park, Jennifer Wong (Asian Dancers), Manoj Sood (Cab Driver), Fatima Robinson (Lori), Gaston Howard, Clay Donahue Fontenot (Maurice's Crew), Ryan Jefferson Lowe (Young Po), Jonross Fong (Young Han), Alonso Oyarzun (Alonso), Samuel Scantlebury (Paperboy), Francois Yip (Motorcycle Fighter), Alvin Sanders (Calvin), William S. Taylor (Harold), Morgan Reynolds (Morgan), David Kopp (Delivery Man), Aaron Joseph (Kid in Boutique), William MacDonald (Officer), Oliver Svensson-Tan (Gate Guard), Candice McClure, Tonjha Richardson (Store Clerks), W.J. Waters (Hardware Store Clerk), Cesar Abraham (Park Bench Kid), Jerry Grant (Bartender), Chic Gibson (Taxi Driver), Jody Vance (Sportscaster), Perry Solkowski (Anchor), Ann Gwathmey (Shopper)

Hearing that his younger brother has been killed as a result of an Asian-African American gang war, ex-cop Han escapes from a Hong Kong jail and heads to America to investigate the crime.

© Warner Bros.

Russell Wong, Jet Li

Isaiah Washington, Delroy Lindo

Jennifer Connelly, Billy Crudup

Billy Crudup, Janet McTeer

WAKING THE DEAD

(USA FILMS) Producers, Keith Gordon, Stuart Kleinman, Linda Reisman; Executive Producer, Jodie Foster; Director, Keith Gordon; Screenplay, Robert Dillon; Based on the novel by Scott Spencer; Co-Producer, Irene Litinsky; Photography, Tom Richmond; Designer, Zoë Sakellaropoulo; Music, Tomandandy; Editor, Jeff Wishengrad; Costumes, Renée April; Casting, Ronnie Yeskel, Richard Hicks; a Gramercy Pictures presentation of an Egg Pictures production; Dolby; Fotokem color; Rated R; 103 minutes; Release date: March 24, 2000

CAST

Fielding Pierce ....Billy Crudup
Sarah Williams..Jennifer Connelly
Juliet Beck...Molly Parker
Caroline Pierce ....Janet McTeer
Danny Pierce ....Paul Hipp
Kim..Sandra Oh
Isaac Green...Hal Holbrook
Francisco Higgens ....Nelson Landrieu
Gisela Higgens ....Ivonne Coll
Governor Kinosis ....Lawrence Dane
Jerry Carmichael...Ed Harris
Angelo Bertelli...Larry Marshall
Fielding's Father ....Stanley Anderson
Fielding's Mother ....Patricia Gage
Father Mileski ....John Carroll Lynch
and Bruce Dinsmore (Tony Dayton), Mimi Kuzyk (Adele Green), Tony Calabretta (Sonny Marchi), Walter Massey (Otto Ellis), Philip Williams (Al), Sharon Washington (Kelly), Bill Haugland (TV Newsman at Bombing), Maxine Guess (Danny's Receptionist), Robert Harding (TV Newsman #2), Don Jordan (Minister with Bertelli on TV), Caroline Sabourin (Little Sarah Look-Alike), Norris Domingue (Congressman at Isaac's Party), Dean Hagopian (Politician at Issac's Party), Bernard Behrens (Father Stanton), Ranee Lee (Woman from Fielding's Campaign), Zoë Sakellaropoulo ("Sarah" in Caroline's Flashback), Scott Spencer (Man with Sarah in Flashback), Alan Fawcett (Reporter at Restaurant), Leah Pinsent (Reporter from Fielding's Past), Karina Iraola (Seny), Marco Ledezma (Gustavo), Walt MacPherson (Sarah's Father), Father John Walsh (Protest Leader Outside Sarah's Funeral), Vlasta Vrana (Priest at Sarah's Funeral), Pascal Petardi, Leonardo Fuica, Qariy Hendrickson (Kids Who Mug Fielding), Sandra Caldwell (Concerned Mom from Letter), Justin Bradley (Adopted Kid from Letter), Richard Hicks (Young Man from Letter), Ed Cambridge (Old Man from Letter)

Billy Crudup, Jennifer Connelly

While campaigning for congress, Fielding Pierce begins having visions of the woman he loved and lost in a car bombing years before, leading him to believe that perhaps she had somehow escaped death, an obsession that threatens to destroy his career.

© USA Films

Hal Holbrook, Billy Crudup

HERE ON EARTH

(20TH CENTURY FOX) Producer, David T. Friendly; Executive Producer, Jeffrey Downer; Director, Mark Piznarski; Screenplay, Michael Seitzman; Photography, Michael D. O'Shea; Designer, Dina Lipton; Editor, Robert Frazen; Costumes, Isis Mussenden; Music, Andrea Morricone; Music Supervisor, Dana Millman; Casting, Nancy Foy; a Fox 2000 Pictures presentation of a David T. Friendly production; Dolby; Deluxe color; Rated PG-13; 96 minutes; Release date: March 24, 2000

CAST

Kelley Morse	Chris Klein
Samantha Cavanaugh	Leelee Sobieski
Jasper Arnold	Josh Hartnett
Malcolm Arnold	Michael Rooker
Betsy Arnold	Annie Corley
Earl Cavanaugh	Bruce Greenwood
Jo Cavanaugh	Annette O'Toole
Jennifer Cavanaugh	Elaine Hendrix
John Morse	Stuart Wilson
Robin Arnold	Ronni Saxon

and Maureen O'Malley (Patty), Tac Fitzgerald (Pete), Jessica Stier (Vanessa), Erik Kristofer (Charlie), Zach Fehst (Steve), Michael Piznarski (Albert), Peter Gregory Thomson (Abel Shiverson), Isabell Monk (Judge Maddick), Garth C. Schumacher (Pastor), Chris Carlson (Paramedic), Jack Walsh (Mr. Lackett), Peter Syvertsen (Vin Pemrose), Stephen Yoakam (Dr. Falco), Eden Bodnar (Amanda Fielding), Mary Woolever (Nurse), Barbara Kingsley (Hospital Nurse)

After a car race between Kelley and Jasper causes the destruction of the town diner, the two are forced to spend the summer helping to rebuild the establishment, during which time Kelley finds himself attracted to Jasper's girlfriend, Samantha.

© Twentieth Century Fox

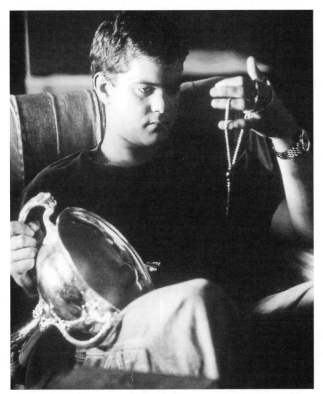

Joshua Jackson

Chris Klein, Leelee Sobieski

THE SKULLS

(UNIVERSAL) Producers, Neal H. Moritz, John Pogue; Executive Producers, William Tyrer, Chris J. Ball, Bruce Mellon; Director, Rob Cohen; Screenplay, John Pogue; Co-Producer, Fred Caruso; Photography, Shan Hurlbut; Designer, Bob Ziembicki; Editor, Peter Amundson; Costumes, Marie-Sylvie Deveau; Music, Randy Edelman; Casting, Mary Vernieu, Anne McCarthy; an Original Film/Newmarket Capital Group presentation of a Neal H. Moritz production; Dolby; Color; Rated PG-13; 106 minutes; Release date: March 31, 2000

CAST

Luke McNamara	Joshua Jackson
Caleb Mandrake	Paul Walker
Will Beckford	Hill Harper
Chloe	Leslie Bibb
Martin Lombard	Christopher McDonald
Detective Sparrow	Steve Harris
Ames Levritt	William Petersen
Litten Mandrake	Craig T. Nelson
Jason Pitcairn	David Asman
Travis Wheeler	Scott Gibson
Dr. Whitney	Nigel Bennett

and Andrew Kraulis (McBride), Derek Aasland (Sullivan), Jennifer Melino (J.J.), Noah Danby (Hugh Mauberson), Mak Fyfe (Laurence Thorne), David Christo (Shawn Packford), Shaw Madison (Chad MacIntosh), Jesse Nilsson (Kent Hodgins), Shawn Mathieson (Jonathan Payne), Steven McCarthy (Sweeney), Matt Taylor (Medic), Henry Alessandroni (Strain), James Finnerty (Preppy Freshman), Cyprian Lerch (Student in Lunch Line), Dominic Kahn (Regatta Judge), Ken Campbell (Starting Judge), Pedro Salvin (Lodge Butler), Derek Boyes (Asst. D.A.), Katherine Trowell (Sanctuary Administrator), Connie Buell (Waitress), Steve Richard (Furniture Mover), Kevin Allen (Sturtevant Security Guard), Paul Walker III (Boxing Coach), Jason Knight (Police Techie), Amanda Goundry (Coed in Caleb's Car), Malin Akerman (Coed in Caleb's Apartment)

College student Luke McNamara and his roommate Will are seduced into joining the Skulls, a secret Ivy League society that offers its inductees the possibility of great power, an offer that seems quite alluring until Will turns up dead.

© Universal Studios

John Cusack, Lili Taylor

John Cusack, Joelle Carter

Jack Black

Jill Peterson, John Cusack, Joan Cusack

Jack Black, Todd Louiso, John Cusack, Lisa Bonet

HIGH FIDELITY

(TOUCHSTONE) Producers, Tim Bevan, Rudd Simmons; Executive Producers, Mike Newell, Alan Greenspan, Liza Chasin; Director, Stephen Frears; Screenplay, D.V. DeVincentis, Steve Pink, John Cusack, Scott Rosenberg; Based upon the novel by Nick Hornby; Co-Producers, John Cusack, D.V. DeVincentis, Steve Pink; Photography, Seamus McGarvey; Designers, David Chapman, Therese Deprez; Editor, Mick Audsley; Costumes, Laura Cunningham Bauer; Music, Howard Shore; Music Supervisor, Kathy Nelson; Casting, Victoria Thomas; a Working Title Films production in association with Dogstar Films/New Crime Productions; Distributed by Buena Vista Pictures; Dolby; Technicolor; Rated R; 114 minutes; Release date: March 31, 2000

John Cusack

CAST

Rob Gordon	John Cusack
Laura	Iben Hjejle
Dick	Todd Louiso
Barry	Jack Black
Marie De Salle	Lisa Bonet
Charlie	Catherine Zeta-Jones
Liz	Joan Cusack
Ian	Tim Robbins
Vince	Chris Rehmann
Justin	Ben Carr
Sarah	Lili Taylor
Penny	Joelle Carter
Caroline	Natasha Gregson Wagner
Alison Jr. High	Shannon Stillo
Rob Jr. High	Drake Bell
Laura's Mom	Laura Whyte
Anaugh	Sara Gilbert
Barry's Customer	Rich Talarico
Beta Band Customer	Matt O'Neill
Middle Aged Customer	Brian Powell
Rob's Mom	Margaret Travolta
Laura's Sister Jo	Jill Peterson
Minister	Dick Cusack
Girl—19 year old	Susan Yoo
Paul	Chris Bauer
Miranda	K.K. Dodds
Alison's Mom	Marilyn Dodds Frank
Kevin Bannister	Duke Doyle
Boy in Park	Aaron Himelstein
Chris Thompson	Jonathan Herrington
Rock Guy	Daniel Lee Smith
Mourners	Leah Gale, David Darlow
Marco	Erik Gundersen
Himself	Bruce Springsteen
Louis	Alex Desert
Man in Store	Alan S. Johnson
Party Guests	Ian Belknap, Andrew Micheli, Polly Noonan, Philip Rayburn Smith, Michele Graff, Susie Cusack
Piano Player	Liam Hayes
Greenday Girl	Damian Rogers
Skateboarder	Robert A. Villanueva
Flea Market Musician	Joe Spaulding
Bartender	Scott A. Martin
Laura's Friend	Heather Norris

Iben Hjejle, John Cusack

When his latest girlfriend takes up with another guy, Rob Gordon, an obsessive music collector and record store owner, looks back on the top five worst break ups of his life.

John Cusack, Jack Black, Todd Louiso, Tim Robbins

PRICE OF GLORY

(NEW LINE CINEMA) Producers, Moctesuma Esparza, Robert Katz, Arthur E. Friedman; Executive Producers, Loretha Jones, Carolyn Manetti, Stephanie Striegel; Director, Carlos Avila; Screenplay, Phil Berger; Co-Executive Producers, Morris Ruskin, Laurie Wagman; Photography, Affonso Beato; Designer, Robb Wilson King; Editor, Gary Karr; Music, Joseph Julian Gonzalez; Music Supervisor, Margaret Guerra Rogers; Costumes, Ruth Carter; Fighter Trainer, Jeff Mulvin; Casting, Rick Pagano; an Esparza-Katz production in association with Arthur E. Friedman Productions; Dolby; Deluxe color; Rated PG-13; 118 minutes; Release date: March 31, 2000

CAST

Arturo Ortega	Jimmy Smits
Rita Ortega	Maria Del Mar
Sonny Ortega	Jon Seda
Jimmy Ortega	Clifton Collins, Jr.
Johnny Ortega	Ernesto Hernandez
Nick Everson	Ron Perlman
Davey Lane	Louis Mandylor
Hector Salmon	Sal Lopez
Mariella Cruz	Danielle Camastra
Pepe	Paul Rodriguez
Young Sonny	Ortega Ulysses Cuadra
Young Jimmy Ortega	Mario Esquivel
Young Johnny Ortega	Gilbert Leal
Chivo	Muni Zano
Marata	Jack Rader
Oscar	Carlos Palomino
Young Arturo Ortega	Matt Cedeno
Mrs. Cruz	Irene De Bari
Luis Cruz	Paco Farias
Little Oscar	Joshua Ponce de Leon
Referee	Jeff Langton
Machado	William Marquez
The Hood	Jose Yenque
Malave	Tony Genaro
Young Hector Salmon	Harley Rodriguez
Azamar	John Verea
Dupree	Patrick Outlaw
TV Announcer	Matthew Kimbrough
Grace Chavez	Michelle Bonilla
Dr. Bill Ward	John La Fayette
Young Rita Ortega	Katrina Gibson
Ring Announcer	Jimmy Lennon, Jr.
Salesman	Tom Simmons
Rex Macon	Craig Love
TV Newscaster	Leyna Nguyen
Priest	John Capodice
Silver Gloves Official	Bill Ryusaki
Angel	Noel Gugliemi
Boxing Official	Clayton Landey
Saraceno	Ernesto Macias
Dr. Cardinal	Zitto Kazann
Ringside Doctor	Larry Strauss

Arturo Ortega, a one-time boxer whose career was unexpectedly interrupted, sees a chance to realize his dream by training his three sons to become championship fighters.

Jon Seda, Jimmy Smits

Jon Seda, Clifton Collins, Jr., Jimmy Smits

Jon Seda

Tulio, Miguel

Chief, Chel

Miguel, Tulio, Chel

Miguel, Tulio

THE ROAD TO EL DORADO

(DREAMWORKS) Producers, Bonne Radford, Brooke Breton; Directors, Erico "Bibo" Bergeron, Don Paul; Executive Producer, Jeffrey Katzenberg; Co-Executive Producer, Bill Damaschke; Screenplay, Ted Elliott, Terry Rossio; Songs, Elton John, Tim Rice; Music Score, Hans Zimmer, John Powell; Designer, Christian Schellewald; Art Directors, Raymond Zibach, Paul Lasaine, Wendell Luebbe; Digital Supervisor, Dan Philips, Senior Supervising Animators, James Baxter, David Brewster, Rodolphe Guenoden, Kathy Zielinski, Frans Vischer, Kristof Serrand; Dolby; Technicolor; Rated PG; 89 minutes; Release date: March 31, 2000

VOICE CAST

Tulio...Kevin Kline
Miguel...Kenneth Branagh
Chel...Rosie Perez
Tzekel-Kan...Armand Assante
Chief...Edward James Olmos
Cortes...Jim Cummings
Altivo..Frank Welker
Zaragoza...Tobin Bell
Acolyte...Duncan Marjoribanks
Kids.....................................Elijah Chiang, Cyrus Shaki-Khan
Narrator...Elton John

A pair of second-rate con men, Tulio and Miguel, travel to the legendary city of gold, El Dorado, where they are proclaimed gods by the High Priest Tzekel-Kan, who hopes to use them as pawns in his attempt to gain power from the chief.

© DreamWorks Pictures

BLACK AND WHITE

(SCREEN GEMS) Producers, Michael Mailer, Daniel Bigel; Executive Producers, Hooman Majd, Ed Pressman, Mark Burg, Oren Koules; Director/Screenplay, James Toback; Line Producer, Jennifer Roth; Associate Producer, Alinur Velidedeoglu; Photography, David Ferrara; Designer, Anne Ross; Editor, Myron Kerstein; Costumes, Jacki Roach; Music Supervisor, Oli "Power" Grant; Casting, Louis DiGiaimo, Stephanie Corsalini; Presented in association with Palm Pictures; Distributed by Sony Pictures Releasing; Dolby; Super 35 Widescreen; Color; Rated R; 100 minutes; Release date: April 5, 2000

Brooke Shields, Elijah Wood, Eddie Kaye Thomas,
Kim Matulova, Method Man

Claudia Schiffer, Allan Houston

CAST

Scotty	Scott Caan
Terry	Robert Downey, Jr.
Sheila	Stacy Edwards
Raven	Gaby Hoffmann
Dean	Allan Houston
Jesse	Kidada Jones
Casey	Jared Leto
Muffy	Marla Maples
Kim	Kim Matulova
Himself	Method Man
Bill King	Joe Pantoliano
Charlie	Bijou Phillips
Rich	Oli "Power" Grant
Cigar	Raekwon
Greta	Claudia Schiffer
Will	William Lee Scott
Sam	Brooke Shields
Mark	Ben Stiller
Marty	Eddie Kaye Thomas
Himself	Mike Tyson
Himself	George Wayne
Wren	Elijah Wood
Themselves	Inspecta Deck, Brett Ratner, Ghostface, Sticky Fingaz, Fredro Starr, Master Killer
Scott	Scott Epstein
Tula	Thaddeus Birkett
Nicky	Chip Banks
Iniko	Hassan Iniko Johnson
Duke	Larry Shaw
Pep	Superb
Tye	Tyrone S. Walker
Richie	Richard Akiva
Victor	Shawn Regtuto
Jus Ske	Justin Ske
Richie V	Richard Voll
Attorney	Steven Beer

and Sabine Lumy, Michelle Dent (Girls in Bed), Frank Pesce (Joey), Richard Ross (Newscaster), Chuck Zito (Chuck), Robert B. Alexander (Darren), Sheila Ball (Sheila), John Bolger (Peter), Joseph Bongiorno (John), Frank Adonis (Frank), Jodi Cohn (Jodi), John Maller (John), Tina Nguyen (Tina), Garry Pastore (Benny Bones), Richard Elms (Driver), Keith Grayson (Krysley), Janine Green (Janine), Cara Hamill (Cara), Katie Hamill (Katie), Michael B. Jordan, Duane McLaughlin. Jade Yorker (Teens), Kristin Klosterman (Christine), Eric Keith McNeil (Combo), Lauren Pratt (Sandy), Shari Raghunati (Shari), Katie Sagona (Katie), Melvin James Shaad (Doorman), Tyree Michael Simpson (Club Security), Patrick Watt (Thomas)

A documentary filmmaker attempts to explore the cultural barriers and interactions between blacks and whites, especially the Caucasian obsession with black hip-hop.

© Screen Gems/Palm Pictures

Power, Raekwon

Stanley Tucci, Ian Holm

Susan Sarandon, Stanley Tucci

JOE GOULD'S SECRET

(USA FILMS) Producers, Charles Weinstock, Elizabeth W. Alexander, Stanley Tucci; Executive Producers, Michael Lieber, Chrisann Verges; Director, Stanley Tucci; Screenplay, Howard A. Rodman; Based on the articles "Professor Seagull" and "Joe Gould's Secret" by Joseph Mitchell; Photography, Maryse Alberti; Designer, Andrew Jackness; Editor, Suzy Elmiger; Costumes, Juliet Polcsa; Music, Evan Lurie; Music Supervisor, Susan Jacobs; Casting, Ellen Lewis, Kathleen Chopin; an October Films presentation of a First Cold Press/Charles Weinstock production; Dolby; DuArt color; Rated R; 104 minutes; Release date: April 7, 2000

CAST

Joe Gould	Ian Holm
Joe Mitchell	Stanley Tucci
Therese Mitchell	Hope Davis
Elizabeth Mitchell	Sarah Hyland
Nora Mitchell	Hallee Hirsh
Sarah	Celia Weston
Harold Ross	Patrick Tovatt
Alice Neel	Susan Sarandon
Vivian Marquie	Patricia Clarkson
Harry Kolis	John Tormey
Chef	Jack O'Connell
Minetta Bartender	Jerry Mayer
Tamar (Hostess)	Nell Campbell
Jack	Ron Ryan
Francis McCrudden	Allan Corduner
Monsieur Gerard	Merwin Goldsmith
Dr. Kim Maxwell	Laura Hughes
Charlie Duell	Steve Martin

and James Hanlon (Mike, Cop at Coffee Shop), David Wohl (Max Gordon), Julie Halston (Sadie Gordon), Aida Turturro (Waitress), Alice Drummond (Helen), Justine Johnson (Mrs. Bagly), Gordon Joseph Weiss (Man at Flophouse), Andrei Belgrader (Teddy), Gabor Morea (Pawnbroker), Ben Shenkman (David), Katy Hansz (Margaret), Mark Cassella (Cop at the Building Site), Harry Bugin (Newsman), Lauren Ward (Anne), Jessica Walling (Betsy), Ted Blumberg (Phil the Writer), Ben Jones (Southern Man at the Party), Peter Francis James (Man at Party), Richard Litt (Bartender), Tom Joseph Foral (Man in Gallery), Leigh Carlson (Janet)

New Yorker reporter Joseph Mitchell befriends and writes a profile of Joe Gould, an eccentric New York vagrant who claims to have written an epic work, "The Oral History of Our Time," the chapters of which are supposedly scattered all over Manhattan.

© USA Films

Patricia Clarkson, Ian Holm

Ian Holm, Allan Corduner, Stanley Tucci

RULES OF ENGAGEMENT

(PARAMOUNT) Producers, Richard D. Zanuck, Scott Rudin; Executive Producers, Adam Schroeder, James Webb; Director, William Friedkin; Screenplay, Stephen Gaghan; Story, James Webb; Co-Producer, Arne Schmidt; Photography, Nicola Pecorini, William A. Fraker; Designer, Robert Laing; Editor, Augie Hess; Costumes, Gloria Gresham; Music, Mark Isham; Stunts, Buddy Joe Hooker; Casting, Denise Chamian; a Richard D. Zanuck/Scott Rudin production, presented in association with Seven Arts Pictures; Dolby; Panavision; Deluxe color; Rated R; 128 minutes; Release date: April 7, 2000

Tommy Lee Jones, Samuel L. Jackson

CAST

Col. Hays Hodges .... Tommy Lee Jones
Col. Terry Childers .... Samuel L. Jackson
Maj. Mark Biggs .... Guy Pearce
Ambassador Mourain .... Ben Kingsley
William Sokal .... Bruce Greenwood
Mrs. Mourain .... Anne Archer
Capt. Lee .... Blair Underwood
Gen. H. Lawrence Hodges .... Philip Baker Hall
General Perry .... Dale Dye
Doctor Ahmar .... Amidou
Capt. Tom Chandler .... Mark Feuerstein
Judge .... Richard McConagle
Colonel Cao .... Baoan Coleman
Hays III .... Nicky Katt
Corporal Hustings .... Ryan Hurst
Harris .... Gordon Clapp
Justin .... Hayden Tank
Jimi .... Ahmed Abounuom
Hodges' Radio Man .... William Gibson
Translator .... Tuan Tran
Lawyer .... John Speredakos
Another Lawyer .... Scott Alan Smith
Little Girl .... Jihane Kortobi
Bailiff—NCO .... David Lewis Hays
Cao's Radio Man .... Peter Tran
Mary Hodges .... Bonnie Johnson
and Jason C. West (Childers' Radio Man), Attifi Mohamed (Tariq), Zouheir Mohamed (Aziz), Chris Ufland (Ambassador Aide), Thom Barry (Chairman Joint Chiefs of Staff), Kevin Cooney (4 Star General), Helen Manning (Sarah Hodges), David Graf (ARG Commander), Conrad Bachmann (Secretary of Defense), Aziz Assimi (Little Boy), Robert Pentz Jr. (Courtroom Spectator), Laird Macintosh (Radio Op), Baouyen C. Bruyere (Col. Cao's Granddaughter), Steven M. Gagnon, Richard F. Whiten, Tom Knickerbocker, Terry Bozeman, Mary Wickliffe, Jody Wood, Elayn Taylor (Jurors), Todd Kimsey, Lawrence Noel Larsen, Stephen Ramsey (Officers), G. Gordon Liddy (Talk Show Host)

Bruce Greenwood

Blair Underwood

Terry Childers, a marine colonel facing trial because of the numerous deaths that occured during a rescue mission at the U.S. Embassy in Yemen, asks that he be represented by Hays Hodges a man of questionable law skills whose life was saved by Childers three decades earlier.

Guy Pearce

Anne Archer, Samuel L. Jackson, Hayden Tank, Ben Kingsley

Robert Loggia, Carroll O'Connor, David Duchovny, Minnie Driver

RETURN TO ME

(MGM) Producer, Jennie Lew Tugend; Executive Producers, C.O. Erickson, Melanie Greene; Director, Bonnie Hunt; Screenplay, Bonnie Hunt, Don Lake; Story, Bonnie Hunt, Don Lake, Andrew Stern, Samantha Goodman; Photography, Laszlo Kovacs; Designer, Brent Thomas; Editor, Garth Craven; Music, Nicholas Pike; Executive Music Producer, Joel Sill; Casting, Mali Finn; a JLT Production; DTS Stereo; Deluxe color; Rated PG; 116 minutes; Release date: April 7, 2000

David Duchovny, Minnie Driver

CAST

Bob Rueland	David Duchovny
Grace Briggs	Minnie Driver
Marty O'Reilly	Carroll O'Connor
Angelo Pardipillo	Robert Loggia
Megan Dayton	Bonnie Hunt
Charlie Johnson	David Alan Grier
Elizabeth Rueland	Joely Richardson
Emmett McFadden	Eddie Jones
Joe Dayton	James Belushi
Sophie	Marianne Muellerleile
Wally Jatczak	William Bronder
Mike	Brian Howe
Jeff	Chris Barnes
Adam Dayton	Adam Tanguay
Karson Dayton	Karson Pound
Tyler Dayton	Tyler Spitzer
Laura Dayton	Laura Larsen
Austin Dayton	Austin Samuel Hibbs
Mr. Bennington	Dick Cusack

and Joey Gian (Singer), Tom Virtue (Dr. Senderak), Holly Biniak (Big Hair), Tamara Tungate (Celia), Kevin Hunt (ER Doctor), Tom Senderak, Jennie Lew Tugend (Paramedics), David Pasquesi (Tony), Claire Lake (ER Nurse), Carol Hunt (Nurse Alice), Patrick Hunt (Danny), Lindsay Allen (Delivery Girl), Don Lake (Transplant Man), Holly Wortell (Marsha), Becky Veduccio (Shari), Peter B. Spector (Valet Guy), Darryl Warren (Father Rudy), Rudy Gabor, William Zirko, Edward Ballog, Angelo Ricco (Italian Singers), Alice Hunt (Nancy), Franklin E. Jones (Chester), Tom Hunt (Tom), Jack Cooper (Ballroom Bartender), Tim O'Malley (Patrick), LaTaunya Bounds (Zebra Girl), Harry Teinowitz (Ice Cream Clerk), Walt Jacobs (M.C.), Alan Gresik's Swing Shift Orchestra (The AG Orchestra), Romano Ghini (Cappucino Man), Gabriella Arena, Paola Sebastiani, Lilliana Vitale (Nuns)

David Alan Grier, David Duchovny

A recent widower, Bob Rueland, finds himself falling in love with Grace Briggs, unaware that Grace's life was saved by a heart transplant due to his late wife.

James Belushi, Bonnie Hunt, Minnie Driver

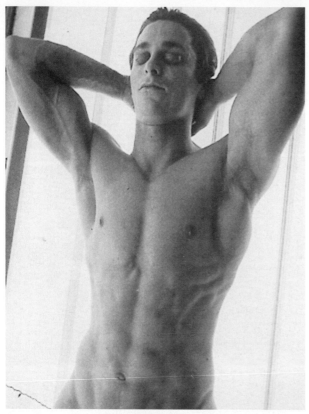

Christian Bale

Christian Bale

AMERICAN PSYCHO

(LIONS GATE) Producers, Edward R. Pressman, Chris Hanley, Christian Halsey Solomon; Executive Producers, Michael Paseornek, Jeff Sackman, Joseph Drake; Director, Mary Harron; Screenplay, Mary Harron, Guinevere Turner; Based on the novel by Bret Easton Ellis; Co-Producers, Ernie Barbarash, Clifford Streit, Rob Weiss; Photography, Andrzej Sekula; Designer, Gideon Ponte; Editor, Andrew Marcus; Costumes, Isis Mussenden; Music, John Cale; Music Supervisors, Barry Cole, Christopher Covert; Casting, Hopkins, Smith & Barden; an Edward R. Pressman production in association with Muse Productions and Christian Halsey Solomon; Dolby; Super 35 Widescreen; Deluxe color; Rated R; 97 minutes; Release date: April 14, 2000

CAST

Patrick Bateman	Christian Bale
Donald Kimball	Willem Dafoe
Paul Allen	Jared Leto
Craig McDermott	Josh Lucas
Courtney Rawlinson	Samantha Mathis
Luis Carruthers	Matt Ross
David Van Patten	Bill Sage
Jean	Chloë Sevigny
Christie	Cara Seymour
Timothy Bryce	Justin Theroux
Elizabeth	Guinevere Turner
Evelyn Williams	Reese Witherspoon
Harold Carnes	Stephen Bogaert
Daisy	Monika Meier
Homeless Man	Reg E. Cathey
Victoria	Marie Dame

and Kelley Harron (Bargirl), Patricia Gage (Mrs. Wolfe), Krista Sutton (Sabrina), Landy Cannon (Man at Pierce & Pierce), Park Bench (Stash), Catherine Black (Vanden), Margaret Ma (Dry Cleaner Woman), Tufford Kennedy (Hamilton), Mark Pawson (Humphrey Rhineback), Jessica Lau (Facialist), Lilette Wiens (Maitre D'), Blair Williams, Glen Marc Silot, Rueben Thompson (Waiters), Charlotte Hunter (Libby), Kiki Buttingnol (Caron), Joyce Korbin (Woman at ATM), Bryan Renfro (Night Watchman), Ross Gibby (Man Outside Store), Christina McKay (Young Woman), Allan McCullough (Man in Stall), Anthony Lemke (Marcus Halberstram), Connie Chen (Gwendolyn Ichiban)

Patrick Bateman, a walking cliche of a 1980s Manhattan yuppie businessman, obsesses with the image of corporate and social perfection to a point where he may or may not have lapsed into a psychotic state, commiting murder to maintain his status.

© Lions Gate Films

Christian Bale, Chloë Sevigny

Christian Bale, Reese Witherspoon, Justin Theroux, Samantha Mathis, Matt Ross

KEEPING THE FAITH

(TOUCHSTONE) Producers, Hawk Koch, Edward Norton, Stuart Blumberg; Executive Producers, Gary Barber, Roger Birnbaum, Jonathan Glickman; Director, Edward Norton; Screenplay, Stuart Blumberg; Photography, Anastas Michos; Designer, Wynn Thomas; Costumes, Michael Kaplan; Editor, Malcolm Campbell; Music, Elmer Bernstein; Casting, Avy Kaufman; a Spyglass Entertainment presentation of a Koch Co./Norton-Blumberg production, a Barber/Birnbaum production; Dolby; Technicolor; Rated PG-13; 127 minutes; Release date: April 14, 2000

Eli Wallach, Anne Bancroft, Ben Stiller, Jenna Elfman

CAST

Jake Schram	Ben Stiller
Father Brian Finn	Edward Norton
Anna Reilly	Jenna Elfman
Ruth Schram	Anne Bancroft
Rabbi Lewis	Eli Wallach
Larry Friedman	Ron Rifkin
Father Havel	Milos Forman
Bonnie Rose	Holland Taylor
Ali Decker	Lisa Edelstein
Rachel Rose	Rena Sofer
Don	Ken Leung
Indian Bartender	Brian George
Debbie	Catherine Lloyd Burns
Ellen Friedman	Susie Essman
Len	Stuart Blumberg

and Sam Goldberg (Jake—Teen), Blythe Auffarth (Anna—Teen), Michael Roma (Brian—Teen), Jonathan Silver (Alan Klein), Brian Anthony Wilson (T-Bone), Juan Piedrahita (Omar), Kelly Deadmon (Woman in Bar), Raphael M. A. Frieder (Cantor), Bodhi Elfman (Casanova), Christopher Gardner, Santi Formosa (Basketball Kids), Francine Beers (Greta Mussbaum), Rena Blumberg (Chaya), Ellen Hauptman (Roz Lentz), Liz Larsen (Leslie), Matt Winston (Matt), Nelson Avidon (Joel), David Wain (Steve Posner), Donna Hanover, Wai Ching Ho (Women in Confessional), Howard Greller (Doctor), Brenda Thomas Denmark (Nurse), Marilyn Cooper ("Don't Walk" Lady), Hawk Koch (Rabbinical Professor), Craig Castaldo (Radio Man), Keith Perry (Old Man Hit with Censor), John Arocho (Bully), Derrick Eason (Co-Worker), Ray Carlson (Monsignor), Barbara Haas (Mother, Synagogue Reception Room), Sunny Keyser, Lorna Lable, Paula Raflo (Mothers), Hillary Brook Canter, Dana Lubotsky, Alexandra Rella (Daughters), Eugene S. Katz (Mohel), Tony Rossi (Hot Dog Vendor), John P. Duffell (Father Duffell), Keith Williams (AIDS Patient)

Ben Stiller, Rena Sofer

Childhood pals, Brian Finn, who has become a priest, and Jake Scharm, who is a rabbi, find themselves competing for the same woman when their long-absent friend Anna Reilly re-enters their lives.

Edward Norton, Jenna Elfman

Ben Stiller, Jenna Elfman, Edward Norton

Sandra Bullock, Viggo Mortensen

Sandra Bullock, Alan Tudyk

28 DAYS

(COLUMBIA) Producer, Jenno Topping; Director, Betty Thomas; Screenplay, Susannah Grant; Photography, Declan Quinn; Designer, Marcia Hinds-Johnson; Editor, Peter Teschner; Music, Richard Gibbs; Music Supervisor, Randall Poster; Co-Producer, Celia Costas; Costumes, Ellen Lutter; Casting, Francine Maisler; a Tall Trees production; Dolby; Deluxe color; Rated PG-13; 103 minutes; Release date: April 14, 2000

CAST

Gwen Cummings...Sandra Bullock
Eddie Boone ....Viggo Mortensen
Jasper ....Dominic West
Lily ....Elizabeth Perkins
Andrea ....Azura Skye
Cornell ....Steve Buscemi
Gerhardt..Alan Tudyk
Oliver ....Michael O'Malley
Roshanda ....Marianne Jean-Baptiste
Daniel ....Reni Santoni
Bobbie Jean ....Diane Ladd
Betty ....Margo Martindale
Evelyn ....Susan Krebs
Guitar Guy ....Loudon Wainwright III
Young Gwen...Katie Scharf
Young Lily..Meredith Deane
Mom ....Elizabeth Ruscio
Aunt Helen..Kathy Payne
Dr. Stavros ....Lisa Sutton
and Joanne Pankow (Saleslady/Night Tech), Corinne Reilly (Vanessa), Andrew Dolan (Groom), Maeve McGuire (Groom's Mother), Jim Moody (Chauffeur), Christina Chang (Bridesmaid), Adam Pervis (Young Boy at Gas Station), Dan Byrd (Older Boy at Gas Station), Ric Reitz (Father at Gas Station), Suellen Yates (Andrea's Mother), Frank Hoyt Taylor (Equine Therapist), Brittani Warrick (Traci), Elijah Kelley (Darnell), Mike Dooly (Marty), Wendee Pratt (Elaine), Bill Anagnos (NY Cabdriver)

Gwen Cummings, a New York writer living in the fast lane, is ordered to spend twenty-eight days at a rehab center after her accessive drinking results in a car accident.

© Columbia Pictures Industries, Inc.

Steve Buscemi, Sandra Bullock

Elizabeth Perkins, Sandra Bullock

Dermot Mulroney, Linda Fiorentino, Paul Newman

Linda Fiorentino, Paul Newman

WHERE THE MONEY IS

(USA FILMS) Producers, Ridley Scott, Charles Weinstock, Chris Zarpas, Christopher Dorr; Executive Producers, Tony Scott, Guy East, Nigel Sinclair, Chris Sievernich, Moritz Borman; Director, Marek Kanievska; Screenplay, E. Max Frye, Topper Lilien, Carroll Cartwright; Story, E. Max Frye; Co-Producer, Beau E.L. Marks; Photography, Thomas Burstyn; Designer, André Chamberland; Costumes, Francesca Chamberland; Editors, Garth Craven, Samuel Craven, Dan Lebental; Music, Mark Isham; Casting, Randi Hiller; a Gramercy Pictures presentation in association with Intermedia Films and Pacifica Film Distribution of a Scott Free/IMF production; Dolby; Deluxe color; Rated PG-13; 89 minutes; Release date: April 14, 2000

Paul Newman

CAST

Henry Manning ....Paul Newman
Carol Ann McKay ....Linda Fiorentino
Wayne McKay ....Dermot Mulroney
Mrs. Foster ....Susan Barnes
Mrs. Tetlow ....Anne Pitoniak
Karl...Bruce MacVittie
Mrs. Galer..Irma St. Paule
Guard..Michel Perron
Mrs. Norton ....Dorothy Gordon
Mrs. Weiler ....Rita Tucket
Kitty..Diane Amos
Cheryl (Wife #2) ....Dawn Ford
Farwell Welk ....T.J. Kenneally
Lloyd the Cop..Roderick McLachlan
Grounds Worker ....Bill Corday
Handyman ....Gordon McCall
and Robert Brewster, Eric Hoziel (Guys), Charles Doucet (Tom), Arthur Holden (Bob), Frank Fontaine (Cop), Richard Jutras (Manager), Janine Theriault (Girl #1), Frankie Faison (Security Guard), Philip Preten (Cop #2), Vlasta Vrana (Jewelry Store Employee), Heather Hiscox (TV Announcer), Michael Brockman (FBI Agent), Emily Wachtel (Waitress), Jayne Eastwood (Connie)

Certain that her patient Henry Manning has faked a stroke to get out of prison, daycare nurse Carol Ann McKay hits on a plan to coax Henry into helping her and her husband plan and pull off a robbery.

© USA Films

Dermot Mulroney, Linda Fiorentino

David Keith

Matthew Settle

Derk Cheetwood

Bill Paxton

Erik Palladino

Thomas Kretschmann

Dave Power

Harvey Keitel

U-571

(UNIVERSAL) Producers, Dino De Laurentiis, Martha De Laurentiis; Executive Producer, Hal Lieberman; Director/Story, Jonathan Mostow; Screenplay, Jonathan Mostow, Sam Montgomery, David Ayer; Photography, Oliver Wood; Designer, Wm. Ladd Skinner, Götz Weidner; Editor, Wayne Wahrman; Costumes, April Ferry; Music, Richard Marvin; Line Producer, Lucio Trentini; Visual Effects Supervisor, Peter Donen; Special Effects Supervisor, Allen Hall; Casting, Carol Lewis; a Studio Canal presentation in association with Dino De Laurentiis; Dolby; Super 35 Widescreen; Deluxe color; Rated PG-13; 116 minutes; Release date: April 21, 2000

T.C. Carson, Will Estes, Matthew McConaughey

CAST

Lt. Andrew Tyler	Matthew McConaughey
Lt. Commander Mike Dahlgren	Bill Paxton
Chief Klough	Harvey Keitel
Lt. Pete Emmett	Jon Bon Jovi
Lt. Hirsch	Jake Weber
Mazzola	Erik Palladino
Ensign Larson	Matthew Settle
Marine Major Coonan	David Keith
Kapitanlieutenant Wassner	Thomas Kretschmann
Wentz	Jack Noseworthy
Eddie	T.C. Carson
Trigger	Thomas Guiry
Tank	Dave Power
Rabbit	Will Estes
Griggs	Derk Cheetwood
Mrs. Dahlgren	Rebecca Tilney
Prudence Dahlgren	Carolyna De Laurentiis
Louise Dahlgren	Dina De Laurentiis
Admiral Duke	Burnell Tucker
Ensign	Rob Allyn
German Chief	Carsten Voigt
Kohl	Gunther Wuerger
German E-Chief	Oliver Stokowski
German Hydrophone Operator	Arnd Klawitter
German Planesman	Kai Maurer
German Engineer	Robert Lahoda
German Lookout	Peter Stark
German Bosun	Erich Redman
Marine Sergeant	Sgt. William John Evans
British Seaman	Robin Askwith
Petty Officer	Jasper Wood
Gunner Officer	Martin Glade
Depth Charge Officer	Oliver Osthus
Other Sergeants	Cpl. John William Falconer, Cpl. Cory Glen Mathews
Mrs. Larson	Valentina Adreatini

Thomas Guiry, Jack Noseworthy, Matthew McConaughey, Jake Weber

During World War II an American submarine crew posing as the enemy boards a German U-boat in order to seize a top secret coding device and find themselves trapped on the foreign sub when their own vessel is destroyed.

2000 Academy Award-winner for Best Sound Editing. This film received an additional Oscar nomination for sound.

© Universal Studios

Matthew McConaughey, Jon Bon Jovi

LOVE AND BASKETBALL

(**NEW LINE CINEMA**) Producers, Spike Lee, Sam Kitt; Executive Producers, Andrew Z. Davis, Jay Stern, Cynthia Guidry; Director/Screenplay, Gina Prince-Bythewood; Photography, Reynaldo Villalobos; Designer, Jeff Howard; Editor, Terilyn A. Shropshire; Music, Terence Blanchard; Music Supervisor, Melodee Sutton; Costumes, Ruth Carter; Casting, Aisha Coley; a 40 Acres and a Mule Filmworks production; Dolby; Fotokem color; Rated PG-13; 124 minutes; Release date: April 21, 2000

CAST

Monica Wright	Sanaa Lathan
Quincy McCall	Omar Epps
Zeke McCall	Dennis Haysbert
Nona McCall	Debbi Morgan
Camille Wright	Alfre Woodard
Nathan Wright	Harry J. Lennix
Lena Wright	Regina Hall
Young Monica	Kyla Pratt
Young Quincy	Glenndon Chatman
Young Lena	Kaykia Harris
Jamal	Jess Willard
Kelvin	Chris Warren, Jr.
Shawnee	Gabrielle Union
Kyra Kessler	Tyra Banks
Felicia	Shar Jackson
Reggie	Charles O'Bannon

and Al Foster (Coach Hiserman), Boris Kodjoe (Jason), Christine Dunford (Coach Davis), Erika Ringor (Sidra O'Neal), April Griffin (Dorsey High School Player), Nathaniel Bellamy (High School Referee #1), Terry Cummings, Chick Hearn, Stu Lantz (Themselves), Jesse Corti (Coach Parra), Leticia Oseguera (Luisa), Kara Brock, Aichi Ali (College Girls), Dion Basco (College Student), Lisa Barkin Oxley (Bank Officer), Rebecca Patterson (Nurse), James Dumont (Reporter), Colleen Matsuhara (UCLA Coach), Andre Bellinger (College Referee), Elimu Nelson (Partygoer), Dick Vitale, Robin Roberts, Trevor Wilson (Themselves), Wendi Levy, Sandra Perez, Carla Houser, Marte Alexander, Sabrina Roberson, Audrey Gomez, Erica Jackson, Valerie Agee (USC Players), Sandra Von Embriqs, Yolanda Higgins (Assistant Coaches), Afton Thompson, Chevana Player, Lorna Monique Clemmons, Carenda Saunder, Chandra Cole, Shawnte Watson, Krystal Braden, Lakesha Willingham, Jenece Johnson, Erika Wilson, Sharon Vigne (Girl's Basketball Team), Major Dennis (Assistant Coach)

Quincy McCall and Monica Wright, who have had a passion for basketball since they were kids, grow into top athletes and, eventually, lovers as they separately pursue their dreams of participating in professional sports.

Omar Epps, Sanaa Lathan

Omar Epps

Sanaa Lathan, Alfre Woodard

Debbi Morgan, Dennis Haysbert

THE VIRGIN SUICIDES

(PARAMOUNT CLASSICS) Producers, Francis Ford Coppola, Julie Costanzo, Dan Halsted, Chris Hanley; Executive Producers, Fred Fuchs, Willi Baer; Director/Screenplay, Sofia Coppola; Based upon the novel by Jeffrey Eugenides; Co-Producers, Fred Roos, Gary Marcus; Photography, Edward Lachman; Designer, Jasna Stefanovic; Editors, Melissa Kent, James Lyons; Costumes, Nancy Steiner; Music, Air (Nicolas Godin, Jean Benoit Dunkel); Music Supervisor, Brian Reitzell; Casting, Linda Phillips-Palo, Robert McGee, John Buchan; an American Zoetrope Production in association with Muse Productions and Eternity Pictures; Dolby; CFI color; Rated R; 97 minutes; Release date: April 21, 2000

CAST

Mr. Lisbon	James Woods
Mrs. Lisbon	Kathleen Turner
Lux Lisbon	Kirsten Dunst
Trip Fontaine	Josh Hartnett
Cecilia Lisbon	Hanna Hall
Bonnie Lisbon	Chelse Swain
Mary Lisbon	A.J. Cook
Therese Lisbon	Leslie Hayman
Dr. Horniker	Danny DeVito
Trip Fontaine '97	Michael Paré
Tim Weiner	Jonathan Tucker
Chase Buell	Anthony DeSimone
Parkie Denton	Noah Shebib
Paul Baldino	Robert Schwartzman
David Barker	Lee Kagan
Peter Sisten	Chris Hale
Dominic Palazzolo	Joe Dinicol
Father Moody	Scott Glenn
Narrator	Giovanni Ribisi
Lydia Perl	Suki Kaiser
Mrs. Scheer	Dawn Greenhalgh
Mr. Scheer	Allen Stewart-Coates
Mrs. Buell	Sherry Miller
Mr. Buell	Jonathan Whittaker
Mrs. Denton	Michele Duquet
Mr. Denton	Murray McRae
Joe Larson	Paul Sybersma
Joe's Mother (Mrs. Larson)	Susan Sybersma
Mrs. Weiner	Roberta Hanley
Trip's Dad	Peter Snider
Donald (Trip's Dad's Friend)	Gary Brennan

and Charles Boyland (Curt Van Osdol), Dustin Ladd (Chip Willard), Kirsten Fairlie (Amy Schraff), Melody Johnson (Julie), Sheyla Molho (Danielle), Ashley Ainsworth (Sheila Davis), Courtney Hawkrigg (Grace), Francois Klanfer (Doctor (Emergency Room)), Mackenzie Lawrenz (Jim Czeslawski), Tim Hall (Kurt Siles), Amos Crawley (John), Andrew Gillies (Principal Woodhouse), Marilyn Smith (Mrs. Woodhouse), John Deans-Buchan (John—Lydia's Boss), Jaya Karsemeyer (Gloria—Reformed Teen), Leah Straatsma (Rannie—Reformed Teen), Marianne Maroney (Teacher intro, Mrs. Woodhouse), Derek Boyes (Football "Grieving Teacher"), Sally Cahill (Mrs. Hedlie), Tracey Ferencz (Nurse), Scott Denton (Mr. O'Connor), Tim Adams (Bozz "Rop" Romano), Joe Roncetti (Kevin Head), Hayden Christensen (Jake Hill Conley), Michael Michaelessi (Park Dept. Foreman), Megan Kennedy (Cheerleader), Sandi Stahlbrand (Meredith Thompson), Neil Girvan (Drunk Man in Pool), Ann Wessels (Woman in Chiffon at Pool), Mark Polley, Kirk Gonnsen (Cemetery Workers), Catherine Swing (Mrs. O'Connor), Sarah Minhas (Wanda Brown)

Tim Weiner looks back on the 1970s when he and his friends were obsessed with the Lisbon Sisters, all of whom left their indelible mark on the boys when circumstances prompted each of them to commit suicide.

© Paramount Classics

Chelse Swain, Kirsten Dunst, Leslie Hayman, A.J. Cook

Kathleen Turner, James Woods

Kirsten Dunst, Josh Hartnett

THE BIG KAHUNA

(LIONS GATE) Producers, Kevin Spacey, Elie Samaha, Andrew Stevens; Executive Producer, Gerard Guez; Director, John Swanbeck; Screenplay, Roger Rueff; Based on his play *Hospitality Suite* ; Photography, Anastas N. Michos; Designer, Kalina Ivanov; Line Producer, Barbara A. Hall; Co-Producer, Joanne Horowitz; Associate Producer, Bernie Morris; Editor, Peggy Davis; Costumes, Katherine Jane Bryant; Music, Christopher Young; Music Supervisors, Anita Camarata, Kaylin Frank; a Franchise Pictures presentation of a Trigger Street production; Dolby; Color; Rated R; 90 minutes; Release date: April 28, 2000

CAST

Larry Mann	Kevin Spacey
Phil Cooper	Danny DeVito
Bob Walker	Peter Facinelli
Bellboy	Paul Dawson

Larry and Phil, a pair of experienced businessmen, join Bob, a young newcomer, at a hotel suite to await the arrival of an important client, leading to a great deal of self-reflection.

© Lions Gate Films

Peter Facinelli, Kevin Spacey

Danny DeVito

Mark Addy, Kristen Johnston, Jane Krakowski, Stephen Baldwin

THE FLINTSTONES IN VIVA ROCK VEGAS

(UNIVERSAL) Producer, Bruce Cohen; Executive Producers, William Hanna, Joseph Barbera, Dennis E. Jones; Director, Brian Levant; Screenplay, Deborah Kaplan, Harry Elfont, Jim Cash, Jack Epps, Jr.; Based on the animated series by Hanna-Barbera Productions, Inc.; Co-Producer, Bart Brown; Photography, Jamie Anderson; Designer, Christopher Burian-Mohr; Editor, Kent Beyda; Costumes, Robert Turturice; Music, David Newman; Song *Viva Rock Vegas* by Doc Pomus and Mort Shuman/performed by Ann-Margret, Alan Cumming; Special Visual Effects/Creature Animation, Rhythm & Hues; a Hanna-Barbera/Amblin Entertainment production; Dolby; Deluxe color; Rated PG; 90 minutes; Release date: April 28, 2000

CAST

Fred Flintstone	Mark Addy
Barney Rubble	Stephen Baldwin
Wilma Slaghoople	Kristen Johnston
Betty O'Shale	Jane Krakowski
Chip Rockefeller	Thomas Gibson
Pearl Slaghoople	Joan Collins
Gazoo/Mick Jagged	Alan Cumming
Colonel Slaghoople	Harvey Korman

and Alex Meneses (Roxie), John Taylor (Keith Rockhard),Tony Longo (Big Rocko), Danny Woodburn (Little Rocko), Taylor Negron (Gazaam/Gazing), Jack McGee, David Jean-Thomas (Bronto Crane Examiners), Brian Coughlin (Bronto Crane Worker), Richard Karron (Bronto Crane), Gary Epp (Dean Agate), Jennifer Simard (Bride-to-Be), Heather McClurg (Tennis Girl), Chene Lawson (Kitty), John Cho (Parking Valet), Nora Burns, Mark Kubr (Party Guests), Cheryl Holdridge-Post (Genvieve), Buck Kartalian (Old Man at Bronton King), Matt Griesser (Booth Worker), Irwin Keyes (Joe Rockhead), Mary Jo Smith (Gambler Woman), Duane Davis (Goon), Kevin Grevioux (Associate Goon), Steven Schirripa (Croupier), John Wills Martin (Casino Security Guard), Lucille M. Oliver (Hotel Worker), Joel Virgil Vierset (Keyboard Player), John Prosky, Rachel Winfree, Ted Rooney, Jim Doughan (Confessors), Jason Kravitz (Choreographer), John Stephenson (Showroom Announcer), Brian Mahoney (Audience Man), Ann Martel Mahoney (Audience Woman), Walter Gertz (Wedding Minister), Beverly Sanders (Photographer), Phil Buckman (Stoney), Jennifer Arden, Jennifer Bachler, Tracie Burton, Teresa Chapman, Jacqueline Case, Betsy Chang, Darlene Dillinger, Kristen Dinsmore, Tracie Hendricks, Helena Hultberg, Katherine Miller, Jessica Page, Kim Timbers-Patteri, Cristal Williams (The Rockettes); William Hanna, Joseph Barbera (Special Appearances); Voices: Mel Blanc (Puppy Dino), Rosie O'Donnell (Octopus Masseuse),

The story of how Fred Flintstone and his best friend Barney Rubble met their future wives, Wilma and Betty, and spent a fun-filled weekend in the prehistoric gambling capital, Rock Vegas. Sequel/prequel to the 1994 Universal release The Flintstones which was also directed by Brian Levant.

© Universal Studios/Amblin Entertainment, Inc.

52

Salma Hayek, Jeanne Tripplehorn

Stellan Skarsgård

TIMECODE

(SCREEN GEMS) Producers, Mike Figgis, Annie Stewart; Director/Story, Mike Figgis; Co-Producers, Dustin Bernard, Gary Scott Marcus; Photography, Patrick Alexander Stewart; Designer, Charlotte Malmlöf; Music, Mike Figgis, Anthony Marinelli; Music Supervisor, Louise Hammar; Casting, Amanda Mackey Johnson, Cathy Sandrich; a Red Mullet production; Distributed by Sony Pictures releasing; Dolby; Color; Rated R; 97 minutes; Release date: April 28, 2000

CAST

Evan Watz	Xander Berkeley
Emma	Saffron Burrows
Rose	Salma Hayek
Therapist	Glenne Headly
Executive	Holly Hunter
Bunny Drysdale	Kyle MacLachlan
Dava Adair	Laurie Metcalf
Joey Z	Alessandro Nivola
Quentin	Julian Sands
Alex Green	Stellan Skarsgård
Lauren Hathaway	Jeanne Tripplehorn
Darren Fetzer	Steven Weber

and Golden Brooks (Onyx Richardson), Viveka Davis (Victoria Cohen), Richard Edson (Lester Moore), Aimee Graham (Sikh Nurse), Andrew Heckler, Daphna Kastner (Auditioning Actors), Holly Houston (Alex's Assistant), Danny Huston (Randy), Patrick Kearney (Drug House Owner), Elizabeth Low (Penny, Evan's Assistant), Mia Maestro (Ana Pauls), Leslie Mann (Cherine), Suzy Nakamura (Connie Ling), Zuleikha Robinson (Lester Moore's Assistant)

Various stories, shown simultaneously on four different parts of the screen, bring together a diverse group of people in Los Angeles in this mostly improvised work.

(top) Salma Hayek; Jeanne Tripplehorn;
(bottom) Stellan Skarsgård; Saffron Burrows and Kyle MacLachlan

Noah Emmerich, Michael Cera, Jim Caviezel

FREQUENCY

(NEW LINE CINEMA) Producers, Hawk Koch, Gregory Hoblit, Bill Carraro, Toby Emmerich; Executive Producers, Robert Shaye, Richard Saperstein; Director, Gregory Hoblit; Screenplay, Toby Emmerich; Photography, Alar Kivilo; Designer, Paul Eads; Editor, David Rosenbloom; Music, Michael Kamen; Costumes, Elisabetta Beraldo; Associate Producer, Patricia Graf; Casting, Amanda Mackey Johnson, Cathy Sandrich; Dolby; Super 35 Widescreen; Deluxe color; Rated PG-13; 117 minutes; Release date: April 28, 2000

CAST

Frank Sullivan	Dennis Quaid
John Sullivan	Jim Caviezel
Jack Shepard	Shawn Doyle
Julia Sullivan	Elizabeth Mitchell
Satch DeLeon	Andre Braugher
Gordo Hersch	Noah Emmerich
Samantha Thomas	Melissa Errico
Johnny Sullivan (6 years)	Daniel Henson
Graham Gibson	Jordan Bridges
Gordo Hersch (8 years)	Stephen Joffe
Commander O'Connell	Jack McCormack
Butch Foster	Peter MacNeill
Gordie, Jr. (10 years)	Michael Cera
Sissy Clark	Marin Hinkle
Chuck Hayes	Richard Sali

and Nesbitt Blaisdell (Fred Shepard), Joan Heney (Laura Shepard), Jessica Meyer (Teenage Runaway), Kirsten Bishopric (Carrie Reynolds), Rocco Sisto (Daryl Adams), Rosemary DeAngelis (Mrs. Finelli), Dick Cavett, Brian Greene (Themselves), Melissa Fitzgerald (Linda Hersch), John DiBenedetto (Con Ed Supervisor), Terry Serpico, Brian Smyj (Con Ed Workers), Nicole Brier (Stoned Teenage Girl), Brantley Bush (Young Intern), David Huband (Lounge Bartender), Timothy Brown (Roof Man Billy), Chuck Margiotta (Pedestal Man Gino), Karen Glave (Lanni DeLeon), Frank McAnulty (Desk Sergeant), Derek Aasland (Stoned Man #1), Jim McAleese (Cozy Bartender), Catherine Burdon, Jennifer Baxter (Young Women), Desmond Campbell (Forensic Tech Hector), Danny Johnson, Colm Magner (Uniformed Cops), Brigitte Kingsley (Bar Waitress), Tucker Robin (Frank, Jr.)

Through a freak occurance caused by electrical static, John Sullivan finds that he is able to jump back in time to 1969 to communicate with his late father through the latter's ham radio kit, leading John to believe that he can keep his dad away from the fire that took his life.

© New Line Cinema, Inc.

Daniel Henson, Dennis Quaid

Elizabeth Mitchell, Andre Braugher

Dennis Quaid

WHERE THE HEART IS

(20TH CENTURY FOX) Producers, Matt Williams, Susan Cartsonis, David McFadzean, Patricia Whitcher; Executive Producers, Carmen Finestra, Rick Leed; Director, Matt Williams; Screenplay, Lowell Ganz, Babaloo Mandel; Based upon the novel by Billie Letts; Photography, Richard Greatrex; Designer, Paul Peters; Costumes, Melinda Eshelman; Editor, Ian Crafford; Music, Mason Daring; Music Supervisor, Lisa Brown; Co-Producers, Gerrit Folsom, Dianne Minter Lewis; Casting, Mali Finn; a Wind Dancer production; Dolby; Deluxe color; Rated PG-13; 120 minutes; Release date: April 28, 2000

Natalie Portman, Ashley Judd

CAST

Novalee Nation	Natalie Portman
Lexie Coop	Ashley Judd
Sister Husband	Stockard Channing
Ruth Meyers	Joan Cusack
Forney Hull	James Frain
Willy Jack Pickens	Dylan Bruno
Moses Whitecotten	Keith David
Mama Lil	Sally Field
Tim	Ray Prewitt
Nicki	Laura House
Rhonda	Karey Green
Girl in Bathroom	Mary Ashleigh Green
Wal-Mart Clerk	Kinna McInroe
Wal-Mart Assistant Manager	Laura Auldridge
Jolene	Alicia Godwin
Sheriff	Dennis Letts
Mr. Sprock	Richard Jones
Mrs. Ortiz	Kathryn Esquivel
Reporter	Mark Mathis
Orderly	John Daniel Evermore

and Linda Wakeman (Hospital Receptionist), David Alvarado (Cellmate), Mark Voges (Religious Man), Angee Hughes (Religious Woman), Todd Lowe (Troy), Margaret Ann Hoard (Mary Elizabeth Hull), Rodger Boyce (Officer Harry), Gabriel Folse (Policeman #2), Mackenzie Fitzgerald (Americus), Natalie Pena (Angela Ortiz), Yvette Diaz (Rosanna Ortiz), TJ McFarland (Ray), Richard Nance (Johnny Desoto), Tony Mann (M.C. of Banquet), John Swasey (Jerry), Scarlett McAlister (Kitty), Kylie Harmon (Praline), Cody Linley (Brownie), Bob Coonrod (Ernie), Heather Kafka (Delphia), Angelina Fiordellisi (Nurse), Cheyenne Rushing (Co-Ed)

Joan Cusack

Dylan Bruno

Novalee Nation, a pregnant teen abandoned by her selfish boyfriend, takes up residence in a Wal-Mart where she gives birth and becomes a celebrity.

© Twentieth Century Fox

Ashley Judd, Natalie Portman, James Frain

Natalie Portman, Stockard Channing

Kristin Scott Thomas, Sean Penn, Anne Bancroft

Kristin Scott Thomas, James Fox

UP AT THE VILLA

(USA FILMS) Producer, Geoff Stier; Executive Producers, Sydney Pollack, Arnon Milchan, Stanley Buchthal; Director, Philip Haas; Screenplay/Editor, Belinda Haas; Based on the novella by W. Somerset Maugham; Co-Executive Producers, Guy East, Nigel Sinclair; Co-Producer, David Brown; Photography, Maurizio Calvesi; Designer/Costumes, Paul Brown; Music, Pino Donaggio; Casting, Celestia Fox; an October Films and Intermedia Films presentation of a Mirage-Stanley Buchthal production; U.S.-British; Dolby; Technicolor; Rated PG-13; 115 minutes; Release date: May 5, 2000

CAST

Mary Panton	Kristin Scott Thomas
Rowley Flint	Sean Penn
Princess San Ferdinando	Anne Bancroft
Sir Edgar Swift	James Fox
Karl Richter	Jeremy Davies
Lucky Leadbetter	Derek Jacobi
Beppino Leopardi	Massimo Ghini
Harold Atkinson	Dudley Sutton
Nina	Lorenza Indovina
Colin Mackenzie	Roger Hammond
Archibald Grey	Clive Merrison
Hilda Grey	Linda Spurrier
Colonel Trail	Ben Aris
Lady Trail	Anne Ridler
Beryl Bryson	Anne Bell
Lulu Good	Barbara Hicks
Peppino	Gianfranco Barra
Isa Mackenzie	Gretchen Given
Dowager	Mary Shipton
Guard	Pierantonio "Noki" Novara

In Florence, Italy, on the eve of World War II, Mary Panton, a recently widowed Englishwoman facing financial hardship, turns to American playboy Rowley Flint for help after a tragedy involving a lovestruck Austrian refugee.

© USA Films

Derek Jacobi, Kristin Scott Thomas

Jeremy Davies, Kristin Scott Thomas

Eva Marie Saint, Kim Basinger

Vincent Perez, Kim Basinger

Garrett Strommen

Liam Aiken, Kim Basinger

I DREAMED OF AFRICA

(COLUMBIA) Producers, Stanley R. Jaffe, Allyn Stewart; Director, Hugh Hudson; Screenplay, Paula Milne, Susan Shilliday; Based upon the book by Kuki Gallmann; Photography, Bernard Lutic; Designer, Andrew Sanders; Editor, Scott Thomas; Music, Maurice Jarre; Costumes, Shirley Russell; Co-Producer, John D. Schofield; Casting, Pat McCorkle, Patsy Pollock; a Jaffilms production; Dolby; Super 35 Widescreen; Technicolor; Rated PG-13; 112 minutes; Release date: May 5, 2000

CAST

Kuki Gallmann..Kim Basinger
Paolo Gallmann...Vincent Perez
Seven Year Old Emanuele..Liam Aiken
Seventeen Year Old Emanuele ....Garrett Strommen
Franca ....Eva Marie Saint
Declan Fielding..Daniel Craig
Simon ....Lance Reddick
Wanjiku ....Connie Chiume
Luka ....James Ngcobo
Mirimuk..Joko Scott
Young Mapengo ....Sabelo Ngobese
Mapengo—Early Teens..Zacharia Phali
Duncan Maitland ....Nick Boraine
Esther Maitland ....Susan Danford
Mike Donovan ....Ian Roberts
Karen Donovan ....Susan Monteregge
Lady Diana Delemere ....Jessica Perritt
Vincenzo..Steven Jennings
Sven...Patrick Lyster

and Winston Ntshona (Old Pokot Chief), John Carson (Pembroke Headmaster), Shannon Esrechowitz (Siri), Michael Brosnihan (14 Year Old Charlie), Theo Landey (21 Year Old Sam), Nick Lorentz (Aiden Whittaker), Valeria Cavalli (Marina), Allison Daugherty (Luciana), Paolo Lorimer (Carlo), Federico Scribani Rossi (Roberto), Sophie Hayden (Gabriella), Giselda Volodi (Rachel), Daniela Foa (Maria), Nathi Khunene, Patrick Bokaba, Dominic Dimba (Bandits), Ernest Ndlovu (Man in Boot), Patrick Mofokeng (Young Police Officer), Kenneth Kambule, Rayburn Sengwayo (Somali Poachers), Emma Vaughan Jones (3 Year Old Sveva), Dixie Cornell (Baby Sveva), Frances Slabolepszy (Hannah Maitland), Frances Nacman (Nurse), Nadine Maharaj (Ema's Friend)

Searching for a change, Kuki Gallmann moves with her husband and son from Italy to the wilds of Africa where she becomes a passionate activist for animal rights.

Forest Whitaker, John Travolta

John Travolta, Kelly Preston

BATTLEFIELD EARTH

(WARNER BROS.) Producers, Elie Samaha, Jonathan D. Krane, John Travolta; Executive Producers, Andrew Stevens, Ashok Amritraj, Don Carmody; Director, Roger Christian; Screenplay, Corey Mandell, J.D. Shapiro; Based on the novel by L. Ron Hubbard; Photography, Giles Nuttgens; Designer/Costumes, Patrick Tatopoulos; Editor, Robin Russell; Music, Elia Cmiral; Visual Effects Supervisor, Erik Henry; Visual Effects, Rhythm and Hues, Gray Matter FX; Co-Producers, Tracee Stanley, James Holt; Casting, Lynn Stalmaster; a Morgan Creek Productions Inc. and Franchise Pictures presentation of a Franchise Pictures-Jonathan D. Krane production-JTP Films production; Dolby; Super 35 Widescreen; Color; Rated PG-13; 117 minutes; Release date: May 12, 2000

CAST

Terl	John Travolta
Jonnie Goodboy Tyler	Barry Pepper
Ker	Forest Whitaker
Carlo	Kim Coates
The Wild Woodsman	Richard Tyson
Chrissy	Sabine Karsenti
Parson Staffer	Michael Byrne
Mickey	Christian Tessier
Sammy	Sylvain Landry
Chirk	Kelly Preston
Processing Clerks	Christopher Freeman, John Topor
Planetship	Shaun Austin-Olsen
Assistant Planetship	Tim Post
Bartender	Earl Pastko
Rock	Michel Perron
District Manager Zeta	Michael MacRae
Psychlo Wrangler	Todd McDougall
Psychlo Hoser	Derrick Damon Reeve
Floyd	Jason Cavalier
Heywood	Sean Hewitt

and Andrew Albert (Labor Supervisor), Alan Legros (Heavy Set Guard), John Topor (One Eyed Guard), Andy Bradshaw (Mason), Jim Meskimen (Blythe), Robert Higden (Supply Clerk), Rejean Denoncourt (Communication Officer), Taft Ruppert (Rodman), Mulumba Tshikuka (Human Pilot), Marie-Josée Croze (Mara), Nadine Corde (Psychlo Babe), Russell Yuen (Speaking Bandit), Andrew Campbell (Leering Grin Bandit), Noel Burton (Clinko)

John Travolta, Barry Pepper

In the distant future when Earth is occupied by the Psychlos, an evil force of giant aliens, Jonnie Goodboy Tyler finds himself captured by the scheming Terl who hopes to use the human species to help him mine gold.

Michael MacRae

HAMLET

(MIRAMAX) Producers, Andrew Fierberg, Amy Hobby; Executive Producers, Jason Blum, John Sloss; Director/Adaptation, Michael Almereyda; Based upon the play by William Shakespeare; Photography, John De Borman; Designer, Gideon Ponte; Line Producer, Callum Greene; Music, Carter Burwell; Music Supervisor, Beth Amy Rosenblatt; Costumes, Luca Mosca, Marco Cattoretti; a Double A Films production; Dolby; Color; Rated R; 112 minutes; Release date: May 12, 2000

Ethan Hawke, Diane Venora, Kyle MacLachlan

CAST

Hamlet	Ethan Hawke
Claudius	Kyle MacLachlan
Gertrude	Diane Venora
Ghost	Sam Shepard
Polonius	Bill Murray
Laertes	Liev Schreiber
Ophelia	Julia Stiles
Horatio	Karl Geary
Marcella	Paula Malcomson
Rosencrantz	Steve Zahn
Guildenstern	Dechen Thurman
Barnardo	Rome Neal
Gravedigger	Jeffrey Wright
Osric	Paul Bartel
Fortinbras	Casey Affleck
Priest	Robert Thurman
Flight Captain	Tim Blake Nelson
Claudius' Bodyguard	John Martin
Blockbuster Clerk	Bernadette Jurkowski
Player King	Robin MacNeil

and D.J. Dara, Sinead Dolan, Paul Ferriter, Larry Fessenden, Sarah Fiol, Tanya Gingerich, Paul Graham, Henry Griffin, India Reed Kotis, Ayun Halliday, Greg Kotis, Barry Manasch, Phillip McKenney, Anne Nixon, Colin Puth, Charles Renfro, Giancarlo Roma, Thomas Roma, Kelly Millicent Sebastien (Special Guest Appearances)

In a modern day take on Shakespeare's classic play, Hamlet broods over the death of his father and the remarriage of his mother to his uncle who has taken control of the powerful Denmark Corporation. Previous screen versions of the play include those starring Laurence Olivier (1948), Richard Burton (1964), Nicol Williamson (1969), Mel Gibson (1990), and Kenneth Branagh (1996).

© Miramax Films

Julia Stiles, Ethan Hawke

Steve Zahn, Dechen Thurman

Bill Murray, Julia Stiles

Amanda Schull, Sascha Radetsky

Zoë Saldana, Ilia Kulik, Sascha Radetsky, Amanda Schull,
Shakiem Evans, Susan May Pratt

Amanda Schull, Ethan Stiefel

CENTER STAGE

(COLUMBIA) Producer, Laurence Mark; Director, Nicholas Hytner; Screenplay, Carol Heikkinen; Photography, Geoffrey Simpson; Designer, David Gropman; Editor, Tariq Anwar; Music, George Fenton; Costumes, Ruth Myers; Co-Producer, Caroline Baron; Choreographer, Susan Stroman; Choreographer of Jonathan's Ballet, Christopher Wheeldon; Casting, Daniel Swee; a Laurence Mark production; Dolby; Panavision; Deluxe color; Rated PG-13; 113 minutes; Release date: May 12, 2000

CAST

Jody	Amanda Schull
Eva	Zoë Saldana
Maureen	Susan May Pratt
Jonathan Reeves	Peter Gallagher
Juliette	Donna Murphy
Nancy	Debra Monk
Cooper	Ethan Stiefel
Charlie	Sascha Radetsky
Sergei	Ilia Kulik
Jim	Eion Bailey
Erik	Shakiem Evans
Audition Teacher	Christine Dunham
Mr. Sawyer	Stephen Stout
Mrs. Sawyer	Maryann Plunkett
Nervous Mother	Laura Hicks
ABA Scouts	Barbara Caruso, Jeffrey Hayenga
Thomas	Victor Anthony
Mother at Audition	Karen Shallo
Eva's Friends	Carlo Alban, Giselle Daly
ABA Girls' Class Teacher	Lisa Leguillo
ABA Pas De Deux Class Teacher	Robert Montano
Anna	Megan Pepin
Emily	Victoria Born
ABA Boys' Class Teacher	Kirk Peterson
Kathleen	Julie Kent
Joan Miller	Elizabeth Hubbard
Gala Patrons	Nancy McDoniel, Sandy Hamilton
ABA Receptionist	Olga Merediz
Salsa Singers	Elvis Crespo, Giselle Tcherniak
Girls at Salsa Club	Jamie Bonelli, Micki Paley
Jim's Friend	Randy Pearlstein
Sergei's Salsa Partner	Nancy Hess

and Sandra Brown, Elizabeth Gaither, Oksana Konobeyeva, Ekaterina Shelkanova (Swan Lake Soloists), Lovette George (Jazz Class Receptionist), Priscilla Lopez (Jazz Class Teacher), Brenda Thomas Denmark (Jonathan's Secretary), Warren Carlyle (Cooper's Assistant), Marcia Jean Kurtz (Emily's Mother), Kari Thompson (Stage Manager), Aesha Ash, Sean Stewart (Jonathan's Ballet Soloists)

ABA Students: Ashley Anderson, Jared Angle, Erin Baiano, Jennifer Balcerzak, Ellen Bar, Tamara Barden, Sant'gria Bello, Dustin Brauneck, Melissa Cabrera, Martine Ciccone, Elena Diner, Nicole Epstein, Alina Faye, Elizabeth Ford, Jason Fowler, Kurt Froman, Kyle Froman, Davena Gross, Natalia Haigler, Craig Hall, Stephen Hanna, Adam Hendrickson, Patrick Howell, Ryan Kelly, Rebecca Krohn, Jessica Kusak, Ryan Lawrence, Riolama Lorenzo, Stephanie Lyons, Deanna McBrearty, Eleena Melamed, Justin Morris, Gillian Murphy, Laura Paulus, Matt Pitcher, Jonathan Porretta, Carrie Lee Riggins, Emilie Schlegel, David Schneider, Chrissy Schultz, Aaron Severini, Kristin Sloan, Jonathan Stafford, Ryan Stewart, Janie Taylor, Pascale Van Kipnis, Jamie Wolf;

Jazz Class Dancers: Julio Augustin, Jim Borstelmann, Liam Burke, Chris Davis, Nina Goldman, Shannon Hammonds, Jack Hayes, Sean Martin Hingston, Joann Hunter, Violetta Klimczewska, Keri Lee, Stephanie Michels, Lisa Nafegar, Michael O'Donnell, Angela Piccinni, Mimi Quillin, John Michael Schert, Lisa Shriver, Scott Taylor, Endalyn Taylor-Shellman, Rocker Verastique, Robert Wersinger

A group of young dancers face various struggles and triumphs during their first year at the American Ballet Academy in New York.

Ethan Stiefel, Amanda Schull, Sascha Radetsky

Elizabeth Hubbard, Ethan Stiefel, Peter Gallagher

Ilia Kulik, Shakiem Evans, Zoë Saldana

Sascha Radetsky

Aladar, Suri, Yar, Plio, Neera

Eema, Url, Aladar, Baylene

Aladar, Kron, Bruton

DINOSAUR

(WALT DISNEY PICTURES) Producer, Pam Marsden; Directors, Ralph Zondag, Eric Leighton; Co-Producer, Baker Bloodworth; Screenplay, John Harrison, Robert Nelson Jacobs; Based on an Original Screenplay by Walon Green; Designer, Walter P. Martishius; Music, James Newton Howard; Editor, H. Lee Peterson; Visual Effects Supervisor, Neil Krepela; Art Director, Cristy Maltese; Digital Effects Supervisor, Neil Eskuri; Story, Thom Enriquez, John Harrison, Robert Nelson Jacobs, Ralph Zondag; Director of Story, Thom Enriquez; Story Artists, Darryl Kidder, Roy Meurin, Frank Nissen, Ray Shenusay, Dick Zondag; Visual Development & Character Designers, Ricardo Delgado, Ian S. Gooding, Mark Hallett, Doug Henderson, David Krentz; Casting, Ruth Lambert, Mary Hidalgo; Distributed by Buena Vista Pictures; Dolby; Technicolor; Rated PG; 82 minutes; Release date: May 19, 2000

VOICE CAST

Aladar

Aladar ....D.B. Sweeney
Plio ....Alfre Woodard
Yar ....Ossie Davis
Zini ....Max Casella
Suri ....Hayden Panettiere
Kron ....Samuel E. Wright
Neera ....Julianna Margulies
Bruton ....Peter Siragusa
Baylene ....Joan Plowright
Eema..Della Reese
and Matt Adler, Sandina Bailolape, Edie Lehmann Boddicker, Zachary Bostrom, Catherine Cavadini, Holly Dorff, Greg Finley, Jeff Fischer, Barbara Iley, David Allen Kramer, Susan Stevens Logan, David McCharen, Tracy Metro, Daran Norris, Bobbi Page, Noreen Reardon, Chelsea Russo, Evan Sabara, Aaron Spann, Melanie Spore, Andrea Taylor, John Walcutt, Camille Winbush, Billy West (Additional Voices)

Aladar, Plio, Eema

Aladar, an orphaned iguanodon raised by a family of lemurs, joins a herd of dinosaurs on a path for a promised paradise after most of the world they know has been devastated by a meteor storm.

© Disney Enterprises

Eema, Aladar, Baylene

Woody Allen, Tracey Ullman

Woody Allen, Michael Rapaport, Jon Lovitz, Tony Darrow

SMALL TIME CROOKS

(DREAMWORKS) Producer, Jean Doumanian; Executive Producer, J.E. Beaucaire; Director/Screenplay, Woody Allen; Co-Executive Producers, Jack Rollins, Charles H. Joffe, Letty Aronson; Co-Producer, Helen Robin; Photography, Zhao Fei; Designer, Santo Loquasto; Editor, Alisa Lepselter; Costumes, Suzanne McCabe; Casting, Juliet Taylor, Laura Rosenthal; a Sweetland Films presentation of a Jean Doumanian production; Dolby; Technicolor; Rated PG; 94 minutes; Release date: May 19, 2000

CAST

Ray Winkler	Woody Allen
Tommy	Tony Darrow
David	Hugh Grant
George Blint	George Grizzard
Benny	Jon Lovitz
May	Elaine May
Denny	Michael Rapaport
Chi Chi Potter	Elaine Stritch
Frenchy Winkler	Tracey Ullman
Candy Salesperson	Carolyn Saxon
Real Estate Agent	Sam Josepher
Dynamite Dealer	Lawrence Levy
Cop	Brian Markinson
TV News Reporter	Dana Tyler
Himself	Steve Kroft
Paul Milton	Brian McConnachie
Winklers' Butler	Riccardo Bertoni
Winklers' Chef	Isaac Mizrahi
Emily Bailey	Kristine Nielsen
Charles Bailey	Larry Pine
Linda Rindelander	Julie Lund

and Diane Bradley, Crystal Field, Cindy Carver, Ray Garvey, Bill Gerber, Olivia Hayman, Laurine Towler, Fanda Nikic (Cookie Store Customers), Teri Black, John Doumanian, Phyllis Burdoe (Winkler Party Guests), Maurice Sonnenberg (Garth Steinway), Richard Mawe (Anthony Gwynne), Karla Wolfangle, Rob Besserer (Modern Dance Performers), Frank Wood (Oliver), Ruth Laredo (Concert Pianist), Julie Halston (Concert Party Guest), Anthony Sinopoli (Frenchy's Chauffeur), Jesse Levy (Church Cellist), Josephine Calabrese, Cindy Wilks, Trevor Moran (Churchgoers), Peter McRobbie, Douglas McGrath (Frenchy's Lawyers), Howard Erskine (Langston Potter), Christine Pipgras, Nick Garfinkle, Kenneth Edelson, Ira Wheeler, William Hill (Potter Party Guests), Ramsey Faragallah (Potters' Waiter), Scotty Bloch (Edgar's Wife), Marvin Chatinover (Dr. Henske)

To cover their intended bank robbery, Ray Winkler and his wife set up a cookie shop as a front, only to have the business unexpectedly take off and turn them into millionaires.

© DreamWorks LLC

Tracey Ullman, Brian Markinson

Hugh Grant, Tracey Ullman

DJ Qualls, Seann William Scott, Breckin Meyer, Paulo Costanzo

Breckin Meyer, Rachel Blanchard

Breckin Meyer, Seann William Scott

ROAD TRIP

(DREAMWORKS) Producers, Daniel Goldberg, Joe Medjuck; Executive Producers, Ivan Reitman, Tom Pollock; Director, Todd Phillips; Screenplay, Todd Phillips, Scot Armstrong; Photography, Mark Irwin; Designer, Clark Hunter; Editor, Sheldon Kahn; Costumes, Peggy Stamper; Music, Mike Simpson; Music Supervisor, Peter Afterman; Casting, Nancy Nayor, Ann Goulder; The Montecito Picture Company presentation of an Ivan Reitman production; Dolby; Technicolor; Rated R; 91 minutes; Release date: May 19, 2000

CAST

Josh	Breckin Meyer
E.L.	Seann William Scott
Beth	Amy Smart
Rubin	Paulo Costanzo
Kyle	DJ Qualls
Tiffany	Rachel Blanchard
Jacob	Anthony Rapp
Earl Edwards	Fred Ward
Barry	Tom Green
Motel Clark	Andy Dick
Ed	Ethan Suplee
French Toast Guy	Horatio Sanz
Tour Group Mom	Rhoda Griffis

and Marla Sucharetza (Sperm Bank Nurse), Ellen Albertini Dow (Barry's Grandma), Edmund Lyndeck (Barry's Grandpa), Jessica Cauffiel (The Wrong Tiffany), Kohl Sudduth (Mark), Wendell B. Harris, Jr. (Professor Anderson), Rini Bell (Carla), Jaclyn DeSantis (Heather), Aliya Campbell (Wendy), Kim Fox (Target Clerk), Patricia Gaul (Cookie Edwards), Richie Dye (Duffy), Mary Lynn Rajskub (Blind Brenda), Tim Ware (Officer Bortz), Julia Wright (Joyce), Paula Claire Jones (Stephanie), Richard Peterson (Michael), Phe Caplan (Boston Coed), Avery Kidd Waddell (Jeff), Omar J. Dorsey (Lawrence), Preston Brant (Chris), Mia Amber Davis (Rhonda), Jimmy Kimmel (Corky the Dog), Bethany Sacks (Lisa), Charlie McWade (Brian), Todd Barry, Bill Rowell (Campus Security), Bill Gribble (Bomb Squad Detective), Guinevere Rodriguez, Al Wiggins, Lisa Chyn, Daniel Taylor, Rachel Marinacci, Bobby Place, Frank Girardeau , Marla Leigh Malcom (Tour Group), Matthew Paul Walsh (Crime Scene Photographer), John Ross Bowie (Waiter), Cristen Coppen (Kim), Cleo King (Woman on Bus), Lori Beth Edgeman, Kellie Garrigan, Rada Phlong, Michael Cornier, Frank Cooper, Mark Bez, Andrew Fowler, Paul Simpson (Party Guests), Raymond DeLoatch, Marc Gordon, Tharon Johnson, Will Aklin, Calvin J. Wilson, Benjamin Booker (Steppers), Bridgett Wise, Aerica D'Amaro (Barry's Girls), Todd Phillips (Foot Lover), Deborah Zoe (E.L.'s Girlfriend), The K.G.B.: Johnny Genius, Moses, Tom Peyton, Ben Kramer, Eric Tobias (Party Band)

Josh and his college friends drive from Ithaca to Austin in an effort to intercept an incriminating video tape that is on its way to Josh's girlfriend.

Mia Amber Davis, DJ Qualls

Tom Cruise, Ving Rhames

MISSION: IMPOSSIBLE 2

(PARAMOUNT) Producers, Tom Cruise, Paula Wagner; Executive Producers, Terence Chang, Paul Hitchcock; Director, John Woo; Screenplay, Robert Towne; Story, Ronald D. Moore, Brannon Braga; Based on the Television Series Created by Bruce Geller; Photography, Jeffrey L. Kimball; Designer, Tom Sanders; Editors, Christian Wagner, Steven Kemper; Costumes, Lizzy Gardiner; Visual Effects Supervisor, Richard Yuricich; Associate Producer, Michael Doven; Music, Hans Zimmer; Mission: Impossible Theme, Lalo Schifrin; Flamenco Choreographer, Antonio Vargas; Casting, Deborah Aquila, Greg Apps, Sarah Halley Finn; Stunts, Brian Smrz; a Cruise/Wagner production; Dolby; Panavision; Deluxe color; Rated PG-13; 126 minutes; Release date: May 24, 2000

Tom Cruise

CAST

Ethan Hunt	Tom Cruise
Sean Ambrose	Dougray Scott
Nyah Hall	Thandie Newton
Luther Strickell	Ving Rhames
Hugh Stamp	Richard Roxburgh
Billy Baird	John Polson
McCloy	Brendan Gleeson
Dr. Nekhorvich	Rade Sherbedgia
Wallis	William Mapother
Ulrich	Dominic Purcell
Michael	Matthew Wilkinson
Boss	Anthony Hopkins
McCloy's Accountant	Nicholas Bell
McCloy's Chemist	Kee Chan
Larrabee	Kim Fleming
Relief Pilot	Dan Luxton
Dr. Gradsky	Christian Manon
Bookie	Lester Morris

and Kelly Ons, Natalie Reis, Nada Rogic, Cristina Brogeras, Adriana Rodriguez, Sandra Rodriguez, Candice Partridge (Flamenco Dancers), Karl McMillan, Alan Lovell, Brett Partridge (Biocyte Security Guards), Nicholas Papademetriou (Prison Guard #2), Daniel Roberts (Co-Pilot), Antonio Vargas (Senor De L'Arena)

Thandie Newton, Dougray Scott

Special Agent Ethan Hunt races against time to retrieve a deadly virus stolen from a Russian biologist by a power-crazed criminal and a pharmaceutical tycoon. Sequel to the 1996 Paramount release Mission: Impossible with Tom Cruise and Ving Rhames reprising their roles.

© Paramount Pictures

Tom Cruise

SHANGHAI NOON

(TOUCHSTONE) Producers, Roger Birnbaum, Gary Barber, Jonathan Glickman; Executive Producers, Jackie Chan, Willie Chan, Solon So; Director, Tom Dey; Screenplay, Alfred Gough, Miles Millar; Co-Producers, Ned Dowd, Jules Daly; Photography, Dan Mindel; Designer, Peter J. Hampton; Editor, Richard Chew; Costumes, Joseph Porro; Music, Randy Edelman; Stunts, Brent Woolsey; Casting, Matthew Barry, Nancy Green-Keyes; a Spyglass Entertainment presentation of a Birnbaum/Barber production in association with a Jackie Chan Films Limited production; Dolby; Panavision; Technicolor; Rated PG-13; 109 minutes; Release date: May 26, 2000

Jackie Chan, Owen Wilson

CAST

Chon Wang	Jackie Chan
Roy O'Bannon	Owen Wilson
Princess Pei Pei	Lucy Liu
Indian Wife	Brandon Merrill
Lo Fong	Roger Yuan
Van Cleef	Xander Berkeley
Imperial Guards	Rong Guang Yu, Cui Ya Hi, Eric Chi Cheng Chen
Wallace	Walton Goggins
Blue	P. Adrien Dorval
Vasquez	Rafael Baez
Hooker in Distress	Stacy Grant
Fifi	Kate Luyben
Andrews	Jason Connery

and Henry O (Royal Interpreter), Russell Badger (Sioux Chief), Simon Baker (Little Feather), Cliff Solomon (Medicine Man), Alan C. Peterson (Saddle Rock Sheriff), Rad Daly (Saddle Rock Deputy), Lee Jay Bamberry, Stephen Strachan, Tim Koetting (Van Cleef Deputies), Rick Ash (Jedadiah), Valerie Planche (Jedadiah's Wife), Tom Heaton (Saloon Bartender), James Baker, Jim Shield, Mike Mitchell, Shayne Wyler (Saloon Gamblers), Ben Salter, Terry King, Michele Fansett (Saddle Rock Townsfolk), Joyce Doolittle, Randy Birch, Andrew Krivanek (Carson City Townsfolk), Christopher Hunt (Apothecary Shopkeeper), Jody Thompson (Margie), Eliza Murbach, Kendall Saunders, Jenafor Ryane (Dream Sequence Hookers), Andrew Bosch, Christy Greene, Brian Gromoff, Jim Finkbeiner (Train Passengers), Chang Tseng (Pei Pei's Father), Sherman Chao (Emperor's Cousin), Regent Or (Emperor), John Heywood, Harold Courchene, George Exelby, John Glawson (Saloon Cowboys), Howard Rothschild (Drunken Doctor), Michael Auger, Stan Isadore, Wacey Labelle, Sam Simon (Chef's Entourage), Tong Lung, Grace Lu, Elise Lew (Chinese Workers), Melvin Skales (Hangman), May Louie, Yeung Kar Kut, Ted Lim, Tik Lun Wong, Kwai Chun Leung, Henry Louie (Opera Performers), Jimmy Carver (Bordello Doorman), Dallas Dorchester, Jason Glass (Blind Drivers), Lisa Stafford (Blonde on Train)

Jackie Chan, Roger Yuan

Chinese Imperial Guard Chong Wang arrives in Wild West America to rescue a kidnapped princess with the reluctant assistant of inept outlaw Roy O'Bannon.

Owen Wilson, Jackie Chan

Lucy Liu, Jason Connery

PASSION OF MIND

(PARAMOUNT CLASSICS) Producers, Carole Scotta, Tom Rosenberg, Ron Bass; Executive Producers, Gary Lucchesi, William Kepper, Ted Tannebaum, Sigurjon Sighvatsson; Director, Alain Berliner; Screenplay, Ron Bass, David Field; Photography, Eduardo Serra; Editor, Anne V. Coates; Music, Randy Edelman; Co-Producer, Andre Lamal; Designer, Pierre-Francois Limbosch; Costumes, Valerie Pozzo Di Borgo; Casting, Deborah Aquila, Sarah Halley Finn; a Lakeshore Entertainment presentation of a Lakeshore Entertainment Production in association with Ron Bass Productions; Dolby; Super 35 Widescreen; Deluxe color; Rated PG-13; 105 minutes; Release date: May 26, 2000

Stellan Skarsgård, Demi Moore

CAST

Marie/Marty ....Demi Moore
William ....Stellan Skarsgård
Aaron ....William Fichtner
Dr. Peters ....Peter Riegert
Jessie ....Sinead Cusack
Jennifer ....Eloise Eonnet
Sarah ....Chaya Cuenot
Kim ....Julianne Nicholson
Dr. Langer ....Joss Ackland
Edward Youngerman ....Gerry Bamman
Danny ....Morgan Hasson
Jean-Pierre ....Hadrian Dagannaud-Brouard
Clerk ....Daniel Hanssens
Girl ....Amanda Spencer

William Fichtner, Demi Moore

A woman who lives two lives, one real and one fantasy, finds herself falling in love with two different men in each of her worlds, a quandry that forces her to seek psychiatric help in hopes of putting an end to her dual lifestyle.

© Paramount Classics

Stellan Skarsgård (back to camera), Chaya Cuenot, Demi Moore, Eloise Eonnet

Nia Long, Jascha Washington, Martin Lawrence

Martin Lawrence

BIG MOMMA'S HOUSE

(20th CENTURY FOX) Producers, David T. Friendly, Michael Green; Executive Producers, Martin Lawrence, Jeffrey Kwatinetz, Rodney Liber, Arnon Milchan; Director, Raja Gosnell; Screenplay, Darryl Quarles, Don Rhymer; Story, Darryl Quarles; Photography, Michael D. O'Shea; Designer, Craig Stearns; Editors, Bruce Green, Kent Beyda; Costumes, Francine Jamison-Tanchuck; Co-Producers, Peaches Davis, David W. Higgins, Aaron Ray; Music Supervisor, Spring Aspers; Music, Richard Gibbs; Special Make-Up Effects Creator, Greg Cannom; Casting, Nancy Klopper; a Regency Enterprises presentation of a David T. Friendly/Runteldat Entertainment production; Dolby; Deluxe color; Rated PG-13; 98 minutes; Release date: June 2, 2000

CAST

Malcolm Turner	Martin Lawrence
Sherry	Nia Long
John	Paul Giamatti
Trent	Jascha Washington
Lester	Terrence Howard
Nolan	Anthony Anderson
Big Momma	Ella Mitchell
Ben	Carl Wright
Sadie	Phyllis Applegate
Miss Patterson	Starletta DuPois
Miss Other Patterson	Jessie Mae Holmes
Lena	Nicole Prescott
Twila	Octavia L. Spencer
Ritha	Tichina Arnold
Reverend	Cedric the Entertainer
Kang	Philip Tan
Basketball Teens	Edwin Hodge, Aldis Hodge
Cazwell	Brian Palermo
Prison Doctor	Brian Paul Stewart
Receptionist	Sarah Zinsser
Cab Driver	Sean Lampkin
Anchorperson	Tony McEwing
Jud	Sean Thibodeau
FBI Agent	Ramsey Luke

and Rosi Rosi, Minnie O. Burton, Rita "Peggy" Fagan-Lewis (Nolan's Volunteers), John Eddins (Police Officer), Louis Archie Shackles, Tameka Holmes (Choir), Ellis Hall (Organist)

In order to trap an escaped con, FBI agent Malcolm Turner sets up a stakeout at the home of a hefty Southern matriarch known as Big Momma, only to discover that he must impersonate the old woman in order to get some information out of the con's ex-girlfriend.

Martin Lawrence, Anthony Anderson

Ella Mitchell, Paul Giamatti

RUNNING FREE

(**COLUMBIA**) formerly *Hoofbeats*; Producer, Jean-Jacques Annaud; Executive Producers, Alisa Tager, Lloyd Phillips; Director, Sergei Bodrov; Screenplay, Jeanne Rosenberg; Story, Jean-Jacques Annaud, Jeanne Rosenberg; Photography, Dan Laustsen; Designer, Wolf Kroeger; Editor, Ray Lovejoy; Costumes, Jo Katsaras-Barklam; Music, Nicola Piovani; Head Animal Trainer, Sled Reynolds; Casting, Janet Meintjies; a Reperage production; Dolby; Widescreen; Deluxe color; Rated G; 81 minutes; Release date: June 2, 2000

CAST

Nyka	Maria Geelbooi
Young Richard	Chase Moore
Boss Man	Jan Decleir
Adult Richard	Arie Verveen
Mine Supervisor	Graham Clarke
Officer	Patrick Lyster
Groom	Morne Visser
Colonel	Daniel J. Robbertse
Boss' Son	Nicholas Trueb
Blacksmith	Robin Smith
Nyka's Friend	Iluce Kgao
Narrator	Lukas Haas

In 1914, a horse, brought to work in an African mining town, is befriended by an orphaned stable boy but must fend for himself when the town's inhabitants are forced to flee due to the encroaching war.

Hamish Linklater, Lola Glaudini

Vince Riverside, Denny Kirkwood

Lucky, Chase Moore

GROOVE

(**SONY PICTURES CLASSICS**) Producers, Danielle Renfrew, Greg Harrison; Executive Producers, Jeff Southard, Michael Bayne; Director/Screenplay/Editor, Greg Harrison; Photography, Matthew Irving; Designer, Chris Ferreira; Costumes, Elizabeth Rodriguez, Kei Hashinoguchi; Music Supervisor, Wade Randolph Hampton; Casting, Maria Ray; a 415 Productions presentation; Dolby; FotoKem Color; Rated R; 84 minutes; Release date: June 9, 2000

CAST

Leyla Heydel	Lola Glaudini
David Turner	Hamish Linklater
Colin Turner	Denny Kirkwood
Harmony Stitts	Mackenzie Firgens
Anthony Mitchel	Vince Riverside
Beth Anderson	Rachel True
Ernie Townsend	Steve Van Wormer
Sgt. Channahon	Nick Offerman
Cliff Rafferty	Ari Gold
Todd Lowman	Angelo Spizzirri
Neil Simonton	Jeff Witzke
Aaron Lubiarz	Bradley Ross
Tobin Claussen	Lew Baldwin
Guy Pritchkin	Dmitri from the Lower Haight (Dimitri Ponce)

and Elizabeth Sun (Maggie McMullen), Chris Ferriera (Bill Neuman), Aaron Langridge (Joe Torres), Jill Jose (Monique Adderly), Chris Stone (Geo Lafont), Karl Ackerman (Shep DeBone), Christoph Klotz (Arty Phipps), Wendy Turner-Low (Lisa Monroe), Bing Ching (DJ Snaz), John Digweed, Forest Green, Monty Luke, Polywog, WishFM (Dance Floor DJ s), Matthew Bernson (Record Store Customer), Jonathan Muller (Crew Member), Eva Christiansen, Sam Trychin (Car Passengers), Jina Park, Jason Zemlicka, Noah Zisman, Sona-Rebecca Klein (Setup Crew), Pete Davison (Cigarette Guy), Brian Behlendorf, No Battles, Shranny (Chill DJ s), Justin Baumrucker (Sticker Kid), Ed Abratowski (Green Haired Guy), Danielle Renfrew (Map Point Betty), Kei Hashinoguchi, Melissa Leebove (Body Painters), Jeffrey Crane (Scammer at Door), Casey Landis, Rob Schroeder (Cops), Matthew Tyreman (Digweed's Roadie), Brian Benson (Toll Booth Operator)

David Turner, a lonely San Francisco writer, is invited by his brother to an all-night rave where he meets up with New York partier Leyla Heydel.

GONE IN SIXTY SECONDS

(TOUCHSTONE) Producers, Jerry Bruckheimer, Mike Stenson; Executive Producers, Jonathan Hensleigh, Chad Oman, Barry Waldman, Denice Shakarian Halicki, Robert Stone, Webster Stone; Director, Dominic Sena; Screenplay, Scott Rosenberg; Based on the motion picture written and directed by Toby Halicki; Photography, Paul Cameron; Designer, Jeff Mann; Costumes, Marlene Stewart; Editors, Tom Muldoon, Chris Lebenzon; Music, Trevor Rabin; Precision Driving Team Coordinators, Bill Young, John McKnight; Casting, Victoria Thomas; Stunts, Chuck Picerni, Jr.; a Jerry Bruckheimer Films presentation; Dolby; Panavision; Technicolor; Rated PG-13; 117 minutes; Release date: June 9, 2000

Nicolas Cage, Giovanni Ribisi

CAST

Randall "Memphis" Raines	Nicolas Cage
Kip Raines	Giovanni Ribisi
Sara "Sway" Wayland	Angelina Jolie
Mirror Man	TJ Cross
Toby	William Lee Scott
Tumbler	Scott Caan
Freb	James Duval
Atley Jackson	Will Patton
Det. Roland Castlebeck	Delroy Lindo
Det. Drycoff	Timothy Olyphant
Donny Astricky	Chi McBride
Otto Halliwell	Robert Duvall
Raymond Calitri	Christopher Eccleston
The Sphinx	Vinnie Jones
Helen Raines	Grace Zabriskie
Kid in Rice Burner	Mike Owen
Blonde in Drag Race	Jaime Bergman
Waitress	Holiday Hopke
Forge	Harry Van Gorkum
Jenny	Grace Una
Cop at Quality Cafe	Jesse Corti
Exotic Car Salesman	Stephen Shellen
DMV Clerk	Alexandra Balahoutis
Car Jacker #1	Rainbow Borden
Worker	Victor Manni
Glass House Guy	Sanjay Pandya
Glass House Girl	Doria Anselmo
Old Woman	Lois Hall
Hype	Dean Rader Duval
Go Cart Kid	C.J. Picerni
Interns	Kevin West, Kevin Weisman
Buddy	Anthony Boswell
Det. Jurgens	Billy Devlin
Fuzzy Frizzel	Bodhi Elfman
James Lakewood	Arye Gross
San Pedro Cop	Greg Collins
Adjacent Mechanic	Cosimo Fusco

Chi McBride, Robert Duvall, Nicolas Cage

and Eddie Mui (Billy Moony), Joseph Patrick Kelly (Snake G.R.A.B.), Scott Burkholder (Rent a Cop), Margaret Kontra Palmer (Televangelist Wife), Charlene Bloom (Swimming Girl), Billy "Sly" Williams (Cop), Alex Walters (Fireman), Lombardo Boyar (Paramedic), Angela Tassoni (Accident Victim), Scott Rosenberg (Private Doctor), Steve Danton (G.R.A.B. Officer #2), Tyler Patton (Security Guard), Carmen Argenziano (Det. Mayhew), Dan Hildebrand (Saul), King Alexander (Bar Dude), Nick Meaney (Thug), Michael A. Pena (Ignacio), Juan Pina (Gang Banger #2), Tim Dezarn (Shotgun Guy), John Carroll Lynch (Impound Manager), Doug Bennett (Wrecker Driver "Mel"), Bob Sattler (C.H.P.)

Master auto thief Memphis Raines is reluctantly drawn back into a life of crime in order to save the life of his younger brother. Remake of the 1974 independent feature that was directed, produced, written by and starred H.B. (Toby) Halicki.

Angelina Jolie, Nicolas Cage

Gloria Reuben, Samuel L. Jackson

Christian Bale, Samuel L. Jackson

SHAFT

(PARAMOUNT) Producers, Scott Rudin, John Singleton; Executive Producers, Adam Schroeder, Paul Hall, Steve Nicolaides; Director, John Singleton; Screenplay, Richard Price, John Singleton, Shane Salerno; Story, John Singleton, Shane Salerno; Based on the novel by Ernest Tidyman, and the MGM motion picture; Photography, Donald E. Thorin; Designer, Patrizia von Brandenstein; Editors, John Bloom, Antonia van Drimmelen; Costumes, Ruth Carter; Co-Producer, Eric Steel; Music, David Arnold; Theme from Shaft by Isaac Hayes; Music Supervisor, Bill Stephney; Stunts, Nick Gillard; Casting, Ilene Starger; a Scott Rudin/New Deal production; Dolby; Panavision; Deluxe color; Rated R; 98 minutes; Release date: June 16, 2000

CAST

John Shaft...Samuel L. Jackson
Carmen Vasquez.....................................Vanessa Williams
Peoples Hernandez.................................Jeffrey Wright
Walter Wade, Jr......................................Christian Bale
Rasaan..Busta Rhymes
Jack Roselli..Dan Hedaya
Diane Palmieri..Toni Collette
(Uncle) John Shaft.................................Richard Roundtree
Jimmy Groves...Ruben Santiago-Hudson
Curt Fleming...Josef Sommer
Carla Howard..Lynne Thigpen
Walter Wade, Sr......................................Philip Bosco
Hon. Dennis Bradford.............................Pat Hingle
Luger..Lee Tergesen
Lt. Kearney...Daniel von Bargen
Lucifer.....................................Francisco "Coqui" Taveras
Alice...Sonja Sohn
Lt. Cromartie...Peter McRobbie
Harrison Loeb.......................................Zach Grenier
Frank Palmieri......................................Richard Cocchiaro
Mike Palmieri..Ron Castellano
Big Raymond...Freddie Ricks
Bonehead..Sixto Ramos
Tattoo..Andre Royo
Dominican...Richard Barboza
Trey Howard...Mekhi Phifer
Cornbread...Gano Grills
Ivy..Catherine Kellner
Uniform Sergeant..................................Philip Rudolph
Mrs. Ann Palmieri.................................Angela Pietropinto
Assistant D.A. Hector Torres................Joe Quintero
Terry..Lanette Ware
Leon..Stu "Large" Riley
and Mark Zeisler (D.A. Andrew Nicoli), Capital Jay (Golem), Bonz Malone (Malik), Ann Ducati (Aunt Toni DeCarlo), Lisa Cooley (News Anchor), John Elsen (Uniform Cop in Metronome), Nadine Mozon (Abused Woman), Lawrence Taylor (Lamont), Caprice Benedetti (Karen), John Cunningham (Judge), Henry G. Thomas, Brian Oswald Talbot, Preston Thomas, Marshall T. Broughton (Malik's Crew), Elizabeth Maresal Mitchell, Scott Lucy (Trey's Friends), Chris Orr, Evan Farmer, Will Chase, Jeff Branson (Walter's Friends), Louie Leonardo, Tony Rhune, Fidel Vicioso (Pistoleros), F. Valentino Morales (Enforcer), Myron Primes, Universal (Young Bloods), Travis Brandon Rosa, Matthew Wallace (Fighting Boys), Luis Torres (Fat Man), John Wojda (Construction Worker), Ahmed Al-Khan, Amer Al-Khan, Rashid Feleyfel (Bystanders at Metronome), Gordon Parks (Lenox Lounge Patron), Gloria Reuben (Sgt. Council)

After New York City detective John Shaft twice arrests spoiled rich kid Walter Wade Jr. for the murder of a young black student, he finds his life in danger by various parties including Dominican drug lord Peoples Hernandez. A continuation of the MGM series that starred Richard Roundtree (Shaft, 1971; Shaft's Big Score, 1972; Shaft in Africa, 1973). Roundtree also appears in this film, as does the director of the first two films, Gordon Parks.

© Paramount Pictures

Samuel L. Jackson, Richard Roundtree, Busta Rhymes

Toni Collette, Samuel L. Jackson

Samuel L. Jackson

Christian Bale, Jeffrey Wright

Ruben Santiago-Hudson, Vanessa Williams, Dan Hedaya, Samuel L. Jackson

Mac, Ginger

Ginger

Nick, Ginger, Fetcher

Rocky (in tub)

The Chickens

Rocky

Mr. Tweedy, Mrs. Tweedy, The Chickens

CHICKEN RUN

(DREAMWORKS) Producers, Peter Lord, David Sproxton, Nick Park; Executive Producers, Jake Eberts, Jeffrey Katzenberg, Michael Rose; Directors/Story, Peter Lord, Nick Park; Screenplay, Karey Kirkpatrick; Photography, Dave Alex Riddett; Line Producer, Carla Shelley; Editor, Mark Solomon; Music, John Powell, Harry Gregson-Williams; Supervising Animator, Loyd Price; Designer, Phil Lewis; Model Production Designer, Jan Sanger; Technical Director, Tom Barnes; Key Animators, Dave Osmand, Merlin Crossingham, Sergio Delfino, Suzy Fagan, Guionne Leroy, Darren Robbie, Jason Spencer-Galsworthy, Jay Grace, Seamus Malone, Ian Whitlock; Casting, Patsy Pollock; an Aardman production, presented in association with Pathé; U.S.-British; Dolby; Technicolor; Rated G; 85 minutes; Release date: June 21, 2000

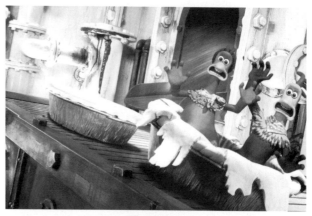

Ginger, Rocky

VOICE CAST

Rocky ....Mel Gibson
Ginger ....Julia Sawalha
Mrs. Tweedy ....Miranda Richardson
Fetcher ....Phil Daniels
Mac ....Lynn Ferguson
Mr. Tweedy...Tony Haygarth
Babs ....Jane Horrocks
Nick ....Timothy Spall
Bunty...Imelda Staunton
Fowler..Benjamin Whitrow

Ginger, a chicken determined to find a way out Tweedy's Egg Farm, sees a ray of hope with the arrival of Rocky, a rooster who claims to know how to fly.

Mac, Ginger, Babs, Bunty

Jim Carrey

ME, MYSELF & IRENE

(20TH CENTURY FOX) Producers, Bradley Thomas, Bobby Farrelly, Peter Farrelly; Executive Producers, Charles B. Wessler, Tom Schulman; Directors, Bobby Farrelly, Peter Farrelly; Screenplay, Peter Farrelly, Mike Cerrone, Bobby Farrelly; Photography, Mark Irwin; Designer, Sidney J. Bartholomew, Jr.; Editor, Christopher Greenbury; Co-Producers, Marc S. Fischer, James B. Rogers, Mark Charpentier; Music, Pete Yorn, Lee Scott; Music Supervisors, Tom Wolfe, Manish Raval; Costumes, Pamela Withers; Casting, Rick Montgomery; a Conundrum Entertainment production; Dolby; Deluxe color; Rated R; 117 minutes; Release date: June 23, 2000

CAST

Charlie Baileygates/Hank Baileygates	Jim Carrey
Irene Waters	Renée Zellweger
Jamaal	Anthony Anderson
Lee Harvey	Mongo Brownlee
Shonté, Jr.	Jerod Mixon
Lieutenant Gerke	Chris Cooper
Whitey	Michael Bowman
Agent Boshane	Richard Jenkins
Colonel Partington	Robert Forster
Officer Stubie	Mike Cerrone
Trooper Finneran	Rob Moran
Dickie Thurman	Daniel Greene
Limo Driver	Tony Cox
Lee Harvey (Age 9)	Andrew Phillips
Jamaal (Age 9)	Jeremy Maleek Leggett
Shonté, Jr. (Age 9)	Justin Chandler

and Zen Gesner (Agent Peterson), Steve Sweeney (Neighbor Ed), Traylor Howard (Layla), Lenny Clarke (Barber Shop Car Owner), Herb Flynn (Herb the Barber), Heather Hodder (Jump Rope Girl), Tracey Abbott (Grocery Store Mom), Jackie Flynn (Trooper Pritchard), Steve Tyler (Maternity Doctor), Googy Gress (Guy on the Street), Joey McGilberry (Helicopter Agent), Sean P. Gildea (Kid's Father), Anna Kournikova (Motel Manager), Mone (Officer Delicato), Richard Tyson (Gun Shop Owner), Dan Murphy (Agent Steve Parfitt), Cam Neely (Trooper Sea Bass), Brian Hayes Currie (Soda Machine Man), Nikkie Tyler Flynn (Trooper Maryann), Mark Leahy (Vermont Police Officer), Kevin J. Flynn (Barber Shop Wiseguy), Conrad Goode (Softball Player), John Mark Andrade (Handsome Barber Shop Guy), Scott T. Neely (Trooper Neely), Shannon Whirry (Beautiful Mom), Jerry Parker (Paramedic), Heather Dyson (Reporter), Christine DiCarlo (TV Reporter), Marc R. Levine (Golfer), John-Eliot Jordan (Pizza Boy), Bob Weekes (Train Conductor), Ezra Buzzington (Disabled Guy), Will Coogan (Disabled Guy's Aide), Rex Allen, Jr. (Narrator)

Charlie Baileygates, a mild-mannered and gullible policeman who is the frequent target of derision and abuse, finally cracks and unleashes Hank, his outspoken and hyper-aggressive alter-ego.

Jim Carrey, Renée Zellweger

Anthony Anderson, Jim Carrey, Jerod Mixon, Mongo Brownlee

Tony Cox, Traylor Howard, Jim Carrey

GETTING TO KNOW YOU

(SUNDANCE CHANNEL) Producers, George LaVoo, Laura Gabbert; Executive Producers, Scott Rosenfelt, Larry Estes, David Skinner; Director, Lisanne Skyler; Screenplay, Lisanne Skyler, Tristine Skyler; Based on three stories ("Getting to Know All About You," "Craps," and "Leila Lee") from *Heat* by Joyce Carol Oates; Co-Producer, Roger Baerwolf; Photography, Jim Denault; Editors, Julie Janata, Anthony Sherin; Music, Michael Brook; Music Supervisor, David Jordan; Line Producer, Per Melita; Designer, Jody Asnes; Costumes, Astrid Brucker; Casting, Jordan Beswick; a ShadowCatcher Entertainment and SearchParty Films presentation of a Gabbert/LaVoo production; Color; Not rated; 91 minutes; Release date: June 28, 2000

CAST

Judith	Heather Matarazzo
Darrell	Mark Blum
Wesley	Zach Braff
Pike	Leo Burmester
Officer Eddie Caminetto	Bo Hopkins
Leila	Mary McCormack
Trix	Bebe Neuwirth
Sonny	Chris Noth
Lamar, Jr.	Jacob Reynolds
Lynn	Sonja Sohn
Bottle Lady	Celia Weston
Jimmy	Michael Weston

and David Aaron Baker (Dr. Clarke), Catherine Anne Hayes (Large Woman), Craig Anthony Grant (Ticket Clerk), Richard Bright (Lotto Man), Tom Gilroy (Jimmy's Father), Tristine Skyler (Irene), Rich T. Alliger (Blackjack Skeptic), Kevin Black (Brady), Dilyn Cassel (Young Mother), Peggy Gormley (Leila's Neighbor), Jonathan Hogan (Trix's Friend)

As sixteen-year old Judith and her brother await their respective buses, they are confronted by a young boy who proceeds to tell them stories of some of the odd characters at the bus station.

© Sundance Channel

Emily Watson, Nick Nolte

Bebe Neuwirth, Mark Blum

TRIXIE

(SONY PICTURES CLASSICS) Producer, Robert Altman; Executive Producer, James McLindon; Director/Screenplay, Alan Rudolph; Story, Alan Rudolph, John Binder; Photography, Jan Kiesser; Designers, Richard Paris, Linda Del Rosario; Editor, Michael Ruscio; Costumes, Monique Prudhomme; Music, Mark Isham, Roger Neill; Casting, Pam Dixon Mickelson; a Pandora presentation of a Sandcastle 5 production; Dolby; Color; Rated R; 117 minutes; Release date: June 28, 2000

CAST

Trixie Zurbo	Emily Watson
Dex Lang	Dermot Mulroney
Sen. Drummond Avery	Nick Nolte
Kirk Stans	Nathan Lane
Ruby Pearli	Brittany Murphy
Dawn Sloane	Lesley Ann Warren
Red Rafferty	Will Patton
Jacob Slotnick	Stephen Lang
Vince Deflore	Mark Acheson
Sid Deflore	Vincent Gale

and Jason Schombing (Ramon), Robert Moloney (Alvin), Troy Yorke (Cleavon Arris), Wendy Noel (Coffee Shop Waitress), David Kopp (Bellboy), Ken Kirzinger (Avery's Bodyguard), Jonathon Young (Gas Attendant), Terence Kelly (Mr. Lang), Karen Elizabeth Austin (Mrs. Lang), Andrew McIlroy (Maitre d'), Dalias Blake, Maria Herrera (Store Guards), Brendan Fletcher (CD Thief), Gina Chiarelli, Stephen E. Miller (Casino Security), Robin Mossley (Casino Pickpocket), Taayla Markell (Casino Call Girl), Michael Puttonen, Kate Robbins (Tourists), Lesley Ewen (Casino Bartender), Darrell Izeard (Casino Guard), Alvin Sanders (Capital Building Custodian), Peter Bryant (Cop #1), Violetta Dobrijevich (Grandma), Rondel Reynoldson (Nurse), Norman Armour (Dr. Gold), Blake Stovin (Valet), Michael Cromien (Legislator on Street), Peter Kufluk (Co-Legislator), Francisco Trujillo (Forum Bartender), Alonso Oyarzun, Tyler Labine, Zak Santiago Alam, Jonathon Sutton (Gang Members), Terry Chen (Waiter), Marke Driesschen, Clay St. Thomas, Claire Riley (Reporters), Raoul Ganeev (Forum Club Chef), Keith Dallas (Detective)

Trixie, an amateur sleuth with a habit of murdering the English language, lands her first big case when she investigates a murder at a casino resort.

© Sony Pictures Entertainment Inc.

THE PATRIOT

Tchéky Karyo, Mel Gibson

Jason Isaacs

Tom Wilkinson

Mel Gibson, Joely Richardson

(COLUMBIA) Producers, Dean Devlin, Mark Gordon, Gary Levinsohn; Executive Producers, William Fay, Ute Emmerich, Roland Emmerich; Director, Roland Emmerich; Screenplay, Robert Rodat; Photography, Caleb Deschanel; Designer, Kirk M. Petruccelli; Editor, David Brenner; Music, John Williams; Costumes, Deborah L. Scott; Co-Producer, Peter Winther; Casting, April Webster, David Bloch; Stunts, R.A. Rondell; a Mutual Film Company production, a Centropolis Entertainment production; Dolby; Panavision; Deluxe color; Rated R; 164 minutes; Release date: June 28, 2000

CAST

Benjamin Martin ....Mel Gibson
Gabriel Martin ....Heath Ledger
Charlotte Selton ....Joely Richardson
Col. William Tavington ....Jason Isaacs
Col. Harry Burwell ....Chris Cooper
Jean Villeneuve...Tchéky Karyo
Rev. Oliver...Rene Auberjonois
Anne Howard ....Lisa Brenner
Gen. Cornwallis..Tom Wilkinson
Dan Scott ....Donal Logue
John Billings...Leon Rippy
Loyalist, Captain Wilkins ....Adam Baldwin
Occam ....Jay Arlen Jones
Peter Howard..Joey D. Vieira
Thomas Martin ....Gregory Smith
Margaret Martin ....Mika Boorem
Susan Martin ....Skye McCole Bartusiak
Nathan Martin ....Trevor Morgan
Samuel Martin ....Bryan Chafin
William Martin ....Logan Lerman
Mrs. Howard ....Mary Jo Deschanel
Captain Bordon ....Jamieson K. Price
Brig. General O'Hara ....Peter Woodward
Redcoat Lieutenant...Grahame Wood
Abigale...Beatrice Bush
Joshua ....Shan Omar Huey
Rollins ....Hank Stone
Skunk ....Kirk Fox
Curly ....Jack Moore
Danvers..Mark Twogood
Colt ....Colt Romberger
General George Washington..Terry Layman
Mrs. Simms ....Shannon Eubanks
Loyalist Simms ....Bill Roberson
Matthew ....Charles Black
and Andy Stahl (General Greene), Kristian Truelsen (Hardwick), Kanin Howell (Postrider), Mark Jeffrey Miller (Wounded Continental), Zach Hanner (British Field Officer), John Curran, Dara Coleman (Redcoat Sergeants), Randall Haynes (Patriot Middleton), John Storey, Greg Good (Cowpens Militiamen), John F. Dzencelowcz II (Continental Soldier), Kyle Richard Engels (Billings' Son), John Bennes (Speaker), Roy McCrerey, P. Dion Moore (Redcoats), Tyler Long (Page Boy), John H. Bush (Abner), Gil Johnson (Militiaman), Scott Miles (Patriot Private), Derrick B. Young (Slave Boy), Le Roy Seabrook (Gullah Minister), Samuel Brown, Jr., Samuel Brown, Sr, Lillie L. Harris, Braima Moiwai (Gullah Musicians), Patrick Tatopoulos (French Naval Officer)

During the American war for independence, former hero of the French and Indian War Benjamin Martin, who has renounced fighting in order to raise his family, finds that he must take up arms again when one of his children is senselessly slaughtered by a British Officer. This film received Oscar nominations for cinematography, sound, and original score.

Logan Lerman, Beatrice Bush, Skye McCole Bartusiak, Mika Boorem, Trevor Morgan, Mel Gibson, Bryan Chafin, Gregory Smith

Mel Gibson, Chris Cooper

Heath Ledger, Mel Gibson

Gregory Smith, Heath Ledger

Heath Ledger

Lisa Brenner

THE ADVENTURES OF ROCKY AND BULLWINKLE

Rene Russo, Jason Alexander, Robert De Niro, Rocky, Bullwinkle

Rene Russo, Robert De Niro, Jason Alexander, Rocky

Rocky, Bullwinkle, Piper Perabo

(UNIVERSAL) Producers, Jane Rosenthal, Robert De Niro; Executive Producers, Tiffany Ward, David Nicksay; Director, Des McAnuff; Screenplay, Kenneth Lonergan; Based on Characters Developed by Jay Ward; Photography, Thomas Ackerman; Designer, Gavin Bocquet; Editor, Dennis Virkler; Co-Producer, Brad Epstein; Music, Mark Mothersbaugh; Executive Music Producer, Joel Sill; Costumes, Marlene Stewart; Visual Effects Producer, Kimberly K. Nelson; Animation Supervisor, David Andrews; Visual Effects Supervisor, Roger Guyett; Casting, Mary Margiotta, Karen Margiotta; a Tribeca Production, presented in association with KC Medien/Capella; Dolby; Deluxe color; Rated PG; 88 minutes; Release date: June 30, 2000

CAST

Natasha Fatale	Rene Russo
Boris Badenov	Jason Alexander
Karen Sympathy	Piper Perabo
Cappy Von Trapment	Randy Quaid
Fearless Leader	Robert De Niro
Rocky	June Foray
Bullwinkle/Narrator	Keith Scott
Minnie Mogul	Janeane Garofalo
P.G. Biggershot	Carl Reiner
Whoppa Chopper Pilot/Ohio Cop with Bullhorn/Jeb	Jonathan Winters
Oklahoma Cop	John Goodman
Lewis	Kenan Thompson
Martin	Kel Mitchell
President Signoff	James Rebhorn
Measures	David Alan Grier
Wossamotta U. President	Norman Lloyd
Schoentell	Jon Polito
Ole	Rod Biermann
Fruit Vendor Twins	Don Novello
Judge Cameo	Whoopi Goldberg
Mattress Salesman	Billy Crystal
General Consternation	John Brandon
General Foods	Harrison Young
General Store	Nigel Gibbs
The Mole	Ed Gale

and Phil Proctor (RBTV Floor Director), Dian Bachar (RBTV Studio Technician), Drena De Niro (RBTV Lackey), Mark Holton (FBI Agent–Potato), Doug Jones (FBI Agent–Carrot), Jane Edith Wilson (FBI Agent–Radish), Lily Nicksay (Sydney), Julia McAnuff (Little Karen), Adam Miller (Little Ole), Steve Rankin (Arrest Cop), Phillip Caruso (Rance), Brian T. Finney (Bailiff), Wesley Mann (Clerk), Jeffrey Ross (District Attorney), Arvie Lowe, Jr (Sharp-Eyed Student), Taraji Henson (Left-Wing Student), T.J. Thyne (Right-Wing Student), Jeremy Maxwell (Angry French Student), Chip Chinery, Ellis E. Williams (Security Guards), David Brisbin (Average Dad), Kristen Lowman (Average Mom), Myrna Niles (Average Grandma), Jack Donner (Average Grandpa), Amanda Brookshire, Patric Brillhart (Average Kids), Jared Doud (Average Teen), Paget Brewster (Jenny Spy), Victor Raider-Wexler (Igor), Robert Bundy, John Campion (Dr. Spies), Max Grodenchik, Eugene Alper (Horse Spies), Alexis Thorpe (Supermodel)

Rocky and Bullwinkle cross from the animated land of Frosbite Falls into the real world in order to put a stop to the villainous Boris and Natasha who, together with criminal mastermind Fearless Leader, are attempting to brainwash the world with Really Bad TV. Based on the animated series that ran on ABC and NBC from 1959 to 1964. June Foray, who did the voice of Rocky for the series, repeats that role for the film.

George Clooney

Mark Wahlberg, George Clooney

The Andrea Gail

Mark Wahlberg

THE PERFECT STORM

(WARNER BROS.) Producers, Paula Weinstein, Wolfgang Petersen, Gail Katz; Executive Producers, Barry Levinson, Duncan Henderson; Director, Wolfgang Petersen; Screenplay, Bill Wittliff; Based on the book by Sebastian Junger; Photography, John Seale; Designer, William Sandell; Editor, Richard Francis-Bruce; Music, James Horner; Costumes, Erica Edell Phillips; Special Visual Effects/Animation, Industrial Light & Magic; Visual Effects Supervisor, Stefen Fangmeier; Stunts, Doug Coleman, Daniel W. Barringer; Casting, Janet Hirshenson, Jane Jenkins; a Baltimore Spring Creek Pictures production in association with Radiant Prods.; Dolby; Panavision; Technicolor; Rated PG-13; 129 minutes; Release date: June 30, 2000

CAST

Billy "Skip" Tyne	George Clooney
Bobby Shatford	Mark Wahlberg
Dale "Murph" Murphy	John C. Reilly
Christine Cotter	Diane Lane
David "Sully" Sullivan	William Fichtner
Michael "Bugsy" Moran	John Hawkes
Alfred Pierre	Allen Payne
Melissa Brown	Karen Allen
Alexander McAnally III	Bob Gunton
Todd Gross	Christopher McDonald
Sgt. Jeremy Mitchell	Dash Mihok
Captain Darryl Ennis	Josh Hopkins
Bob Brown	Michael Ironside
Edie Bailey	Cherry Jones
Irene "Big Red" Johnson	Rusty Schwimmer
Ethel Shatford ("Ma")	Janet Wright
Captain Linda Greenlaw	Mary Elizabeth Mastrantonio

and Todd Kimsey (Lt. Rob Pettit), Chris Palermo (Flight Engineer Borgers), Wiley Pickett (Sgt. Millard Jones), Hayden Tank (Dale Murphy, Jr.), Merle Kennedy (Debra Murphy), Jennifer Sommerfield (Alfred Pierre's Girlfriend), Joseph D. Reitman (Douglas Kosco), Sandy Ward (Quentin), Melissa Samuels (Pam, Todd Gross' Assistant), Steve Barr (Commander Brudnicki), J. Scott Shonka (Communications Officer), Patrick Foley (Falcon Jet Pilot), Lloyd Malone (Falcon Jet Co-Pilot), Billy Mayo (C-130 Pilot), Mark Adams (C-130 Co-Pilot), Tim Trotman (C-130 Navigator), Barry Rutstein (C-130 Engineer), Patrick Stinson, Terry Anzur (TV Newscasters), Katelyn C. Brown, Miles Schneider (Carrot Top Kids), James Lee (Helmsman), Jim Argenbright (Quartermaster), Michael Spaseff (Look-Out)

The true story of how a group of Gloucester fisherman ventured far into the Atlantic ocean to secure a major haul only to find themselves confronted by a fierce storm of unprecedented magnitude. This film received Oscar nominations for visual effects and sound.

© Warner Bros.

Bruce Willis, Spencer Breslin

DISNEY'S THE KID

(**WALT DISNEY PICTURES**) Producers, Jon Turteltaub, Christina Steinberg, Hunt Lowry; Executive Producers, Arnold Rifkin, David Willis; Director, Jon Turteltaub; Screenplay, Audrey Wells; Photography, Peter Menzies, Jr.; Designer, Garreth Stover; Editors, Peter Honess, David Rennie; Costumes, Gloria Gresham; Music, Marc Shaiman; Casting, Marcia Ross, Donna Morong, Gail Goldberg; a Junction Entertainment production; Dolby; Technicolor; Rated PG; 104 minutes; Release date: July 7, 2000

Spencer Breslin, Emily Mortimer

CAST

Russ Duritz	Bruce Willis
Rusty Duritz	Spencer Breslin
Amy	Emily Mortimer
Janet	Lily Tomlin
Deirdre Lafever	Jean Smart
Kenny	Chi McBride
Sam Duritz	Daniel von Bargen
Dr. Alexander	Dana Ivey
Giselle	Susan Dalian
Bob Riley	Stanley Anderson
Kenny's Grandmother	Juanita Moore
Clarissa	Esther Scott
Governor	Deborah May
Newsstand Cashier	Vernee Watson Johnson
Newsstand Tourist	Jan Hoag
Sky King Waitress	Melissa McCarthy
Gloria Duritz	Elizabeth Arlen
Flight Attendant	Alexandra Barreto
Hot Dog Vendor	John Apicella

Lily Tomlin, Spencer Breslin

and Brian McGregor (Vince), Reiley McClendon (Mark), Brian Tibbetts (Herbert), Brian McLaughlin (George), Steve Tom (Lawyer Bruce), Marc Copage (Lawyer Jim), Rod McLachlan (Lawyer Seamus), Scott Mosenson (Wedding Guest), Brian Fenwick (Governor's Aide), Dusan Fager (Governor's Other Aide), Toshiya Agata (Sushi Chef), Joshua Finkel (Josh), Lou Beatty, Jr. (General Manager), E.J. Callahan (Principal), Daryl Anderson (Janet's Husband), Darrell Foster (Best Man), Michael Wajacs (Security Guard), John Travis (Chef Mike), Larry King (Himself), Jeri Ryan, Nick Chinlund (Larry King's Guests), Stuart Scott, Rich Eisen, Harold Greene (Themselves), Kevon Edmonds (Wedding Singer), Julia Waters, Maxine Waters, Stephanie Sprull (Backup Singers), Matthew Perry (Long-Haired Client)

Russ Duritz, a successful image consultant, is confronted by his eight-year-old self, an awkward kid who is no more impressed by his older self than Russ is by the kid who represents everything he's glad he left behind.

Spencer Breslin, Bruce Willis

BUT I'M A CHEERLEADER

(LIONS GATE) Producers, Andrea Sperling, Leanna Creel; Executive Producers, Michael Burns, Marc Butan, Peter Locke, Donald Kushner; Director, Jamie Babbit; Screenplay, Brian Wayne Peterson; Photography, Jules LaBarthe; Designer, Rachel Kamerman; Costumes, Alix Friedberg; Editor, Cecily Rhett; Music, Pat Irwin; Casting, Sheila Jaffe, Georgianne Walken, Julia Kim; an Ignite Entertainment production, in association with the Kushner-Locke Co. and HKM Films; Dolby; Deluxe color; Rated R; 81 minutes; Release date: July 7, 2000

Clea DuVall, Natasha Lyonne

CAST

Megan Bloomfield	Natasha Lyonne
Graham Eaton	Clea DuVall
Mary J. Brown	Cathy Moriarty
Peter	Bud Cort
Nancy	Mink Stole
Mike	RuPaul Charles
Rock Brown	Eddie Cibrian
Dolph	Dante Brasco
Hilary	Melanie Lynskey
Lloyd Morgan-Gordon	Wesley Mann
Larry Morgan-Gordon	Richard Moll
Lipstick Lesbian	Julie Delpy

and Joel Michaely (Joel Goldberg), Kip Pardue (Clayton Dunn), Katrina Phillips (Jan), Douglas Spain (Andre), Katharine Towne (Sinead Laren), Brandt Wille (Jared), Michelle Williams (Kimberly), Ione Skye (Kelly), Katie Donahue, Danielle Reneau (Cheerleaders), Kyle Thatcher (Joel's Father), Robert Pine (Mr. Eaton), Rachelle Carson (Graham's Stepmom), Charles Braden (Bruce)

When high schooler Megan Bloomfield's straight-laced parents suspect her of having lesbian tendencies, they ship her off to a gay rehab camp.

© Lions Gate Films

Carmen Electra

SCARY MOVIE

(MIRAMAX) Producers, Eric L. Gold, Lee R. Mayes; Executive Producers, Brad Grey, Peter Safran, Bo Zenga, Bob Weinstein, Harvey Weinstein, Cary Granat, Peter Schwerin; Director, Keenen Ivory Wayans; Co-Producer, Lisa Suzanne Blum; Screenplay, Shawn Wayans, Marlon Wayans, Buddy Johnson, Phil Beauman, Jason Friedberg, Aaron Seltzer; Associate Producer, Robb Wilson King; Visual Effects Supervisor, Brian Jennings; Photography, Francis Kenny; Editor, Mark Helfrich; Music, David Kitay; Music Supervisor, Michael Dilbeck; Costumes, Darryle Johnson; Casting, Mary Vernieu, Anne McCarthy, Christine Sheaks; a Dimension Films presentation of a Wayans Bros. Entertainment, Gold-Miller, Brad Grey Pictures presentation; Dolby; Super 35 Widescreen; Deluxe color; Rated R; 88 minutes; Release date: July 7, 2000

CAST

Ray	Shawn Wayans
Shorty	Marlon Wayans
Gail Hailstorm	Cheri Oteri
Buffy	Shannon Elizabeth
Cindy Campbell	Anna Faris
Bobby	Jon Abrahams
Greg	Lochlyn Munro
Brenda	Regina Hall
Doofy	Dave Sheridan
Drew Decker	Carmen Electra
Sheriff	Kurt Fuller
Principal Squiggy	David L. Lander

and Frank B. Moore (Not Drew's Boyfriend), Giacomo Baessato, Kyle Graham, Leanne Santos (Trick or Treaters), Mark McConchie (Drew's Dad), Karen Kruper (Drew's Mom), Rick Ducommun (Cindy's Dad), Lloyd Berry (Homeless Man), Matthew Paxman (Annoying Guy), Chris Robson (KOMQ Reporter), Susan Shears, Peter Bryant, Nicola Crosbie, Ian Bliss (Reporters), Andrea Nemeth (Heather), Craig Brunanski (Road Victim), Dan Joffre (Cameraman Kenny), Kelly Coffield (Teacher), Reg Tupper (Beauty Pageant MC), Tanja Reichert (Miss Congeniality), Kendall Saunders (Miss Thing), D.M. Babe Dolan (Grandma), David Neale, Nels Lennarson (Policemen), Chris Wilding (Shorty's Roommate), Trevor Roberts (Dookie), Glynis Davies (Buffy's Mom), Jayne Trcka (Miss Mann), Peter Hanlon (Suicidal Teacher), Ted Cole (Older Man in Theater), Doreen Ramus (Old Lady in Theater), Lee R. Mayes (Amistad II Captain), Mark Hoeppner (Whipmaster), Jessica Van Der Veen (Woman in Theater), Jim Shepard (Young Man in Theater), Marissa Jaret Winokur (Garage Victim), Dexter Bell (Shorty's Friend), Ted Gill (Store Clerk), James Van Der Beek (Guy at Window)

A group of worthless teenagers is stalked by a crazed killer.

© Dimension Films

Hugh Jackman, James Marsden, Patrick Stewart, Halle Berry, Famke Janssen

Anna Paquin, Hugh Jackman

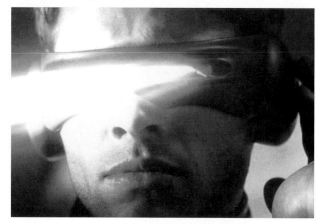

James Marsden

Ray Park

Halle Berry, Tyler Mane

X-MEN

(20TH CENTURY FOX) Producers, Lauren Shuler Donner, Ralph Winter; Executive Producers, Avi Arad, Stan Lee, Richard Donner, Tom DeSanto; Director, Bryan Singer; Screenplay, David Hayter; Story, Tom DeSanto, Bryan Singer; Based upon the Marvel Comics comic book series created by Stan Lee; Photography, Newton Thomas Sigel; Designer, John Myhre; Editors, Steven Rosenblum, Kevin Stitt, John Wright; Co-Producers, Joel Simon, William S. Todman, Jr.; Music, Michael Kamen; Visual Effects Supervisor, Michael Fink; Special Makeup Designer, Gordon Smith; Costumes, Louise Mingenbach; Casting, Roger Mussenden; The Donners' Company/Bad Hat Harry production, presented in association with Marvel Entertainment Group; Dolby; Panavision; Deluxe color; Rated PG-13; 97 minutes; Release date: July 14, 2000

Patrick Stewart, Ian McKellen

CAST

Logan/Wolverine	Hugh Jackman
Professor Charles Xavier	Patrick Stewart
Magneto (Erik Lehnsherr)	Ian McKellen
Jean Grey	Famke Janssen
Cyclops	James Marsden
Storm	Halle Berry
Rogue	Anna Paquin
Sabretooth	Tyler Mane
Toad	Ray Park
Mystique	Rebecca Romijn-Stamos
Senator Robert Kelly	Bruce Davison
Henry Guyrich	Matthew Sharp
Young Magneto	Brett Morris
Magneto's Mother	Rhona Shekter
Magneto's Father	Kenneth McGregor
Rogue's Boyfriend	Shawn Roberts
Rogue's Mother	Donna Goodhand
Rogue's Father	John E. Nelles
Trucker	George Buza
Contender	Darren McGuire
Waterboys	Carson Manning, Scott Leva
Emcee	Aaron Tager
Stu	Kevin Rushton
Bartender	Doug Lennox
Newscasters	David Nichols, Nanette Barrutia-Harrison, Dan Duran, Dave Allen Clark
Stu's Buddy	Malcolm Nefsky
Kitty	Sumela Kay
Bobby	Shawn Ashmore
Jubilee	Katrina Florece
John	Alexander Burton

Halle Berry

and Quinn Wright (Lily Pond Kid), Daniel Magder (Boy on Raft), Matt Weinberg (Tommy), Madison Lanc (Tommy's Sister), Stan Lee (Hot Dog Vendor), Adam Robitel (Guy on Line), Dave Brown (Lead Cop), Ben P. Jensen (Sabretooth Cop), Tom DeSanto (Toad Cop), Todd Dulmage (Coast Guard), Elias Zarou (U.N. Secretary General), David Black (President), Robert R. Snow (Secret Service), David Hayter (Museum Cop), Cecil Phillips (Security Guard), Deryck Blake (Plastic Prison Guard), Ilke Hincer, Ron Sham, Jay Yoo, Gregori Miakouchkine, Eleanor Comes, Guiseppe Gallaccio, Rupinder Brar, Abi Ganem (Translators), Joey Purpura, Manuel Verge, Wolfgang Muller, Ralph Zuljan, Andy Grote (German Soldiers)

Wolverine and Rogue, two "gifted" youngsters with unusual powers, are welcomed into Professor Xavier's school for nuturing their skills, an institution threatened by a U.S. Senator's war on mutants and by Xavier's nemesis, Magneto, who hopes to use his own group of "specialized" students to bring destruction to mankind.

© Twentieth Century Fox

Hugh Jackman, Rebecca Romijn-Stamos

Mike White, Lupe Ontiveros

Beth Colt, Chris Weitz

CHUCK & BUCK

(ARTISAN) Producer, Matthew Greenfield; Executive Producers, Jason Kliot, Joana Vicente; Director, Miguel Arteta; Screenplay, Mike White; Photography, Chuy Chávez; Designer, Renée Davenport; Editor, Jeff Betancourt; Music, Joey Waronker, Tony Maxwell, Smokey Hormel; Co-Producers, Scott M. Cort, Beth Colt; Costumes, Elaine Montalvo; Co-Executive Producers, Thomas Brown, Charles J. Rusbasan, Judith Zarin, Michael Escott; Casting, Meredith Tucker, Miranda Thompson; a Blow Up Pictures presentation of a Flan De Coco film; Dolby; Color; Rated R; 96 minutes; Release date: July 14, 2000.

Mike White, Chris Weitz

CAST

Buck O'Brien ....Mike White
Charlie "Chuck" Sitter ....Chris Weitz
Beverly ....Lupe Ontiveros
Carlyn ....Beth Colt
Sam ....Paul Weitz
Jamila ....Maya Rudolph
Diane ....Mary Wigmore
Barry ....Paul Sand
Tommy ....Gino Buccola
Tommy's Mom ....Annette Murphy
Witch ....Glory Simon
Mark ....Doug Kieffer
Jake ....Jonathan Brown
Dorothy ....Ruthie Bram
Scarecrow ....Giovanni Gieco
Bank Teller ....Linda Lichter
Jolie ....Meredith Tucker
Josh Weintraub ....Zak Penn
Melissa Booth ....Dana Baratta
Buck's Mom ....Pamela Gordon
Pilar ....Josephina J. Rocha
and T.J. Wilkins, Ezra Pugh, Erin Espinoza, Megan McCaw (Theatre Kids), Tony Maxwell, Vince Duffy (Themselves), Jesse Lee Thomas (Young Chuck—Photos), Caleb Wilson (Young Chuck—Film), Nathaniel Olderman (Young Buck), Chuy Chávez, Adam Storms Parker, Paul Gelfman, James Mooney, Damon Huss, Jamie Hook (Actors), Miranda Thompson (Cocktail Waitress), Ron Yerxa (Minister), Yehuda Maayan (Man at Wedding)

After the death of his mother, Buck, a grown man with the emotional maturity of a child, moves to Los Angeles in hopes of re-establishing his childhood friendship with Chuck, a now-successful record producer who feels uncomfortable about Buck's neediness and inability to let go of the past.

Glory Simon, Paul Weitz

LOSER

(COLUMBIA) Producers, Amy Heckerling, Twink Caplan; Executive Producer, John M. Eckert; Director/Screenplay, Amy Heckerling; Photography, Rob Hahn; Designer, Steven Jordan; Editor, Debra Chiate; Music, David Kitay; Music Supervisor, Elliot Lurie; Costumes, Mona May; Casting, Lynn Kressel; a Cockamamie production; Dolby; Deluxe color; Rated PG-13; 95 minutes; Release date: July 21, 2000

Jason Biggs, Mena Suvari

CAST

Paul Tannek	Jason Biggs
Dora Diamond	Mena Suvari
Adam	Zak Orth
Chris	Tom Sadoski
Noah	Jimmi Simpson
Prof. Edward Alcott	Greg Kinnear
Dad	Dan Aykroyd
Gena	Twink Caplan
Sal	Bobby Slayton
Victor	Robert Miano
Annie	Mollee Israel
Homeless Woman	Colleen Camp
Another City Worker	Andy Dick
Panty Hose Customer	Steven Wright

and Brian Backer (Doctor), Meredith Scott Lynn (Dog Loving Girl), Stuart Cornfeld (Foreman), Taylor Negron (Photographer), Andrea Martin (Professor), Scott Thompson (Cell Phone Guy), Kedar Brown (Jay), David Spade (Video Store Clerk), Catherine Black (Military Jacket Girl), Rick Demas (Bouncer), Sanjay Talwar (Convenience Cashier), Tracy Dawson (Drug Saleswoman), Carolyn Goff (Kristen), Mike Beaver (Boy at Concert), Richard Blackburn (Security Guard), Billy Otis (Prisoner), Jenny Kim (Student Worker), Alison Sealy-Smith (University Official), Martin Roach (Veterinarian), Heidi Weeks (Saks Saleswoman), Daniela Olivieri (Store Tailor), Kavita Persaud, Corwin Hall, Andrew Storms, Serena Lea (Hi Ro Students), Nicholas Michael Bacon (Beer Store Clerk), Valerie Boyd, Colleen Reynolds (Aunts), Jack Jessop (Grandfather), Mallory Margel (Paul's Sister), Patrick Mark (Bloody Nose Guy), Tanja Jacobs, Darrin Brown (Party Goers), James Barret (Guy), Robert Tinkler (Bar Patron), Katherine Shekter, Robinne Fanfair, Clare Preuss, Sadie Leblanc, Silvana Kane, Kerri Michalica (College Girls), Geoffrey Antoine (Coffee Counter Guy), Danny Truelove, Marc McMulkin, Jonathon Fernandes, Tiffany Leonardo (Dancing Kids)

Jason Biggs

Paul Tannek, a good-natured scholarship student whose naivete makes him the brunt of abuse among the ultra-cynical denizens at a New York City college, falls for Dora Diamond, who is already having an affair with her English lit professor.

© Columbia Pictures Industries Inc.

Tom Sadoski, Zak Orth, Jimmi Simpson

Mena Suvari, Greg Kinnear

Michelle Pfeiffer, Harrison Ford

Katharine Towne, Michelle Pfeiffer

WHAT LIES BENEATH

(DREAMWORKS/20TH CENTURY FOX) Producers, Steve Starkey, Robert Zemeckis, Jack Rapke; Director, Robert Zemeckis; Screenplay, Clark Gregg; Story, Sarah Kernochan, Clark Gregg; Executive Producers, Joan Bradshaw, Mark Johnson; Photography, Don Burgess; Designers, Rick Carter, Jim Teegarden; Editor, Arthur Schmidt; Costumes, Susie DeSanto; Music, Alan Silvestri; Visual Effects Supervisor, Robert Legato; Casting, Ellen Lewis, Marcia DeBonis; an Imagemovers production; Dolby; Panavision; Technicolor; Rated PG-13; 126 minutes; Release date: July 21, 2000

CAST

Norman Spencer ....Harrison Ford
Claire Spencer ....Michelle Pfeiffer
Jody ....Diana Scarwid
Dr. Drayton ....Joe Morton
Warren Feur ....James Remar
Mary Feur ....Miranda Otto
Madison Elizabeth Frank ....Amber Valletta
Caitlin Spencer ....Katharine Towne
Beatrice ....Victoria Bidewell
Teddy ....Eliott Goretsky
Dr. Stan Powell ....Ray Baker
Elena ....Wendy Crewson
Mrs. Templeton ....Sloane Shelton
Dean Templeton ....Tom Dahlgren
Mrs. Frank...Micole Mercurio
EMT Worker ....Donald Taylor
PhD Students ....Dennison Samaroo, Jennifer Tung,
Rachel Singer, Daniel Zelman

A year after Dr. Norman Spencer has ended an extra-marital affair, his wife Claire begins to experience mysterious voices and visions in their home.

© DreamWorks LLC/Twentieth Century Fox

Michelle Pfeiffer

Diana Scarwid, Michelle Pfeiffer

NUTTY PROFESSOR II: THE KLUMPS

(UNIVERSAL) Producer, Brian Grazer; Executive Producers, Jerry Lewis, Eddie Murphy, Tom Shadyac, Karen Kehela, James D. Brubaker; Director, Peter Segal; Screenplay, Barry W. Blaustein, David Sheffield, Paul Weitz, Chris Weitz; Story, Steve Oedekerk, Barry W. Blaustein, David Sheffield; Photography, Dean Semler; Designer, William Elliott; Editor, William Kerr; Co-Producers, James Whitaker, Michael Ewing; Visual Effects Supervisor, Jon Farhat; Special Makeup Effects, Rick Baker; Costumes, Sharen Davis; Music, David Newman; Music Supervisors, Gary Jones, Happy Walters; Casting, Pamela Basker, Joanne Koehler; an Imagine Entertainment presentation of a Brian Grazer production; Dolby; Deluxe color; Rated PG-13; 106 minutes; Release date: July 28, 2000

Eddie Murphy, Janet Jackson

CAST

Sherman Klump/Buddy Love/ Granny Klump/Mama Klump/ Papa Klump/Young Papa Klump/ Ernie Klump/Lance Perkins	Eddie Murphy
Denise Gaines	Janet Jackson
Dean Richmond	Larry Miller
Jason	John Ales
Denise's Father	Richard Gant
Denise's Mother	Anna Maria Horsford
Leanne Guilford	Melinda McGraw
Ernie Klump, Jr.	Jamal Mixon
Isaac	Gabriel Williams
Restaurant Manager	Chris Elliott
Restaurant Trainee	Duffy Taylor
Dr. Knoll	Earl Boen
Ms. Stamos	Nikki Cox
Claudine	Freda Payne
Old Willie	Sylvester Jenkins
Chantal	Wanda Sykes
Stripper	George King
Preacher	Charles Walker
Bridesmaid	Enya Flack
Party Guest/Bridesmaid	Andrea C. Robinson
Party Guest	Kym E. Whitley
Mrs. Dudikoff	Selma Stern
Receptionist	Julia Schultz
Men in Bathroom	Barry W. Blaustein, David Sheffield
Zeke	Ralph Drischell
Baby Buddys	Myles Mason, Jeffrey Michael Freeman, Maurice Colquitt
Boardroom Members	Bill Applebaum, Harry S. Murphy,

Eddie Murphy

and Tom Jourden (Guy in Elevator), Shawnette Heard, Kelly Konno, Laurie Sposit, Nadine Ellis (Dancers), Kevin Michael Mondane (Buddy at 15), Viola Kates Stimpson (Sweet Old Lady), Naomi Kale (Buxom Student), Kente Scott (Fraternity Student), Justin Urich (Lecture Student), Sonya Eddy (Heavyset Woman), James D. Brubaker (Krusty Reporter), Richie Palmer (Cab Driver), Charles Napier (Four Star General), Steve Kehela, Miguel A. Nunez, Jr. (Scientists), Renee Tenison (Dog Owner), Richard Saxton (American Newscaster), Peter Segal, William Kerr (Scared Popcorn Men), Michael Ewing (Hot Dog Vendor), Nicole Segal (Scared Little Girl)

Professor Sherman Klump, determined to rid himself of his alter-ego, Buddy Love, experiments with extracting Buddy's DNA from his system, only to have the randy troublemaker show up full-bodied and determined to get his hands on Klump's revolutionary youth serum. Sequel to the 1996 Universal film The Nutty Professor with Eddie Murphy, Larry Miller, John Ales, and Jamal Mixon repeating their roles.

Jamal Mixon, Eddie Murphy, Eddie Murphy, Eddie Murphy, Eddie Murphy, Eddie Murphy

Piper Perabo, Adam Garcia

LeAnn Rimes, Piper Perabo

COYOTE UGLY

(TOUCHSTONE) Producers, Jerry Bruckheimer, Chad Oman; Executive Producers, Mike Stenson, Scott Gardenhour; Director, David McNally; Screenplay, Gina Wendkos; Photography, Amir Mokri; Designer, Jon Hutman; Editor, William Goldenberg; Costumes, Marlene Stewart; Music, Trevor Horn; Music Supervisors, Kathy Nelson, Bob Badami; Choreographer, Travis Payne; Casting, Bonnie Timmerman; a Jerry Bruckheimer Films presentation; Dolby; Panavision; Technicolor; Rated PG-13; 100 minutes; Release date: August 4, 2000

CAST

Violet Sanford	Piper Perabo
Kevin O'Donnell	Adam Garcia
Lil	Maria Bello
Gloria	Melanie Lynskey
Cammie	Izabella Miko
Rachel	Bridget Moynahan
Zoe	Tyra Banks
Lou	Del Pentecost
Danny	Michael Weston
Bill Sanford	John Goodman
Herself	LeAnn Rimes
Romero	Bud Cort

and Jeremy Rowley (William Morris Receptionist), Ellen Cleghorne (Music Publishing Receptionist), John Fugelsang (Richie the Booker), Grant Tuskerud, Eddie Anisko, Jason Jacobs, Patrick Yonally (Finale Club Lead-In Band), Robert Ahlers, Orlando Sims, Barry Michael Duff, William Ritter III, Chanda Bailey (Finale Club Back-Up Musicians), Freeze Luv (Fiji Mermaid Club Bouncer), Alex Band, Miles Mosley, Aaron Kamin, Vic Vanacore (Fiji Mermaid Club Band), Greg Pitts (Fiji Mermaid Waiter), Whitney Dylan (Fiji Mermaid Worker), Marvin Krueger (Surgeon), Victor Argo (Pete), Peter Appel, John Mondin (Pizza Customers), Frank Medrano (Walt), Elizabeth Beckwith (Office Receptionist), Diane Hudock (Open Mic Woman), Tara McLean (Open Mic Singer), Eric Ritter, Thomas R. Martin (Audience Members), Ken Campbell (Biker), Jorgen De Mey (Coyote Ugly Customer), Jimmy Shubert, Greg Ginther (Coyote Ugly Drunks), Jeff Michalski (Fire Marshal), Kaitlin Olsen, Jennifer Jean, Susan Yeagley, Jill Gettelson (Bidding Customers), Jack McGee (Pitcher), Paul Davis-Miller (Sam Ash Salesman), Johnny Zander (Roy the Busboy), Wali Collins (Critch), Scott Russo, Rob Brewer, Steve Morris, Wade Youman, Patrick Kim (Elbow Room Band Members), Natasha Reulet, Sarah Morris, Jennifer Day, Nava Plotsky, Alicia Sorell, Jennifer Manalo (Girls at the Surprise Party), Nicole Ghastin (Lyndsay Morgan), Jonathan Klein (Manager), Alexandra Balahoutis (Hostess), Johnny Knoxville, Chris Wylde (College Guys), Mandy Amano, Carla Alaponte, Stephanie Hodge, Allison Ford, Kathy Nowrey (Dancing Girls in Bar), Michael Bay (Photographer), Chip Chinery, Nick Vallelonga (Cops), Joseph Patrick Kelly, Greg Collins (Coyote Ugly Bar Patrons), Stephen Snedden (Customer—Fancy Drinks), Chris Soldevilla (Man Ordering Shots), Joseph Bucaro III, James T. Sale (Finale Club Drunks), Heather Shannon Ryan (Sorority Girl), Biljana Filipovic (Bar Fight Girlfriend)

Violet Sanford moves to New York to pursue her dream of becoming a songwriter only to find herself tending bar at the hottest, sexiest waterhole in town, the Coyote Ugly.

© Touchstone Pictures/Jerry Bruckheimer Inc.

(clockwise from center) Piper Perabo, Tyra Banks, Maria Bello, Bridget Moynahan, Izabella Miko

John Goodman, Piper Perabo

HOLLOW MAN

Kevin Bacon, Josh Brolin, Elisabeth Shue, Greg Grunberg

(COLUMBIA) Producers, Douglas Wick, Alan Marshall; Executive Producer, Marion Rosenberg; Director, Paul Verhoeven; Screenplay, Andrew W. Marlowe; Story, Gary Scott Thompson, Andrew W. Marlowe; Photography, Jost Vacano; Designer, Allan Cameron; Editor, Mark Goldblatt; Music, Jerry Goldsmith; Co-Producer, Stacy Lumbrezer; Costumes, Ellen Mirojnick; Senior Visual Effects Supervisor, Scott E. Anderson; Special Visual Effects, Sony Pictures Imageworks, Inc., Tippett Studio; Computer Graphics Imagery and Video Display, Banned from the Ranch Entertainment; Make-Up Effects Designers and Creators, Alec Gillis, Tom Woodruff, Jr.; Casting, Howard Feuer; a Douglas Wick production; Dolby; Deluxe color; Rated R; 114 minutes; Release date: August 4, 2000

CAST

Linda McKay	Elisabeth Shue
Sebastian Caine	Kevin Bacon
Matthew Kensington	Josh Brolin
Sarah Kennedy	Kim Dickens
Carter Abbey	Greg Grunberg
Frank Chase	Joey Slotnick
Janice Walton	Mary Randle
Dr. Kramer	William Devane
Sebastian's Neighbor	Rhona Mitra
Warehouse Guard	Pablo Espinosa
Mrs. Kramer	Margot Rose
Wino	Jimmie F. Skaggs
Boy in Car	Jeffrey George Scaperotta
Girl in Car	Sarah Bowles
Mom	Kelli Scott
Dad	Steve Altes
General Caster	J. Patrick McCormack
Gate Guard	Darius A. Sultan
Isabelle the Gorilla	Tom Woodruff, Jr.
Gorilla Vocals	Gary Hecker

A team of scientists creates an invisibility serum which their leader, Sebastian Caine, tries on himself, only to find that the procedure cannot be reversed as hoped. This film received an Oscar nomination for visual effects.

© Columbia Pictures Industries, Inc.

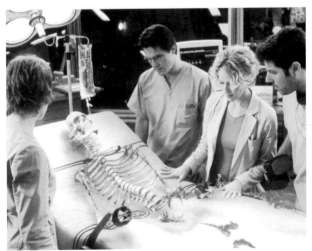

Kim Dickens, Bacon bits, Josh Brolin, Elisabeth Shue, Greg Grunberg

Elisabeth Shue, Kevin Bacon

Clint Eastwood, Tommy Lee Jones

James Garner, Tommy Lee Jones, Donald Sutherland, Clint Eastwood

SPACE COWBOYS

(WARNER BROS.) Producers, Clint Eastwood, Andrew Lazar; Executive Producer, Tom Rooker; Director, Clint Eastwood; Screenplay, Ken Kaufman, Howard Klausner; Photography, Jack N. Green; Designer, Henry Bumstead; Editor, Joel Cox; Music, Lennie Niehaus; Costumes, Deborah Hopper; Aerial Unit/2nd Unit Director, Craig Hosking; Visual Effects Supervisor, Michael Owens; Special Visual Effects/Animation, Industrial Light & Magic; Casting, Phyllis Huffman, Liz Keigley, Sari E. Keigley; a Malpaso and Mad Chance production, presented in association with Village Roadshow Pictures/Clipsal Films; Dolby; Panavision; Technicolor; Rated PG-13; 129 minutes; Release date: August 4, 2000

CAST

Frank D. Corvin...Clint Eastwood
Hawk Hawkins..Tommy Lee Jones
Jerry O'Neill...Donald Sutherland
Tank Sullivan..James Garner
Bob Gerson...James Cromwell
Sara Holland..Marcia Gay Harden
Eugene Davis ....William Devane
Ethan Grace...Loren Dean
Roger Hines ....Courtney B. Vance
General Vostov ....Rade Sherbedgia
Barbara Corvin..Barbara Babcock
Dr. Anne Caruthers...Blair Brown
Himself ....Jay Leno
Tiny.. Nils Allen Stewart
Cocktail Waitress ....Deborah Jolly
Young Frank D. Corvin ....Toby Stephens
Young Hawk Hawkins ....Eli Craig
Young Jerry O'Neill ....John Asher
Young Tank Sullivan ....Matt McColm
Young Bob Gerson ....Billie Worley
Jason..Chris Wylde
Jason's Girlfriend...Anne Stedman
Capcom..James MacDonald
Astronauts ....Kate McNeil, Karen Mistal, John K. Linto
Mission Control Tech ....Mark Thomason
Jerry's Girlfriend..Georgia Emelin
State Department Official ....Rick Scarry
JBC Security Guard ....Paul Pender
Qualls...Tim Halligan
1958 Press Reporter ....Manning Mpinduzi-Mott
Waiter..Steve Monroe
Centrifuge Tech ....J.M. Henry
Construction Tech...Steven West
Trajectory Engineer ....Cooper Huckabee
Andrew...Hayden Tank
Press Reporters ....Jock MacDonald, Artur Cybulski
T-38 Pilot ....Gerald Emerick
Little Girl ....Reneé Olstead
NASA Doctor ....Don Michaelson
and Gordon Owens (Simsupe), Steve Stapenhorst (Vice President), Lauren Cohn (Teacher), Michael Louden, Jon Hamm (Young Pilots), Deborah Hope, Erica Grant (Engineers), Lamont Lofton (KSC Guard), Alexander Kuznetsov (Russian Engineer)

Four flyers who were rejected by the space program back in 1958, are given a second chance forty-some years later when the team's leader, Frank Corvin, is summoned by NASA to fix a Russian communications satellite containing a guidance system he designed. This film received an Oscar nomination for sound editing.

© Warner Bros. Pictures/Village Roadshow Films

Clint Eastwood

James Garner, Tommy Lee Jones, Clint Eastwood, Donald Sutherland

Clint Eastwood, Tommy Lee Jones

James Cromwell, Clint Eastwood

Clint Eastwood, William Devane

Loren Dean, Clint Eastwood

Margaret Cho

PSYCHO BEACH PARTY

(STRAND) Producers, Ginny Biddle, Jon Gerrans, Marcus Hu, Victor Smyris; Executive Producer, John Hall; Director, Robert Lee King; Screenplay, Charles Busch, based on his play; Photography, Arturo Smith; Designer, Franco-Giacomo Carbone; Costumes, Camille Jumelle; Editor, Suzanne Hines; Music, Ben Vaughn; Music Supervisor, Howard Parr; a Strand/New Oz and Red Horse Films presentation; Dolby; Color; Not rated; 95 minutes; Release date: August 4, 2000

CAST

Chicklet/Florence Forrest ....Lauren Ambrose
Kanaka ....Thomas Gibson
Starcat ....Nicholas Brendon
Bettina/Diane ....Kimberly Davies
Lars/Larry ....Matt Keeslar
Capt. Monica Stark ....Charles Busch
Mrs. Forrest ....Beth Broderick
Berdine ....Danni Wheeler
Yo Yo...Nick Cornish
Provoloney..Andrew Levitas
Marvel Ann ....Amy Adams
Rhonda...Kathleen Robertson
T.J. ....Nathan Bexton
Junior ....Buddy Quaid
Cookie...Jenica Bergere
and Channon Roe (Wedge Riley), Ruth Williamson (Pat), David Chokachi (Eddie), John Cirigliano (Vince), Jolie Jenkins (Angie), Mike Malin (Bobby), Charlie Finn (Pea Brain), Nick D'Agosto (Counterman), Richard Fancy (Dr. Wentworth/Dr. Edwards), Michael Manasseri (Boy), Rona Benson (Girl), Tera Bonilla (Go-Go Girl), Stephen Wozniak (Johnny), Madison Eginton (Young Florence), Los Straight Jackets: Daniel W. Amis, Peter Curry, Edward Heeran, James K. Lester (Band), Reggie Lee, Mark Stephens, Andrew McKay, Danny Brewington, Larry Sullivan Jr., Angus Kennedy, James Leo Ryan, John Willford (Dancers)

Virginal Florence (Chicklet) joins the beach-happy teens for a summer of surf and sand, until their hi-jinks are disrupted by a series of gruesome murders.

I'M THE ONE THAT I WANT

(CHO TAUSSIG PRODS.) Producer, Lorene Machado; Executive Producers, Margaret Cho, Karen Taussig; Director, Lionel Coleman; Screenplay, Margaret Cho; Line Producer, Dennis Sugasawara; Editor, Robyn T. Migel; Music, Joan Jett & the Blackhearts; Color; Not rated; 94 minutes; Release date: August 4, 2000

IN CONCERT

Margaret Cho

Matt Keeslar, Lauren Ambrose

Nicholas Brendon

Donal Logue, Greer Goodman

THE TAO OF STEVE

Donal Logue

(SONY PICTURES CLASSICS) Producer, Anthony Bregman; Executive Producer, Ted Hope; Co-Producer, Alton Walpole; Director, Jenniphr Goodman; Screenplay, Duncan North, Greer Goodman, Jenniphr Goodman; Story, Duncan North; Photography, Teodoro Maniaci; Designer, Rosario Provenza; Editor, Sarah Gartner; Music, Joe Delia; Music Supervisor, Tracy McKnight: Costumes, Birgitta Bjerke; Casting, Nicole Arbusto, Joy Dickson, Teresa Neptune; a Good Machine production in association with Thunderhead Productions, LLC; Dolby; Technicolor; Rated R; 88 minutes; Release date: August 4, 2000

CAST

Dex ....Donal Logue
Syd ....Greer Goodman
Dave ....Kimo Wills
Beth ....Ayelet Kaznelson
Rick ....David Aaron Baker
Maggie ....Nina Jaroslaw
Ed...John Hines
Chris ....Selby Craig
Matt ....Craig D. Lafayette
Jeremy ....Matthew Hotsinpiller
Priest ....John Harrington Bland
Julie ....Dana Goodman
Jill ....Sue Cremin
Sarah ....Roxanne DeMien
Diane...Jessica Bohan
and Jessica Gormley, Mercedes Herrero, Cheryl Anne Jaroslaw (Gossipy Women); Everly Reunion Band: Dave Bynum (Bass), Matt Nader (Guitar/Vocals), Dave Terry (Vocals/Guitar); Tristan Bennett (Tris), Duncan North (Duncan), Zak Garcia (Zak), Jacob Sanchez (Blond Card Shark), Cira Sandoval (Vanessa), Shane Hamashige (Corey), Jeannie Bauder (Secretary), Nicholas Ballas (Doctor), Malaika Amon (Kinko's Chick), Garland Hunter (Kelly), Astro the Dog (Himself)

Greer Goodman, Donal Logue

Dex, once the most popular guy in college, now lives by the tao of all things Steve, a seemingly foolproof theory of dating that is put to the test when he meets the very independent Syd.

Donal Logue, Greer Goodman

CECIL B. DEMENTED

(ARTISAN) Producers, John Fiedler, Joe Caracciolo, Jr., Mark Tarlov; Executive Producers, Anthony DeLorenzo, Fred Bernstein; Director/Screenplay, John Waters; Photography, Robert Stevens; Designer, Vincent Peranio; Costumes, Van Smith; Editor, Jeffrey Wolf; Music, Zoë Poledouris, Basil Poledouris; Casting, Pat Moran, Billy Hopkins, Suzanne Smith & Kerry Barden; a Polar Entertainment production; Presented in association with Le Studio Canal+; U.S.-French; Dolby; Alpha Cine color; Rated R; 88 minutes; Release date: August 11, 2000

CAST

Honey Whitlock	Melanie Griffith
Cecil B. DeMented (Sinclair Stevens)	Stephen Dorff
Cherish	Alicia Witt
Lyle	Adrian Grenier
Lewis	Larry Gilliard, Jr.
Raven	Maggie Gyllenhaal
Rodney	Jack Noseworthy
Petie	Michael Shannon
Dinah	Harriet Dodge
Chardonnay	Zenzele Uzoma
Fidget	Eric M. Barry
Pam	Erika Lynn Rupli

Stephen Dorff

and Mink Stole (Mrs. Sylvia Mallory), Ricki Lake (Libby), Patricia Hearst (Fidget's Mother), Kevin Nealon, Roseanne (Themselves), John Michaelson (Charles), Eric Roberts (Honey's Ex-Husband), Judith Knight Young (Ticket Seller), Mark Bernier (Studio Executive), Ray Felton (Roy Stillings), Jewel Orem (Maid), Bill Grimmett (Mayor Adam Fenwick), Jeffrey Wei (William, Boy in Wheelchair), Sloane Brown (Newscaster), Billy Green, Mia Walker, James Klingenberg (Children), Ginger Tipton (Box Office Lady), Nathan Stolpman (Ticket Taker), Melanie Gorombol (Candy Counter Girl), Gary Wheeler (Theatre Manager), Joyce Flick Wendl (Puker), Tyler Mason Buckalew (Teen Boy), Tara Garwood (Charles Theater Girl), Marty Lodge (Film Commissioner), James Byrne Reed (Producer), Patsy Grady Abrams, Rhea Felken, Shana Gelbard (Family Women), Susan Lowe, Mary Vivian Pearce (Family Ladies), Michael Gabel (Film Delivery Driver), Mark Joy (Fidget's Dad), Alan J. Wendl (Security Teamster), Peter Gil (Director), Eric Richardson (Director of Photography), Jean Pierre), Marybeth Wise (Assistant Director), Cynthia Webb-Manley (Large Lady), Channing Wilroy (Shop Steward), Dan Morgan, Delaney Williams, Frank Ferrara, Steve Mack, Michael Willis (Teamsters), O. Lee Fleming (Sniffles), Scott Morgan (Groupie), Tim Caggiano (Porno Fan), Tyler Miller (Fan A), Geoffrey I. Grissett (Boy Fan), Brooke Houghton (Girl Fan), Joshua Billings (Drive-In Manager), Nat Benchley, Dave Trovato (SWAT Cops), Billy Tolzman (Petie's Trick), Jonathan Fiorucci (Raven's Groupie), Conrad Karlson (The Psychiatrist), Rosemary Knower (Cecil's Mom), Terry McCrea, Jeff Perryson (Jocks), Doug Roberts (Cecil's Dad), John Waters (Reporter in Honey's Hotel Room)

A crazed director and his team of cinema terrorists kidnap Hollywood film star Honey Whitlock and force her to star in their underground movie.

Melanie Griffith

Alicia Witt

Jack Noseworthy, Melanie Griffith, Stephen Dorff, Larry Gilliard, Jr.

BLESS THE CHILD

(**PARAMOUNT**) Producer, Mace Neufeld; Executive Producers, Bruce Davey, Robert Rehme; Director, Chuck Russell; Screenplay, Tom Rickman, Clifford Green, Ellen Green; Based on the novel by Cathy Cash Spellman; Photography, Peter Menzies, Jr.; Designer, Carol Spier; Editor, Alan Heim; Co-Producer, Stratton Leopold; Music, Christopher Young; Costumes, Denise Cronenberg; Visual Effects, MVFX; Visual Effects Supervisors, Joel Hynek, Glenn Neufeld; Makeup and Creature Effects, Keith Vanderlaan's Captive Audience Productions; Casting, Deborah Aquila, Sarah Halley Finn; an Icon Productions presentation of a Mace Neufeld production; Dolby; Panavision; Deluxe color; Rated R; 107 minutes; Release date: August 11, 2000

CAST

Maggie O'Connor	Kim Basinger
John Travis	Jimmy Smits
Eric Stark	Rufus Sewell
Reverend Grissom	Ian Holm
Jenna	Angela Bettis
Cody	Holliston Coleman
Cheri	Christina Ricci
Dahnya	Dimitra Arlys
Sister Rosa	Lumi Cavazos

and Michael Gaston (Bugatti), Eugene Lipinski (Stuart), Anne Betancourt (Maria), Helen Stenborg (Sister Joseph), Matthew Lemche (New Dawn Kid at Van), Dan Warry-Smith, Elisabeth Rosen, Tony Del Rio, Nicole Lyn, Michael McLachlan, Jonathan Malen (New Dawn Kids), Vincent Corazza (Reverend's Asst.), David Eisner (Dr. Ben), Gary Hudson (Maggie's Date), Samantha O'Dwyer (Cody, 3 years old), Nicolas Martí Salgado (Martin Casillas), Marcia Bennett (Head Nurse), Peter Mensah (Good Samaritan Janitor), Yan Birch (Good Samaritan on Bridge), Alexa Gilmour (Good Samaritan in Subway), Wanda Lee Evans (Woman on Bus), Cedric Smith (Pediatric Doctor), Dwayne McLean (Homeless Man), Brenda Devine (Woman with Sick Daughter), Lauren Spring (Daughter), Christopher Redman (New Dawn Intern), Jovanni Sy (Code Blue Doctor), Trevor Bain (Task Force Investigator), Brian Heighton (Techie), Chris Marren, Todd William Schroeder (Diner State Trooper), John Healy (Diner Local Policeman), Dylan Harman (Boy in Playground), David Sparrow (Crawford), Michael Copeman (Police Lt.), Neil Girvan, Carol Lempert, Kelvin Wheeler, Tony Meyler (Detectives), Richard Carmichael (Task Force Detective), Roman Podhora (Desk Sgt.), Dean Gabourie, Arnold Pinnock (Alley Officers), Teresa Pavlinek (Dentist's Receptionist), Jeffrey Caudle (Boy in Dentist's Chair), Catherine Fitch (Sister Helena), Neville Edwards (Pier Cop), John Shepherd (Mr. Czernik), Norma Edwards (Mrs. Czernik), Leeza Gibbons (Herself), Dan Duran, Sandi Stahlbrand (Reporters), Mia Lee (Newscaster), Matt Birman (Upstate Cop), Meredith McGeachie (Nurse), Henry Alessandroni (Hospital Cop), Austin Reed, Corrina Reed, Brianna Reed (Baby Cody)

Maggie O'Connor's irresponsible sister Jenna dumps an autistic newborn on her, only to return six years later with a new husband who kidnaps the child. It soon becomes evident that the child has incredible powers that evil forces are hoping to control for their own means.

© Paramount Pictures

Kim Basinger

Christopher Walken

THE OPPORTUNISTS

(**FIRST LOOK**) Producers, John Lyons, Tim Perell; Executive Producers, Peter Saraf, Jonathan Demme, Edward Saxon, David Forrest, Beau Rogers; Director/Screenplay, Myles Connell; Photography, Teodoro Maniaci; Editor, Andy Keir; Designer, Debbie DeVilla; Costumes, Kasia Walicka Maimone; Line Producer, William Perkins; Co-Producers, Martin Fink, Richard E. Johnson; Music, Kurt Hoffman; Casting, Kathleen Chopin; a Flashpoint presentation in association with Prosperity Pictures of a Eureka Pictures/Clinica Estetico/Kalkaska production; Dolby; Color; Rated R; 89 minutes; Release date: August 11, 2000

CAST

Victor Kelly	Christopher Walken
Michael Lawler	Peter McDonald
Sally Mahon	Cyndi Lauper
Miriam Kelly	Vera Farmiga
Pat Duffy	Donal Logue
Jesus Del Toro	Jose Zuniga
Mort Stein	Tom Noonan
Aunt Diedre	Anne Pitoniak
Ted Walikaki	Olek Krupa
Dylan	Paul D'Amato
Harry	Wally Dunn
Kevin	Patrick Fitzgerald

and Chuck Cooper (Arnon Morris), Claudia Shear (Gladys), Kate Burton (Rest Home Sister), Jim Mayzie (Rest Home Priest), Jerry Grayson (Tom Hansome), John Ortiz (Ismail Espinoza), Rosalyn Coleman (Kevin's Partner), Lawrence R. Leritz (Arresting Officer), Steve Nuke (Thug #1), Joey Perillo (Precinct Desk Officer), Marilyn Torres (Amanda Del Toro), Brandon Vega (Tony Del Toro)

Victor Kelly, an ex-con trying to leave his criminal past behind, is forced into one last safe-cracking job by a man claiming to be Victor's cousin.

© First Look Pictures

AUTUMN IN NEW YORK

Winona Ryder, Richard Gere

Richard Gere, Winona Ryder

(MGM) Producers, Amy Robinson, Gary Lucchesi, Tom Rosenberg; Executive Producers, Ted Tannebaum, Ron Bozman; Director, Joan Chen; Screenplay, Allison Burnett; Photography, Changwei Gu; Designer, Mark Friedberg; Editor, Ruby Yang; Costumes, Carol Oditz; Music, Gabriel Yared; Music Supervisor, Peter Afterman; Co-Producer, Andre Lamal; Casting, Sheila Jaffe, Georgianne Walken; a Lakeshore Entertainment, Gary Lucchesi/Amy Robinson production, presented in association with Lakeshore Entertainment; Dolby; Deluxe color; Rated PG-13; 103 minutes; Release date: August 11, 2000

CAST

Will Keane	Richard Gere
Charlotte Fielding	Winona Ryder
John	Anthony LaPaglia
Dolly	Elaine Stritch
Lisa	Vera Farmiga
Sarah	Sherry Stringfield
Lynn	Jill Hennessy
Dr. Grandy	J.K. Simmons
Simon	Sam Trammell
Dr. Sibley	Mary Beth Hurt
Shannon	Kali Rocha
Alberto	Steven Randazzo
Autumn Woman #1	Toby Poser
Netto	George Spiel Vogel III
Fakir	Ranjit Chowdhry
Eriko	Audrey Quock
Melissa	Tawny Cypress
458 Waiters	Gabriel Portuondo, Laurent Schwaar, Patrick Price
458 Bartenders	Ted Koch, Alvin Einbender
Models at Bar	Daniella Van Graas, Rachel Nichols
458 Customers	Steven Ravid, Ron Emanuel, Dan Camins, John Guidera, Russell Hunston, Nik Pjeternikaj
Charlotte's Birthday Friends	Paige Handler, Liza Lapira
Little Girl at Playground	Sarah Burns
Michael (Doorman)	Bill Raymond
Will's Driver	Earl Carroll
Taxi Driver	David Filippi
Michelle	Becca Lee
Old Frail Lady	Estelle Robinson
Little Girl at Museum	Brittney Bunkis
Librarian	Delores Mitchell
Clown at Halloween Party	Hatsumi Yoshida
50's Girl at Halloween Party	Kristi Lee Guinness
Vampire at Halloween Party	Luca Waldman
Twins	Daniella Cantermen, Deanna Cantermen
Choirmaster	Harry Burney
Boy at Rockefeller	Cheyne M. Hansen
Nurse at Cleveland Heart Institute	Pamela Twyble
Nurse at New Haven Hospital	Iris Flick
St. Vincent's Nurse	Kathleen Goldpaugh
Grubby Man	Robert Plunkett

A famous, womanizing New York restauranteur, Will Keane, prepares for yet another short-term, commitment-free affair when he begins dating young Charlotte Fielding, until he is confronted with the fact that she is seriously ill.

© Metro-Goldwyn-Mayer Pictures, Inc.

THE REPLACEMENTS

(WARNER BROS.) Producer, Dylan Sellers; Executive Producers, Erwin Stoff, Jeffrey Chernov, Steven Reuther; Director, Howard Deutch; Screenplay, Vince McKerwin; Photography, Tak Fujimoto; Designer, Dan Bishop; Costumes, Jill Ohanneson; Editors, Bud Smith, Seth Flaum; Music, John Debney; Associate Producer, Elena Spiotta; Stunts and Football Coordinator, Allan Graf; Casting, Mary Gail Artz, Barbara Cohen; a Bel-Air Entertainment presentation of a Dylan Sellers production; Dolby; Technicolor; Rated PG-13; 118 minutes; Release date: August 11, 2000

CAST

Shane Falco	Keanu Reeves
Jimmy McGinty	Gene Hackman
Clifford Franklin	Orlando Jones
Bateman	Jon Favreau
Annabelle Farrell	Brooke Langton
Nigel "The Leg" Gruff	Rhys Ifans
Edward O'Neil	Jack Warden
Jamal	Faizon Love
Andre	Michael "Bear" Taliferro
Fumiko	Ace Yonamine
Walter Cochran	Troy Winbush
Brian Murphy	David Denman
Wilkinson	Michael Jace
Pilachowski	Gailard Sartain
Banes	Art LaFleur
Eddie Martel	Brett Cullen
Lindell	Keith David
Wilson Carr	Archie L. Harris, Jr.
Malcolm La Mont	Evan Dexter Parke
Themselves	John Madden, Pat Summerall
Dallas Head Coach	Allan Graf
Refs	Al Brown, Richard Pilcher
Mrs. O'Neil	Robyn Peterson
Dwight Edwards	Gregory Williams
Detroit Quarterback	Kevin Reid
Biker	William J. McKeon

and Cliff McMullen (Policeman), Zachary I. Young (Kid in Liquor Store), Kenward Lee (Korean Store Owner), Sarah Ann Morris (Heather), Caroline Keenan (Dawn), Elisa Jacobs (Red-Haired Cheerleader), Stella Choe (Asian Cheerleader), John Clark (Dallas Defender), Tyrone Roy, Todd Champagne (Detroit Linebackers), Eric Miller (Detroit Lineman), Kel Watkin (San Diego Quarterback), Michael Brinkman (Phoenix Head Coach), Peter Ohnegian (Washington Center), Jesper Inglis (Washington Player), Mark Ellis (San Diego Head Coach), Dylan Sellers (League Commissioner), Stephen F. Schmidt (Maryland Corrections Officer), Marty Wright (Butler), Todd Eric Yeaman (Washington Offensive Tackle), Jon Garcia (O'Neil's Assistant), Tom Berry (Mini-Mart Customer), Rhonda Overby (Sideline Reporter), James Black, Jon K. Farless (Reps), Edward M. Beckford, Jr. (News Reporter), E. Dawn Samuel, Craig Sechler, Robert Shepherd, Markus Alexander (Reporters), Robert Vique, Doug Olear (Men on Street), Paul Morella, Bobby DeAngelo, Seymour Horowitz (Gangsters), Dave Cureton (Matheson), Thomas Korzeniowski, Gregory B. Goossen (Drunks), Christian Lyon, Marc C. Geschwind (Bartenders), Michelle Johnson (Fumiko's Girl), Elliot Balis, Laura L. Cottrel, Amber Dulski, Tim Estep, Levis Francis, Colett Hillman, Milinda A. Jefferson, Renee Latimore, Ken Martin, Melissa Mustotto, Emily Roberts, Chris Stabile, Stephanie Sutch, Justin L. Wilson, Seanna Zimmerman (Sentinal Cheerleaders), Marcia Dor (Doris Horner), Nicole Schiro, Heather Pederson, Michelle Courtney, Gemma Roskam, Andrea Graham, Leni Greenblatt, Mia Reeves, Margie Tompros, Royan Miller, Maria Berman, Jaya Kamal, Leanna Foglia, Russell Marcum, Mary Ann Walsh (Wannabee Cheerleaders), Paul M. Clary (Platform Camera Man), Jessica Lynn Johnson (Channel 3 WWEN News Sportscaster), Doug O'Lear (Union Man Interviewed on News), Danny Scalf (Sideline Photographer), Ryan Slattery (Ticket Tacker), David Smolar (Psycho Fan), Pearl Myers (Cheerleader)

A team of second-rate football has-beens and wannabees is recruited to fill in during a pro football strike.

Gene Hackman, Keanu Reeves

Brooke Langton, Keanu Reeves

Jon Favreau, Rhys Ifans

Jennifer Lopez

Vince Vaughn, Jennifer Lopez

THE CELL

(NEW LINE CINEMA) Producers, Julio Caro, Eric McLeod; Executive Producers, Donna Langley, Carolyn Manetti; Director, Tarsem Singh; Screenplay, Mark Protosevich; Co-Producers, Mark Protosevich, Stephen J. Ross; Photography, Paul Laufer; Designer, Tom Foden; Editors, Paul Rubell, Robert Duffy; Music, Howard Shore; Visual Effects Supervisor, Kevin Tod Haug; Costumes, Eiko Ishioka, April Napier; Casting, Ronna Kress; a Caro-McLeod/Radical Media production; Dolby; Super 35 Widescreen; Deluxe color; Rated R; 107 minutes; Release date: August 18, 2000

CAST

Catherine Deane	Jennifer Lopez
FBI Agent Peter Novak	Vince Vaughn
Carl Stargher	Vincent D'Onofrio
Dr. Miriam Kent	Marianne Jean-Baptiste
FBI Agent Gordon Ramsey	Jake Weber
Henry West	Dylan Baker
Teddy Lee	James Gammon
Lucien Baines	Patrick Bauchau
Julia Hickson	Tara Subkoff
Anne Marie Vicksey	Catherine Sutherland
Young Carl Stargher	Jake Thomas
Edward Baines	Colton James
Dr. Cooperman	Gerry Becker
Ella Baines	Musetta Vander
Cole	Dean Norris
Mrs. Hickson	Lauri Johnson
Agent Stockwell	John Cothran, Jr.
Agent Brock	Jack Conley
Officer Alexander	Kamar De Los Reyes
Swat Team Member	Christopher Janney
FBI Technician	Nicholas Cascone
FBI K-9 Agent	Joe La Piana
Dr. Reid	Pruitt Taylor Vince

and Kim Chizevsky-Nicholls, Jennifer Dawn Day, Alanna Vicente, Aja Echols, Vanessa Branch, Elena Maddalo (Stargher's Victims), Gareth Williams (Stargher's Father), Glenda Chism (Woman in Tub), Monica Lacy, Joy Creel Liefeld, Leanna Creel (Mothers)

The FBI turns to scientist Catherine Deane to utilize her radical new chemical therapy to enter the mind of unconscious serial killer Carl Stargher and find out where he has imprisoned his last, living victim. This film received an Oscar nomination for makeup.

Vincent D'Onofrio

Jennifer Lopez

THE ORIGINAL KINGS OF COMEDY

(PARAMOUNT) Producers, Walter Latham, David Gale, Spike Lee; Executive Producer, Van Toffler; Director, Spike Lee; Co-Producer, Butch Robinson; Associate Producers, Rylyn Demaris, Angelia Price; Photography, Malik Sayeed; Designer, Wynn P. Thomas; Editor, Barry Alexander Brown; Executive Music Producer, Alex Steyermark; an MTV Films and Latham Entertainment presentation of a 40 Acres and a Mule Filmworks production; Dolby; Color; Rated R; 115 minutes; Release date: August 18, 2000

IN CONCERT

Steve Harvey, D.L. Hughley, Cedric the Entertainer, Bernie Mac

Bernie Mac, Cedric the Entertainer, D.L. Hughley, Steve Harvey

Vincent D'Onofrio, Janeane Garofalo

Jeanne Tripplehorn, Vincent D'Onofrio

STEAL THIS MOVIE

(LIONS GATE) Producers, Robert Greenwald, Jacobus Rose; Director, Robert Greenwald; Executive Producers, Jon Avnet, Vincent D'Onofrio, Ken Christmas; Co-Producers, Elizabeth Selzer Lang, Bradley H. Gordon; Screenplay, Bruce Graham; Based on the books *To America With Love: Letters from the Underground* by Abbie Hoffman and Anita Hoffman, and *Abbie Hoffman: American Rebel* by Marty Jezer; Photography, Denis Lenoir; Designers, Richard Paris, Linda Del Rosario; Editor, Kimberly Ray; Music, Mader; Music Supervisor, Evyen Klean; Makeup, James Ryder, Marilyn Terry, Edelgard Pfluegel; Casting, Jeanne McCarthy; a Greenlight production in association with Ardent Films; Dolby; Deluxe color; Rated R; 107 minutes; Release date: August 18, 2000

CAST

Abbie Hoffman ....Vincent D'Onofrio
Anita Hoffman ....Janeane Garofalo
Johanna Lawrenson ....Jeanne Tripplehorn
Gerry Lefcourt...Kevin Pollak
Stew Albert ....Donal Logue
Jerry Rubin ....Kevin Corrigan
David Glenn ....Alan Van Sprang
Tom Hayden ....Troy Garity
Judy Albert ....Ingrid Veninger
Louis Wertzel ....Stephen Marshall
and Joyce Gordon (Florence Hoffman), Bernard Kay (John Hoffman), Jean Daigle (Sheriff), Johnie Chase (Josh), Joshua Dov (Hippie Kid–NYC), Michael Cera (America Hoffman–at 6), Craig Ryan (America Hoffman–at 16), James Binkley, Walter Masko, Brian King (Crew Cuts), Merwin Mondesir (Private Kendall), Derek Murchie (Undercover Cop), Joey Pomanti (Juror), Shawn Lawrence (Stahl), Jim Codrington (Soldier), Tony Meyler, Nick Bacon (Cops), Trevor Bain (Medic), Shane Daley (Chicago Cop), Kent Staines (Richard Schultz), Ken Kramer (Judge Julius Hoffman), David Eisner (William Kunstler), Todd Kozan (Rennie Davis), Panou (Bobby Seale), Timm Zemanek (David Dollinger), Keith Jones (John Froines), Marc Aubin (Lee Weiner), Dom Fiore (Jury Foreman), Chad Willet (Sky), Tyagi Schwartz (Wannabe Hippie), Demore Barnes (Student Leader), Robert Smith (Ad Exec), Jeana MacIsaac (Unknown Woman), Scott Wickware (FBI Agent Kells), Kevin Hare (FBI Agent), Shaun Smyth (Paul Held), Jody Racicot (Cardozo), Aaron Steele (Sambini), Stuart Clow (FBI Agent in Filing Room), Rhona Shekter, Kim Roberts (Auditors), Beatriz Pizano (Mrs. Ramos), Michael Capellupo (Studio Exec), Andy Marshall (Security Guard), Jeff Pustil (Dr. Oscar Janiger), June Whiteman (Mayor at Yacht Club), Carolyn Goff (Hippie Girl), Donald Tripe, Christina Donatelli (Newscasters), Philip Craig (Police Chief), Toni Ellewind (Mother), Robert Ward (FBI Agent in Boiler Room)

The true story of sixties activist and revolutionary Abbie Hoffman, whose protest against the Vietnam War at the 1968 Democratic Convention in Chicago, brought him fame and notoriety.

Clare Kramer, Rini Bell, Kirsten Dunst

Kirsten Dunst, Jesse Bradford

BRING IT ON

(UNIVERSAL) formerly *Cheer Fever*; Producers, Marc Abraham, Thomas A. Bliss; Executive Producers, Armyan Bernstein, Max Wong, Caitlin Scanlon, Paddy Cullen; Director, Peyton Reed; Screenplay, Jessica Bendinger; Photography, Shawn Maurer; Designer, Sharon Lomofsky; Editor, Larry Bock; Music, Christophe Beck; Music Supervisor, Billy Gottlieb; Costumes, Mary Jane Fort; Choreographer, Anne Fletcher; "Clovers" Routines Creator, Hi-Hat; Cheerleading Coordinator, Brent Devarne; Casting, Joseph Middleton; a Beacon Pictures presentation; Dolby; Fotokem color; Rated PG-13; 98 minutes; Release date: August 25, 2000

CAST

Torrance Shipman	Kirsten Dunst
Missy Pantone	Eliza Dushku
Cliff Pantone	Jesse Bradford
Isis	Gabrielle Union
Courtney	Clare Kramer
Whitney	Nicole Bilderback
Darcy	Tsianina Joelson
Kasey	Rini Bell
Jan	Nathan West
Les	Huntley Ritter
Lava	Shamari Fears
Jenelope	Natina Reed
Lafred	Brandi Williams
Aaron	Richard Hillman
Big Red	Lindsay Sloane
Carver	Bianca Kajlich
Bruce Shipman	Holmes Osborne
Christine Shipman	Sherry Hursey
Justin Shipman	Cody McMains
Sparky Polastri	Ian Roberts
Toros Tight End	David Edwards
Toros Quarterback	Ashley Howard
New Pope Cheerleaders	Nikole Lee Amateau, Clementine Ford
Costa Mesa Quarterback	Grant Thompson
Costa Mesa Linebacker	Leonard Clifton
Argumentative Girl	Marie Wise
Been-Crying-for-Hours Girl	Dru Mouser
Rappin' White Girl	Tracy Pacheco
Be Aggressive Girl	Alicia Michelle Sassano
Start-Over Girl	Natasha Soll
Theatre Boy	Ryan Drummond
Tiny Tot Cheerleader	Paullin Wolfe
Emcees	David E. Willis, Beth LaMure
Event Coordinator	Anne Fletcher

and Doug Waldo (UCA Official), Annie Hinton (High-Strung Mom), Louise Gallagher (Class Monitor), Edmond Clay (Football Announcer), Daniella Kuhn (T.V. Reporter), Aloma Wright (Pauletta),Paul Bloom (T.V. Commentator), Melanie Atmadja (Jamie), Silencio Por Favor (Mime), Jodi Harris (Cheer Coach), Nectar Rose (Nervous Cheerleader), Hilary Salvatore (Toothless Cheerleader), Elizabeth Johnson (Confident Cheerleader), Riley Smith (Guy Cheerleader), Carla Mackauf (Aaron's Lover), Anna Lisa Mendiola (Clover Cheerleader)

San Diego high schooler Torrance Shipman achieves her dream of becoming the captain of the cheerleading squad, only to discover that their routines had been stolen by their former captain from the Clovers, a hip-hop cheer squad from East Compton.

© Universal Studios

Natina Reed, Brandi Williams, Gabrielle Union, Shamari Fears

Kirsten Dunst, Eliza Dushku

(top row down) Kirsten Dunst, Clare Kramer, Eliza Dushku, Rini Bell, Gabrielle Union, Lindsay Sloane, Nathan West, Jesse Bradford, Tsianina Joelson, Huntley Ritter

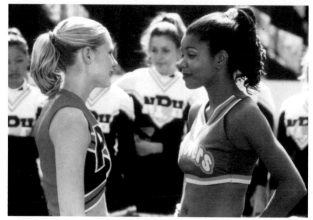

Kirsten Dunst, Gabrielle Union

Kirsten Dunst, Nathan West, Eliza Dushku, Huntley Ritter

THE CREW

(TOUCHSTONE) Producers, Barry Sonnenfeld, Barry Josephson; Executive Producers, George Litto, Michael S. Glick; Director, Michael Dinner; Screenplay, Barry Fanaro; Photography, Juan Ruiz-Anchia; Designer, Peter Larkin; Editor, Nicholas C. Smith; Costumes, Betsy Cox; Co-Producer, Zane Weiner; Music, Steve Bartek; Music Supervisor, Dondi Bastone; Casting, Junie Lowry Johnson; a George Litto Pictures production, a Sonnenfeld/Josephson Worldwide Entertainment production; Dolby; Technicolor; Rated PG-13; 87 minutes; Release date: August 25, 2000

CAST

Bobby Bartellemeo	Richard Dreyfuss
Joey "Bats" Pistella	Burt Reynolds
Mike "The Brick" Donatelli	Dan Hedaya
Tony "Mouth" Donato	Seymour Cassel
Det. Olivia Neal	Carrie-Anne Moss
Ferris "aka Maureen" Lowenstein	Jennifer Tilly
Pepper Lowenstein	Lainie Kazan
Raul Ventana	Miguel Sandoval
Det. Steve Menteer	Jeremy Piven
Young Bobby Bartellemeo	Casey Siemaszko
Young Joey "Bats" Pistella	Matt Borlenghi
Young Tony "Mouth" Donato	Billy Jayne
Young Mike "The Brick" Donatelli	Jeremy Ratchford

and Mike Moroff (Jorge), Jose Zuniga (Escobar), Carlos Gomez (Miguel), Louis Guss (Jerry "The Hammer" Fungo), Joe Rigano (Frankie "Rash" Decuello), Ron Karabatsos (Fat Pauly), Frank Vincent (Marty), Manuel Estanillo (Louis Ventana), Marc Macaulay (Driver), Cullen Douglas (Young Man), Jim Coleman (Paramedic), Louis Lombardi (Jimmy Whistles), Aaron Elbaz (Young Joey), Vince Cecere, Allan Nicholls (Wiseguys), Dana Daurey (Model Girl), Jeremy Shore (Model Guy), Hope Pomerance (Realtor), Penelope Alexitch, Christy Tummond (Girls), Evelyn Brooks (Grandmother), Don Williams (Elderly Husband), Jill Beach (Newscaster), Lorri Bagley (Sofa Girl), Antoni Cornacchione (Officer), Ian Marioles (Security Guard), Fyvush Finkel (Sol Lowenstein), Mal Jones (Dr. Ward), Ru Flynn (Mommy), Ginger Southall (Reporter), Gino Salvano (Raul Guy #2), Elizabeth Powers (Girl), Jay Cannistraci (Tommy "Shakes"), John Archie (Doctor), Christa Campbell (Nurse), Adam Cronan (Burger King Manager), Judith Delgado (Judge), April Engel (Ferris Dancer), Patrick Fox (Jet Ski Kid), Daniel A. Leone (Barber Shop Guy), Yoset Rosenberg (Rabbi), Fabian Hernandez (Bus Boy), David H. Steel (Coach), Susie Park (Asian Masseuse), Carlo Perez Allen (Latino Mobster), George Fisher (Tony the Torch), Harry Boykoff (Louie the Lip)

When four former mobsters find themselves facing eviction from their senior citizen hotel, they hatch a plan to save their residence, a scheme that goes awry and finds them in trouble with a powerful drug lord.

© Buena Vista Pictures Distribution/George Litto Pictures, Inc.

Richard Dreyfuss, Seymour Cassel, Dan Hedaya, Burt Reynolds

Dan Hedaya, Burt Reynolds, Richard Dreyfuss

Richard Dreyfuss, Seymour Cassel, Burt Reynolds, Dan Hedaya

Carrie-Anne Moss, Lainie Kazan, Jennifer Tilly, Jeremy Piven

DARK DAYS

(PALM PICTURES) Producer/Director/Photography, Marc Singer; Executive Producers, Paolo Seganti, Randall Mesdon, Morton Swinsky, Gordon Paul; Co-Producer, Ben Freedman; Editor, Melissa Neidich; Music, DJ Shadow; Associate Producers, Christopher Griffith, Richard Giles, Mette Jensen, Avra Jain, David Wike, Scott Bradley, Giancarlo Bonati, Charlotte Stockdale; a Wide Angle Pictures and Palm Pictures presentation of a Picture Farm production in association with the Sundance Channel and Sputnik7; Dolby; Color; Not rated; 82 minutes; Release date: August 30, 2000. Documentary on a community of homeless people living in a train tunnel beneath Manhattan, featuring Ralph, S. Henry, Dee, Esteban, Henry, Atoulio, Tommy, Cathy, Brian, Joe, Bernard, Tito, Lee, The Twins, Jose, Greg, Ronnie, Ozzy, Marayah, Maria, Mike, and Jasmine.

James Spader

Marisa Tomei

Henry, Tommy

THE WATCHER

(UNIVERSAL) Producers, Christopher Eberts, Elliot Lewitt, Jeff Rice, Nile Niami; Executive Producers, Patrick Choi, Paul Pompian; Director, Joe Charbanic; Screenplay, David Elliot, Clay Ayers; Story, Darcy Meyers, David Elliot; Photography, Michael Chapman; Designers, Brian Eatwell, Maria Caso; Editor, Richard Nord; Music, Marco Beltrami; Casting, Jane Alderman; a Lewitt/Eberts-Choi/Niami production; Presented in association with Interlight; Dolby; Deluxe color; Rated R; 96 minutes; Release date: September 8, 2000

CAST

Joel Campbell	James Spader
Polly	Marisa Tomei
David Allen Griffin	Keanu Reeves
Ibby	Ernie Hudson
Hollis	Chris Ellis
Mitch	Robert Cicchini
Lisa	Yvonne Niami
Diana	Jennifer McShane
Sharon	Gina Alexander
Ellie	Rebakah Louise Smith

and Joe Sikora (Skater), Jillian Peterson (Jessica), Michelle Dimaso (Rachel), Andrew Rothenberg (Jack Fray), David Pasquesi (Norton), Dana Kozlov (Anchorwoman), Butch Jerinic (Flower Girl), Marilyn Dodds Frank (Wanda), Rebekah Arthur (Business Woman), Sheila Lahey (Wanda's Sister), Jason Wells (Computer Tech), Lisa Velten (Photo Store Employee), Frederick Garcia (Coffee Store Clerk), Mindy Bell (Supervising Agent), Ryan Oliver (Waiter), Varen Black (Reporter), Tamara Tungate (Young Woman), Quinn Yancy (Campbell's Secretary), Jennifer Anglin (Television Reporter), Peter Reinemann (Motel Clerk), Michael Nicolosi (Passerby), Rich Komenich (Bloody Guy), Michael Guido (Mendel), Janelle Snow (Waitress), Joe Forbrich (Bennigan Manager), Scott Benjaminson (Guest)

After years of tracking various psychotic killers, FBI Agent Jack Campbell moves to Chicago to get away from his past life only to be faced with a series of murders that seem to have been committed by a man who had previously eluded his capture.

Ryan Phillippe, Benicio Del Toro

Juliette Lewis

Nicky Katt, Ryan Phillippe, Taye Diggs

THE WAY OF THE GUN

(ARTISAN) Producer, Kenneth Kokin; Executive Producer, Russ Markowitz; Director/Screenplay, Christopher McQuarrie; Photography, Dick Pope; Designer, Maia Javan; Editor, Stephen Semel; Costumes, Genevieve Tyrrell, Heather Neely McQuarrie; Music, Joe Kraemer; Casting, Lynn Kressel, Cate Praggastis; an Aqaba production; Dolby; Deluxe Color; Rated R; 118 minutes; Release date: September 8, 2000

CAST

"Parker"	Ryan Phillippe
"Longbaugh"	Benicio Del Toro
Robin	Juliette Lewis
Jeffers	Taye Diggs
Obecks	Nicky Katt
Hale Chidduck	Scott Wilson
Joe Sarno	James Caan
Dr. Allen Painter	Dylan Kussman
Francesca Chidduck	Kristin Lehman
Abner	Geoffrey Lewis
Federales	Mando Guerrero, Andres Orozco, Jose Perez
Interviewer	Neil Pollock
P. Whipped	Henry Griffin
Raving Bitch	Sarah Silverman
Sloppy Prostitute	Irene Santiago
Receptionist	Jan Jensen

A pair of gunmen get into more trouble than they bargained for when they abduct a young pregnant woman who has been hired as a surrogate mother by a wealthy couple.

Benicio Del Toro, James Caan

NURSE BETTY

(USA FILMS) Producers, Gail Mutrux, Steve Golin; Executive Producers, Philip Steuer, Stephen Pevner, Moritz Borman, Chris Sievernich; Director, Neil LaBute; Screenplay, John C. Richards, James Flamberg; Story, John C. Richards; Photography, Jean Yves Escoffier; Designer, Charles Breen; Costumes, Lynette Meyer; Editors, Joel Plotch, Steven Weisberg; Music, Rolfe Kent; Casting, Heidi Levitt; a Gramercy Pictures presentation in association with Pacifica Film Distribution of a Propaganda Films/AB'-Strakt Pictures/IMF production; Dolby; Super 35 Widescreen; Technicolor; Rated R; 108 minutes; Release date: September 8, 2000

Chris Rock, Morgan Freeman, Renée Zellweger

CAST

Charlie	Morgan Freeman
Betty Sizemore	Renée Zellweger
Wesley	Chris Rock
George McCord (Dr. David Ravell)	Greg Kinnear
Del Sizemore	Aaron Eckhart
Rosa Herrera	Tia Texada
Roy Ostrey	Crispin Glover
Sheriff Ballard	Pruitt Taylor Vince
Lyla	Allison Janney
Sue Ann	Kathleen Wilhoite
Chloe	Elizabeth Mitchell
Darlene	Susan Barnes
Ellen	Harriet Sansom Harris
Jasmine	Sung Hi Lee
Dr. Lonnie Walsh	Laird Macintosh
Blake	Steven Gilborn
Mercedes	Jenny Gago
Joyce	Sheila Kelley
Merle	Matthew Cowles

and Wayne Tippit (Doctor), George D. Wallace (Grandfather), Lesley Woods (Grandmother), Cynthia Martells (Chief Nurse), Alfonso Freeman (ER Doctor), Kevin Rahm, Steven Culp (Friends), Deborah May (Gloria Walsh), Michael Murphy (Studio Guard), Tina Smith (Waitress), Mike Kennedy (Cook), Irene Olga Lopez (Rosa's Mother), Steve Franken (Administrator), Kelwin Hagen (Deputy), Joshua Dotson (Parking Valet), Dona Hardy (Patient), Paul Threlkeld (Grip), Jose Vasquez (Gang Member), Jack Jacobson (Stagehand), Elaine Corral-Kendall (Anchor)

Morgan Freeman, Renée Zellweger

After witnessing her husband's brutal murder, Betty loses all sense of reality and takes off for Los Angeles to meet her favorite soap opera character, Dr. David Ravell, whom she believes is a real person.

© Universal Studios Inc.

Renée Zellweger, Aaron Eckhart

Renée Zellweger, Greg Kinnear

Patrick Fugit, Kate Hudson

Philip Seymour Hoffman, Patrick Fugit

Patrick Fugit

Zooey Deschanel, Michael Angarano, Frances McDormand

Jason Lee, John Fedevich, Noah Taylor, Billy Crudup, Mark Kozelek

ALMOST FAMOUS

(DREAMWORKS/COLUMBIA) Producers, Cameron Crowe, Ian Bryce; Director/Screenplay, Cameron Crowe; Photography, John Toll; Designers, Clay A. Griffith, Clayton R. Hartley; Costumes, Betsy Heimann; Editors, Joe Hutshing, Saar Klein; Co-Producer, Lisa Stewart; Music, Nancy Wilson; Music Supervisor, Danny Bramson; Casting, Gail Levin; a Vinyl Films production; Dolby; Technicolor; Rated R; 122 minutes; Release date: September 13, 2000

CAST

Russell Hammond	Billy Crudup
Elaine Miller	Frances McDormand
Penny Lane	Kate Hudson
Jeff Bebe	Jason Lee
William Miller	Patrick Fugit
Anita Miller	Zooey Deschanel
Young William	Michael Angarano
Dick Roswell	Noah Taylor
Ed Vallencourt	John Fedevich
Larry Fellows	Mark Kozelek
Sapphire	Fairuza Balk
Polexia Aphrodisia	Anna Paquin
Beth From Denver	Olivia Rosewood
Dennis Hope	Jimmy Fallon
Lester Bangs	Philip Seymour Hoffman
Leslie	Liz Stauber
Estrella Starr	Bijou Phillips
Mrs. Deegan	Alice Marie Crowe
Roadie Scully	J.J. Cohen
Roadie Gregg	Gary Douglas Kohn
Roadie Mick	Ray Porter
Freddy	Mark Pellington
Jann Wenner	Eion Bailey
Ben Fong-Torres	Terry Chen
David Felton	Rainn Wilson
Alison the Fact Checker	Erin Foley
Darryl	Jesse Caron
Principal	Charles Walker
Vic Munoz	Jay Baruchel
Alice Wisdom	Pauley Perrette
Reg	Peter Frampton

and Zack Ward (The Legendary Red Dog), Mitch Hedberg (Eagles Road Manager), Devin Corey, (The Who Road Manager), Pete Droge, Elaine Summers (Hyatt Singers), Eric Stonestreet (Sheldon the Desk Clerk), Marc Maron (Angry Promoter), Shane Willard (Ticket Scalper), Chris McElprang (Aaron Amedori), John Patrick Amedori (Himself), Kate Peckham (Quiet Girl), Julia Schuler (Waving Girl), Brian Vaughan (Real Topeka Kid), Anthony Martelli (Poolside Provocateur), Zach Clairville (Acid Kid), Ian Ridgeway, Isaac Curtiss, Chris Lennon Davis (Topeka Partiers), Scott N. Stevens (Co-Pilot), Kevin Sussman (Lenny), Reathel Bean (Warwick Hotel Clerk), Tom Riis Farrell (Plaza Doctor), Laura Bastianelli (Nurse), Samuel Aaron Roberson, Brian Andreasen, Jared Hren, Mary Dragicevich, Aura Barry (High School Band), Daniel Wilson (Journalism Teacher), William Barillaro (Bus Driver), Holly Maples (Flight Attendant), Matt Griesser (PSA Co-Pilot), Susan Yeagley (Have a Nice Day Stewardess), Nicole Spector (Hippie Girl at Airport), Patrick Irmen (Wanna Get High Guy), Nick Swardson (Insane Bowie Fan), Cindy Weber, Kris Weber, Kaitlyn Weber, Kimberly Weber, Kristin Weber (Shocked Elevator Family), Samer Sourakli (Mustache Boy), Michelle Moretti (Swingo's Desk Clerk), Ana Maria Quintana, Lisa Buchignani (Arizona Housekeepers)

15-year-old music fan William Miller gets his big chance at making his name in the world of rock journalism when he goes on the road with the up-and-coming band Stillwater.

2000 Academy Award-winner for Best Original Screenplay. This film received additional Oscar nominations for supporting actresses (Frances McDormand, Kate Hudson), and editing.

Noah Taylor, Patrick Fugit, Kate Hudson, Billy Crudup, Fairuza Balk, Jason Lee, Anna Paquin, Mark Kozelek, Olivia Rosewood, John Fedevich

Michael Angarano

Anna Paquin, Fairuza Balk, Bijou Phillips

DUETS

Gwyneth Paltrow, Huey Lewis

Andre Braugher, Paul Giamatti

(HOLLYWOOD PICTURES) Producers, Kevin Jones, Bruce Paltrow, John Byrum; Executive Producers, Lee R. Mayes, Neil Canton, Tony Ludwig, Alan Riche; Director, Bruce Paltrow; Screenplay, John Byrum; Photography, Paul Sarossy; Designer, Sharon Seymour; Costumes, Mary Claire Hannan; Editor, Jerry Greenberg; Music, David Newman; Music Supervisors, Richard Rudolph, Maya Rudolph; Casting, Francine Maisler; a Kevin Jones production, presented in association with Seven Arts Pictures and Beacon Pictures; Distributed by Buena Vista Pictures; Dolby; Technicolor; Rated R; 112 minutes; Release date: September 15, 2000

CAST

Suzi Loomis	Maria Bello
Reggie Kane	Andre Braugher
Todd Woods	Paul Giamatti
Ricky Dean	Huey Lewis
Liv	Gwyneth Paltrow
Billy Hannon	Scott Speedman
Harriet Cahagan	Marian Seldes
Candy Woods	Kiersten Warren
Arlene	Angelina Phillips
Blair	Angie Dickinson
Ronny Jackson	Lochlyn Munro
Beth the Hostess	Carol Alexander
Tulsa Bartender	Michael Rogers
Redhead	Amanda Kravat

and Ian Robison, Roger Haskett, John Payne (Sales Guys), Tom Bougers (Desk Sergeant), Steve Oatway (Ralph Beckerman), Erika von Tagen (Julie), Laura Murdoch (Dead Showgirl), Roman Danylo (Albuquerque Desk Clerk), Keegan Tracy (Sheila), Ann Warn Pegg (Taffy), Ron Small (Old Homeless Man), Tony Marr (Japanese Business Man), Brian Jensen (Cincinnati Bartender), Tom Heaton (Charlie), Andrew Johnston (Shop Manager), Wyley Vlahovic (Desert Joint Man), Beverly Elliott (Desert Joint Woman), Diane Brown (Desert Joint Hostess), Warren Takeuchi (Texas Trooper #1), Aaron Pearl (Buddy), J.B. Bivens (Clark), Candus Churchill (Karaoke Woman), Brent Butt (Kansas Motel Clerk), David Neale (Desk Manager), Mike "Mitch" Mitchell (K.C. Gas Station Attendant), Iris Quinn (K.S. Hostess), Brenda Crichlow (Omaha Clerk), Maya Rudolph (Omaha Karaoke Hostess), Marlaina Andre, Michael Bublé, "Karaoke Karl" Detken, Dan Joffre, Nicole Parker-Smith, Erin Wright (Finale Singers), Anita Dutton (Tonia Kasper), Larry Dutton (Hobie Kasper), Gary Hetherington (Omaha Police Captain), John Pinette (John), Susan Campbell (Airline Representative)

Six different people, hoping to find some meaning in their lives, head for a major Karaoke contest in Omaha, Nebraska.

© Buena Vista Pictures Distribution

Maria Bello, Scott Speedman

Kiersten Warren, Paul Giamatti

URBANIA

(LIONS GATE) Producers, Jon Shear, Stephanie Golden, J. Todd Harris; Co-Producers, Meta Puttkammer, Douglas Hunter; Director, Jon Shear; Screenplay, Jon Shear, Daniel Reitz; Based on the play *Urban Folk Tales* by Daniel Reitz; Photography, Shane F. Kelly; Designer, Karyl Newman; Costumes, David Matwijkow; Music, Marc Anthony Thompson; Music Supervisor, David Falzone; Editors, Randolph K. Bricker, Ed Marx; Casting, Jordan Beswick; a Commotion Picures and Daly/Harris Productions presentation; Color; Rated R; 104 minutes; Release date: September 15, 2000

Dan Futterman, Alan Cumming

CAST

Charlie	Dan Futterman
Brett	Alan Cumming
Chris	Matt Keeslar
Matt	Josh Hamilton
Bill	Lothaire Bluteau
Chuck	Bill Sage
Clara	Barbara Sukowa
Cassandra, the Kidney Thief	Paige Turco
Deedee	Megan Dodds
Ron	Gabriel Olds
Dean	Samuel Ball

and Scott Denny (Ken, Cassandra's Victim), Sanjeev Jhaveri (Cassandra's Helper), James Simon (Sam), David Wheir (Gary), Cheryl Brubacker (Pam), Paul Dawson (The Bloodied Man), Marylouise Burke (Yvette, the Poodle Lady), Pamela Shaw (Judy, the Photo Lady), Rich Clayton (Cashier), David Catalano (Frat Guy); The One Night Stands: Joe Danisi (Vin), Melinda Wade (Nadine); The Window Couple: Christopher Bradley (Efraim), Brian Keane (Neil); Gerry Bamman (Don)

Dan Futterman

Charlie, trying to recover from a traumatic experience, spots a mysterious stranger whom he believes holds the key to his recovery, sending him on a nocturnal journey through Manhattan.

© Lions Gate Films

Matt Keeslar, Dan Futterman

BAIT

(WARNER BROS.) Producer, Sean Ryerson; Executive Producers, Tony Gilroy, Jaime Rucker King; Director, Antoine Fuqua; Screenplay, Andrew Scheinman, Adam Scheinman, Tony Gilroy; Photography, Tobias Schlessler; Designer, Peter Jamison; Editor, Alan Edward Bell; Co-Producer, Joseph Boccia; Music, Mark Mancina; Visual Effects, Spin Entertainment; Stunts, John Stoneham, Jr.; a Castle Rock Entertainment presentation; Dolby; Panavision; Technicolor; Rated R; 119 minutes; Release date: September 15, 2000

CAST

Alvin Sanders ....Jamie Foxx
Edgar Clenteen ....David Morse
Bristol..Doug Hutchison
Lisa Hill ....Kimberly Elise
Agent Wooly..David Paymer
Stevie Sanders...Mike Epps
Agent Blum ....Jamie Kennedy
Agent Boyle ....Nestor Serrano
Ramundo...Kirk Acevedo
Julio ....Jeffrey Donovan
Agent Walsh..Megan Dodds

and Tia Texada (Tika), Neil Crone (Supervisor), Robert Pastorelli (John Jaster), Matthew Witherly, Jason Jones (Guards), Bill Lynn (Night Watchman), Glyn Thomas (Chem-Tech Agent), Victor A. Young, Don Allison (Senators), Paul Miller (Dr. Harris), Gouchy Boy, Arnold Pinnock, Cle Bennet, Desmond Campbell (Convicts), Shawn Lawrence (Warden Clay), Lee Rumohr, Norm Spencer (Bound Guards), Tom Cappadona (Cab Driver), Jonathan Hadary (Cafe Owner), Ritchie Coster (Buyer), Stan Coles (General), Larry Block (Customer), Billy Otis (Odd Inmate), Navaco Bernice Downey (Girl in Club), John Berger (Medical Examiner), Joe Pingue, Martin Roach (Cops), John Harper (Running Man), Dylan Bierk (Police Photographer), Bruce Beaton (Agent with Coffee), Ron Kennell, Conrad Bergschneider (Mobile Agents), Nick Pjoternicky (Agent), Ron Bell (Trucker), Joanna Polley (Rhonda Glimsher's Voice), Lorraine McNeil (Woman Looking in Car Window)

The U.S. Treasury department uses two-bit thief Alvin Sanders as after he is given confidential information by his dying prison cellmate pertaining to the whereabouts of some stolen gold.

Jamie Foxx, David Morse

Monica Keena, Vincent Kartheiser

CRIME + PUNISHMENT IN SUBURBIA

(UNITED ARTISTS) Producers, Pamela Koffler, Larry Gross, Christine Vachon; Director, Rob Schmidt; Screenplay Larry Gross; Photography, Bobby Bukowski; Designer, Ruth Ammon; Costumes, Sophie de Rakoff Carbonell; Music, Michael Brook; Music Supervisor, Liza Richardson; Editor, Gabriel Wrye; Associate Producer, Sara Rose; Co-Producer, Dara Weintraub; Casting, Susan Shopmaker, Matthew Barry; a Killer Films production; Distributed by MGM Distribution Co.; Dolby; Deluxe color; Rated R; 99 minutes; Release date: September 15, 2000

CAST

Roseanne Skolnik ....Monica Keena
Vincent ....Vincent Kartheiser
Maggie Skolnik..Ellen Barkin
Fred Skolnik...Michael Ironside
Jimmy ....James DeBello
Chris ....Jeffrey Wright
Moznick..Blake C. Shields
Bella..Conchata Ferrell
Coach ....Marshall Teague
Cecil ....Nicki Aycox
Dean ....Christian Payne

and Anthony C. Chow (Teacher), Bonnie Somerville (Stuck Up Girl), Lucinda Jenney (Vincent's Mom), Jim Boyce (Mr. Dwyer), Matt Champagne (Counselor Lord), Jim Swanson (Rat Fink Neighbor), Tommy Perna (Officer Lambert), Tommy Bush (Chief Judson), Susan Davis (Grandmother), Brad Greenquist (Calvin Berry), Dennis Liss (Bailiff), Jeff Lawrence (Judge Jack), Valerie Wildman (Prosecutor), Jack Angel (Russ)

Roseanne, a popular high school teen, talks her boyfriend into helping her kill her abusive stepfather.

UNDER SUSPICION

(LIONS GATE) Producers, Lori McCreary, Anne Marie Gillen, Stephen Hopkins; Executive Producers, Morgan Freeman, Gene Hackman, Maurice Leblond, Ross Grayson Bell; Director, Stephen Hopkins; Screenplay, Tom Provost, W. Peter Iliff; Based on the film *Garde á Vue*, written by Claude Miller, Jean Herman, Michael Audiard, based on the book *Brainwash* by John Wainright; Photography, Peter Levy; Designer, Cecilia Montiel; Editor, John Smith; Costumes, Francine Jamison-Tanchuck; Music, BT; Music Supervisor, George Acogny; Line Producer, Llewellyn Wells; Casting, Reuben Cannon, Eddie Dunlop; a Revelations Entertainment and TFI International presentation; U.S.-French; Dolby; Technicolor; Rated R; 111 minutes; Release date: September 22, 2000

Joseph McIntyre, Jean Louisa Kelly

CAST

Henry Hearst	Gene Hackman
Captain Victor Benezet	Morgan Freeman
Detective Felix Owens	Thomas Jane
Chantal Hearst	Monica Bellucci
Isabella	Nydia Caro
Superintendent	Miguel A. Suárez
Detective Castillo	Pablo Cunqueiro
Camille Rodriguez	Isabel Algaze
Maria Rodriguez	Jackeline Duprey
Paco Rodriguez	Luis Caballero

and Patricia Beato (Darlita), Sahyly Yamile (Reina), Hector Travieso (Peter), Marisol Calero (Sgt. Arias), Vanessa Shenk (Sue Ellen Huddy), Gelian Cotto (Paulina Valera), Myron Herrick (Mr. Ricardi), Vanesa Millán, Zina Ponder Pistor (Wives), Willie Denton (Ben), Ramon Saldaña (Raymond), Conchita Vicens (Ruthanne), Rene Cervoni (Thomas), Frank Rose (Drunken Acquaintance), Mike Gomez, Luisa Leschin, Vanessa Marquez, Norma Maldonado, Richard Miró, Odalys Nanin, Al Rodrigo, Marcelo Tubert (Singers)

Veteran police captain Victor Benezet interrogates wealthy tax attorney Henry Hearst whom he believes might be responsible for the murder of two young girls.

Jean Louisa Kelly, Joseph McIntyre

THE FANTASTICKS

(UNITED ARTISTS) Producers, Michael Ritchie, Linne Radmin; Executive Producer, Art Schaefer; Director, Michael Ritchie; Screenplay, Tom Jones, Harvey Schmidt, based on their musical play; Photography, Fred Murphy; Designer, Douglas W. Schmidt; Costumes, Luke Reichle; Editor, William S. Scharf; Music, Harvey Schmidt; Lyrics, Tom Jones; Choreographer, Michael Smuin; Casting, Rick Pagano; Distributed by MGM; 1995; Dolby; Panavision; Deluxe color; Rated PG; 86 minutes (cut from previous 110 minute print); Release date: September 22, 2000

CAST

Amos Babcock Bellomy	Joel Grey
Henry	Barnard Hughes
Luisa Bellomy	Jean Louisa Kelly
Matt Hucklebee	Joseph McIntyre
El Gallo	Jonathon Morris
Hucklebee	Brad Sullivan
Mortimer	Teller

and Arturo Gil (The Bavarian Baby), Tony Cox (His Assistant), Victoria Stevens (Jo Jo, the Chicken Lady), Trayne Thomas (Tattooed), Shaunery Stevens, Dyrk Ashton (Roustabouts), Gregory Amato, Lee Bell, Celia Fushille-Burke, Marjorie Grundvig, Tiffany Heft, Jennifer Jaffe, Mark Anthony Lopez, Julian Montaner, Rika Onizuka, Joseph Woelfel (Dancers)

A pair of young lovers meet secretly, believing that their fathers would disapprove of their coupling, when in fact the two old men have been conspiring to get their children together for years. The Off-Broadway musical opened on May 5, 1960 at the Sullivan Street Theatre where it was still playing at the time of the film's release.

Gene Hackman, Morgan Freeman

Penélope Cruz

Harold Perrineau, Jr., Penélope Cruz

WOMAN ON TOP

(FOX SEARCHLIGHT) Producer, Alan Poul; Executive Producers, Bronwen Hughes, Fina Torres; Director, Fina Torres; Screenplay, Vera Blasi; Photography, Thierry Arbogast; Designer, Philippe Chiffre; Editor, Leslie Jones; Co-Producer, Nancy Paloian-Breznikar; Music, Luis Bacalov; Music Supervisor, Frankie Pine; Costumes, Elisabeth Tavernier; Casting, Alexa L. Fogel, Laura Folger, Ruy Brito; an Alan Poul production; Dolby; Super 35 Widescreen; Deluxe Color; Rated R; 83 minutes; Release date: September 22, 2000

CAST

Isabella Oliveira...Penélope Cruz
Toninho Oliveira..Murilo Benício
Monica Jones ....Harold Perrineau, Jr.
Cliff Lloyd ....Mark Feuerstein
Alex Reeves ....John De Lancie
TV Director..Anne Ramsay
Claudia Hunter ....Ana Gasteyer
Isabella's Mother...Eliana Guttman
Isabella's Father ....Eduardo Mattedi

and Analu De Castro (Little Isabella—age 2), Thais De Sá Curvelo (Little Isabella—age 5), Ana Paula Oliveira (Cook), Marilice Santos (Sexy Neighbor), Giba Conceiçào, Joaquim Pinto, Vevé Calazans (Troubadours), June A. Lomena (Zeke), Bob Greene (Nikos), Lázaro Ramos (Max), Wagner Moura (Rafi), Cléa Simões (Serafina), Tom Curti (Matire'D), John Crook (Seafood Restaurant Manager), Jonas Bloch (Pierre Laroche), Michel Bercovitch (Academy Student), Carlos Gregório (Melvin), Malu Pessin (Esther), Daniele Suzuki (Yoko), Luis Careca (Thor), Jerry Penacoli (Tom Kelly), Inaldo Santana (Angry Fisherman), Jorge Maia (Yemanja Waiter), Dizoneth Santos (Prison Officer), Phil (Gaffer), Roberta Kennedy (Bar Waitress), Jeff Scott Flores, Gordon Hansen (Bar Regulars), Roger Stoneburner (Bartender), Sergio Maciel (Flower Delivery Man), B. Chico Purdiman, Bob Saenz (Guards), Thomas Hieatt (Hippie Prisoner), David Herman (Photographer), Edlon Tupi (Jail Guard), Otávio Martins (P.A.), Inês Cardoso (Food Stylist), Alan Poul, Jim Freeman (The "Suits"), Adele Proom (Nikos' Mother)

Isabella escapes from her stifling marriage in Brazil and ends up in San Francisco where her mystical culinary skills have men falling under her spell.

Murilo Benício

Penélope Cruz, Mark Feuerstein

BEST IN SHOW

(WARNER BROS.) Producer, Karen Murphy; Executive Producer, Gordon Mark; Director, Christopher Guest; Screenplay, Christopher Guest, Eugene Levy; Photography, Roberto Schaefer; Designer, Joseph T. Garrity; Editor, Robert Leighton; Music, Jeffrey CJ Vanston; Costumes, Monique Prudhomme; Casting, Stuart Aikins; a Castle Rock Entertainment production; Dolby; Technicolor; Rated PG-13; 90 minutes; Release date: September 27, 2000

Eugene Levy, Catherine O'Hara with Winky

CAST

Sheri Ann Cabot	Jennifer Coolidge
Harlan Pepper	Christopher Guest
Scott Donlan	John Michael Higgins
Hamilton Swan	Michael Hitchcock
Gerry Fleck	Eugene Levy
Christy Cummings	Jane Lynch
Stefan Vanderhoof	Michael McKean
Cookie Fleck	Catherine O'Hara
Meg Swan	Parker Posey
Buck Laughlin	Fred Willard
Dr. Theodore W. Millbank III	Bob Balaban
Leslie Ward Cabot	Patrick Cranshaw
Graham Chissolm	Don Lake
Dr. Chuck Nelken	Jay Brazeau
Fay Berman	Linda Kash
Max Berman	Larry Miller
Zach Berman	Cody Gregg
Hotel Manager	Ed Begley, Jr.
Malcolm	Malcolm Stewart
Trevor Beckwith	Jim Piddock

and Carrie Aizley (Fern City Show Spectator), Lewis Arquette (Fern City Show Spectator), Dany Canino (Fern City Show Judge), Will Sasso, Stephen E. Miller (Fishin' Hole Guys), Colin Cunningham (New York Butcher), Jehshua Barnes (Scott's Wild Date), Scott Williamson, Deborah Theaker, Rachael Harris (Winky's Party Guests), Fulvio Cecere (Airport Passerby), Teryl Rothery, Dave Cameron (Philly AM Hosts), Tony Alcantar (Philly AM Chef), Camille Sullivan (Philly AM Assistant), Lynda Boyd, Madeleine Kipling, Merrilyn Gann, Andrew Johnston (Cabot Party Guests), Jay-Lyn Green (Leslie's Nurse), Earlene Luke (Mayflower Hound Judge), Carmen Aguirre (Taft Hotel Maid), Harold Pybus (Mayflower Toy Judge), Hiro Kanagawa (Pet Shop Owner), Cleo A. Laxton (Mayflower Terrier Judge), Corrine Koslo (Mayflower Sporting Judge) Andrew Wheeler (Mayflower Ring Steward), Don Emslie (Mayflower Non-Sporting Judge), Don S. Davis (Mayflower Best in Show Judge), Steven Porter (Bulge), Melanie Angel (American Bitch Photo Editor), Doane Gregory (Terry the Photographer)

Various obsessive dog owners converge at the annual Mayflower Dog Show to have their beloved pets compete for the top prize.

© Castle Rock Entertainment

Christopher Guest, Hubert

Fred Willard, Jim Piddock

Michael McKean with Tyrone, John Michael Higgins with Miss Agnes

Burgess Jenkins

Nicole Ari Parker

Ryan Hurst

Wood Harris

Will Patton, Denzel Washington

Ryan Gosling

Kate Bosworth

Donald Faison

Ethan Suplee

REMEMBER THE TITANS

(WALT DISNEY PICTURES) Producers, Jerry Bruckheimer, Chad Oman; Executive Producers, Mike Stenson, Michael Flynn; Director, Boaz Yakin; Screenplay, Gregory Allen Howard; Photography, Philippe Rousselot; Designer, Deborah Evans; Costumes, Judy Ruskin Howell; Editor, Michael Tronick; Music, Trevor Rabin; Music Supervisors, Kathy Nelson, Bob Badami; Casting, Ronna Kress; Presented in association with Jerry Bruckheimer Films; Distributed by Buena Vista Pictures; Dolby; Panavision; Technicolor; Rated PG; 113 minutes; Release date: September 29, 2000

Hayden Panettiere, Denzel Washington

CAST

Coach Herman Boone ....Denzel Washington
Coach Bill Yoast ....Will Patton
Big Ju (Julius Campbell) ....Wood Harris
Gerry Bertier ....Ryan Hurst
Petey Jones ....Donald Faison
The Rev (Jerry Harris) ....Craig Kirkwood
Lewis Lastik ....Ethan Suplee
Sunshine (Ronnie Bass) ....Kip Pardue
Sheryl Yoast ....Hayden Panettiere
Carol Boone ....Nicole Ari Parker
Emma Hoyt ....Kate Bosworth
Blue (Daryl) Stanton ....Earl C. Poitier
Alan Bosley ....Ryan Gosling
Ray Budds ....Burgess Jenkins
Glascoe ....Neal Ghant
Cook ....David Jefferson, Jr.
Jerry Buck ....Preston Brant
Kirk Barker ....Michael Weatherly
Coach Paul "Doc" Hinds ....Gregalan Williams
Coach Tyrell ....Brett Rice
A.D. Watson ....Richard Fullerton
Executive Director ....J. Don Ferguson
Nicky Boone ....Krystin Leigh Jones
Mr. Campbell ....Afemo Omilami
Col. Bass ....Andrew Masset
Mr. Bosley ....Tim Ware
Captain Hal ....Tom Turbiville
Coach Ed Henry ....Tom Nowicki
Coach Taber ....Jim Grimshaw
Coach Tolbert (Groveton)..David Dwyer
Kip Tyler (Groveton)...Walter Benjamin Keister
Ferdinand Day ....Lou Walker
Mrs. Bertier ....Marion Guyot
Radio Announcer ....Rhubarb Jones
Colorman...Bob Neal
Doctor...Dan Albright
Cop ....Mike Pniewski
Nurse ....Sharon Blackwood
and Paula Claire Jones, Kelly C. Cheston (White Girls), Walker Jones (White Kid #1), Ronald L. Connor, Courtney James Stewart (Black Kids), EY Coley, John Wesley Register (Officials), B. Keith Harmon (Crooked Official), Andy Francis (Quarterback), Stuart Greer (Marshall Assistant Coach), Derick Marshall (Davis), Scott Miles (Fred Alderson), Kevin Dankofsky, David Chandley, Scott Slade, Ric Reitz (Reporters), Steve Barnes (Titan Supporter), Rory Griffin, Ryan Kowalske, Thomas Elliott, C. Stephen Browder, Jameel Jackson, Randy D. Patman, Jr., Jemal L. Webb, Shawn Cummings, Michael Rouby, Ray Stoney (Titans), Shanda Besler (Emma's Friend), David Devries (Parent), Andrew Collins (Black Newspaper Man), Steve Martin, Matt Adams (Hecklers), Marcus M. Moore (Special Teams Coach), Ryan Duncan (Opposition Quarterback)

Kip Pardue

In 1971, an Alexandria high school is forced to integrate, a controversial decision that is further heightened when black coach Herman Boone is hired to preside over the football team.

Earl C. Poitier, Wood Harris, Donald Faison, Ryan Gosling, Craig Kirkwood, Ethan Suplee, Kip Pardue

GIRLFIGHT

(SCREEN GEMS) Producers, Sarah Green, Martha Griffin, Maggie Renzi; Executive Producers, John Sayles, Jonathan Sehring, Caroline Kaplan; Director/Screenplay, Karyn Kusama; Photography, Patrick Cady; Editor, Plummy Tucker; Designer, Stephen Beatrice; Costumes, Luca Mosca, Marco Cattoretti; Music, Theodore Shapiro; Music Supervisors, Susan Jacobs, Gary Harris, Louis DiLivio; Casting, Orpheus Group, Maria E. Nelson, Ellyn Long Marshall; The Independent Film Channel Productions presentation of a Green/Renzi production; Dolby; Technicolor; Rated R; 113 minutes; Release date: September 29, 2000

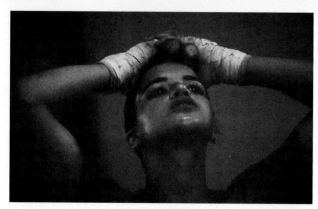

Michelle Rodriguez

CAST

Diana Guzman	Michelle Rodriguez
Hector	Jaime Tirelli
Sandro Guzman	Paul Calderon
Adrian	Santiago Douglas
Ricki Stiles	Alicia Ashley
Ira	Thomas Barbour
Marisol	Elisa Bocanegra
Don	Louis Guss
Mr. Price	J.P. Lipton
Ms. Martinez	Iris Little-Thomas
Cal	Herb Lovelle
Pawnbroker	Jack R. Marks
Gym Coach	Diane Martella
Karina	Belqui Ortiz
Edward	Dadi Pinero
Al	Jose Rabelo
Tino	Anthony Ruiz
Tiny Guzman	Ray Santiago
Science Teacher	John Sayles
Ray	Victor Sierra
Veronica	Shannon Walker Williams

and Graciella Ortiz (Student), Chuck Hickey (Gym Janitor), José Espinal (Ray's Friend), Yiyo Guzman (Ray's Corner Man), Michael Bentt (Fight Pro), Gus Santorella, Courtney Krause (Fight Pro Posse), Edgardo Claudio, Allan Gropper, Danny Gant (Referees), Millie Tirelli (Candice), Josephine Pignataro (Wife), Sanford Redock (Announcer), Allie Woods, Jr. (Janitor), Ricky Colon, Andre Eason, Angel Gonzalez, Gabby Guzman, Andee Hernandez, Carlos Hernandez Jr., Carlos Hernandez Sr., Daniel Judah, Christian Leyba, Paul Maldonado, Angel Osvaldo, Ralphie Rivera, Donnell Smith, Angel Torres, Angel Vega (Boxers)

Michelle Rodriguez, Santiago Douglas

A hot-tempered young woman living in poverty in Brooklyn, finds a way out of her dead-end existence through the world of boxing.

Michelle Rodriguez, Jaime Tirelli

Santiago Douglas, Michelle Rodriguez

Kathleen Robertson, Ali Landry, Minnie Driver

Kathleen Turner

BEAUTIFUL

(DESTINATION) Producers, John Bertolli, B.J. Rack; Executive Producers, Dick Vane, Kate Driver, Wendy Japhet, Barry London, Brent Baum, Steve Stabler, Marty Fink, David Forrest, Beau Rogers; Director, Sally Field; Screenplay, Jon Bernstein; Photography, Robert Yeoman; Designer, Charles Breen; Editor, Debra Neil-Fisher; Music, John Frizzell; Costumes, Chrisi Karvonides-Dushenko; Co-Producers, Mark Morgan, Jon Bernstein, Jade Ramsey; Casting, Amanda Mackey Johnson, Cathy Sandrich; a 2 Drivers/Fogwood Films production, presented in association with Flashpoint Limited and Prosperity Pictures; Dolby; Technicolor; Rated PG-13; 112 minutes; Release date: September 29, 2000

CAST

Mona Hibbard	Minnie Driver
Ruby	Joey Lauren Adams
Vanessa	Hallie Kate Eisenberg
Verna Chickle	Kathleen Turner
Joyce Parkins	Leslie Stefanson
Lorna Larkin (Miss Texas)	Bridgette L. Wilson
Wanda Love (Miss Tennessee)	Kathleen Robertson
Lance DeSalvo	Michael McKean
Miss American Hiss Host	Gary Collins
Nedra	Linda Hart
Lurdy	Brent Briscoe
Mona at 12	Colleen Rennison
Ruby at 12	Jacqueline Steiger
Alberta	Sylvia Short
Clara	Herta Ware
Belindy Lindbrook	Ali Landry

and Robin Reneé (Miss Alabama), Chuti Tiu (Miss Hawaii), Samantha Harris (Miss Minnesota), Dawn Heusser (Miss West Virginia), Julie Condra (Miss Iowa), Jessica Collins (Miss Lawrenceville), Deborah Kellner (Reigning Miss Illinois), Brent Huff (Miss Illinois Local Pageant Host), Charles Dougherty (Director), Shawn Christian (Wink Hendricks), Margaret Emery (Pageant P.A.), Irene Roseen (Official), Mark Christensen (Production Assistant), William Forward (Orthodontist), Liz Lang (Dental Nurse), Alexander Folk (Tom the Grocer), Lu Elrod (Neighbor Woman), Adilah Barnes (Home Economics Teacher), Cindy Montoya-Picker (Dance Teacher), Landry Allbright (Summer), Lorna Scott (Mother in Diner), Earl B. Schuman, Mary E. Thompson (Elderly Couple in Restaurant), Rosine Ace Hatem (Theresa), Claire Benedek, Dale Raoul (Shoppers), Robert Phelps (Mr. Willoughby), Jordan Lund (Detective), Warren Munson (Judge), Keli Daniels, Susan Segal (Fitness Club Ladies), Annabella Price (Mother at Slumber Party), Sydney Berry (Little Girl at Slumber Party), Ken Baldwin (E.I. Crew Member), Spice Williams (Prisoner)

Minnie Driver

Mona Hibbard makes it her goal to rise to the top of the beauty pageant circuit while trying to keep her illegitimate daughter a secret from the media and pageant coordinators.

Hallie Kate Eisenberg, Joey Lauren Adams

Timothy Olyphant, Ben Weber

Dean Cain

THE BROKEN HEARTS CLUB: A ROMANTIC COMEDY

(SONY PICTURES CLASSICS) Producers, Mickey Liddell, Joseph Middleton; Line Producer, Connie Dolph; Co-Producers, Julie Plec, Sam Irvin; Director/Screenplay, Greg Berlanti; Photography, Paul Elliott; Designer, Charlie Daboub; Costumes, Mas Kondo; Editor, Todd Busch; Music, Christophe Beck; Music Supervisor, Julianne Kelley; Casting, Joseph Middleton; a Banner Entertainment production; Super 35 Widescreen; Color; Rated R; 94 minutes; Release date: September 29, 2000

CAST

Benji	Zach Braff
Cole	Dean Cain
Kevin	Andrew Keegan
Leslie	Nia Long
Jack	John Mahoney
Anne	Mary McCormack
Howie	Matt McGrath
Dennis	Timothy Olyphant
Taylor	Billy Porter
Marshall	Justin Theroux
Patrick	Ben Weber
Purple Guy	Robert Arce
Kip Rogers	Michael Bergin
Larry	Chris Payne Gilbert
Shopper	Nora Burns
Mickey	John Brandon
Josephine	Diane McBain
Cop	Robert Peters
Russian Woman	Leeza Vinnichenko
J. Crew Guy	Chris Wiehl
Betty	Jennifer Coolidge
Catcher	Kerr Smith
Umpire	Ken Kerman
Brian	Brian Gaskill
Idaho Guy	Chris Kane
Barry	David Youse
Director	Chris Weitz

A group of gay friends residing in the Los Angeles area go through various ups and downs while looking for love, sex and friendship.

© Sony Pictures Entertainment

Matt McGrath, Ben Weber, Zach Braff

Matt McGrath, Justin Theroux

(back row) Matt McGrath, Ben Weber, Timothy Olyphant, Zach Braff, John Mahoney; (front) Andrew Keegan, Dean Cain, Billy Porter

John Mahoney

Nia Long

Mary McCormack

Matt McGrath, Ben Weber, Andrew Keegan

121

Jada Pinkett-Smith, Damon Wayans

Savion Glover

Cartier Williams, Savion Glover, Tyheesha Collins

Tommy Davidson, Savion Glover

BAMBOOZLED

(NEW LINE CINEMA) Producers, Jon Kilik, Spike Lee; Director/Screenplay, Spike Lee; Photography, Ellen Kuras; Designer, Victor Kempster; Costumes, Ruth Carter; Editor, Sam Pollard; Music, Terence Blanchard; Music Supervisor, Alex Steyermark; Choreographer, Savion Glover; Associate Producer, Kisha Imani Cameron; Casting, Aisha Coley; a 40 Acres and a Mule Filmworks production; Dolby; Color; Rated R; 135 minutes; Release date: October 6, 2000.

CAST

Pierre Delacroix (Peerless Dothan)	Damon Wayans
Manray (Mantan)	Savion Glover
Sloan Hopkins	Jada Pinkett-Smith
Womack (Sleep 'N Eat)	Tommy Davidson
Dunwitty	Michael Rapaport
Honeycutt	Thomas Jefferson Byrd
Junebug	Paul Mooney
Dot	Sarah Jones
Verna	Gillian Iliana Waters
Orchid Dothan	Susan Batson

Mau Mau's:

Big Black	Mos Def
1/16th Black	M.C. Serch
Double Black	Gano Grills
Mo Black	Canibus
Jo Black	DJ Scratch
Smooth Black	Charli Baltimore
Hard Black	Mums

Pickaninny's:

Topsy	Dormeshia Sumbry-Edwards
Aunt Jemima	Tyheesha Collins
Lil' nigger Jim	Cartier Williams
Jungle Bunny	Jason Bernard
Sambo	Baakari Wilder
Rastus	Sekou Torbet

and Mantan's Writing Staff: Anna Hsieh (Joan), Kris Park (Fish), Cheryl Lynn Bowers (Mona), Julie Dretzin (Beth), Steven McElroy (Seth), Stephen Kunken (David), Katie MacNichol (Anna), Joshua Weinstein (Kirk), A.D. Miles (Aaron), Daniel Milder (Peter), Jason Winther (Jeff), also: Alabama Porch Monkeys: Ahmir "?uestlove" Thompson, James "Kamal" Gray, Leonard "Hub" Hubbard, Kyle "Scratch" Jones (The Roots), Tariq Trotter (Levi—Musical Director); Christopher Wynkoop (Massa Charlie), Jani Blom (Jukka Laks), Dina Pearlman (Myrna Goldfarb), Imhotep Gary Byrd, Johnnie L. Cochran Jr., Rev. Al Sharpton, Mira Sorvino, Matthew Modine (Themselves), Arthur Nascarella (Police Chief), Liza Jessie Peterson (Ruth—Casting Director), Don Ezzard Peavy II (Auditioning Dancer), Tony Arnaud (Auditioning "Digeroo-Doo Player"), Tuffy Questell (Auditioning "Singer"), David Wain (Bunning), Ron Lawrence (Mau Mau's Engineer), Al Palagonia (Bobby), Mildred Clinton (Louise), Ephraim Benton (Tre), Tanesha Marie Gary (Stacy), Shannon Walker Williams (Young Black Woman), Matthew Cole Weiss (Young White Man), Coati Mundi (Papo), La Bruja (Cuca), Rodney "Bear" Jackson, Rafael Osorio (Stage Security Guards), Ed Blunt, Renton Kirk (CNS Security Guards), Kim Director, Connie Freestone (Starlets), Rayietta Hill (Hottie), John Wallace, Arthur Thomas (Dawgs), Lisa Ferreira, Kiki Haynes, Judah Jacobs, Light Eyes, Chyna, Luz Whitney (Da Bomb Girls), Danny Hoch (Timmi Hillnigger).

Frustrated at his efforts to get some quality programs on the air, black television writer Pierre Delacroix comes up with an outrageous idea for a modern day "minstrel show" hoping the suggestion will get him fired, only to find out that the network is eager to produce the show which becomes a nationwide hit.

Tommy Davidson, Savion Glover

Michael Rapaport

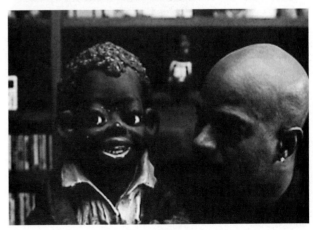

Damon Wayans

MEET THE PARENTS

Ben Stiller

Robert De Niro, Ben Stiller

(UNIVERSAL/DREAMWORKS) Producers, Nancy Tenenbaum, Jane Rosenthal, Robert De Niro, Jay Roach; Director, Jay Roach; Screenplay, Jim Herzfeld, John Hamburg; Story, Greg Glienna, Mary Ruth Clarke; Co-Producers, Amy Sayres, Shauna Weinberg; Photography, Peter James; Designer, Rusty James; Editor, Jon Poll; Associate Producers, Greg Glienna, Emo Phillips, Jim Vincent; Costumes, Daniel Orlandi; Music, Randy Newman; Music Supervisor, Randall Poster; Song: "A Fool in Love" written and performed by Randy Newman; Casting, Ellen Chenoweth; a Nancy Tenenbaum Films presentation of a Tribeca Production; Dolby; Deluxe color; Rated PG-13; 108 minutes; Release date: October 6, 2000

CAST

Jack Byrnes	Robert De Niro
Greg Focker	Ben Stiller
Pam Byrnes	Teri Polo
Dina Byrnes	Blythe Danner
Debbie Byrnes	Nicole Dehuff
Denny Byrnes	Jon Abrahams
Bob Banks	Tom McCarthy
Linda Banks	Phyllis George
Larry Banks	James Rebhorn
Kevin Rawley	Owen Wilson
Flight Attendant	Kali Rocha
Norm the Interrogator	Bernie Sheredy
Pharmacy Clerk	Judah Friedlander
Animal Shelter Worker	Peter Bartlett
Chicago Airport Security	John Elsen
Hospital Patient	Mark Hammer
Ticket Agent	Amy Hohn
Father O'Boyle	William Severs
Kinky	John Fiore
Lost Luggage Clerk	Marilyn Dobrin
Courier	Frank Santorelli
Late Night Courier	Russell Hornsby
Little Girl	Patricia Cook
Little Boys	Cody Ahrens, Cole Hawkins, Spencer Breslin
Wedding Worker	Ina Rosenthal
Nurse	Kim Rideout
Airport Policeman	Kresimir Novakovic
Cops	John Joseph Gallagher, G.A. Aguilar
Security Guard	Lynn Ann Castle

Greg Focker hopes to make an impression on the parents of his girlfriend Pam, only to find that his every move spells disaster during a visit to attend the wedding of Pam's sister. This film received an Oscar nomination for original song ("A Fool in Love").

© Universal Studios/DreamWorks LLC

Teri Polo, Robert De Niro, Blythe Danner

Robert De Niro, Ben Stiller

Ben Stiller, Teri Polo

Robert De Niro, Owen Wilson, Teri Polo, Ben Stiller

Blythe Danner, Robert De Niro

Colin Farrell

Matthew Davis, Colin Farrell

Shea Whigham, Colin Farrell, Matthew Davis, Clifton Collins, Jr., Russell Richardson, Thomas Guiry

Afemo Omilami, Colin Farrell

TIGERLAND

(20th CENTURY FOX) Producers, Arnon Milchan, Steven Haft, Beau Flynn; Executive Producer, Ted Kurdyla; Director, Joel Schumacher; Screenplay, Ross Klavan, Michael McGruther; Photography, Matthew Libatique; Designer, Andrew Laws; Editor, Mark Stevens; Music, Nathan Larson; a Regency Enterprises presentation of a Haft Entertainment/New Regency production; Dolby; Deluxe color; Rated R; 109 minutes; Release date: October 6, 2000

CAST

Roland Bozz	Colin Farrell
Jim Paxton	Matthew Davis
Miter	Clifton Collins, Jr.
Cantwell	Thomas Guiry
Wilson	Shea Whigham
Johnson	Russell Richardson
Captain Saunders	Nick Searcy
Sergeant Landers	Afemo Omilami
Sergeant Thomas	James McDonald
Sergeant Oakes	Keith Ewell
Sergeant Eveland	Matt Gerald
Sergeant Drake	Stephen Fulton
Sergeant MP	Tyler Cravens
Hit the Break Driver	Michael Edmiston
Sheri	Arian Ash
Claudia	Haven Gaston
Training Sergeant Filmore	Michael Shannon
Killed Truck Driver	Roger Floyd
Bartender	Ronnie Schafer
Bargirl	Frances Taylor
Sniffling Soldier	Matt White

and Christy McKee, Karolyn Arnold (Hookers), James Lessick, Jr. (Hobo Vet), Daniel Martin (Range Officer), Marc MacCulay (Tigerland CO), Cole Hauser (Sergeant Cota, aka NCO), Nubia (Girl with Bandana), Jack Newman (Sergeant Gordon), Neil Brown (Keams), Tory Kittles (Ryan), Rhynell Brumfield (Dickson), Chris Huvane (Barnes), Shamari Lewis (Lukins), Dane Northcutt (Hicks), Gerald Jackson, Jr. (New Orleans Drag Queen), Jonathan Hill (Drew), Jeff Hephner (McManus), Drew Gardner (Drunk Nixon), Dennis Benatar (Gate to Tigerland Sergeant)

Roland Bozz, a defiant and individualistic soldier, rebels against the inhumane treatment he and his fellow recruits receive during the final stages of infantry training before they are shipped off to Vietnam.

© Monarchy Enterprises B.V./Regency Entertainment (USA), Inc.

TWO FAMILY HOUSE

(LIONS GATE) Producers, Anne Harrison, Alan Klingenstein; Executive Producers, Jim Kohlberg, Adam Brightman; Director/Screenplay, Raymond De Felitta; Photography, Michael Mayers; Designer, Teresa Mastropierro; Editor, David Leonard; Music, Stephen Endelman; Music Supervisor, Susan Jacobs; Songs Performed by John Pizzarelli Trio; Costumes, Liz McGarrity; Casting, Sheila Jaffe, Georgianne Walken, Julia Kim; a Filbert Steps production; Dolby; Color; Rated R; 104 minutes; Release date: October 6, 2000

Michael Rispoli, Kelly Macdonald

CAST

Buddy Visalo	Michael Rispoli
Mary O'Neary	Kelly Macdonald
Estelle Visalo	Katherine Narducci
Jim O'Neary	Kevin Conway
Chipmunk	Matt Servitto
Laura	Michele Santopietro
Donato	Louis Guss
Marie	Rosemary DeAngelis
Danny	Anthony Arkin
Anthony	Saul Stein
Angelo	Vincent Pastore
Gloria	Sharon Angela
Tina	Ivy Jones
Mr. Cicco	Victor Arnold
Mr. Brancaccio	Richard B. Shull

and Nick Tosches (Hotel Clerk), Jack O'Connell (Mr. Mahoney), Gerry Bamman (Mr. Pine), Barbara Haas (Mrs. Genova), Marshall Efron (Tiny), Joseph R. Gannascoli (Counter Guy), Robert Fitch (Drunken Guy), Peggy Gormley (Miss Dimunjik), Richard Licata (Mr. Asippi), John McLaughlin (Arthur Godfrey), John Pizzarelli (Julius LaRosa)

Buddy Visalo, still hoping to fulfill his dream of becoming a successful singer, comes up with an idea to buy a two family house and convert the ground floor into a neighborhood bar where he can perform.

Michael Rispoli

Katherine Narducci

Vincent Pastore, Michael Rispoli

Jennifer Connelly, Jared Leto

Ellen Burstyn

REQUIEM FOR A DREAM

(ARTISAN) Producers, Eric Watson, Palmer West; Executive Producers, Nick Wechsler, Beau Flynn, Stefan Simchowitz; Co-Executive Producer, Ben Barenholtz; Co-Producers, Randy Simon, Jonah Smith, Scott Vogel, Scott Franklin; Director, Darren Aronofsky; Screenplay, Hubert Selby, Jr., Darren Aronofsky; Based on the novel by Hubert Selby, Jr.; Photography, Matthew Libatique; Designer, James Chinlund; Costumes, Laura Jean Shannon; Editor, Jay Rabinowitz; Music, Clint Mansell; Visual Effects Designers/Supervisors, Jeremy Dawson, Dan Schrecker; Casting, Freddy Luis, Jennifer Lindesmith; a Thousand Words presentation of a Sibling/Protozoa production in association with Industry and Bandeira Entertainment; Dolby; Deluxe color; Not rated; 102 minutes; Release date: October 6, 2000

CAST

Sara Goldfarb	Ellen Burstyn
Harry Goldfarb	Jared Leto
Marion Silver	Jennifer Connelly
Tyrone C. Love	Marlon Wayans
Tappy Tibbons	Christopher McDonald
Ada	Louise Lasser
Rae	Marcia Jean Kurtz
Mrs. Pearlman	Janet Sarno
Mrs. Scarlini	Suzanne Shepherd
Mrs. Ovadia	Joanne Gordon
Mrs. Miles	Charlotte Aronofsky
Mr. Rabinowitz	Mark Margolis
Dr. Pill	Peter Maloney
Dr. Spencer	Ben Shenkman
Big Tim	Keith David
Southern Doctor	Dylan Baker
Donut Cop	Mike Kaycheck
Corn Dog Stand Boss	Jack O'Connell
Lyle Russell	Chas Mastin
Mailman	Ajay Naidu
Arnold the Shrink	Sean Gullette
Nurse Mall	Samia Shoaib
King Neptune	Abraham Abraham
Alice	Aliya Campbell
Young Tyrone	Te'ron A. O'Neal

and Heather Litteer, Jenny Decker, Ami Goodheart, Nina Zavarin (Big Tim Party Girls), Scott Bader, Jim Centofanti, Scott Chait, Daniel Clarin, Ben Cohen, Eric Cohen, Brett Feinstein, Ricky Fier, John Getz, Andrew Kessler, Ross Lombardo, Carter Mansbach, Scott Miller, Todd Miller, Joshua Pollack, Craig Rallo, Geordan Reisner, Keith Scandore, David Seltzer, Chris Varvaro, Ricardo Viñas, Chad Weiner, Jesse Weissberger, Greg Weissman (Party Animals)

In Brighton Beach, Brooklyn, junkie Harry Goldfarb finds his life spiralling out of control from drug abuse, little aware that his mother has also lost her grip on reality, becoming dangerously addicted to diet pills while trying to lose weight for a television appearance. This film received an Oscar nomination for actress (Ellen Burstyn).

© Artisan Entertainment, Inc.

Marlon Wayans, Jared Leto

Jared Leto, Jennifer Connelly

Jennifer Connelly

Jared Leto

Marlon Wayans

Ellen Burstyn, Jared Leto

GET CARTER

(WARNER BROS.) Producers, Mark Canton, Elie Samaha, Neil Canton; Executive Producers, Andrew Stevens, Don Carmody, Bill Gerber, Ashok Amritraj, Steve Bing, Arthur Silver; Director, Stephen Kay; Screenplay, David McKenna; Based on the novel *Jack's Return Home* by Ted Lewis; Photography, Mauro Fiore; Designer, Charles J.H. Wood; Costumes, Julie Weiss; Editor, Jerry Greenberg; Music, Tyler Bates; Co-Producers, Dawn Miller, James Holt, John Goldstone; Associate Producer, Kevin King; Stunts, David Jacox; Casting, Amanda Mackey Johnson, Cathy Sandrich; a Morgan Creek Productions, Inc. and Franchise Pictures presentation of a Franchise Pictures and Canton Company production; Dolby; Panavision; Deluxe color; Rated R; 104 minutes; Release date: October 6, 2000.

CAST

Jack Carter	Sylvester Stallone
Gloria	Miranda Richardson
Doreen	Rachael Leigh Cook
Geraldine	Rhona Mitra
Eddie	Johnny Strong
Con McCarty	John C. McGinley
Jeremy Kinnear	Alan Cumming
Cliff Brumby	Michael Caine
Thorpey	John Cassini
Cyrus Paice	Mickey Rourke
Jim Davis	Mark Boone Junior
Les Fletcher	Garwin Sanford

and Darryl Scheelar (Security Guard), Crystal Lowe, Lauren Smith (Girls), John Moore (Priest), Tyler Labine (Bud #1), Michel Cook (Richard Carter), Morgan Brayton (Waitress), Yves Cameron (Peter), Alexander Pervakov (Jimmy), Chris Duggan (Bouncer), Michael Rumain (Big Mike), Rob Lee (Simkins), Nathanial Deveaux (Vorhees)

A Vegas money collector returns to Seattle for his brother's funeral, hoping to make amends for his past, only to realize that his brother was probably murdered, prompting him to seek revenge. Remake of the 1971 MGM film Get Carter which starred Michael Caine, who also appears in this film, and of the 1972 MGM film Hit Man with Bernie Casey.

Sylvester Stallone, Michael Caine

THE LADIES MAN

(PARAMOUNT) Producer, Lorne Michaels; Executive Producers, Erin Fraser, Thomas K. Levine, Robert K. Weiss; Director, Reginald Hudlin; Screenplay, Tim Meadows, Dennis McNicholas, Andrew Steele; Photography, Johnny E. Jensen; Designer, Franco De Cotiis; Editor, Earl Watson; Associate Producer, Albert Botha; Costumes, Eydi Caines-Floyd; Music, Marcus Miller; Music Supervisors, Heidi Smith, Bill Stephney; Casting, Rick Montgomery; a Lorne Michaels production, presented in association with SNL Studios; Dolby; Deluxe color; Rated R; 84 minutes; Release date: October 13, 2000

CAST

Leon Phelps	Tim Meadows
Julie	Karyn Parsons
Lester	Billy Dee Williams
Scrap Iron	John Witherspoon
Candy	Jill Talley
Barney	Lee Evans
Lance	Will Ferrell
Cheryl	Sofia Milos
Bucky	Eugene Levy
Frank	David Huband
Hal	Ken Campbell
Mail Man	Kevin McDonald
Teresa	Tamala Jones
Audrey	Julianne Moore

and Tiffany Thiessen (Honey DeLune), Rocky Carroll (Cyrus), Brett Heard, Arnold Pinnock, Shaun Majumder, Diego Fuentes (VSA Members), Sean Thibodeau (Hugh Hefner), Mark McKinney (Mr. White), Chris Parnell (Phil Swanson), J'Mari Luke, J'Avie Luke (Newborn Leon), Taye Thomas, Treye Thomas (Baby Leon), Ryan Field (Leon, 12 Yrs.), Patrick Patterson, Diane Fabian (Older Lovers), Susan Aceron, Philip Guerrero (Young Lovers), April Mullen, Dennis McNicholas (Teen Lovers), Ardon Bess (Stage Manager), Robin Ward (Gil Stewart), Joan Massiah (Nun), Hadley Sandiford (Merle), Barbara Barnes Hopkins (Edna), Sal Scozzari, Stephen Greig, D.J. O'Keefe, William Yong, Troy Liddell, Shawn Byfield (VSA Dancers), John Stoneham, Jr. (VSA Driver), Boyd Banks (C&W Station Manager), Jim Codrington (Soul Station Manager), Arthur Eng (Silver Suit Man), Aaron Philip Berg (Brian), Michelle Maria Silveira (Houseboat Cutie), Inna Korobkina (Hef's Girl), Rebecca Weinberg (Hef's Best Girl), Robyn Palmer (Playboy Bunny), Simone Stock (Playboy Photographer), Reginald Hudlin (Aloysius), Destri Yap (Leon, Jr.)

After being fired from his radio show for being too provocative, love advice disc jockey Leon Phelps goes on a search for the mysterious woman who has sent a letter offering herself and her fortune.

Tim Meadows

DR. T & THE WOMEN

(ARTISAN) Producers, Robert Altman, James McLindon; Executive Producer, Cindy Cowan; Director, Robert Altman; Screenplay, Anne Rapp; Photography, Jan Kiesser; Designer, Stephen Altman; Co-Producers, David Levy, Tommy Thompson; Editor, Geraldine Peroni; Costumes, Dona Granata; Music, Lyle Lovett; Casting, Pam Dixon Mickelson; a Sandcastle 5 production; Dolby; Panavision; Deluxe color; Rated R; 121 minutes; Release date: October 13, 2000

CAST

Helen Hunt, Richard Gere

Laura Dern

Farrah Fawcett

Dr. T (Sullivan Travis)..Richard Gere
Bree ....Helen Hunt
Kate ....Farrah Fawcett
Peggy..Laura Dern
Carolyn...Shelley Long
Connie..Tara Reid
Dee Dee ....Kate Hudson
Marilyn ....Liv Tyler
Harlan ....Robert Hays
Bill...Matt Malloy
Eli ....Andy Richter
Dr. Harper..Lee Grant
Dorothy...Janine Turner
Joanne ....Holly Pellham-Davis
and Jeanne Evans (First Exam Patient), Ramsey Williams (Menopausal Patient), Dorothy Deavers (Patient with Cane), Ellen Locy (Tiffany), Cameron Cobb, Mike Scott (Golf Pro Shop Boys), Irene Cortez (Maria), Clara Peretz (Lacey), Mackenzie Fitzgerald (Amber), Juliette Loraine Gauntt (Kristin), Susan McLaughlin (Hospital Receptionist), Oliver Tull (Psychiatric Ward Nurse), Kelli Finglass (Cheerleader Director), Judy Trammell (Cheerleader Choreographer), Wren Arthur, Scarlett McAlister, Angee Hughes, Tina Parker, Marsha McClelland (Dr. T's Staff), Angie Bolling, Nancy Drotning, Shawne Fielding, Andrea Lynch, Meagan Mangum, Lyn Montgomery, Laurel Whitsett, Morgana Shaw, Louanne Stephens, Sarah Wallace, Gail Cronauer, Pam Dougherty, Candace Evans, Greta Ferrell, Susana Gibb, Yvonna Lynn, Shawna McGovern, Andrea Moore, Riley Kirk, Jane Simoneau , Libby Villari, Kim Terry (Dr. T's Patients), Gina Hope, Katherine Bongfeldt, Hollie Stenson, Erin McGrew, Linda Comess (Psychiatric Patients), Robert Elliott, Cynthia Dorn (City Council), Chris Abbott, Audrea Ulmer, Sara Overall, Nance Watkins, Elizabeth Ware, Nina Austin (Wedding Party), Uta Acosta, Norma Clayton, Irene Gonzalez, Dijonee Macias, Shaylene Ruiz, Angela Landini (Mexican Village), Eric Ryan (Birth Baby)

Successful Dallas gynecologist Sullivan Travis finds some solace in his out-of-control life when he begins an affair with Bree, a golf pro.

Liv Tyler, Kate Hudson

Shelley Long, Richard Gere

Robin Thomas, Joan Allen, Jeff Bridges, Sam Elliott, Saul Rubinek

Mike Binder, Joan Allen, Saul Rubinek, Sam Elliott

THE CONTENDER

(DREAMWORKS) Producers, Marc Frydman, Douglas Urbanski, Willi Baer, James Spies; Executive Producers, Dr. Rainer Bienger (Cinerenta), Gary Oldman; Director/Screenplay, Rod Lurie; Photography, Denis Maloney; Designer, Alexander Hammond; Editor, Michael Jablow; Costumes, Matthew Jacobsen; Music, Larry Groupé; Co-Producers, Scott Shiffman, Steve Loglisci; Casting, Mary Jo Slater; a Cinerenta/Cinecontender presentation of a Battleground production in association with the SE8 Group; U.S.–German; Dolby; Foto-Kem color; Rated R; 126 minutes; Release date: October 13, 2000

CAST

Shelly Runyon	Gary Oldman
Laine Hanson	Joan Allen
President Jackson Evans	Jeff Bridges
Reginald Webster	Christian Slater
Kermit Newman	Sam Elliott
Jack Hathaway	William Petersen
Jerry Toliver	Saul Rubinek
Oscar Billings	Philip Baker Hall
Lewis Hollis	Mike Binder
William Hanson	Robin Thomas
Cynthia Lee	Mariel Hemingway
Paige Willomina	Kathryn Morris
Fiona Hathaway	Kristen Shaw
Makerowitz	Douglas Urbanski
Timmy	Noah Fryrear
Dierdra	Angelica Torn
Paul Smith	Joe Taylor
Congressman Skakle	Kevin Geer
Congressman Harding	Doug Roberts
Congressman Marshall	Bev Appleton
Glenda	Sandra Register
Peter Crenshaw	Tony Booth
Steve Poullet	Andrew Boothby
Maggie Runyon	Irene Ziegler
Director Friend	Del Driver
Wilke	Sean Pratt
Anchorman	Bill Bevins
Show Producer	Ed Sala
Stevenson	Kirk Penberthy
Stagehand	Justin Dray
Reporter #4	Jackie Laubacher
Aide	David Bridgewater

and Kevin Grantz (Secret Service Chief), Michael Kennedy (Congressman Fletcher), David Londoner (Congressman Jones), Billy Dye (Waiter), Larry King (Himself), Amit Mehta (Abu Hunter), Greg Cooper (Ted Edwards), J. Scott Shonka (Cappy), Scoot Powell (Attorney), Catherine Schaffner (Patricia Lavameer), Stan Kelly (Alan), William L. Chandler (Personal Waiter), Liz Marks (Sheila), Robert Harvey, Steve Hurwitz (Lobbyists), Ric Young, Sherri Richmond, Teresa Wells Jones, Lynn West, Dave Guertler, Michael Goodwin (Reporters), Heather Rosebeck (Elaine Bidwell), Roderick Jimenez (Trevor), Donald Campen (Sergeant at Arms), Justin Lewis (Producer), Fred Iacovo (Joe Smith), Dawn Westbrook (Secretary), Jolene Carroll (Maid)

After the death of the vice president, President Jackson Evans appoints a woman, Senator Laine Hanson, to fill the position, a controversial decision that causes political adversary Shelly Runyon to dig into Hanson's past in order to discredit her. This film received Oscar nominations for actress (Joan Allen) and supporting actor (Jeff Bridges).

© DreamWorks LLC

Mike Binder, Joan Allen

Gary Oldman

William Petersen

Christian Slater

BEDAZZLED

Elizabeth Hurley, Brendan Fraser

(20TH CENTURY FOX) Producers, Trevor Albert, Harold Ramis; Director, Harold Ramis; Screenplay, Larry Gelbart, Harold Ramis, Peter Tolan; Based on the motion picture *Bedazzled* with screenplay by Peter Cook, from a story by Peter Cook and Dudley Moore; Executive Producer, Neil Machlis; Photography, Bill Pope; Designer, Rick Heinrichs; Editor, Craig P. Herring; Costumes, Deena Appel; Co-Producer, Suzanne Herrington; Visual Effects Supervisor, Richard Edlund; Music, David Newman; Music Supervisor, Dawn Solér; a Regency Enterprises presentation of a Trevor Albert production; Dolby; Panavision; Deluxe color; Rated PG-13; 93 minutes; Release date: October 20, 2000

CAST

Elliot Richards ....Brendan Fraser
The Devil ....Elizabeth Hurley
Alison Gardner/Nicole...Frances O'Connor
Carol/Penthouse Hostess ....Miriam Shor
Dan/Esteban/Beach Jock/
Sportscaster/African Party Guest ....Orlando Jones
Bob/Roberto/Beach Jock/Sportscaster/
Lincoln Aide...Paul Adelstein
Jerry/Alejandro/Beach Jock/Sportscaster/Lance........................Toby Huss
Elliot's Cellmate ....Gabriel Casseus
Priest..Brian Doyle-Murray
Desk Sergeant ....Jeff Doucette
and Aaron Lustig (Synedyne Supervisor), Rudolf Martin (Raoul), Julian Firth (John Wilkes Booth), David Bain (McDonald's Employee), William Salyers (Elegant Devil), Tom Woodruff, Jr (Biggest Devil), William Marquez (Eduardo), Ilya Morelle (Russian Drug Dealer), Paul Simon (Police Officer), R.M. Haley (Mover), Ray Haratian (Pablito), Iain Rogerson, Biddy Hodson, Roger Hammond, William Osbourne (Play Actors), Laurel A. Ward, Beverly Wiles, Robert Ambrose, Suzanne Herrington (Tech Support Advisors), Bonnie Somerville, Sadie Kratzig (Girls at Beer Garden), Mickey Victor (Drug Factory Foreman), Stephán A. McKenzie (DV8 Bouncer), Lindsay Albert, Joanna Bacalso, Anderson Bourell, Cara Michelle Meschter, Jessica Anne Osekowsky (DV8 Clubgoers), Christine Cameron (DV8 Waitress), Michelle Boehle, Brigid Burns, Gigi Chavoshi, Natalie Hohalek, Eboni Y. Nichols, Katy Quinealty, Gloria Rodriguez, Susie Shoemaker, Joelene Walker, Hope Wood (Cheerleaders/Dancers)

Desperate to make co-worker Alison Gardner his girlfriend, socially inept Elliot Richards makes a pact with the Devil to receive seven wishes in order to obtain his goal. Remake of the 1967 20th Century-Fox film Bedazzled, that starred Peter Cook, Dudley Moore, and Eleanor Bron.

Frances O'Connor, Brendan Fraser

Brendan Fraser

Elizabeth Hurley, Brendan Fraser

James Caan, Joaquin Phoenix

Joaquin Phoenix, Mark Wahlberg

Mark Wahlberg

Charlize Theron, Joaquin Phoenix

THE YARDS

(MIRAMAX) Producers, Nick Wechsler, Paul Webster, Kerry Orent; Executive Producers, Bob Weinstein, Harvey Weinstein, Jonathan Gordon; Director, James Gray; Screenplay, James Gray, Matt Reeves; Co-Producers, Matt Reeves, Christopher Goode; Photography, Harris Savides; Editor, Jeffrey Ford; Costumes, Michael Clancy; Designer, Kevin Thompson; Music, Howard Shore; Music Supervisor, Dana Sano; Casting, Douglas Aibel; a Paul Webster/Industry Entertainment production; Dolby; Panavision; Deluxe color; Rated R; 115 minutes; Release date: October 20, 2000

CAST

Leo Handler	Mark Wahlberg
Willie Gutierrez	Joaquin Phoenix
Erica Stoltz	Charlize Theron
Frank Olchin	James Caan
Val Handler	Ellen Burstyn
Kitty Olchin	Faye Dunaway
Bernard Stoltz	Chad Aaron
Raymond Price	Andrew Davoli
Arthur Mydanick	Steve Lawrence
Seymour Korman	Tony Musante
Paul Lazarides	Victor Argo
Manuel Sequiera	Tomas Milian
Hector Gallardo	Robert Montano

and Victor Arnold, Louis Guss (Nathan Grodner), Domenick Lombardozzi (Todd), Joe Lisi (Elliot), David Zayas (Officer Jerry Rifkin), Joseph Ragno (Parole Officer), Teresa Yenque (Maid), Jose Soto (Orderly), John Tormey (Contract Officer), Teddy Coluca (Terry), Jack O'Connell (Sal Disipio), Dan Grimaldi (Executive One), Garry Pastore (Detective Tommasino), Ron Brice (Detective Boulett), Gene Canfield (Queensborough Policeman), Keith Hernandez (Baseball Celebrity), Allan Houston (Basketball Celebrity), Andi Shrem (Belva), Joe Dimare (Dante), Barry Wetcher (Young Doctor), Oscar Colon (Well-Dressed Man), Jack Kent (Young Italian Man), Brandon Danziger (Neil), Doug Barron (Doctor), Floyd Resnick (Hospital Cop), Chris Edwards, Raymond Seiden (Police Officers), Annika Pergament (Reporter), Maximiliano Hernandez (Bartender), Kip Evans (Guy), John Elsen, Douglas Crosby (Officers), Scott Nicholson (Policeman #1), Kim Merritt (Todd's Girlfriend), Erin Walls (Dante's Girlfriend), Tyree Simpson (Doorman), Peter Vallone (Councilman), Irwin Gray (Lawyer), Denise Traficanti (Secretary), Roma Torre, Louis Dodley, Ernie Anastos (News Anchors)

Leo Handler, returning from a stretch in prison for taking the fall for some friends, hopes to start life anew. Instead he finds himself drawn back into a world of corruption when he is given a job by his influential uncle at the New York City subway yards.

Kevin Spacey, Haley Joel Osment

Helen Hunt, Haley Joel Osment, Kevin Spacey

PAY IT FORWARD

(WARNER BROS.) Producers, Steven Reuther, Peter Abrams, Robert L. Levy; Executive Producers, Mary McLaglen, Jonathan Treisman; Director, Mimi Leder; Screenplay, Leslie Dixon; Based on the novel by Catherine Ryan Hyde; Photography, Oliver Stapleton; Music, Thomas Newman; Designer, Leslie Dilley; Costumes, Renee Ehrlich Kalfus; Editor, David Rosenbloom; Casting, Geraldine Leder; a Tapestry Films production, presented in association with Bel-Air Entertainment; Dolby; Technicolor; Rated PG-13; 122 minutes; Release date: October 20, 2000

CAST

Eugene Simonet	Kevin Spacey
Arlene McKinney	Helen Hunt
Trevor McKinney	Haley Joel Osment
Chris Chandler	Jay Mohr
Jerry	James Caviezel
Ricky	Jon Bon Jovi
Grace	Angie Dickinson
Sidney	David Ramsey
Thorsen	Gary Werntz
Woman on Bridge	Colleen Flynn
Adam	Marc Donato
Bonnie	Kathleen Wilhoite
Michelle	Liza Snyder
Nurse	Jeannetta Arnette
Thorsen's Daughter	Hannah Werntz
Principal	Tina Lifford
Rough Kids	Loren D. Baum, Nico Matinata, Zack Duhame
Shawn	Shawn Pyfrom
Alexandra	Alexandra Kotcheff
Jordan	Bradley White
Christi	Christi Colombo

and Phillip Stewart (Phillip), Justin Parsons (Justin), Myeshia Dejore Walker (Myeshia), Brenae Suzanne Davey (Brenae), Molly Kate Bernard (Molly), Andrew Patrick Flood (Andy), Tameila N. Turner (Tameila), Julian Correa (Julian), Carrie Ann Sullivan (School Girl), Patricia Deanda (Change Girl), Ryan Berti, Gabriela Rivas (Hallway Kids), Carrick O'Quinn (Man in Window), Stephanie Feury (Woman in Window), Bernard White (Cop), Tom Bailey, Tim Dezarn, Jonathan Nichols (Liquid Men), Ron Keck, John Powers (Lowlifes), Bob McCracken (Creepy Middle-Aged Man), Frank Whiteman (Doctor), Eugene Osment (Cop Who Gives Directions), Kendall Tenney, Sue Tripathy (Newscasters), Rusty Meyers (News Stand Guy), Leslie Dilley (The Governor)

Young Trevor responds to his teacher's class project to change the world by coming up with a plan in which he will help three people who will, in turn, help three others, in hopes of starting a chain of improvement in society.

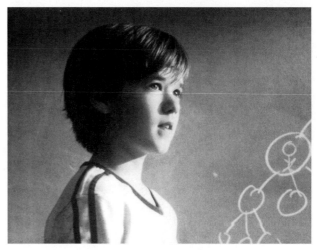

Haley Joel Osment

Haley Joel Osment, Helen Hunt

ANIMAL FACTORY

(SILVER NITRATE) Producers, Julie Yorn, Elie Samaha, Steve Buscemi, Andrew Stevens; Executive Producers, Allan Cohen, Barry Cohen; Co-Producer, Tracee Stanley, Edward Bunker, Danny Trejo; Director, Steve Buscemi; Screenplay, Edward Bunker, John Steppling; Based on the novel *The Animal Factory* by Edward Bunker; Photography, Phil Parmet; Designer, Steven Rosenzweig; Costumes, Lisa Parmet; Editor, Kate Williams; Line Producer, Tim Moore; Music, John Lurie; Music Supervisor, Lynn Geller; Casting, Sheila Jaffe, Georgianne Walken; a Franchise Pictures presentation of a Phoenician Entertainment/Industry Entertainment/Arts Production Group production; Dolby; Color; Rated R; 95 minutes; Release date: October 20, 2000 (This film had its premiere on Cinemax in July, 2000)

CAST

Earl Copen	Willem Dafoe
Ron Decker	Edward Furlong
Vito	Danny Trejo
Paul Adams	Mark Boone Junior
Lt. Seeman	Seymour Cassel
Jan the Actress	Mickey Rourke
Buck Rowan	Tom Arnold
James Decker	John Heard
A.R. Hosspack	Steve Buscemi

and Chris Bauer (Bad Eye), Rockets Redglare (Big Rand), Jake Labotz (Jesse), Mark Engelhardt (T.J.), Edward Bunker (Buzzard), Victor Pagan (Psycho Mike), Ernest Harden, Jr. (Richland), Afemo Omilami (Capt. Knight), Michael Buscemi (Mr. Harrell), J.C. Quinn (Ivan McGhee), Steven Randazzo (Jacob Horvath), Mark Webber (Tank), Jonny Spanish (Billy), Vincent Laresca (Ernie), Larry Fessenden (Benny), Mark Amitin (Bifocals Man), Sal Mazzotta (Florizzi), John Lumia (Wayne), Antony (Toni Johnson), John Knox (Stoneface), Rick Walls (Iron Man), Richard Burton, Jeffrey Dwayne Cousar (Prisoners), James Johnson (Deputy in Courtroom), Judge Paul P. Panepinto (Judge), Wendee Pratt, Anika Hawkins (Prosecutors), Jim Goodall (Jesse's Drummer), Will Holshouser (Accordionist), Hahn Rowe (Violinist), Francisco Sandoval (Hispanic Con), Brian Anthony Wilson (Ponchio), Sixto Ramos (Sgt. Perez), James Martin Kelly (Sgt. Armstrong), Christopher Long (Guard), Sean P. Anderson (B Section Guard), Patrick F. McDade (D.A. McDonald), Damali Mason (Escorting Guard), Joliet Harris (Court Guard), Paul L. Nolan (Deputy), Vince Mancini (Warden Coburn), Vincent Yates (Robert Knowles), Ed Hodson (Trash Truck Driver)

A young drug dealer is sentenced to prison where he is taken under the protective wing of an influential con.

© Franchise Pictures/Silver Nitrate

Edward Furlong, Willem Dafoe

Candace Evanofski, Donald Holden

Curtis Cotton III, Paul Schneider

GEORGE WASHINGTON

(COWBOY BOOKING) Producers, David Gordon Green, Sacha W. Mueller, Lisa Muskat; Executive Producer, Sam Froelich; Director/Screenplay, David Gordon Green; Co-Producers, Erin Aldridge, Craig Zobel; Photography, Tim Orr; Editors, Steven Gonzales, Zene Baker; Music, Michael Linnen, David Wingo, others; Art Director, Richard Wright; a Blue Moon Productions and Code Red presentation; Cinemascope; Color; Not rated; 89 minutes; Release date: October 27, 2000

CAST

Nasia	Candace Evanofski
George	Donald Holden
Buddy	Curtis Cotton III
Damascus	Eddie Rouse
Rico Rice	Paul Schneider
Vernon	Damian Jewan Lee
Sonya	Rachael Handy
Euless	Jonathan Davidson
Ruth	Janet Taylor
Augie	Scott Clackum
Lancaster	Jason Shirley
Tyler	Christian Gustoitis
Rico's Father	Beau Nix

In a rural Southern town, young George, in an effort to escape from his miserable life at home, takes to hanging out with some other kids in an abandoned amusement park, where a tragedy occurs.

© Cowboy Booking Intl.

ONCE IN THE LIFE

(LIONS GATE) Producers, David Bushell, Helen Sugland, Laurence Fishburne; Executive Producers, Larry Meistrich, Stephen Carlis, Donald C. Carter; Director/Screenplay, Laurence Fishburne; Based on his play *Riff Raff*; Photography, Richard Turner; Designer, Charley Beal; Costumes, Darryle Johnson; Music, Branford Marsalis; Music Supervisors, Barry Cole, Christopher Covert; Editor, Bill Pankow; Associate Producers, Keith Abell, Joseph T. DiMartino; Line Producer, Ray Angelic; Casting, Bonnie Timmermann; a Shooting Gallery presentation in association with Cinema Gypsy Prods.; Dolby; Technicolor; Rated R; 107 minutes; Release date: October 27, 2000

CAST

20/20 Mike	Larry Fishburne
Torch	Titus Welliver
Tony	Eamonn Walker
Freddie Nine Lives	Dominic Chianese, Jr.
Manny Rivera	Paul Calderon
Ruffhouse	Gregory Hines
Maxine	Annabella Sciorra
Buddha	Michael Paul Chan
Hector	Andres "Dres" Titus
Chino	Tiger Chen
Mike Murphy	Nick Chinlund

and Tim White (Little Billy), Wanda De Jesus (Jackie), Justin Pierre Edmund (Little Mickey), Huey Morgan (Carlos), Madison Riley (Precious), Sue Costello (Sergeant Kneely), Alan Francis (Strip Club Patron)

Tony is dispatched by a drug dealer to dispose of his friend 20/20 Mike and Mike's half-brother, Torch, as punishment for stealing heroin from him, an assignment that results in conflicting loyalties between the three men.

© Lions Gate Films

Laurence Fishburne, Titus Welliver

Eamonn Walker, Dominic Chianese, Jr.

John Travolta, Lisa Kudrow

LUCKY NUMBERS

(PARAMOUNT) Producers, Andrew Lazar, Jonathan D. Krane, Sean Daniel, Nora Ephron; Director, Nora Ephron; Screenplay, Adam Resnick; Executive Producer, G. Mac Brown; Photography, John Lindley; Designer, Dan Davis; Editor, Barry Malkin; Costumes, Albert Wolsky; Co-Producer, Donald J. Lee, Jr.; Music, George Fenton; Music Supervisor, Nick Meyers; Casting, Francine Maisler, Kathleen Driscoll-Mohlar; a Studio Canal presentation of a Jonathan D. Krane production, a Mad Chance production, in association with Alphaville; Dolby; Deluxe color; Rated R; 100 minutes; Release date: October 27, 2000

CAST

Russ Richards	John Travolta
Cyrstal Latroy	Lisa Kudrow
Gig	Tim Roth
Dick	Ed O'Neill
Dale	Michael Rapaport
Chambers	Daryl Mitchell
Lakewood	Bill Pullman
Jerry Green	Richard Schiff
Walter	Michael Moore
Chief Troutman	Sam McMurray

and Michael Weston (Larry), Maria Bramford (Wendy), Caroline Aaron (Nurse Sharpling), John F. O'Donohue (Bobby), Colin Mochrie (Jack), Nick Loren (Father), Jake Fritz (Sam), Emmy Laybourne (Process Server), Ken Jenkins (Dan Schuff), Andrea Walters (Heidi Zimmer), Denalda Williams (Dottie), Ginger Williams (Larry's Girlfriend), Craig Lally (Cop), Andy Siegel (Kippy), Frank Riccardi, Jr. (Dale's Partner), Carol Androsky (Judy), Pat Jordan (Larry's Mother), Scott Mosenson (Paramedic), Dawn McMillan (Carol), Katrina Law, Kim Stutzman, Susie Ewing (Teen Girls), Nancy Hopewell, Carmen Ashby (Waltzing Crab Patrons), Chris Palmer (Mitch Robertson), Margaret Travolta, Toya A. Brown (Nurses), Tony Carreiro, Stephanie Erb, Alfonso Gomez-Rejon (Reporters), J.J. Sacha (Game Show Announcer), Etty Lau, Lindsley Allen, Kelly Devine, Tomasina Parrott, Tracy Phillips, Kiva Dawson (Dancers), Floyd Peterson (Voice Over Announcer)

A Pennsylvania tv weather man, down on his luck, enlists the station's lotto ball girl to help him fix the lottery in his favor, a scheme that goes disastrously awry.

© Paramount Films

CHARLIE'S ANGELS

(COLUMBIA) Producers, Leonard Goldberg, Drew Barrymore, Nancy Juvonen; Executive Producers, Betty Thomas, Jenno Topping, Joseph M. Caracciolo; Director, McG; Screenplay, Ryan Rowe, Ed Solomon, John August; Based on the television series created by Ivan Goff and Ben Roberts; Photography, Russell Carpenter; Designer, J. Michael Riva; Editors, Wayne Wahrman, Peter Teschner; Music, Edward Shearmur; Music Supervisor, John Houlihan; Costumes, Joseph G. Aulisi; Choreographer, Marguerite Derricks; Casting, Justine Baddeley, Kim Davis-Wagner; a Leonard Goldberg/Flower Films/Tall Trees Production; Dolby; Deluxe color; Rated PG-13; 92 minutes; Release date: November 3, 2000

Drew Barrymore, Bill Murray, Lucy Liu, Cameron Diaz

CAST

Natalie	Cameron Diaz
Dylan	Drew Barrymore
Alex	Lucy Liu
Bosley	Bill Murray
Eric Knox	Sam Rockwell
Vivian Wood	Kelly Lynch
Roger Corwin	Tim Curry
Thin Man	Crispin Glover
Jason	Matt LeBlanc
Mr. Jones	LL Cool J
Chad	Tom Green
Pete	Luke Wilson
Pasqual	Sean Whalen
Flight Attendant	Tim Dunaway
Himself	Alex Trebek
Reform Officer	Raleigh Wilson
Fencing Opponent	Mark Ryan
Driving Instructor	Bobby Ore
DJ	Guy Oseary
UPS Delivery Guy	Joe Duer
Red Star Systems Techies	Matthew Frauman, Reggie Hayes
Doris	Melissa McCarthy
Red Star Systems Directors	Bob Stephenson, Ned Bellamy
Director's Buddy	Raymond Patterson
Red Star Systems Security Guard	Bjorn Flor
Boys	Gaven E. Lucas, Michael Barryte
Corwin's Driver	Andrew Wilson
Assistant Director	Branden Williams
Stuntwoman	Michiko Nishiwaki
Accordionist	Frank Marocco
Partygoer	Darrell Pfingsten
Bouncers	Jimmy Calloway, Kevin Grevioux
Bathroom Thug	Michael Papajohn
Shooters	Jim Palmer, Shawn Woods
Getaway Drivers	Kenny Endoso, Tom Garner

and Isaac C. Singleton, Jr. (Kidnapper), Paul Eliopoulos, Tim Gilbert, Al Goto, Steven Ito, Felipe Savahge, Mike Smith, Jerry Trimble (Knox Thugs), John Forsythe (Voice of Charlie)

Lucy Liu, Cameron Diaz, Drew Barrymore

Three dynamic female private investigators are hired to find the kidnapped founder of Knox Technologies who has designed a valuable voice-identification software. Based on the television series that ran on ABC from 1976 to 1981 and originally starred Kate Jackson, Farrah Fawcett-Majors, Jaclyn Smith, and David Doyle, then later featured Cheryl Ladd, Shelley Hack, and Tanya Roberts. John Forsythe repeats his television role here as the voice of Charlie.

Drew Barrymore, Cameron Diaz, Lucy Liu

THE LEGEND OF BAGGER VANCE

(DREAMWORKS/20TH CENTURY FOX) Producers, Robert Redford, Michael Nozik, Jake Eberts; Executive Producer, Karen Tenkhoff; Director, Robert Redford; Screenplay, Jeremy Leven; Based on the novel by Steven Pressfield; Co-Producers, Chris Brigham, Joseph Reidy; Photography, Michael Ballhaus; Designer, Stuart Craig; Editor, Hank Corwin; Music, Rachel Portman; Costumes, Judianna Makovsky; Visual Effects Supervisor, Richard Chuang; Casting, Debra Zane; a Wildwood/Allied production; Dolby; DuArt color; Rated PG-13; 127 minutes; Release date: November 3, 2000

CAST

Bagger Vance	Will Smith
Rannulph Junuh	Matt Damon
Adele Invergordon	Charlize Theron
Walter Hagen	Bruce McGill
Bobby Jones	Joel Gretsch
Hardy Greaves	J. Michael Moncrief
Neskaloosa	Peter Gerety
Grantland Rice	Lane Smith
O.B. Keeler	Michael O'Neill
Spec Hammond	Thomas Jay Ryan
Frank Greaves	Trip Hamilton
Dougal McDermott	Dermot Crowley
John Invergordon	Harve Presnell
McManus	Danny Nelson
Laidlaw	Bob Penny
Delahunty	Michael McCarty
Idalyn Greaves	Carrie Preston
Eugene James	Turner Green
Wilbur Charles	Blake King
Mary Jones	Andrea Powell
Older Hardy	Jack Lemmon

and John Bennes, Jonathan Green, Shane Brown, J. Don Ferguson (Citizens), F. Roger Mitchell (Aaron), Charles Riffenberg IV, Leon Lamar, Cory Carbaugh, Charles Seabrook, Bilaal Salaam (Card Players), Charles Ward, George Green (Men), Julie Jones (Woman #1), Valanie Lang (Girl #1), Bernard Hocke (News Photographer), Dan Beene (Willy), Elliott Street (Carter), Wilbur T. Fitzgerald (Roy), Sonny Seiler (Sonny the Bartender), Joseph Reidy (Photographer), Tannis Stoops (Anna Mae), Dearing Paige Hockman, Erika Mounts (Hagen Girls), Neil Gonzaga, Ronald Steppe, Hugh Baggett (Bar Patrons), Jabulani Brown (Jones' Caddy), Vijay Patel (Hagen's Caddy)

A once-prominent golfer comes out of a decade-long period of inactivity to compete in a special match, coached by a mysterious caddie named Bagger Vance. This was the final film appearance of Jack Lemmon who died on June 27, 2001.

J. Michael Moncrief, Will Smith, Matt Damon

J. Michael Moncrief

Joel Gretsch, Matt Damon, Bruce McGill

Charlize Theron, Matt Damon

LITTLE NICKY

(NEW LINE CINEMA) Producers, Robert Simonds, Jack Giarraputo; Executive Producers, Adam Sandler, Michael De Luca, Brian Witten, Robert Engelman; Director, Steven Brill; Screenplay, Tim Herlihy, Adam Sandler, Steven Brill; Photography, Theo Van De Sande; Designer, Perry Andelin Blake; Editor, Jeff Gourson; Costumes, Ellen Lutter; Visual Effects Supervisor, John Sullivan; Music, Teddy Castellucci; Music Supervisor, Michael Dilbeck; Casting, Roger Mussenden; a Happy Madison production in association with The Robert Simonds Company; Dolby; Deluxe color; Rated PG-13; 90 minutes; Release date: November 10, 2000

Patricia Arquette, Adam Sandler

CAST

Nicky	Adam Sandler
Valerie	Patricia Arquette
Dad	Harvey Keitel
Adrian	Rhys Ifans
Cassius	Tommy "Tiny" Lister, Jr.
Lucifer	Rodney Dangerfield
Todd	Allen Covert
Peter	Peter Dante
John	Jonathan Loughran
Voice of Beefy	Robert Smigel
Holly	Reese Witherspoon
Referee	Dana Carvey
Peeper	Jon Lovitz
Gatekeeper	Kevin Nealon
Chief of Police	Michael McKean
Deacon	Quentin Tarantino
Chubbs	Carl Weathers
Jimmy the Demon	Blake Clark
The Townie	Rob Schneider
Street Vendor	John Witherspoon
Nipples	Clint Howard
Christa	Leah Lail
Jenna	Jackie Titone
Harlem Globetrotters Coach	Mannie Jackson
Alumni Hall Announcer	Frank Sivero
Cardinal	Lewis Arquette
Mayor	George Wallace
Hitler	Christopher Carroll
Mom	Ellen Cleghorne
Dad	Reggie McFadden
Son	Philip D. Bolden
Mrs. Dunleavy	Laura Harring
Scottie Dunleavy	Isaiah Griffin
Baby Zacariah	Brandon Rosenberg
Fitzie	Kevin Grady
Sal the Demon	Sal Cavaliere

and Orlando Antigua, Matthew Jackson, Curley "Bo" Johnson, Herbert Lang, William Stringfellow, Lou Dunbar (Harlem Globetrotters), Erinn Bartlett (Fenner), Henry Winkler, Ozzie Ozbourne, Bill Walton, Regis Philbin, Sylvia Lopez (Themselves), Sid Ganis (Weatherman), Todd Holland, Gerard "Sheck" Bugge (Reformed Demons), Mary Brill (Church Woman), Suzanne Frydman (Pregnant Woman), John Kirk (Young Man), Tom McNulty (Screaming Man), Mike Giarraputo (Half Court Shot Fan), Fred Wolf, Gwendolyn G. Yeager (Fans), Jana Sandler, Kalie Stewart Conner, Stephanie Chad, Kimberly Velez, Tracey Ostrand (Angels), David Sardi (Popeyes Cashier), Tom Winkler, John Farley (Human Dartboards), Tim Young (Cop), Troy Brown (Beating Cop), Eli Wolstan (Vendor Cop), Michael Charles Roman, Peter Tambakis, John White (Kids), Jeff Imada (Chinese Delivery Guy), Radioman (Bum in Alley), Mary Diveny (Lady in Park), Stuart Rudin (Bus Shelter Bum), Ng Thanh Nhan (Korean Vendor), Peter Linardi (Fat Guy), Ricco Bueno (Gardener), Lynn Wilson (Mother with Carriage), Lillian Adams (Old Lady at Game), Andrew L. Mensch (Boy), Joe Griffo (Evil Little Person), Cindy Sorenson (Female Little Person), Jake McKinnon (Big Bird), Michael Deak (Gary the Monster), Agustin Alvardo, David Michael John Castner, Dana Moir, Paul Tanksley, Jr. (Men in Church), J. Graysen Stubbs (Church Kid), Ruth Annesi (Woman in Audience), Vincenetta Gunn (Angry Woman), Jess Harnell (Gary the Monster, Voice Over)

Rodney Dangerfield, Harvey Keitel

When the Devil refuses to turn over his throne to his two eldest sons, they decide to cause havoc in New York City, prompting Satan to send his awkward son Nicky to Earth to stop them.

Tommy "Tiny" Lister, Jr., Rhys Ifans

Robert De Niro, Cuba Gooding, Jr.

MEN OF HONOR

(20TH CENTURY FOX) formerly *Navy Divers*; Producers, Robert Teitel, Bill Badalato; Executive Producers, Bill Cosby, Stanley Robertson; Director, George Tillman, Jr.; Screenplay, Scott Marshall Smith; Based upon the life of Carl Brashear; Photography, Anthony B. Richmond; Designer, Leslie Dilley; Editor, John Carter; Costumes, Salvador Perez; Music, Mark Isham; Underwater Director of Photography, Pete Romano; 2nd Unit Director/Stunts, Ernie Orsatti; a Fox 2000 Pictures presentation of a State Street Pictures production; Dolby; J-D-C Widescreen; Deluxe color; Rated R; 129 minutes; Release date: November 10, 2000

CAST

Billy Sunday	Robert De Niro
Carl Brashear	Cuba Gooding, Jr.
Gwen	Charlize Theron
Jo	Aunjanue Ellis
Mr. Pappy	Hal Holbrook
Snowhill	Michael Rapaport
Captain Pullman	Powers Boothe
Captain Hartigan	David Keith
Rourke	Holt McCallany
Isert	Joshua Leonard
Boots	Dennis Troutman

and Joshua Feinman (DuBoyce), Theo Pagones (Mellegrano), Ryan Honey (Yarmouth), David Conrad (Hanks), Chris Warren, Jr. (Young Carl), Lester B. Hanson (Admiral Yon), Jack Frazier (Rear Admiral French), David Richard Heath (Medical Officer), Demene E. Hall (Mrs. Biddle), Alimi Ballard (Coke), Shawn Michael Howard (Junie), Troy Lund (Blonde Gate SP), Henry Harris (Rescued Pilot), Matt Dotson (Marine Guard), Carl Lumbly (Mac, Carl's Father), Lonette McKee (Ella, Carl's Mother), Glynn Turman (Chief Floyd), David Meyers (Dr. Cudahy), Richard Perry Turner (Dr. Dinkins), George "Chick" Rankins (Cab Driver), Richard Sanders (Bartender), Nasir Najieb (Black Inductee), Dennis Bateman (Navy Instructor), Eric Newsome (Naked Grunt), Steven Clark Pachosa (Navy Recruiter), Marilyn Faith Hickey (Pinch-Faced Woman), Bruce Burkhartsmeier (Presiding Officer), Michael Tyrone Williamson (Waiter), Michelle Guthrie (Therapist), Michael Patrick Egan (Sailor), Scott Kraft (Ropelski), Tim Monsion (News Reporter), Dulé Hill (Red Tail), Timothy McCuen Piggee (School Master), John J. Polce (Hospital Security), The Count (Band Leader), Allen Gerbino, Art Gotsar (Pilots), Robert Blanche (Shore Patrolman #2), Ivory L. Dilley (Frantic Girl), Chad W. Smathers (Drowning Boy), Wayne Morse (Navy Orderly), Rachel Jahn (Candy Striper), Jon Du Clos (Sunday's Assistant), Leon Russom (Decker), Richard Radecki (Fan Tail Chief), Randy Flagler (Bomb Chief), Jeremy Taylor (Deckhand), Jason Bailey (Sonar Man)

The true story of how Carl Brashear overcame opposition and prejudice to become a top navy diver.

© Twentieth Century Fox

Cuba Gooding, Jr.

Robert De Niro, Cuba Gooding, Jr.

Cuba Gooding, Jr., Charlize Theron

Mark Ruffalo, Rory Culkin

Laura Linney, Mark Ruffalo

Laura Linney, Mark Ruffalo

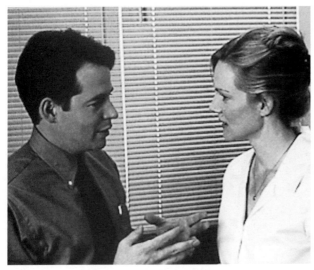

Matthew Broderick, Laura Linney

YOU CAN COUNT ON ME

(PARAMOUNT CLASSICS) Producers, Larry Meistrich, Barbara De Fina, John N. Hart, Jeffrey Sharp; Executive Producers, Martin Scorsese, Steve Carlis, Donald C. Carter, Morton Swinsky; Director/Screenplay, Kenneth Lonergan; Co-Producers, Keith Abell, Julian Iragorri; Line Producer, Jill Footlick; Photography, Stephen Kazmierski; Editor, Anne McCabe; Designer, Michael Shaw; Costumes, Melissa Toth; Music, Lesley Barber; Music Supervisors, Christopher Covert, Barry Cole; Associate Producers, Robert Kravis, Rachel Peters; Casting, Lina Todd; a Shooting Gallery and Hart Sharp Entertainment presentation in association with Cappa Productions; Dolby; Color; Rated R; 111 minutes; Release date: November 10, 2000

CAST

Sammy	Laura Linney
Terry Prescott	Mark Ruffalo
Brian	Matthew Broderick
Rudy	Rory Culkin
Bob	Jon Tenney
Mabel	J. Smith-Cameron
Mrs. Prescott	Amy Ryan
Mr. Prescott	Michael Countryman
Sheriff Darryl	Adam LeFevre
Amy	Halley Feiffer
Young Sammy	Whitney Vance
Young Terry	Peter Kerwin
Minister	Betsy Aidem
Sheila	Gaby Hoffmann
Waitress	Lisa Altomare
Ron	Kenneth Lonergan
Nancy	Nina Garbiras
Plumber	Richard Hummer
Rudy Sr.'s Girlfriend	Kim Parker
Rudy Sr.	Josh Lucas
Older Cop	Allan Gill
Young Cop	Brian Ramage

Sammy, a single mother raising her eight-year-old son, is visited by her drifter brother Terry with whom she has maintained a close bond despite their disparate lives.

This film received Oscar nominations for actress (Laura Linney), and original screenplay.

© Paramount Classics

Kelley, Jim Carrey

DR. SEUSS' HOW THE GRINCH STOLE CHRISTMAS

(UNIVERSAL) Producers, Brian Grazer, Ron Howard; Executive Producer, Todd Hallowell; Director, Ron Howard; Screenplay, Jeffrey Price, Peter S. Seaman; Based on the book by Dr. Seuss; Photography, Don Peterman; Designer, Michael Corenblith; Editors, Dan Hanley, Mike Hill; Associate Producers, Aldric La'Auli Porter, Louis Velis, David Womark; Costumes, Rita Ryack; Special Makeup Effects, Rick Baker; Music, James Horner; Music Supervisor, Bonnie Greenberg; Song: "Where Are You Christmas" by James Horner, Will Jennings, Mariah Carey; Visual Effects Supervisor, Kevin Mack; Special Visual Effects and Digital Animation, Digital Domain; Casting, Jane Jenkins, Janet Hirshenson; an Imagine Entertainment presentation of a Brian Grazer production; Dolby; CFI color; Rated PG; 105 minutes; Release date: November 17, 2000

CAST

Grinch	Jim Carrey
Cindy Lou Who	Taylor Momsen
Max	Kelley
May Who	Jeffrey Tambor
Martha May Whovier	Christine Baranski
Lou Lou Who	Bill Irwin
Betty Lou Who	Molly Shannon
Drew Lou Who	Jeremy Howard
Stu Lou Who	T.J. Thyne
Christina Whoterberry	Lacey Kohl
Junie	Nadja Pionilla
Officer Wholihan	Jim Meskimen
Whobris	Clint Howard
Customer	Michael Dahlen
Elderly Timekeeper	Rance Howard
Biker Who	David Costabile
Miss Rue Who	Mary Stein
Crazy Mose	James Ritz
Post Office Clerk	Deep Roy
Sophie	Jessica Sara
Who Boy	Mason Lucero
8-Year Old May Who	Ben Bookbinder
School Girl	Michaela Gallo
8-Year Old Martha	Landy Allbright
8-Year Old Whobris	Reid Kirchenbauer
8-Year Old Grinch	Josh Ryan Evans
Tree Trimmer	Kevin Isola
Narrator	Anthony Hopkins

and Rachel Winfree (Rose), Mindy Sterling (Clarnella), Gavin Grazer (Yodeler), Walter Franks (Clerk), Verne J. Troyer (Band Member), Clay Martinez (Cook), Q'Orianka Kilcher (Little Choir Member), Reid Kirchenbauer (Kid), Caroline Williams (Tiny Who Woman), John Short (Tiny Who Man), Grainger Esch (Near Miss Who), Eva Burkley (Pudding Chef), Bryce Howard (Surprised Who), Charles Croughwell (Balloon Who), Frank Welker (Voice of Max), Rebecca Chace, Suzanne Krull, Steve Kehela, Lillias White, Rain Pryor, John Alexander (Shoppers)

Tired of the happiness the citizens of Whoville get from Christmas, the curmudgeonly Grinch decides to put a stop to the festivities by stealing the holiday away from them.

2000 Academy Award-winner for Best Makeup. This film received additional Oscar nominations for costume design and art direction.

© Universal Studios

Taylor Momsen, Jim Carrey

Taylor Momsen, Jim Carrey

Jim Carrey, Kelley

Jim Carrey

Christine Baranski, Jim Carrey, Jeffrey Tambor

Jim Carrey

Kelley, Jim Carrey

Taylor Momsen, Jim Carrey

THE 6TH DAY

Arnold Schwarzenegger, Michael Rapaport

Tony Goldwyn, Robert Duvall

(COLUMBIA) Producers, Mike Medavoy, Arnold Schwarzenegger, Jon Davison; Executive Producers, Daniel Petrie, Jr., David Coatsworth; Director, Roger Spottiswoode; Screenplay, Cormac Wibberley, Marianne Wibberley; Photography, Pierre Mignot; Designers, James Bissell, John Willett; Editors, Mark Conte, Dominique Fortin, Michel Arcand; Costumes, Trish Keating; Music, Trevor Rabin; Make-Up Effects, Alec Gillis, Tom Woodruff, Jr.; Special Effects Supervisor, Michael Lantieri; Casting, Judith Holstra; a Phoenix Pictures presentation of a Jon Davison production; Dolby; Color; Rated PG-13; 124 minutes; Release date: November 17, 2000

CAST

Adam Gibson	Arnold Schwarzenegger
Hank Morgan	Michael Rapaport
Michael Drucker	Tony Goldwyn
Robert Marshall	Michael Rooker
Talia Elsworth	Sarah Wynter
Natalie Gibson	Wendy Crewson
Wiley	Rod Rowland
Vincent	Terry Crews
Speaker Day	Ken Pogue
Tripp	Colin Cunningham
Dr. Griffin Weir	Robert Duvall
Katherine Weir	Wanda Cannon
Clara Gibson	Taylor Anne Reid
Virtual Girlfriend	Jennifer Gareis
RePet Salesman	Don McManus
Johnny Phoenix	Steve Bacic
Police Lieutenant	Christopher Lawford
RePet Spokesman	Mark Brandon

and Ellie Harvie (Rosie), Don S. Davis (Cardinal de la Jolla), Jennifer Sterling (Virtual Attorney), Walter Von Huene (Virtual Psychiatrist), Chris Cound (Snowboarder #1), Ben Bass (Bodyguard), Robert Clarke, Michael Budman (Zealots), Warren T. Takeuchi, Claudine Grant, Alex Castillo (Reporters), D. Neil Mark, Colin Lawrence, Mark Gibbon, Brian Jensen, Crawford James (Security Guards), Peter Kent (Duty Officer), Hiro Kanagawa (Team Doctor), Mi-Jung Lee (Newscaster), Gillian Barber (Doctor), Gerard Plunket (Technician), Claire Riley (Webcaster), Andrew McIlroy (Scott Moore), Norma Jean Wick, Paul Carson (Announcers), Graham Andrews (Cab Driver), Benita Ha (Teacher), Andrea Libman (Voice of SimPal Cindy)

In the future, when the cloning of animals is possible but the replication of humans forbidden, pilot Adam Gibson returns home one evening to find that he has been duplicated by a sinister organization that wants the real Adam dead once they realize they've cloned the wrong man.

© Columbia Pictures Industries Inc./Phoenix Pictures

Terry Crews, Michael Rooker, Sarah Wynter, Rod Rowland

Sarah Wynter, Arnold Schwarzenegger, Michael Rooker

Angelica Pickles, Lil Deville, Chuckie Finster,
Dil Pickles, Tommy Pickles

(foreground) Tommy Pickles, Chuckie Finster, Angelica Pickles, Phil
Deville, Lil Deville, (behind) Charlotte and Charles Pickles, Dil, Didi,
Drew, and Stu Pickles, Howard and Betty Deville

Angelica Pickles, Jean-Claude, Dil Pickles, Tommy Pickles, Chuckie
Finster, Phil Deville, Lil Deville

Phil Deville, Lil Deville, Spike, Chuckie Finster, Angelica Pickles,
Tommy Pickles, Dil Pickles, Kimi Watanabe

RUGRATS IN PARIS—THE MOVIE

(PARAMOUNT) Producers, Arlene Klasky, Gabor Csupo; Executive Producers, Albie Hecht, Julia Pistor, Eryk Casemiro, Hal Waite; Directors, Paul Demeyer, Stig Bergqvist; Screenplay, J. David Stem, David N. Weiss, Jilly Gorey, Barbara Herndon, Kate Boutilier; Based on the characters created by Arlene Klasky, Gabor Csupo, Paul Germain; Co-Producers, Tracy Kramer, Terry Thoren, Norton Virgien; Line Producer, Sean Lurie; Designer, Dima Malanitchev; Editor, John Bryant; Music, Mark Mothersbaugh; Music Supervisor, George Acogny; Sequence Directors, John Eng, Raul Garcia, John Holmquist, Andrei Svislotski, Greg Tiernan; Voice Casting, Barbara Wright; a Nickelodeon Movies presentation of a Klasky/Csupo production; Dolby; Deluxe color; Rated G; 78 minutes; Release date: November 17, 2000

VOICE CAST

Tommy Pickles...E.G. Daily
Dil Pickles..Tara Charendoff
Angelica Pickles ....Cheryl Chase
Chuckie Finster...Christine Cavanaugh
Susie Carmichael ....Cree Summer Franck
Betty Deville/Lil Deville/Phil Deville....................................Kath Soucie
Drew Pickles/Chas Finster ....Michael Bell
Charlotte Pickles ....Tress MacNeille
Wedding DJ ....Casey Kasem
Grandpa Lou Pickles ....Joe Alasky
Lulu Pickles ....Debbie Reynolds
Stu Pickles ....Jack Riley
Coco La Bouche ....Susan Sarandon
Jean-Claude...John Lithgow
and Julia Kato (Kira Watanabe), Melanie Chartoff (Didi Pickles), Margaret Smith (Stewardess), Phillip Simon (Animatronic Bus Driver), Phil Proctor (Howard Deville), Paul Demeyer (Dog Catcher/Street Cleaner), Mako (Mr. Yamaguchi), Marlene Mitsuko Wamene, Darrell Kunitomi, Goh Misawa (Villagers "Princess Spectacular"), Tim Curry, Kevin Michael Richardson, Billy West (Sumo Singers), Dionne Quan (Kimi Watanabe), Richard Michael (French Worker), Philippe Benichou (Ninja), Darryl Wright (Café Owner), Lisa McClowry (Princess), Charles Fathy (Photographer), Dan Castellaneta (Priest), Charlie Adler (Inspector), Roger Rose (Finster Wedding DJ), Hannah Makragelidis, Shannon Stephens, Ben Sunderland (Pre-School Kids)

Chuckie Finster and his friends and family travel to Paris where Stu Pickles has been summoned to work on his new invention for EuroReptarland, a new amusement park, and where Chuckie hopes to find a new mom for his dad. Sequel to the 1998 Paramount film The Rugrats Movie.

© Paramount Pictures/Viacom International, Inc.

Ben Affleck, Gwyneth Paltrow

Gwyneth Paltrow, Ben Affleck

BOUNCE

(MIRAMAX) Producers, Steve Golin, Michael Besman; Executive Producers, Bob Weinstein, Harvey Weinstein, Bob Osher, Meryl Poster; Director/Screenplay, Don Roos; Co-Producers, Alan C. Blomquist, Bobby Cohen; Photography, Robert Elswit; Designer, David Wasco; Editor, David Codron; Music, Mychael Danna; Music Supervisor, Randall Poster; Costumes, Peter Mitchell; Casting, Patrick J. Rush, Sharon Klein; a Steve Golin and Michael Besman production; Dolby; Deluxe color; Rated PG-13; 106 minutes; Release date: November 17, 2000

CAST

Buddy Amaral	Ben Affleck
Abby Janello	Gwyneth Paltrow
Jim Weller	Joe Morton
Mimi	Natasha Henstridge
Greg Janello	Tony Goldwyn
Seth	Johnny Galecki
Prosecuting Attorney Mandel	David Paymer
Scott Janello	Alex D. Linz
Janice Guerrero	Jennifer Grey
Donna Heisen	Caroline Aaron
Joey Janello	David Dorfman
Ron Wachter	Edward Edwards
Carol Wilson	Lisa Carpenter Prewitt
TV Announcer	Lisa Joyner
CNN Reporter	Richard Saxton
Kevin Walters	Juan Garcia
Ellen Seitz	Mary Ellen Lyon
Karen	Thea Mann
Luke	Matthew Frauman
Todd Exner	Sam Robards
Josh	Ty Murphy
Narrator, Infinity Commercial	Dave McCharen
Zola	Julianne Christie
Emcee	Jeff Garlin

and Nicole Tocantins (Dionne), Ashley Montgomery (Prom Girl), Eric Aude (Prom Boy), Scott Alan Smith (Jack), Mark Ankeny (Tom), Julia Campbell (Sue), Michael Laskin (Frank Steadman), Michael Ayala (Court TV Reporter), David St. James (Judge), Don Amendolia (Infinity Attorney), John Levin (Janice's Attorney), Chris Harrison (Chicago Anchor)

After her life is shattered when her husband is killed in a plane crash, Abby Janello tenuously begins a romance with Buddy Amaral, unaware that Buddy had swapped airline tickets with her husband just before the fatal event.

© Miramax Films

Ben Affleck, Joe Morton

Gwyneth Paltrow, Alex D. Linz, David Dorfman

WHAT'S COOKING?

(LIONS GATE) Producer, Jeffrey Taylor; Executive Producers, Abe Glazer, Beau Rogers, David Forrest; Director, Gurinder Chadha; Screenplay, Gurinder Chadha, Paul Mayeda Berges; Photography, Jong Lin; Designer, Stuart Blatt; Editor, Janice Hampton; Music, Craig Pruess; Costumes, Eduardo Castro; Casting, Cathy Henderson-Martin, Dori Zuckerman; a Flashpoint presentation with Jeffrey Taylor, Ethan Hurt and Steven D. Kravitz for Because Entertainment; Dolby; Color; Rated PG-13; 106 minutes; Release date: November 17, 2000

CAST

The Avilas
Elizabeth Avila .... Mercedes Ruehl
Javier Avila .... Victor Rivers
Anthony Avila .... Douglas Spain
Sofia Avila .... Maria Carmen
and Isidra Vega (Gina Avila), Elena Lopez (Grandma Avila), A Martinez (Daniel), Richard Yniguez (Robert Avila), Eva Rodriguez (Auntie Eva), Adrian Armas (Avila Cousin), Caz (Gordo)

The Nguyens
Trinh Nguyen .... Joan Chen
Duc Nguyen .... Francois Chau
Jimmy Nguyen .... Will Yun Lee
Jenny Nguyen .... Kristy Wu
and Brennan Louie (Joey Nguyen), Jimmy Pham (Gary Nguyen), Kieu Chinh (Grandma Nguyen), Chao-Li Chi (Grandpa Nguyen), Chad Todhunter (Luke), Scotty Nguyen (Don)

The Seeligs
Ruth Seelig .... Lainie Kazan
Herb Seelig .... Maury Chaykin
Rachel Seelig .... Kyra Sedgwick
Carla .... Julianna Margulies
and Albie Selznick (Art Seelig), Suzanne Carney (Sarah Seelig), Estelle Harris (Aunt Bea), Ralph Manza (Uncle David), Andrew Heckler (Jerry), Marty (Max)

The Williams
Audrey Williams .... Alfre Woodard
Ronald Williams .... Dennis Haysbert
Michael Williams .... Eric K. George
Kristen Williams .... Brittany Jean Henry
and Ann Weldon (Grace Williams), Shareen Mitchell (Paula Moore), Gregory Itzin (James Moore), Mariam Parris (Monica Moore); with Frank Novak (Governor Rhodes), Margie Loomis (Woman in Airport), Gwendolyn Oliver (TV Reporter), Charles Constant (TV Announcer), Bruce Dobos (Turkey Man), Darren O'Bannon, Jeremy Berger, Alexandra Castro (Students)

A look at four different Thanksgiving gatherings: a Latino reunion in which the family's philandering patriarch shows up; a couple welcoming their daughter and her female lover; a Vietnamese woman hoping to bring her divided family together; and a successful African-American couple trying to come up with a dinner to impress their yuppie guests.

© Trimark Pictures

Julianna Margulies, Lainie Kazan, Kyra Sedgwick

Alfre Woodard

Joan Chen, Kristy Wu, Kieu Chinh

Maria Carmen, Mercedes Ruehl, Eva Rodriguez, Elena Lopez

ONE DAY IN SEPTEMBER

(SONY PICTURES CLASSICS) Producers, Arthur Cohn, John Battsek; Director, Kevin MacDonald; Executive Producer, Lillian Birnbaum; Photography, Alwin Kuchler, Neve Cunningham; Special Stills Photography, Raymond Depardon; Editor, Justine Wright; Associate Producer, Andrew Ruhemann; Music, Alex Heffes, Craig Armstrong; Narrator, Michael Douglas; a Redbus Film Distribution presentation of an Arthur Cohn & a Passion Pictures production; Dolby; Color; Rated R; 92 minutes; Release date: November 17, 2000; This movie had its American premiere on HBO earlier in the year. Documentary on the murder of two Israeli athletes by a group of Palestinian terrorists during the Munich Olympics, on September 5, 1972.

WITH

Ankie Spitzer, Jamal Al Gashey, Gerald Seymour, Alex Springer, Gad Zabari, Shmuel Lalkin, Manfred Schreiber, Walther Troger, General Ulrich K. Wegener, Hans-Dietrich Genscher, Schlomit Romano, Magdi Gohary, Zvi Zamir, Dan Shillon, Heinz Hohensinn, Esther Roth, Hans Jochen Vogel, Anouk Spitzer.

1999 Academy Award-winner for Best Documentary.

© Sony Pictures Entertainment Inc.

Libyan Terrorist

102 DALMATIANS

(WALT DISNEY PICTURES) Producer, Edward S. Feldman; Director, Kevin Lima; Screenplay, Kristen Buckley, Brian Regan, Bob Tzudiker, Noni White; Story, Kristen Buckley, Brian Regan; Based upon the novel *The One Hundred and One Dalmatians* by Dodie Smith; Photography, Adrian Biddle; Designer, Assheton Gorton; Editor, Gregory Perler; Costumes, Anthony Powell; Music, David Newman; Co-Producers, Paul Tucker, Patricia Carr; Visual Effects Supervisor, Jim Rygiel; Animal Coordinator, Gary Gero; Casting, Priscilla John; Stunts, Steve Dent; Distributed by Buena Vista Pictures; Dolby; Technicolor; Rated G; 101 minutes; Release date: November 22, 2000

CAST

Cruella De Vil	Glenn Close
Jean Pierre Le Pelt	Gerard Depardieu
Kevin Shepherd	Ioan Gruffudd
Chloe Simon	Alice Evans
Alonso	Tim McInnerny
Ewan	Ben Compton
Agnes	Carol Macready
Mr. Torte	Ian Richardson
Detective Armstrong	Jim Carter
Mr. Button	Ron Cook
Judge	Timothy West

and David Horvitch (Doctor Pavlov), Dick Brannick (Pavlov's Assistant), Mike Hayley (Constable), Nicholas Hutchison (Reporter), Tim Willcox (ITN Reporter), June Watson (Prison Warden), Tony Bluto (Photocopier Repairman), Tessa Vale (Ticket Seller), John Styles (Punch & Judy Man), Kerry Shale, Thierry Lawson (Le Pelt's Assistants), Hugh Futcher (Brakeman), Charles Simon (Lord Carnivore), Dorothea Phillips (Mrs. Mirthless), Delphine Annaiis (Paris Poodle Lady), Eric Idle (Voice of Waddlesworth)

Released from prison, onetime dognapper Cruella De Vil appears to be a changed woman when she buys a failing dog shelter, when in fact she is plotting with French fashion designer Jean Pierre Le Pelt to snatch enough dalmatian puppies to make the ultimate coat. Sequel to the 1996 Disney feature 101 Dalmatians with Glenn Close and Tim McInnerny repeating their roles. This film received an Oscar nomination for costume design.

© Disney Enterprises

Gerard Depardieu, Glenn Close

Alice Evans, Ioan Gruffudd

Samuel L. Jackson, Bruce Willis

Samuel L. Jackson

Robin Wright Penn, Bruce Willis

Bruce Willis

UNBREAKABLE

(TOUCHSTONE) Producers, M. Night Shyamalan, Barry Mendel, Sam Mercer; Executive Producers, Gary Barber, Roger Birnbaum; Director/Screenplay, M. Night Shyamalan; Photography, Eduardo Serra; Designer, Larry Fulton; Editor, Dylan Tichenor; Costumes, Joanna Johnston; Music, James Newton Howard; Casting, Douglas Aibel; a Blinding Edge Pictures/Barry Mendel production; Dolby; Technicolor; Rated PG-13; 107 minutes; Release date: November 22, 2000

CAST

David Dunn ....Bruce Willis
Elijah Price ....Samuel L. Jackson
Audrey Dunn ....Robin Wright Penn
Joseph Dunn ....Spencer Treat Clark
Elijah's Mother ....Charlayne Woodard
Dr. Mathison ....Eamonn Walker
Kelly ....Leslie Stefanson
Elijah at 13 ....Johnny Hiram Jamison
Babysitter ....Michaelia Carroll
Comic Book Clerk ....Bostin Christopher
School Nurse ....Elizabeth Lawrence
David Dunn at 20 ....David Duffield
Audrey Inverso at 20 ....Laura Regan
Orange Suit Man ....Chance Kelly
ER Doctor ....Michael Kelly
Businessman ....Firdous Bamji
Saleswoman ....Johanna Day
Priest ....James Handy
Ancient Personnel Secretary ....Sally Parrish
Noel ....Richard E. Council
and Damian Young (Green Army-Jacketed Man), Sherman Roberts (Physician), Whitney Sugarman (Physical Therapist), Dianne Cotten Murphy (Mother Walking By), M. Night Shyamalan (Stadium Drug Dealer), Sasha Neulinger (Thermometer Boy), Jose L. Rodriguez (Truck Driver), Samantha Savino (Peering Girl on Train), Ukee Washington (Radio Announcer), Susan Wilder (Shoplifter), Greg Horos (Slicked-Hair Man), Todd Berry (Frat Party Boy), Angela Eckert (Frat Party Girl), Anthony Lawton (Hostage Father), Julia Yorks (Hostage Girl), John Patrick Amedori (Hostage Boy), John Morley Rusk (Security Dispatcher), Joey Hazinsky (Five-Year-Old Boy), Bill Rowe (Bar Patron), Marc H. Glick (EastRail Engineer), Kim Thomas (Hostage Woman)

David Dunn's survival of a devastating train wreck in which every other passenger was killed, invokes the interest of a mysterious stranger who may hold the key to why David not only lived through the crash but why he walked away without so much as a minor injury.

© Touchstone Pictures

Geoffrey Rush

Kate Winslet

Michael Caine, Amelia Warner

Geoffrey Rush, Kate Winslet

Joaquin Phoenix

Geoffrey Rush

Kate Winslet, Joaquin Phoenix

QUILLS

(**FOX SEARCHLIGHT**) Producers, Julia Chasman, Nick Wechsler, Peter Kaufman; Executive Producers, Des McAnuff, Sandra Schulberg, Rudolf Wiesmeier; Director, Philip Kaufman; Screenplay, Doug Wright, based upon his play; Photography, Rogier Stoffers; Designer, Martin Childs; Editor, Peter Boyle; Costumes, Jacqueline West; Co-Producer, Mark Huffam; Music, Stephen Warbeck; an Industry Entertainment/a Walrus & Associates, Ltd. production in association with Hollywood Partners; Dolby; Deluxe color; Rated R; 120 minutes; Release date: November 22, 2000

Kate Winslet, Geoffrey Rush

CAST

The Marquis de Sade	Geoffrey Rush
Madeleine	Kate Winslet
Abbé Coulmier	Joaquin Phoenix
Dr. Royer-Collard	Michael Caine
Madame Leclerc	Billie Whitelaw
Delbené	Patrick Malahide
Simone	Amelia Warner
Renee Pelagie	Jane Menelaus
Prouix	Stephen Moyer
Valcour	Tony Pritchard
Cleante	Michael Jenn
Pitou	Danny Babington
Dauphin	George Yiasoumi
Bouchon	Stephen Marcus
Charlotte	Elizabeth Berrington
Franval	Edward Tudor-Pole
Orvolle	Harry Jones
Madame Bougival	Bridget McConnel
Mademoiselle Clairwil	Pauline McLynn
Michette	Rebecca Palmer
Louison	Toby Sawyer
Guerin	Daniel Ainsleigh
Gaillon	Terry O'Neill
Mademoiselle Renard (Girl on Guillotine)	Diana Morrison
Sister Noirceuil	Carol Macready
The Horseman	Tom Ward
Fop	Richard Mulholland
Napoleon	Ron Cook
Pawnbroker	Julian Tait
Sister Flavie	Tessa Vale
Vendors	Howard Lew Lewis, Andrew Dunford
Prostitute	Lisa Hammond
Lunatic Band Member	Matthew Fraser
Lunatic at Play	Jamie Beddard

Michael Caine

Imprisoned at the Charenton insane asylum, the Marquis de Sade continues to write his controversial, sexually sensationalistic prose which he has laundress Madeleine smuggle to a publisher, invoking the wrath of the asylum's new chief doctor. This film received Oscar nominations for actor (Geoffrey Rush), costume design, and art direction.

Joaquin Phoenix, Kate Winslet

VERTICAL LIMIT

(**COLUMBIA**) Producers, Lloyd Phillips, Robert King, Martin Campbell; Executive Producer, Marcia Nasatir; Director, Martin Campbell; Screenplay, Robert King, Terry Hayes; Story, Robert King; Photography, David Tattersall; Designer, Jon Bunker; Editor, Thom Noble; Costumes, Graciela Mason; Music, James Newton Howard; 2nd Unit Director/Stunts, Simon Crane; Visual Effects Supervisor, Kent Houston; Casting, Pam Dixon Mickelson; Dolby; Deluxe color; Rated PG-13; 126 minutes; Release date: December 8, 2000

CAST

Peter Garrett	Chris O'Donnell
Elliot Vaughn	Bill Paxton
Annie Garrett	Robin Tunney
Montgomery Wick	Scott Glenn
Monique Aubertine	Izabella Scorupco
Major Rasul	Temuera Morrison
Royce Garrett	Stuart Wilson
Grunge Climbers	Tom Struthers, Leos Stransky
Aziz	Augie Davis
Colonel Amir Salim	Roshan Seth
Sergeant Asim	Alejandro Valdes-Rochin
Tom McLaren	Nicholas Lea
Ali Hasan	Rod Brown
Cyril Bench	Steve Le Marquand
Malcolm Bench	Ben Mendelsohn
Himself	Ed Viesturs
Skip Taylor	Robert Taylor
Kareem Nazir	Alexander Siddig
WNN Cameraman	Clinton Beavan

and David Hayman (Frank "Chainsaw" Williams), Robert Mammone (Brian Maki), Nicole Whippy (Spanish Climber), Colin Moy, Ian Bolt, Nicolette Kenny, Ross McKellar (Technicians), Tiffany De Castro (Crying Woman), Campbell Cooley ("Campbell"), Alistair Browning ("Ali"), Jo Davidson (Italian Team Member), Tamati Rice, Sally Spencer Harris, Craig Walsh Wrightson (Party Goers), Leela Patel (Mayama Wick), Gavin Craig (Summit Air Pilot), Shahid Zafar (Prayer Leader)

Mountain climber Peter Garrett races against time to save his sister who is trapped, along with her summit climbing team, atop K2, the world's second tallest peak.

Scott Glenn

Bill Paxton, Scott Glenn, Izabella Scorupco,
Chris O'Donnell, Robin Tunney

Robin Tunney, Nicholas Lea

Chris O'Donnell, Izabella Scorupco

Meg Ryan, Russell Crowe

PROOF OF LIFE

Meg Ryan, Russell Crowe

(WARNER BROS.) Producers, Taylor Hackford, Charles Mulvehill; Executive Producers, Steven Reuther, Tony Gilroy; Director, Taylor Hackford; Screenplay, Tony Gilroy; Inspired by the Vanity Fair article "Adventures in the Ransom Trade" by William Prochnau and by the book *Long March to Freedom* by Thomas Hargrove; Photography, Slawomir Idziak; Designer, Bruno Rubeo; Editors, John Smith, Sheldon Kahn; Music, Danny Elfman; Casting, Nancy Klopper; a Castle Rock Entertainment presentation in association with Bel-Air Entertainment of an Anvil Films production; Dolby; Super 35 Widescreen; Technicolor; Rated R; 135 minutes; Release date: December 8, 2000

CAST

Alice Bowman	Meg Ryan
Terry Thorne	Russell Crowe
Peter Bowman	David Morse
Janis Goodman	Pamela Reed
Dino	David Caruso
Ted Fellner	Anthony Heald
Jerry	Stanley Anderson
Eric Kessler	Gottfried John
Wyatt	Alun Armstrong
Ian Havery	Michael Kitchen
Ivy	Margo Martindale
Fernandez	Mario Ernesto
Sanchez Juaco	Pietro Sibille
Maria	Vicky Hernandez
Norma	Norma Martinez
Eliodoro	Diego Trujillo
Sandro	Aristoteles Picho
Cinta	Sarahi Echeverria

and Carlos Blanchard (Carlos), Raul Rodriguez (Tomas), Mauro Cueva (Rico), Alejandro Cordova (Rambo), Sandro Bellido (Mono), Miguel Iza (ELT Officer), Roberto Frisone (Calitri), Tony Vazquez (Fred/Marco), Claudia Dammert (Ginger), Rowena King (Pamela), Michael Byrne (Luthan), Jaime Zevallos (Nino), Gilberto Torres (Raymo), Flora Martinez (Linda), Laura Escobar (Cara), Marcos Bustos (Alex), Jorge Medina (Berto), Gerard Naprous (Pierre Lenoir), Alexander Balueyev (Russian Colonel), Dimitri Shevchenko (Russian Sergeant), Zbigniew Zamachowski (Terry's Driver), Said K. Saralijen (Chechen Leader), Oscar Carrillo, Pedro Martinez Laya, Wolframio Benavides (Trial Honchos), Alonso Alegria (Master of Ceremonies), Merlin Hanbury-Tenison (Terry's Son), Stefan Gryff (Bank Official), Yolanda Vazquez (Notary)

David Caruso

David Morse

Peter Bowman, an American engineer working in Latin America, is kidnapped for a $3 million dollar ransom, a figure his employer refuses to pay, prompting Peter's wife Alice to enlist the help of kidnap and ransom expert Terry Thorne to get the job done.

Meg Ryan, Russell Crowe

SPRING FORWARD

(IFC) Producers, Jim McKay, Gill Holland, Tom Gilroy, Paul Mezey; Executive Producers, Jonathan Sehring, Caroline Kaplan, William Gilroy, Michael Stipe; Director/Screenplay, Tom Gilroy; Photography, Terry Stacey; Designer, Susan Block; Editor, James Lyons; Music, Hahn Rowe; Costumes, Catherine Thomas; Associate Producers, Paul Oliva, John S. Johnson, Michael Morley, Kevin Chinoy, Liev Schreiber; Casting, Bonnie Finnegan; an Independent Film Channel Prods. presentation of a C-Hundred Film Corp./CineBLAST! production; Color; Rated R; 110 minutes; Release date: December 8, 2000

Ned Beatty, Liev Schreiber

CAST

Murphy	Ned Beatty
Paul	Liev Schreiber
Fredrickson	Campbell Scott
Fran	Ian Hart
Georgia	Peri Gilpin
Don Reagan	Bill Raymond
Dawn	Catherine Kellner
Hope	Hallee Hirsh
Bobby	Justin Laboy
Kristin	Kristin Laboy
Boy with Snowblower	David Roland Frank

An ex-con takes a job working for the parks and recreation department of a small New England town where he slowly develops a friendship with a veteran employee on the verge of retirement.

© IFC Films

Rae Dawn Chong, Hill Harper, Terrell Mitchell, Billy Dee Williams

Hill Harper, Marla Gibbs

THE VISIT

(URBANWORLD) Producer/Director/Screenplay, Jordan Walker-Pearlman; Based on the play by Kosmond Russell; Executive Producers, Vicky Pike, Morris Ruskin, Stacy Spikes; Photography, John Ndiaga Demps; Designer, John Larena; Costumes, Carlos Rosario; Editors, Alison Learned, Jordan Walker-Pearlman; Music, Michael Bearden, Stefán Dickerson, Ramsey Lewis, Wallace Roney, Stanley A. Smith; Presented in association with Dawa Movies; Ultra-Stereo; Color; Rated R; 107 minutes; Release date: December 15, 2000

CAST

Alex Waters	Hill Harper
Tony Waters	Obba Babatundé
Felicia McDonald	Rae Dawn Chong
Henry Waters	Billy Dee Williams
Lois Waters	Marla Gibbs
Dr. Coles	Phylicia Rashad
Marilyn Coffey	Talia Shire
Bill Brenner	David Clennon
Al Rheingold	Glynn Turman

and Efrain Figueroa (Max Cruz), Amy Stiller (Julie Bronsky), Jascha Washington (Young Alex), Christopher Babers (Young Tony), Jennifer Nicole Freeman (Young Felicia), Tim Dezarn (Guard Enheim), Charmin Lee White (Mrs. Tony Waters), Terrell Mitchell (Tony's Son), Enoh Essien (Tony's Daughter), Hugh Dane (Mr. McDonald), Jordan Lund (Photographer), Drew Reukewitz (Prison Guard), Kirk Acevedo (Parolee), Lyne Odums (Crackhouse Woman), Jaime Perry (Drug Dealer), David Roberson (Corrections Officer), Javier Silcock (Lamar)

Alex Waters, dying of AIDS while serving a prison sentence for a crime he claims he did not commit, decides to confront his estranged family and heal old wounds.

© Urbanworld Films

Pacha, Kuzco

Pacha, Kuzco Llama

Pacha, Kuzco Llama

Kuzco, Kronk, Yzma

THE EMPEROR'S NEW GROOVE

(WALT DISNEY PICTURES) Producer, Randy Fullmer; Executive Producer, Don Hahn; Director, Mark Dindal; Screenplay, David Reynolds; Story, Chris Williams, Mark Dindal; Based on an original story by Roger Allers and Matthew Jacobs; Music, John Debney; Songs, Sting, David Hartley; Associate Producer, Patricia Hicks; Art Director, Colin Stimpson; Editor, Pamela Ziegenhagen-Shefland; Co-Art Director, Thomas Cardone; Artistic Supervisors: Story, Stephen Anderson; Layout, Jean-Christophe Poulain; Background, Natalie Franscioni-Karp; Clean-Up, Vera Pacheco; Visual Effects, Mauro Maressa; Character Design, Joseph C. Moshier; Production Designer, Paul Felix; Layout Stylists, Kevin Nelson, Robh Ruppel; Casting, Ruth Lambert, Mary Hidalgo; Distributed by Buena Vista Pictures; Dolby; Technicolor; Rated G; 79 minutes; Release date: December 15, 2000

VOICE CAST

Kuzco/Kuzco Llama ....David Spade
Pacha ....John Goodman
Yzma...Eartha Kitt
Kronk ....Patrick Warburton
Chicha ....Wendie Malick
Chaca ....Kellyann Kelso
Tipo...Eli Russell Linnetz
Bucky ....Bob Bergen
Theme Song Guy ....Tom Jones
Waitress ....Patti Deutsch
Old Man...John Fiedler
Official...Joe Whyte
and Stephen Anderson, Rodger Bumpass, Rob Clotworthy, Jennifer Darling, Miriam Flynn, Geri Lee Gorowski, Jess Harnell, Sherry Lynn, Danny Mann, Mickie McGowan, D.F. Reynolds, Andre Stojka, Steve Susskind (Additional Voices)

Kuzco, a selfish, egocentric emperor, is turned into a llama by a power-hungry sorceress, forcing him to bond with Pacha, a peasant, in order to find his way home and restore himself to human form. This film received an Oscar nomination for original song ("My Funny Friend and Me").

© Disney Enterprises

CHOCOLAT

Juliette Binoche

Johnny Depp

(MIRAMAX) Producers, David Brown, Kit Golden, Leslie Holleran; Executive Producers, Bob Weinstein, Harvey Weinstein, Meryl Poster, Alan C. Blomquist; Director, Lasse Hallström; Screenplay, Robert Nelson Jacobs; Based on the novel by Joanne Harris; Co-Producer, Mark Cooper; Photography, Roger Pratt; Designer, David Gropman; Editor, Andrew Mondshein; Costumes, Renée Ehrlich Kalfus; Co-Executive Producer, Michelle Raimo; Music, Rachel Portman; Music Supervisor, Bob Last; Choreographer, Scarlett Mackmin; Chocolate Expert, Walter Bienz; Casting, Billy Hopkins, Suzanne Smith, Kerry Barden, John Hubbard, Ros Hubbard, Amy Maclean; a David Brown production; Dolby; Technicolor; Rated PG-13; 121 minutes; Release date: December 15, 2000

CAST

Vianne Rocher	Juliette Binoche
Armande Voizin	Judi Dench
Comte de Reynaud	Alfred Molina
Josephine Muscat	Lena Olin
Roux	Johnny Depp
Serge Muscat	Peter Stormare
Caroline Clairmont	Carrie-Anne Moss
Madame Audel	Leslie Caron
Guillaume Bierot	John Wood
Pere Henri	Hugh O'Conor
Anouk Rocher	Victoire Thivisol
Luc Clairmont	Aurèlien Parent Koenig
Jean-Marc Drou	Antonio Gil-Martinez
Françoise Drou	Hélène Cardona
Dedou Drou	Harrison Pratt
Didi Drou	Gaelan Connell
Yvette Marceau	Elisabeth Commelin
Alphonse Marceau	Ron Cook
Baptiste Marceau	Guillaume Tardieu
Madame Rivet	Michele Gleizer
Madame Pouget	Dominique MacAvoy
George Rocher	Arnaud Adam
Chitza	Christianne Gadd
Gati	Marion Hauducoeur
Thin Grizzled Man	Esteban Antonio
Musicians	J.J. Holiday, Jeffrey Poskin, Malcolm Ross, Ged Barry, Iain Stoddard
Storyteller	Tatyana Yassukovich
Charly the Dog	Sally

Vianne Rocher and her young daughter arrive in the small French village of Lansquenet where she opens a chocolaterie, offering an irresistible collection of sweets that awaken the inhabitants' desires and incur the wrath of the self-righteous town nobleman, Comte de Reynaud. This film received Oscar nominations for picture, actress (Juliette Binoche), supporting actress (Judi Dench), screenplay adaptation, and original score.

© Miramax Films

Alfred Molina, Juliette Binoche

Juliette Binoche, Judi Dench

Johnny Depp, Juliette Binoche

Juliette Binoche, Lena Olin

Alfred Molina, Carrie-Anne Moss

Lena Olin

Ed Harris

Bud Cort, Ed Harris

Jennifer Connelly

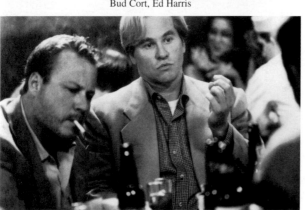

John Heard, Val Kilmer

Amy Madigan

POLLOCK

(SONY PICTURES CLASSICS) Producers, Fred Berner, Ed Harris, Jon Kilik; Executive Producers, Peter M. Brant, Joseph Allen; Director, Ed Harris; Screenplay, Barbara Turner, Susan J. Emshwiller; Based on the book *Jackson Pollock: An American Saga* by Steven Naifeh; Photography, Lisa Rinzler; Designer, Mark Friedberg; Editor, Kathryn Himoff; Music, Jeff Beal; Painting Coach, Lisa Lawley; Costumes, David C. Robinson; Casting, Todd Thaler; a Peter M. Brant and Joseph Allen production in association with Zeke Productions and Fred Berner Films; Dolby; Widescreen; Color; Rated R; 117 minutes; Release date: December 15, 2000

Ed Harris, Marcia Gay Harden

CAST

Jackson Pollock	Ed Harris
Lee Krasner	Marcia Gay Harden
Peggy Guggenheim	Amy Madigan
Ruth Kligman	Jennifer Connelly
Clement Greenberg	Jeffrey Tambor
Howard Putzel	Bud Cort
Tony Smith	John Heard
Willem DeKooning	Val Kilmer
Helen Frankenthaler	Stephanie Seymour
Dan Miller	Tom Bower
Sande Pollock	Robert Knott
Reuben Kadish	Matthew Sussman
Stella Pollock	Sada Thompson
Hans Namuth	Norbert Weisser
Edith Metzger	Sally Murphy
Arloie Pollock	Molly Regan
Ted Dragon	Moss Roberts
Alfonso Ossorio	Eduardo Machado
Harold Rosenberg	John Rothman
May Rosenberg	Annabelle Gurwitch
Mercedes Matter	Isabelle Townsend
Vita Peterson	Claire Beckman
William Baziotes	Kenny Scharf
Betty Parsons	Barbara Garrick
James Johnson Sweeney	Everett Quinton
Jay Pollock	Stephen Beach
Alma Pollock	Jill Jackson
Charles Pollock	David Leary
Elizabeth Pollock	Donna Mitchell
11-Year-Old Jeremy Pollock	Sondra Jablonski
Frankie Pollock	Frank Wood
Marie Pollock	Julia Anna Rose
8-Year-Old Jonathan Pollock	Kyle Smith

A look at the life of self-destrucitve painter Jackson Pollock whose radical style revolutionized the art world in the post-war era.

2000 Academy Award-winner for Best Supporting Actress (Marcia Gay Harden). This film received an additional Oscar nomination for actor (Ed Harris).

© Sony Pictures Entertainment, Inc.

Ed Harris

Stephanie Seymour, Jeffrey Tambor

Mel Gibson

Helen Hunt, Mel Gibson

WHAT WOMEN WANT

(PARAMOUNT) Producers, Nancy Meyers, Bruce Davey, Matt Williams, Susan Cartsonis, Gina Matthews; Executive Producers, Stephen McEveety, David McFadzean, Carmen Finestra; Director, Nancy Meyers; Screenplay, Josh Goldsmith, Cathy Yuspa; Story, Josh Goldsmith, Cathy Yuspa, Diane Drake; Co-Producer, Bruce A. Block; Photography, Dean Cundey; Designer, Jon Hutman; Editors, Stephen A. Rotter, Thomas J. Nordberg; Music, Alan Silvestri; Music Supervisor, Bonnie Greenberg-Goodman; Choreographer, Keith Young; Casting, Howard Feuer, Deborah Aquila; an Icon Productions presentation of an Icon/Wind Dancer production; Dolby; Deluxe color; Rated PG-13; 126 minutes; Release date: December 15, 2000.

CAST

Nick Marshall	Mel Gibson
Darcy Maguire	Helen Hunt
Lola	Marisa Tomei
Dan Wanamaker	Alan Alda
Alex Marshall	Ashley Johnson
Morgan Farwell	Mark Feuerstein
Gigi	Lauren Holly
Eve	Delta Burke
Margo	Valerie Perrine
Dr. Perkins	Bette Midler
Erin	Judy Greer
Annie	Sarah Paulson
Sue Cranston	Ana Gasteyer
Dina	Lisa Edelstein
Flo	Loretta Devine
Stella	Diana-Maria Riva
Cameron	Eric Balfour
Office Intern/Inner Voice Actress	Andrea Taylor
Truck Driver	John Frazier
Men on Street	Joe Petcka, Brian Callaway, Coby Goss, Christian Michel
Ogling Man	Perry Cavitt
Unimpressed Women	Crystal McKinney, Jeanne Renick
Gigi's Friend	Kathrin Lautner
Little Nick	Logan Lerman
Showgirls	Kelly Cooper, Palmer Davis, Katie Miller
Nick's Mom	Dana Waters
Male Role Model	Gregory Cupoli
Woman in Sweater	Alexondra Lee
Counter Girl	Aviva Gale

and Shirley Prestia, T.J. Thyne (Coffee Shop Customers), Norman H. Smith (Norm), Audrey Wasilewski (Secretary with Danish), Angela Oh (Dan's Secretary), Robert Briscoe Evans (Ted), Chris Rolfes, Katie Kneeland, Jeanine O'Connell, Kelley Hazen, Brooke Elliott, Kristina Martin (Women in Park), Harmony Rousseau (Sloane/Curtis Receptionist), Lisa Long (Sloane/Curtis Executive), Heidi Helmer, Marla Martensen, Sally Meyers-Kovler, Ashley Quirico, Regan Rhode, Liz Tannebaum, Leshay Tomlinson (Marshall Fields Shoppers), Cristine Rose (Sloan/Curtis Attorney), Arden Myrin (Darcy's Assistant), Rachel Duncan, Alex McKenna (Alex's Friends), Regiane Gorski (Yoga Instructor), Juliandra Gillen, Lisa Anne Hillman, Tracy Pacheco (Women in Library), Jamie Gutterman (Jogger by Lake), Maggie Egan, Juanita Jennings, Robin Pearson Rose (Kitchen Secretaries), Hallie Meyers Shyer, Laura Quicksilver (Girls at Lunch Counter), Kate Asner, Caryn Greenhut, Jennifer Greenhut, Marnie Mosiman, Sierra Pecheur (Women at Lunch Counter), Nnenna Freelon (Nightclub Singer), Gil Hacohen (Haim), Nancy Monsarat, Jacqueline Thomas, Rory Rubin (Nike Executives), Chris Emerson (Mail Room Kid), Victoria Kelleher (Secretary), Gertrude Wong (Woman in Chinatown), Andi Eystad (Girl at Prom)

A freak accident allows self-proclaimed ladies man Nick Marshall to hear the inner-thoughts of every woman he comes into contact with.

Ashley Johnson, Robert Briscoe Evans, Lauren Holly, Mel Gibson

Helen Hunt, Mel Gibson

Mel Gibson

Mel Gibson, Mark Feuerstein

Delta Burke, Mel Gibson, Valerie Perrine

Marisa Tomei, Mel Gibson

Seann William Scott, Ashton Kutcher

DUDE, WHERE'S MY CAR?

(20TH CENTURY FOX) Producers, Wayne Rice, Broderick Johnson, Andrew A. Kosove, Gil Netter; Director, Danny Leiner; Screenplay, Philip Stark; Photography, Robert Stevens; Designer, Charles Breen; Editor, Kimberly Ray; Co-Producer, Nancy Paloian-Breznikar; Music, David Kitay; Music Supervisors, Dana Millman, Dave Jordan; Visual Effects Supervisor, Rich Thorne; Casting, Ronnie Yeskel, Richard Hicks; a Wayne Rice/Gil Netter production; Dolby; Deluxe color; Rated PG-13; 83 minutes; Release date: December 15, 2000

CAST

Jesse	Ashton Kutcher
Chester	Seann William Scott
Wanda	Jennifer Garner
Wilma	Marla Sokoloff
Nelson	David Herman
Nordic Dudes	Christian Middlethon, David W. Bannick
Tommy	Charlie O'Donnell
Christie Boner	Kristy Swanson
Tania	Teressa Tunney
Zoltan	Hal Sparks
Jumpsuit Chicks	Mitzi Martin, Nichole M. Hiltz, Linda Kim, Mia Trudeau, Kim Marie Johnson
Big Cult Guys	Bill Chott, Michael Ray Bower
Jeff	Turtle
Zellner	Kevin Christy
Zilbor	Kristoffer Winters
Zelmina	Mary Lynn Rajskub
Zarnoff	Robert Clendenin
Mrs. Crabbleman	Linda Porter
Gene	"Stuttering" John Melendez

and Joanna Bacalso (Redheaded Bartender), Katherine Baker (Stripper #1), Keone Young (Chinese Tailor), Marc Lynn (Ray Cop), Christopher Darga (Anderson Cop), Pat Finn (Rick Cop), Dwight Armstrong (Fun O'Rama Employee), Cinco Paul (Counselor), Brendan Ian Hill (Stuart), Jona Kai Jacobsen (Anthony), Cleo King (Penny), Big Johnson (Birthday Father), Galvin Chapman (Birthday Son), John Toles-Bey (Mr. Pizzacoli), Jodi Ann Paterson (Super Chick), Freda Foh Shen (Chinese Food Lady), Brent Spiner (Pierre), Andy Dick (Mark), Melissa Messmer, Misty Atkinson, Veronica Gomez, Melissa Burleson, Annette Pursley, Melissa Copen, Linda Maria Balver, Cheryl Tsai (Dancers), Fabio (Himself), Claudine Barros (Patty), Dominic Capone (Mr. Pizzacoli, Jr.), Erik Aude, Ryan Christian, Blaise Fitzgerald, William H. Gray (Muscle Heads) Sydney (Jackal)

Two incredibly stupid stoners try to figure out where their car disappeared to while they were stoned.

Seann William Scott, Ashton Kutcher

Ashton Kutcher, Seann William Scott

Marla Sokoloff, Seann William Scott, Ashton Kutcher, Jennifer Garner

FINDING FORRESTER

(COLUMBIA) Producers, Laurence Mark, Sean Connery, Rhonda Tollefson; Executive Producers, Dany Wolf, Jonathan King; Director, Gus Van Sant; Screenplay, Mike Rich; Photography, Harris Savides; Designer, Jane Musky; Editor, Valdis Oskarsdottir; Costumes, Ann Roth; Casting, Francine Maisler, Bernard Telsey, David Vaccari; a Laurence Mark production in association with Fountainbridge Films; Dolby; Panavision; Deluxe color; Rated PG-13; 136 minutes; Release date: December 19, 2000

Sean Connery, Rob Brown

CAST

William Forrester	Sean Connery
Jamal Wallace	Rob Brown
Professor Robert Crawford	F. Murray Abraham
Claire Spence	Anna Paquin
Terrell	Busta Rhymes
Ms. Joyce	April Grace
Coleridge	Michael Pitt
Dr. Spence	Michael Nouri
Matthews	Richard Easton
Massie	Glenn Fitzgerald
Damon	Zane R. Copeland, Jr.
Janice	Stephanie Berry
Fly	Fly Williams III
Kenzo	Damany Mathis
Clay	Damien Lee
Coach Garrick	Tom Kearns

and Matthew Noah Word (Hartwell), Charles Bernstein (Dr. Simon), Matt Malloy (Bradley), Matt Damon (Sanderson), Jimmy Bobbitt (Rapper), Capital Jay (Opposing Player), James T. Williams II (Student), Cassandra Kubinski (Claire's Friend), Sophia Wu (Librarian), Gerry Rosenthal (Student Speaker), Tim Hall (Student Manager), Tom Mullica (Old Money Man), David Madison (Kid in the Hall), Joey Buttafuoco (Night Man), Jaime McCaig, William Modeste (Referees), Daniel Rodriguez (Hallway Boy), Samuel Tyson (Creston Player), Vince Giordano (Big Band Leader), Gregory Singer (Violinist), Dean Pratt, Kerry MacKillop (Trumpet Players), Harvey Tibbs (Trombone Player), Jack Stuckey, Mark Lopeman, Mark Phaneuf, Larry Wade (Sax Players), Conal Fowkes (Piano Player), Matt Munisteri (Guitarist), John Meyers (Drummer), Ron Morgan (Mailor Priest), Allison Folland (Jeopardy Contestant), Alex Trebek (Himself)

A brilliant young scholar-athlete, recruited by an elite Manhattan prep school, befriends a reclusive one-time author who helps the teen develop his writing skills.

© Columbia Pictures Industries, Inc.

F. Murray Abraham

Rob Brown, Busta Rhymes

Anna Paquin, Rob Brown

THE GIFT

(PARAMOUNT CLASSICS) Producers, James Jacks, Tom Rosenberg, Gary Lucchesi; Executive Producers, Sean Daniel, Ted Tannebaum, Gregory Goodman, Rob Tapert; Director, Sam Raimi; Screenplay, Billy Bob Thornton, Tom Epperson; Photography, Jamie Anderson; Designer, Neil Spisak; Editors, Arthur Coburn, Bob Murawski; Costumes, Julie Weiss; Music, Christopher Young; Co-Producer, Richard S. Wright; Casting, Deborah Aquila; a Lakeshore Entertainment presentation of a Lakeshore/Alphaville production; Dolby; Deluxe color; Rated R; 112 minutes; Release date: December 20, 2000

Cate Blanchett, Greg Kinnear

CAST

Annie Wilson	Cate Blanchett
Buddy Cole	Giovanni Ribisi
Donnie Barksdale	Keanu Reeves
Jessica King	Katie Holmes
Wayne Collins	Greg Kinnear
Valerie Barksdale	Hilary Swank
Gerald Weems	Michael Jeter
Linda	Kim Dickens
David Duncan	Gary Cole
Annie's Granny	Rosemary Harris
Sheriff Pearl Johnson	J.K. Simmons
Kenneth King	Chelcie Ross
Albert Hawkins	John Beasley
Mike Wilson	Lynnsee Provence
Miller Wilson	Hunter McGilvray
Ben Wilson	David Brannen

and Nathan Lewis (Cornelius), Benjamin Peacock (Tommy), Alex Lee (Paul Dean), Clay James (Stanley), Russell Durham Comegys (Ben Sr.), Janell McLeod (Mrs. Francis), Robby Preddy (Lady #2), Lucky Lawrence (Handsome Man at Bar); The Souvenirs: Mo, Lucky Lawrence, Boots Kutz, Buck Edwards, D.J. Pawlak (The Band); Kipp Chambers (Boy at Dance), Dallas Johnson (Dallas), Stuart Greer (Officer Huggins), Jeff Bragg (Jed Barksdale), Danny Elfman (Tommy Lee Ballard), S.D. Stephens (Deputy on Shore), Samuel E. Parlin, Jr. (Deputy in Boat), Ed Reddick (Judge), Rebecca Koon (Buddy's Mother), Erik Cord (Buddy's Father)

Annie Wilson, a psychic in a small Southern town, uses her powers in hopes of finding out who murdered the young fiancee of the high school principal.

Giovanni Ribisi

Keanu Reeves

Hilary Swank

MISS CONGENIALITY

(WARNER BROS.) Producer, Sandra Bullock; Executive Producers, Marc Lawrence, Ginger Sledge, Bruce Berman; Director, Donald Petrie; Screenplay, Marc Lawrence, Katie Ford, Caryn Lucas; Photography, Laszlo Kovacs; Designer, Peter Larkin; Editor, Billy Weber; Music, Edward Shearmur; Music Supervisor, Steve Schnur; Choreographer, Scott Grossman; Stunts, Jack Gill; a Castle Rock Entertainment presentation in association wtih Village Roadshow Pictures and NPV Entertainment of a Fortis Films production; Dolby; Deluxe color; Rated PG-13; 109 minutes; Release date: December 22, 2000

Michael Caine, Sandra Bullock, Benjamin Bratt

CAST

Gracie Hart	Sandra Bullock
Victor Melling	Michael Caine
Eric Matthews	Benjamin Bratt
Stan Fields	William Shatner
McDonald	Ernie Hudson
Agent Clonsky	John DiResta
Kathy Morningside	Candice Bergen
Cheryl "Rhode Island"	Heather Burns
Karen "New York"	Melissa De Sousa
Frank Tobin	Steve Monroe
Mary Jo "Texas"	Deirdre Quinn
Leslie "California"	Wendy Raquel Robinson
Alana "Hawaii"	Asia DeMarcos
Agent Harris	Ken Thomas
Agent Grant	Gabriel Folse
Agent Jensen	Christopher Shea
Young Gracie	Mary Ashleigh Green
Tough Boy	Cody Linley
Alan	Eric Ian Goldberg
Krashow	Daniel Kamin
Ivan	Konstantin Selivanov
Russian Waitress	Mona Lee
Russian Bodyguards	Sergei Levtsuk, Johnny Caan
Pageant Announcer	Debbie Nelson
Pageant Director	Don Cass
Assistant Director	Laurie Guzda
Backstage Security Guard	Jimmy Graham
Security Guard	Ruperto Reyes, Jr.
Pageant Matron	Bernadette Nason
Bartender	Stephen Bruton
Beth	Jessica Holcomb
Tina	Jennifer Gareis
Herself	Ellen Schwartz
Starbucks Cop	Cassandra L. Small
Starbucks Guy	Marco Perella
Preliminary Judge	Cynthia Dorn
Newscaster	Catenya McHenry
Warehouse Dentist	Paige Bishop
Warehouse Hair Stylist	Lucien Douglas

William Shatner, Sandra Bullock

and Georgia Foy (Miss United States), LeeAnne Locken (Nebraska), Pei-San Brown (Alaska), Isamari White (Florida), Kimberly Crawford (Maine), Jamie Drake Stephens (Maryland), Dyan Conner (Massachusetts), Kelly Bright (Minnesota), Dee Dee Adams (Missouri), Shana McClendon (Nevada), Janie Terrazas (New Mexico), Holly Mills (Ohio), Angela VanDe Walle (Oregon), Tarah Bartley (South Carolina), Farah White (Tennessee), Summyr Miller (Utah), Jessica Hale (Vermont), Pam Green (Washington).

FBI agent Gracie Hart goes undercover as a contestant in the Miss United States Pageant in order to nab a psychopath who has threatened to cause havoc at the event.

Michael Caine, Sandra Bullock, Candice Bergen

Andrea Di Stefano, Javier Bardem

Olatz Lopez Garmendia

BEFORE NIGHT FALLS

(FINE LINE FEATURES) Producer, Jon Kilik; Executive Producers, Julian Schnabel, Olatz Lopez Garmendia; Director, Julian Schnabel; Screenplay, Cunningham O'Keefe, Lázaro Gómez Carriles, Julian Schnabel; Based on the memoir *Antes que anochezca* by Reinaldo Arenas; Photography, Xavier Pérez Grobet, Guillermo Rosas; Designer, Salvador Parra; Editor, Michael Berenbaum; Music, Carter Burwell, Lou Reed, Laurie Anderson; Music Supervisors, Olatz Lopez Garmendia, Susan Jacobs; Costumes, Mariestela Fernandez; Associate Producer, Matthias Ehrenberg; a Grandview Pictures/El Mar Pictures production; Dolby; Technicolor; Rated R; 132 minutes; Release date: December 22, 2000

CAST

Reinaldo Arenas	Javier Bardem
Lázaro Gómez Carilles	Olivier Martinez
Pepe Malas	Andrea Di Stefano
Bon Bon/Lieutenant Victor	Johnny Depp
Cuco Sanchez	Sean Penn
Herberto Zorilla Ochoa	Michael Wincott
Fina Correa	Najwa Nimri
Virgilio Piñera	Hector Babenco
Reinaldo's Mother	Olatz Lopez Garmendia
Teenage Reinaldo	Vito Maria Schnabel
Professor	Jerzy Skolimowski
Reinaldo's Father	Sebastian Silva
Young Reinaldo	Giovani Florido
Reinaldo's Grandmother	Lolo Navarro
Teacher	Carmen Beato
Smallest School Children	Cy Schnabel, Olmo Schnabel
Reinaldo's Grandfather	Pedro Armendáriz
Carlos	Diego Luna
Lolin	Lia Chapman
Translator	Aquiles Benites
Pretty Blonde Student	Eva Piaskowska
Maria Teresa Freye de Andrade	Patricia Reyes Spindola
Women in Car	Marlene Diaz, Olga Borayo
Tomas Diego	Santiago Magill
Faustino	Manolo Garcia
Girl with Keys	Lola Schnabel
Landlady	Ofelia Medina
Woman (UNEAC)	Lois Barragan
Nightclub Singer	Eduardo Antonio
Valeria	Stella Schnabel
José Lezama Lima	Manuel González
Nicolas Abreu	Maurice Compte

and Claudette Maille (María Luis Lima), John Ortiz (Juan Abreu), Vincent Laresca (Jose Abreu), Rene Rivera (Recruit Driver), Chanel Puertas (Blonde on Beach), Manolo Rivero (Royal Gay), Nemo (Pedro the Bus Driver), Andrea Fassler (French Tourist), Magda (Santeria Dancer), Julian Bucio (Violent Soldier), Jorge Zaráte (Prosecutor), Francisco Gatorno (Jorge Camacho), Marisol Padilla Sanchez (Margarita Camacho), Jorge Zamora (Kid with Kite), Noel Medina (Policeman on Beach), Julyan Diaz, Eduardo Arroyuelo (Teenagers), Antonio Zavala (Stranger in Lenin Park), Eloy Ganuza (State Security in Lenin Park), Khotan (Young Man with Bird), René Pereira (Antonio), Abel Woolrich (Hungry Inmate), Mario Oliver (Gay Inmate), Robertico Valdez (Singing Prisoner), Claudio Osorio (Guard at El Morro), Alfredo Villa (Armando Garcia), Diahnne Déa (Blanca Romero), Caridad Martinez (Dancer in the Convent), Zulema Cruz (Zulema), Annie Gil (Blanca's Teenage Daughter), Filiberto Estrella (Dwarf), Juan Cristobal Murillo (Immigration Officer), Filiberto Hebra (Man at Mariel Harbor), Matthias Ehrenberg (Officer at Mariel Harbor), Jack Schnabel (Mr. Greenberg), Esther Schnabel (Mrs. Greenberg), Xavier Domingo (Death), Eric Springer (Orderly), Jimmy Nugent (Taxi Driver)

The true story of Cuban poet Reinaldo Arenas, who faced persecution from the Castro regime because of his homosexuality. This film received an Oscar nomination for actor (Javier Bardem).

Javier Bardem, Johnny Depp

Javier Bardem

Johnny Depp

Javier Bardem, Olivier Martinez

Javier Bardem

Javier Bardem, Andrea Di Stefano

Tom Hanks

Tom Hanks

CAST AWAY

(20TH CENTURY FOX/DREAMWORKS) Producers, Steve Starkey, Tom Hanks, Robert Zemeckis, Jack Rapke; Executive Producer, Joan Bradshaw; Director, Robert Zemeckis; Screenplay, William Broyles, Jr.; Photography, Don Burgess; Designer, Rick Carter; Editor, Arthur Schmidt; Costumes, Joanna Johnston; Music, Alan Silvestri; Visual Effects Supervisor, Ken Ralston; Casting, Victoria Burrows; an Imagemovers/Playtone production; Dolby; Deluxe color; Rated PG-13; 143 minutes; Release date: December 22, 2000

CAST

Chuck Noland	Tom Hanks
Kelly Frears	Helen Hunt
Stan	Nick Searcy
Jerry Lovett	Chris Noth
Bettina Peterson	Lari White
Ramon	Paul Sanchez
Fyodor	Leonid Citer
Dick Peterson	David Allen Brooks
Beautiful Russian Woman	Yelena Papovic
Russian Babushka	Valentina Ananyina
Nicolai	Semion Sudarikov
Yuri	Peter von Berg
Lev	Dimitri S. Boudrine
French FedEx Loader	François Duhamel
Pilot Jack	Michael Forest
Pilot Green	Viveka Davis
Memphis State Student	Jennifer Choe
Kelly's Mother	Nan Martin
Anne Larson	Anne Bellamy
Dennis Larson	Dennis Letts
Wendy Larson	Wendy Worthington
Skye Larson	Skye McKenzie
Virginia Larson	Valerie Wildman
John Larson	John Duerler
Steve Larson	Steve Monroe
Lindsey Larson	Ashley & Lindsey Trefger
Katie Larson	Alyssa, Kaitlyn & Lauren Gainer
Gregory Larson	Albert & Gregory Pugliese
Matt Larson	Brandon & Matthew Reinhart
Lisa Madden	Lisa Long
Lauren Madden	Lauren Birkell
Elden Madden	Elden Henson
Morgan Stockton	Timothy Stack
Alice Stockton	Alice Vaughn
Chase Stockton	Chase Bebak
Gage Stockton	Gage Bebak
Amanda Stockton	Amanda & Andrea Cagney
Fred Stockton	Fred & Peter Semmer
Joe Wally	Joe Conley
Ralph Wally	Aaron Rapke
Pilot Al	Vin Martin
Pilot Blaine	Garret Davis
Pilot Peter	Jay Acovone
Pilot Kevin	Christopher Kriesa
Himself	Fred Smith
FedEx Anchors	Michelle Robinson, Tommy Cresswell
Becca Twig	Jenifer Lewis
Maynard Graham	Geoffrey Blake
FedEx Manager	Rich Sickler
Taxi Driver	Derick Alexander

FedEx systems engineer Chuck Noland boards a plane for a routine business flight and finds himself stranded alone on a remote island when the plane crashes, killing the remainder of the crew. This film received Oscar nominations for actor (Tom Hanks) and sound.

Tom Hanks

Tom Hanks

Helen Hunt, Tom Hanks

Tom Hanks

Tom Hanks

O BROTHER, WHERE ART THOU?

(TOUCHSTONE/UNIVERSAL) Producer, Ethan Coen; Executive Producers, Tim Bevan, Eric Fellner; Director, Joel Coen; Screenplay, Ethan Coen, Joel Coen; Based upon *The Odyssey* by Homer; Co-Producer, John Cameron; Photography, Roger Deakins; Designer, Dennis Gassner; Costumes, Mary Zophres; Music, T-Bone Burnett, Carter Burwell; Editors, Roderick Jaynes (Ethan Coen, Joe Coen), Tricia Cooke; Casting, Ellen Chenoweth; Presented in association with Studio Canal; a Working Title Production; Dolby; Super 35 Widescreen; Deluxe color; Rated PG-13; 107 minutes; Release date: December 22, 2000

CAST

Ulysses Everett McGill...George Clooney
Pete Hogwallop ....John Turturro
Delmar O'Donnel...Tim Blake Nelson
Big Dan McTeague ....John Goodman
Penny Wharvey ....Holly Hunter
Tommy Johnson..Chris Thomas King
Pappy O'Daniel..Charles Durning
Junior O'Daniel...Del Pentecost
George Nelson...Michael Badalucco
Pappy's Staff...J.R. Horne, Brian Reddy
Homer Stokes ....Wayne Duvall
The Little Man ....Ed Gale
Vernon T. Waldrip..Ray McKinnon
Sheriff Cooley..Daniel Von Bargen
Man with Bullhorn...Royce D. Applegate
Wash Hogwallop ....Frank Collison
Boy Hogwallop...Quinn Gasaway
Blind Seer..Lee Weaver
Pomade Vendor ....Milford Fortenberry
Radio Station Man...Stephen Root
Mr. French ....John Locke

and Gillian Welch (Soggy Bottom Customer), A. Ray Ratliff (Record Store Clerk), Mia Tate, Musetta Vander, Christy Taylor (Sirens), April Hardcastle (Waitress), Michael W. Finnell (Interrogator), Georgia Rae Rainer, Marianna Breland, Lindsey Miller, Natalie Shedd (Wharvey Girls), John McConnell (Woolworths Manager), Isaac Freeman, Wilson Waters, Jr., Robert Hamlett (Gravediggers), Willard Cox, Evelyn Cox, Suzanne Cox, Sidney Cox (Cox Family), Buck White, Sharon White, Sheryl White (White Family), Ed Snodderly, David Holt (Village Idiots)

In depression-era Mississippi, three men escape from a prison chain gang and head towards the promise of a fortune in buried treasure. This film received Oscar nominations for screenplay adaptation and cinematography.

© Touchstone Pictures/Universal Studios

John Turturro, Tim Blake Nelson, George Clooney

George Clooney, Holly Hunter

John Goodman

Tim Blake Nelson, John Turturro, George Clooney

Nicolas Cage, Téa Leoni

Téa Leoni, Nicolas Cage

THE FAMILY MAN

(UNIVERSAL) Producers, Marc Abraham, Zvi Howard Rosenman, Tony Ludwig, Alan Riche; Executive Producers, Armyan Bernstein, Thomas A. Bliss, Andrew Z. Davis; Director, Brett Ratner; Screenplay, David Diamond, David Weissman; Photography, Dante Spinotti; Designer, Kristi Zea; Editor, Mark Helfrich; Costumes, Betsy Heimann; Casting, Matthew Barry, Nancy Green-Keyes; a Beacon Pictures presentation of a Riche/Ludwig-Zvi Howard Rosenman-Saturn production; Dolby; Panavision; Deluxe color; Rated PG-13; 126 minutes; Release date: December 22, 2000

Nicolas Cage, Makenzie Vega

CAST

Jack Campbell	Nicolas Cage
Kate	Téa Leoni
Cash	Don Cheadle
Arnie	Jeremy Piven
Alan Mintz	Saul Rubinek
Lassiter	Josef Sommer
Annie	Makenzie Vega
Josh	Jake Milkovich, Ryan Milkovich
Evelyn	Lisa Thornhill
Big Ed	Harve Presnell
Adelle	Mary Beth Hurt
Paula	Amber Valletta
Lorraine	Francine York
Mrs. Peterson	Ruth Williamson
Tony the Doorman	John O'Donahue
Frank the Security Man	Daniel Whitner
Executives	Lucy Lin, Lisa Lo Cicero

and Wass Stevens (Trader), Thomas James Foster (Joe the Valet), Irene Roseen (Mintz's Assistant), Ken Leung (Deli Clerk), Mak Fai (Grandfather in Deli), Maggi-Meg Reed (Lady in Deli), Kate Walsh (Jeannie), Ray Valentine (Evelyn's Husband), Gianni Russo (Nick), Tom McGowan (Bill), Joel McKinnon Miller (Tommy), Tanya Newbould (Nick's Wife), Hilary Adahms (Party Guest), Troy Hall (Kenny), Kathleen Doyle (Big Ed's PA Voice), Mary Civiello (CNBC Reporter), Paul Keith (Suit Salesman), Elisabeth Sjoli (Hostess), Philippe Bergeron (Waiter), Christopher Breslin (Restaurant Patron), Si Picker (Tire Customer), Lisa Guzman (Girl at Market), Robert Downey, Sr. (Man in House), P.J. Barry (Limo Driver), Nina Barry (Kate's Assistant), Ellis (Lucy the Dog)

Jack Campbell, a high-powered Wall Street executive who believes he has everything in life he needs, awakes one morning to discover that he is suddenly living a middle-class existence in suburbia and married to the woman he parted from thirteen years earlier.

© Universal Studios

Nicolas Cage, Don Cheadle

Rebecca Pidgeon, Philip Seymour Hoffman

Julia Stiles, William H. Macy, Linda Kimbrough

STATE AND MAIN

(FINE LINE FEATURES) Producer, Sarah Green; Executive Producers, Jon Cornick, Alec Baldwin; Co-Producers, Mark Ordesky, Rachel Horovitz, Alan Mruvka, Joseph Nittolo; Director/Screenplay, David Mamet; Photography, Oliver Stapleton; Designer, Gemma Jackson; Costumes, Susan Lyall; Editor, Barbara Tulliver; Music, Theodore Shapiro; Casting, Avy Kaufman; a Green/Renzi production in association with El Dorado Pictures, presented in association with Filmtown Entertainment; Dolby; DuArt color; Rated R; 106 minutes; Release date: December 22, 2000

CAST

Bob Barrenger	Alec Baldwin
Mayor George Bailey	Charles Durning
Douglas Mackenize	Clark Gregg
Joseph Turner White	Philip Seymour Hoffman
Sherry Bailey	Patti LuPone
Walt Price	William H. Macy
Claire Wellesley	Sarah Jessica Parker
Marty Rossen	David Paymer
Ann Black	Rebecca Pidgeon
Carla Taylor	Julia Stiles
Doc Wilson	Michael Higgins
Priest	Michael Bradshaw
Bunky	Morris Lamore
Spud	Allen Soule
Jack	Ricky Jay
Hotel Clerk	Matt Malloy

and Tony V (Water Delivery Man), Tony Mamet (Electrician), Jack Wallace (Bellhop), Michael James O'Boyle (Chuckie), Carlotte Potok (Maude), Christopher Kaldor (Officer Cal Thompkin), Rick Levy (Gun Store Owner), J.J. Johnston (Stationmaster), Richard L. Friedman (Postman), Kolbie McCabe (Girl on Scooter), Emma Norman (Fisherwoman), Dee Nelson (Decorator), Brian Howe (Bartender), Robert Walsh, Ken Cheeseman (Troopers), G. Roy Levin (Salesman with Rubber Duck), Matthew Pidgeon (BBC TV Reporter), Daniel B. Hovanesian (Bailiff), Jerry Graff (Fake Judge), Timothy Jernigan-Smith (Billy on Bike), Paul Butler (Real Judge), Alexandra Kerry (Television Director), Jordan Lage (Doc Morton), Lionel Mark Smith (Bill Smith), Vincent Guastaferro (Uberto Pazzi-Sforzo), Linda Kimbrough (Courteney), Jim Frangione (Tommy Max), Lana Bilzerian, Josh Marchette (Production Assistants), Laura Silverman (Secretary), Jonathan Katz (Howie Gold)

A Hollywood film crew descends upon a small Vermont town to shoot a film, causing havoc with the locals because of their thoughtless actions.

Sarah Jessica Parker, Alec Baldwin

Clark Gregg, Alec Baldwin, Robert Walsh, David Paymer

DRACULA 2000

(DIMENSION) Producers, W.K. Border, Joel Soisson; Executive Producers, Wes Craven, Marianne Maddalena, Bob Weinstein, Harvey Weinstein, Andrew Rona; Director, Patrick Lussier; Screenplay, Joel Soisson; Story, Joel Soisson, Patrick Lussier; Co-Producers, Dan Arredondo, Ron Schmidt; Photography, Peter Pay; Designer, Carol Spier; Costumes, Denise Cronenberg; Editors, Patrick Lussier, Peter Devaney Flanagan; Visual Effects Supervisor, Erik Henry; Makeup Effects Creator, Gary J. Tynnicliffe; Music, Marco Beltrami; Music Supervisor, Ed Gerrard; Casting, Randi Hiller, Sarah Halley Finn; Presented by Wes Craven in association wtih Neo Art & Logic; Distributed by Miramax Films; Dolby; Color; Rated R; 99 minutes; Release date: December 22, 2000

CAST

Simon Sheppard	Jonny Lee Miller
Mary Heller	Justine Waddell
Dracula	Gerard Butler
Lucy (Vitamin C)	Colleen Ann Fitzpatrick
Solina	Jennifer Esposito
Nightshade	Danny Masterson
Valerie Sharpe	Jeri Ryan
Eddie	Lochlyn Munro
Trick	Sean Patrick Thomas
Marcus	Omar Epps
Abraham Van Helsing	Christopher Plummer
Dax	Tig Fong

and Tony Munch (Charlie), Shane West (JT), Nathan Fillion (Father David), Tom Kane (Anchor Man), Jonathan Whittaker (Gautreaux), Robert Verlaque (Dr. Seward), Randy Butcher, Bill Davidson, Peter Cox, Chris Lamon, Duncan McLeod (Stakemen), Wayne Downer (Desk Guard), Robert Racki (Door Guard), William Prael (Parade Cop), Karon Briscoe (Teen Co-Worker), Scarlett Huntley (Blood Doll), Harold Short (Black Angel of Death), David J. Francis (Jesus), Shimmy Silverman (Barker)

A group of thieves opens a crypt unleasing Dracula upon the 21st Century, prompting the vampire to head to New Orleans in search of the daughter of his nemesis, Abraham Van Helsing

© Dimension Films

Gerard Butler

Brían F. O'Byrne, Anna Friel, Barry McEvoy

AN EVERLASTING PIECE

(DREAMWORKS/COLUMBIA) Producers, Barry Levinson, Paula Weinstein, Mark Johnson, Louis DiGiaimo, Jerome O'Connor; Executive Producer, Patrick McCormick; Director, Barry Levinson; Screenplay, Barry McEvoy; Photography, Seamus Deasy; Designer, Nathan Crowley; Editor, Stu Linder; Music, Hans Zimmer; Music Supervisor, Allan Mason; Costumes, Joan Bergin; Hair Piece Consultant, Hugh McAllistair; Casting, John Hubbard, Ros Hubbard; a Bayahibe Films production in association with Baltimore/Spring Creek Pictures productions; Dolby; Technicolor; Rated R; 103 minutes; Release date: December 25, 2000

CAST

Colm O'Neill	Barry McEvoy
George	Brían F. O'Byrne
Bronagh	Anna Friel
Gerty	Pauline McLynn
Mrs. O'Neill	Ruth McCabe
Mickey	Lauren Kinlan
Scalper	Billy Connolly
Mr. Black	Des McAleer
IRA Man	Colum Convey
Milker	Ian Cregg

and David Pearse (Comrade), Seamus Ball (Mr. Duggan), Enda Oates (Detective), Des Braiden (Vicar), George Shane (Billy King), Brendan Costelloe (English Patient), Simon Delaney (Orderly), Olivia Nash (Eileen McGivern), Kathleen Bradley (Bronagh's Cousin), MacLean Stewart, A.J. Kennedy (Masked Men), Darren Lawless (Smok Mullen), Peter Quinn (Que McKeever), David Howarth (British Officer), Mark Carruthers (TV Anchor), Nevan Finnegan (Dixieland Man), Samuel Bright (Wee Messer), Philip Young (Man in Cinema), Conor Bradford (News Reporter), Martin Nicholl (Hard Man), Michael Fieldhouse (Barrister), Bryan McCaugherty (Creeped Youth), Jack Quinn (Bronagh's Dad), Frank O'Keefe (Professor), Paul Clancy (Butcher), Little John Nee, Jonathan Shankey (Toupee Men), Paul McFetridge (IRA Man's Wife)

In early 1980s Belfast, a pair of barbers, Colm, a Catholic, and George, a Protestant, team up to make a killing in the toupee market in Northern Ireland.

© DreamWorks LLC

ALL THE PRETTY HORSES

(MIRAMAX/COLUMBIA) Producer, Robert Salerno, Billy Bob Thornton; Executive Producers, Sally Menke, Jonathan Gordon; Director, Billy Bob Thornton; Screenplay, Ted Tally; Based on the novel by Cormac McCarthy; Co-Producers, Bruce Heller, Mary Ann Madden; Photography, Barry Markowitz; Designer, Clark Hunter; Editor, Sally Menke; Music, Marty Stuart; Costumes, Doug Hall; Casting, Mary Vernieu, Anne McCarthy; Dolby; Panavision; Deluxe color; Rated PG-13; 117 minutes; Release date: December 25, 2000

Matt Damon, Penélope Cruz

CAST

John Grady Cole	Matt Damon
Lacey Rawlins	Henry Thomas
Alejandra	Penélope Cruz
Jimmy Blevins	Lucas Black
Rocha	Ruben Blades
Dona Alfonsa	Miriam Colon
Judge	Bruce Dern
Cole	Robert Patrick
J.C. Franklin	Sam Shepard
Captain	Julio Oscar Mechoso
Luisa	Angelina Torres
Grandfather	J.D. Young
Mother	Laura Pope
Girl	Yvette Diaz
Girl's Mom	Imelda Colindres
Manuel	Augustin Solis
Maria	Elizabeth Ibarra
Esteban	Lonnie Rodriguez
Lieutenant	Fredrick Lopez
Orlando	Denes Lujan

and Daniel Lanois, Raul Malo (Singers), Ferron Lucero, Jr., Manuel Sanchez (Lieutenant's Men), Edwin Figueroa (Charro), Matthew E. Montoya (Indian), Julian Prada (Prison Singer), Roberto Enrique Pineda (Doctor), Vincente Ramos (Commandante), George R. Lopez (Clapping Man), J.D. Garfield (Carlos), Julio Cedillo (Campesino), Marc Miles (Deputy Smith), Brian Orr (Man at Car)

Henry Thomas

Hoping to start a new life after his mother sells the ranch on which he's spent his whole life, Texan John Grady Cole takes off with best friend Lacey Rawlins for Mexico. There he finds himself in a great deal of trouble after crossing paths with teen misfit Jimmy Blevins, and after falling in love with the daughter of a powerful landowner.

© Miramax Films

Lucas Black

Matt Damon

THIRTEEN DAYS

(NEW LINE CINEMA) Producers, Armyan Bernstein, Peter O. Almond, Kevin Costner; Executive Producers, Ilona Herzberg, Michael De Luca, Thomas A. Bliss, Marc Abraham; Director, Roger Donaldson; Screenplay, David Self; Based on the book *The Kennedy Tapes: Inside the White House During the Cuban Missile Crisis*, edited by Ernest R. May, Philip D. Zelikow; Photography, Andrzej Bartkowiak; Designer, Dennis Washington; Editor, Conrad Buff; Costumes, Isis Mussenden; Music, Trevor Jones; Co-Producers, Paul Deason, Mary Montiforte; Casting, Dianne Crittenden; Presented in association with Beacon Pictures; Dolby; Deluxe color; Rated PG-13; 145 minutes; Release date: December 25, 2000

Steven Culp, Bruce Greenwood, Kevin Costner

CAST

Kenny O'Donnell	Kevin Costner
John F. Kennedy	Bruce Greenwood
Robert F. Kennedy	Steven Culp
Robert McNamara	Dylan Baker
Adlai Stevenson	Michael Fairman
Dean Rusk	Henry Strozier
McGeorge Bundy	Frank Wood
General Curtis LeMay	Kevin Conway
Ted Sorenson	Tim Kelleher
Dean Acheson	Len Cariou
General Maxwell Taylor	Bill Smitrovich
Arthur Lundahl	Dakin Matthews
Adm. George Anderson	Madison Mason
Cmmdr. William B. Ecker	Christopher Lawford
Gen. Marshall Carter	Ed Lauter
Anatoly Dobrinyn	Elya Baskin
Alexander Fomin	Boris Lee Krutonog
John McCrone	Peter White
George Ball	James Karen
Scotty Reston, Journalist	Timothy Jerome
Andrei Gromyko	Olek Krupa
Helen O'Donnell	Lucinda Jenney
Valerian Zorin	Oleg Vidov
U2 Pilot	Shawn Driscoll
Mark O'Donnell	Drake Cook

and Caitlin Wachs (Kathy O'Donnell), Jon Foster (Kenny O'Donnell, Jr.), Matthew Dunn (Kevin O'Donnell), Kevin O'Donnell (NPIC Photo Interpreter), Janet Coleman (Evelyn Lincoln), Bruce Thomas (Floyd), Stephanie Romanov (Jacqueline Kennedy), Liz Sinclair, Colette O'Connell (Kennedy's Assistants), Karen Ludwig (Operator Margaret), Audrey Rapoport, Marliese K. Schneider (White House Operators), Walter Adrian (Lyndon Johnson), Daniel Ziskie (Gen. Walter "Cam" Sweeney), Kelly Connell (Pierre Salinger), Jack McGee (Mayor Daly), Lamar Smith (Aide), John Aylward (Orville Dryfoos), Vivien Straus (White House Aide), David O'Donnell (Lt. Bruce Wilhemy), Gene Del Bianco (Petty Officer), Ben Koldyke (RF-8 Pilot), Daniel Vergara (OAS President), Reuben Moreno (Argentine Diplomat), Thomas Roberts (Sonar Operator), Sean Bergin (Chief Sonarman), Alan Francis (Executive Officer of USS Pierce), Robert Munstis, Joseph Repoff, Alex Veadov (Radio Room Operators), Michael Gaston (Captain of USS Pierce), J. Tucker Smith (Captain of USS Kennedy), Chris Henry Coffey (Officer of Destroyer), Radu Gavor (Romanian Delegate), Zitto Kazann (Chilean Delegate), Jack Blessing (John Scali), Tom Everett (Walter Sheridan), Karl Makinen (Young FBI Agent), Charles Esten (Major Rudolph Anderson), Charles Barrett (Air Force NCO), Darryl Smith (Football Coach), Allan Graf (Football Referee), Robert Miranda (RFK'S Driver), Todd Sible (RFK's Staffer), Marya Kazakova (Soviet Woman), Craig Hosking (Pilot)

When U.S. spy planes reveal missiles in Cuba, President Kennedy and his staff spend thirteen tense days trying to keep the country from engaging in nuclear war with Russia.

© New Line Cinema, Inc.

Dylan Baker, Steven Culp

Tim Kelleher, Steven Culp, Kevin Costner, Ed Lauter, Bill Smitrovich, Bruce Greenwood, Peter White, Henry Strozier

Michael Douglas, Erika Christensen

Catherine Zeta-Jones

Luis Guzman, Miguel Ferrer, Don Cheadle

Topher Grace, Vonte Sweet, Michael Douglas

Benicio Del Toro, Jacob Vargas

TRAFFIC

(USA FILMS) Producers, Edward Zwick, Marshall Herskovitz, Laura Bickford; Executive Producers, Richard Solomon, Mike Newell, Cameron Jones, Graham King, Andreas Klein; Director, Steven Soderbergh; Screenplay, Stephen Gaghan; Based on the mini-series *Traffik* created by Simon Moore, originally produced by Carnival Films for Channel 4 Television; Photography, Peter Andrews (Steven Soberbergh); Designer, Philip Messina; Editor, Stephen Mirrione; Costumes, Louise Frogley; Music, Cliff Martinez; Casting, Debra Zane; a Bedford Falls/Laura Bickford production, presented in association with Initial Entertainment Group; Dolby; CFI color; Rated R; 147 minutes; Release date: December 27, 2000

CAST

Robert Wakefield	Michael Douglas
Montel Gordon	Don Cheadle
Javier Rodriguez	Benicio Del Toro
Ray Castro	Luis Guzman
Arnie Metzger	Dennis Quaid
Helena Ayala	Catherine Zeta-Jones
Carlos Ayala	Steven Bauer
Caroline Wakefield	Erika Christensen
Francisco Flores	Clifton Collins, Jr.
Eduardo Ruiz	Miguel Ferrer
Seth Abrahms	Topher Grace
Barbara Wakefield	Amy Irving
General Arturo Salazar	Tomas Milian
Ana Sanchez	Marisol Padilla Sanchez
Manolo Sanchez	Jacob Vargas
Chief of Staff	Albert Finney
Jeff Sheridan	D.W. Moffett
General Ralph Landry	James Brolin
Attorney Michael Adler	Peter Riegert
ADA Dan Collier	John Slattery
Juan Obregon	Benjamin Bratt

and Andrew Chavez, Michael Saucedo (Desert Truck Drivers), Jose Yenque (Salazar Soldier/The Torturer), Emilio Rivera (Salazar Soldier #2), Michael O'Neill (Lawyer Rodman), Russell G. Jones (Clerk), Lorene Hetherington, Eric Collins (State Capitol Reporters), Leticia Bombardier (Ruiz's Secretary), Carl Ciarfalio (Ruiz's Assistant), Steve Lambert (Van Driver), Gilbert Rosales (Van Passenger), Corey Spears (Fucked-up Bowman), Majandra Delfino (Vanessa), Alec Roberts (David Ayala), Dean Faulkner (Parking Valet), Daniella Kuhn (Tourist Woman), Brandon Keener (Tourist Man), Beau Holden, Peter Stader, James Lew, Jeremy Fitzgerald, Russell Solberg (DEA Agents, CalTrans), Don Snell, Enrique Murciano, Gary Carlos Cervantes (DEA Agents, Trailer), Rick Avery, Mario Roberts, Eileen Weisinger, Ken Johnston, Mike Watson, Kurt Lott, Lincoln Simonds, Steve Tomaski, Buck McDancer, John Callery, Ousaun Elam, Brian Avery (DEA Agents, Public Storage), Rena Sofer, Stacey Travis, Jennifer Barker (Helena's Friends), Governor Bill Weld, Senator Don Nickles, Senator Harry Reed, Jeff Podolsky, Senator Barbara Boxer, Senator Orrin Hatch, Senator Charles Grassley (Themselves), George Blumenthal, Jewelle Bickford, Dave Hager, Tucker Smallwood (Partygoers), Stephen Dunham (Lobbyist), Margaret Travolta (Economist), Victor Quintero, Toby Holguin, Ramiro Gonzalez (Salazar Soldiers), Viola Davis (Social Worker), James Pickens, Jr. (Prosecutor Ben Williams), Elaine Kagan (Judge Reed), Jim Ortega (Arrested Man in Apartment), Greg Boniface, Tom Rosales (Tackled Men), Rudy M. Camacho (Customs Official), Yul Vazquez (Tigrillo/Obregon Assassin), Jack Conley (Agent Hughes), Eddie Velez (Agent Johnson), Craig N. Chretien (Director of EPIC), John Brown (Assistant Director of EPIC), Mike Siegel (DEA Representative), Joel Torres (Porfilio Madrigal), Steve Rose (Marty), Kimber Fritz (Rehab Counselor), Harsh Nayyar, Mary Pat Gleason (Witnesses), Vincent Ward (Man on Street), Jesu Garcia (Pablo Obregon), Gregory Estevane (Polygraph Administrator), Alex Procopio (Polygraph Assistant), Rita Gomez (Mrs. Castro), Kaizaad Navroze Kotwal (Teacher), David Jensen ("John"), Jay Fernando Krymis, Mike Malone (Waiters), Rena Pereyra (Doctor), Kymberly S. Newberry (Press Secretary), Carroll Schumacher (Ayala Secretary), Michael Showers (Meeting Leader), Salma Hayek (Mistress of Juarez Druglord)

Three concurrent stories involving the drug trade: a Mexican policeman hopes to expose a powerful drug dealer; the U.S. government's newly appointed drug czar is stunned to discover that his teenage daughter is a drug addict; an upscale San Diego housewife tries desperately to help her husband after he is arrested for trafficking drugs on the side.

2000 Academy Award-winner for Best Supporting Actor (Benicio Del Toro), Director, Screenplay Adaptation, and Editing. This film received an additional Oscar nomination for picture.

Michael Douglas, Amy Irving

Dennis Quaid, Catherine Zeta-Jones

Erika Christensen, Topher Grace

Ryan Daugherty in *Trans* © Cowboy Booking

Eric Mabius, Samantha Buck in *Wirey Spindell* © WinStar Cinema

TRANS (Cowboy Booking) Producer, Michael Robinson; Director/Screenplay, Julian L. Goldberger; Photography, Jesse Rosen; Designer, Sarah Wagoner; Editor, Alfonso Goncalves; Music, Fat Mama and Her Trans World Orchestra; Associate Producer, Martin Garner; a Yid Panther and Down Home Pictures presentation in association with Cowboy Booking International; Color; Not rated; 78 minutes; Release date: January 7, 2000. CAST: Ryan Daugherty (Ryan Kazinski), Justin Lakes, Jon Daugherty, Michael Gulnac, Stephanie Davis, Edge, Jeremiah Robinson, Elijah Smith, Trevor Thomas, Charles Walker

CREATURE (Seventh Art) Producer, Don Lepore; Director/Editor, Parris Patton; Photography, John Travers; Music, Chad Smith; a Grapevine Films production, in association with In Motion Pictures, Planet Inc., and Randazzo Films; Colo; Not rated; 64 minutes; Release date: January 14, 2000. Documentary on Stacey "Hollywood" Dean, a pre-op transsexual, and his/her life in Los Angeles; featuring Butch Dean, Dusty Dean, Filberto "Barbarella" Ascencio.

THE REUNION (Good Medicine) Producers, Paul Corvino, Leticia Gomez, Dallas Hartnett; Executive Producers, Sean P. Casey, Joseph S. DiMarco; Director, Larry Eudene; Screenplay, Paul Corvino; Photography, Patrick Capone; Designer, Zeljka Pavlinovic; Music, Kirsten Vogelsang; Editors, Glenn Conte, Robert Fitzgerald; Casting, Kelly Blake, Liz Lewis; from Asylum Pictures, Esquire Films; Black and white/color; Not rated; 84 minutes; Release date: January 19, 2000. CAST: Timothy Devlin (Louis Witkowski), Elizabeth P. McKay (Felicia), Patrick Ferraro (Joey), Leila Sbatini (Ashley), Jack Mulcahy (Hal Coleman), Mimi Langeland (Caroline), Kristopher Medina (Elden), Edouard DeSoto (Santiago)

Stacey "Hollywood" Dean in *Creature* © Seventh Art Releasing

WIREY SPINDELL (WinStar Cinema) Producers, Eric Schaeffer, Dolly Hall, Lloyd Segan, Terence Michael; Director/Screenplay, Eric Schaeffer; Executive Producers, Bruce Greenfield, Van Greenfield; Photography, Kramer Morgenthau; Designer, Mark Helmuth; Music, Amanda Kravat, Peter Millrose; Editor, Mitch Stanley; Costumes, Amanda Silberstein, Bootsy Holler; Casting, Sheila Jaffe, Georgianne Walken; a Five Minutes Before The Miracle production; Dolby; Technicolor; Not rated; 101 minutes; Release date: January 21, 2000. CAST: Eric Schaeffer (Wirey Spindell), Eric Mabius (Wirey at 17), Devin Matthews-Johnson (Wirey—Junior High), Zane Adlum (Wirey—6 Years Old), Baby John Henry (Baby Wirey), Callie Thorne (Tabatha), Samantha Buck (Samantha), Jennifer Wiltsie (Wirey's Mom—Young), Peggy Gormley (Wirey's Mom—Mature), John Doman (Wirey's Father), Caroline Strong (Judy), Erica Bergsmeds (Helena), Don Creech (Teacher, Mean-Gray Hair), Laura Chen (Little Chinese Girl), Billie Greenfield (Brooke Swarthen), Corey Michael (Greg—6 Years Old), Kaleigh Palazzo (Cousin Betsy), John Deyle (Principal Dickens), Silvan Sennon (Robby—7th Grade), Bryan Callen (Robby—Present Day), George Bass (Raphael), Michael Pallotia (Gabe), Paul Frediani (Calhoun Coach), Stefan Niemczyk (Lapper), Edward J. Moore (Lapper Teacher/Coach), Anthony Tavaglione (Mean Kid—Jr. High), Chuck Bradley (Mean Kid Spy), Gerry Rosenthal (Mike Johnson), Kerilynn Pratt (First Date), Bill Weeden (Bill), Carolyn Swift (Mary), John C. Haynes, Jim Gaffigan (Announcers), Retania Alda (Bratelboro Coach's Wife), Jenna Stern (Roxanne), Jan Greenfield (Teenage Girl), Sarah Ziff (Sarah), Leanne Whitney (Beth), Mathew Brown (Bass Player), Ian O'Donnel (Dave), Greg Haberny (Niles), Lisa Lang (Stephanie), Michelle Hurst (Arlene), Eric E. Demski (Kikos), Hamilton Deoliveira (Bloody Cross Guy, Jiz), David Healy (Yuppie Guy), Dionne Ford Kurth (Model, Danny), Kenneth P. Strong (Shrink), Adam Ernster (Spike), Ingrid Kogin (Russian Hooker), Steven Bradbury (Teacher—Shop Class), Mark Kachersky (Football Coach), Angela Bullock (Tabatha's Girlfriend), Stacey Leigh Ivey (Stripper Waitress), Melvin Rodriguez (Worker—Doorman), William Charles Mitchell (FBI Man), Jorge Pupo, Michael Patterson, Ray Fitzgerald (Scouts), Irma St. Paule (Angel Lady), Tara Kruse (Sally)

HELLHOUNDS ON MY TRAIL: THE AFTERLIFE OF ROBERT JOHNSON (Nonfiction Films/Mug-Shot Prods.) Producers, Jeff Sanders, Robert Mugge; Director/Editor, Robert Mugge; from Cowboy Booking; Color/Black and white; Not rated; 95 minutes; Release date: January 21, 2000. Documentary tributing blues musician Robert Johnson, featuring Stephen C. Le Vere, Bob Weir, Robert Lockwood Jr., Alvin Youngblood Hart, Rob Wasserman, David "Honeyboy" Edwards, Henry Townsend, Tracy Nelson, Marcia Ball, Irma Thomas, Peter Green, Nigel Watson, Joe Louis Walker, Billy Branch, Keb' Mo', Chris Whitley, G. Love and Special Sauce, Guy Davis, Gov't Mule, Roy Rogers, Rory Block, Sonny Landreth, Bill Morrissey, Billy Hector Trio.

Joe Louis Walker, Billy Branch in *Hellhounds on My Trail*
© Nonfiction Films

Tyne Daly, Irma St. Paule in *A Piece of Eden* © FilmAcres

THE BOONDOCK SAINTS (Franchise/Indican) Producers, Chris Brinker, Rob Fried, Elie Samaha, Lloyd Segan;Executive Producers, Ashok Amritraj, Don Carmody, David Della Rocco, Andrew Stevens; Director/Screenplay, Troy Duffy; Photography, Adam Kane; Designer, Robert de Vico; Editor, Bill DeRonde; Costumes, Mary McLeod; Music, Jeff Danna; Casting, Tina Gerussi, Kevin Fennessy; a Franchise Pictures presentation of a Blood Syndicate production in association with Fried Films, the Lloyd Segan Co. and Chris Brinker Prods.; Dolby; FotoKem color; Rated R; 110 minutes; Release date: January 21, 2000. CAST: Willem Dafoe (Paul Smecker), Sean Patrick Flanery (Conner MacManus), Norman Reedus (Murphy MacManus), David Della Rocco (Rocco), Billy Connolly (Il Duce), David Ferry (Det. Dolly), Brian Mahoney (Det. Duffy), Bob Marley (Det. Greenly), Richard Fitzpatrick (The Chief), William Young (Monsignor), Robert Pemberton (Mackiepenny), Bill Craig (McGerkin), Dorothy-Marie Jones (Rosengurtie), Scott Griffith (Ivan Checkov), Layton Morrison (Vladdy), James Binkley (Officer Newman), Matthew Chaffee (Officer Chaffey), Robert Vernon Eaton (Officer Langley), Kym Kristalie (Beat-up Woman), Gerard Parkes (Doc), Peter Windrem, Elizabeth Brown (Reporters), Todd Schroeder (Russian Mobster), Jeffrey R. Smith (Bartender), Jonathan Higgins (Officer Michaell), Anthony Chrysostom (Judge), Lizz Alexander (Virginal Woman), Derek Murchie, Robert B. Kennedy (Media Men), Carlo Rota (Yakavetta), Ron Jeremy Hyatt (Vincenzo Lipazzi), Tom Barnett (Irish Gun Dealer), Glenn Marc Silot (Rueben), Victor Pedtchenko (The Fat Man), Lauren Piech (Donna), Gina Sorell (Rayvie), Jeanna Fine (Dancer), Sergio Di Zio (Oly), Angelo Tucci (Vinnie), Jimmy Tingle (The Priest), Dick Callahan (Sal), Morris Santia (Drug Dealer), Carmen DiStefano (Augustus), Darren Marsman (Pimp), Christopher Flockton (Mr. Cobb), Roberta Angelica (Forensic Woman #1), Markus Parilo (Sick Mob Man), Gary Nicholson (Correctional Officer), Joe Pingue (Geno), Kevin Chapman (Chappy), Nicholas Pasco (Hojo), Pat Riccio (Mafia Man), Chris Brinker, Don Carmody (Mafioso), Ryan Parks (Langley)

A PIECE OF EDEN (FilmAcres) formerly *Tredici*; Producer/Director, John D. Hancock; Executive Producer, Bob Hiler; Screenplay, Dorothy Tristan; Co-Producer, Ken Kitch; Photography, Misha Suslov; Music, Angelo Badalamenti; Editor, Dennis O'Connor; Casting, Susan Willett; Color; Not rated; 109 minutes; Release date: February 4, 2000. CAST: Marc Grapey (Bob Tredici), Rebecca Harrell (Happy Buchanan), Tyne Daly (Aunt Aurelia), Frederic Forrest (Paulo Tredici), Andreas Katsulas (Giuseppi Tredici), Robert Breuler (Franco Tredici), Tristan Rogers (Victor Hardwick), Irma St. Paule (Maria), Marshall Efron (Andres), Jeff Puckett (Greg Tredici), Julia Swart (Claire Tredici), Rengin Altay (Maria at 30), Lara Phillips (TV Reporter), Jeannette Washluske (Nurse), James Ferguson (Teenage Franco), Tracy Lopresto (Bob's Mother), Jesse Giuliani (Young Franco), Kevin Hundt (Young Paolo), Annastecia Spano (Young Aurelia), Matthew T. Mender (Bob at 9), Kiva Wenig (Bob at 4), Brittany Miser (Nikki), Christian Porod (Anthony), Gabriel Escobedo, Martin González, José Vargas, Roy Reyalado (Farm Workers), Beth Behler (Mr. Hardwick's Assistant), Mary Wagner (Ms. Hofmeister), Claudette Harrison (Hofmeister Daughter), Glenn Hutchinson (Farm Salesman), Don Varda (Computer Delivery Man), Jim Quartuccio

(Chauffeur), Brooks B. Barnes (Fish Truck Driver), Diana Glasgow (Shirley), Theresa Bowen (Fan), Colleen Davenport, Ted Grice (Customers), James R. Lewis (Big Jack Hurley), Jake Christner (Teeange Paulo), Brandi Keehn (Teenage Aurelia)

KNOCKOUT (Renegade Pictures) Producers, Lorenzo Doumani, Simone Sheffield; Director, Lorenzo Doumani; Screenplay, Mark Stevens, Lorenzo Doumani; Photography, Hisham Abed; Designer, John Hernandez; Costumes, Sylvia Vega-Vasquez; Editor, Dayle Mustain; Music, Sidney James; Boxing Choreographer, Terry Claybon; Casting, Katy Wallin, Thom Klohn; a DMG Pictures presentation; Dolby; Deluxe color; Rated PG-13; 99 minutes; Release date: February 4, 2000. CAST: Sophia-Adella Hernandez (Belle Alvarado), Eduardo Vañez (Mario Rodriguez), Tony Plana (Chuck Alvarado), Paul Winfield (Ron Regent), William McNamara (Michael DeMarco), Maria Conchita Alonso (Carmen Alvarado), Gina LaPiana (Sandra Lopez), Fredia Gibbs (Tanya "Terminator" Tessaro), Tony Burton (Sergeant Hawkins), Brittany Parkyn (Young Isabelle), Dora Weber (Farmer's Daughter), Mike Moroff (Officer Stark), Erick Vazquez (Enrique), Ralph Cooper (Regent's Assistant), Mike Rad (Street Punk), Tracy Caymen (Officer), Raoul N. Rizik (Priest), Jackie Kallen (WFBA Official), Jim Jenkins, Shane Mosley (Fight Commentators), Ben Lira (Referee), Lou Filippo (Main Fight Referee), Alex Espindola (Boy Boxer), Oscar Peralta (Young Hood), Karen Ingram (DeMarco's Assistant), Gary Santangelo (Ring Guy), Victoria Aguio, Addie Avalos, Amanda Briones, Ali Cunningham, Cheryl Elizaga, Joanne Metallo, Sha'ri Pendleton, Bridget A. Reese, Marcia E. Valley (Boxers)

Sophia-Adella Hernandez, William McNamara in *Knockout*
© Renegade Pictures

Cameron Van Hoy, Mischa Barton in *Pups* © Allied Entertainment

Ann Zupa, David Lee Wilson, Chris Jarecki in *Pariah* © Indican

PUPS (Allied Entertainment Group) Producers, Ash, Daniel M. Berger; Director/Screenplay, Ash; Executive Producers, Kazuyoshi Okuyama, Sachie Oyama; Photography, Carlos Arguello; Costumes, Merrie Lawson; Designer, Daniel M. Berger; Editor, Michael D. Schultz; Casting, Stephanie Chao; Presented in association with Kazuyoshi Okuyama & Team Okuyama & Five Heart Films Inc.; Dolby; Color; Not rated; 103 minutes; Release date: February 11, 2000. CAST: Cameron Van Hoy (Stevie), Mischa Barton (Rocky), Burt Reynolds (Daniel Bender), Adam Farrar (Wheelchair Man), David Alan Graf (Bank Manager), Kurt Loder (Himself), James Gordon (J.P.), Darling Narita (Joy), Ed Metzger (Mr. Edwards), Suzie Horton (Rio), Jonathan Coogan (Bank Security Guard), Uri Ryder (Pizza Man), Mathew Fairchild (Rocky's Dad), Hsa Mann, Johnny Hawaiian (Puppy Sellers), Kevin Kennedy (Field Reporter), David N. Preston, Stanley B. Herman (Studio Reporters), Beatie Pompa (Studio Reporter #2/Senator), Hardia Madden (Agent Hardy), C.C. Betchloff (Agent C.C.), James Gordon (TV Preacher), Alex Lui (Officer #1), Matt Roth (Bank Worker #1), Natascha Cobar (Bank Customer), Matthew C. Dunn (MTV Cameraman), Dara Tomanovic (Bender's Wife/Stevie's Mom), Ashley Darrow (Phoebie)

TROIS (Rainforest) Producer, William Packer; Executive Producers, Aaron Goodwin, Eric Goodwin, Madison Gray; Director/Screenplay, Rob Hardy; Story, Will Power; Photography, Charles Mills; Costumes, Jeanette Guillermo; Music, Steven Gutheinz; Editor, Griff Thomas; TRF Productions; Color; Rated R: 93 minutes; Release date: February 11, 2000. CAST: Gary Dourdan (Jermaine Davis), Gretchen Palmer (Jade Owens), Kenya Moore (Jasmine Davis), Solomon K. Smith (Terrance/Eric), Thomas Jefferson Byrd (Thomas), Chrystale Wilson (Tammy), Bryce Wilson (Robert), Jay Jones (Charles Givens), Tariq Holloway (Derrick Givens), Donna Biscoe (Ms. Paul), George Williams (Judge Cummings),

Gretchen Palmer, Gary Dourdan, Kenya Moore in *Trois*
© Rainforest Films

Ron N. Binder (Wilson), Gregory W. Anderson (Det. Anderson), Tom Rowley (Det. Smith), Chato Waters (Rosalyn), Heather Roxanne Ferguson (Bar Lesbian), Kishawnna Terry, Deionne Gibson (Lesbians), Roxane T. Mims (Jasmine's Mother), Carl Anthony (Jasmine's Father), Keanna Henson (Club Singer), El Rock, Avery Johnson, Billy Odum, Melvin Baldwin (The Chronicle Band), Rob Hardy (MC), William Packer (Man in Club), Wendy Delouche (Charles' Wife), Tory Hunter (Charles' Lawyer), Ryan McNally, Susan Stevens (Lawyer), Luchia Ashe (Woman in Car), Terry Bello, Kelue Ray (Radio Voices), Janet Jack (Radio Caller), Thomasina McCoy (Bar Waitress), Dori Hunter (Car Accident Witness)

SEX: THE ANNABEL CHONG STORY (Strand) Producers, Hugh F. Curry, David Whitten, Gough Lewis; Executive Producers, Kathleen Curry, Suzanne Bowers Whitten; Director, Gough Lewis; Photography, Jim Michaels, Kelly Morris, Gough Lewis, Tony Morone; Music, Bruce Fowler, Peter Mundinger; Editor, Kelly Morris; a Greycat Releasing presentation of a Coffee House Films production; U.S.-Canadian; Dolby; Color; Not rated; 86 minutes; Release date: February 11, 2000. Documentary on Annabel Chong, an under-graduate student who made it her goal to set a record by having sex with 251 men in a period of ten hours. Featuring Annabel Chong/Grace Quek, John Bowen, Ed Powers, Dr. Walter Williams, Charles Conn, Dick James, Monica Moran, Steve Austin, Jim South, Al Goldstein, Ron Jeremy, Lanisha Shanthi Easter, Mr. and Mrs. Quek, Allen Wong, Frank Sanford, Seymore Butts, Ona Zee, Chi Chi LaRue, Michael J. Coxx, Calvin Teo, Robert Black, Israel Gonzales, Donna Warner, Jack Hammer, David Carr, Chuck Zane, Jasmin St. Claire, Elana Craig, Dick Nasty, Raynard Tan, Susan James

PARIAH (Indican) Producers, Shaun Hill, Vince Rotonda; Executive Producers, David Hill, Elaine Hill; Director/Screenplay, Randolph Kret; Photography, Nils Erickson; Music/Co-Producer, Scott Grusin; Additional Music, Anthony St. Sinclair; Editor, Bill DeRonde; Costumes, Carrie Niccol; Line Producer, Dave Bennett; a Poor Boy Prods. presentation; Dolby; Eastman color; Not rated; 105 minutes; Release date: February 18, 2000. CAST: Damon Jones (Steve), Dave Ward (Crew), David Lee Wilson (David Lee), Aimee Chaffin (Sissy), Angela Jones (Angela), Anna Padgett (Lex), Dan Weene (Joey), Ann Zupa (Babe), Brandon Slater (Doughboy), Jason Posey (Kevin), Chris Jarecki (Tall Guy), Terence Washington (Mario), Tyrone Young (Ty), Orlando Estrada (Aaron), Robert Hargett (Rob), Elexa Williams (Sam), Tupelo Jereme (Rachel), Ray Wadsworth (Bobby), Kelly McCrary (Steve's Sister), Joe Wood (Crew's Father), Clint Curtis (The Preacher), Lynn Odell (David Lee's Mother), Michael Turner (Ray), Candy Ass (The Drag Queen)

THE WAITING GAME (Seventh Art) Producers, Mirjam Goldberg, Ken Liotti; Director, Ken Liotti; Screenplay, Kirk Lavine, Ken Liotti; Music, Jim Farmer; Designer, Sonya Gropman; an Absolute Films production; Color; Not rated; 81 minutes; Release date: February 24, 2000. CAST: Will Arnett (Lenny), Debbon Ayer (Merris), Dwight Ewell (Joe), Eddie Malavarca (Derek), Terumi Matthews (Andi), Michael Raynor (Franco), Daniel Riordan (Dan), Taylor Stanley (Shannon), Donald Williams (Nick

Eddie Malavarca, Dwight Ewell in *The Waiting Game* © Seventh Art

Colm Meaney, Katrin Cartlidge in *Claire Dolan* © MK2/Serene Films

the Cook), Alice Spivak (Customer from Hell), Chris Lawford (Barfly), Howard Spiegel (LA Director), Amy Marcs (Casting Director), Leslie Lyles (Therapist), Scott Wojcik (Cliff), Pam Wilterdink (Cynthia), Harvey Waldman (Ralph), John McKay (Bathroom Customer)

BROWN'S REQUIEM (Avalanche) Producers, Tim Youd, David Scott Rubin; Director/Screenplay, Jason Freeland; Based on the novel by James Ellroy; Executive Producers, John J. McDonnell III, Marc Ezralow, Theodore J. Farnsworth III; Photography, Seo Mutarevic; Designer, Marc Rizzo; Editor, Toby Yates; Music, Cynthia Millar; Costumes, Mimi Melgaard; Casting, Joseph Middleton; a J&T Productions presentation, in association with Savvy Lad, Inc.; Dolby; Deluxe color; Rated R; 105 minutes; Release date: February 25, 2000. CAST: Michael Rooker (Fritz Brown), Selma Blair (Jane), Valerie Perrine (Marguerita Hansen), Harold Gould (Solly K), Tobin Bell (Stan the Man), Brad Dourif (Edwards), Brion James (Cathcart), William Sasso (Fat Dog), Kevin Corrigan (Walter), Jack Conley (Ralston), William Newman (Augie), Barry Newman (Jack Skolnick), Jack Wallace (Bud Myers), Big Daddy Wayne (Leotis McCarver), Ron Barker (Bartender), David Labiosa (Henry Cruz), Al Rodrigo (Sandoval), Lisa Koch (Lulu), Lee Weaver (Wino), Kevin Jackson (Mark Swirkal), Rolando Molina (Ernie), Danny Mora (Armando), Jennifer Coolidge (Helen), Christopher Meloni (Cavanaugh), John Prosky (Larkin)

CLAIRE DOLAN (Film Society of Lincoln Center) Producer, Ann Ruark; Director/Screenplay, Lodge Kerrigan; Photography, Teodoro Maniaci; Designer, Sharon Lomofsky; Editor, Kristina Boden; Music, Ahrin Mishan, Simon Fisher Turner; Costumes, Laura Jean Shannon; Casting, Avy Kaufman; a Marin Karmitz presentation of an MK2 Productions and Serene Films production, 1998; Dolby; Color; Not rated; 95 minutes; Release date: February 25, 2000. CAST: Katrin Cartlidge (Claire Dolan), Patrick Husted (George), Muriel Maida (Claire's Mum), Lizabeth MacKay (Administrator), Colm Meaney (Roland Cain), Svetlana Jovanovich (Eve), Madison Arnold (Priest), Brenda Thomas Denmark (Woman at Book Stand), Jim Frangione (Man in Bar), Ed Hodson (Driver), Sean Powers (Driver's Friend), Sally Stark (Waitress at Newark Diner), Maryann Plunkett (Mary Egan), Sarah Rose Hendrickson (Siobhan), Candy Buckley, Lola Pashalinski (Salon Clients), Vincent D'Onofrio (Elton Garrett), Babo Harrison (Salon Owner), Marian Quinn (Woman in Park), Missy Yager (Cathy), John Doman (Cain's Friend), Henry Morales-Ballet, Gary Warner, Mark Zimmerman, Jonathan Smit (Tricks), Miranda Stuart Rhyne (Angela), Alan Davidson (Man in Diner), John Ventimiglia, Dominic Marcus (Newark Cab Drivers), Adrianna Sevan (Woman at Cab Stand), Tom Gilroy ($1000 Trick), Michael Laurence (Elton's Fare), Blaise Corrigan (Gunman), Joan Buddenhagen (Airport Ticket Agent), David Little (Man in Chicago Cafe), Bruce MacVittie (Obstetrician), Kate Skinner (Madeline Garrett)

3 STRIKES (MGM) Producer, Marcus Morton; Executive Producers, Julio Caro, Benny Medina, Brad Krevoy; Director/Screenplay, D.J. Pooh; Co-Producer, Jeremiah Samuels; Photography, John W. Simmons; Designer, Thomas Fichter; Editor, John Carter; Music Supervisors, Aaron Anderson, Andrew Shack; Costumes, Tracey White; Casting, Kim Williams; an Absolute Entertainment/Motion Picture Corporation of America production in association with Lithium Entertainment Group; Dolby; FotoKem color; Rated R; 82 minutes; Release date: March 1, 2000. CAST: Brian Hooks (Rob Douglas), N'Bushe Wright (Juanita), Faizon Love (Tone), E40 (Mike), Starletta DuPois (Moms), George Wallace (Pops), David Alan Grier (Jenkins), Dean Norris (Officer Roberts), Barima McKnight (Blue), Meagan Good (Buela), Mo'Nique (Dahlia), De'Aundre Bonds (J.J.), Antonio Fargas (Uncle Jim), Harmonica Fats (Grandpa), Mike Epps (Dee), Kurt "Big Boy" Alexander (Dre), Angela Wright (Joaney), Vincent Schiavelli (Cortino), Phil Morris (Mr. Libowitz), Jerry Dunphy (Himself), D.J. Pooh (Trick Turner/Taxi Driver), John Verea (Saldamo), Richard Fancy (Captain), Kam, Layback, Roger White, Terrence Stephens (Inmates), David Leisure (District Attorney), Gerald O'Loughlin (Judge), Dennis Howard (Governor), Shawn Fonteno (Big Mo), Rashaan Nall (T-Bird), Yolanda Whitaker (Charita), Melanie Comarcho (Woman in Police Station), Angela Tracy (Fly Female), Bennet Guillory (Stan Wilson), Marcus Morton (Taxi Driver), Michele Maika (Hotel Concierge), Rod Garr (Hospital Guard), Lydell Cheshier (Orderly), Regino Montes (Old Man), Jeffrey Garcia (Valet), Bruce Fairburn, Kevin Finn, Terence Winter (Patrol Officers), Christel Cottrell (Receptionist), Jascha Washington (Little Boy), Darreck D. Burns (Barber), King T (Liquor Store Thug), Cherry, Sacha Kemp, Elan Carter, Avonté Cherie (Aerobic Video Girls)

Brian Hooks in *3 Strikes* © Absolute Entertainment

Stephanie Knight, Kirk Harris in *My Sweet Killer* © FilmKitchen.com

Sammi Davis in *Soft Toilet Seat*s © STS Productions, Inc.

MY SWEET KILLER (FilmKitchen.com/Method Fest Releasing) Producers, Jack Rubio, Doug Lindeman; Executive Producers, Justin Dossetti, Dale Warner; Director, Justin Dossetti; Screenplay, Kirk Harris; Photography, Bragi Thor Henriksson; Music, Sean Abreu; Editor, Jane Allison Fleck; Color; Not rated; 77 minutes; Release date: March 2, 2000. CAST: Kirk Harris (Charlie Cavenaugh), Jack Rubio (Dave "Buck" Buckler), Clifton Collins, Jr. (Horton), Art Chudabala (Quote), Luis Guizar (Jerry), Stephanie Knight (Pasqua), Del Zamora (Mr. Lincock), Jonathon Chaus (Dr. Resner)

LOUIS PRIMA: THE WILDEST (Historic Films) Producer, Joe Lauro; Director, Don McGlynn; Executive Producers, Celia Zaentz, Don McGlynn; Photography, Steve Wacks, Randy Drummond, Alex Vlacos; Editors, Christian Moltke-Leth, Don McGlynn; Color/black and white; Not rated; 82 minutes; Release date: March 3, 2000. Documentary on trumpeter-singer Louis Prima, featuring Keely Smith, Sam Butera, Gia Maione, Jimmy Vincent, Lou Sineaux, Bruce Raeburn, Will Friedwald, Leon Prima, Madeline Prima, Louis Prima Jr., Lena Prima

SOFT TOILET SEATS (Phaedra Cinema) Producer, Shirley Craig; Executive Producer, Dave Stauffacher; Director/Screenplay, Tina Valinsky; Photography, Stephen Timberlake; Designer, Gabriella A. Goor; Costumes, Maral Kalinian; Editors, Lynel Moore Cioffi, Nancy Rosenbum, John Refoua, Robbie Adler; Music, Louis Durra, Jeffrey R. Gund; Casting, Aaron Griffith; a Shirley Craig production; Dolby; FotoKem color; Not rated; 112 minutes; Release date: March 10, 2000.

CAST: David Alex Rosen (Arne Steinberg), Alexa Jago (Tilly Rensley), Sammi Davis (Annie Ashland), Jonathan Aubé (Joey Carpini), Michael Greene (Det. Colson), Margaret Blye (Margaret Lennox), Savannah Henderson (Melissa Planko), Harris Laskaway (George Planko), Terri Hoyos (The Gaswoman), Jim Golden (The Bartender), Lisa Passero (Mrs. Carpini)

GOD'S ARMY (Zion Films) Producer/Director/Screenplay, Richard Dutcher; Photography, Ken Glassing; Art Director, Heath Houseman; Editor, Michael Chaskes; Music, Miriam Cutler; Casting, Jennifer Buster; Dolby; Color; Rated PG; 107 minutes; Release date: March 10, 1999. CAST: Matthew Brown (Elder Allen), Richard Dutcher (Elder Dalton), Jacque Gray (Sister Fronk), DeSean Terry (Elder Banks), Michael Buster (Elder Kinegar), Luis Robledo (Elder Sandoval), Jeff Kelly (Elder Mangum), John Pentecost (President Beecroft), Lynn Carr (Sister Beecroft), Kelli Coleman (Sister Monson), Anthony Anselmi (Elder Harmer), Todd Davis (Elder Stokes), Peter Jackson (Elder Downey), Seamus Hurley (Elder Rex), Francine Riber (Connie), Fawn Perez (Laura), Lorena Mena (Lyla), Louie Olivos, Jr. (Laura's Father), Lance Johnson (Brother Rose), Jennifer Christopher (Karla), Erica Clare (Sindy), Doug Stewart (Benny), Elaine Hill (Elaine), Darron Johnson (Lionel), Malayika Singley (Jenna), Dominique Dumas, Jeremiah Dumas (Jenna's Boys), John Kraemer (Tim), Taz Brighton Dodge, Eli Dutcher, Kiki Kehoe (Tim's Kids), Paul Downey (Paramedic), Albert Cabrera (Ambulance Driver), Scott Sandler (Nurse), Gwen Dutcher (Sexy Mormon Lady),

Louis Prima in *Louis Prima: The Wildest* © Historic Films

Jacque Gray, Matthew Brown in *God's Army* © Zion Films

George Condo in *Condo Painting* © USA Films

The Lifestyle © Seventh Art

Ethan Dutcher, Lucas Dutcher (Beach Kids), Paul Vito Abato (Old Man), Sherri Boyzsa (Dragon Lady), Soledad St. Hilaire (Latina), Jim Thiel (Bathroom Man), Cody Rosenberg (Coroner), Larry Bagby, Richard Radstone (Cops), Rob Consoli (Perp), Lance Schmidt (Mortician), James Powell (Gene Dalton), Cade Kleven, A.J. Desveaux (Little Pops)

CONDO PAINTING (USA Films) Producer, Dana Giacchetto; Director/Photography, John McNaughton; Screenplay, George Condo, John McNaughton; Co-Producer, Mark Pollard; Editors, Elena Maganini, Tom Keefe; Music Supervisor, Jim Sampas; Animation, Gary Leib Animation; an October Films presentation of a Pod Squad Productions presentation; from October Films; Dolby; Foto-Kem color; Not rated; 87 minutes; Release date: March 10, 2000. Documentary on New York artist George Condo and his muses, the Anitpodal Beings, featuring George Condo, Patrick Achdjian, William S. Burroughs, Anna Condo, Eleonore Condo, Raphaelle Condo, Allen Ginsberg, Dana Sunshine, Eric Barnes, John Sampas, Pasquale Condo, Muriel Condo, Jim Sampas, Karin Weiner, Bernard Picasso.

THE LIFESTYLE (Seventh Art) Producer, Dan Cogan; Executive Producers, Ted Hope, James Schamus, Mary Jane Skalski; Director, David Schisgall; Photography/Associate Producer, Peter Hawkins; Editor, Andrew Hafitz; Music, Byron Estep, Edward Sperry; Color; Not rated; 78 minutes; Release date: March 16, 2000. Documentary on suburban middle-class, middle-aged couples who engage in group sex, featuring Sarah and Orin, Carmen and John, Pat and Ric, Gina and John, Wild Bill Goodwin, Dr. Robert McGinley, Jim and Shery, Hugh and Karen, CJ and George, Jeanne and Bright, Dante Amore.

TREASURE ISLAND (King Pictures) Producer, Adrienne Gruben; Director/Screenplay/Photography, Scott King; Music, Chris Anderson; Designer, Nathan Marsak; Editor, Dody Dorn; Casting, Nicole Arbusto; Black and white; Not rated; 86 minutes; Release date: March 17, 2000. CAST: Lance Baker (Frank), Nick Offerman (Samuel), Jonah Blechman (The Body), Pat Healy (Clark), Suzy Aiko Nakamura (Yo-Ji), Rachel Singer (Anna), Stephanie Ittleson (Stella), Daisy Hall (Penny), Caveh Zahedi (Harold), Becket Cook (The Gent), Scot Thomas Robinson (Jimmy), Bob Byington (Thomas), Guinevere Turner (Evelyn), J.P. Manoux (Officer Hughes), Lisa Papineau (Diedre), Paul Gutrecht (Some Guy), Richard Schave (Preacher Man), Nigel Cox (Enid), Rio Hackford (Hans), James Donovan (John)

SPECTRES OF THE SPECTRUM (Other City Prods.) Producer/Director/Screenplay, Craig Baldwin; Photography/Editor, Bill Daniel; Music, John Watermann, Korla Pandit, Dominic Frontiere, DJ Spooky; Designers, Matt Day, Thad Povey, Chris Santeramo, Molli Simon; Color/Black and white; Not rated; 84 minutes; Release date: March 17, 20000. Documentary collage, featuring Sean Kilcoyne (Yogi), Caroline (Boo Boo), Beth Lisick

MY AMERICAN VACATION (Santa Monica Pictures) Producers, Frank Gargani, V.V. Dachin Hsu, Cindy Sison; Director/Screenplay, V.V. Dachin Hsu; Photography, Dean Lent; Designer, Fu Ding Cheng; Music, Joel Iwataki; Editors, Marc Grossman, Clarinda Wong; from Winn Entertainment; Color; Not rated; 89 minutes; Release date: March 17, 2000. CAST: Tsai Chin (Grandma Lee), Dennis Dunn (Henry), Roger Fan (Ming-Yee-Ba), Sasha Hsuczyk (Melissa), Kim Miyori (Ming Yee), Deborah Nishimura (Ming Na)

BUDDY BOY (Independent Pictures) Producers, Cary Woods, Gina Mingacci; Director/Screenplay, Mark Hanlon; Executive Producer, Elliot Lewis Rosenblatt; Photography, Hubert Taczanowski; Designer, Robert Morris; Editor, Hughes Winborne; Costumes, Sara Jane Slotnick; Music, Graeme Revell; Casting, Dan Shaner, Michael Testa; an IP Production; Dolby; Color; Rated R; 103 minutes; Release date: March 24, 2000. CAST: Aidan Gillen (Francis), Emmanuelle Seigner (Gloria), Susan Tyrrell (Sal), Mark Boone Junior (Vic), Harry Groener (Father Gillespie), Hector Elias (Mr. Salcedo), Jon Huertas (Omar), Richard Assad (Haroonian), Kelly Waymire (Ireland), Tim Dekay (Ken), Darryl Henriques (Doctor), Micheal Halsey (Brian), Pamela Gordon (Marilyn), Tom McCleister (Mr. Jones), Irene Roseen (Navajo Clad Woman), Jessica Goana (Love Pendant Girl), Thomas Prisco (Yoga Man), Joyce Guy (Another Woman), Ernie Lee Banks (Earl)

Aidan Gillen in *Buddy Boy* © Independent Pictures

Marla Sokoloff, James Franco, Jodi Lyn O'Keefe, Shane West
in *Whatever It Takes* © Columbia Pictures Industries, Inc.

John Waters, Divine, Danny Mills, Mary Vivian Pearce
in *Divine Trash* © WinStar Cinema

WHATEVER IT TAKES (Columbia) Producer, Paul Schiff; Co-Producers, Matt Berenson, Mark Schwahn; Executive Producers, Bill Brown, Vicki Dee Rock; Director, David Raynr; Screenplay, Mark Schwahn; Photography, Tim Suhrstedt; Designer, Edward T. McAvoy; Costumes, Leesa Evans; Editor, Ronald Roose; Music, Edward Shearmur; Music Supervisor, Amanda Scheer-Demme; Casting, Randi Hiller; a Phoenix Pictures presentation of a Paul Schiff production; Dolby; Deluxe color; Rated PG-13; 92 minutes; Release date: March 24, 2000. CAST: Shane West (Ryan Woodman), Marla Sokoloff (Maggie), Jodi Lyn O'Keefe (Ashley Grant), James Franco (Chris), Aaron Paul (Floyd), Colin Hanks (Cosmo), Manu Intiraymi (Dunleavy), Julia Sweeney (Kate Woodman), Kip Pardue (Harris), Scott Vickaryous (Stu), Richard Schiff (P.E. Teacher), Kevin Ruf (Security Guard), Erin Champaign, Rachel Zerko (Shower Girls), Eric Kushnick (Stoner), Christine Lakin (Sloane), Nicole Tarantini (Marnie), Shyla Marlin (Shyla), Vanessa Evigan (Vanessa), Julie Garibaldi (Stuck Up Girl), Chantal Abbey (Swim Coach), Joe Gieb (Octopus Ride Operator), Tyrone Granderson Jones (Toothless Carnie), Mason Lucero (Sweet Kid), Stan Sellars (Teacher), Jeff Sanders (Large Football Player), Marge Anderson (Old Woman), Sam Menning (Old Man), Nick Cannon (Chess Club Kid), Hubert Hodgin (Waiter), Rachel Kaber (Miranda), Caroline Kindred (Little Girl), Romy Rosemont (Cosmo's Date), Mami Nakamura (Noriko), Jay Harrington (Cop), David Koechner (Virgil Doolittle)

Cynthia Ngewu in *Long Night's Journey Into Day* © Iris Films

LONG NIGHT'S JOURNEY INTO DAY (Iris Films/Cinemax Reel Life) Producer, Frances Reid; Directors, Frances Reid, Deborah Hoffmann; Screenplay, Antjie Krog; Photography, Frances Reid, Ezra Jwili; Editor, Deborah Hoffmann; Associate Producer, Johnny Symons; Color; Not rated; 94 minutes; Release date: March 29, 2000. Documentary on South Africa's Truth and Reconciliation Commission, featuring Peter Biehl, Linda Biehl, Mongezi Manqina, Evelyn Manqina, "Easy" Nofemela, Eric Taylor, Nomonde Calata, Nyameka Goniwe, George Bizos, Robert McBride, Sharon Welgemoed, Cynthia Ngewu, Edith Mjobo, Thapelo Mbelo, Tony Weaver, Jann Turner, Desmond Tutu, Glena Wildschut, Mary Burton, Pumla Gobodo-Madikizela, Isabel Cilliers. (This film received an Oscar nomination for documentary feature).

DIVINE TRASH (WinStar) Producers, Cindy Miller, Steve Yeager; Executive Producers, Caroline Kaplan, Jonathan Sehring, Tim Kahoe, Brooks Moore, Thomas W. Yeager; Director, Steve Yeager; Screenplay, Kevin Heffernan, Steve Yeager; Photography, Jeff Atkinson, Jim Harris, Steve Yeager; Music, Don Barto; Editors, Terry Campbell, Tim Kahoe, Steve Yeager; a Divine Trash production; Dolby; Color; Not rated; 105 minutes; Release date: March 31, 2000. Documentary on filmmaker John Waters, featuring John Waters, Jeanine Basinger, Steve Buscemi, Hal Hartley, J. Hoberman, Ken Jacobs, Jim Jarmusch, Laurence Kardish, George Kuchar, Mike Kuchar, Herschell Gordon Lewis, David Lochary, Edith Massey, Jonas Mekas, Glenn Milstead/Divine, Frances Milstead, Paul Morrissey, Mary Vivian Pearce, Vince Peraino, John Pierson, Robert Shaye, Van Smith, Mink Stole, John Waters Sr., Patricia Waters, Steve Waters

READY TO RUMBLE (Warner Bros.) Producers, Bobby Newmyer, Jeffrey Silver; Executive Producers, Steven Reuther, Mike Tollin; Director, Brian Robbins; Screenplay, Steven Brill; Based on WCW Characters; Photography, Clark Mathis; Designer, Jaymes Hinkle; Editor, Ned Bastille; Music, George S. Clinton; Casting, Marci Liroff; Presented in association with Bel-Air Entertainment; an Outlaw production, in association with Tollin/Robbins productions; Dolby; Technicolor; Rated PG-13; 107 minutes; Release date: April 7, 2000. CAST: David Arquette (Gordie Boggs), Oliver Platt (Jimmy King), Scott Caan (Sean Dawkins), Bill Goldberg, Diamond Dallas Page, Steve "Sting" Borden (Themselves), Rose McGowan (Sasha), Richard Lineback (Mr. Boggs), Chris Owen (Isaac), Joe Pantoliano (Titus Sinclair), Martin Landau (Sal Bandini), Caroline Rhea (Eugenia King), Tait Smith (Buddy King), Ellen Albertini Dow (Mrs. MacKenzie), Kathleen Freeman (Jane King), Lewis Arquette (Fred King), Ahmet Zappa (Cashier), Chad Carr, Darby Wilson, Joey Deters (8 Year Old Kids), Max Daniels (Stu), John Ennis (Stan), Jill Ritchie (Brittany), Melanie Deanne Moore (Wendy), Catherine Paolone (Mrs. Boggs), Wendy Jean Wilkins (Gabby Boggs), Ric Mancini, Bruce-Robert Serafin (Front Row Fans), Greg Collins (Crusty Veteran Cop), David Ursin (Fire Chief), Earl H. Bullock (Cop #1), Maryedith Burrell, Anne Christianson, Jody Hahn, Marne Dupere (Nuns), Floyd Levine (Floor Manager), Peter Blincoe (Video Cameraman), Richard Karron (Sanitation Guy), Alex Skuby (Young Doctor), Tim Sitarz (Fireman Fred),

Oliver Platt, David Arquette in *Ready to Rumble*
©Warner Bros./Bel-Air Pictures

Stacy Valentine in *The Girl Next Door* © VCA Pictures

Tony Pennello (Gus), Jeff Podgurski (The Chewer), Adam Tomei, Jason Kassin (Siamese Twins), Philip Pavel (Happy Young Man), Julia Schultz (Kitty), Rosalie Vega, Taylor Bernard (King Sexy Girls), Bam Bam Bigelow, Gorgeous George, Juventud Guerrero, Van Hammer, Curt Hennig, Prince Iaukea, Disco Inferno, Billy Kidman, Konnan, Rey Mysterio Jr., Saturn, Randy Savage, Booker T., Sid Vicious, Chae, Fyre, Spice, Storm, Tygress, Gene Okerlund, Tony Schiavone, Mike Tenay, Michael Buffer, Charles Robinson (Themselves), William E. Daley (Bill Silverman)

THIS IS NOT AN EXIT: THE FICTIONAL WORLD OF BRET EASTON ELLIS (First Run Features) Producer, Julian Ozanne; Director, Gerald Fox; Photography, Richard Numeroff, Simon Fanthorpe, Les Young; Music, Stefan Girardet; Editors, Melvyn Bragg, Tony Webb; Presented by Melvyn Bragg; a Marquee Film and Television Production for LWT/NVC; Color; Not rated; 80 minutes; Release date: April 7, 2000. CAST: Dechen Thurman (Patrick Bateman), Rachel Weisz (Lauren Hynde), Jason Bushman (Clay), Paul Blackthorne (Victor Ward), Marieclaire (Hollywood Housewife), Kelly Rogers (Evelyn), Noelle McCutchen (Blair), Natalie Avital (Anne), David Monahan (Hamlin), Michael Cavalier (Reeves), Huger Foote (MTV VJ), John Bryan (Clay's Father), Justine Melman (Junkie), Cory Travalena (Poolboy), Tamsin Pike, Vered Halkin (Girls), Casey Schacter (Muriel); Bret Easton Ellis, Jay McInerney, Will Self, Morgan Entrekin, Blake Morrison.

THE GIRL NEXT DOOR (Indican) Producers, Christine Fugate, Adam Berns, Eren McGinnis; Executive Producer, Michael Berns; Director, Christine Fugate; Editors, Kate Amend, Christine Fugate; Music, Denis M. Hannigan; Music Supervisor, Michele Wernick; GND Productions presentation of a Cafe Sisters production; Color; Not rated; 82 minutes; Release date: April 14, 2000. Documentary on the life of porn performer Stacy Valentine.

AMERICAN GYPSY: A STRANGER IN EVERYBODY'S LAND (Independent) Producer/Director, Jasmine Dellal; Photography, Michele Zaccheo, Jasmine Dellal; Editors, Joseph De Francesco, Jasmine Dellal; Associate Producers, Nora Cadena, Gail Firth; Stereo; Color; Not rated; 80 minutes; Release date: April 21, 2000. Documentary on American gypsies, featuring Ian Hancock, the families of Grover & Lippie Marks, Jimmy and Jane Marks, William Duna

Dechen Thurman in *This Is Not an Exit* © First Run Features

Jimmy Marks in *American Gypsy*

James Marsden in *Gossip* © Warner Bros./Village Roadshow

Heather Graham, Goran Visnjic in *Committed* © Miramax Films

GOSSIP (Warner Bros.) Producers, Jeffrey Silver, Bobby Newmyer; Executive Producers, Joel Schumacher, Bruce Berman; Director, David Guggenheim; Screenplay, Gregory Poirier, Theresa Rebeck; Story, Gregory Poirier; Photography, Andrzej Bartkowiak; Designer, David Nichols; Editor, Jay Cassidy; Co-Producer, John M. Eckert; Music, Graeme Revell; Costumes, Louise Mingenbach; Casting, Lora Kennedy; an Outlaw production; Presented in association with Village Roadshow Pictures and NPV Entertainment; Dolby; Panavision; Technicolor; Rated R; 91 minutes; Release date: April 21, 2000. CAST: James Marsden (Derrick Webb), Lena Headey (Cathy Jones), Norman Reedus (Travis), Kate Hudson (Naomi Preston), Marisa Coughlan (Sheila), Sharon Lawrence (Det. Kelly), Eric Bogosian (Prof. Goodwin), Edward James Olmos (Det. Curtis), Joshua Jackson (Beau Edson), Kwok-Wing Leung (Chinese Man), Mif (Doorman), Poe (Singer), Vicky Lambert, Kenya Massey (Club Dancers), Noam Jenkins (Bartender), Stephanie Mills (Rebecca Lewis), Raven Dauda (Andrea), Krstin Booth (Diane), Novie Edwards (Ms. Waters), Shanly Trinidad (Marie), Samantha Espie (Leslie), Christopher Ralph (Bill), Kris Holdenried (Bruce), Deborah Pollitt (Gina), Balázs Koós (Rick), Robin Brûlé (Louise), Sadie Leblanc (Erica), Elizabeth Guber (Grace), Roman Podhora (Det. Ayres), Marc Hickox (Paul), Jessica Greco (Charlene), Alexia Landeau (Sasha), Bill Lake (Lt. Miles), David Nichols (Prof. Vindaloo), Sanjay Talwar (Taxi Driver), Timm Zemanek (High School Principal), Norma Dell'Agnese (Danbury Typist), Mairon Bennett (Vlasta), Marc Cohen (Officer Stevens), Charles Guggenheim (Derrick's Father), Marion Guggenheim (Derrick's Mother), John Wills Martin (The Stranger)

FAMILY TREE (Independent Artists) Producers, Mike Curb, Carole Curb Nemoy; Director, Duane Clark; Screenplay/Associate Producer, Paul Canterna; Executive Producers, Clifford Webber, Quinn Coleman; Photography, John Peters; Music, Mike Curb, Randy Miller; Designer, Katherine Vallin; Costumes, Dorothy Amos; Casting, Rough Diamond Casting; a WarnerVision Films presentation of a Curb Entertainment production; Color; Rated G; 90 minutes; Release date: April 21, 2000. CAST: Robert Forster (Henry Musser), Naomi Judd (Sarah Musser), Andrew Lawrence (Mitch "Mess" Musser), Matthew Lawrence (Mark Musser), Cliff Robertson (Larry), Krystal Benn (Jessica), Genevieve Butler (Diane), Kate Forster (Ms. Krynock), Susan Gayle Watts (Mayor Margaret Jones), D. Elliot Woods (Councilman Jordan), Tony Tarantino (Dr. Stevens), Tyler Hoechlin (Jeff Jo), Jeffrey Pace (Shawn), Corbin Bleu (Ricky), Quinn Beswick (Duffy), George Murdock (Big Wig), Gregg Binkley (Bill Belko), Eddie Ebell (Luigi), Faith McDevitt (Mrs. Ferguson), Jack Donner (Joseph), Hamilton Camp (Bob), Ken Johnson (Store Owner), Leonardo Termo (Vince), David Carpenter (Dirt Jo), Steve Wilde, John Mastando (Surveyors), Alan David Gelman (Ed), Beecey Carlson (Connie), Ken Duncan (George), William Dennis Hurley (Mayor's Aide), Brendan B. Dawson (Truck Driver), Austin Stout (Allen)

COMMITTED (Miramax) Producers, Dean Silvers, Marlen Hecht; Executive Producers, Harvey Weinstein, Bob Weinstein, Jonathan Gordon, Amy Slotnick; Director/Screenplay, Lisa Krueger; Photography, Tom Krueger; Editors, Curtiss Clayto, Colleen Sharp; Costumes, Beth Pasternak; Designer, Sharon Lomofsky; Music, Calexico; Casting, Billy Hopkins, Suzanne Smith, Kerry Barden; a Dean Silvers/Marlen Hecht production; Dolby; Deluxe color; Rated R; 98 minutes; Release date: Apr. 28, 2000. CAST: Heather Graham (Joline), Luke Wilson (Carl), Casey Affleck (Jay), Goran Visnjic (Neil), Alfonso Arau (Grampy), Patricia Velasquez (Carmen), Clea DuVall (Mimi), Mark Ruffalo (T-Bo), Summer Phoenix (Meg), Art Alexakis (Car Thief), Kim Dickens (Jenny), Mary Kay Place (Psychiatrist), Dylan Baker (Carl's Editor), Wood Harris (Chicky), Laurel Holloman (Adelle), Robert Acoto (Pierced Man), Davina Lane (Pierced Woman), William Marsh (Hyundai Man), Kyme McMahan (Hyundai Woman), Robert Holguin (El Paso Times Photographer), The Chairez Brothers (Mexican Seranaders), Benjamin Jacob Lewis (Toby), Javier Renteria, Rafael Anaya (Cops), Forrest Silvers, Tyler Silvers (Wedding Guests), Jon Stewart (Dean)

LEFTOVERS (Troma) Producers, Patric Z, Margo Romero; Executive Producers, Dave Parker, Lionel Luna; Director/Screenplay, Jason Phillips; Co-Producers, Travis Daking, Billy Hamilton; Photography, Cory Christiansen; a Lloyd Kaufman and Michael Herz presentation; Color; Not rated; 90 minutes; Release date: April 28, 2000. CAST: Mark Fite (Zack), Timothy DiPri (Dean), Todd Stanton (Frank), Jason Oliver (Buzz)

Matthew Lawrence, Andrew Lawrence, Naomi Judd, Robert Forster
in *Family Tree* © Curb Entertainment Intl.

Robert Karl Burke, Peter Coyote in *The Basket* © North by Northwest Ent.

Rob Morrow, Claire Forlani in *Into My Heart* © Jean Doumanian Prods.

SPIN THE BOTTLE (CineBlast! Prods.) Producers, Jamie Yerkes, Kris Homsher; Executive Producers, Gill Holland, Kevin Chinoy; Director/Story, Jamie Yerkes; Screenplay, Amy Sohn; Photography, Harlan Bosmajian; Designer, Johanna Belson; Music, Ed Tomney; Editors, Josh Apter, Jamie Yerkes; Casting, Mary Clay Boland, Catherine Riggs; DuArt color; Not rated; 82 minutes; Release date: May 4, 2000. CAST: Mitchell Riggs (Ted), Kim Winter (Bev), Jessica Faller (Alex), Heather Goldenhersh (Rachel), Holter Graham (Jonah), Michael Conn (Young Jonah), Allison Gervais (Young Bev), April Harvey (Young Alex), Zachary Newland (Young Ted), Kristen Way (Young Rachel)

THE BASKET (North by Northwest Entertainment) Producer/Director, Rich Cowan; Executive Producers, Marc Dahlstrom, Dave Holcomb, Greg Rathvon, Dave Tanner; Screenplay, Don Caron, Rich Cowan, Frank Swoboda, Tessa Swoboda; Photography, Dan Heigh; Designer, Vincent De Felice; Music, Don Caron; Costumes, Nanette Acosta; Casting, Robin Nassif, Michael Greer; from Privileged Communications; Color; Rated PG; 101 minutes; Release date: May 5, 2000. CAST: Peter Coyote (Martin Conlon), Karen Allen (Bessie Emery), Robert Karl Burke (Helmut Brink), Amber Willenborg (Brigitta Brink), Jock MacDonald (Nicholas Emery), Eric Dane (Tom Emery), Brian Skala (Nathan Emery), Casey Cowan (Samuel Emery), Tony Lincoln (Pastor Simms), Patrick Treadway (Frederick Treadway), Ellen Travolta (Agnes Barnes), Jack Bannon (Marcus Danielson), Elwon Bakly (Ben Emery), Joey Travolta (Charlie Cohn), Paul Hostetler (Old Helmut Brink), Kelly Eviston (Nancy Danielson), Cole Gamble (Erik Danielson), Jeff Waggoner (George Haines), Michael Van Gelder (Lewis Tinsley), MacKenzie Koppa (Katie Danielson), Heidi Nelson (Sara Barnes), Jamie Flanery (David Tinsley), John Rustan (Gregory Ranson), Michael Ferguson (Daniel Haines), Ron Varela (Mel Hester), Sara Edlin (Immigration Officer), Gordon Grove (Referee), Rick Burkhart, Scott McQuilken, Jess Walter, Bryan Smelcer, Jason Pulliam (Spokane Basketball Players), Terry Sticka (Kai Brink), Mark Forman (Bartender), Leslie Laursen (Mrs. Tinsley), Lindsey Kiehn (Sara Barnes), Jerry Fleming, Tim Sanger (American Soldiers), Steven Smith (Dr. Naismith), Cecil Ellsworth (Janitor), Stan Calder (Train Conductor), Henry Swoboda (Basketball Timekeeper), Mike Shaw, Chuck Anderson, John Graham, Jim Buckley, Ross Niblock (Bar Customers), Molly (Chester)

INTO MY HEART (Jean Doumanian Productions) Producer, Jean Doumanian; Executive Producer, J.E. Beaucaire; Co-Executive Producer, Letty Aronson; Directors/Screenplay, Anthony Stark, Sean Smith; Photography, Michael Barrow; Editors, Merril Stern, Robert Reitano; Music, Michael Small; Designer, Ford Wheeler; Costumes, Stephanie Maslansky; Casting, Sheila Jaffe, Georgianne Walken; Color; Not rated; 93 minutes; Release date: May 5, 2000. CAST: Rob Morrow (Ben), Claire Forlani (Nina), Jake Weber (Adam), Jayne Brook (Kat), Sebastian Roche (Chris), Nora Ariffin (Waitress), Nelson Martinez (Doorman), John Doumanian (Chestnut Vendor), Harvey Madonick M.D. (Paramedic), Owen Smith (Owen)

LUMINARIAS (New Latin Pictures) Producer, Sal Lopez; Executive Producers, Sal Lopez, Evelina Fernandez, Jose Luis Valenzuela, Joel Ehrlich; Director, Jose Luis Valenzuela; Screenplay, Evelina Fernandez; Photography, Alex Phillips; Designer, Patssi Valdez; Editors, Terilyn Shropshire, Jeff Koontz; Associate Producer, Pepe Serna; Co-Producer, Mina Vasquez; a Sleeping Giant production; Dolby; Color; Rated R; 100 minutes; Release date: May 5, 2000. CAST: Evelina Fernandez (Andrea), Scott Bakula (Joseph), Marta Du Bois (Sofia), Angela Moya (Lilly), Dyana Ortelli (Irene), Seidy Lopez (Cindy), Robert Beltran (Joe), Sal Lopez (Pablo), Cheech Marin (Jesus), Fidel Gomez (Joey), Angelina Estrada (Tia Concha), Lupe Ontiveros (Tia Tonia), Mike Gomez (Frank Chavez), Liz Torres (Judge Sanchez), Geoffrey Rivas (Carlos/Carmela), Andrew C. Lim (Lu), Pepe Serna (Rick), Richard Coca (Tony), Ayisha Sinclair (Laura), Sab Shimono (Lu's Father), June Kim (Lu's Mother), Barbara Niven (Jan)

Scott Bakula, Evelina Fernandez in *Luminarias* © New Latin Pictures

Nia Long, Jamie Foxx in *Held Up* © Trimark Pictures

Bonnie Root in *Coming Soon* © Unapix

THE LOVE MACHINE (Olympia Pictures) Director, Gordon Eriksen; Photography, Hiro Wakiya; No other credits available; from As1; Color; Not rated; minutes; Release date: May 11, 2000. CAST: Mariana Carreno (Cecilia), Marlene Forte (Becca Campbell), Chip Garner (Chip), Will Keenan (Mike), Tomo Omori (Shino), Gary Perez (Julio), Al D. Rodriguez (Javier), Jun Suenaga (Akira), Kayoko Takahashi (Kyoko)

HELD UP (Trimark) Producers, Neal H. Moritz, Jonathon Komack Martin, Stokely Chaffin; Executive Producers, Mark Amin, Devin DeWalt; Director, Steve Rash; Screenplay, Jeff Eastin; Story, Jeff Eastin, Erik Fleming; Co-Producers, Jay Heit, Jaime Rucker King; Photography, David A. Makin; Designer, Rick Roberts; Music, Robert Folk; Editor, Jonathan Chibnall; Costumes, Eduardo Castro; Casting, Mary Vernieu, Anne McCarthy; a Minds Eye Pictures presentation; Dolby; Fotokem color; Rated PG-13; 91 minutes; Release date: May 12, 2000. CAST: Jamie Foxx (Michael Dawson), Nia Long (Rae), Barry Corbin (Pembry), John Cullum (Jack), Jake Busey (Beaumont), Michael Shamus Wiles (Biker), Eduardo Yanez (Rodrigo), Sarah Paulson (Mary), Diego Fuentes (Sal), Roselyn Sanchez (Trina), Julie Hagerty (Gloria), Sam Gifaldi (Rusty), Dalton James (Sonny), Sam Vlahos (Jose), Billy Morton (Delbert), Herta Ware (Alice), Harper Roisman (Howard), Natalia Cigliuti (Wilma), Gary Owen (Clute), David Deveau (Delinquent), Kimberly Karpinski (Reporter), Tim Dixon (Leon), Alvaro Gonzalo (Electrician), Grant Boulon (Cameraman), Andrew Jackson (Billy), Cabral Rock (Messenger), Kathryn Winslow (Pilot), Chris Scott (Gladys), Ian Black (Man), Ron Sauve (No Teeth), Gerry Quigley (Horace), Lane Price (Cowboy), Alex Docking (TV Newscaster)

SCREWED (Universal) Producer, Robert Simonds; Executive Producers, Brad Grey, Ray Reo; Directors/Screenplay, Scott Alexander, Larry Karaszewski; Photography, Robert Brinkmann; Designer, Mark Freeborn; Editor, Michael Jablow; Music, Michel Colombier; Co-Producers, Fitch Cady, Julia Dray; a Robert Simonds/Brad Grey production; Dolby; Deluxe color; Rated PG-13; 81 minutes; Release date: May 12, 2000. CAST: Norm Macdonald (Willard Fillmore), Dave Chappelle (Rusty P. Hayes), Elaine Stritch (Miss Crock), Danny DeVito (Grover Cleaver), Daniel Benzali (Det. Tom Dewey), Sherman Hemsley (Chip Oswald), Sarah Silverman (Hillary), Malcolm Stewart (Roger), Lochlyn Munro (Officer Richardsen), Brent Chapman, Brian Jensen, Shawn Macdonald, Kelly Fiddick (Danes), Helena Yea ("Aunt Mabel"), Lorenzo Campbell (Tito), Damon Thornton (Tito's Henchman), Lorena Gale (Angry Momma), Sue Astley (Morgue Operator), Mark Acheson (Mr. Kettle), Joanna Piros (National Anchor Woman), Samantha Ferris (Local Anchorwoman), Brian Arnold (News Anchorman), Ted Friend, Claire Riley, April Telek (News Reporters), Lois Dellar (Policewoman), Ken Kirzinger, Charles André (Cops), Camille Sullivan (Flower Shop Clerk), D. Harlan Cutshall (Sharp Shooter), Ben Derrick (Cop at Pile Up), Ann Warn Pegg (Meter Maid), Brent Butt, Anthony Harrison (Buddies), Robert Moloney (Vice President), Lloyd Berry (Willard's Uncle), Dee Jay Jackson (Garbage Man), Tygh Runyan (Cussing Guy), Georgina Hegedos (Russian Lady), Khaira Le (Ticket Agent), Laurie Bekker (Chicken Girl), Martin Amado (Chicken Shack Worker), Irene Miscisco (Lady in Beauty Shop), Tom Heaton (Morgue Janitor), "Bam Bam" (Muffin), Tony Morelli, Jim R. Dunn (ND Cops)

COMING SOON (Unapix) Producers, Beau Flynn, Stefan Simchowitz, Keven Duffy; Executive Producers, Thomas Augsberger, Matthias Emcke; Director, Colette Burson; Screenplay, Colette Burson, Kate Robin; Photography, Joaquin Baca-Asay; Designer, Anne Stuhler; Editor, Norman Buckley; Costumes, Melissa Toth; Casting, Marcia Shulman; a Key Entertainment production in association with Bandeira Entertainment; Dolby; FotoKem color; Rated R; 91 minutes; Release date: May 12, 2000. CAST: Tricia Vessey (Nell Kellner), Gaby Hoffmann (Jenny Simon), Bonnie Root (Stream Hodsell), James Roday (Chad), Mia Farrow (Judy Hodsell), Ryan Reynolds (Henry Lipschitz), Spalding Gray (Mr. Jennings), Kevin Corrigan (Sid), Peter Bogdanovich (Bartholomew), Ryan O'Neal (Dick), Bridget Barkan (Polly), Seth Michael May (Freckled Kid), Ramsey Faragallah (Wahid), Ellen Pompeo (Upset Girl), Dmitry Lipkin (Young Teacher), Jared Ryan (Petrus), Leslie Lyles (Vivien Simon), Candy Buckley (Madame Aurevoir), Abigail Revasch (Renee), Ranjit Chowdhry (Afshin), Sarah Trelease (Stash), Ashton Kutcher (Louie), Tim Cunningham (Frank), Rhasaan Orange (Sincere Boy), Anna Heins (Volunteer), Mary Diveny (Blind Lady, Joan), Irma St. Paule (Blind Lady #2), Victor Argo (Mr. Neipris), Timothy D. Stickney (Suave Man), Rebecca Nelson (Ms. Metcalf), Jessie Munch (Very Young Model), Ruthanna Hopper (Intense Woman), Yasmine Bleeth (Mimi), David Eigenberg (Andy), Elzbieta Czyzewska (Dr. Luft), Kevin Fitzgerald Corrigan (Sid), James McCaffrey (Dante), Xenia (Liza)

Norm Macdonald, Sarah Silverman, Dave Chappelle, Elaine Stritch
in *Screwed* © Universal Studios

SHADOW BOXERS (Swerve Films) Producer/Director/Screenplay/Editor, Katya Bankowsky; Photography, Anthony Hardwick, Tony Wolberg; Music, Zoël; Black and white/color; Not rated; 72 minutes; Release date: May 12, 2000. Documentary on women's boxing, featuring Lucia Rijker.

ACHILLE'S LOVE (Castle Hill) Producer, Chris T. McIntyre; Executive Producers/Screenplay, John C. Mouganis, Heidi Haaland; Director, Meredith S. Cole; Photography, Stephen Shank; Designer, John Lindsey McCormick; Costumes, Cynthia Albert; Editor, Anne McCabe; Music, Emmanuel Kiriakou; Choreographers, Dimitrio Pantzoulas, Andrea L. Reichenfeld; an Achilles' Heel Partners & Pittsburgh Pictures presentation; Color; Not rated; 90 minutes; Release date: May 12, 2000. CAST: Mather Zickel (Ike Mannis), Claudia Besso (Lucy Boxwell), John C. Mouganis (Connan Charles), Harry O'Toole (Old George), Elias Ganias (Young George), Fred McCarren (Trevor), Doug Mertz (Malcolm), Sheila McKenna (Amanda), André Koslowski (Pascal), Scott Kerschbaumer (Howard), Zachary Mott (Michael), Alex Coleman (Constantine Zoras), Erriette Linas (Sofia Zoras), Kathryn Watkins (Sandy), Anthony Stakis (Stavro), Julianne Shinto (Candace), Bob Tracey (Mansfield), Anthony Zaras (Socrates), Candace Michel (Mrs. Winthrop), Beatrice Mouganis (Mrs. Campbell), Kimberly Paroline (Lindsay), Rhea Seehorn (Heather), Maria Hnarakis (Penny), Sylvia Hanna (Helen), Ruel Davis (Jesus), John Hanna (Manni), Connan McManus (Brian Struthers), Janet Helms (Jane Struthers), J.P. Nutini (Stage Manager), Chris Passodelis (Mario), Jack Donahue (Bartender), Nancy Wehrheim, Thelma Edmunds, Lisa Cangialosi, Bruce Fox (Judges)

LUMINOUS MOTION (Artistic License) Producers, Anthony Bregman, Ted Hope; Director, Bette Gordon; Screenplay, Robert Roth, Scott Bradfield; Based on the novel *The History of Luminous Motion* by Scott Bradfield; Executive Producer, Eric Rudin; Photography, Teodoro Maniaci; Designer, Lisa Albin; Editor, Keiko Deguchi; Music, Lesley Barber; Co-Producer, Elyse Goldberg; Line Producer, Dara Weintraub; Costumes, Melissa Toth; Casting, Ellen Parks; a Good Machine production; Dolby; Technicolor; Not rated; 94 minutes; Release date: May 19, 2000. CAST: Eric Lloyd (Phillip), Deborah Kara Unger (Mom), Terry Kinney (Pedro), Jamey Sheridan (Dad), James Berland (Rodney), Paz de la Huerta (Beatrice), June Stein (Ethel), Bruce MacVittie (Norman), Patrick Fitzgerald, Con Horgon, Martin Alvin, P.J. Brown (Men)

Eric Lloyd, Deborah Kara Unger in *Luminous Motion* © Artistic License

BETTER LIVING THROUGH CIRCUITRY (Seventh Art) Producers, Brian McNelis, Stuart Swezey; Executive Producer, Brian Perera; Director, Jon Reiss; Screenplay, Jon Reiss, Stuart Swezey, Brian McNelis; Photography, Jon Reiss, Steven Janas, Byron Shah, Michael Bartowski, Lee Abbot, Joe Plonsky, John Preibe; Editor, Eric Zimmerman; Computer Animation, OVT Visuals, Dots Per Minute, Glen Grillo/Nighttribe; a Cleopatra Pictures presentation of a Parasite production; Color; Not rated; 88 minutes; Release date: May 26, 2000. Documentary on the electronic dance community and the rave culture it has produced, featuring The Crystal Method, DJ Spooky, Carl Cox, Moby, Superstar DJ Keoki, Scanner, Heather Hart, Genesis P'Orridge of Psychic TV, BT, Roni Size & Reprazent, Frankie Bones, Electric Skychurch, Wolfgang Flur of Kraftwerk, Jack Dangers/Meat Beat Manifesto, Pure Children, Atomic Babies, Mike Szabo, Chris Decker/Medicine Drum, Jason Bently, Freaky Chakra, Juno Reactor, Adam X, Simply Jeff, Uberzone, Loop Guru, Lords of Acid, Phillip Blaine, System 7

Claudia Besso, Mather Zickel in *Achille's Love* © Castle Hill

Better Living Through Circuitry © Seventh Art Releasing

Wilhamenia Dickens in *Thirteen* © Film Society of Lincoln Center

THIRTEEN (Film Society of Lincoln Center/Independent Feature Project) Producer/Director/Screenplay/Photography/Editor, David Williams; Music, Shep Williams, Cecil Hooker, Carlos Garza; from Bellevue Films; 1997; Color; Not rated; 87 minutes; Release date: June 2, 2000. CAST: Wilhamenia Dickens (Nina), Lillian Foley (Lillian), Don Semmens (Artist), Michael Aytes (Michael), Michael Jeffrey, Dawn Tinsley (Social Workers), David Scales (Lillian's Male Freind), Doug Washington (Nina's Uncle), Anisa Dickens (Kiki), Thomas Shelton (Man Working in Lillian's Yard), Mary Aytes ("Babysis"), Marguerita Austin (Woman Married a Long Time), Shelby Ware (Woman Worried About Boyfriend), Nathalie Le Floch (Dog Owner), Brenda Parker (Teacher), Samuel Flynn (Insurance Salesman), Chichie Tascoe (Canine Designer), Wanda Dickens (Wanda)

AMERICAN BABYLON (Stone Productions) Producers/Conception, David Heilbroner, Robert Stone; Director/Photography, Robert Stone; Executive Producer, Anthony Horn; Music, Joel Harrison; from RS Productions in association with Court TV; Color; Not rated; 86 minutes; Release date: June 2, 2000. Documentary on detective Jeff Fauntleroy, an heroic Atlantic City cop in the city's more devastated areas; featuring Jeff Fauntleroy and Lonell Jones.

Lonell Jones, Jeff Fauntleroy in *American Babylon* © Robert Stone

POP & ME (Seventh Art) Producers, Richard Roe, Chris Roe; Executive Producers, Richard Roe, Chris Moore; Director, Chris Roe; Additional Story Development, Erik Arnesen; Editors, Jesse Negron, Chris Roe; Additional Editing, Juliann Jannus, Mark Hornweibel; Photography, Erik Arnesen, Chris Roe; Music, Steve Edwards, Mazatl Galindo; Co-Producers, Tony Hiernan, Walter Buckley; a Fish Eggs presentation; Color; Not rated; 90 minutes; Release date: June 9, 2000. Documentary on father and sons, featuring the filmmaker, Chris Roe, and his dad, Richard Roe.

CATFISH IN BLACK BEAN SAUCE (Iron Hill Pictures) Producer/Director/Screenplay, Chi Muoi Lo; Co-Producer, Stanley Yung; Photography, Dean Lent; Designer, Skyler J.D. Adler; Music, Stanley A. Smith; Editor, Dawn Hoggatt; Costumes, Maral Kalinian; Casting, Eileen Mack Knight, Meredith Behrend; from Black Hawk Entertainment; Dolby; FotoKem color; Rated PG-13; 110 minutes; Release date: June 9, 2000. CAST: Paul Winfield (Harold Williams), Mary Alice (Dolores Williams), Chi Muoi Lo (Dwayne), Lauren Tom (Mai), Kieu Chinh (Thanh), Sanaa Lathan (Nina), Tyler Christopher (Michael), Tzi Ma (Vinh), George Wallace (James), Wing Chen (Samantha), Amy Tran (Young Mai), Kevin Lo (Young Dwayne), Kevin D'Arcy, Rosey Brown (Guards), Ron Galbraith (Doctor), Calvin Nguyen (Teacher), Richard F. Whiten (Motorcycle Cop), Lalanya Masters (Bank Teller), Mark Daniel Cade (Asst. Bank Mgr.), Jedda Jones (Agnes), Roxanne Reese (Nadine), Saachiko Magwili (Mother), William Thomas (Douglas), April Tran (Interpreter), Tom Ryan (Lt. Davis), Carol Kiernan (Nurse), Thu Hong (Opera Singer), Ho Lo (Man at Airport), Vien Hong (Transvestite), Pamela Gordon (Jasmine's Voice), Christy House (Lang's Voice), Bandit (Jasmine), Mango (Kitten)

AMERICAN PIMP (Seventh Art) Producers, Allen Hughes, Albert Hughes, Kevin Messick; Directors, The Hughes Brothers (Allen Hughes, Albert Hughes); Photography, Albert Hughes; Co-Producer, Spencer Franklin; Editor, Doug Pray; an Underworld Entertainment presentation; Dolby; CFI color; Not rated; 86 minutes; Release date: June 9, 2000. Documentary on pimps and the prostitution profession, featuring Rosebudd, Schauntte, Bradley, C-Note, Ken Ivy, Charm, R.P., Fillmore Slim, Sir Captain, Payroll, Gorgeous Dre, Bishop Don Magic Juan, Mel Taylor, Kenny Red, Danny Brown, Dennos Hof (Pimps), Too Short (Rapper), Jade, Samantha & Monica, Latrice, Spicy (Prostitutes)

DREAMERS (Dark Lantern Pictures) Producer, Artie Glackin; Executive Producers, Peiti Feng, Yang-Wen Lu, Carl L. Fredericks, Henry Zhao; Director/Screenplay, Ann Lu; Associate Producers, Matt Compton,

Richard Roe, Julian Lennon, Chris Roe in *Pop & Me*
© Seventh Art Releasing

Chi Muoi Lo, Mary Alice, Paul Winfield in *Catfish in Black Bean Sauce* © Black Hawk Entertainment

Jeremy Jordan, Mark Ballou in *Dreamers* © Dark Lantern

Jeremy London; Co-Producer, Craig Hall; Photography, Neal L. Fredericks; Designer, Jordan Steinberg; Editor, Andrea Zondler; Music, Bob Mithoff; an Artie Glackin production, an American Anvil presentation; FotoKem color; Not rated; 93 minutes; Release date: June 9, 2000. CAST: Jeremy Jordan (Dave), Courtney Gains (Mike), Portia Dawson (Patricia), Ruth De Sosa (Valerie), Camille Gaston (Matt), Brian Krause (Pete), Paul Bartel (Larry), Mark Ballou (Ethan), Lauralinda Bedell (Angelle), Broc Benedict (Young Dave), Rina Bennett (Doctor in White Room), Kelly Biddlecome (Kathy), Glenda Morgan Brown (Barbara), Linda Castro (Jane), Robert Cavanaugh (David), Joseph Cohen (Bully), Keith Coogan (Rob), Tracy Dali (Nancy), Anastasia Drake (Rachel), Peiti Feng (Asian Hooker), Taimak Guari (Sam), Steven Anthony Lawrence (Matthew), Amy Lindsay (Fantasy Girl), Leann Love Maldonado (Mandy), James Margolin (Guy Mullane), Fay Playsted (Ronda), Philip Arthur Ross (Phil), Steven Robert Ross (Steve), Dana Rossi (Diane), Sarah Rubano (Wardrobe), Nicholle Sabel (Jenny), Sam Saletta (Young Ethan), Amber Rose Sealey (Michelle), Mary Lou Secor (Grandma), Fusako Shiotani (Japanese Tour Guide), Stephanie Sterns (Universal Tour Guide), Ken Takemoto (Yasujiro), Barbara Vidinha-Tyler (Hispanic Mom), Jesse Vint (Carl), Jason Wolk (Todd), Kiyoko Yamaguchi (Pei), Yukyo (Lilly), Doreen Zetterlund (Rosa)

THE WOMAN CHASER (Inwood Films) Producer, Soly Haim; Executive Producer, Joe McSpadden; Director/Screenplay, Robinson Devor; Based on the novel by Charles Willeford; Photography, Kramer Morgenthau; Designer, Sandrine Junod; Editor, Mark Winitsky; Music, Daniel Luppi; Casting, Rosemary Welden; a Tarmac Films presentation; Black and white; Not rated; 87 minutes; Release date: June 14, 2000. CAST: Patrick Warburton (Richard Hudson), Emily Newman (Laura), Eugene Roche (Used Car Dealer), Lynette Bennett (Mother), Joe Durrenberger (Chet Wilson), Ron Morgan (Bill), Pat Crowder (Salvation Army Lady), Mel Hampton (Flaps Hartwell), Marilyn Rising (Becky), Paul Malevitz (Leo Steinberg), Ernie Vincent (The Man), Laura Witty (Mrs. Shantz), Keith van Straaten (Dickie J. Hewlett), Delaina Mitchell (The Man's Secretary), Josh Hammond (Young Richard), Leslie Lauten (Bathing Cap Girl), Barry Sigismondi (Pool Attendant), John Maynard (Moderator), Ezra Buzzington (Piano Player), Larry DeLassus (Waiter at Bar), Danny Allen (Good Samaritan), Charles Deering (Highway Cop), Tom Morris (Arresting Officer), Thien H. Nguyen (Chinese Waiter), Estelle Cohen (Office Secretary), Laicie Manrelle (Little Girl in Field), Christopher Young (Motel Night Clerk)

American Pimp © Seventh Art Releasing

Patrick Warburton in *The Woman Chaser* © Inwood Films

Cale, Akima in *Titan A.E.* © Twentieth Century Fox

Frankie Negron, Val Lik in *Boricua's Bond* © USA Films

BOOKWARS (Avatar Films) Producer/Director/Editor, Jason Rosette; Co-Producers, Michel Negroponte, James and John Montoya; Music, Rich Goldstein and Little Muddy; Color; Not rated; 79 minutes; Release date: June 9, 2000. Documentary on New York's street booksellers, featuring Peter Whitney, Rick Sherman, Marvin, Everett Shaprio, Polish Joe, Al Mappo, Margueritte, Ron Harris, Jason Rosette

TITAN A.E. (20th Century Fox) Producer, David Kirschner, Gary Goldman, Don Bluth; Directors, Don Bluth, Gary Goldman; Screenplay, Ben Edlund, John August, Joss Whedon; Story, Hans Bauer, Randall McCormick; Music, Graeme Revell; Designer, Philip A. Cruden; Art Director, Kenneth Valentine Slevin; Director of Animation, Len Simon; Executive Producer, Paul Gertz; Directing Animators, Troy Saliba, Renato Dos Anjos, John Hill, Edison Goncalves, Robert Fox, Paul Newberry; Casting, Marion Levine; a Gary Goldman production in association with David Kirschner productions; Dolby; Cinemascope; Technicolor; Rated PG; 95 minutes; Release date: June 16, 2000. VOICE CAST: Matt Damon (Cale), Bill Pullman (Korso), John Leguizamo (Gune), Nathan Lane (Preed), Janeane Garofalo (Stith), Drew Barrymore (Akima), Ron Perlman (Prof. Sam Tucker), Alex D. Linz (Young Cale), Tone-Loc (Tek), Jim Breuer (The Cook), Chris Scarabosio (Queen Drej), Jim Cummings (Chowquin), Charles Rocket (Firrikash/Slave Trader Guard), Ken Campbell (Po), Tsai Chin (Old Woman), Crystal Scales (Drifter Girl), David L. Lander (The Mayor)

BOYS AND GIRLS (Dimension) Producers, Jay Cohen, Lee Gottsegen, Murray Schisgal; Executive Producers, Bob Weinstein, Harvey Weinstein, Jill Sobel Messick, Jeremy Kramer; Director, Robert Iscove; Screenplay, The Drews (Andrew Lowery, Andrew Miller); Co-Producer, Sue Baden-Powell; Photography, Ralf Bode; Designer, Marcia Hinds-Johnson; Editor, Casey O. Rohrs; Music, Stewart Copeland; Choreographer, Jerry Evans; Costumes, April Ferry; Casting, Joseph Middleton; a Punch 21 production; Distributed by Miramax Films; Dolby; Deluxe color; Rated PG-13; 94 minutes; Release date: June 16, 2000. CAST: Freddie Prinze, Jr. (Ryan), Claire Forlani (Jennifer), Jason Biggs (Hunter), Amanda Detmer (Amy), Heather Donahue (Megan), Alyson Hannigan (Betty), Monica Arnold (Katie), Brendon Ryan Barret (Young Ryan), Gay Thomas-Wilson (N.Y. Flight Attendant), Raquel Beaudene (Young Jennifer), David Smigelski (King), Blake Shields (Knight), Sean Maysonet (Michael), John X (D.J.), Tsianina Joelson (Girl in Bar), Kristofer Mickelson (Big Guy), Matt Carmody (Kirt), Richard Hillman (Frat Guy), Tim Griffith (Timmy), Timi Prulhiere (Andie), Eric Rutherford (Noah), Matt Schulze (Paul), Angela Oh (Waitress), Brian Poth (Guy in Diner), Mimi Rose (Girl in Diner), David Correia (Shuttle Driver), Lisa Eichhorn (Shuttle Passenger), Lee Garlington (L.A. Flight Attendant), John Henry Redwood (Businessman), Barbara Spiegel (Saleswoman), Kylie Bax, Kristy Hinze, Ines Rivero, Renate Verdaam (Supermodels), Susan Kellerman (Therapist)

EASTSIDE (Hollywood Independents) Producer, Mark Roberts; Executive Producer, Ravi Chopra; Director, Lorena David; Screenplay, Eric P. Sherman; Photography, Lisa Wiegand; Line Producer, Justin Conley; Designer, Clare Brown; Costumes, Luellen Harper Thomas; Casting, Sharon Nederlander; a Candlelight Films presentation of a Kingsize Entertainment; Dolby; Color; Not rated; 94 minutes; Release date: June 21, 2000. CAST: Mario Lopez (Antonio Lorez), Elizabeth Bogush (Clare Gabriel), Mark Espinoza (Horatio Lopez), Efrain Figueroa (Armando De La Rosa), Gulshan Grover (Gulshan), Maurice Compte (Toad), Richard Lynch (Mihalas Gabriel), Molly O'Leary (Nurse), Carlos Gallardo (Luis), William Marquez (Factory Manager), Marc Daniel Brandon (Pee Wee), Robert Rincon (Vincent), Christine Avila (Vincent's Mother), Bob Koherr (Paramedic), John Michael Morgan (Hospital Guard), Corbin Timbrook (Doctor), Jonathan Klein (Male Nurse), Harley Zumbrum (Mysterious Man), Tracy Lynn Cruz (Woman), Jorge Cervera, Jr. (Attorney), Richard Livingston (Financial Consultant), Fitz Houston (Car Wash Manager), Mary Portser (Receptionist), Tony Ceravantes (De La Rosa's Soldier)

Claire Forlani, Freddie Prinze, Jr. in *Boys and Girls* © Dimension Films

Gutterpunks in *The Decline of Western Civilization: Part III*
© Abbey Entertainment

Melissa Leo, Sam Trammell in *Fear of Fiction* © PowWow Prods.

BORICUA'S BOND (USA Films) Producer, Greg Scheinman; Director/Screenplay/Casting, Val Lik; Executive Producers, Alan Novich, Pharmboys Partners; Photography, Brendan Flynt; Editor, Doug Abel; Co-Producers, Robyn Karp, Val Lik, Akivah Bloom; an October Films presentation of a Rogue Pictures presentation in association with MIA; Dolby; Cinemascope; DuArt color; Rated R; 95 minutes; Release date: June 21, 2000. CAST: Frankie Negron (Tommy), Val Lik (Allen), Ramses Ignacio (Axel), Jorge Gautier (Wilson), Jesglar Cabral (Antonio), Geovanny Pineda (Avery), Erica Torres (Christine), Kaleena Justiniano (Rose), Robyn Karp (Susan Miller), Marco Sorisio (Officer Highlander), Jeff Asencio (Paco), Michael "2-smove" Demitro (Sammy), Pietro Gonzalez (Diner Owner), Manuel Jesus Cabral (Tommy's Father), Elsa Canals (Tommy's Mother), Maurice Phillips (Santa), Edison Torres (Priest), Vanessa Del Sol (Princess), Jack "JDS" Da Silva (Blinky), Footprintz (Seta), Paul Manion (Det. Chroney), Freddie Lopez (Singer on the Street), Luis Torres (Christine's Father), Lissette Montolio (Christine's Mother), Olga Lebron (Christine's Aunt), Gerson Munoz (Christine's Trick), Yanira Canals (Hazel), Ileana Rodriguez (Lady in Window), Daniel Ruiz, Carlos Ruiz (Bouncers), Austin Stark (Willie), Jeffrey Karp (Diner Customer)

SURVIVING PARADISE (New Light Entertainment) Producers, Bahman Maghsoudlou, Kamshad Kooshan; Director/Screenplay, Kamshad Kooshan; Executive Producers, Fred Afshar, Torange Yeghiazarian, Kambiz Kuschan; Photography, Paul Mayne; Designer, Jay Vetter; Music, Richard Herrera Lopez; Editor, Rick LeCompt; Color; Not rated; 90 minutes; Release date: June 30, 2000. CAST: Shohreh Aghdashloo (Pari), Keyan Arman Abedini (Sam), Lauren Parissa Abedini (Sara), Joe Alvarez (Mr. F), David Wissak (Mr. Z), David Barry (Mr. A), Saba Altomeh (Saba), Anahid Avanesian (Afi), Bruce Bailey (Sgt. McCoy), Verton Banks (Lionel), James Carretta (Young Man), Jimmy Cruise (Carlos), Paris Davari (Mr. Mohajer), Lunden De Leon (Phyllis), Otis Freeman (Lou), Shalizeh Imankhan (Booseh), Negar Khoshkhram (Nikoo), Steven Kondo (Chinese Man), Shahrokh Mashayekh (Bobak), Behzad Masrour (Jalal), David Naderi (Dr. Moniri), Porsche Norman (Ayiesha), Justin Norman (Rashad), Vahik Pirhamzei (Mo), Tiger Reel (Writer), Fariba Salarkia (Roya), Fatemeh Shogaeinia (Khanoom Bozorg), Estrella Vazquez (Latino Girl), Brad Vickery (Police Officer), Torange Yeghiazarian (Fereshteh)

THE DECLINE OF WESTERN CIVILIZATION: PART III (Abbey Entertainment) Producer, Scott Wilder; Director, Penelope Spheeris; Photography, Jamie Thompson; Editor, Ann Trulove; Co-Producer, Ross Albert; Music, Phil Suchomel; Music Supervisor, Stephen E. Smith; a Spheeris Films, Inc. presentation; Foto-Kem Color; Not rated; 88 minutes; Release date: July 7, 2000. Documentary on the Los Angeles punk scene, featuring Final Conflict, Litmus Green, Naked Aggression, The Resistance.

FEAR OF FICTION (PowWow Prods.) Producers, Gerry Kagan, Charlie Ahearn; Director/Screenplay, Charlie Ahearn; Line Producer, Jake Myers; Photography, John Foster; Designer, Mark White; Editor, Christina Boden; Music, Evan Lurie, Lee Ranaldo; Casting, Judy Henderson, Robyn Knol; Color; Not rated; 99 minutes; Release date: July 13, 2000. CAST: Melissa Leo (Sigrid Anderssen), Sam Trammell (Red Hopkins/Tom Hopkins), Penn Jillette (Albert), Reno (Master of Ceremonies), David Wheir (Victor), Stephen Pearlman (Mr. Basketball Head), Irma St. Paule (Gertrude), Clark Johnson (Gary), Linda Larkin (Liz), Annie Giobbe (Debbie), Lee Bryant (Mrs. Hopkins), Talmadge Lowe (George), Jay Devlin (Ray), Myra Carter (Mrs. Anderssen)

CHUTNEY POPCORN (Mata Films) Producers, Susan Carnival, Nisha Ganatra, Sarah Vogel, Kelley Forsyth; Executive Producer, Trina Wyatt; Director, Nisha Ganatra; Screenplay, Nisha Ganatra, Susan Carnival; Photography, Erin King; Editor, Jane Pia Abromowitz; Music, Karsh Kale; Designer, Jody Kipper; Costumes, Robin Shane; Casting, Judy Henderson & Associates; a Seneca Falls presentation; DuArt color; Not rated; 92 minutes; Release date: July 14, 2000. CAST: Jill Hennessy (Lisa), Nisha Ganatra (Reena), Nick Chinlund (Mitch), Madhur Jaffrey (Meenu), Sakina Jaffrey (Sarita), Ajay Naidu (Raju), Cara Buono (Janis), Daniella Rich (Tiffany), Eliza Foss (Dr. Brendel), Priscilla Lopez (Loretta), Alisa Mast (Becca), Amy Veltman (Jet)

Jill Hennessy, Nisha Ganatra, Cara Buono in *Chutney Popcorn*
© Mata Prods. Inc.

Joan Allen, Gary Sinise in *It's the Rage* © All the Rage, Inc.

Peter Weller, Balthazar Getty in *Shadow Hours* © CanWest Films

IT'S THE RAGE (Silver Nitrate) a.k.a. *All the Rage* ; Producers, James D. Stern, Peter Gilbert, Ash R. Shah, Anne McCarthy, Mary Vernieu; Executive Producers, Will Tyrer, Chris Ball, Gary Levinsohn, Mark Vernieu; Director, James D. Stern; Screenplay, Keith Reddin; Photography, Alex Nepomniaschy; Designer, Jerry Fleming; Costumes, Edi Giguere; Music, Mark Mothersbaugh; Editor, Tony Lombardo; from Scanbox Entertainment; Dolby; Color; Rated R; 97 minutes; Release date: July 14, 2000. CAST: Joan Allen (Helen Harding), Andre Braugher (Tim Sullivan), Josh Brolin (Tennel), Jeff Daniels (Warren Harding), Robert Forster (Tyler), Anna Paquin (Annabel Lee), Giovanni Ribisi (Sidney Lee), David Schwimmer (Chris), Gary Sinise (Norton Morgan), Bokeem Woodbine (Agee), Wayne Morse (Clerk), January Jones (Janice Taylor), Deborah Offner (Secretary), Barb Wallace (Diana), Kevin Crowley (Ed), Robert Peters (Phil), Alex Watson (Guard One), Muse Watson (Todd), Dan Anders (Coroner), Dan Pettersson (Ambulance Driver)

THE NIGHT LARRY KRAMER KISSED ME (FilmNext) Producers, Michael Caplan, Kirkland Tibbels; Director, Tim Kirkman; Screenplay, David Drake; Photography, James Carman; Editor, Caitlin Dixon; from Montrose Pictures; Color; Not rated; 79 minutes; Release date: July 14, 2000. David Drake's 1992 one-man Off-Broadway show about a gay man's journey to self-discovery is captured on film.

David Drake in *The Night Larry Kramer Kissed Me* © Buck

SHADOW HOURS (CanWest Entertainment) Producers, Peter McAlevey, Isaac H. Eaton; Executive Producer, Michael Thomas Shannon; Director/Screenplay, Isaac H. Eaton; Photography, Frank Byers; Designer, Francis J. Pezza; Music, Brian Tyler; Costumes, Luke Reichle; Co-Producers, Balthazar Getty, Shon Greenblatt; Casting, Cathy Henderson-Martin, Dori Zuckerman; a Newmark Films presentation in association with 5150 Productions, Inc.; Dolby; CFI color; Rated R; 93 minutes; Release date: July 14, 2000. CAST: Balthazar Getty (Michael Holloway), Peter Weller (Stuart Chappell), Rebecca Gayheart (Chloe Holloway), Peter Greene (Det. Steve Adrianson), Frederic Forrest (Sean), Brad Dourif (Roland Montague), Michael Dorn (Det. Thomas Greenwood), Corin Nemec (Vincent), Johnny Whitworth (Tron), Arroyn Lloyd (Mickey), Clayton Landey (Announcer), Richard Moll (Homeless Man), Julie Brown (Speaker), Chris Doyle (Sweeny), Tane McClure (Keesha), Cheryl Dent (Serena), Sonny King (Manager, Nude Bar), Benjamin Lum (Mr. Ming), Steve Hulin (Willie Wilson), Mark Ginther (Eli Houston), Monty Freeman, De'Voreaux White, Joseph Reilich (Transvestites), Aloma Wright (Nurse Johnson), Yareli Arizmendi (Dr. Marshall), Josephine Bailey (Desk Clerk), Phillip Bergeron (Antoine), Daniel Faraldo (Santos Armando), Gregory Scott Cummins (Johnny), Daniel Alexander (Pete), Beau Starr (Jeremiah Walker), Leroy Thompson (Dealer), Byron Chief Moon (Chatuga), Ilia Volok (Russian), E.J. Callahan (Man with Handicap Sign), Maral Nigolian (Neighbor), Hans Howe (Bum), Frank Novak (Husband), Diane Robin (Wife), Chris Weber (Hitchhiker), Charles Sergis (KFWC Newscaster), Eric Strausz (Cop with Bullet Proof Vest); Performance Artists: Ron Athey (Man with Hooks in Face), Crystal Cross, Stosh J. Fila (Women in Suspension Room), Bernard Eismere (Man in Suspension Room), Cyril Kuhn, Tom Bliss (Huffers), Daryl Carlton (Guard), Kari French (Tripper), Jake Miller (Fingered Man), Mistress Ilsa (Elegant Woman), Pleasant Gehman (Lingerie Woman), Marcy Johnston (Nazi Mistress), Joey Jaramillo (Bavarian Puppet Boy), Luke Reichle (Butler), Selene Moreno (Small Woman), Amber Cannon (Pale Woman), Jade Semiprecious (Chopsticks Woman), Russ Glazer (Man Sucking Toes), Michelle Muloney (Seductress), Chris Colvin (Boy Toy), Alex Livingston (Chamber Boy), Abby Travis Foundation (Punk Rock Band), Ginger Moon, Austin St. Croix (Exotic Dancers)

SWEET JANE (Phaedra) Producers, W.K. Border, Clark Hunter; Executive Producers, Joel Soisson, Michael Leahy; Director/Screenplay, Joe Gayton; Photography, Greg Littlewood; Designer, Clark Hunter; Editor, Jennifer Lane; Music, Walter Werzowa; Costumes, Merrie Lawson; Casting, Mark Tillman; a NEO Motion Pictures presentation; Dolby; FotoKem color; Not rated; 83 minutes; Release date: July 14, 2000. CAST: Samantha Mathis (Jane), Joseph Gordon-Levitt (Tony), William McNamara (Stan Bleeker), Bud Cort (Dr. Geller), Mary Woronov (Saleslady), Phil Fondacarro (Bob), Daniel Roebuck (Kellygreen), Nicki Micheaux (Martielle), Derek Webster (Darryl), Michelle Johnston (Alice), Kimberly Scott (Dr. Gordon), Barbara Pilavin (Old Woman Patient), Russell Gray (Silhouette), Rex Ryan (Clemenzo), Gary Bullock (Figure), Milton Quon (Korean Clerk), Jodi Ross, Lucia Vincent (Reporters), Bonnie Arrons (Waitress), Michael Albala (John)

Samantha Mathis, Joseph Gordon-Levitt in *Sweet Jane* © Phaedra Films

Benjamin in *Benjamin Smoke* © Cowboy Booking

THE IN CROWD (Warner Bros.) Producer, James G. Robinson; Executive Producers, Jonathan A. Zimbert, Michael Rachmil; Director, Mary Lambert; Screenplay, Mark Gibson, Philip Halprin; Photography, Tom Priestley; Designer, John D. Kretschmer; Costumes, Jennifer L. Bryan; Editor, Pasquale Buba; Music, Jeff Rona; Casting, Pam Dixon Mickelson; a Morgan Creek production; Dolby; Color; Rated PG-13; 104 minutes; Release date: July 19, 2000. CAST: Susan Ward (Brittany Foster), Lori Heuring (Adrien Williams), Matthew Settle (Matt Curtis), Nathan Bexton (Bobby), Ethan Erickson (Tom), Laurie Fortier (Kelly), Kim Murphy (Joanne), Katharine Towne (Morgan), Daniel Hugh Kelly (Dr. Henry Thompson), Tess Harper (Dr. Amanda Giles), Jay R. Ferguson (Andy), A.J. Buckley (Wayne the Gardner), Charlie Finn (Greg), Erinn Bartlett (Sheila), Peter Mackenzie (Bob Mead), Heather Stephens (Tanya), Joanne Pankow (Milena), Taylor Negron (Louis), David Reinwald (Dr. Beck), Scot M. Sanborn (Jack Simmers), Tonya Smalls, Julia Wright (Pedicurists), Michael J. Young (Diner Patron), Ron Clinton Smith (Desk Guard), Brenda Onhaizer (Nurse), Ronald McCall (EMS Technician), Teresa Lynn O'Toole (Fighting Chicken Girl), Keith Kuhl (Dancer at Club), Leland L. Jones (Photographer), Mary Elias (Dr. Thompson's Date)

BENJAMIN SMOKE (Cowboy Booking) Producers/Directors, Jem Cohen, Peter Sillen; Executive Producer, Noah Cowan; Photography, Jem Cohen, Peter Sillen, Sarah Cawley; Editors, Nancy Roach, Jem Cohen, Peter Sillen; Music, Smoke; a co-production of Gravity Hill Films and Pumpernickel; a C-Hundred Film Corp presentation; Color/Black and white; Not rated; 80 minutes; Release date: July 21, 2000. Documentary on HIV-positive, drag queen musican Benjamin and his band, Smoke; featuring Smoke: Benjamin, Tim Campion, Brian Halloran, Coleman Lewis, Bill Taft.

THE EYES OF TAMMY FAYE (Lions Gate) Producers, John Hoffman, Fenton Bailey, Randy Barbato; Directors, Fenton Bailey, Randy Barbato; Executive Producer, Sheila Nevins; Executive in Charge of Production, Harry Knapp; Photography, Sandra Chandler; Editor, Paul Wiesepape; Post Production Supervisor, Eduardo Magaña; Associate Producers, Thairin Smothers, Gabriel Rotello; Music, Jimmy Harry; Narrator, RuPaul Charles; a World of Wonder Productions, Inc. in association with Channel Four & Cinemax Reel Life presentation; U.S.-British; Dolby; Color; Rated PG-13; 79 minutes; Release date: July 21, 2000. Documentary on one-time Christian evangelists Jim and Tammy Faye Bakker, featuring Tammy Faye Bakker-Messner, Roe Messner, Jim Bakker, Jamie Bakker, Rev. Mel White, Pat Boone, Tammy Sue Bakker Chapman, Steven Chao, Jim J. Bullock, Roseanne, Greg Gorman, Charles Sheperd, James Albert.

Susan Ward, Nathan Bexton, Lori Heuring in *The In Crowd*
© Morgan Creek Productions, Inc.

Tammy Faye Bakker-Messner in *The Eyes of Tammy Faye*
© Lions Gate Films

Charlie Spradling in *Spent* ©Regent Entertainment

Olympia Dukakis, Roy Scheider in *Better Living* © Golden Heart

SPENT (Regent) Producers, Rana Joy Glickman, Jordan Summers, Gil Cates Jr.; Executive Producers, Joe Cates, Jordan Zevon; Director/Screenplay, Gil Cates Jr.; Photography, Robert D. Tomer; Designer, Aaron Osborne; Editor, Jonathan Cates; Music, Stan Ridgway; Costumes, Mimi Maxmen; a Trademark Entertainment/Rana Joy Glickman production; Dolby; FotoKem color; Not rated; 91 minutes; Release date: July 21, 2000. CAST: Jason London (Max), Charlie Spradling (Brigette), Phill Lewis (Doug), Erin Beaux (Nathan), James Parks (Grant), Richmond Arquette (Jay), Barbara Barrie (Mrs. Walsh), Gilbert Cates (Mr. Walsh), Rain Phoenix (Kimberly), Margaret Cho (Shirley), Jonathan Ethan Blechman (Scott), Yale Summers (Max's Father), Kim Winter (Forum Waitress)

THOMAS AND THE MAGIC RAILROAD (Destination) Producers, Britt Allcroft, Phil Fehrle; Executive Producers, Charles Falzon, Nancy Chapelle, Barry London, Brent Baum, John Bertolli; Director/Screenplay, Britt Allcroft; Photography, Paul Ryan; Designer, Oleg Savytski; Editor, Ron Wisman; Costumes, Luis M. Sequeira; Music, Hummie Mann; Original "Thomas" Music & Songs, JNR Campbell, Mike O'Donnell; Songs, Hummie Mann, Don Black, Sue Ennis; Visual Effects Supervisor, Bill Neil; Casting, Karen Margiotta, Mary Margiotta, Ross Clydesdale, Juli-Ann Kay; a Gullane Pictures, Barry London/Brent Baum presentation; Presented in association with Isle of Man Film Commission; U.S.-British; Dolby; Deluxe color; Rated G; 89 minutes; Release date: July 26, 2000. CAST: Alec Baldwin (Mr. Conductor), Peter Fonda (Grandpa Burnett Stone), Mara Wilson (Lily), Russell Means (Billy Twofeathers), Didi Conn (Stacy), Michael E. Rodgers (Junior), Cody McMains (Patch), Jared Wall (Young Burnett), Laura Bower (Young Tasha), Lori Hallier

(Lily's Mother), Michael E. Rodgers (Mr. C. Junior); VOICE CAST: Eddie Glen (Thomas), Neil Crone (Diesel 10/Splatter/Gordon), Colm Feore (Toby), Linda Ballantyne (Percy), Kevin Frank (Dodge/Henry/Bertie/Harold), Shelley Elizabeth Skinner (Annie & Clarabel), Britt Allcroft (Lady)

THE ST. FRANCISVILLE EXPERIMENT (Trimark) Producer, Dana Scanlan; Videographer, Todd Richard; Editors, Tom Vater, Jeff Bradley; from the Kushner-Locke Company; Color; Rated R; 79 minutes; Release date: July 28, 2000. CAST: Tim Baldini (Videographer), Madison Charap (Psychic), Paul Palmer (Ghost Hunter), Ryan Larson (Historian), Troy Taylor (Ghost Authority), Paul J. Salamoff (Producer), Sarah Clifford (Psychic in St. Francisville), Ava Kay Jones (Voodoo Priestess). Katherine Smith (Paranormal Expert)

BETTER LIVING (Goldheart Pictures) Producers, Ron Kastner, Lemore Syvan; Co-Producer, Melissa Marr; Director, Max Mayer; Screenplay, Max Mayer, George F. Walker; Based on the play by George F. Walker; Photography, Kurt Lennig; Designer, Mark Ricker; Costumes, Laura Bauer; Editor, Steve Silkenson; Casting, Walken Jaffe Casting; Color; Not rated; 95 minutes; Release date: August 4, 2000. CAST: Olympia Dukakis (Nora), Roy Scheider (Tom), Edward Herrmann (Jack), Deborah Hedwall (Elizabeth), Catherine Corpeny (Maryann), Wendy Hoopes (Gail), James Villemaire (Junior), Phyllis Somerville (Nellie), Scott Cohen (Larry), Jamie Gonzalez (Pock), Dan Moran (Dan), Brian Tarantina (Danny), Myra Lucretia Taylor (Waitress), Jessy Terrero, Gary Zazulka (Bikers)

Alec Baldwin in *Thomas and the Magic Railroad*
© Destination Film Distribution Company

Christopher George Marquette, Polly Draper in *The Tic Code* © Avalanche

Dominique Swain in *Intern* © L'Intern, LLC.

Tyne Daly in *The Autumn Heart* © Arrow Releasing

THE TIC CODE (Avalanche) Producers, Michael Wolff, Karen Tangorra; Executive Producers, Steve Sherman, Bob Van Ronkel; Director, Gary Winick; Screenplay, Polly Draper; Co-Producers, Paulette Bartlett, First Artists; Line Producer, Diana Schmidt; Photography, Wolfgang Held; Designer, Rick Butler; Music, Michael Wolff; Editors, Bill Pankow, Kate Sanford; Costumes, Karen Perry; Casting, Sheila Jaffe, Georgianne Walken; Presented in association with Gun for Hire Films; Dolby; Color; Rated R; 91 minutes; Release date: August 4, 2000. CAST: Gregory Hines (Tyrone Pike), Polly Draper (Laura), Christopher George Marquette (Miles), Carol Kane (Miss Gimpole), Desmond Robertson (Todd), Carlos McKinney (Chester), Dick Berk (Dick), John B. Williams (Spanky), Tony Shalhoub (Phil), Robert Iler (Denny), Bill Nunn (Kingston), Fisher Stevens (Morris), James McCaffrey (Michael), Allison Nurse (Blonde #1), Peter Appel, Michael Wolff (Engineers), Pat Moya (Belinda), Ismail Bashey (Indian Man), David Johansen (Marvin), Camryn Manheim (Mrs. Swensrut), Blair Ashlee Swanson (Confident Girl) (Note: This movie had its U.S. premiere on cable television in April, 1999)

INTERN (Moonstone Entertainment/Giv'en Films) Producers, Galt Neiderhoffer, Etchie Stroh, Daniela Soto-Tahplin; Executive Producer, Randy Simon; Director, Michael Lange; Screenplay, Caroline Doyle, Jill Kopelman; Photography, Rodney Charters; Designer, Jody Asnes; Editor, Anita Brandt-Burgoyne; Music, Jimmy Harry; Color; Not rated; 90 minutes; Release date: August 11, 2000. CAST: Dominique Swain (Jocelyn Bennett), Ben Pullen (Paul Rochester), Kathy Griffin (Cornelia Crisp), Joan Rivers (Dolly Bellows), Peggy Lipton (Roxanne Rochet), Paulina Porizkova (Chi Chi Chemise), David Deblinger (Richard Sinn), Billy Porter (Sebastian Niederfarb), Anna Thompson (Antoinette De la Paix), Leilani Bishop (Resin), James Urbaniak (Olivier), Anson Scoville (Alex), Bill Raymond (Deep Throat), Rocco Sisto (Pierre), Victor Varnado (Messenger), Alexia Landeau (Bianca), Gwyneth Paltrow, Andre Leon Talley, Elizabeth Saltzman, Tommy Hilfiger, Frederic Fekkai, Rebecca Romijn-Stamos, Narciso Rodriguez, Kevyn Aucoin, Stella McCartney, Cynthia Rowley, Marc Jacobs, Donna Hanover, John Bartlett, Nell Campbell, Diane von Furstenberg, Donna Karan, Kenneth Cole, Simon Doonan, Philip Block, Amy Ashley, Gretchen Gunlocke, Marina Rust, Deda Coben, Glenda Bailey, Richard Sinnott, Jennifer Jackson, Susan Kittenplan, Carmen Bogonova, Cricket Burns, Pamela Fiori, Pauline Alguilera (Themselves)

THE AUTUMN HEART (Film Cellar) Producers, Jerri Sher, Kelley A. McMahon; Executive Producers, Marc Chabot, Lisa Marie Schiller; Director, Steven Maler; Screenplay, Davidlee Wilson; Photography, John Leuba; Editor, Joel Hirsch; Designer, Susan Zeeman Rogers; Music, Sheldon Mirowitz; Casting, Susan Willett; Color; Not rated; 109 minutes; Release date: August 11, 2000. CAST: Ally Sheedy (Deb), Davidlee Wilson (Daniel), Jack Davidson (Lee), Marla Sucharetza (Diane), Marceline Hugot (Donna), John Fiore (Bill Sullivan), Tyne Daly (Ann), Ariel Gabino Martinez Gonzalez (Steve), Julian Sands, Lisa Keller, Willy O'Connell

SUNSET STRIP (20th Century Fox) Producers, Art Linson, John Linson; Executive Producer, James Dodson; Director, Adam Collis; Screenplay, Randall Jahnson, Russell Degrazier; Story, Randall Jahnson; Photography, Ron Fortunato; Designer, Cynthia Charette; Editor, Bruce Cannon; Music, Stewart Copeland; Costumes, Ha Nguyen; Choreographer, Toni Basil; Casting, Don Phillips; a Fox 2000 Pictures presentation of a Linson Films production; Dolby; Deluxe color; Rated R; 90 minutes; Release date: August 11, 2000. CAST: Simon Baker (Michael), Anna Friel (Tammy), Nick Stahl (Zach), Rory Cochrane (Felix), Adam Goldberg (Shapiro), Tommy J. Flanagan (Duncan), Darren Burrows (Bobby), John Randolph (Mr. Niederhaus), Stephanie Romanov (Christine), Jared Leto (Glen), Mary Lynn Rajskub (Eileen), Maurice Chasse (Nigel), Mike Rad (Badger), Josh Richman (Barry Bernstein), Sebastian Robertson (Busboy), Dori Brenner (Doctor), Krista Allen (Jennifer), Matthew Frauman (Hobbit), Justin Ashforth (Joel), Robin Moxey (Ronny), Rainbow Borden (Butch), Marcus Johnson (Toussaint), André Roberson (Leroy), Dave Lafa (Malcolm), Garland R. Spencer (Darryl), Ron De Roxtra (Vito), Turtle (Turner's Counter Clerk), Kellie Waymire (Mary), Brian Gattas (Production Asst.), Michelle Beaudoin (Girl with Frizzy Red Hair), Anna Berger (Older Waitress), Judy Greer (Younger Waitress), Paul Weiss (Guitar Counter Clerk), Nowldar Alexander Winterhawk (Guitar Store Clerk #2), Ryan "Rhino" Michaels (Doorman at Duncan's), Jimmie F. Skaggs (Guitar Center Owner), Ralph P. Martin (Motel Pool Man), Linda Lawson (Mrs. Canter)

Nick Stahl, Simon Baker in *Sunset Strip* © Twentieth Century Fox

199

Ramblin' Jack Elliott in *The Ballad of Ramblin' Jack* © Lot 47 Films

Derick Martini, Steven Martini in *Smiling Fish and Goat on Fire*
© Stratosphere Entertainment

THE BALLAD OF RAMBLIN' JACK (Lot 47) Producers, Aiyana Elliott , Paul Mezey, Dan Partland; Executive Producers, Hunter Grayler Brodie, Jesse Crawford; Director/Photography, Aiyana Elliott; Screenplay, Aiyana Elliott, Dick Dahl; Co-Producer, Dick Dahl; Editors, David Baum, Susan Littenberg; a Plantain Films presentation in association with Crawford Communications; Color; Not rated; 112 minutes; Release date: August 16, 2000. Documentary on folk legend Ramblin' Jack Elliott, featuring Ramblin' Jack Elliott, Arlo Guthrie, Martha Elliott, Janice Windsor Currie, Dave Van Ronk, Gill Gross, David Adnopoz, Elanore Snyder, Jerry Kay, Nora Guthrie, Pete Seeger, June Shelley, Wizz Jones, Victor Maymudes, Izzy Young, Harold Leventhal, Ed Pearl, Kris Kristofferson, Odetta, Michael Green, Barbara Dodge

LOVE & SEX (Lions Gate) Producers, Timothy Scott Bogart, Brad Wyman, Martin J. Barab, Darris Hatch; Executive Producer, Mark Damon; Director/Screenplay, Valerie Breiman; Photography, Adam Kane; Designer, Sarah Sprawls; Editor, Martin Apelbaum; Line Producer, Michelle Ledoux; Costumes, Sara Jane Slotnick; Music, Billy White Acre, Pierpaolo Tiano; Casting, Dan Shaner, Michael Testa; an MDP Worldwide presentation of a Bogart/Barab/Wyman/Hatch production; Dolby; Color; Not rated; 83 minutes; Release date: August 25, 2000. CAST: Famke Janssen (Kate Welles), Jon Favreau (Adam Levy), Noah Emmerich (Eric), Cheri Oteri (Mary), Ann Magnuson (Ms. Steinbacher), Josh Hopkins (Joey Santino), Robert Knepper (Gerard), Vincent Ventresca (Richard), Kristen Zang (Savannah), David Steinberg (Tiny Man), Elimu Nelson (Jerome Davis), Don Brunner (Police Officer), Yvonne Zima (Kate, aged 9), Melissa Fitzgerald (Melanie), Rob Swanson (Blind Date), Will Rothhaar (Bobby, aged 9), Rance Howard (Earl), Ron Kochevar (Man), Angela Marsden (Peaches), Troy Blendell (Frank), Nicolette Little (Michelle, aged 6), David Schwimmer (Rob, Jehovah's Witness)

FASTPITCH (Artistic License) Producer/Director/Screenplay, Jeremy Spear; Screenplay, Jeremy Spear, Juliet Weber, Fred Kaufman; Executive Producer, Cathrine Stickney Steck; Co-Producer, Michel Negroponte; Photography, Elia Lyssy; Editor, Juliet Weber; Music, William "Spaceman" Patterson; from Shortstop Films Inc; Dolby; Color; Not rated; 90 minutes; Release date: August 25, 2000. Documentary on fast-pitch softball, featuring Jeremy Spear, Shane Hunuhunu, Nick McCurry, Peter J. Porcelli, Jr., Darren Zack.

SMILING FISH AND GOAT ON FIRE (Stratosphere) formerly *Goat on Fire & Smiling Fish;* Producers, Derick Martini, Kevin Jordan, Steven Martini; Executive Producers, Sheliah Goldman, Tommy Lynch, Richard Abramowitz, Ronna Wallace, Michael Silberman; Director, Kevin Jordan; Screenplay, Kevin Jordan, Derick Martini, Steven Martini; Photography, Fred Iannone; Set Designers, Karyn Burgner, Deana Aho; Editors, Kevin Anderson, Ryan Rothmaier; Music, Chris Horvath; a Martin Scorsese presentation of a Martini/Jordan and Red Horse production; Dolby; Color; Rated R; 90 minutes; Release date: August 25, 2000. CAST: Derick Martini (Chris Remi), Steven Martini (Tony Remi), Christa Miller (Kathy), Amy Hathaway (Alison), Bill Henderson (Clive Winter), Rosemarie Addeo (Anna), Heather Jae Marie (Nicole), Nicole Rae (Natalie), Wesley Thompson (Burt Winter), Jeff Kern (Mike)

Jon Favreau, Famke Janssen in *Love & Sex* © Lions Gate Films

Johnnie Reese, Don Bajema in *Chalk* © Damian Smith

Trey Anastasio, Mike Gordon in *Bittersweet Motel* © Danny Clinch

Brian Van Holt, Amanda Peet in *Whipped*
© Destination Film Distribution Company

CHALK (Tenderloin Action Group/Pacific Rim Media) Producers, Rand Crook, Ethan Sing; Director, Rob Nilsson; Screenplay, Don Bajema, Rob Nilsson; Photography, Mickey Freeman; Art Director, Lee Patzer; Editor, David Schickele; Music, Tim Alexander; Associate Producer, Drew Fellman; Produced with the cooperation of Sue Backman and Chalkers Billiard Club; a Project of the Tides Center; Color; Not rated; 134 minutes; Release date: August 25, 2000. CAST: Edwin Johnson (Watson), Johnnie Reese (Jones), Kelvin Han Yee (TC), Don Bajema (Dorian), Denise Concetta Cavaliere (Lois), John Tidwell (Johnnie), Destiny Costa (Wanda)

BITTERSWEET MOTEL (Image Entertainment) Producer/Director, Todd Phillips; Executive Producer, Joshua Plank; Photography, Elia Lyssy; Editor, Alan Oxman; a Stranger Than Fiction presentation of a Bittersweet Films production, released in association with Aviva Entertainment and Little Villa Features; Dolby; DuArt color; Not rated; 82 minutes; Release date: August 25, 2000. In concert with rock band Phish: Trey Anastasio (guitar), Jon Fishman (drums), Mike Gordon (bass), Page McConnell (keyboards)

WHIPPED (Destination) Producer/Director/Screenplay, Peter M. Cohen; Executive Producers, Anthony Armetta, Taylor MacCrae, Barry London, Brent Baum, Brad Jenkel; Co-Producers, Zorie Barber, Andrew R. Shakman; Photography, Peter B. Kowalski; Designer, Katherine M. Szilagyi; Editor, Tom McArdle; Costumes, Karen Kozlowski; Line Producer, Jill Rubin; Music, Michael Montes; Casting, Jodi Collins; Presented in association with Hi-Rez Films; Dolby; Technicolor; Rated R; 82 minutes; Release date: September 1, 2000. CAST: Amanda Peet (Mia), Brian Van Holt (Brad), Judah Domke (Eric), Zorie Barber (Zeke), Jonathan Abrahams (Jonathan), Callie Thorne (Liz), David J. Cohen, Dave Heyman, George Song, Bo Bazylevsky, Marc Courtiol, Marcus Ho (Stiffs), Linda Udd, Beth Ostrosky (Chicks), Kurt Williams (Cab Driver), Kristin Di Spaltro, Heather Liebl, Jamie Donahue, Elaina Erika Davis (Girls), Bridget Moynahan (Marie), Aviva Gale (Stacey), Taryn Reif (Bristol), Leslie Cohen, Amy Karl, Kashanna Evans, Susanna Spies (Amanda's Girlfriends), Monte Viader (Hot Girl in Park), Peter M. Cohen (Pizza Delivery Guy), Sarah Isenberg, Tanya Brown (Lesbian Dancers), Karen Kozlowsky (Hoover Hana), Natalie Jovan, Jen (Two Hot Freaks), Tony Javed (Italian Bicycler), Lyle Kanouse (Plumber), Neriah Davis (Dreamgirl), Billy Cordon (Geeky Boy)

WILDFLOWERS (Fries Film Group) Producers, Timothy Bird, Thomas Garvin, Zachary Matz; Executive Producers, Daryl Hannah, Christine Vachon; Director/Screenplay, Melissa Painter; Photography, Paul Ryan; Editor, Brent White; Music, Sam Bisbee; Designer, Andrea Soeiro; from Filmsmith Productions; Color; Rated R; 93 minutes; Release date: September 1, 2000. CAST: Daryl Hannah (Sabine), Clea DuVall (Cally), Eric Roberts (Jacob), Tomas Arana (Wade), Richard Hillman (Graham), Eric Yetter (Dylan), Robert Haas (Poet), John Doe (Teacher), Sheila Tousey (Martha), Irene Bedard (Ruby), James Burnett (Tailor), David Graham (Trip), Alan Gelfant (Wolf), Justin Vue (Bear), Johanna

Mattox (Julie), Heather Mathieson (Teacher's Wife), John Roble (Coulter), David Fine (Bolinas Roofer)

HIGHLANDER: ENDGAME (Dimension) Producers, Peter Davis, William Panzer; Executive Producers, Bob Weinstein, Harvey Weinstein, Cary Granat; Director/Screenplay, Douglas Aarniokoski; Photography, Doug Milsome; Designer, Jonathan Carlson; Co-Producer, Patrick Peach; Co-Executive Producers, H. Daniel Gross, Beth Anne Calabro; Editors, Christopher Blunden, Michael N. Knue, Robert A. Ferretti; Music, Nick Glennie-Smith; Casting, Michelle Guish; Stunts, Joe Dunne; Martial Arts Choreographer, Donnie Yen; a Davis/Panzer production; Distributed by Miramax Films; Dolby; Widescreen; Deluxe color; Rated R; 88 minutes; Release date: September 1, 2000. CAST: Christopher Lambert (Connor MacLeod), Adrian Paul (Duncan MacLeod), Bruce Payne (Jacob Kell), Lisa Barbuscia (Faith/Kate), Donnie Yen (Jin Ke), Edge (Rogue Highwayman), Sheila Gish (Rachel Ellenstein), Mihnea Trusca (Villager), Beatie Edney (Heather), June Watson (Caiolin MacLeod), Donald Douglas (Father Rainey), Liviu Timus (Executioner), Oris Erhuero (Winston), Christopher Leps (Hooded Monk), Ian Paul Cassidy (Cracker Bob), Damon Dash (Carlos), Vernon Rieta (Manny), John Medlen (Monk #1), Douglas Aarniokoski (Kirk), Thomas Lockyer (Matthew Hale), Peter Wingfield (Methos), Charmian May (Lady), Paul Bigley (Knave), Daniel Parker (Puffer), Jim Byrnes (Dawson), Jessica Mann (Rachel #1, 8 years old), Robert Hewett (Photographer), Kananu Kimiri (Faith's Assistant), David Nicholls (Drunk Friend), Abigail Kinsbury (Rachel #2, 12 years old), Candace Hallinan (Rachel #3, 19 years old), Wendy Partridge (Colleague)

Bruce Payne in *Highlander: Endgame* © Dimension Films

Memphis Bleek, Jay-Z in *Backstage* © Dimension Films

Jennifer Jordan Day, Michael Patrick Gaffney in *Clouds*
© IN Pictures

BACKSTAGE (Dimension) Producer, Damon Dash; Executive Producers, Bob Weinstein, Harvey Weinstein, Cary Granat, Lyor Cohen; Director, Chris Fiore; Photography, Elena "EZ" Sorre, Mark Peterson, Lenny Santiago; Editors, Chris Fiore, Richard Calderon; Presented in association with Roc-a-Fella Records and the Island Def Jam Music Group; Distributed by Miramax Films; Dolby; Color; Rated R; 86 minutes; Release date: September 6, 2000. Documentary of rapper Jay-Z's 1999 "Hard Knock Life" tour, featuring Jay-Z, DMX, Method Man, Redman, Beanie Sigel, Memphis Bleek, DJ Clue, Amil, Ja Rule.

TURN IT UP (New Line Cinema) Producers, Guy Oseary, Happy Walters; Executive Producers, Gary Ventimiglia, Lennox Parris, Lester Parris; Director/Screenplay, Robert Adetuyi; Based on a story by Ray "Cory" Daniels, Chris Hudson, Kelly Hilaire; Co-Producers, Pras Michel, E. Bennett Walsh; Photography, Hubert Taczanowski; Designer, Ina Mayhew; Editor, Jeff Freeman; Music, Frank Fitzpatrick; Costumes, Mimi Melgaard; Casting, Robi Reed-Humes; Dolby; Deluxe Color; Rated R; 83 minutes; Release date: September 6, 2000. CAST: Pras (Diamond), Elain Graham (Rose), Chris Messina (Baz), Eugene Clark (Marshall), Harry-O (Master Mix), Ja Rule (Gage), Patrice Goodman (Jane), John Ralston (Mr. White), Jason Statham (Mr. B), Chang Tseng (Mr. Chang), Tamala Jones (Kia), Jeff Jones (Minister), Vondie Curtis Hall (Cliff), Melyssa Ford (Deborah), Derwin Jordan (Seamus), Leroy Allen (Security Guard), Faith Evans (Natalie), DJ Skribble (DJ), Shinehead (Smiley), Conrad Dunn (Urie), Juliana Stojkic (Pregnant Slavic Woman), Ted Clark (Crusher), Errol Gee (Tyrone), Cam Natale (Slick), Robert Dodds (JT)

Pras, Ja Rule in *Turn It Up* © New Line Cinema, Inc.

THE BULLS' NIGHT OUT (Cobra Communications) Producer, Arun Vir; Executive Producers, Lindley Farley, Raymond Nieves, Randy Jurgensen; Director/Screenplay, Lindley Farley; Story, Lindley Farley, Pasquale Gaeta; Photography, Cornelius Schultze-Kraft; Editors, Elizabeth Bouiss, Dipu Mehta, Lindley Farley; Music, Frank Foster; Casting, Ragland & Assoc.; 1995; Color; Not rated; 82 minutes; Release date: September 6, 2000. CAST: Jack Marnell (George Wall), Steve Kasprzak (Louie Esposito), A.J. Johnson (J.J. Clark), J.J. Flash (Paul "Zap" Zachry), Russ Romano (Bill Wilson), David Harman (Captain Ralph Abruzzi), Roslyn Ziff (Audrey), Jayne A. Larson (Ruby Wall), Shane Barbanel (Jeremy), Steve Roberts (Wachter, the Baker), Mark Llewellyn (Bandit), Charles Daniels (Blow-up), Rubi Hochland (Sonny Edwards), Glenn Vitale (Marco Salvo), Kirk Williams Sr., Caesar Campbell (Dealers), Ron G. Jones (Sonny's Lt.), Theo Perry (Shabazz), Gerard Catus (Homeless Man), Chris Mordecai, Gregory B. Jones (Night Patrolmen), Patrick Landers (Junkie), Mike Calderone, Lucas Pena (Cop Bar Patrons)

CLOUDS (IN Pictures) Producers, Don Thompson, Gary Lindsay; Executive Producer, Wayne Moore; Director/Screenplay, Don Thompson; Co-Producers, Will Arntz, E. Ted Prince, Walter Goodwin; Photography/Editor, Gary Lindsay; Designer, Gordon Halloran; Music, Nawang Khechog, The Rosenbergs; Presented in association with nextPix and Pacific Grove Productions; Dolby; Color; Not rated; 95 minutes; Release date: September 8, 2000. CAST: Michael Patrick Gaffney (Robert St. John), Jennifer Jordan Day (Beatrice), Richard Barrows (Tab), Patricia Ann Rubens (Mrs. Martin), Ryan Mickels (St. John as a Child), Amy Leonard (Little Girl), Sandy Rouge Anderson (Juanita), Dick Kellogg (Prof. Steiner), Jamuna Llewellyn (Woman St. John Meets in Restaurant), Rob Nilsson (Frank), Christine Stafford (Vera), Hans Larson (Vera's Boyfriend), Bill Lindsay, Marilyn Lindsay (People in Restaurant), Jaz Halloran, Tim Furness (Boys at Video Arcade), Rex Gardiner, Rita Gardiner (People in Park), Amy Champ (Fellini Woman in Park/Woman at Bar/Woman in Riverwalk), Chloe West (Cinderella Girl), Caitlin Hicks (Cinderella Mom), Linda Bennett (Woman at Bar), Cora Gwynn (Woman at Bar St. John Looks At), "Jewel" Sandoval (Mouth Harp Player), Zeke Wheeler (Man in Riverwalk), Sashalai Stanger (Young Girl at Accident), "Pinky" (Accident Witness), Lori Halloran (Newscaster)

MY 5 WIVES (Artisan) Producers, Rodney Dangerfield, John Curtis; Executive Producers, Eric Thom, Walter Josten, Pieter Kroonenburg; Director, Sidney J. Furie; Screenplay, Rodney Dangerfield, Harry Basil; Photography, Curtis J. Petersen; Designer, Graeme Murray; Costumes, Monique Warren; Music, Robert Carli; Line Producer, Tracey Boyd; Editor, Saul Pincus; from Blue Rider Pictures, My Five Wives (B.C.) Films Inc.; U.S.-Canadian; Dolby; Color; Rated R; 100 minutes; Release date: September 8, 2000. CAST: Rodney Dangerfield (Monte Peterson), Andrew Dice Clay (Tony Morano), John Byner (Preston Gates), Molly Shannon (Dr. Barbara Van Dyke), Jerry Stiller (Don Giovanni), John Pinette (Stewart), Rob DeLeeuw (Shuffles), Fred Keating (Ray), Judy Tylor (Stephanie), Angelika Baran (Emily), Kate Luyben (Virginia),

Jon Cryer, Rick Stear in *Went to Coney Island...* © Phaedra Cinema

Albrecht Becker (left) in *Paragraph 175* © Telling Pictures

Emmanuelle Vaugier (Sarah), Anita Brown (Megan), Karin Konoval (Janet), Brandy Sanders (Blanche), Anaya Farrell (Louise), Peter Hanlon (J.B. Caldwell), Don MacKay (Judge Roberts), Kevin Blatch (Bailiff), Mary McDonald (Miss Jennings), Douglas Newell (Brother Andrew), Laurie Murdoch (Brother Joseph), Sarah Deakins (Gwen Gates), Lee Jay Bamberry (Auctioneer), Paul McGillion (Waiter), Ralph J. Alderman (Farmer), Jim Shepard (Bookstore Keeper), Kasper Michaels (Merchant), Bill Dow (Sheriff), Richard Cox (Deputy), Gavin Buhr (Truck Driver), Jason Griffith (Worker), Rheta Hutton (Old Lady), Lloyd Berry (Old Man), Laurie Brunetti (Romeo), Stefanie von Pfetten (Hotel Desk Clerk), Peter Kelamis (Gambler), D. Harlan Cutshall (Pit Boss), Ona Grauer (Poolside Cocktail Waitress), Alannah Stewartt, Amy Stiller (Vegas Divorcees), Kelly Dean Sereda (Valet), Dean Paul Gibson (Cab Driver), Alexander Pervakov (Bouncer), Zahf Hajee (Deejay), Garrett Doray, Tim Wilson, Gordon Laxton (Dancers), Mark Schooley (Man), L. Harvey Gold (Captain)

WENT TO CONEY ISLAND ON A MISSION FROM GOD ... BE BACK BY FIVE (Phaedra) Producers/Screenplay, Jon Cryer, Richard Schenkman; Director, Richard Schenkman; Photography, Adam Beckman; Designer, Bill Stabile; Editor, Richard LaBrie; Music, Midge Ure; Costumes, Deirdra Elizabeth Govan; Associate Producers, Dailey Kennedy, Anne R. Flocco; Line Producer, Lawrence Elmer, Jr.; Casting, Mark Saks; an Evenmore Entertainment production; Color; Rated R; 94 minutes; Release date: September 8, 2000. CAST: Jon Cryer (Daniel), Rick Stear (Stan), Rafael Baez (Richie), Ione Skye (Gabby), Frank Whaley (Skee-ball Weasel), Peter Gerety (Maurice), Akili Prince (Julie), Aesha Waks (Cindy Goldclang), Susan Foster (Jennifer), Dominic Chianese (Mickey, the Photographer), William Wise (Sexy Larry, the Store Owner), Patricia Mauceri (Mrs. Munoz), Leslie Hendrix (The Bearded Lady), Jesse Lenat (Jojo), Brandon Espinoza (12 year old Stan), Timmy Reifsnyder (12 year old Daniel), Richard Acosta (12 year old Richie), Laura Breckenridge (12 year old Gabby), Judy Reyes (Waitress), Robert Levine (Sol), Helmar Augustus Cooper (Bumper Car Operator), Justin Pierre Edmund (Kid), Fernando Lopez (Richie's Brother), Richard Schenkman (Freak Show Guy), Norbert Butz (Pawnbroker), Marceline Hugot (Homeless Woman), Roz Ryan (Nurse), Peggy Pope (Mrs. Bernstein, Teacher), May Lin Pultar (Consuela), Wilson Jermaine Heredia (Darcy), Diane Cheng (Mrs. Liu), Eugene Byrd (Teenage Fiend)

PARAGRAPH 175 (New Yorker) Producers, Rob Epstein, Jeffrey Friedman, Michael Ehrenzweig, Janet Cole; Directors, Rob Epstein, Jeffrey Friedman; Narration Written by Sharon Wood; Co-Producer, Howard Rosenman; Photography, Bernd Meiners; Director of Research/Associate Producer, Klaus Muller; Editor, Dawn Logsdon; Music, Tibor Szemzo; Narrator, Rupert Everett; a Telling Pictures/HBO Theatrical Documentary Production; Color/Black and white; Not rated; 81 minutes; Release date: September 13, 2000. Documentary on how homosexuality was made a crime under the aegis of "Paragraph 175" after the Nazis took power in Germany.

THE DREAM CATCHER (Redeemable Features) Producers, Julia Reichert, Steven Bognar, Ed Radtke; Director, Ed Radtke; Screenplay, Ed Radtke, M.S. Nieson; Photography, Terry Stacey; Designer, Sally Petersen; Editor, James Klein; Music, Georgiana Gomez; Casting, Alison Kennedy Maier, Jonathan Platt; a Film Society of Lincoln Center & the Independent Feature Project presentation from American Independent Vision, in association with Time Warner Cable and the Sundance Channel; DuArt Color; Not rated; 99 minutes; Release date: September 15, 2000. CAST: Maurice Compte (Freddy), Paddy Connor (Albert), Jeanne Heaton (Katherine), Joseph F. Arthur (Freddy's Father), Patrick Shining Elk (Caretaker), Larry John Meyers (Freddy's Uncle), David Reece (Deer Hunter), Leslie Orr (Woman at ATM), Amanda Lanier (Rhea), Danny Morris (Jerry), Buck Truitt (Cashier), Sean Wolf Hill (Threatening Driver), Michael Conn (Pisser), Tom Wamsley (Trucker in Bathroom), Rohn Thomas (Raymond), Melanie Johnson (Brenda), Fred Gloor (Fisherman), Kim Tuvin (Nursing Home Nurse), Temba Ngqakayi (Irate Driver), Chris Miller (Marine), Lonna D. Kingsbury (Cafeteria Worker), Jeff Carter (Principal), Frank R. Lewis (Garage Attendant), Robin Mullins (Albert's Mom), Richard E. Corey (Carny), Howard Shook (Lead Thug), Kevin Rotramel, Dan Kiger (Thugs), Zuella "Babes" Murray (Caretaker's Wife), Andrew John, Dallas James Naljahih (Caretaker's Kids), Miya Cerno (Infant), Les Paul, Patricia Martinez (People in Pick-up Truck), Gary Zweig (Store Manager), Robert Grant Elkins (Old Cop), Stephen M. Francia, Jr. (Young Cop), Matt Miller (Lieutenant), Jason Love, William D. Young, Jr., Patricia McUey, Terry Alton Inlow (Police Officers), Bob Barnes (Diner Owner), Tony Darnell-Davis (Carl), Roger Winkler, James Taylor, Val Worbman (Diner Regulars), Dalton Bybee, Dylan Bybee (Kids in Van), Henley Green, Stuart Klorfine (Parents in Van)

Paddy Connor, Maurice Compte in *The Dream Catcher*
© Redeemable Features

John Ventimiglia, Michael Imperioli in *On the Run* © Phaedra Cinema

Rob Lowe in *The Specials* © Regent Entertainment

ON THE RUN (Phaedra) Producers, Tino Navarro, Bruno De Almeida; Director, Bruno De Almeida; Screenplay, Joseph Minion; Based on a story by Bruno De Almeida, Jonathan Berman; Photography, Igor Sunara; Designer, Andy Bernard; Costumes, Cat Thomas; Music, Frank London; Editor, Beatrice Sisul; Casting, Georgianne Walken, Sheila Jaffe; an MGN Filmes production in association with Arco Films and CLT-UFA International in co-production with Sunday Films and RTP with the financial support of ICAM and the participation of Canal+, a Tino Navarro production; U.S-Portuguese, 1998; Color; Not rated; 94 minutes; Release date: September 15, 2000. CAST: Michael Imperioli (Albert De Santis), John Ventimiglia (Louie Salazar), Drena De Niro (Rita), Agnés Jaoui (Kirstin), Joaquim de almeida (Ignacio), Suzanne Shepherd (Lady in Travel Agency), Sara Graca (Vicky), Victor Argo (Man Shaving), Jason Pabon (Young Albert), Saul Negron (Young Louie), Tony Zacarro (Cop in Apartment), Tino Navarro (Homeless), Arthur Nascarella (Irwin), Tim Gilroy (Tom), Kate Lunsford (Waitress), L.B. Williams (Cop in Coffee Shop), Sharon Angela (Tina), Joel Rooks (Bartender), Luis Fontes, Miguel Ferreira (Bodyguards), Gary Perez (Cop in Havana Club), Dwight Ewell (Rasta), Joseph R. Gannascoli (Burly Guy), Paul Lazar (Cabbie), Nick Sandow (Jack), Anna Kohler (Anna), John Frey (George), Bronson Dudley (Dr. Shapiro), Paolina Weber (Nurse), Eddie Branquinho, David Callegati (Cops in Hospital)

30 DAYS (Arrow) Producers, Matthew Rego, Michael Rego, Arielle Tepper; Director/Screenplay, Aaron Harnick; Photography, David Tumblety; Designer, Michael Fagin; Costumes, Juliet A. Polcsa; Editor, Sean Campbell; Associate Producer, Hank Unger; Music Supervisor, Brian Ross; Casting, Andra Reeve; an Arielle Tepper/Araca Group production; Color; Not rated; 87 minutes; Release date: September 15, 2000. CAST: Ben Shenkman (Jordan Trainer), Arija Bareikis (Sarah Meyers),

Barbara Barrie, Jerry Adler, Ben Shenkman in *30 Days* © Arrow Releasing

Alexander Chaplin (Mike Charles), Bradley White (Tad Star), Thomas McCarthy (Brad Drazin), Catherine Kellner (Lauren), Jerry Adler (Rick Trainer), Barbara Barrie (Barbara Trainer), Arden Myrin (Stacey), Mark Feuerstein (Actor), Lisa Edelstein (Danielle), Tina Holmes (Jenny), Meghan Stranger (Maria)

THE GODS OF TIMES SQUARE (Glass Eye Pix/Scorpio Dogs) Producer/Director/Photography, Richard Sandler; Associate Producer, Larry Fessenden; Editor, Dan Brown; Color; Not rated; 94 minutes; Release date: September 20, 2000. Documentary on Times Square's sidewalk preachers and philosophers.

THE SPECIALS (Regent) Producers, Dan Bates, Mark A. Altman, Rick Mischel; Executive Producers, Mark & Ellie Gottwald; Director, Craig Mazin; Screenplay, James Gunn; Photography, Eliot Rockett; Designer, Dorian Vernacchio; Costumes, Nickolaus Brown; Editor, Stephen Garrett; Special Visual Effects, Foundation Imaging; Casting, Christine Sheaks; a Mindfire Entertainment Production in association with Brillstein/Grey Entertainment; Dolby; FotoKem color; Rated R; 82 minutes; Release date: September 22, 2000. CAST: Rob Lowe (The Weevil), Jamie Kennedy (Amok), Thomas Haden Church (The Strobe), Paget Brewster (Ms. Indestructible), Kelly Coffield (Power Chick), Judy Greer (Deadly Girl), James Gunn (Minute Man), Sean Gunn (Alien Orphan), Jordan Ladd (Nightbird), Mike Schwartz (U.S. Bill), Barry Del Sherman (Zip Boy), Michael Weatherly (Verdict), Jim Zulevic (Mr. Smart), John Doe, Abdul Salaam El Razzac, Lauren Cohn, Tom Dorfmeister, Greg Erb, Brian Gunn, Chuti Tiu (Eight), Matt Champagne (Tippin), Ellie Cornell (Linda), Chase Masterson (Moira Murphy), Frank Medrano (Orestes), Melissa Joan Hart (Sunlight Girl), Christopher Shea, Lee Kirk (Reporters), Jenna Fischer (College Girl)

PRINCE OF CENTRAL PARK (Keystone) Producer, Julius R. Nasso; Executive Producers, Abe Hirschfeld, John P. Gulino, Karen Poindexter, Philip B. Goldfine; Director/Screenplay, John Leekley; Based on the novel by Evan H. Rhodes, and the play by Evan H. Rhodes, Donald Sebesky, Gloria Nissenson; Photography, Jonathan Herron; Designer, Deana Sidney; Music, Ted Shapiro; Editor, Philip Steinman; Casting, Ellen Parks; a Seagal-Nasso production; Dolby; Color; Rated PG-13; 109 minutes; Release date: September 22, 2000. CAST: Kathleen Turner (Rebecca Cairn), Danny Aiello (Noah Cairn), Harvey Keitel (The Guardian), Cathy Moriarty (Mrs. Ardis), Frankie Nasso (JJ Somerled), Lauren Velez (Rosa Sanchez), Jerry Orbach (Businessman), Mtume Gant (Easy), Tina Holmes (Annalisse Somerled), Carmen Moreno (Sophia), Svetlana Efremova (Sophia's Mom), Francesco Vittorio (Young JJ), Michael Moran (Security Guard), Stephanie Beny (School Principal), Frank Anthony (Carousel Operator), Larry Clarke, Vincent Rocco (Cops), Daniel Ziskie (City Planner), John P. Gulino (Deputy Mayor), Victor Rojas, Greg Russell Cook, Rick Gonzalez, Arthur Acuña, Ryan Bondoc (Gangbangers), Ted Arcidi (Construction Worker), Philippe Mao (Maitre D'), Martha Ryan (Nurse Yeager), Pamela Stewart (Nurse Kohanek), Jaliyl Lynn (Dominique), Frank Bongiorno (Judge), Lexie Sperduto (Little Girl)

Cathy Moriarty, Danny Aiello, Frankie Nasso, Kathleen Turner
in *Prince of Central Park* © Keystone

Eva Mendes, Jennifer Morrison in *Urban Legends: Final Cut*
© Columbia Pictures/Phoenix Pictures

ALMA (Alma Pictures) Producer/Director, Ruth Leitman; Executive Producer, Peter Wentworth; Photography, Mark Petersen; Editors, Anna Husaini, Ruth Leitman, Darcy Bowman; Music, Connie Hanes, Steve Dixon; Music Supervisor, Margie Thorpe; Color; Not rated; 94 minutes; Release date: September 22, 2000. Documentary on the dysfunctional Thorpe family, featuring Alma Thorpe, Margie Thorpe, James Thorpe, RuPaul, Now Explosion.

URBAN LEGENDS: FINAL CUT (Columbia) Producers, Neal H. Moritz, Gina Matthews, Richard Luke Rothschild; Executive Producers, Nicholas Osborne, Brad Luff; Director, John Ottman; Screenplay, Paul Harris Boardman, Scott Derrickson; Photography, Brian Pearson; Designer, Mark Zuelzke; Editors, John Ottman, Rob Kobrin; Music, John Ottman; Costumes, Marie-Sylvie Deveau, Trysha Bakker; Casting, Randi Hiller; a Phoenix Pictures presentation of a Neal H. Moritz/Gina Matthews production; Dolby; Deluxe color; Rated R; 94 minutes; Release date: September 22, 2000. CAST: Jennifer Morrison (Amy Mayfield), Matthew Davis (Travis/Trevor), Hart Bochner (Prof. Solomon), Loretta Devine (Reese), Joseph Lawrence (Graham), Anson Mount (Toby), Eva Mendes (Vanessa), Jessica Cauffiel (Sandra), Anthony Anderson (Stan), Michael Bacall (Dirk), Marco Hofschneider (Simon), Derek Aasland (P.A. Kevin), Jacinda Barrett (Lisa), Peter Millard (Dr. Fain), Chas Lawther (Dean Patterson), Chuck Campbell (Geek in Plane), Yani Gellman (Rob),

Jeannette Sousa (Libby), Rory Feore (Killer Flight Attendant), Shauna Black (Blonde Girlfriend), Leland Tilden, Joel Gorson (Jocks on Plane), David Cook, Bianca Muller, Jenny Kim, Nicole Crozier (Student Screamers), Pat Kelly (Crony in Screening Room), Stephanie Moore (Girl in 16mm Film), Kevin Hare, David Sparrow (Police Officers), Clare Martina Preuss (Clapper Girl), Santo (Vicious Dog)

UNINVITED GUEST (Trimark) Producer, Larry "Spud" Raymond; Executive Producer, Kevin D. Hightower; Director/Screenplay, Timothy Wayne Folsome; Photography, Wayne Sells; Designer, Cory Woiculevicz; Editor, Edward R. Abroms; Music, Gregory D. Smith; from Picture Me Rollin' Productions; Color; Rated R; 116 minutes; Release date: September 22, 2000. CAST: Mekhi Phifer (Silk), Mari Morrow (Debbie), Malinda Williams (Tammy), Mel Jackson (Howard), William-Christopher Stephens (Trey), Kim Fields (Store Owner), Wayna Morris (Mo), Lisa France (Art Instructor)

Alma Thorpe in *Alma* © Alma Pictures

Mekhi Phifer in *Uninvited Guest* © Trimark Pictures

Rufus Read, Noah Fleiss, Cassandra Morris in *Double Parked*
© Fierce Films

Ed Robertson, Steven Page in *Barenaked in America* © Shooting Gallery

DOUBLE PARKED (Castle Hill) Producers, Stephen Kinsella, Matthew Myers; Executive Producer, Mark Montgomery; Director/Story, Stephen Kinsella; Screenplay, Stephen Kinsella, Paul Solberg; Photography, Jim Denault; Designer, Anthony Gasparro; Music, Craig Hazen, David Wolfert; Costumes, Monica Willis; Editor, Seth E. Anderson; Casting, Adrienne Stern; a Fierce Films presentation of a 44th Street Films Production; Dolby; Color; Not rated; 97 minutes; Release date: September 22, 2000. CAST: Callie Thorne (Rita Ronaldi), William Sage (Karl Severson), Noah Fleiss (Bret), Rufus Read (Matt Ronaldi), Cassandra Morris (DiDonna), P.J. Brown (Warren), Michelle Hurd (Lola), Eileen Galindo (Dolores Gonzalez), Lanny Flaherty (Louie), Ruth Williamson (Marge), Ed Wheeler (Officer McBride), Anthony De Sando (Angel Gonzalez), Paul Solberg (Wig Salesman), Stephen "Peabo" Peabody (Angry Delivery Man), Gerri Igarashi (Angry Asian Woman), Sally Mayes (Angry Rich Woman), Blaze Jackson (Matt—age 2), Nicholas Jackson (Bret—age 4), Anonette Schwartzberg (Old Lady Across the Street), John Arocho, Allan Lindo, Patrick J.P. Duffy (Bullies on Playground)

TWILIGHT: LOS ANGELES (Off Line) Producers, Ezra Swerdlow, Anna Deavere Smith; Director, Marc Levin; Conceived/Written by Anna Deavere Smith; Photography, Maryse Alberti; Editor, Robert Eisenhardt; Music, Camara Kambon; Produced in association with PBS and Thirteen/WNET; Color; Not rated; 85 minutes; Release date: September 27, 2000. A filmed translation of Anna Deavere Smith's one-woman performance piece *Twilight: Los Angeles, 1992.*

BARENAKED IN AMERICA (Shooting Gallery) Producers, Cheryl Teetzel, Susanne Tabata; Executive Producer, Pierre Tremblay; Director, Jason Priestley; Photography, Danny Nowak; Editor, Al Fleet; Music, Barenaked Ladies; a Nettfilms Production; Dolby; Color; Not rated; 90 minutes; Release date: September 29, 2000. Documentary on the Canadian pop group Barenaked Ladies, featuring Ed Robertson, Steven Page, Jim Creeggan, Kevin Hearn, Tyler Stewart.

THE GREAT DANCE: A HUNTER'S STORY (Off the Fence Prods.) Producer, Ellen Windemuth; Executive Producer, James Hersov; Directors/Photography, Craig Foster, Damon Foster; Screenplay, Jeremy Evans; Editor, Damon Foster; Music, Barry Donnelly; Aardvark/Earthrise/Liquid Pictures; Color; Not rated; 78 minutes; Release date: September 29, 2000. Documentary on the !Xo San bushmen of the Kalahari desert in southern Africa.

RUNNING ON THE SUN (Galaxy Entertainment) Producers, Leland Hammerschmitt, Mel Stuart; Executive Producers, Kirk Friedman, Richard Houghton; Director, Mel Stuart; Photography, John Malvino, Kevin O'Brien, David West; Music, Michel Colombier; Editor, Greg Byers; from Qualcomm Productions; Dolby; Color; Not rated; 100 minutes; Release date: September 29, 2000. Documentary on a 135-mile marathon race held at the height of summer in Death Valley, featuring Adam Bookspan, Angelika Castaneda, Eric Clifton, Maria De Jesus, Jack Denness, Gabriel Flores, Daniel Jensen, Kirk Johnson, Ben Jones, William Curt Maples, Chris Moon, Nick Palazzo, Ephraim Romesburg, Lisa Smith

Anna Deavere Smith in *Twilight: Los Angeles* © Off Line

Josh Evans, Sticky Fingaz in *The Price of Air* © Artistic License Films

Paul Hipp, Boyd Kestner in *Cleopatra's Second Husband* © Indican

Marc Palmieri, Nicol Zanzarella in *Too Much Sleep* © Open City

THE PRICE OF AIR (Artistic License) Producers, Zachary Matz, Thomas Garvin, Michael Madsen; Executive Producers, Lauren Wild, Lisa Larrivee; Director/Screenplay, Josh Evans; Photography, Rufus Standefer; Designer, Karin Haase; Editors, Sabine El Chamaa, Fritz Feick; Costumes, Jacqueline Aronson; Music, Goldie; Casting, Cathy Henderson-Martin & Dori Zuckerman; an M. & J.K. presentation of a Zachary Matz production; Color; Not rated; 85 minutes; Release date: September 29, 2000. CAST: Josh Evans (Paul), Charis Michelsen (Anne), Michael Madsen (Mr. Ball), Dick Van Patten (Mr. Rye), Michelle Phillips (Mrs. Rye), Sticky Fingaz (D), Goldie (Greaser), Allison Lange (Amy Rye), Alexis Arquette (Willy), Jenna Hoffman (Thumpy), Badja Djola (Sugar), Gary Chazen (Sr. Dontra), George Randall (Zuma)

CLEOPATRA'S SECOND HUSBAND (Indican) Producers, Jill Goldman, David Scott Rubin, Jacqui de la Fontaine, Jon Reiss; Executive Producers, Peter Getty, Linda Stewart, Claire Best; Director/Screenplay, Jon Reiss; Photography, Matt Faw; Designers, John Di Minico, Thomas Thurnauer; Costumes, Scott Freeman; Music, Cary Berger; Editor, Toby Yates; Casting, Lindsay D. Chag; a Cucoloris Films presentation of a Flying Cow production; Color; Not rated; 92 minutes; Release date: September 29, 2000. CAST: Paul Hipp (Robert Marrs), Boyd Kestner (Zack Taylor), Bitty Schram (Hallie Marrs), Radha Mitchell (Sophie), Alexis Arquette (Alex), Jonathan Penner (Jon), Nancye Ferguson (Asti)

TOO MUCH SLEEP (Angelika/Open City) Producers, Jason Kliot, Joana Vicente; Director/Screenplay, David Maquiling; Co-Producers, Michele Medina, David Maquiling; Photography, Robert Mowen; Editor, Jim Villone; Music, Mitchell Toomey; Presented in association with Arrowhead Productions; Ultra Stereo; Color; Not rated; 86 minutes; Release date: October 6, 2000. CAST: Marc Palmieri (Jack Crawford), Pasquale Gaeta (Eddie), Nicol Zanzarella (Kate), Philip Galinsky (Andrew), Judy Sabo Podinker (Judy), Gage Dehesa (Boy), John Stonehill (Frankie), Martin Pfeifercorn (Man on Street), Anita Orlacchio (Woman at Car Wash), Nicole Orlacchio, Alexis Orlacchio (Children), Paul Sena, George Masters, Ted Boehler, Vic Hyer (Men at Deli), Joan Maquiling (Jack's Mother), Jack Mertz (Judy's Father), Ruth Kaye (Gert), Jon Langione (Tom Coffee), Stan Carp (Male Nurse), Martin Epstein (Social Critic), Glenn Zarr (Mel), Michael Hernando, Alan Podinker (Dancers), Jeff Morris (Bartender), Brett Podinker (Waiter), R.G. Rader (Jonathan), Mary Ann Riel (Sandy), John Medina, Rocco Paolo (Bouncers), Raj Kanithi (Mr. Raj), Peggy Lord Chilton (Mrs. Bruner), Temme Davis (Lucy), Laurie Eng (Restaurant Hostess), Sally Stat (Agnes Janarone), Anthony Trentacost (Chris Bruner), Katie Rossi (Girl)

LOST SOULS (New Line Cinema) Producers, Nina R. Sadowsky, Meg Ryan; Executive Producers, Donna Langley, Michael De Luca, Betsy Stahl, Pierce Gardner; Director, Janusz Kaminski; Screenplay, Pierce Gardner; Story, Pierce Gardner, Betsy Stahl; Photography, Mauro Fiore; Designer, Garreth Stover; Editors, Anne Goursaud, Andrew Mondshein; Costumes, Jill Ohanneson; Music, Jan A.P. Kaczmarek; Special Make-Up and Animatronic Effects, Stan Winston Studio; Visual Effects and Animation, Cinesite; Casting, Mindy Marin; a Prufrock Pictures production; Dolby; Deluxe color; Rated R; 97 minutes; Release date: October 13, 2000. CAST: Winona Ryder (Maya Larkin), Ben Chaplin (Peter Kelson), Sarah Wynter (Claire Van Owen), Philip Baker Hall (Father James), John Hurt (Father Lareaux), Elias Koteas (John Townsend), Brian Reddy (Father Frank), John Beasley (Mike Smythe), John Diehl (Henry Birdson), Paul Kleiman (Paramedic), Robert Clendenin (Mental Patient), Oliver Clark (Mr. Silberman), Michael Mantell (Kleiman), Brad Greenquist (George Viznik), Ming Lo (Michael Kim), Anna Gunn (Sally Prescott), W. Earl Brown (William Kelson), Cyd Strittmatter (Susan Kelson), James Lancaster (Father Jeremy), Susan Mosher (Receptionist), Maureen Grady (Secretary), Anne Betancourt (Mrs. Quintana), Robert Castle (Josef the Doorman), Anna Berger (Mrs. Levotsky), Kai Ephron (Guard), Lil Henderson (Cranky Woman), John Prosky (Orderly), Rob Moore (Young Man), Ursula Brooks (Lauren), Rainer Judd, Uri Ryder (Party People), Ashley Edner (Gina), Connie Ray (Mother), Jan Triska (Melvin Szabo), Ayo Haynes (Day Care Worker), Joe Clark (Store Owner), Victor Slezak (Father Thomas), Cynthia Darlow (Directionless Woman), Joseph Lyle Taylor (Irked Motorist), Julie Ariola (Reader), Kaity Tong (Herself), Tom McCleister (Father Malcolm), Dan Finnerty (Technical Director), Xanthia Decaux (Production Assistant), Eden Byrd (Waitress), Charlotte L. Fleming (School Secretary), Daniel Jones (School Kid), Kim Harris Ornitz (Joe the Orderly), Victor Ralys (Lithuanian Priest), Norman Smith (Waiter), Terry Van Zandt (Mental Patient #2), Buddy Quaid (Buddy the Waiter), Jamie Denbo (Sharon, Leslie Grant Show), Jodi Daley (Leslie Grant), David Raymond Wagner (Joe, Leslie Grant Show), K.K. Dodds (Deputy), Drew Snyder (Doctor), Kate Beahan (Flirtatious Girl), Rebecca Hobbs (Publicist), Jon Stahl (Voice of Psychiatrist), Alfre Woodard (Police Supervisor)

Ben Chaplin, Winona Ryder in *Lost Souls* © New Line Cinema Inc.

Sam Trammell, Jessica Prunell in *Followers* © Castle Hill

Whispers in *Whispers: An Elephant's Tale* © Disney Enterprises, Inc.

FOLLOWERS (Castle Hill) Producers, Jonathan M. Flicker, Dennis Gossett, Jr.; Director/Screenplay/Editor, Jonathan M. Flicker; Photography, William M. Miller; Designer, Jason Fetvedt; Music, Joe Kurasz; Associate Producers, Stuart Ginsberg, Naiem Mohammed; Casting, Adrienne Stern; a Wildgoose Productions film; Color; Not rated; 87 minutes; Release date: October 13, 2000. CAST: Sam Trammell (John Dietrich), Eddie Robinson (Steve Trayer), Mark Dobies (Jake Tyler), Jessica Prunell (Cynthia Gordon), Jerry Laurino (Allen Phillips), Cary Phillips (Terry Graham), Crew Hoakes (T.J. O'Malley), Willie T. Carpenter (Mr. Trayer), Carol Clarke (Mrs. Trayer), Teja Frank (Shannen Trayer), Robert Flicker (Mr. Dietrich), Paul Raggio (Lawyer), Jonathan M. Flicker (Jeff Portnoy), Dave Hugas (Fredricks), Marino Wecer (Frank), Jason Fuscellaro, Chris Danielle, Greg Martin, Frank Fuscellaro, Mark Forlenza, Eugene Mazzola, Eric Leifer, Paul Viggiano, Ali Ghavami, Eric Traber, Pat Costello, Dave Hugas, Greg Nelson, Chris Jaworski, Steve Wisniewski, Matt Fornale, Michael Growney, Ray Murta, Jason Case, John Sautter, David Sylvester (KPL Brothers & Pledges), Douglas Eldridge, Peter Catenacci (Police Officers), Brian Lubroth, Peter Catenacci (Paramedics), William M. Miller (Witness), Steve Moreno (Bartender), Naiem Mohammed (Guy Walking with Steve), Dave Frigerio (Jerk at Party), Piper Perabo, Robin Eads (Girls at Party), Lisanne Franco (Subway Voice), Ego (Betty the Dog)

JUST LOOKING (Sony Classics) formerly *Cherry Pink*; Producer, Jean Doumanian; Executive Producer, J.E. Beaucaire; Co-Executive Producers, Letty Aronson, John Logigian; Co-Producer, Michael A. Jackman; Director, Jason Alexander; Screenplay/Associate Producer, Marshall Karp; Photography, Fred Schuler; Designer, Michael Johnston; Costumes, Karen Perry; Music, Michael Skloff; Music Supervisors, Kenny Vance, Ken Weiss; Editor, Norman Hollyn; Casting, Sheila Jaffe, Georgianne Walken; a Jean Doumanian Productions presentation; Dolby; Color; Rated R; 94 minutes; Release date: October 13, 2000. CAST: Ryan Merriman (Lenny), Joseph Franquinha (John), Peter Onorati (Phil), Gretchen Mol (Hedy), Patti LuPone (Sylvia), Amy Braverman (Alice), Ilana Levine (Norma), Richard Licata (Polinsky), Allie Spiro-Winn (Barbara), John Bolger (Dr. Flynn), Robert Weil (Guido), Alex Sobel (Marty), Deirdre O'Connell (Mrs. Braverman), Colin Martin (Driver), Chevi Colton (Mrs. Crescetelli), Marcell Rosenblatt (Mrs. Edelberg), Shirl Bernheim (Mrs. Glantz), Heather Hopwood (Myrna), Bart DeFinna (John's Dad), Christopher Spitzer (Hookup Guy)

WHISPERS: AN ELEPHANT'S TALE (Walt Disney Pictures) Producers/Story, Beverly Joubert, Dereck Joubert; Director/Photography, Dereck Joubert; Screenplay, Dereck Joubert, Jordan Moffet, Holly Goldberg Sloan; Editor, Nena Olwage; Music, Trevor Rabin; Voice Casting, Marion Levine; a Dereck and Beverly Joubert production; Dolby; Color; Rated G; 72 minutes; Release date: October 13, 2000. VOICE CAST: Angela Bassett (Groove), Joanna Lumley (Half Tusk), Anne Archer (Gentle Heart), Debi Derryberry (Whispers), Kevin Michael Richardson (Adult Whsipers), Alice Ghostley (Tuskless), Betty White (Round), Kat Cressida (Princess), Joan Rivers (Spike), John DiMaggio (Tough-Tusk/Fulla Bull), Tone Loc (Macho Bull), Jeannie Elias (Stranger/Herd Elephant); and Jim Black, Joseph Molekoa, David Mabukane, Sandor Carter (Poachers)

Ryan Merriman, Gretchen Mol in *Just Looking*
© Sony Pictures Entertainment Inc.

Jason Cairns in *One* © Shooting Gallery

Gwen Somers. Kimberly Johnson, Gaelle Comparat, Jennifer Marks, Catherine Brewton in *Hot Wax Zombies on Wheels!* © Phaedra Cinema

Joelle Carter, Guillermo Diaz in *Just One Time* © Cowboy Booking

ONE (Shooting Gallery) Producer/Designer, Wendy Cary; Executive Producers, Jeff Boortz, John Sideropoulos, Johnny Wow, Mickey Cottrell; Director, Tony Barbieri; Screenplay, Tony Barbieri, Jason Cairns; Photography, Matthew Irving; Editor, Jeffery Stephens; a Two Nine Prods. presentation, in association with 3 Ring Circus; Color; Not rated; 88 minutes; Release date: October 13, 2000. CAST: Kane Picoy (Nick Razca), Jason Cairns (Charlie O'Connell), Autumn Macintosh (Sarah Jenkins), Ed Lynch (Johnny the Bartender), Gabriell Ruvolo (Iris Razca), Paul Herman (Ted Razca), Muhammed Hasan (Dan the Parole Officer), Willie La Nere (Coach Gus), Cassandra Braden (Helen), Kara Michaels (Joan), Rainy Jo Stout (Nancy), Heather Gomoll (Girl with Balloon), Robbie Lanzone (Small Boy on Couch), Kathryn Matthews (Small Girl in Wheelchair), Colette Ibanez (Stripper), Tito Barbieri, Rick Bruno, Mike Gilliam (Scouts), Jonsen Vitug (Faceless), Tom Williamson, Socrates Delianides (Dice Players)

HOT WAX ZOMBIES ON WHEELS! (Phaedra) Producers, Mike J. Roush, Bob Yesk; Executive Producers, Jim Zimbler, Bruce T. Dugan; Director, Mike J. Roush; Screenplay, Elizabeth S.J. Bergholz; Photography, Mark Combs; Editor, Kenn Kashima; Designer, Robert Poe; Costumes, Alison Achauer; Music, Ken Jones, Bobby Buontempo; a Blue Sky Entertainment Inc. Film in association with Wax Rhapsodic LLC; Color; Not rated; 88 minutes; Release date: October 13, 2000. CAST: Jill Miller (Sharon), Tre Lovell (Sven), Jon Briddell (Mick), Gwen Somers (Yvonne Wayne), Kimberly Johnson (Carrie), N.A. Stewart (Martin), Randall St. George (Obadiah), John Rawling (Zebadiah), Forrest G. Wood (Matt the Mayor), Joe Babicki (Self-Serve Ted), Skip Belyea (Bancroft Hutchenreuther), Lynne Hatcher (Marian), Catherine Brewton (Nurse Lydia), Bill Blum (Frank "Press" Miller), Robyn Lewis (Manicurist Ruby), Robert Ciancimino (Big F—king Deal Desk Cop), Ed Herbstman (DJ), Greg Albanese (Engineer), John-Michael Vaughn (Ken the Mailman), Gaelle Comparat (Teddi), Jennifer Marks

JUST ONE TIME (Cowboy Booking) Producers, Lane Janger, Jasmine Kosovic, Exile Ramirez; Executive Producers, Marcus Hu, Charlotte Mickie, David R. Ginsburg; Director/Story, Lane Janger; Screenplay, Lane Janger, Jennifer Vandever; Photography, Michael St. Hilaire; Designer, Stephen J. Beatrice; Costumes, Melissa Bruning; Editor, Mitch Stanley; Music, Edward Bilous; Casting, Billy Hopkins, Suzanne Smith, Kerry Barden; a Code Red Film, Alliance Atlantis presentation in association with Danger Filmworks; Color; Not rated; 111 minutes; Release date: October 20, 2000. CAST: Joelle Carter (Amy), Guillermo Diaz (Victor), Jennifer Esposito (Michelle), Lane Janger (Anthony), Vincent Laresca (Nick), Domenick Lombardozzi (Cyrill), David Lee Russek (Dom), Pat Moya (Mona)

MVP: MOST VALUABLE PRIMATE (Keystone) Producer, Ian Fodie; Executive Producers, Robert Vince, Michael Strange, Anne Vince; Director, Robert Vince; Screenplay, Anne Vince, Robert Vince; Photography, Glen Winter; Music, Brahm Wenger; Editor, Kelly Herron;

Costumes, Cali Newcomen; Key Animal Trainers, Carol Lille, Greg Lille; Casting, Ellie Kanner, Lorna Johnson; a Keystone Family Pictures presentation; Dolby; Color; Rated PG-13; 93 minutes; Release date: October 20, 2000. CAST: Kevin Zegers (Steven Westover), Jamie Renée Smith (Tara Westover), Oliver Muirhead (Dr. Peabody), Rick Ducommun (Coach Marlowe), Lomax Study (Dr. Kendall), Stanley Katz (Einsteen), Russell Ferrier (Darren), Philip Granger (Mark Westover), Ingrid Tesch (Susie Westover), Dave Thomas (Willy Drucker), Ray Galletti (Magoo), Aaron Smolinski (Pete the Captain), Shane Vajda (Moose), Trevor Roberts (Larry), Bernie, Mac, Louie (Jack), Alexa Benette Fox (Jane), Jane Sowerby (Julie Beston), Myles Ferguson (Waterboy), Patrick Cranshaw (Super Fan), David Lewis (Organist), Miles McNamara (University Dean), Nick Misura (Ticket Master), John B. Lowe (Conductor), Kirby Morrow (Tiger #1), Debra Donohue (Reporter #1), Dolores Drake, Christine Willes (Ladies), Jay Brazeau (Harry), Darryl Davis (Referee), Ralph Alderman (Fred), Frank C. Turner (Bart), Ann Warn Pegg (Lucy), Campbell Lane (Melvin), Lois Dellar (Teacher), John Harris (Vikings Coach), Helen Honeywell (Secretary), Robert Lee (Ticket Agent), Jim Hughson (Don)

RECKLESS INDIFFERENCE (Utopia Films) Producers, William Gazecki, Dale Rosenbloom; Executive Producers, Henry Bloomstein, Gene Schwam; Co-Producers, W. Scott Goldie, Randall Sullivan; Director/Editor, William Gazecki; Photography Eric Reiner; Music, Ashley Witt; Color; Not rated; 89 minutes; Release date: October 20, 2000. Documentary, featuring Alan M. Dershowitz, Tom Hayden.

Kevin Zegers in *MVP: Most Valuable Primate* © Keystone Pictures, Inc.

Cameron Dye, Kevin Geer in *The Tavern* © Castle Hill

Live Nude Girls Unite! © First Run Features

THE TAVERN (Castle Hill) Producer/Director/Screenplay, Walter Foote; Executive Producers, James Cooper, Lin Chen Tien; Photography, Kurt Lennig; Designer, Gonzalo Cordoba; Costumes, Lisa Padovani; Editor, Josh Apter; Music, Bill Lacey, Loren Toolajian; Casting, Jerry Beaver; from Foote Speed Productions in association with Redeemable Features; Color; Not rated; 88 minutes; Release date: October 20, 2000. CAST: Cameron Dye (Ronnie), Kevin Geer (Dave), Carlo Alban (Tommy), Kym Austin (Sharon), Gary Perez (Miguel), Nancy Ticotin (Gina), Greg Zittel (Kevin), Steven Marcus (Jerry), Frank Girardeau (Ronnie's Father), Jennifer Harmon (Ronnie's Mother), Margaret Cho (Carol), Tyler Foote, Lillian Foote (Dave's Children), Phyllis Esposito (Angela), Tom Ryan (Jimmy), Michael Baker (Freddie), Pete Zias (Boy #1), Edward K. Thomas (Cliff), Don Creech (Shank), Donald Roman Lopez (Waiter), Al Espinoza (Busboy), Jesse Doran (Marino), La Donna Mabry (INS Clerk), Bruce Katzman (George), Richard Mover (Killer), David Runco (Jackie's Fiancée), Simon Jutras (Frenchman), Heather King (Jeannette), Susan Cella (Irate Woman), Carol Goodheart (Real Estate Agent), Richard Petrocelli (Sal), Robert Turano (Nick), Sharon Mayberry (Interviewer), Harold Alvarez (Tavern Busboy), Bernie McInerney (John Mahoney), Henry Strozier, Eric Kornfeld, John Pero (Customers), The Saw Doctors: Davy Carton, Leo Moran, Pearse Doherty, John Donnelly, Derek Murray (Subway Band)

MY GENERATION (Cabin Creek Films) Producer/Director, Barbara Kopple; Photography, Tom Hurwitz; Editor, Tom Haneke; Supervising Producer, Linda Saffire; Color; Not rated; 103 minutes; Release date: October 20, 2000. Documentary on the Woodstock Festivals of 1969, 1994, and 1999.

LIVE NUDE GIRLS UNITE! (First Run Features) Producers, Julia Query, John Montoya; Executive Producer, Gini Reticker; Director/Screenplay, Julia Query, Vicky Funari; Photography, Julia Query, John Montoya, Sarah Kennedy, Vicky Funari; Co-Producers, Sarah Kennedy, Avilla Peterson; Editors, Vicky Funari, Heidi Rahlmann Plumb; Music, Allison Hennessy, Kali, others; a Query? production; Color; Not rated; 70 minutes; Release date: October 20, 2000. Documentary on a talent strike at San Francisco's Lusty Lady strip club.

SOUND AND FURY (Artistic License) Producer, Roger Weisberg; Director, Josh Aronson; Photography, Brian Danitz, Cordy Waterman; Coordinating Producers, Jackie Roth, Julie Sacks; Music, Mark Suozzo; Editor, Ann Collins; a Ronald Guttman and Nora Coblence presentation of a Production of Aronson Film Associates and Public Policy Productions in association with Next Wave Films; Color; Not rated; 80 minutes; Release date: October 25, 2000. Documentary on the controversy within the deaf community regarding the development of cochlear implants to help the hearing impaired. (This film received an Oscar nomination for documentary feature).

BOOK OF SHADOWS: BLAIR WITCH 2 (Artisan) Producer, Bill Carraro; Executive Producers, Daniel Myrick, Eduardo Sanchez; Director, Joe Berlinger; Screenplay, Dick Beebe, Joe Berlinger; Photography, Nancy Schreiber; Editor, Sarah Flack; Costumes, Melissa Toth; Music, Carter Burwell; Associate Producer, Kevin Foxe; Casting, Bernard Telsey, Will Cantler, David Vaccari; Dolby; Color; Rated R; 90 minutes; Release date: October 27, 2000. CAST: Kim Director (Kim), Jeffrey Donovan (Jeff), Erica Leerhsen (Erica), Tristen Skyler (Tristen), Stephen Barker Turner (Stephen), Bruce Reed, Lynda Millard, Deb Burgoyne, Andrea Cox

My Generation © Cabin Creek Films

Heather Artinian in *Sound and Fury* © Artistic License

Erica Leerhsen, Stephen Barker Turner, Tristen Skyler, Jeffrey Donovan in *Book of Shadows* © Artisan Entertainment

Sandrine Holt, Hill Harper in *Loving Jezebel* © Shooting Gallery

(Burkittsville Residents), Joe Berlinger, Sara Phillips (Burkittsville Tourists), Lanny Flaherty (Sheriff Cravens), Pete Burris, Ed Sala, Robert M. Kelly (MBI Men), Briton Green, Erik Jensen (Stoners), Peggy K. Chang, Tony Tsang, Anja Baron (Foreigners), Kevin Murray (Doctor), Keira Naughton (Nurse), Lauren Hulsey (Eileen Treacle), Tyler Zeisloft, Richard Kirkwood, Justin Fair (Teenagers), Raynor Scheine (Rustin Parr), Brilane Bowman (Ham Lady), Kennen Sisco (Peggy), Dina Napoli (Reporter, WBAL), Landra Booker (Reporter, Fox 45), Jacqui Allen (Reporter), Sloane Brown (Reporter, WJZ 13), Kurt Loder, Chuck Scarborough (Themselves)

THE SCULPTRESS (Phaedra) Producer, Tony DiDio; Executive Producer, Denis Shusterman; Director/Screenplay, Ian Merrick; Photography, David Scardina; Editor, Jeffery Stephens; Designer, Don Day; Costumes, Marianna Astrom de Fina; Music, Tim Jones; Casting, Erica Arnold, Mia Levinson; a Plus Entertainment presentation of a D&S Screen Production; Dolby; Color; Rated R; 96 minutes; Release date: October 27, 2000. CAST: Jeff Fahey (Dobie), Patrick Bauchau (Prof. Giraud), Katie Wright (Sarah), Emmanuelle Vaugier (Sylvie), Allen Cutler (Chris), Vivis Colombetti (Madame Cleo), Miriam Babin (Mrs. Borelli), Katriona Browne (Isabelle), Johanna Falls (Marie), Bridget Nelson (Celeste), Stone Man (Bill)

LOVING JEZEBEL (Shooting Gallery) Producer, David Lancaster; Director/Screenplay, Kwyn Bader; Photography, Horacio Marquinez; Designer, Franckie Diago; Editor, Tom McArdle; Music, Tony Prendatt; Line Producer, Franny Baldwin; Costumes, Arjun Bhasin; Casting, Billy Hopkins, Suzanne Smith, Kerry Barden, Mark Bennett; a Universal Focus and Shooting Gallery presentation of a Starz! Encore Entertainment production in association with Bet Movies of a David Lancaster production; Dolby; Color; Rated R; 85 minutes; Release date: October 27, 2000. CAST: Hill Harper (Theodorous), Justin Pierre Edmund (Little Theodorus), David Moscow (Gabe), Laurel Holloman (Samantha), Nicole Ari Parker (Frances), Sandrine Holt (Mona), Lysa Aya Trenier (June), Andre Blake (Necco), Jean-Christophe Emo (Francois), Larry Gilliard, Jr. (Walter), John Doman (Pop Melville), Phylicia Rashad (Alice Melville), Elisa Donovan (Salli McDonnell), Heather Gottlieb (Nina Clarise), Diandra Newlin (Nikki Noodleman), Faith Greer (Mrs. Harp), Barry Yourgrau (Mr. Leone), Eugene Ashe (Man in Car), Makeda Christodoulos, Abigail Rose Revasch (Israeli Girls), Judah Domke, Jason Hefter (Customers), Gregory Grove (Waiter), Angel Brown (Rita), Ray Frazier (Skip), Crystal Rose (Beth), Bryant Clifford (Steve)

COLLECTORS (Abject Films) Producers, Julian P. Hobbs, Christopher Trent; Director, Julian P. Hobbs; Photography, Nigel Kinnings; Editor, Ralph Pioreck; Music Director, Don Dinicola; Color; Not rated; 80 minutes; Release date: October 27, 2000. Documentary on the artwork of various serial killers and those who collect it, featuring Rick Stanton, Tobias Allen, Harold Schechter, Elmer Wayne Henley, Walter Scott, Andy Kahan, Joe Coleman

DOWN 'N DIRTY (Po' Boy Film) Producers, Roger Mende, Fred Williamson, Linda Williamson; Director, Fred Williamson; Photography, James M. LeGoy; Music, Johnny Ross; from Golden Lion productions; Rated R; 102 minutes; Release date: October 27, 2000. CAST: Fred Williamson (Dakota Smith), Bubba Smith (Det. Jerry Cale), Gary Busey (D.A. Mickey Casey), Tony Lo Bianco (Det. Dan Ward), Beverly Johnson (Sandra Collins), Randy J. Goodwin (Nick Gleem), David Carradine (Gil Garner), Charles Napier (Capt. Jerry Teller), Andrew Divoff (Jimmy), Suzanne von Schaack (Lisa Stevens), David Novak (Det. Bob Mahoney), Lou Casal (Det. Pete Jones), Rod McCary (Chief Block), Frank Pesce (Kingpin), Sam Jones (Stanton James), DC Ford (Detective)

MERCY STREETS (Providence) Producers, Kevin Downes, Bobby Downes, Geoff Ludlow, Jon Gunn, David White, Travis Mann; Executive Producers, Marta Wells, Dan Wells, Karen Bowerman, Greg Bowerman; Director, Jon Gunn; Screenplay, John Mann, Jon Gunn; Photography, Chris Magee; Designer, Michael Pearce; Costumes, Mila Hermanovski; Editors, Jeffrey Lee Hollis, Jon Gunn, Brett Winn; from Signal Hill Pictures; Dolby; FotoKem color; Rated PG-13; 106 minutes; Release date: October 31, 2000. CAST: David White (John/Jeremiah), Eric Roberts (Rome), Cynthia Watros (Samantha), Shiek Mahmud-Bey (Tex), Robert La Sardo (TJ), Stacy Keach (Father Tom), Lawrence Taylor (Father Dan), Koji Kataoki (Mr. Takashi), Kevin Downes (Peter), Lisa Furst (Sunny), Mark Twogood (Prison Guard), Bill Capizzi (Hot Dog Vendor), Brad Heller (Vendor's Buddy), Michael Villani (Sgt. Griffin), Brian C. Bennetts (Concerned Driver), Lory Bennetts, Nancy Bennetts (Neighborhood Couple), Robert Lyon Rasner (Concerned Passerby), Brendan Norton (Voice of Young John/Jeremiah), Nell Buttolph (Woman in Red Dress), Jon Ramos, Jasun Ramos (Young Twins), Rachel Perlin, Alexis Peña, Hailey Pemelton, Rachel Pemelton (Kids on Street), Trevor Ludlow, Trevor Dodge (Young Boys in Street)

David White, Stacy Keach in *Mercy Streets* © Providence

Ben Gazzara, Rita Moreno in *Blue Moon* © Paradise Pictures/Castle Hill

Carrie-Anne Moss, Val Kilmer in *Red Planet*
© Warner Bros./Village Roadshow

BLUE MOON (Castle Hill) Producers, Ronnie Shapiro, Sylvia Caminer; Executive Producer, Norman Chanes; Director/Screenplay, John A. Gallagher; Story, Stephen Carducci; Photography, Craig DiBona; Designer, Wing Lee; Costumes, Catherine Thomas; Editors, Craig McKay, Naomi Geraghty; Music, Stephen Endelman; Casting, Bonnie Timmermann, Judy Henderson; a Paradise Pictures presentation of a Blue Moon production; Technicolor; Rated PG-13; 89 minutes; Release date: November 3, 2000. CAST: Ben Gazzara (Frank), Rita Moreno (Maggie), Alanna Ubach (Peggy), Brian Vincent (Mac), Burt Young (Bobby), Vincent Pastore (Joey), Heather Matarazzo (Donna), Victor Argo (Tony), David Thornton (Frank's Father), Lillo Brancato, Jr. (Pete), Shawn Elliot (The Ambassador), Maggie Wagner (Angela)

LOOKING FOR AN ECHO (Regent) Producers, Martin Davidson, Paul Kurta; Director, Martin Davidson; Executive Producer, Steve Tisch; Screenplay, Jeffrey Goldenberg, Robert Held, Martin Davidson; Photography, Charles Minsky; Editor, Jerrold L. Ludwig; Music Supervisor, Kenny Vance; Associate Producers, Tim Christenson, Joel Tuber; Co-Producers, Mary Jo Slater, Anthony Esposito; a Steve Tisch/Paul Kurta production; Dolby; Color; Rated R; 97 minutes; Release date: November 10, 2000. CAST: Armand Assante (Vince), Diane Venora (Joanne), Joe Grifasi (Vic), Tom Mason (Augie), Tony Denison (Nappy), Johnny Williams (Pooch), Edoardo Ballerini (Anthony), Christy Romano (Tina), David Vadim (Tommie), Monica Trombetta (Francine), David Margulies (Dr. Ludwig), Fanni Green (Nurse Fowler), Paz De La Huerta (Nicole), Gena Scriva (Arlene), Gayle Scott (Renee), Llana Levine (Sandi), Cleveland Still (Dereuct), Peter Jacobson (Marty Pearlstein), Murray Winstock (Orchid Blue Lead), Amanda Homi, Machan Notarile

(Orchid Blue Singers), Michael Cooke Kendrick (Jason), Kresimir "Crash" Novakovic (Waiter), Mike J. Alpert (Street Vendor), Uri "Teddy" Dallal (Public Access Drums), Jorge Pequero (Public Access Bass), Eva Giangi (Public Access Keyboard), Lisa France (Nuftse), Rick Faugno (Young Vince), Johnny Giacalone (Young Vic), Tommy Michaels (Young Augie), Eric Meyersfield (Young Nappy), Danny Gerard (Young Pooch), Norbert Butz (Vocals for Anthony), Gary Bonner, Eddie Hokenson, Kenny Vance, Murray Weinstock (Singers)

RED PLANET (Warner Bros.) Producers, Mark Canton, Bruce Berman, Jorge Saralegui; Executive Producers, Charles J.D. Schissel, Andrew Mason; Director, Antony Hoffman; Screenplay, Chuck Pfarrer, Jonathan Lemkin; Story, Chuck Pfarrer; Photography, Peter Suschitzky; Designer, Owen Paterson; Costumes, Kym Barrett; Editors, Robert K. Lambert, Dallas S. Pruett; Music, Graeme Revell; Visual Effects Supervisor, Jeffrey A. Okun; Casting, Lora Kennedy; a Mark Canton production, presented in association with Village Roadshow Pictures and NPV Entertainment; Dolby; Panavision; Technicolor; Rated PG-13; 105 minutes; Release date: November 10, 2000. CAST: Val Kilmer (Gallagher), Tom Sizemore (Burchenal), Carrie-Anne Moss (Kate Bowman), Benjamin Bratt (Santen), Simon Baker (Pettengil), Terence Stamp (Chantilas), Jessica Morton, Caroline Bossi (Website Fans), Bob Neill (Voice of Houston)

REBELS WITH A CAUSE (Zeitgeist) Producer/Director/Screenplay/Editor, Helen Garvy; Photography, Emiko Omori; Associate Producer, Robert Pardun; a Shire Films production; Color; Not rated; 110 minutes; Release date: November 10, 2000. Documentary on the social

Joe Grifasi, Edoardo Ballerini, Armand Assante in *Looking for an Echo*
© Regent Entertainment

Rebels With a Cause © Zeitgeist Films

Gertrude Elion in *Me and Isaac Newton* © First Look Pictures

Angel Moore, Mack Moore in *Angel's Ladies*
© Picture This! Entertainment

changes of the sixties, ranging from the civil rights movement to the protests against the United States' involvement in the Vietnam War, featuring Jane Adams, Bill Ayers, Carolyn Craven, Carl Davidson, Bernardine Dohrn, Alice Embree, Dick Flacks, Todd Gitlin, Carol Glassman, Juan Gonzalez, Alan Haber, Casey Hayden, Tom Hayden, Sharon Jeffrey Lehrer, Mark Kleiman, Sue Eanet Klonsky, Steve Max, Carl Oglesby, Robert Pardun, Bob Ross, Vivian Leburg Rothstein, Judy Schiffer Perez, Jeff Shero Nightbyrd, Mike Spiegel, Marilyn Salzman Webb, Elizabeth Stanley, Cathy Wilkerson, Junius Williams

ME AND ISAAC NEWTON (First Look) Producers, Jody Patton, Eileen Gregory; Director, Michael Apted; Photography, Maryse Alberti; Line Producer, Steven Wren; Editor, Suanne Rostock; Music, Patrick Seymour; a Clear Blue Sky production, presented by Paul G. Allen; Color; Not rated; 105 minutes; Release date: November 10, 2000. Documentary on seven distinguished modern day scientists, Gertrude Elion, Ashok Gadgil, Michio Kaku, Maja Mataric, Steven Pinker, Karol Sikora, Patricia Wright.

ANGEL'S LADIES (Cowboy Booking) Producers, Doug Lindeman, Straw Weisman; Director/Conceived by, Doug Lindeman; Executive Producer, Ron Habakus; Videography, Brad Laven, Doug Lindeman, Rick Lunn; Editor, Rick Lunn; a FilmKitchen.com in association with Marquee Productions presentation; Color; Not rated; 80 minutes; Release date: November 10, 2000. Documentary on "Angel's Ladies," a brothel owned by former funeral parlor owners Mack and Angel Moore.

THE WEEKEND (Strand) Producer, Ian Benson; Executive Producers, Pippa Cross, Janette Day; Director/Screenplay, Brian Skeet; Based on the novel by Peter Cameron; Line Producer, Richard Turner; Photography, Ron Fortunato; Designer, Bob Shaw; Costumes, Edi Giguere; Music, Dan Jones, Sarah Class; Editor, Chris Wyatt; a Granada presentation of a Lunatics & Lovers/Granada Film production; Color; Not rated; 97 minutes; Release date: November 22, 2000. CAST: Gena Rowlands (Laura Ponti), Deborah Kara Unger (Marian Kerr), Brooke Shields (Nina), David Conrad (Lyle), James Duval (Robert), Gary Dourdan (Thierry), D.B. Sweeney (Tony), Jared Harris (John Kerr)

POOR WHITE TRASH (Hollywood Independents) Producers, Mark Roberts, Lorena David; Executive Producer, Michael Lawrence; Director/Screenplay, Michael Addis; Co-Producer, Justin Conley; Photography, Peter Kowalski; Designer, Clare Brown; Editor, Tom McArdle; Costumes, Luellen Harper Thomas; Music, Tree Adams; Casting, Katy Wallin; a Kingsize Entertainment production, presented in association with Filmstar; Color; Not rated; 86 minutes; Release date: December 1, 2000. CAST: Sean Young (Linda Bronco), William Devane (Ron Lake), Jason London (Brian Ross), Tony Denman (Mike Bronco), Jacob Tierney (Lennie Lake), Jaime Pressly (Sandy Lake), M. Emmet Walsh (Judge Pike), Tim Kazurinsky (Carlton Rasmeth), Richard Livingston (Prosecutor Machado), Kerri Randles (Suzi), Danielle Harris (Suzy), Patrick Renna (Ricky Kenworthy), Craig Patton (Ken Kenworthy), Todd Babcock (Darrin Haggard), Fred Belford (Cops), Charles Soloman, Jr. (Baliff)

Deborah Kara Unger in *The Weekend* © Strand Releasing

Jacob Tierney, Sean Young, William Devane, Tony Denman
in *Poor White Trash* © Hollywood Independents

Henry Thomas in *A Good Baby*

Justin Whalin, Marlon Wayans, Zoe McLellan in *Dungeons & Dragons*
© New Line Cinema

A GOOD BABY (Independent Feature Project/Film Society of Lincoln Center) Producers, Lianne Halfon, Tom Carouso; Director/Screenplay/Editor, Katherine Dieckmann; Story, Leon Rooke; Photography, Jim Denault; Designer, Debbie DeVilla; Costumes, Kathryn Nixon; Casting, Avy Kaufman; Music, David Mansfield; a Kardana Films presentation; Dolby; DuArt color; Not rated; 98 minutes; Release date: December 1, 2000. CAST: Henry Thomas (Raymond Toker), David Strathairn (Truman Lester), Cara Seymour (Josephine Priddy), Danny Nelson (Hindmarch), Jayne Morgan (Sarah), Allison Glenn (Sister), Jerry Foster (Trout), Jerry Rushing (Wallace), Emilie Jacobs (Lena), Hannah Grady (Baby), Danny Vinson (Cal), Lance Holland, Bob Post (Men Fixing Truck), Palma Kauppert (Woman Shaking Rug), April Chapman (Farm Woman), Chester Ervin, Chris Levi (Men in Passing Car), Rhoda Griffis (Mother in Shack), Caroline Hunter Wallis (Mother's Baby), Kia Baden, Alexandra Gates, Christen Glenn, Kendal Kulp (Mother's Children), Neva Howell (Woman at Mailboxes), Toby Huss (Voice of AmeriShine), Leslie Riley (Suburban Customer), Ashley & Andrea Roberts (Suburban Baby), Emily Johnson-Erday (Ashley Jean), Ralph Gates (Man on Tractor), Bonnie Mackenzie (Customer in Cal's), Nathaniel & Perry Cheremka (Additional Good Babies)

PANIC (Roxie) Producers, Andrew Lazar, Lori Miller, Matt Cooper; Executive Producer, David Cooper; Director/Screenplay, Henry Bromell; Photography, Jeffry Jur; Designer, Dan Bishop; Costumes, Susan Matheson; Editors, Lynzee Klingman, Cindy Mollo; Music, Brian Tyler; Casting, Matthew Barry; a Vault/Mad Chance production; Dolby;

Widescreen; Color; Rated R; 88 minutes; Release date: December 1, 2000. CAST: William H. Macy (Alex), John Ritter (Josh Parks), Neve Campbell (Sarah), Donald Sutherland (Michael), Tracey Ullman (Martha), Barbara Bain (Deidre), David Dorfman (Sammy), Tina Lifford (Dr. Leavitt), Bix Barnaba (Louie), Thomas Curtis (Alex at 7), Andrea Taylor (Candice), Stewart J. Zully (Eddie), Miguel Sandoval (Larson), Nicholle Tom (Tracy), Erica Ortega (Rachel), Greg Pitts (Alex at 20), Steve Moreno (Sean), Steve Valentine, Nick Cassavetes (This movie made its U.S. premiere on Cinemax cable channel on Aug. 27, 2000).

DUNGEONS & DRAGONS (New Line Cinema) Producers, Courtney Solomon, Kia Jam, Tom Hammel; Executive Producers, Joel Silver, Allan Zeman, Nelson Leong; Director, Courtney Solomon; Screenplay, Topper Lilien, Carroll Cartwright; Based on the property owned by Wizards of the Coast Inc.; Co-Producers, Station X Studios, LLC, Steve Richards; Photography, Doug Milsome; Designer, Bryce Perrin; Editor, Caroline Ross; Costumes, Barbara Lane; Music, Justin Caine Burnett; Visual Effects Supervisor, Joan Collins Carey; Special Mechanical Effects Supervisor, George Gibbs; Casting, Elisa Goodman, Abra Edelman, Jeremy Zimmerman; a Sweetpea Entertainment/Silver Pictures production; Dolby; Deluxe color; Rated PG-13; 107 minutes; Release date: December 8, 2000. CAST: Justin Whalin (Ridley Freeborn), Marlon Wayans (Snails), Jeremy Irons (Profion), Zoe McLellan (Marina Pretensa), Thora Birch (Empress Savina), Kristen Wilson (Norda), Richard O'Brien (Xilus), Tom Baker (Halvarth), Lee Arenberg (Elwood Gutworthy), Edward Jewesbury (Vildan Vildir), Robert Miano (Azmath),

William H. Macy in *Panic* © Roxie Releasing

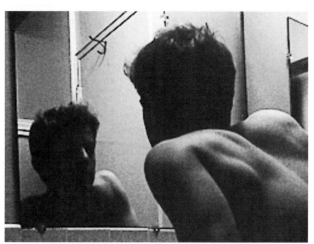

Erik MacArthur in *Boys Life 3* © Strand Releasing

Bill Bourier, Jennifer Christopher in *Strippers*
© Ameer Jorge Prods.

Dwight Yoakam, Bridget Fonda in *South of Heaven, West of Hell*
© Phaedra Cinema

Bruce Payne (Damodar), Tomas Havrlik (Mage), Martin Astles, Matthew O'Toole (Orcs), David O'Kelly (Three Eyes), Kia Jam, Nicolas Rochette, David Mandis (Thieves), Robert Henny (Crimson Brigade), Stanislav Ondricek (Another Mage), Roman Hemala (Council Mage), Andrew Blau, Marta Urbanova (Elves), Jiri Machacek (Loyalist General)

BOYS LIFE 3 (Strand) *Majorettes in Space:* Director/Screenplay, David Fourier; Photography, Pierre Stoeber; Editor, Fabrice Rouaud; a Haut et Court production with the support of Procirep; CAST: Cleo Delacruz, Aurelien Bianco, Jean-Marc Delacruz, Elise Laurent, Olivier Laville, Philippe Bianco.*hITCH:* Director/Screenplay, Bradley Rust Gray; Photography, Sarah Levy, Bradley Rust Gray; Music, Mike Rechner; CAST: Drew Wood (Jason), Jason Herman (Porp). *Inside Out:* Producers, Thom Fennessey, Jason Gould; Director/Screenplay, Jason Gould; Photography, Sharone Meir; Editor, Christopher Holmes; Music, Michael Skloff; CAST: Alexis Arquette (Adam), Katie Asner (Susan), Charlie Brill (Winkler), Christina Crawford (Herself), Anne DeSalvo (Phyllis), Steve Flynn (Michael), Elliott Gould (Aaron's Father), Jason Gould (Aaron), Sam Gould (Simon), Tara Karsian (Woman at Group), Jordan Ladd (Summer), Ken Lerner (Judge Levin), Jon Polito (Paparazzi), Luis Raul (Autograph Seeker), Judy Toll (Rochelle). *Just One Time:* Producers, Exile Ramirez, Lane Janger; Director/Screenplay, Lane Janger; Photography, Tim Naylor; Editor, Francois Keraudren; Music, David Frank; CAST: Joelle Carter (Amy), Guillermo Diaz (Victor), Jennifer Esposito (Michelle), Lane Janger (Anthony). *$30:* Producers, Line Postmyr, Gregory Cooke, Christopher Landon; Director, Gregory Cooke; Screenplay, Christopher Landon; Photography, Dermott Downs; Editor, Lorne Morris; Music, Peter Rafelson; CAST: Sara Gilbert (Emily), Erik MacArthur (Scott), Greg Itzin (Scott's Father); Color; Not rated; 80 minutes; Release date: December 8, 2000.

STRIPPERS (Hollywood Independents) Producers, Jorge Ameer, Janine Gosselin, Marianne Marx, John Greenlaw, Rochelle Jefferson; Executive Producers, Jorge Ameer, John Greenlaw; Director/Screenplay/Designer, Jorge Ameer; Photography, Aaron Kirsch, Gary Tachell; Costumes, Elize Salzman; Music, Paul McCarty; Editor, Rollin Olson; Cast ing, Antonio Saviour; Presented in association with A.J. Productions; Color; Not rated; 75 minutes; Release date: December 8, 2000. CAST: Tony Tucci, John Greenlaw (Alan Gardner), Jorge Ameer (Kevin), Kerrie Clark (Susan), Jeff Seal (Harry), JD Roberto (David), Linda Graybel (Violet), Kirsten Holly Smith (Bank Rep), Jane Grogan (Betty), Bob Nellis (Tadpole), Elena Zaretsky (Nurse), Danny Rhosenfeld (Mark), Linda Nile (Psychic), Michel Swiney (Repo Man), Lisa Marx (Credit Rep), Jennifer Christopher, Bill Bourier (Models), Shaun McDowell (Security), Wesley Paris (Parking Attendant), Smitty Smith (Bar Owner), Chika Marx (Barmaid), Scott Kaufman (Bar Security)

SOUTH OF HEAVEN, WEST OF HELL (Phaedra) Producers, Gray Frederickson, Darris Hatch; Director/Music, Dwight Yoakam; Screenplay, Dwight Yoakam, Stan Bertheaud; Story, Dwight Yoakam, Dennis Hackin, Otto Felix; Photography, James Glennon; Designer, Siobhan Roome; Costumes, Le Dawson; Editor, Robert A. Ferretti; Casting, Linda Phillips-Palo, Robert McGee; Dolby; Color; Rated R; 131 minutes; Release date: December 15, 2000. CAST: Dwight Yoakam (Valentine Casey), Vince Vaughn (Taylor), Billy Bob Thornton (Brigadier Smalls), Bridget Fonda (Adalyne Dunfries), Peter Fonda (Shoshonee Bill), Paul Reubens (Arvid), Bud Cort (Agent Otts), Bo Hopkins (Doc Angus Dunfries), Matt Clark (Burl Dunfries), Noble Willingham (Sheriff Harris), Scott Wilson (Clete Monroe), Luke Askew (Leland), Joe Unger (Nogales), Michael Jeter (Uncle Jude), Ritchie Montgomery (Harold), Matt Maloy (Harvey), Natalie Canerday (Sissy), Otto Felix (Tim "The Wrist" Simms), Joe Ely (Petrified Paul), Terry McIlvain (U.S. Christmas), Amber Taylor (Tess Bonaventure), Charles Burba (Preacher), Audrey Lowe (Jenny), Maria Daleo (Heddie Monroe), Marta Santamaria (Rosana), Warren Zevon (Babcock), Corky Wimberly (Jesco Lynch), Flecia Beard (Margaret), Warner McKay (Eli Combs)

HOOVER (Pamplin-Fisher Co.) Producers, Robert W. Fisher, Rick Pamplin; Executive Producers, Ernest Borgnine, William L. Whitacare; Co-Producers, Joseph T. Lyons, Matt Green; Co-Executive Producers, Lynda Bensky, Harry Flynn, Pamela Sweet Flynn; Director, Rick Pamplin; Screenplay, Robert W. Fisher, Rick Pamplin; Photography, Stephen F. Campbell; Editor, Oliver Peters; Music, Rick Silanskas; Art Director, Holly Payberg; Century III Surroundsound; Color; Not rated; 93 minutes; Release date: December 25, 2000. CAST: Ernest Borgnine (J. Edgar Hoover), Cartha D. "Deke" Deloach (Interviewee)

PROMISING NEW ACTORS OF 2000

Jamie Bell
(*Billy Elliot*)

Erika Christensen
(*Traffic*)

Kate Hudson
(*Almost Famous, Dr. T & The Women, Gossip*)

Colin Farrell
(*Tigerland*)

Patrick Fugit
(*Almost Famous*)

Sanaa Lathan
(*Love and Basketball*)

Amanda Peet
(*Isn't She Great, The Whole Nine Yards, Whipped*)

Adam Garcia
(*Coyote Ugly, Bootmen*)

Hugh Jackman
(*X-Men*)

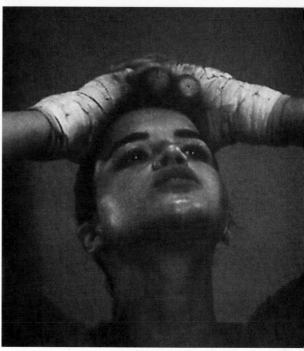

Michelle Rodriguez
(*Girlfight*)

Zhang Ziyi
(*Crouching Tiger, Hidden Dragon*)

Mark Ruffalo
(*You Can Count on Me*)

ACADEMY AWARDS FOR 2000

PRESENTED SUNDAY, MARCH 25, 2001

Russell Crowe

Russell Crowe, Djimon Hounsou

Gladiator © Dreamworks LLC/Universal Pictures

GLADIATOR

Connie Nielsen, Russell Crowe

Joaquin Phoenix (center)

Russell Crowe

(DREAMWORKS/UNIVERSAL) Producers, Douglas Wick, David Franzoni, Branko Lustig; Executive Producers, Walter F. Parkes, Laurie MacDonald; Director, Ridley Scott; Screenplay, David Franzoni, John Logan, William Nicholson; Story, David Franzoni; Photography, John Mathieson; Designer, Arthur Max; Editor, Pietro Scalia; Costumes, Janty Yates; Music, Hans Zimmer, Lisa Gerrard; Visual Effects Supervisor, John Nelson; Stunts, Phil Neilson; Casting, Louis DiGiaimo; a Douglas Wick production in association with Scott Free Productions; Dolby; Super 35 Widescreen; Technicolor; Rated R; 154 minutes; Release date: May 5, 2000.

CAST

Maximus ....Russell Crowe
Commodus...Joaquin Phoenix
Lucilla..Connie Nielsen
Proximo..Oliver Reed
Marcus Aurelius...Richard Harris
Gracchus ....Derek Jacobi
Juba...Djimon Hounsou
Falco..David Schofield
Gaius..John Shrapnel
Quintus ....Tomas Arana
Hagen...Ralf Moeller
Lucius...Spencer Treat Clark
Cassius ....David Hemmings
Cicero ....Tommy Flanagan
Tiger ....Sven-Ole Thorsen
Slave Trader ....Omid Djalili
Praetorian Officer..Nicholas McGaughey
Scribe ....Chris Kell
Assassins ....Tony Curran, Mark Lewis
Valerius..John Quinn
Praetorian Guard #1 ....Alun Raglan
Engineer...David Bailie
German Leader...Chick Allen
Giant Man...Dave Nicholls
Rome Trainer #1 ....Al Hunter Ashton
Narrator..Billy Dowd
Lucius' Attendant...Ray Calleja
Maximus' Wife ....Giannina Facio
Maximus' Son ....Giorgio Cantarini

Realizing that his father, the emperor, favors popular Roman general Maximus as his successor, the power crazy Commodus orders the general and his family to be executed. When Maximus escapes his fate, he is sold into slavery where he becomes a gladiator, thereby paving the way for his revenge. This was the final film of Oliver Reed who died during production on May 2, 1999.

2000 Academy Award-winner for Best Picture, Actor (Russell Crowe), Visual Effects, Sound, and Costume Design. This film received additional Oscar nominations for supporting actor (Joaquin Phoenix), director, cinematography, editing, original screenplay, original score, and art direction.

Oliver Reed, Ralf Moeller, Djimon Hounsou, Russell Crowe

Connie Nielsen, Joaquin Phoenix

Joaquin Phoenix, Russell Crowe

Russell Crowe

Richard Harris, Russell Crowe

RUSSELL CROWE

in *Gladiator* © DreamWorks LLC/Universal Pictures
ACADEMY AWARD FOR BEST ACTOR OF 2000

JULIA ROBERTS

in *Erin Brockovich* © Universal Studios
ACADEMY AWARD FOR BEST ACTRESS OF 2000

BENICIO DEL TORO

in *Traffic* © USA Films
ACADEMY AWARD FOR BEST SUPPORTING ACTOR OF 2000

MARCIA GAY HARDEN

in *Pollock* © Sony Pictures Entertainment, Inc.
ACADEMY AWARD FOR BEST SUPPORTING ACTRESS OF 2000

ACADEMY AWARD NOMINEES FOR BEST ACTOR

Javier Bardem in *Before Night Falls*

Tom Hanks in *Cast Away*

Ed Harris in *Pollock*

Geoffrey Rush in *Quills*

ACADEMY AWARD NOMINEES FOR BEST ACTRESS

Joan Allen in *The Contender*

Juliette Binoche in *Chocolat*

Ellen Burstyn in *Requiem for a Dream*

Laura Linney in *You Can Count on Me*

ACADEMY AWARD NOMINEES FOR BEST SUPPORTING ACTOR

Jeff Bridges in *The Contender*

Willem Dafoe in *Shadow of the Vampire*

Albert Finney in *Erin Brockovich*

Joaquin Phoenix in *Gladiator*

ACADEMY AWARD NOMINEES FOR BEST SUPPORTING ACTRESS

Judi Dench in *Chocolat*

Kate Hudson in *Almost Famous*

Frances McDormand in *Almost Famous*

Julie Walters in *Billy Elliot*

ACADEMY AWARD WINNER FOR BEST FOREIGN LANGUAGE FILM

Zhang Ziyi, Chow Yun Fat

Michelle Yeoh

CROUCHING TIGER, HIDDEN DRAGON

(SONY PICTURES CLASSICS) Producers, Bill Kong, Hsu Li-kong, Ang Lee; Executive Producers, James Schamus, David Linde; Director, Ang Lee; Screenplay, Wang Hui Ling, James Schamus, Tsai Kuo Jung; Based on the novel by Wang Du Lu; Co-Producers, Zheng Quan Gang, Dong Ping; Associate Producers, Philip Lee, Chui Po Chu; Photography, Peter Pau; Designer/Costumes, Tim Yip; Editor, Tim Squyres; Action Choreographer, Yuen Wo Ping; Music, Tan Dun; Cello Solos, Yo-Yo Ma; Theme Song *A Love Before Time* by Jorge Calandrelli and Tan Dun (music), James Schamus (lyric)/Performed by Coco Lee; Martial Arts Coordinators, Ku Huen Chiu, Wong Kim Wai; Special Visual Effects, MVFX, Los Angeles; a Columbia Pictures Film Production Asia presentation in association with Good Machine International of an Edko Films, Zoom Hunt International production in collaboration with China Film Co-Production Corp. and Asian Audio Visual and Cultural Co., Ltd.; Hong Kong-Tiawanese; Dolby; Super 35 Widescreen; Technicolor; Rated PG-13; 120 minutes; American release date: December 8, 2000

CAST

Li Mu Bai	Chow Yun Fat
Yu Shu Lien	Michelle Yeoh
Jen Yu	Zhang Ziyi
Lo	Chang Chen
Sir Te	Lung Sihung
Jade Fox	Cheng Pei Pei
Governor Yu	Li Fa Zeng
Bo	Gao Xian
Madam Yu	Hai Yan
Tsai	Wang Deming
May	Li Li
Auntie Wu	Huang Su Ying
De Lu	Zhang Jin Ting
Maid	Yang Rui
Gou Jun Pei	Li Kai
Gou Jun Sinung	Feng Jian Jua
Shop Owner	Du Zhen Xi
Captains	Xu Cheng Lin, Lin Feng
Gangster A	Wang Wen Sheng
Gangster B	Song Dong
Mi Biao	Ma Zhong Xuan
Fung Machete Chang	Li Bao Cheng
Monk Jing	Yang Yong De
Performers	Zhang Shao Jun, Ma Ning
Waiter	Zhu Jian Min
Homeless Man	Don Chang Sheng
Waitress	Shih Yi
Servant	Chen Bin
Nightman	Chang Sao Chen

Li Mu Bai, a powerful martial arts warrior intent on following a new path in life, bestows his legendary sword upon Sir Te, only to have it stolen by a mysterious thief who may be in league with the deadly Jade Fox.

2000 Academy Award-winner for Best Foreign Language Film, Cinematography, Art Direction, and Music Score. This film received additional Oscar nominations for picture, director, editing, screenplay adaptation, costume design, and original song (A Love Before Time).

Zhang Ziyi

Chang Chen

Zhang Ziyi, Michelle Yeoh

Zhang Ziyi

Michelle Yeoh

Zhang Ziyi, Chang Chen

Michelle Yeoh

INTO THE ARMS OF STRANGERS: STORIES OF THE KINDERTRANSPORT

(WARNER BROS.) Producer, Deborah Oppenheimer; Director/Screenplay, Mark Jonathan Harris; Photography, Don Lenzer; Editor, Kate Amend; Music, Lee Holdridge; Archival Researcher, Corrinne Collett; Narrator, Judi Dench; a Sabine Films production, in co-operation with the U.S. Holocaust Memorial Museum; Dolby; Black and white/color; Rated PG; 122 minutes; Release date: September 15, 2000. Documentary on the Kindertransport, Great Britain's effort during World War II to take in over 10,000 Jewish children from Germany, Austria, and Czechoslovakia.

2000 Academy Award-winner for Best Documentary Feature.

©Warner Bros. Pictures

TOP BOX OFFICE FILMS OF 2000

1. Dr. Seuss' How the Grinch Stole Xmas (Univ/Nov) $260,100,000
2. Cast Away (20th-DW/Dec) $233,540,000
3. Mission: Impossible 2 (Par/May).....................$214,140,000
4. Gladiator (DW-Univ/May)............................$187,610,000
5. What Women Want (Par/Dec) $182,760,000
6. The Perfect Storm (WB/Jun) $182,610,000
7. Meet the Parents (Univ-DW/Oct) $165,560,000
8. X-Men (20th/Jul) $157,230,000
9. Scary Movie (Mir/Jul) $156,870,000
10. What Lies Beneath (DW-20th/Jul) $155,390,000

Izabella Scorupco, Chris O'Donnell in *Vertical Limit*
©Columbia Pictures Industries, Inc.

Jim Carrey in Dr. Seuss' *How the Grinch Stole Christmas* ©Universal Studios

11. Dinosaur (BV/May)................................$137,560,000
12. Crouching Tiger, Hidden Dragon (Sony/Dec) $127,730,000
13. Charlie's Angels (Col/Nov)..........................$125,310,000
14. Erin Brockovich (Univ-Col/Mar)......................$125,100,000
15. Traffic (USA/Dec)..................................$124,100,000
16. Nutty Professor II: The Klumps (Univ/Jul) $122,210,000
17. Big Momma's House (20th/Jun) $117,440,000
18. Remember the Titans (BV/Sep) $115,610,000
19. The Patriot (Col/Jun) $113,310,000
20. Chicken Run (DW/Jun)..............................$106,400,000
21. Miss Congeniality (WB/Dec)........................$106,210,000
22. Gone in Sixty Seconds (BV/Jun) $101,600,000
23. Unbreakable (BV/Nov)..............................$94,950,000
24. Space Cowboys (WB/Aug)...........................$90,400,000
25. Me, Myself & Irene (20th/Jun) $90,300,000

26. The Emperor's New Groove (BV/Dec) $89,270,000
27. Scream 3 (Dimension-Mir/Feb) $88,100,000
28. U-571 (Univ/Apr) $77,130,000
29. Rugrats in Paris—The Movie (Par/Nov)...............$75,940,000
30. The Family Man (Univ/Dec)..........................$75,800,000
31. Hollow Man (Col/Aug)..............................$73,180,000
32. Chocolat (Mir/Dec)................................$71,160,000
33. Shaft (Par/Jun)...................................$70,180,000
34. Disney's The Kid (BV/Jul) $69,640,000
35. Road Trip (DW/May) $68,390,000
36. Bring It On (Univ/Aug)............................$68,380,000
37. Vertical Limit (Col/Dec) $68,340,000
38. 102 Dalmatians (BV/Nov) $66,910,000
39. The Cell (NL/Aug) $61,240,000
40. Rules of Engagement (Par/Apr) $61,100,000

Piper Perabo, Adam Garcia in *Coyote Ugly* ©Touchstone Pictures

Mel Gibson in *The Patriot* ©Columbia Pictures Industries, Inc.

41. Mission to Mars (BV/Mar) $60,810,000
42. Coyote Ugly (BV/Aug)..............................$60,710,000
43. Fantasia 2000 (BV/Jan)............................$60,520,000
44. Snow Day (Par/Feb) $59,970,000
45. The Whole Nine Yards (WB/Feb) $57,110,000
46. Next Friday (NL/Jan)..............................$57,200,000
47. Shanghai Noon (BV/May) $56,370,000
48. Romeo Must Die (WB/Mar) $55,800,000
49. Final Destination (NL/Mar) $53,340,000
50. Finding Forrester (Col/Dec) $51,710,000

51.	The Road to El Dorado (DW/Mar)	$50,870,000
52.	Men of Honor (20th/Nov)	$48,780,000
53.	Dude, Where's My Car? (20th/Dec)	$46,410,000
54.	The Tigger Movie (BV/Feb)	$45,480,000
55.	O Brother, Where Art Thou?(BV-Univ/Dec)	$45,100,000
56.	The Replacements (WB/Aug)	$44,700,000
57.	Frequency (NL/Apr)	$44,430,000
58.	Pokemon the Movie 2000 (WB/Jul)	$43,670,000
59.	The Beach (20th/Feb)	$39,610,000

Leonardo DiCaprio in *The Beach* ©20th Century Fox

60.	The Exorcist (WB/reissue, Sep)	$39,500,000
61.	Little Nicky (NL/Nov)	$39,380,000
62.	Pitch Black (USA/Feb)	$39,190,000
63.	The Original Kings of Comedy (Par/Aug)	$38,150,000
64.	Bedazzled (20th/Oct)	$37,830,000
65.	Autumn in New York (MGM/Aug)	$37,580,000
66.	Keeping the Faith (BV/Apr)	$36,820,000
67.	Bounce (Mir/Nov)	$36,810,000
68.	28 Days (Col/Apr)	$36,640,000
69.	Hanging Up (Col/Feb)	$35,750,000
70.	The Flintstones in Viva Rock Vegas (Univ/Apr)	$35,270,000
71.	The Skulls (Univ/Mar)	$35,100,000
72.	The 6th Day (Col/Nov)	$36,470,000
73.	Thirteen Days (NL/Dec)	$34,600,000
74.	My Dog Skip (WB/Jan)	$34,140,000
75.	Pay It Forward (WB/Oct)	$33,370,000

Brendan Fraser, Elizabeth Hurley in *Bedazzled* ©Twentieth Century Fox

Renée Zellweger in *Nurse Betty* ©Universal Studios

76.	Dracula 2000 (Mir/Dec)	$33,100,000
77.	Proof of Life (WB/Dec)	$32,580,000
78.	Almost Famous (DW/Sep)	$32,280,000
79.	Where the Heart Is (20th/Apr)	$32,100,000
80.	Return to Me (MGM/Apr)	$32,120,000
81.	The Legend of Bagger Vance (DW-20th/Nov)	$30,710,000
82.	The Art of War (WB/Aug)	$30,110,000
83.	Bless the Child (Par/Aug)	$30,100,000
84.	Snatch (Screen Gems/Dec)	$29,100,000
85.	The Watcher (Univ/Sep)	$28,710,000
86.	Love and Basketball (NL/Apr)	$26,630,000
87.	High Fidelity (BV/Mar)	$26,580,000
88.	The Adventures of Rocky & Bullwinkle (Univ/Jun)	$25,960,000
89.	Book of Shadows: Blair Witch 2 (Artisan/Oct)	$25,340,000
90.	Nurse Betty (USA/Sep)	$25,150,000
91.	Reindeer Games (Dim-Mir/Feb)	$22,920,000

Tobey Maguire in *Wonder Boys* ©Paramount Pictures Corp.

92.	Titan A.E. (20th/Jun)	$22,680,000
93.	Billy Elliot (Univ/Oct)	$21,770,000
94.	Battlefield Earth (WB/May)	$21,450,000
95.	Urban Legends: Final Cut (Col/Sep)	$21,430,000
96.	Down to You (Mir/Jan)	$19,970,000
97.	Boys and Girls (Mir/Jun)	$19,920,000
98.	Wonder Boys (Par/Feb)	$19,380,000
99.	Best in Show (WB/Sep)	$18,520,000
100.	The Ninth Gate (Artisan/Mar)	$18,440,000

FOREIGN FILMS RELEASED IN THE U.S. IN 2000

THE TERRORIST

(PHAEDRA CINEMA) Producers, Shree Prasad, Jit Joshi; Executive Producers, Ravi Sunil Doshi, Vikram Singh, Mark Burton; Director/Photography/Story, Santosh Sivan; Screenplay, Santosh Sivan, Ravi Deshpande, Vijay Deveshwar; Designer, Shyam Sunder; Editor, Sreekar Prasad; Music, Sonu Sisupal, Rajamani; a John Malkovich presentation of a Moderne Gallerie Motion Picture/WonderFilms in association with Indian Image Productions; Indian, 1998; Dolby; Gemini color; Not rated; 95 minutes; American release date: January 14, 2000

CAST

Malli	Ayesha Dharkar
Thyagu	Vishnu Vardhan
Perumal	Bhanu Prakash
Lover	K. Krishna
Leader	Sonu Sisupal
Lotus	Vishwas
Sumitra	Anuradha
Old Lady	Bhavani
Vasu	Parmeshwaran
Gopal	Gopal
Commando	Bala
Traitor	Saravana
Photographer	Anna Durai

and Kanya, Swetha, Sheela, Sarajini, Devi, Ishwarya (Terrorist Girls), Gop, Ramanan, Bablu, Shailesh, Shyam, Parthib (Boys)

Malli, a nineteen year old girl, is chosen for a coveted suicide mission in which she is instructed to assassinate a prominant politican, an assignment she begins to question as she draws closer to her target.

© Phaedra Cinema

Ewan McGregor

Ayesha Dharkar, Vishwas

EYE OF THE BEHOLDER

(DESTINATION) Producers, Nicolas Clermont, Tony Smith; Director/Screenplay, Stephan Elliott; Executive Producers, Hilary Shor, Mark Damon; Co-Producer, Al Clark; Line Producer, Manon Bougie; Photography, Guy Dufaux; Designer, Jean-Baptiste Tard; Costumes, Lizzy Gardiner; Music, Marius De Vries; Editor, Sue Blainey; Casting, Vera Miller, Nadia Rona; a Behaviour Worldwide in association with Village Roadshow-Ambridge Film Partnership presentation of a Hit &Run/Filmline International production; Canadian-British; Dolby; Super 35 Widescreen; Color; Rated R; 110 minutes; American release date: January 28, 2000

CAST

The Eye	Ewan McGregor
Joanna Eris	Ashley Judd
Alex	Patrick Bergin
Dr. Brault	Genevieve Bujold
Hilary	K.D. Lang
Gary	Jason Priestley
Lucy	Ann-Marie Brown, Kaitlin Brown
Mike	David Nerman
Paul	Steven McCarthy
Hugo	Vlasta Vrana
Nathy	Janine Theriault
Toohey	Don Jordan
Ms. Keenan	Maria Revelins

and Lisa Forget (Nurse), Gayle Garfinkle (HeadWaitress), Russell Yuen, Stephane Levasseur (Federal Agents), Al Vandecruys, Sam Stone (Alaskan Federal Agents), Mauro Venditelli (Boss), Josa Maule (Receptionist), Carole Collin (Secretary), Stephanie Sbrega (Sandra), Philip Le Maistre (Gas Attendant), Michel Perron (Fat Businessman), Maria Bircher (Waitress), Howard Bilerman (Waiter), Cara Reynolds (Young Joanna), Leonard Farlinger (Young Joanna's Father), Jason Baerg (Gay Man), Michelle Sweeney (Salvo), Donovan Reiter, Erik Johnson (Locals), Amanda Davis (Girl), Carl Crevier (Chauffeur), Dr. Erwin Goldberg (Doctor), Garth Gilker (Airport Guard), James Hieminga (Wade), Bob Brewster (Cop), Charles Powell (Prisoner), Thomas Karle (Fat Man), Louis Negin (Bartender), Al Clark (Redneck), Una Kay (Hilary's Mother), Merlee Shapiro (Reva Desk Clerk), Vera Miller, Nadia Rona (Tea Trolley Ladies)

The Eye, a lonely British intelligence agent is assigned to track a suspected blackmailer, Joanna Eris, a woman he becomes increasingly fascinated by once he realizes she is actually a murderer.

© Destination Film Distribution Company, Inc.

Godu Lama

Orgyen Tobgyal

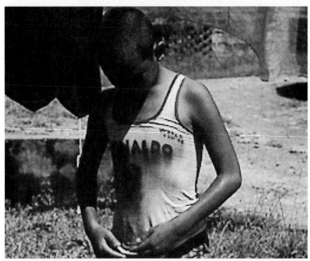

Jamyang Lodro

THE CUP

(FINE LINE FEATURES) Producers, Malcolm Watson, Raymond Steiner; Executive Producers, Hooman Majd, Jeremy Thomas; Director/Screenplay, Lhyentse Norbu; Photography, Paul Warren; Music, Douglas Mills, Phillip Beazley; Editor, John Scott; Designer, Raymond Steiner; a Palm Pictures presentation of a Coffee Stain production; Bhutanese-Australian, 1999; Dolby; Fujicolor; Rated G; 93 minutes; American release date: January 28, 2000

CAST

Geko	Orgyen Tobgyal
Lodo	Neten Chokling
Orgyen	Jamyang Lodro
Abbot	Lama Chonjor
Old Lama	Godu Lama
Tibetan Layman	Thinley Nudi
Cook Monk	Kungang
Palden	Kunsang Nyima
Nyima	Pema Tshundup
Vajra Master	Dzigar Kongtrul
TV Shop Owner	Dhan Pat Singh
Abbot's Attendant	Oga
Taxi Driver	Raj Baboon
Sleeping Monk	Jamyang Nyima

and Pema Wangchen, Namgyal Wangchuk (Storytelling Monks), Dundrup Gyamtso (Tea Monk), Orgyen Tsering (Football Can Monk), Rigzin Wangchuk (TV Watch Monk), Palden Gyatso, Ngawang Gelek (Satellite Dish Monks), Kelsang (Magazine Monk), Tupten Loday, Drakpa Tenzin, Gaday Tsering (Lights Out Monks), Cheying Pading (Leather Sandal Monk), Pema Kunchap (Tractor Monk), Tracy Mann (Newsreader), Shanti Steiner (Aerobics Instructors), Dickey Wangmo (Tibetan Woman—Voice Over), Pema Yonten (Tibetan TV Bouncer)

Palden, a new arrival at a Tibetan monestary, is surprised to find that many of its members are obsessed soccer fans, to a point where one of its more rebellious members has devised an elaborate scheme to see the 1998 World Cup final.

© Fine Line Features

Jamyang Lodro

OUTLAW!

(ADRIANA CHIESA ENTERPRISES) Producer, Gianfranco Piccioli; Executive Producer, Mino Barbera; Director/Story, Enzo Monteleone; Screenplay, Enzo Monteleone, Angelo Orlando; Based on the book *Ormai è fatta!: Cronaca di un'evasione* (*In the Bag!: Chronicle of an Escape*) by Horst Fantazzini; Photography, Arnaldo Catinari; Designer, Simona Garotta; Costumes, Andrea Viotti; Editor, Cecilia Zanuso; Music, Pivio & Aldo de Scalzi; a Hera International Film production in collaboration with RAI-Radiotelevisione Italiana; Italian, 1999; Color; Not rated; 95 minutes; American release date: February 2, 2000

CAST

Horst Fantazzini	Stefano Accorsi
Lance Corporal Di Gennaro	Giovanni Esposito
Brigadiere Lo Iacono	Emilio Solfrizzi
Wife	Fabrizia Sacchi
Assistant Public Prosecutor	Antonio Catania
Colonel Tagliaferri	Paolo Graziosi
Marshal Juliano	Andrea Lolli
Manager	Antonio Petrocelli
Lawyer Mazza	Alessandro Haber
Father	Francesco Guccini
Calimero	Fabio Ferri
Brigadiere Santillo	Alessandro Lombardo

The true story of gentleman bandit, Horst Fantazzini, a man who robbed banks with a toy gun, but found himself in deeper trouble when he inadvertently wounded two guards during his aborted prison escape.

Stefano Accorsi (center)

Stefano Accorsi

Yaël Abecassis, Yoram Hattab

Meital Barda, Sami Hori

KADOSH

(KINO) Producers, Michel Propper, Amos Gitaï, Laurent Truchot; Director, Amos Gitaï; Screenplay, Amos Gitaï, Eliette Abecassis, Jacky Cukier; Photography, Renato Berta; Editors, Monica Coleman, Kobi Netanel; a coproduction of Agav Hafakot, M.P. Productions and Le Studio Canal+; Israeli, 1999; Color; Not rated; 110 minutes; American release date: February 16, 2000

CAST

Rivka	Yaël Abecassis
Meir	Yoram Hattab
Malka	Meital Barda
Yossef	Uri Ran Klausner
Rav Shimon	Yussef Abu Warda
Yaakov	Sami Hori
Elisheva	Lea Koenig
Gynecologist	Rivka Michaeli
Uncle Shmouel	Samuel Calderon
Man in Bar	Amos Gitai

In Mea Shearim, the Orthodox Jewish section of Jerusalem, Meir and Rivka find their marriage in jeopardy when it is declared illegal by Meir's father, the community Rabi, because they are unable to have children.

© Kino International

NOT ONE LESS

(SONY PICTURES CLASSICS) Producer, Zhao Yu; Executive Producer, Zhang Weiping; Director, Zhang Yimou; Screenplay, Shi Xiangsheng; Photography, Hou Yong; Designer, Cao Jiuping; Costumes, Dong Huamiado; Editor, Zhai Ru; Music, Sam Bao; a Columbia Pictures Film Production Asia presentation of a Guangxi Film & Beijing New Picture; Chinese, 1998; Dolby; Color; Rated G; 106 minutes; American release date: February 18, 2000

CAST

Themselves	Wei Minzhi, Zhang Huike, Sun Zhimei
Mayor Tian	Tian Zhenda
Teacher Gao	Gao Enman
TV Station Receptionist	Feng Yuying
TV Host	Li Fanfan
Mr. Zhang	Zhang Yichang
Brick Factory Owner	Xu Zhanqing
Zhang Huike's Mother	Liu Hanzhi
Bus Station Man	Ma Guolin
TV Station Manager	Wu Wanlu

and Liu Ru (Train Station Announcer), Wang Shulan (Stationery Store Clerk), Fu Xinmin (TV Station Director), Bai Mei (Restaurant Owner), Zhang Mingshan, Ming Xinhong, Jiao Jie, Tian Xuewei, Rong Huimin, Li Mei, Sun Zhiwei, Li Lingyu, The Students of Shuiquan Primary School in Zhenningbao Village.

When Teacher Gao takes a month off from school to visit his ailing mother, 13-year-old Wei Minzhi is given the job of overseeing the class, with the condition that none of the 28 students drops out of school during her stay.

© Sony Pictures Entertainment, Inc.

Rosalind Ayres, Charlotte Coleman, Edin Dzandzanovic, Charles Kay

Steve Sweeney, Danny Nussbaum, Jay Simpson

Tian Zhenda, Wei Minzhi

BEAUTIFUL PEOPLE

(TRIMARK) Producer, Ben Woolford; Executive Producers, Roger Shannon, Ben Gibson; Director/Screenplay, Jasmin Dizdar; Photography, Barry Ackroyd; Designer, Jon Henson; Editor, Justin Krisch; Line Producer, Christopher Collins; Costumes, Louise Page; Music, Garry Bell; Casting, Suzanne Crowley, Gilly Poole; a Tall Stories production in association with the Arts Council of England and the Merseyside Film Production Fund with the participation of BSKYB and British Screen, of a presentation of The British Film Institute and Channel Four; British, 1999; Dolby; Color; Rated R; 109 minutes; American release date: February 18, 2000

CAST

Portia Thornton	Charlotte Coleman
George Thornton	Charles Kay
Nora Thornton	Rosalind Ayres
Roger Midge	Roger Sloman
Felicity Midge	Heather Tobias
Griffin Midge	Danny Nussbaum
Kate Higgins	Siobhan Redmond
Jerry Higgins	Gilbert Martin
Dr. Mouldy	Nicholas Farrell
Jim	Steve Sweeney
Sister	Linda Bassett
Croat	Faruk Pruti
Serb	Dado Jehan
Edward Thornton	Julian Firth
Joseph Thornton	Edward Jewesbury
Tim Mouldy	Bobby Williams
Tom Mouldy	Joseph Williams
Bigsy	Jay Simpson
Pero Guzina	Edin Dzandzanovic
Mrs. Mouldy	Melee Hutton

and Thomas Goodridge (Youth with Mobile Phone), Tony Peters (Bus Driver), Elizabeth Isiorho (African Woman), Dev Sagoo (DSS Clerk), Vera Jakob (Waitress), Louise Breckon-Richards (Policewoman), Sharon D. Clark (Nurse Tina), Jessica Brandon (Chloe Higgins), Martin Alderdice (BBC Camera Man), Nicholas McGaughey (Welshman), Walentine Giorgiewa (Dzemila Hadzibegovic), Radoslav Youroukov (Ismet Hadzibegovic), Niall Ivers (Hashim), Raules Davies (UN Soldier), Alan Cowan (Immigration Official), Jonny Phillips (Brian North), Craig Stokes (Hospital Security Guard), Kenan Hudaverdi (Railway Worker), Annette Badland (Psychologist), Peter Harding (Detective), Andrew Logan (Hypnotherapist), Antony Carrick (Retired MP)

In London several characters find their lives intersecting under unexpected circumstances including a delinquent, a free-thinking middle class doctor who falls for a penniless Bosnian refugee, and a troubled doctor who attempts to help a Bosnian couple.

© Trimark Pictures

MIFUNE

(SONY PICTURES CLASSICS) Producers, Birgitte Hald, Morten Kaufmann; Director, Søren Kragh-Jacobsen; Screenplay, Søren Kragh-Jacobsen, Anders Thomas Jensen; Story, Søren Kragh-Jacobsen; Photography, Anthony Dod Mantle; Editor, Valdis Oskarsdottir; Music, Nulle and Verdensorkestret; Casting, Stine Brüel; a Nimbus Film presentation in cooperation with Zentropa Entertainments, DRTV and SVT Drama with support from Nordisk Film & TV Pond and the Danish Film Institute; Danish, 1999; Dolby; Color; Rated R; 99 minutes; American release date: February 25, 2000

CAST

Kresten	Anders W. Berthelsen
Liva	Iben Hjejle
Rud, Kresten's Brother	Jesper Asholt
Claire, Kresten's Wife	Sofie Gråbøl
Bjarke, Liva's Brother	Emil Tarding
Gerner	Anders Hove
Pernille	Paprika Steen
Nina	Mette Bratlann
Hanne	Susanne Storm
Lykke	Ellen Hillingsø
Bibbi	Sidse Babett Knudsen
The Voice	Søren Fauli
Palle the Pimp	Søren Malling
Claire's Father	Keld Nørgaard
Claire's Mother	Kirsten Vaupel
Greying John	Torben Jensen
Priest	Klaus Bondam

and Lene Laub Oksen, Line Kruse (Hookers), Sofie Stougaard (Woman in Bakery), Rasmus Haxen, Ole Møllegaard (Gerner's Friends), Esben Pedersen (The Dead Father), Christian Sievert (Herning), Arthur Jensen, Albert Pedersen, Morten Flyverbom (Rud's Friends), Christian Grønvall (Bartender), Jens Basse Dam (Fat Redneck Businessman), Peter Rygaard, Dan Paustian (Horny Business Types)

Kresten, a successful businessman determined to keep his lower-class family a secret from his wife, hires a housekeeper to take care of his mentally handicapped brother Rud, unaware that the woman is a former prostitute on the run from her pimp.

© Sony Pictures Entertainment

Anders W. Berthelsen, Iben Hjejle

THE CLOSER YOU GET

(FOX SEARCHLIGHT) Producer, Uberto Pasolini; Director, Aileen Ritchie; Screenplay, William Ivory; Story, Herbie Wave; Photography, Robert Alazraki; Designer, Tom McCullagh; Costumes, Kathy Strachan; Music, Rachel Portman; Co-Producers, Polly Leys, Mark Huffam; Editor, Sue Wyatt; Casting, Maureen Hughes; a Redwave production; Irish-British-U.S.; Dolby; Deluxe color; Rated PG-13; 90 minutes; American release date: February 25, 2000

CAST

Kieran O'Donnagh	Ian Hart
Ian	Sean McGinley
Kate	Niamh Cusack
Mary	Ruth McCabe
Pat	Ewan Stewart
Sean	Sean McDonagh
Siobhan	Cathleen Bradley
Ollie	Pat Shortt
Ella	Deborah Barnett
Father Hubert Mallone	Risteard Cooper
Dollie	Maureen O'Brien
Giovanni	Pat Laffan
Brian	Frank Laverty

and Joan Sheehy (Joan), Britta Smith (Mrs. Duncannon), Patricia Martin (Mrs. Lock), Doreen Keough (Mrs. Giovanni), Pauline Hutton (Deirdra), Nuala O'Neill (Molly), Dessie Gallagher (Mickey), Michael McDougall (Liam), Nora Keneghan (Mrs. Campbell), Antonio Sierra, Massimo Marraccini, Tito Heredia, Thomas Timoney, Philippe Buret (Spanish Sailors), Brian Cannon (Bus Driver), Nikki Fox, Karen Noble, Regina Ford (American Girls), Jackie Quinn (Jackie Fitzpatrick)

The male population of a shrinking Irish village, bemoaning the lack of eligible women in their midst, hatch a plan to place an ad in a U.S. newspaper to entice American women overseas.

© Fox Searchlight Pictures

Ian Hart, Cathleen Bradley, Risteard Cooper

THE LITTLE THIEF

(NEW YORKER) Producer, Pierre Chevalier; Executive Producer, Gilles Sandoz; Director, Erick Zonca; Screenplay, Erick Zonca, Virginie Wagon; Photography, Pierre Milon, Catherine Pujol; Designer, Kristina Zonca; Editor, Jean-Robert Thomann; Costumes, Cecile Berges; an AGAT Films & Cie. production in association with La Sept-Arte; French, 1999; Color; Not rated; 65 minutes; American release date: March 1, 2000

CAST

"S"	Nicolas Duvauchelle
Barruet	Yann Tregouet
The Eye	Jean-Jérôme Esposito
Chacal	Martial Bezot
Mathias	Jean-Armand Dalomba
Tony	Joe Prestia
Leila	Ingrid Preynat
Tina	Véronique Balme
Vampire	Olivier Gerby
Sandra	Emilie Lafarge
Bakery Chef	Dominique Abellard
Employee at Bakery	Gilbert Landreau

Brooding and restless, "S" loses his job and winds up doing menial tasks for a group of young thieves whom he hopes to impress enough to be made part of the gang.

© New Yorker Films

Nicolas Duvauchelle

Nicolas Duvauchelle

Johnny Depp

THE NINE GATE

(ARTISAN) Producer/Director, Roman Polanski; Executive Producers, Wolfgang Glattes, Michel Cheyko; Co-Producers, Iñaki Nuñez, Antonio Cardenal, Alain Vannier; Line Producer, Suzanne Wiesenfeld; Screenplay, John Brownjohn, Enrique Urbizu, Roman Polanski; Based on the novel *El Club Dumas* by Arturo Pérez-Reverte; Photography, Darius Khondji; Designer, Dean Tavoularis; Editor, Hervé de Luze; Music, Wojciech Kilar; Costumes, Anthony Powell; Special Effects, Gilbert Pieri; Casting, Howard Feuer; a RP Productions/Orly Films/TF1 Filmproduction co-production with the participation of BAC Films/Canal+/Kino Visión/Origen Producciones Cinematográficas with the participation of Via Digital; French-Spanish-U.S., 1999; Dolby; Super 35 Widescreen; Color; Rated R; 133 minutes; American release date: March 10, 2000

CAST

Dean Corso	Johnny Depp
Liana Telfer	Lena Olin
Boris Balkan	Frank Langella
Bernie	James Russo
Victor Fargas	Jack Taylor
Pablo & Pedro Ceniza	José López Rodero
Witkin	Allen Garfield
Baroness Frieda Kessler	Barbara Jefford
The Girl	Emmanuelle Seigner

and Tony Amoni (Liana's Bodyguard), Andrew Telfer (Willy Holt), Jacques Dacqmine (Old Man), Joe Sheridan (Old Man's Son), Rebecca Pauly (Daughter-in-Law), Catherine Benguigui (Concierge), Maria Ducceshi (Secretary), Jacques Collard (Gruber), Dominique Pozzetto (Desk Clerk), Emmanuel Booz (Baker), Lino Riberio de Sousa (Hotel Porter), José López Rodero (1st & 2nd Workman), Asii Rais (Cabby), Bernard Richier, Marinette Richier (Cafe Owners)

A rare books specialist is hired by a demonologist to authenticate a book said to unlock the door to the underworld.

© Artisan Entertainment

ORPHANS

(SHOOTING GALLERY) Producer, Francs Higson; Executive Producer, Paddy Higson; Director/Screenplay, Peter Mullan; Photography, Grant Scott Cameron; Designer, Campbell Gordon; Editor, Colin Monie; Costumes, Lynn Aitken; Music, Craig Armstrong; Casting, Doreen Jones; a Channel Four Films presentation in association with the Scottish Arts Council, National Lottery Fund, and the Glasgow Film Fund of an Antoinine Green Bridge production; British-Scottish, 1998; Dolby; Color; Not rated; 101 minutes; Release date: March 10, 2000

CAST

Thomas	Gary Lewis
Michael	Douglas Henshall
Sheila	Rosemarie Stevenson
John	Stephen McCole
Tanga	Frank Gallagher
Hanson	Alex Norton
Carole	Laura O'Donnell
Uncle Ian	Dave Anderson
DD Duncan	Malcolm Shields
Ed	John Comerford
Alison	Deirdre Davis
Melissa	Debbie Walsh
Anne Marie	Lee-Ann McCran
Bernadette	Donna Chalmer
Father Fitzgerald	Seamus Ball
Lenny	Paul Doonan ,
Young Michael	Fraser Campbell
Young Thomas	Paul McNamara
Frank	Gilbert Martin
Henry	Laurie Ventry
Minnie	Maureen Carr
Rose	Annie Swan

and Steven Singleton (Seamus), Kate Brailsford (Bullet Boy Mum), Stephen Docherty (Alastair), Judith A. Williams (Amanda), June Brogan (Mona), Eric Barlow (Mr. Bell), Frances Carrigan (Mrs. Bell), Sheila Donald (Mrs. Finch), Robert Carr (Mr. Leitch), Luka Kennedy (Fraser), Catherine Connell (Angela), Lenny Mullan (Julian), Martha Leishman (Alice), Jim Twaddale (Liam), Joel Strachan (Neil), Dorothy Jane Stewart (Margaret), Tam White (Alistair), Linda Cuthbert (Elvelyn), Louise Dunn (Moira), Jan Wilson (Sandra), Helen Devon (Jessica), Vanya Eadie (Maria)

The Flynn siblings return home to Glasgow to attend the funeral of their mother, a gathering that brings about various hostilities and misunderstandings.

© Shooting Gallery

Greta Scacchi, James Wilby

Douglas Henshall, Stephen McCole

COTTON MARY

(UNIVERSAL) Producers, Nayeem Hafizka, Richard Hawley; Executive Producer, Paul Bradley; Director, Ismail Merchant; Screenplay, Alexandra Viets; Photography, Pierre L'Homme; Costumes, Sheena Napier; Music, Richard Robbins; Editor, John David Allen; Designer, Alison Riva; Casting, Celestia Fox; a Merchant Ivory Production; from United International Pictures; British-French-U.S., 1999; Dolby; Technicolor; Not rated; 124 minutues; Release date: March 15, 2000

CAST

Lily Macintosh	Greta Scacchi
Cotton Mary	Madhur Jaffrey
John Macintosh	James Wilby
Blossom	Neena Gupta
Mrs. Evans	Sarah Badel
Mrs. Smythe	Joanna David
Rosie	Sakina Jaffrey
Mrs. Davids	Gemma Jones
Mattie	Nadira
Abraham	Prayag Raaj
Gwen	Surekha Sikri
Theresa Macintosh	Laura Lumley

and Matteo Piero Mantegazza, Olivia Caesar (Baba), Riju Bajaj (Mugs), Cuckoo Parameswaran, Beena Manoj, Maggie Arthasery (Nurses), Gerson Da Cunha (Doctor Correa), Mahabanoo Mody-Kotwal (Matron), Harshiya Rafiq (Mira), Vinnie D'Souza (Guitar Player), Captain Raju (Inspector Ramiji Raj), Chinappa, Ashok Koshy (Tea Workers), Firdausi Jussawalla (Mr. Panamal), Shirly Somasundaram, Shobha Vijay, Jaya George (Ayahs), Philip Tabor (Jack), Luke Jones (Charlie), Susan Malick (Bunny Rogers), Hamza (Fisherman), Virendra Saxena (Joseph), Poornima Mohan (Receptionist), Caroline Charlety, Ranjini Haridas, Gayatri Krishnan (Stylists), Txuku Iriarte Solana (Sylvie D'Costa)

In 1954 India, a British radio correspondent and his wife invite an Anglo-Indian nurse, Mary, into their lives after she helps tend for their new-born child, only to have the woman slowly take control of the household.

© Universal Studios

WINTERSLEEPERS

(WINSTAR) Producer, Stefan Arndt; Director, Tom Tykwer; Screenplay, Tom Tykwer, Anne-Françoise Pyszora; Photography, Frank Griebe; Designer, Alexander Manasse; Editor, Katja Dringenberg; Music, Tom Tykwer, Johnny Klimek, Reinhold Heil; Costumes, Aphrodite Kondos; Line Producer, Malinka Comfort; from X-Filme Creative Pool GmbH, Bavaria Film International; German, 1997; Cinemascope; Color; Not rated; 124 minutes; American release date: March 17, 2000

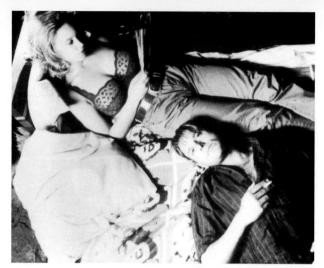

Floraine Daniel, Heino Ferch

CAST

René	Ulrich Matthes
Laura	Marie-Lou Sellem
Rebecca	Floriane Daniel
Marco	Heino Ferch
Theo	Josepf Bierbichler
Nina	Laura Tonke
Marita	Sofia Dirschel
Otto	Sebastian Schipper
Anna	Saskia Vester

and Werner Schnitzer (Senior Consultant), Renee Schoenberg (Gerd), Simon Donatz (Peter), Jacob Donatz (Luis), Agathe Teffershofer (Edith), Robert Meyer (Keibl), Harry Taschner (Kuhn)

In a snowy German skiing village the lives of five of its inhabitants intersect.

Paul Cook, Sid Vicious, Johnny Rotten, Steve Jones

Marie-Lou Sellem

Johnny Rotten, Steve Jones

THE FILTH AND THE FURY

(FINE LINE) Producers, Anita Camarata, Amanda Temple; Executive Producers, Eric Gardner, Jonathan Weisgal; Director, Julien Temple; Editor, Niven Howie; Researcher, John Shearlaw; Film Grading/Picture Effects, The Farm; a FilmFour Ltd.presentation in association with the Sex Pistols/Jersey Shore/Nitrate Film Prods.; British-U.S.; Dolby; Deluxe color; Rated R; 108 minutes; American release date: March 29, 2000. Documentary on the punk band The Sex Pistols (Paul Cook, Steve Jones, Glen Matlock, Johnny Rotten, Sid Vicious).

Hossein Mahjub, Mohsen Ramezani

Farahnaz Safari, Mohsen Ramezani, Elham Sharim

Mohsen Ramezani, Elham Sharim

THE COLOR OF PARADISE

(SONY PICTURES CLASSICS) a.k.a. *The Color of God*; Producer, Mehdi Karimi; Executive Producers, Ali Kalij, Mehdi Karimi; Director/Screenplay, Majid Majidi; Photography, Mohammad Davoodi; Designer/Costumes, Asghar Nezhadeimani; Music, Alireza Kohandairi; Editor, Hassan Hassandoost; a Varahonar Company production; Iranian, 1999; Color; Rated PG; 81 minutes; American release date: March 31, 2000

CAST

Mohammad	Mohsen Ramezani
Hashem, Mohammad's Father	Hossein Mahjub
Granny	Salime Feizi
Hanyeh, Mohammad's Sister	Elham Sharim
Bahareh, Mohammad's Sister	Farahnaz Safari
Blind Center Teachers	Mohammad Rahmaney, Zahra Mizani
Blind Center Dean	Kamal Mirkarimi
Carpenter	Morteza Fatemi
Young Woman	Masoomeh Zeinati
Young Woman's Father	Ahmad Aminian
Village School Dean	Moghadam Behbahani
Village Teacher	Behzad Rafeiey
Villager	Johnali Khorami

Hashem, a poor coal miner in Northern Iran, hopes to remarry but finds his blind 8-year-old son an obstacle in his plans for a new life, prompting him to try to unload the boy on others. This film received an Oscar nomination for foreign language film, 1999.

© Sony Pictures Entertainment, Inc.

243

Grégorie Colin, Denis Lavant

Michel Subor

Denis Lavant

BEAU TRAVAIL

(NEW YORKER) a.k.a. Good Work; Executive Producer, Jerome Minet; Director, Claire Denis; Screenplay, Claire Denis, Jean-Pol Fargeau; Inspired by Herman Melville's novella *Billy Budd, Sailor*; Photography, Agnès Godard; Designer, Arnaud de Moleron; Music, Charles Henry de Pirrefeu, Eran Tzur; Editor, Nelly Quettier; Costumes, Judy Shrewsbury; Casting, Nicolas Lublin; a La Sept Arte/Pathe Television/S.M. films production; French, 1999; Dolby; Color; Not rated; 93 minutes; American release date: March 31, 2000

CAST

Sergeant Galoup...Denis Lavant
Commandant Bruno Forestier ....Michel Subor
Gilles Sentain ....Grégoire Colin
Young Woman..Marta Tafesse Kassa
and Richard Courcet, Nicolas Duvauchelle, Adiatou Massidi, Mickeal Rakovski, Dan Herzberg, Giuseppe Molino, Gianfranco Poddighe, Marc Veh, Thong Duy Nguyen, Jean-Yves Vivet, Bernardo Montet, Dimitri Tsiapkinis, Djamel Zemali, Abdelkader Bouti (Legionnaires)

At a Foreign Legion post in the gulf of Djibouti in East Africa, the company's routine is disrupted by the appearance of a young new recruit who becomes favored for his goodness and generosity, much to the discomfort of the post's brooding young commander.

Denis Lavant

EAST-WEST

(SONY PICTURES CLASSICS) Producer, Yves Marmion; Director, Regis Wargnier; Screenplay, Roustam Ibraguimbek, Serguei Bodrov, Louis Gardel, Regis Wargnier; Photography, Laurent Dailland; Designers, Vladimir Svetozarov, Alexei Levtchenko; Costumes, Pierre-Yves Gayraud; Editor, Herve Schneid; Music, Patrick Doyle; Line Producers, Gerard Crosnier, Andrei Belous; a UGC YM-NTV Profit-Mate Productions-Gala Film-France 3 Cinéma with the participation of Canal+-Sofica Sofinergie 5 with the support of Euroimages; French-Russian-Spanish-Bulgarian, 1999; Dolby; Color; Rated PG-13; 121 minutes; American release date: April 7, 2000

CAST

Marie	Sandrine Bonnaire
Alexei Golovine	Oleg Menchikov
Gabrielle	Catherine Deneuve
Sacha	Serguëi Bodrov, Jr.
Serioja (at 7 years)	Ruben Tapiero
Serioja (at 14 years)	Erwan Baynaud
Pirogov	Grigori Manoukov
Olga	Tatiana Doguileva
Colonel Boiko	Bogdan Stupka
Nina Fiodorovna	Meglena Karalambova
Viktor	Atanass Atanassov
Alexandrovna	Tania Massalitinova
Volodia Petrov	Valentin Ganev
Serguei Koslov	Nikolai Binev

and René Féret (French Ambassador), Daniel Martin (Turkish Captain), Hubert Saint-Macary (Embassy Advisor), Jauris Casanova (Fabiani), Joel Chapron (Theatre Interpreter)

When Stalin launches an amnesty campaign in order to get Russian emigrants to return to their home country, Alexei Golovine and his family return home after years of living in France, only to find out that they have been tricked by falses promises. This film received an Oscar nomination for foreign language film, 1999.

Sandrine Bonnaire, Oleg Menchikov

Serguëi Bodrov, Jr., Sandrine Bonnaire

Serguëi Bodrov, Jr., Sandrine Bonnaire

Catherine Deneuve, René Féret

ME MYSELF I

(SONY PICTURES CLASSICS) Producer, Fabien Liron; Director/Screenplay, Pip Karmel; Executive Producer, Les Films Du Loup; Line Producer, Vicki Popplewell; Photography, Graham Lind; Designer, Murray Picknett; Co-Producer, Andrena Finlay; Editor, Denise Haratzis; Music, Charlie Chan; Costumes, Paul Warren, Ariane Weiss; Casting, Shauna Wolifson, Mullinars Consultants; a Gaumont presentation; Australian-French, 1999; Dolby; Color; Rated R; 104 minutes; American release date: April 7, 2000

CAST

Pamela Drury (Pamela One and Two) .... Rachel Griffiths
Robert .... David Roberts
Ben .... Sandy Winton
Stacey .... Yael Stone
Douglas .... Shuna Loseby
Rupert .... Trent Sullivan
Terri .... Rebecca Frith
Geoff .... Felix Williamson
Janine .... Ann Burbrook
Max .... Maeliosa Stafford
Allen .... Terence Crawford
Deirdre .... Christine Stephen-Daly
Sally .... Kirstie Hutton
and Donal Forde (Young Christian), Frank Whitten (Charlie), Mariel McClorey (Harriet), Maurice Morgan (Stripper), Adam Ray (Restaurant Photographer), Lucinda Armour (Pregnant Woman), Lynne McGimpsy (Security Guard), Peter Brailey (Roger), Andrew Caryofyllis (Harry), Anthony Issa (Passing Student), Lenore Munro (Sophie), Phaedra Nicolaidis, Billie Prichard (Self Defence Girls), Mishka Martin, Jennifer Kontominas, Marteen Stroh, Natalie Gilroy, Nubia Santos, Jessica Orcsik, Melanie Alaura, Claire Langmore, Stephanie Doherty (Credit Girls), Spud (Brandy the Dog), Lyndon Wilkinson (Pamela's Mother—voice), Lisa Rock (Pamela Double)

Pamela Drury, a woman unhappy with her place in life, meets up with her alternate self, Pamela Two, who has taken the path Pamela One feels she should have by marrying the man Pamela One turned down thirteen-years ago.

Rachel Griffiths, David Roberts

Karin Vanasse

SET ME FREE (EMPORTE-MOI)

(MERCHANT IVORY FILMS/ARTISTIC LICENSE) Producers, Lorraine Richard, Alfi Sinniger, Carole Scotta; Executive Producer, Louis Laverdière; Director, Léa Pool; Screenplay, Léa Pool, Nancy Huston, Monique H. Messier; Photography, Jeanne Lapoirie; Art Director, Serge Bureau; Music, ECM; Costumes, Michèle Hamel; Editor, Michel Arcand; Casting, Lucie Robitaille; Produced by Cité-Amérique Cinéma Télévision Inc./Catpics/Haut et Court; Canadian, 1999; Dolby; Color; Not rated; 94 minutes; American release date: April 14, 2000

CAST

Hanna .... Karine Vanasse
Paul .... Alexandre Mérineau
The Mother .... Pascale Bussières
The Father .... Miki Manojlovic
Laura .... Charlotte Christeler
The Teacher .... Nancy Huston
The Grandmother .... Monique Mercure
The Prostitute .... Anne-Marie Cadieux
The Landlady .... Marie-Hélène Gagnon
Sébastien .... Sébastien Burns
and Neil Kroetsch (Pawnbroker), Gary Boudreault (Baker), Jacques Brouillet (The Priest), Jérome Leclerc-Couture (Claudio), Suzanne Garceau (Nurse), Frédéric Zacharek (Young Grocery Store Clerk), Sandrine Michon (Sandra), Guy Héroux (Man Who Moves), Marie-Josée Tremblay (Student—Elyse), Normand Canac-Marquis (Customer), Paul Kunigis (Chess Player)

A thirteen-year old girl, growing up in an unhappy household, becomes entranced by a character she sees in a film, finding a similarity between this fictional woman and a teacher with whom she hopes to form a friendship.

EAST IS EAST

Linda Bassett, Om Puri

Archie Panjabi

(MIRAMAX) Producer, Leslee Udwin; Executive Producer, Alan J. Wands; Director, Damien O'Donnell; Screenplay, Ayub Khan-Din, based on his play; Photography, Brian Tufano; Designer, Tom Conroy; Associate Producer, Stephanie Guerrasio; Editor, Michael Parker; Costumes, Lorna Marie Mugan; Music, Deborah Mollison; Line Producer, Shellie Smith; Hair and Make-up Designer, Penny Smith; Casting, Toby Whale, Joan McCann; a Filmfour presentation of an Assassin Films production; British, 1999; Dolby; Color; Rated R; 96 minutes; American release date: April 14, 2000

CAST

George Khan	Om Puri
Ella Khan	Linda Bassett
Sajid Khan	Jordan Routledge
Meenah Khan	Archie Panjabi
Maneer Khan	Emil Marwa
Saleem Khan	Chris Bisson
Tariq Khan	Jimi Mistry
Abdul Khan	Raji James
Nazir Khan	Ian Aspinall
Auntie Annie	Lesley Nicol
Earnest	Gary Damer
Mr. Moorhouse	John Bardon
Stella Moorhouse	Emma Rydal
Peggy	Ruth Jones
Poppa Khalid	Kriss Dosanjh
Priest	Ben Keaton
Mullah	Kaleem Janjua
Abdul Karim	Albert Moses
Helen Karim	Rosalind March
Mr. Shah	Madhav Sharma
Mrs. Shah	Leena Dhingra
Iyaaz Ali Khan	Jimmi Harkishin
Zaid	Saikat Ahamed
Doctor	Ralph Birtwell
Etienne Francois	Thierry Harcourt
Mark	Gary Lewis
Fat Twat	Roger Morlidge
Bouncer	Bruce McGregor
Receptionist	Margaret Blakemore

In 1970s Britain, George Khan finds that his traditional Pakistani ways are in opposition to the values of his growing offspring who rebel against his harsh dominance of their lives.

© Miramax Films

Emil Marwa, Raji James, Chris Bisson, Archie Panjabi, Jordan Routledge, Ruth Jones, Jimi Mistry, Emma Rydal

Emma Rydal, Jimi Mistry

CROUPIER

(SHOOTING GALLERY) Producer, Jonathan Cavendish; Executive Producer, James Mitchell; Director, Mike Hodges; Screenplay, Paul Mayersberg; Co-Producer, Christine Ruppert; Line Producer, Jake Lloyd; Photography, Mike Garfath; Editor, Les Healey; Music, Simon Fisher Turner; Designer, Jon Bunker; Costumes, Caroline Harris; Casting, Leo Davies; a Channel Four Films presentation in association with Filmstiftung NRW, WOR and La Sept Cinema and Arte; British-German, 1998; Dolby; Color; Not rated; 91 minutes; American release date: April 21, 2000.

Clive Owen

CAST

Jack Manfred	Clive Owen
Marion Neil	Gina McKee
Jani de Villiers	Alex Kingston
David Reynolds	Alexander Morton
Bella	Kate Hardie
Matt	Paul Reynolds
Giles Cremorne	Nick Reding
Jack Snr.	Nicholas Ball
Mr. Tchai	Ozzi Yue
Detective Inspector Ross	Tom Mannion
Gordon	James Clyde
Fiona	Emma Lewis
Chloe	Kate Fenwick

and Ciro De Chiara (Arabic Man, Cheat), Barnaby Kay (Car Dealer), Sheila Whitfield (Manicurist), John Radcliffe (Barber), Eddie Osei (West Indian Punter), Doremy Vernon, Claudine Carter (Women), George Khan (Coughing Man), David Hamilton (Casino Supervisor), Carol Davis (Table Supervisor), Ursula Alberts (Madame Claude), Neville Phillips (White-Haired Man), Joanna C. Drummond (Agnes), Manfred Holden (McTachi's Bodyguard), Rhona Mitra (Girl with Joint), John Baker, Vida Garman (Couple in Toilet), Christine Niemöller (Pat), Claudia Barth (Waitress), Arnold Zarom (Habib the Terrorist), Rosemarie Dunham (Jewish Woman), Magnus Hastings (Gigolo), John Surman (Loser), Mark Long, Michail Golzarandi (Gangsters), Karl-Heinz Ciba (Accusing Punter), Loretta Parnell (Lucy)

Aspiring writer Jack Manfred takes a job as a croupier in the London gambling world, where he begins to enjoy the power he holds over the customers.

© Shooting Gallery

Clive Owen, Alex Kingston

THE LAST SEPTEMBER

(TRIMARK) Producer, Yvonne Thunder; Executive Producers, Nik Powell, Neil Jordan, Stephen Woolley, Peter Fudakowski; Director, Deborah Warner; Screenplay, John Banville; Based upon the novel by Elizabeth Bowen; Photography, Slawomir Idziak; Designer, Caroline Amies; Costumes, John Bright; Music, Zbigniew Preisner; Editor, Kate Evans; Co-Producer, Marina Gefter; Casting, Leo Davis; a Matrix Films and Scala presentation in association with Bord Scannan na hÉireann/The Irish Film Board and Radio Telefis Eireann; British-Irish-French; Dolby; Deluxe color; Rated R; 103 minutes; American release date: April 21, 2000

CAST

Lady Myra Naylor	Maggie Smith
Sir Richard Naylor	Michael Gambon
Francie Montmorency	Jane Birkin
Marda Norton	Fiona Shaw
Hugo Montmorency	Lambert Wilson
Lois Farquar	Keeley Hawes
Captain Gerald Colthurst	David Tennant
Peter Connolly	Gary Lydon
Daventry	Richard Roxburgh
Laurence Carstairs	Jonathan Slinger
Livvy Connolly	Emily Nagle
O'Brien	Tom Hickey
Maids	Maeve Kearney, Francine Mulrooney, Christina Wilson
Doreen Hartigan	Catherine Walsh
Nora Hartigan	Bernie Downes
Sergeant Wilson	Mikel Murfi

and Arthur Riordan (Black and Tan Soldier), Kieran Ahern (Daniel Connolly), Miles Horgan (Postman), Aaron Harris (Captain Vermont), Lesley McGuire (Mrs. Vermont), Mal Whyte (Second Officer), Tamsin MacCarthy (Marcie Mangan)

In 1920s Ireland, Lois Farquar, an restless 19-year-old from an aristocratic family, finds herself being courted by a British Army captain, while being attracted to an Irish freedom fighter whom she discovers hiding on her relative's estate.

© Trimark Pictures

Maggie Smith, Jane Birkin, Lambert Wilson, Michael Gambon

Amy Irving, Antonio Fagundes

BOSSA NOVA

(SONY PICTURES CLASSICS) Producer, Lucy Barreto; Executive Producer/Director, Bruno Barreto; Screenplay, Alexandre Machado, Fernanda Young; Based on the story *A Senhorita Simpson (Mrs. Simpson)* by Sergio Sant'Anna; Photography, Pascal Rabaud; Art Directors, Cássio Amarante, Carla Caffé; Editor, Ray Hubley; Music, Eumir Deodato; Costumes, Emília Duncan; Casting, Sheila Jaffe, Georgianne Walken, Fernanda Ribas, Marcela Altberg; a Luiz Carlos Barreto production in association with Globo Filmes; Brazilian-U.S.; Dolby; Super 35 Widescreen; Color; Rated R; 95 minutes; American release date: April 28, 2000

CAST

Mary Ann Simpson	Amy Irivng
Pedro Paulo	Antonio Fagundes
Acácio	Alexandre Borges
Tânia	Débora Bloch
Nadine	Drica Moraes
Sharon	Giovanna Antonelli
Vermont	Rogério Cardoso
Gordo	Sérgio Loroza
Peçanha	Flávio São Thiago
Juan	Alberto De Mendoza
Roberto	Pedro Cardoso
Trevor	Stephen Tobolowsky
Wan-Kim-Laua	Kazuo Matsui
Reporter	Cássia Linhares
English School Receptionist	Kate Lyra
Tailor Shop Receptionist	Mara Carvalho

An American English teacher, living in Rio de Janiero since the death of her husband, falls in love with a lawyer who has recently ended his seven-year marriage.

© Sony Pictures Entertainment, Inc.

Lorraine Pilkington, Nicola Reynolds

HUMAN TRAFFIC

Danny Dyer

(MIRAMAX) Producers, Allan Niblo, Emer McCourt; Executive Producer, Renata S. Aly; Co-Executive Producers, Nigel Warren-Green, Michael Wearing, Kevin Menton; Director/Screenplay, Justin Kerrigan; Associate Producers, Rupert Preston, Arthur Baker; Photography, David Bennett; Designer, Dave Buckingham; Editor, Patrick Moore; Music, Rob Mello, Mathew Herbert; Music Supervisor, Pete Tong; Makeup & Hair Design, Tony Lilley; Costumes, Claire Anderson; Casting, Sue Jones, Gary Howe; an Irish Screen presentation of a Fruit Salad Film production; Irish-British, 1999; Dolby; Fujicolor; Rated R; 99 minutes; American release date: May 5, 2000

John Simm, Lorraine Pilkington

CAST

Jip	John Simm
LuLu	Lorraine Pilkington
Koop	Shaun Parkes
Nina	Nicola Reynolds
Moff	Danny Dyer
Lee	Dean Davies
LuLu's Uncle Eric	Peter Albert
Karen Benson	Jan Anderson
Moff's Father	Terence Beesley
Moff's Grandmother	Anne Bowen
Asylum Doorman	Neil Bowens
Matt	Peter Bramhill
Reality	Jo Brand
Fleur	Stephanie Brooks
Andy	Richard Coyle
Pablo Hassan	Carl Cox
Inca	Roger Evans
Tyler	Bradley Freegard

and Elizabeth Harper, Sarah Blackburn , Nicola Davey (Jip's Exes), Carol Harrison (Moff's Mother), Jennifer Hill (Jip's Secretary), Tyrone Johnson (Hip Hop Junkie), Justin Kerrigan (Ziggy Marlon), Nicola Heywood-Thomas (TV Interviewer), Nick Kilroy (Herbie), Andrew Lincoln (Felix), Howard Marks (Himself), Robert Marrable (Casey), Louis Marriot (Cardiff Bad Boy), Danny Midwinter (Tyrone), Millsy in Nottingham (Millsy from Roath), Robbie Newby (Karen Benson's Boyfriend), Ninjah (Tom Tom's MC), Cadfen Roberts (Jip's Mother's Client), Mad Doctor X (Koop's Workmate), Phillip Rosch (Jip's Manager), Jason Samuels (Bad Boy), Mark Seaman (Jeremy Faxman), Lynne Seymour (Connie), Patrick Taggart (Luke), Giles Thomas (Martin), Menna Trussler (LuLu's Auntie Violet), Larrington Walker (Koop's Father), Anna Wilson (Boomshanka), Eilian Wyn (Doctor), Tim Hamilton (Breakdancer/Bodypopper), Alicia Ferraboschi, Sherena Flash, Marat Khairoullu, Adam Pudney, Mark Seymore, Algernon Williams, Colin Williams, Frank Wilson (Bodypoppers).

A group of friends compensate for the boredom of their dead-end jobs with their hell-raising weekends of drinking, partying and drugging.

Shaun Parkes, John Simm

KIKUJIRO

(SONY PICTURES CLASSICS) Producers, Masayuki Mori, Takio Yoshida; Director/Screenplay/Editor, Takeshi Kitano; Photography, Katsumi Yanagishima; Music, Joe Hisaishi; Art Director, Norihiro Isoda; Costumes, Fumio Iwasaki; Line Producer, Shinji Komiya; Casting, Takefumi Yoshikawa; Presented by Bandai Visual, Tokyo FM, Nippon Herald, Office Kitano; Japanese, 1999; Dolby; Color; Rated PG-13; 116 minutes; American release date: May 26, 2000

Beat Takeshi, Yusuke Sekiguchi

CAST

Kikujiro	Beat Takeshi
Masao	Yusuke Sekiguchi
Miki, Kikujiro's Wife	Kayoko Kishimoto
Masao's Mother	Yuko Daike
Masao's Grandmother	Kazuko Yoshiyuki
Man at Bus Stop	Beat Kiyoshi
Biker/Fatso	Great Gidayu
Biker/Baldy	Rakkyo Ide
Traveling Man	Nezumi Imamura
Juggler Girl	Fumie Hosokawa
Scary Man	Akaji Maro
Yakuza Boss	Daigaku Sekine

and Yoji Tanaka, Makoto Inamiya, Hisahiko Murasawa (Yakuzas), Taro Suwa, Hidehisa Ejiri (Hucksters), Kenta Arai (Masao's Friend)

The obnoxious, irresponsible Kikujiro is reluctantly assigned to accompany nine-year old Masao on his journey to visit the mother he has never met.

© Sony Pictures Entertainment, Inc.

John Standing, Kirina Mano, Matthew Delamere

Polly Walker, Matthew Delamere

8 1/2 WOMEN

(LIONS GATE) Producer, Kees Kasander; Co-Producers, Terry Glinwood, Bob Hubar, Denis Wigman; Director/Screenplay, Peter Greenaway; Photography, Sacha Vierny; Designer, Wilbert Van Dorp; Editor, Elmer Leupen; Makeup Artist, Sara Meerman; Costumes/Designer (Japan), Emi Wada; Casting, Danielle Roffe, Aimi O (Japan); a Woodline Productions Ltd., Movie Masters B.V., Delux Productions s.a. and Continent Film Gmbh presentation; German-Luxembourg-Dutch-British, 1999; Dolby; Color; Rated R; 121 minutes; American release date: May 26, 2000

CAST

Philip Emmenthal	John Standing
Storey Emmenthal	Matthew Delamere
Kito	Vivian Wu
Simato	Shizuka Inoh
Clothilde	Barbara Sarafian
Mio	Kirina Mano
Griselda	Toni Collette
Beryl	Amanda Plummer
Giaconda	Natacha Amal
Giulietta/Half Woman	Manna Fujiwara
Palmira	Polly Walker
Celeste	Elizabeth Berrington
Marianne	Myriam Muller
Simon	Don Warrington
Philip's Wife	Claire Johnston

and Paul Hoffmann, Tony Kaye, Ann Overstall (Mourners), Malcolm Turner (Undertaker), Patrick Hastert (Man in Street), Julian Vincent, Ciaran Mulhern, John Overstall (Men in Cinema), Derek Kueter, Jules Werner, Sophie Langevin (Debt Collectors), Denise Gregoire (Sister Nun), Sascha Ley, Bettina Scheuritzel, Radica Jovicic, Jill Mercedes (Nuns), Dean Harrington (American Businessman), Noriyuki Konishi (Korean Businessman), Jean-Gabriel Dupuy, Stéphane Prevot (French Businessmen), Katsuya Kobayashi (Simato's Father), Ryota Tsuchiya (Simato's Brother), Takumi Matsui (Simato's Finacee), Kiyoshi Ishiguro (Fiancee's Brother), Hairi Katagiri (Half Woman Companion), Yurika Sano (Half Woman, 8 Years Old), Satomi Meguro (Half Woman, 10 Years Old), Sachiko Meguro, Hisayuki Yoshioka, Hanji Mishima (Mio's Companions), Toyonosuke Fujima (Kabuki Father), Kango Fujima, Senyoichi Nishikawa (Kabuki Sons)

A recently widowed man and his son decide that they will establish a collection of women whom they will help financially while receiving sexual services from them.

© Lions Gate Films

Natascha McElhone, Kenneth Branagh

Nathan Lane, Stefania Rocca

LOVE'S LABOUR'S LOST

(MIRAMAX) Producers, David Barron, Kenneth Branagh; Executive Producers, Guy East, Nigel Sinclair, Harvey Weinstein, Bob Weinstein, Alexis Lloyd; Director/Adaptation, Kenneth Branagh; Based on the play by William Shakespeare; Photography, Alex Thomson; Designer, Tim Harvey; Costumes, Anna Buruma; Editors, Neil Farrell, Dan Farrell; Music, Patrick Doyle; Music Producer, Maggie Rodford; Choreographer, Stuart Hopps; Casting, Randi Hiller, Nina Gold; an Intermedia Films and Pathé Pictures presentation in association with the Arts Council of England, Le Studio Canal+ of a Shakespeare Film Company production; British; Dolby; Panavision; Technicolor; Rated PG; 93 minutes; American release date: June 9, 2000

CAST

Berowne	Kenneth Branagh
Nathaniel	Richard Briers
Boyet	Richard Clifford
Maria	Carmen Ejogo
Mercade	Daniel Hill
Costard	Nathan Lane
Dumaine	Adrian Lester
Longaville	Matthew Lillard
Rosaline	Natascha McElhone
Holofernia	Geraldine McEwan
Katherine	Emily Mortimer
King	Alessandro Nivola
Moth	Anthony O'Donnell
Jaquenetta	Stefania Rocca
Princess	Alicia Silverstone

Timothy Spall (Don Armado), Jimmy Yuill (Dull), Alfred Bell (Gaston), Daisy Gough (Isabelle), Graham Hubbard (Eugene), Paul Moody (Jaques), Yvonne Reilly (Beatrice) Iain Stuart Robertson (Hippolyte), Emma Scott (Celimene), Amy Tez (Sophie), and Nikki Abraham, Colin Barrett, Jonathan Blazer, Catherine Dugdale, Michele Du Verney, Richard Joseph, Trudi Swift, Bryn Walters (Dancers)

The King of Navarre and his three friends swear to give up women only to have their vow challenged by the arrival of the Princess of France and her three attendants.

© Miramax Films

Emily Mortimer, Carmen Ejogo, Natascha McElhone, Alicia Silverstone

Alessandro Nivola, Alicia Silverstone, Matthew Lillard, Adrian Lester, Emily Mortimer, Kenneth Branagh, Natascha McElhone

Kenneth Branagh, Matthew Lillard, Alessandro Nivola, Adrian Lester

James Frain, Jennifer Ehle, Ralph Fiennes

Molly Parker, Ralph Fiennes

James Frain, Ralph Fiennes, Rosemary Harris

Ralph Fiennes, Deborah Kara Unger

SUNSHINE

(PARAMOUNT CLASSICS) Producers, Robert Lantos, Andras Hamori; Executive Producers, Rainer Kölmel, Jonathan Debin; Director, István Szabó; Screenplay, István Szabó, Israel Horovitz; Story, István Szabó; Photography, Lajos Koltai; Designer, Atila F. Kovacs; Costumes, Györgyi Szakács; Editors, Dominique Fortin, Michel Arcand; Music, Maurice Jarre; Casting, Deirdre Brown; an Alliance Atlantis and Serendipity Point Films in association with Kinowelt presentation; Hungarian-German-Canadian-Austrian, 1999; Dolby; Color; Rated R; 180 minutes; American release date: June 9, 2000

Rachel Weisz, Ralph Fiennes

CAST

Ignatz Sonnenschein/Adam Sors/Ivan Sors	Ralph Fiennes
Valerie Sors	Rosemary Harris
Greta Sors	Rachel Weisz
Valerie Sonnenschein	Jennifer Ehle
Major Carola Kovacs	Deborah Kara Unger
Andor Knorr	William Hurt
Hannah Sors (Wippler)	Molly Parker
Gustave Sonnenschein	James Frain
Gustave Sors	John Neville
Rose Sonnenschein	Miriam Margolyes
Emmanuel Sonnenschein	David de Keyser
Istvan Sors	Mark Strong
Emmanuel at 12	Ádám László
Aaron Sonnenschein	Balázs Hantos
Josefa Sonnenschein	Kathleen Gati
Rabbi Bettelheim	Vilmos Kun
Mr. Hackl	Jácint Juhász
Mrs. Hackl	Flóra Kádár
Kato	Katja Studt
Landlady in Vienna	Kati Sólyom
Dr. Emil Vitak	Joachim Bissmeier
Notary	Tamás Fodor
Rabbi at Wedding	Tamás Raj
Minister of Justice	Bill Paterson
Doctors	Dr. Zoltán Bognár, Sándor Simó, János Vészi
Count Forgach	Attila Löte
Emperor	Frederick Treves
Dr. Lanyi	István Hirtling
Man at Synagogue	Zoltán Gera
Footman	András Fekete
Istvan at 18	Bálint Trunkó
Adam at 17	János Nemes
Commander of Lenin Boys	Tamás Juranics
Red Guard	András Stohl
Boys	Tamás Keresztes, Bence Kotány
Anselmi	Péter Andorai
General Jakofalvy	Rüdiger Vogler
Lugosy	Zsolt László
Priest at Conversion	Gábor Mádi Szabó
Hungler	István Szilágyi
Baron Margittay	Hanns Zischler
Rossa	László Gálfi
Tersikovsky	Zoltán Seress
Saray	István Bubik

Ralph Fiennes

and Eszter Ónodi (Secretary at Officer's Club), Sándor Dánffy (Policeman), Buddy Elias (Mr. Brenner), Károly Mécs (Defense Secretary), Ádám Rajhona (Caretaker), Péter Takács (Stefano Sarto), Mari Törocsik (Kato), László Szepesi (Olympic Judge), János Kulka (Molnar), János Nemes (Ivan at 16), Lajos Kovács (Military Police in Camp), Gábor Máté (Rosner), Israel Horovitz (Poet), Andrea Fullajtár (Agota Hofer), György Kézdy (Outraged Man), Trevor Peacock (Comrade General Kope), Péter Halász (Wild Duck), Tamás Jordán (Sommer), István Fonyó (Warehouse Guard), József Fonyó (Prison Sergeant), Frigyes Hollósi (Mr. Ledniczky), Ila Schütz (Mrs. Ledniczky), Ica Gurnik (Woman in Hospital), Éva Igó (Policewoman)

A look at the tumultuous political changes in 20th century Hungary as seen through the eyes of the Sonnenschein family, who built their fortune on a passed-down recipe for an elixir known as "A Taste of Sunshine."

William Hurt, Ralph Fiennes

HUMANITÉ

Emmanuel Schotté, Philippe Tullier

(WINSTAR) Executive Producers, Jean Bréhat, Rachid Bouchareb; Director/Screenplay, Bruno Dumont; Photography, Yves Cape; Sets, Marc-Philippe Guerig; Costumes, Nathalie Raoul; Editor, Guy Lecorne; Music, Richard Cuvillier; a 3B Productions/ARTE France Cinema/CR-RAV co-production; French, 1999; Dolby; Cinemascope; Color; Not rated; 148 minutes; American release date: June 14, 2000

CAST

Pharaon de Winter	Emmanuel Schotté
Domino	Séverine Caneele
Joseph	Philippe Tullier
Commandant	Ghislain Ghesquiere
Eliane	Ginette Allegre
Nurse	Daniel Leroux
Conservationist	Arnaud Brejon de la Lavergnee
Jean, the Cop	Daniel Pétillon
English Cop	Robert Bunzl
Angry Worker	Dominique Pruvost
CRS	Jean Luc Dumont

and Diane Gray, Paul Gray (British Travelers), Sophie Vercamer, Murielle Houche, Pascaline Guyot, Lilianne Facq, Myriam Dehaine (Workers), Jean Beulque (The Guide), Bernard Catrycke (Nadege's Father), Marthe Vandenberg (Grandmother), Amanda Goemaere, Honorine Douche (Children), Marie Therese Cadet, Denis Claerebout (Parents), Suzanne Berteloot (Nurse), Sylvie Perel (Domino's Friend), Malik Haquem (The Dealer), Alain Beaufrome, Pierre-Olivier Thery (Pharaon's Colleagues), Frederic Engelaere (Young Worker), Pierre Harrisson (Man in Pyjamas), Marie Helene Aernout (Aline), Lucien Hallynck (Man Wearing Beret), Andre Geloen (Gardener), Jean-Francois Carpentier (Fisherman), Theophile Boidin, Jerome Pollet, Sebastion Muselet (Bathers), Gery Laforce (Bus Driver), Gregory Ryckewaert, Hamid Bouderja (Museum Technicians), Stephanie Wyts (Barmaid), Philippe Duriez, Ivanne Duriez, Alexis Duriez (Customers)

Pharaon, a sensitive police detective in northern France, agonizes over solving the brutal and disturbing rape-murder of an eleven year-old girl, while simulataneously struggling to cope with his unrequited love for factory worker Domino.

Séverine Caneele

Emmanuel Schotté

Philippe Tullier, Séverine Caneele, Emmanuel Schotté

Billy Crudup

Samantha Morton, Billy Crudup

Billy Crudup

JESUS' SON

(LIONS GATE) Producers, Elizabeth Cuthrell, Lydia Dean Pilcher, David Urrutia; Executive Producer, Steven Tuttleman; Director, Alison Maclean; Screenplay, Elizabeth Cuthrell, David Urrutia, Oren Moverman; Based on the book by Denis Johnson; Co-Producer, Margot Bridger; Associate Producer, Oren Moverman; Photography, Adam Kimmel; Designer, David Doernberg; Costumes, Kasia Walicka Maimone; Music, Joe Henry; Music Supervisor, Randall Poster; Casting, Laura Rosenthal, Ali Farrell; an Alliance Atlantis presentation of an Evenstar Films production; Canadian-U.S.; Dolby; Super 35 Widescreen; Technicolor; Rated R; 108 minutes; American release date: June 16, 2000.

CAST

FH (Fuckhead)	Billy Crudup
Michelle	Samantha Morton
Wayne	Denis Leary
Georgie	Jack Black
John Smith	Will Patton
Dr. Shanis	Greg Germann
Mira	Holly Hunter
Bill	Dennis Hopper
Salesman	Robert Michael Kelly
Car Crash Driver	Torben Brooks
Driver's Wife	Dierdre Lewis
Car Crash Doctor	Jimmy Moffit
Dead Man's Wife	Antoinette Lavecchia
Richard	Steve Buck
Tom	Ben Shenkman
Stan	Scott Oster
Beatle	Brooke Shive
Jack Hotel	Mark Webber
McInnes	John Ventimiglia

and Jesse Weaver Jr. (Carl), Michael Shannon (Dundun), Todd Berry, Bill Thompson (College Kids), Elizabeth Cuthrell (Diner Waitress), Joanne Bradley (Mary), Evita Sobel (Bartender), Ronald Croy (Big Guy in Fight), Yvette Mercedes (E.R. Nurse), Denis Johnson (Terrance Weber), Christine Mourad, Katie Rimmer (ICU Nurses), John Clement (Medical Assistant), Carol Florence (Abortion Clinic Nurse), Ron Van Lieu (Counsellor), Alan Davidson (Snakeskin), William Salera (Man in Laundromat), Miranda July (Black Eyed Nurse), Omar Koury (E.R. Doctor), Lee Golden (Isaac), Boris McGiver (Max), Susanne Case-Sulby (Beverly Home Head Nurse), Kevin Carroll (Chris), Michael Bove (Interpreter), Clista Townsend, David Tuttleman (AA People), Rebecca Kimball (Mennonite Woman), David Urrutia (Mennonite Husband), Christine Cowin (Young Nurse)

FH, an amiable, optimistic drug addict and drifter, ends up at a nursing home where he finally puts his desire to assist other unfortunate people to good use.

Billy Crudup, Dennis Hopper

Manuel Lozano, Fernando Fernán Gómez

Manuel Lozano, Fernando Fernán Gómez

BUTTERFLY

(MIRAMAX) formerly *Butterfly's Tongue*; Executive Producers, Fernando Bovaira, José Luis Cuerda; Director, José Luis Cuerda; Screenplay, Rafael Azcona; Based on the book *Qué Me Quieres, Amor?* by Manuel Rivas; Photography, Javier Salmones; Art Director, Josep Rosell; Associate Producer, José María Besteiro; Editor, Nacho Ruiz Capillas; Music, Alejandro Amenábar; Line Producer, Emiliano Otegui; Costumes, Sonia Grande; a Sogetel-Las Producciones del Escorpión production with the collaboration of Canal+ Spain, TVE and TVG; Spanish, 1999; Dolby; Panavision; Color; Rated R; 95 minutes; American release date: June 16, 2000

Manuel Lozano

CAST

Don Gregorio	Fernando Fernán Gómez
Moncho	Manuel Lozano
Rosa	Uxia Blanco
Ramón	Gonzalo Uriarte
Andés	Alexis de los Santos
D. Avelino	Jesús Castejón
Otis	Guillermo Toledo
Carmiña	Elena Fernández
Roque	Tamar Novas
Roque's Father	Tatán
Boal	Roberto Vidal
Marcías	Celso Parada
Cura	Celso Bugallo
Alcalde	Tucho Lagares
Nena	Milagros Jiménez
Aurora	Lara López
Jose Maria	Alberto Castro
Romualdo	Diego Vidal

and Xosé Manuel Olveira (Accordion Player), Manuel Piñiero (Trumpet Player), Alfonso Cid, Manuel Seara (Sax Players), José Ramón Vieira (String Bass), Antonio Pérez (Singer), Eduardo Gómez (Wise Man), Eva Maria Fernández, Feli Manzano (Neighbors), José F. Expolio (Tightrope Walker), Golfo (Tarzán)

On the eve of the Spanish Civil War, Don Gregorio an elderly schoolmaster with strong liberal views, befriends young Moncho, whose father faces troubled from the rising nationalists because of his own loyalty to the Republican government.

© Miramax Films

Manuel Lozano, Fernando Fernán Gómez

TIME REGAINED

(KINO) Producer, Paulo Branco; Director, Raul Ruiz; Screenplay, Gilles Taurand, Raul Ruiz; Based on the novel *Remembrance of Things Past /In Search of Lost Time* by Marcel Proust; Photography, Ricardo Aronovich; Music, Jorge Arriagada; Designer, Bruno Beauge; Costumes, Gabriella Pescucci, Caroline de Vivaise; ; Editor, Denise de Casabianca; Casting, Richard Rousseau; a Gemini Films, France 2 Cinéma, Les Films du Lendemain, Blu Cinematografica production in association with Madraoga Filmes with the participation of Canal+, CNC; French-Italian, 1999; Dolby; Color; Not rated; 158 minutes; American release date: June 16, 2000

CAST

Odette de Crecy	Catherine Deneuve
Gilberte	Emmanuelle Béart
Morel	Vincent Perez
Charlus	John Malkovich
Saint-Loup	Pascal Greggory
Madame Verdurin	Marie-France Pisier
Bloch	Christian Vadim
Madame de Farcy	Arielle Dombasle
The Narrator	Marcello Mazzarella
Albertine	Chiara Mastroianni
Voice of Marcel Proust	Patrice Chereau
Oriane de Guermantes	Edith Scob
Rachel	Elsa Zylberstein
Madame Cottard	Dominique Labourier
Monsieur Cottard	Philippe Morier-Genoud
Le Prince de Foix	Melvil Poupaud
Céleste	Matilde Seigner
Jupien	Jacques Pieller
Marcel	Andre Engel
Françoise	Helene Sugere
Marcel Enfant	George Du Fresne
Grandmother of Marcel	Monique Melinand
Father of Marcel	Laurence Fevrier
Uncle Adolphe	Jean-François Balmer
Marcel (adolescent)	Pierre Mignard
Prince of Guermantes	Lucien Pascal
Monsieur Verdurin	Jerome Prieur
Charles Swann	Bernard Paitrat
Goncourt	Alain Robbe-Grillet
La Princess Russe	Ingrid Caven
Duke of Guermantes	Jean-Claude Jay
Monsieur Bontemps	Alain Rimoux
Gilberte	Camille Du Fresne
The Great Designer	Alain Guillo
Guermante's Butler	Pierre-Alain Chapuis
Cafe de la Paix's Head Waiter	Jean-Francois Lapalus
Gaspard, Cafe de la Paix's Cook	Darrien O'Doul
Hotel Manager, Balbec	Daniel Isoppo
Young Waiter, Balbec	Patrice Juiff
Hotel Bellhop, Balbec	Pascal Tokatlian
Morel's Friend	Marine Delterme
Rachel's Husband	Jean Badin
Maurice	Laurent Schwar
Monsiuer Leon	Mess Hattou
Louis (Military Man)	Alexandre Soulie

and Sebastien Libessart (Military Man #2), Fabrice Cals, Jean-Pierre Allain (Workmen at Jupien), Carl de Miranda (Sailor at Jupien), Herve Falloux (Monsiquer Redingote), Philippe Lehembre (General), Vanzetta (Officer), Rosita Mital (Old Maid), Tatie Vauville (Old Maid's Mother), Michel Armin (Distinguished Client at Jupien), Pierre Vilanova (Monsieur Rene), Andre Delmas (Priest at Jupien), Philippe Gauguet (Jupien's Chauffeur), Serge Brincat (Cade de la Paix's Waiter), Yann Classen, Bruno Guillot, Emmanuel Crepin (Military Men, Cafe de la Paix), Francis Leplay (Jupien's Employee), Isabelle Auroy (Madame de Sainte Euverte), Jacques-François Zeller (Marcel's Grandfather), Serge Delcramer (Marcel's Father), Suzy Marquis (Old Woman at Gilberte), Laure de Clermont-Tonnerre (Gilbert's Daughter), Laetitia Colon-Vialaziex (Lea), Maxime Nourissat (Leo), Romain Sellier (Charles' Friend, Cafe de la Paix), Pierre Pitrou (Photographer), Alexandre Boussat (Rene, Morel's Friend), Sheila Irubacek (Vicomtesse de Saint-Fiacre), Bernard Barberet (One Legged Man), Alain Declos (Uncle Adolphe's Valet), Diane D'Assigny (Pianist, Bal de Tete), Guillaume Choquet (Violinist, Bal de Tete), Manuela Morgaine (Reader), Christian Magis (Blind Man)

As author Marcel Proust lay dying, he looks back on his own life, which becomes intertwined with characters from his novels.

Vincent Perez, Marie-France Pisier

Catherine Deneuve

Emmanuelle Béart

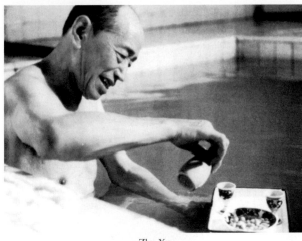

Zhu Xu

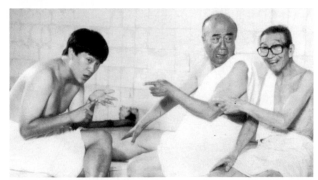

He Bing, Li Ding, Feng Shun

Pu Cun Xin

SHOWER

(SONY PICTURES CLASSICS) Producer, Peter Loehr; Executive Producer, Sam Duann; Director, Zhang Yang; Screenplay, Zhang Yang, Liu Fen Dou, Huo Xin, Diao Yi Nan, Cai Xiang Jun; Photography, Zhang Jian; Music, Ye Xiao Gang; Art Director, Tian Meng; Editors, Zhang Yang, Yang Hong Yu; Costumes, Hao Ge; a Xi'an Film Studio/Zhang Peimin presentation of an Imar Film Co. production; Chinese, 1999; Dolby; Color; Rated PG-13; 92 minutes; American release date: July 7, 2000

CAST

Master Liu	Zhu Xu
Liu Daming	Pu Cun Xin
Liu Erming	Jiang Wu
He Zheng	He Bing
Zhang Jinhao	Hu Bei Bei
Lao Lin	Li Ding
Lao Wu	Feng Shun
Miao Zhuang	Du Peng
Wang Fang	Sui Yongqing

Daming, a successful business man, returns to Beijing where his fast-living seems at odds with his father's more genteel way of living, as represented by the out-dated bathhouse that serves as a kind of community center for its elderly customers.

© Sony Pictures Entertainment, Inc.

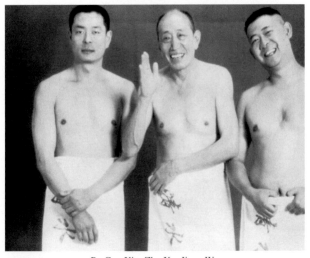

Pu Cun Xin, Zhu Xu, Jiang Wu

THE FIVE SENSES

(FINE LINE) Producers, Camelia Frieberg, Jeremy Podeswa; Executive Producers, Charlotte Mickie, Ted East, David R. Ginsburg; Director/Screenplay, Jeremy Podeswa; Photography, Gregory Middleton; Designer, Taavo Soodor; Costumes, Gersha Phillips; Editor, Wiebke von Carolsfeld; Music, Alex Pauk, Alexina Louie; Associate Producer, Shimmy Brandes; an Alliance Atlantis presentation of a Five Senses Production with the participation of Alliance Atlantis Pictures; Produced in association with the Canadian Broadcasting Corporation; Canadian, 1999; Dolby; Color; Rated R; 104 minutes; American release date: July 14, 2000

CAST

Rona	Mary-Louise Parker
Richard	Philippe Volter
Ruth	Gabrielle Rose
Robert	Daniel MacIvor
Rachel	Nadia Litz
Anna Miller	Molly Parker
Gail	Pascale Bussiéres
Roberto	Marco Leonardi
Rupert	Brendan Fletcher
Raymond	Richard Clarkin
Rebecca	Tara Rosling
Amy Lee Miller	Elize Frances Stolk
Carl	Clinton Walker
Richard's Patient	Astrid Van Wieben
Richard's Doctor	Paul Bettis
Justin	James Allodi

and Gavin Crawford (Airport Clerk), Sandi Stahlbrand, Ola Sturik (TV Reporters), Amanda Soha (Sylvie), Gisele Rousseau (Odile), Damon d'Oliveira (Todd), Sonia LaPlante (Monica), Janet Van De Graaff (Policewoman), Paul Soles (Mr. Bernstein), Clare Coulter (Clare), Roman Podhora, Greg Ellwand (Policemen), Shaun O'Mara, Glen Peloso (Park Cruisers), Tracy Wright (Alex), Darren O'Donnell (Medic), Daniel Taylor (Singer)

Several inter-related stories involving various Toronto residents and their obsessions with the five senses, take place around the disappearance of a young child.

© Fine Line Features

Mary-Louise Parker, Marco Leonardi

Alexis Loret, Juliette Binoche

ALICE AND MARTIN

(USA FILMS) Producer, Alain Sarde; Director, André Téchiné; Screenplay, André Téchiné, Gilles Taurand; Photography, Caroline Champetier; Designer, Ze Branco; Costumes, Elisabeth Tavernier; Editor, Martine Giordano; Music, Philippe Sarde; Line Producers, Jean-Jacques Albert, Yvon Crenn; Casting, Michel Nasri, Stephane Foenkinos, Jacques Grant, Benedicte Guiho; from October Films; a Les Films Alain Sarde, France 2 Cinéma, France 3 Cinéma/Vertigo Films (Spain) production, with the participation of Canal+, Studio Images 4; French-Spanish, 1998; Dolby; Color; Rated R; 123 minutes; American release date: July 21, 2000

CAST

Alice	Juliette Binoche
Martin Sauvagnac	Alexis Loret
Benjamin Sauvagnac	Mathieu Amalric
Jeanine Sauvagnac	Carmen Maura
Frederic Sauvagnac	Jean-Pierre Lorit
Lucie	Marthe Villalonga
Robert	Roschdy Zem
Victor Sauvagnac	Pierre Maguelon
Francois Sauvagnac	Eric Kreikenmayer
Martin (child)	Jeremy Kreikenmayer
Christophe	Kevin Goffette
Laurence	Christiane Ludot

and Veronique Rioux, Corinne Hache, Mauricio Angarita, Lilite Guegamian, Thierry Barone (Musicians), Ruth Malka-Viellet (Tania), Jocelyn Henriot (Tania's Assistant), Patrick Goavec (The Doctor), Emmanuel Marcandier (The Young Groom), Thomas Vallegeas (The Neighbor), Eric Hewson-Schmit (The Photographer), Nathalie Vignes (The Nurse), Franck de la Personne (The Examining Magistrate)

Martin, a troubled young man from a broken home, journeys to Paris to stay with his half-brother, Benjamin, and ends up falling for Benjamin's roommate, Alice.

© USA Films

NEW WATERFORD GIRL

(ALLIANCE ATLANTIS) Producers, Jennifer Kawaja, Julia Sereny; Executive Producers, Christopher Zimmmer, Ted East, Victor Loewy; Director, Allan Moyle; Screenplay, Tricia Fish; Photography, Derek Rogers; Designer, Emanuel Jannasch; Music, Geoff Bennett, Longo Hai, Ben Johannesen; Editor, Susan Maggi; a Sienna Films/Imagex production; Canadian, 1999; Color; Not rated; 97 minutes; American release date: July 26, 2000

CAST

Mooney Pottie	Liana Balaban
Lou Benzoa	Tara Spencer-Nairn
Frances Pottie	Nicholas Campbell
Cookie Pottie	Mary Walsh
Midge Benzoa	Cathy Moriatry
Cecil Sweeney	Andrew McCarthy
Dr. Hogan	Mark McKinney
Joey	Kevin Curran
Darlene Pottie	Cassie MacDonald
Betty Anne Pottie	Krista MacDonald
Sandra	Susan Laney Dalton
Lisa	Stacy Smith
Lexter Pottie	Darren Kaey
Felix Pottie	Adrian Dixon
Darcy Benzoa	Patrick Joyce
Father Madden	Lorne Purdy
Meeker	Zach Fraser
Mickey	Jody Richardson
Pickles Kavanaugh	Dave Frances

and Patricia Zentilli (Patty), Sarah Whittier (Tammy), Mike MacPhee (Derek), Lori LeDrew (Bonnie), Ida Donovan (Mrs. Roach), Rudy Pilchie (Karl), John Dunsworth (Roddy), Gordon White (Angelo the Bootlegger's Son), Maynard Morrison (Fry Cook), Bette MacDonald (Fry Cook Screamer), Gordon Gammie (The Businessman), Marguerite MacNeil (Boxing Mom), Tricia Fish (Noreen), John Goodrich (Twitchy Guy), Stephen Troy Gillis (Guy #1), Laurel MacDonald (Charlene), Colleen MacIsaac (Canteen Clerk), Sarah Loveridge (Red-Haired Woman), Aaron Armstrong (Sandy MacPhee), Blair Boone (Referee), Ashley MacIsaac (Town Fiddler), Sam White (Boxing Announcer)

Mooney, a restless fifteen year old girl living a dead-end existence in a small mining town, sees her chance for escape when she befriends Lou, a fiesty new girl from the Bronx.

© Alliance Atlantis

Liana Balaban

WONDERLAND

(USA FILMS) Producers, Michele Camarda, Andrew Eaton; Executive Producers, Stewart Till, David M. Thompson; Director, Michael Winterbottom; Screenplay, Laurence Coriat; Line Producer, Anita Overland; Co-Producer, Gina Carter; Photography, Sean Bobbitt; Designer, Mark Tildesley; Costumes, Natalie Ward; Editor, Trevor Waite; Music, Michael Nyman; Casting, Wendy Brazington; a Universal Pictures International and BBC Films presentation of a Kismet Film Company and Revolution Films production; British, 1999; Dolby; Panavision; Color; Rated R; 108 minutes; American release date: July 29, 2000

CAST

Debbie	Shirley Henderson
Nadia	Gina McKee
Molly	Molly Parker
Dan	Ian Hart
Eddie	John Simm
Tim	Stuart Townsend
Eileen	Kika Markham
Bill	Jack Shepherd
Darren	Enzo Cilenti
Melanie	Sarah-Jane Potts
Franklyn	David Fahm
Donna	Ellen Thomas
Jack	Peter Marfleet
Alex	Nathan Constance

and Anton Saunders (Bloke in Bed with Debbie), Abby Ford (Nurse), Michelle Jolly (Midwife), Rebecca Lenkiewicz (Policewoman), Vanessa Pratt (Kelly), Michael Hodgson (Kitchen Shop Father), Emma Sear (Kitchen Shop Mother), Megan Sear (Kitchen Shop Baby), Nuno Vaz (Portuguese Neighbor)

A look at three generations of one family during a chilly November week-end in London, during which their lives intersect in various surprising and emotional ways.

© Universal Studios, Inc.

Shirley Henderson, Gina McKee, Molly Parker

GIRL ON THE BRIDGE

(PARAMOUNT CLASSICS) Producer, Christian Fechner; Executive Producer, Herve Truffaut; Director, Patrice Leconte; Screenplay, Serge Frydman; Photography, Jean-Marie Dreujou; Designer, Ivan Maussion; Costumes, Annie Périer; Editor, Joellë Hache; a Films Christian Fechner/UGCF/France 2 Cinéma production, with the participation of Sofinergie 5 and Canal+; French, 1998; Dolby; Panavision; Black and white; Rated R; 92 minutes; American release date: July 29, 2000

Daniel Auteuil, Vanessa Paradis

CAST

Gabor	Daniel Auteuil
Adele	Vanessa Paradis
Suicide Victim	Claude Aufaure
TGV Waiter	Farouk Bermouga
Kusak	Bertie Cortez
Mr. Loyal	Nicolas Donato
Italian Megaphone	Enzo Etoyko
Barker	Giorgios Gatzios
Takis	Demetre Gerogalas
Irene	Catherine Lascault
TGV Ticket Collector	Didier Lemoine
Firemen	Pierre-François Martin-Laval, Jean-Paul Rouvray
Italian Waiter	Stéphane Metzger
Intern	Franck Monsigny
Miss Memory	Mireille Mossé
The Barman	Boris Napes
Stage Manager	Luc Palun
Bride	Isabelle Petit-Jacques
Contortionist	Frédéric Pflüger
Guy in T-Shirt	Jacques Philipson
Hotel Concierge	Philippe Sire
Nurse	Natascha Solignac
Casino Woman	Isabelle Spade
Clown	Jacques Vertan
Casino Neighbor	Bruno Villien

Daniel Auteuil

A fading performer in search of a partner for his knife-throwing act, finds the ideal woman in Adele whom he has just stopped from throwing herself in the Seine.

Vanessa Paradis

Vanessa Paradis

SAVING GRACE

(**FINE LINE**) Producer/Story, Mark Crowdy; Executive Producers, Cat Villiers, Xavier Marchand; Director, Nigel Cole; Screenplay, Craig Ferguson, Mark Crowdy; Line Producer, Steve Clark-Hall; Co-Producers, Craig Ferguson, Torsten Leschly; Photography, John de Borman; Designer, Eve Stewart; Costumes, Annie Symons; Music, Mark Russell; Editor, Alan Strachan; Hair & Makeup Designer, Roseann Samuel; Casting, Gail Stevens; a Portman Entertainment presentation in association with Sky Pictures and Wave Pictures of a Homerun Production; British; Dolby; Widescreen; Deluxe color; Rated R; 93 minutes; American release date: August 4, 2000.

Martin Clunes, Valerie Edmond

CAST

Grace Trevethan	Brenda Blethyn
Matthew	Craig Ferguson
Dr. Bamford	Martin Clunes
Jacques	Tchéky Karyo
Nicky	Valerie Edmond
Margaret	Phyllida Law
Vicar	Leslie Phillips
Harvey Sloggit	Tristan Sturrock
China McFarlane	Jamie Foreman
Vince	Bill Bailey
Quentin	Clive Merrison
Honey	Diana Quick
Diana	Linda Kerr Scott
Mrs. Hopkins	Denise Coffey
Charlie	Paul Brooke
Sgt. Alfred	Ken Campbell
Melvyn	John Fortune
Nigel	Philip Wright
Terry	Darren Southworth
Tony	Magnus Lindgren
Bob	Dean Lennox Kelly
Removal Boss	Johnny Bamford
Postman	Bill Hallet
Secretary	Alison Dillon
John Trevethan	Bill Weston
Presenters	Jonathan Kydd, Mark Crowdy
Master of Ceremonies	Jay Benedict
Man at Checkout	Ben Cole

Following her husband's death, Grace Trevethan faces financial ruin until her gardener, Matthew, talks her into using her horticultural skills to grow marijuana for profit.

© Fine Line Features

Phyllida Law, Linda Kerr Scott

Martin Clunes, Craig Ferguson, Paul Brooke, Brenda Blethyn, Tristan Sturrock

Brenda Blethyn, Craig Ferguson

Juliane Köhler, Maria Schrader

Maria Schrader, Juliane Köhler

AIMÉE & JAGUAR

(ZEITGEIST) Producers, Günter Rohrbach, Hanno Huth; Director, Max Färberböck; Screenplay, Max Färberböck, Rona Munro; Based on the book by Erica Fischer; Associate Producer, Gerhard von Halem; Line Producer, Stefaan Schieder; Photography, Tony Imi; Set Designers, Albrecht Konrad, Uli Hanisch; Costumes, Barbara Baum; Editor, Barbara Hennings; Casting, Risa Kes Casting; a Günter Rohrbach/Senator Film production; German, 1999; Dolby; Color; Not rated; 125 minutes; American release date: August 11, 2000.

CAST

Felice Schragenheim (Jaguar)	Maria Schrader
Lilly Wust (Aimée)	Juliane Köhler
Ilse	Johanna Wokalek
Klärchen	Heike Makatsch
Lotte	Elisabeth Degen
Günther Wust	Detlev Buck
Lilly (Today)	Inge Keller
Ilse (Today)	Kyra Mladeck
Mrs. Jäger	Margit Bendokat
Werner Lause	Jochen Stern
Editor in Chief Keller	Peter Weck
Stefan Schmidt	H.C. Blumenberg
Father Kappler	Klaus Manchen
Mother Kappler	Sarah Camp
Erika	Desirée Nick
Maria	Patrizia Moresco
Marlene	Karin Friesecke
Fritz Borchert	Dani Levy
Grandma Hulda	Lya Dulitzkaya
Mr. Ude	Klaus Koennecke
Mrs. Ude	Barbara Focke
Tanja	Dorkas Kiefer

and Werner Rehm (Conductor), Rüdiger Hacker (Ernst Biermösl), Peer Jäger (Mr. Pohl), Anette Felber (Mrs. Pohl), Bastian Trost (Lieutenant), Rosel Zech (Blonde Woman), Carl Heinz Choynski (Brummer), Ulrich Matthes (Eckert).

Maria Schrader

In war torn Germany, Lilly, a married woman with children enjoying privileges under the Nazi rule, begins a dangerous affair with Felice, a Jewish member of the underground.

© Zeitgeist Films

Juliane Köhler, Maria Schrader

AN AFFAIR OF LOVE

(FINE LINE) a.k.a. *A Pornographic Affair*; Producer, Patrick Quinet; Director, Frédéric Fonteyne; Screenplay, Philippe Blasband; Photography, Virginie Saint Martin; Designer, Véronique Sacrez; Editor, Chantal Hymans; Costumes, Anne Schotte; Music, Jeannot Sanavia, André Dziezuk, Marc Mergen; Presented in association with Patrick Quinet and Artémis Productions; French-Swiss-Belgium-Luxembourg, 1999; Dolby; Color; Rated R; 80 minutes; American release date: August 11, 2000

CAST

Her ....Nathalie Baye
Him ....Sergi López
Mr. Lignaux ....Paul Pavel
Mrs. Lignaux ....Sylvie van den Elsen
Interviewer..Jacques Viala
Hotel Receptionist ....Pierre Geranio
Ambulance Driver ....Hervé Sogne
Hospital Employee ....Christophe Sermet

A man and woman are interviewed separately about their past sexual encounters with one another, the result of an ad she had placed seeking a partner to act out her fantasy.

© Fine Line Features

Nathalie Baye, Sergi López

Catherine Deneuve, Jean-Pierre Bacri

Catherine Deneuve, Emmanuelle Seigner

PLACE VENDÔME

(EMPIRE) Executive Producer, Alain Sarde; Director, Nicole Garcia; Screenplay, Nicole Garcia, Jacques Fieschi; Photography, Laurent Dailland; Associate Producer, Christine Gozlan; Costumes, Nathalie Du Roscoat; Elisabeth Tavernier; Editors, Luc Banner, Françoise Bonnot; Music, Richard Robbins; Casting, Frederique Moidon, Lucie Boulting; a Les Film Alain Sarde/TF1 Films Production/Les Films de l'Etang/Alhena Films/Angel's Company production, with the participation of Canal+, CNC and Studio Images 3; French, 1998; DTS; Widescreen; Color; Not rated; 117 minutes; American release date: August 18, 2000.

CAST

Marianne Malivert..Catherine Deneuve
Nathalie..Emmanuelle Seigner
Jean-Pierre ....Jean-Pierre Bacri
Battistelli ....Jacques Dutronc
Vincent Malivert ....Bernard Fresson
Eric Malivert ....Francois Berleand
Janos ....Dragan Nikolic
Samy ....Otto Tausig
Charlie Rosen...Laszlo Szabo
Pierson ....Elisabeth Commelin
Kleiser...Philippe Clevenot
Sam's Son...Malik Zidi
Phillipe Ternece ....Eric Ruf
Saliha ....Nidal Al-Askhar
Christopher Makos...Larry Lamb
Wajman..Julian Fellowes
and Monem Abel (Indian Diamond Businessman), Michael Culkin, Nick Ellsworth, Antoine Blanquefort (De Beers Men), Coralie Seyrig, Carmen Román (Malvert Employees), Martine Erhel (Louise), Arnaud Xainte, Aristide Demonico, Paolo Capisano (Malivert Employees), Germaine Labarthe (Shop Customer), Eric Landau (Diamond Expert), James Oliver (Advocate), Sylvie Fleep, Hélène Otternaud, Saliha Fellahi (Clinic Nurses), Pierre Mottet (The Doctor), Michel Hulby, Paul Chevillard, Catherine Cretin (Dinner Guest), Delphine Blamont (Chambermaid at the Ritz), Pierre-Jean le Gregan (Bellhop), Pascal Renault (The Hunter), Mykhael Georges-Schar (Hilton Concierge), Phillipe Giblin (Jean-Pierre's Assistant), Arno Feffer (Musician Behind with the Rent), Cecile Camp (His Wife), Mehdi Mengal (His Son), Jean-Claude Perrin (The Priest), Albert Goldberg (Poker Player), David George, Henry Leon Bakon (Samy's Friends), Béatrice Demachy (Rosen's Secretary), Jacques Michel (Kleiser's Associate), Patrick Colucci (Cafe Manager), Paul Kawan (Broker at Antwerp Exchange)

Marianne Malivert, the unhappy, alcoholic wife of a noted jewelry expert, finds herself left in possession of five very valuable gems after her husband's suicide. When she realizes the diamonds are desired by various parties she seizes this opportunity to pull her life back together and use them to her advantage.

© Empire Pictures

SOLOMON & GAENOR

Ioan Gruffudd

Mark Lewis Jones

(SONY CLASSICS) Producer, Sheryl Crown; Executive Producers, Andy Porter, David Green; Director/Screenplay, Paul Morrison; Photography, Nina Kellgren; Designer, Hayden Pearce; Costumes, Maxine Brown; Music, Illona Sekacz; Editor, Kant pan; Casting, Joan McCann; an S4C and Filmfour with the Arts Council of England and the Arts Council of Wales presentation of an Apt Film and Television production in association with September Films; British, 1999; Dolby; Deluxe color; Rated R; 102 minutes; U.S. release date: August 25, 2000.

CAST

Solomon	Ioan Gruffudd
Gaenor	Nia Roberts
Gwen	Sue Jones Davies
Idris	William Thomas
Crad	Mark Lewis Jones
Rezl	Maureen Lipman
Isaac	David Horovitch
Bronwen	Bethan Ellis Owen
Thomas	Adam Jenkins
Ephraim	Cyril Shaps
Philip	Daniel Kaye
Benjamin	Elliot Cantor
Noah Jones	Steffan Rhodri
Reverend Roberts	Emyr Wyn
Wyn	Julian Lewis Jones
Huw	Arwyn Davies
Geraint	Dai Morgan
Rhys	Rhys Evans
Aunt Myfanwy	Helen Griffin
Trefor Lloyd	Gwyn Vaughan Jones
Uncle Mennasseh	Alan Schwartz
Aunt Sadie	Anne Sessions
Naomi	Olivia Simova
Mannie Silvergilt	Barry Davies
Rabbi Wolfe	Rabbi Daniel Levy

and Derek Smith (Jewish Man), Jane Manuel (Jewish Woman), Daniel Pruchnie (Jewish Child), Ri Richards (Glass Woman), Gill Griffiths (First Woman), Manon Eames (Welsh Woman at Door), Dafydd Wyn Roberts (Old Tramp), Ceri Evans (Ceridwen), Huw Emlyn (Barman Alun), Winston Evans (Postman), Sion Hopkins (Sleepy John)

In a Welsh mining village in 1911, Gaenor falls in love with Solomon who refuses to disclose his Jewish background for fear of losing her. This film received an Oscar nomination for foreign language film, 1999.

© Sony Pictures Entertainment, Inc.

Ioan Gruffudd, Nia Roberts

Nia Roberts, Ioan Gruffudd

THE ART OF WAR

(WARNER BROS.) Producer, Nicolas Clermont; Executive Producers, Elie Samaha, Dan Halsted, Wesley Snipes; Director, Christian Duguay; Screenplay, Wayne Beach, Simon Davis Barry; Story, Wayne Beach; Photography, Pierre Gill; Designer, Anne Pritchard; Editor, Michel Arcand; Music, Normand Corbeil; Co-Producer, Richard Lalonde; Casting, Rosina Bucci, Vera Miller, Nadia Rona; a Morgan Creek Productions, Inc. and Franchise Pictures and Amen Ra Films presentation of a Filmline International production; Canadian-U.S.; Dolby; Super 35 Widescreen; Color; Rated R; 118 minutes; American release date: August 27, 2000

CAST

Neil Shaw	Wesley Snipes
Eleanor Hooks	Anne Archer
Cappella	Maury Chaykin
Julia Fang	Marie Matiko
David Chan	Cary-Hiroyuki Tagawa
Bly	Michael Biehn
Douglas Thomas	Donald Sutherland
Novak	Liliana Komorowska
Ambassador Wu	James Hong
Ray	Paul Hopkins
Ochai	Glen Chi Ying-Ming
Ming	Ron Yuan
Anna	Bonnie Mak
Tina Chan	Uni Park
Hong Kong Reporter	Erin Selby
Zeng Zi	Fernando Chien
Shades	Paul Wu
Alex Wingate	Noel Burton

and Andrew Peplowski, Andrew Nichols (TNN Reporters, UN), Mike Tsarouchas (NYPD Lieutenant), Steve Park (Tatoo), Yardly Kavanagh (Reporter at Chan's Hotel), Frank Schorpion (TWN News Anchorman), Fred Bessa, Terry Simpson (NY Cops), Tony Calabretta (Detective #2), Fred Lee (Doctor Chin), Tang Weifeng, Huy Phong Doan (Triad Hoods), Phil Chiu (Triad Hood, Driver), Jeniene Phillips (TWN Reporter), Frank Cavallaro (Reporter #6), Michelle Sweeney (Diner Waitress), Richard Jutras (Larry, Hook's Secretary), Jeff Ward (FBI Agent, Times Square), Ken Tran (Triad Bruiser), Marlon Sterling Long (FBI Agent #1, Athletic Club), Han Zhenhu (Athletic Club Shopkeeper), Danny Blanco-Hall (NY Cop #2, Athletic Club Kitchen), Paul Stewart (American Ambassador), Jason Cavalier (Security Guard), Tracey McKee (Times Square Reporter), Toula Bassanoff (FBI Agent, Elderly Chinese Hobo)

Covert UN agent Neil Shaw is framed to take the blame for the assassination of a Chinese ambassador, making him the target of the actual conspirators.

© Filmline International Inc.

Marie Matiko, Wesley Snipes

Julie Walters, Aingeal Grehan

TITANIC TOWN

(SHOOTING GALLERY) Producers, George Faber, Charles Pattinson; Executive Producers, David M. Thompson, Robert Cooper, Rainer Mockert; Director, Roger Michell; Screenplay, Anne Devlin; Based on the novel by Mary Costello; Line Producer, Sally French; Photography, John Daly; Designer, Pat Campbell; Editor, Kate Evans; Costumes, Hazel Pethig; Music, Trevor Jones; a Company Pictures production, of a Pandora Cinema and BBC Films presentation in association with Hollywood Partners, supported by the Arts Council of Northern Ireland through its National Lottery Fund with the participation of British Screen; British-Irish, 1998; Dolby; Color; Not rated; 96 minutes; American release date: September 1, 2000.

CAST

Bernie McPhelimy	Julie Walters
Aidan McPhelimy	Ciaran Hinds
Annie McPhelimy	Nuala O'Neill
Thomas McPhelimy	James Loughran
Brenda McPhelimy	Barry Loughran
Sinead McPhelimy	Elizabeth Donaghy
Dino/Owen	Ciaran McMenamin
Patsy French	Jaz Pollock
Niall French	Caolan Byrne
Deirdre	Aingeal Grehan
Whittington	Oliver Ford Davies
Immonger	Nick Woodeson
Finnbar	Des McAleer
Cahir	BJ Hogg
Nora	Doreen Hepburn
Kathleen	Ruth McCabe
Mary McCoy	Veronica Duffy

and Timmy McCoy (Colm), Lorcan Cranitch (Tony), Cathy White (Rosaleen), Malcolm Rodgers (Uncle James), Tracey Wilkinson (Lucy), Kelly Flynn (Bridget), Cheryl O'Dwyer (Maureen), Magie Shevlin (Mrs. Morris), Billy Clark (Gunman), Fo Cullen (Miss Savage), Simon Fullerton (Jimmy Kane), Duncan Marwick (Lionel Thirston), John Drummond (Sergeant), Paul Trussell (Lanky Soldier), Lee Netteingham, Neil Maskell, Peter Ferdinando, Mark Mooney (Soldiers), Darren Bancroft (Corporal), Claire Curran (Niuala Curran), Julia Dearden (Mrs. Gilroy), Mairead Redmond (Mairead Curran), Andrew Havill (Officer), Paula Hamilton (Mrs. Brennan), Mike Dowling (Butcher), Robert Calvert (Bus Driver), Jeananne Crowley (Mrs. Lockhart), Peter Ballance (Fergus), Richard Clements (Brian), Colum Convey (Interviewer), Amanda Hurwitz (Night Nurse), Tony Rohr (Cork Driver), Richard Smedley (Patrol Leader), Alan McKee (Reporter), Tony Devlin (Republican Youth), Andrew Downs (Ambulance Driver), Breffni McKenna (Paramedic), John Quinn (Republican), Packy Lee (Hijack Youth), Catriona Hinds (TV Journalist), Christina Nelson, Gerard McCartney (Journalists), Karen Staples (Nurse), Kieran Aherne (Father Clancy), Brenda Winter (Mrs. Duffy), Richard Orr (Man in Black Jacket), Chris Parr (1st Radio Interviewee)

After a friend of hers is killed in crossfire, Bernie McPhelimy starts her own personal crusade against the IRA occupation of her Northern Ireland town, an act that incurs the wrath of her neighbors who feel she has betrayed the cause.

© Shooting Gallery

MADADAYO

(WINSTAR) Producer, Hisao Kurosawa; Executive Producers, Yo Yamamoto, Yuzo Irie; General Producers, Yasuyoshi Tokuma, Gohei Kogure; Director/Screenplay, Akira Kurosawa; Based on the book by Hyakken Uchida; Photography, Takao Saito, Masaharu Ueda; Art Director, Yoshiro Muraki; Costumes, Kazuko Kurosawa; Music, Shin'Ichiro Ikebe; English Subtitles, Jeanette Amano; Japanese, 1993; Dolby; Color; Not rated; 134 minutes; American release date: September 1, 2000

CAST

Professor Hyakken Uchida	Tatsuo Matsumura
Professor's Wife	Kyoko Kagawa
Takayama	Hisashi Igawa
Amaki	George Tokoro
Kiriyama	Masayuki Yui
Sawamura	Akira Terao
Rev. Kameyama	Asei Kobayashi
Dr. Kobayashi	Takeshi Kusaka

After he retires from teaching to concentrate on his writing, a beloved German professor is visited each year on his birthday over a 17-year period by his former students. This was the final film directed by Akira Kurosawa who died on Sept. 6, 1998.

© Winstar Cinema

Marisa Pitarresi, Philippe Torreton

IT ALL STARTS TODAY

(INDEPENDENT ARTISTS) Producers, Alain Sarde, Frédéric Bourboulon; Director, Bertrand Tavernier; Screenplay, Dominique Sampiero, Tiffany Tavernier, Bertrand Tavernier; Photography, Alain Choquart; Art Director, Thierry François; Costumes, Marpessa Djian; Editors, Sophie Brunet, Sophie Mandonnet; Music, Louis Sclavis; from Le Studio Canal+; Little Bear/Les Films Alain Sarde/TF1 Films productions; French, 1999; Color; Not rated; 117 minutes; American release date: September 8, 2000

CAST

Daniel	Philippe Torreton
Valeria	Maria Pitarresi
Samia	Nadia Kaci
Mrs. Lienard	Veronique Ataly
Cathy	Nathalie Bécue
Mrs. Tiévaux	Emmanuelle Bercot
Mrs. Delacourt	Françoise Bette
Mrs. Baudoin	Christine Citti
Sophie	Christina Crevillen
Gloria	Sylviane Goudal
The Inspector	Didier Bezace

and Betty Teboulle (Mrs. Henry), Gérard Giroudon (The Mayor), Marief Guittier (Daniel's Mother), Daniel Delabesse (Marc), Jean-Claude Frissung (Director's Colleague), Thierry Gibault (Police Detective), Philippe Meyer (Municipal Official), Gérald Cesbron (Mr. Henry), Michelle Goddet (Mother of Abused Child), Stefan Elbaum (Abused Child's Uncle), Nathalie Desprez (Mrs. Bry), Françoise Miquelis (Mrs. Duhem), Frédéric Richard (Mr. Bacheux), Johanne Cornil-Leconte (Mrs. Bacheux), Sylvie Delbauffe (Woman with Baby), Lambert Marchal (Remi), Kelly Mercier (Laetitia), Mathieu Lenne (Jimmy), Rémi Henneuse (Kevin), Corinne Agthe (Mrs. Paquotte), Dominique Bouchard (Doctor for 4-Year-Old Check-Up), Benoit Constant (Daniel's Father), Patrick Courteix (Mrs. Henry's Neighbor), Veronique Dargent (Mrs. Loiseau), Valerie Dermagne (The Nurse), Lilyane Discret (Young Mother), Leila Duhem (Mrs. Polliaert), Yamina Duvivier (Mrs. Chimot), Severine Fernand (Angeline's Mother), Catherine Gorosz (Mrs. Daumise), Christophe Guichet (Daniel's Brother), Nadia Ikisse (Mrs. Mimouni), Marie-Madeleine Langlois (Neighbor Lady), Nelly Larachiche (Mrs. Legrand), France Leroy (Cafe Owner), Claude Lienard (Mrs. Henry's Doctor), Marcelle Loutre (Guegdan's Mother), Jacky Meunier (Valeria's Father), Cecile Montagnon (Mrs. Lamart), Michele Niewrzeda (Mrs. Bornat), Vincenza Orologio (Valeria's Mother), Marie-Francoise Prette (Mrs. Marchal), Linda Prudhomme (Mrs. Dupuis), Monique Quivy (Lunch Room Lady), Claude Ronnaux (Colleague), Francoise Sage (Mrs. Meriaux), Pascale Verdiere (Wet Nurse)

A look at the life of a preschool principal in a depressed region of France.

Tatsuo Matsumura

Kyoko Kagawa, Hisashi Igawa, Tatsuo Matsumura, George Tokoro

POLA X

(WINSTAR) Producer, Bruno Pesery; Executive Producers, Albert Prevost, Raimond Goebel; Director, Leos Carax; Screenplay, Leos Carax, Lauren Sedofsky, Jean-Pol Fargeau; Based on the novel *Pierre or the Ambiguities* by Herman Melville; Photography, Eric Gautier; Designer, Laurent Allaire; Editor, Nelly Quettier; Costumes, Esther Walz; Music, Scott Walker; a production of Arena Films, Pola Production, Théo Films, France 2 Cinéma, Pandora Filmproduktion, Euro Space, and Vega Film; French-German-Japanese-Swiss, 1999; Dolby; Color; Not rated; 124 minutes; American release date: September 8, 2000.

CAST

Pierre	Guillaume Depardieu
Isabelle	Katerina Golubeva
Marie	Catherine Deneuve
Lucie	Delphine Chuillot
Razerka	Petruta Catana
The Child	Mihaella Silaghi
Thibault	Laurent Lucas
Margherite	Patachou
The Chief	Sharunas Bartas
Fred	Samuel Dupuy
Augusto	Miguel Yeco

and Mathias Miekuz (TV Presenter), Dine Souli (Taxi Driver), Khireddine Medjoubi (Cafe Owner's Son), Mark Zak (Romanian Friend), Anne Richter (Chef's Wife), Myriam Defremont, Michel B. Duperial, Pascal Parmentier, Jean-Jacques Colin (Policemen)

A man leading a seemingly idyllic life with his mother in a Normandy chateau, comes face to face with a mysterious woman who has been appearing in his dreams, and is stunned to find out that she is his half-sister.

Guillaume Depardieu, Delphine Chuillot

Catherine Deneuve, Guillaume Depardieu

SOLAS

(GOLDWYN/FIREWORKS) Producer, Antonio P. Pérez, Eduardo Santana; Director/Screenplay, Benito Zambrano; Photography, Tote Trenas; Art Director, Lala Obrero; Editor, Fernando Pardo; Music, Antonio Meliveo; a Maestranza Films (Sevilla) production in association with Via Digital and Canal Sur TV, presented in association with Canwest Entertainment; Spanish, 1999; Dolby; Color; Not rated; 98 minutes; American release date: September 8, 2000.

CAST

María	Ana Fernandez
Mother	María Galiana
Father	Paco De Osca
Neighbor	Carlos Alvarez-Novoa
Juan	Juan Fernández
Doctor	Antonio Perez Dechent
The Fat Man	Miguel Alobar

and Pilar Sanchez, Concha Galán (Cleaning Women), Paco Tous (Partner of Juan), Rosario Lara (Boss of Cleaning Women), Estrella Távora (Nurse), José Manuel Seoa (Nightwatchman), Magdalena Barrero (Sick Woman), Sebastián Herrero (Sick Man), Praxedes Nieto (Butcher), Manolo Linares (Blind Man)

A bitter woman's unhappy, troubled life is given solace when her loving mother comes to stay with her.

Ana Fernandez

Jose Coronado, Mariel Verdú

Jose Coronado

Francisco Rabal

GOYA IN BORDEAUX

(SONY PICTURES CLASSICS) Producer, Andrés Vincent Gómez; Co-Producer, Fulvio Lucisano; Director/Screenplay, Carlos Saura; Photography, Vittorio Storaro; Art Director, Pierre-Louis Thèvenet; Costumes, Pedro Moreno; Music, Roque Baños; Editor, Julia Juániz; an Andrés Vincent Gómez production for Lolafilms in co-production with Italian International Film, in collaboration with RAI-Radiotelevisione Italiana, and with the collaboration of Via Digital Television Espanol S.A.; Spanish-Italian, 1999; Dolby; Univision; Color; Rated R; 102 minutes; American release date: September 15, 2000.

CAST

Francisco de Goya	Francisco Rabal
Goya as a Young Man	Jose Coronado
Rosarito	Dafne Fernández
Duchess of Alba	Mariel Verdú
Leocadia Zorilla de Weiss	Eulalia Ramón
Moratín	Joaquín Climent
Pepita Tudó	Cristina Espinosa
Godoy	Jose María Pou
Priest/San Antonia	Saturnino García
Juan Valdés	Carlos Hipólito
José de la Cruz	Emilio Gutiérrez Caba
Salcedo	Manuel de Blas
Braulio Poe	Pedro Azorin
Novales	Joan Valles
Asensio	Paco Catalá

and Franco Di Francescantonio (Doctor in Andalucía) José Antonio (Dancer, Duke de Osuna), Mario de Candia (Bayeu), La Fura dels Baus (Los Desastres de la Guerra), Concha Leza (Woman in Andalucía), Jaime Losada (Gaulon), Aihnoa Suarez (Rosarito, Aged 6), José Reche (Murdered Corpse), José Sainz (Guilty Gravedigger), Demetrio Julian (San Antonio's Father), Stephane Salom (Young French Man), Roberto Arcilla (Chubby French Man), Lorena Pellarini (French Woman), Azucena de la Fuente (Josefina Bayeu), Bartolomé Moreno, Francisco Jesús Santillana, José Luis Chavarria, Luis Llamas (Men), Natalie Pinot (Piano Teacher), Olivier D'Belloch (Gaulon's Assistant), Borja Elgea (Goya's Friend)

Eighty-two-year old artist Francisco de Goya, living in exile in Bordeaux, recounts his turbulent life to his daughter.

© Sony Pictures Entertainment, Inc.

HUMAN RESOURCES

(SHOOTING GALLERY) Producers, Caroline Benjo, Carole Scotta; Director/Screenplay, Laurent Cantet; Line Producer, Barbara Letellier; Photography, Matthieu Poirot Delpech; Art Director, Romain Denis; Editor, Robin Campillo; Casting, Constance Demontoy; a co-production of Haut et Court-La Sept ARTE/Unité de Programmes Fictions, Pierre Chevalier with the support of Centre National de la Cinématographie Procirep, Media Program of European Union and BBC Films; French-British; Dolby; Color; Not rated; 103 minutes; American release date: September 15, 2000.

CAST

Frank	Jalil Lespert
The Father	Jean-Claude Vallod
The Mother	Chantal Barré
Sylvie	Véronique de Pandelaère
Olivier	Michel Begnez
Chief Executive	Lucien Longueville
Mrs. Arnoux	Danielle Mélador
Head of HR	Pascal Sémard
Alain	Didier Émile-Woldemard
Betty	Françoise Boutigny
Félix	Félix Cantet
Marie	Marie Cantet
Christian	Stéphane Tauvel

Young Frank, fresh out of business school, lands a job in the human resources department at the factory where his father works and finds himself opposing his father in a labor management dispute.

© Shooting Gallery

Adam Monty, Isabella Rosselini

Laura Fraser, Marianne Sägebrecht

Jalil Lespert, Jean-Claude Vallod

LEFT LUGGAGE

(CASTLE HILL) Producers, Ate de Jong, Hans Pos, Dave Schram; Director, Jeroen Krabbé; Screenplay, Edward de Vries; Based on the novel by Carl Friedman; Co-Executive Producers, Craig Haffner, Brad Wilson; Photography, Walther vanden Ende; Co-Producers, Dirk Impens, Rudy Verzyck; Music, Henny Vrienten; Editor, Edgar Burcksen; Costumes, Bernadette Corstens, Yan Tax; Casting, Susie Figgis; a Trident Releasing presentation; Dolby; Cine Color; Belgian-Netherlands-U.S.; Not rated; 100 minutes; Release date: September 22, 2000

CAST

Chaja Silberschmidt	Laura Fraser
Simcha	Adam Monty
Mrs. Kalman	Isabella Rosselini
Mr. Kalman	Jeroen Krabbé
Mr. Apfelschnitt	Chaim Topol
Mrs. Silberschmidt	Marianne Sägebrecht
Mr. Silberschmidt	Maximilian Schell
Concierge	David Bradley
Sofie	Heather Weeks
Mrs. Goldman	Miriam Margolyes
Mr. Goldman	Lex Goudsmit

and Krijn ter Braak (Grandfather), Mieke Verheyden (Grandmother), Noura Van der Berg (Selma), Lana Broekaert (Chaya—7 years), Koen de Bouw (Father Chaya—20 years), Edwin de Vries, Bart de Vries (Hasids), Benjamin Broekaert (Dov), Ben Glanz (Avrum), Bloeme Cohen, Marlies Claissen (Tsivjas), Ann Petersen (Landlady), Luc Van Mello, Gideon Rijnders (Police Officers), Luc D'Heu (Restaurant Owner), Marc Lauwrys, Ben Van Ostade (Cooks), Ben Rottiers (Resistance Fighter), Alex de Jong (Cantor), Antonie Kamerling (Peter), Michael Pas (The Cook)

In 1970s Belgium, Chaja, the daughter of Holocaust survivors, takes a job as a nanny for a Hasidic Jewish family and forms a special bond with their son, Simcha, a boy who will not speak.

© Castle Hill

Björk, Catherine Deneuve

Catherine Deneuve

DANCER IN THE DARK

(FINE LINE) Producer, Vibeke Windeløv; Executive Producers, Peter Aalbæk Jensen; Director/Screenplay, Lars von Trier; Photography, Robby Müller; Designer, Karl Juliusson; Costumes, Manon Rasmussen; Music, Björk; Lyrics, Lars von Trier, Sjón Sigurdsson; Choreographer/Dance Director, Vincent Paterson; Editors, Molly Malene Stensgaard, François Gedigier; Casting, Avy Kaufman; a Zentropa Entertainments4, Trust Film Svenska, Film I Väst and Liberator Productions presentation; Danish-Swedish-French; Dolby; Widescreen; Color; Rated R; 137 minutes; U.S. release date: September 23, 2000.

CAST

Selma Jezková ....Björk
Kathy ....Catherine Deneuve
Bill ....David Morse
Jeff ....Peter Stormare
Oldrich Novy ....Joel Grey
Samuel ....Vincent Paterson
Linda..Cara Seymour
Norman ....Jean-Marc Barr
Gene ....Vladica Kostic
Brenda ....Siobhan Fallon
District Attorney ....Zeljko Ivanek
Dr. Porkorny ....Udo Kier
Morty..Jens Albinus
Judge ....Reathel Bean
Receptionist..Mette Berggren
Defense Attorney ....Lars Michael Dinesen
Suzan ....Katrine Falkenberg
Angry Man..Michael Flessas
Detective ....John Randolph Jones
Officer of the Court ....Noah Lazarus
Visitor ....Sheldon Litt
Clerk of the Court ....Andrew Lucre
and John Martinus (Chairman), Luke Reilly (New Defense Council), T.J. Rizzo (Boris), Stellan Skarsgård (Doctor), Sean Michael Smith (Person in Doorway), Paprika Steen (Woman on Night Shift), Eric Voge (Officer), Nick Wolf (Man with Hood), Timm Zimmermann (Guard)

A simple-minded factory worker, trying to save up enough money for an operation to ensure that her young son will not lose his eyesight as she is, escapes from her drab life in a fantasy world of imaginary musical numbers. This film received an Oscar nomination for original song ("I've Seen It All").

© Fine Line Features

David Morse, Björk

David Morse, Peter Stormare

Christopher Horsey, Adam Garcia, Matt Lee, Lee McDonald

BOOTMEN

(FOX SEARCHLIGHT) Producer, Hilary Linstead; Executive Producer/Director/Choreographer, Dein Perry; Screenplay, Steve Worland; Story, Steve Worland, Hilary Linstead, Dein Perry; Co-Producer, Antonia Barnard; Photography, Steve Mason; Designer, Murray Picknett; Editor, Jane Moran; Costumes, Tess Schofield; Music, Cezary Skubiszewski; Music Design & Production, Lawrence Maddy; Casting, Christine King; a Hilary Linstead/Dein Perry production, presented in association with the Australian Film Finance Corp.; Australian; Dolby; Deluxe color; Rated R; 92 minutes; American release date: October 6, 2000

Adam Garcia, Sam Worthington

CAST

Sean Okden	Adam Garcia
Linda	Sophie Lee
Mitchell Okden	Sam Worthington
Walter	William Zappa
Gary Okden	Richard Carter
Sara	Susie Porter
Huey	Anthony Hayes
Angus	Christopher Horsey
Colin	Andrew Kaluski
Johnno	Matt Lee
Derrick	Lee McDonald
Young Sean	Vaughan Sheffield
Young Mitchell	Christian Patterson
Mrs. Okden	Lisa Perry
Williams	Bruce Venables
Kim	Justine Clarke
Gerard Ball	Andrew Doyle
Huey's Mates	Craig Anderson, Jonno Zissler
Footy Player	Harry Dakanalis

and Gateshead Rugby Club (Football Team), Dein Perry (Anthony Ford), Kelly Aykers (Ford's Girlfriend), Ian Sandercoe, Paul Elliot, David Carter, Craig Lancaster (Pub Band—Sandercoe), Reid Perry (Mitch Jr.)

Sophie Lee

Sean Okden, a steel mill worker eager to make more of his life, enlists some friends to help him put on a show, utilizing a different style of industrial-strength tap dancing.

Andrew Kaluski, Christopher Horsey, Adam Garcia, Matt Lee,
Lee McDonald

YI YI (A ONE AND A TWO)

(WINSTAR) Producers, Kawai Shinya, Tsukeda Naoko; Director/Screenplay, Edward Yang; Photography, Yang Weihan; Designer/Music, Peng Kaili; Editor, Chen Bowen; Associate Producers, Yu Weiyen, Kubota Osamu; Casting, Alex Yang; a 1+2 Seisaku Iinkai, Pony Canyon Inc. & Omega Project Inc. & Hakuhodo Inc. presentation of an Atom Films production; Taiwanese-Japanese; Dolby; Eastman color; Not rated; 173 minutes; American release date: October 6, 2000

Elaine Jin, Jonathan Chang

CAST

NJ Jian...Wu Nienjen
Mr. Ota...Issey Ogata
Min-Min...Elaine Jin
Ting-Ting...Kelly Lee
Yang-Yang...Jonathan Chang
A-Di...Chen Xisheng
Sherry Chang-Breitner...Ke Suyun
Da-Da...Michael Tao
Xiao-Yen...Xiao Shushen
Lili...Adrian Lin
"Fatty"...Yupang Chang
Grandma...Tang Ruyun
Mrs. Jiang, Lily's Mother...Xu Shuyuan
Yun-Yun...Zeng Xinyi
Migo...Li Yongfeng
Nancy...Jin Shihui
Wu Jie...Wu Jie
Shu Ge...Shu Guozhi
Liren...Dai Liren
NJ's Neighbor...You Meiyun
Xiao Yan's Uncle...You Qidong
Young Soldier...Ke Yulun
Dean...Liu Liangzuo
Lili's English Tutor...Chen Lihua
Policeman...Chen Yiwen
Young Banker...Song Shaoqing
Boss Huang...Luo Bei-An
Piano Bar Pianist...Antonio Lee

and Danny Deng, Fan Reijun, Cheng Jianxiong, Zhen Yuancheng, Cai Ruying, Sun Fajun, Jay Miao (A-Di's Friends), Tang Congsheng, Wang Qizan, Li Jianchang (Punks at NY Bagel Cafe), Tsuda Kenjiro (Robata Restaurant Waiter), Wu Weining (The "Concubine"), Zhang Huiling (Huiling), Xu Guiying (NJ's Secretary), Allen Lu (Mrs. Jiang's Boyfriend), Yang Shiping, Ye Ziyan (Grandma's Doctors), Yang Jinhua (Doctor's Wife), Li Wanyun, Lin Xiaowei (Xiao Yan's Assistants), Wu Yiting (The Baby), Xu Wenjuan (Da-Da's Wife), Wang Zhengkai (Security Guard), Xie Nianzu (Policeman), Chen Shiqi, Xiang Guangting, Lin Yanchun (Yang-Yang's Classmates).

Xiao Shushen, Chen Xisheng

On the day of her brother's marriage, Min-Min sees her seemingly perfect middle-class family life begin to unravel.

© Winstar Cinema

Kelly Lee, Tang Ruyun

Jonathan Chang, Elaine Jin

Jamie Bell

Jamie Bell

Jamie Draven

Stuart Wells

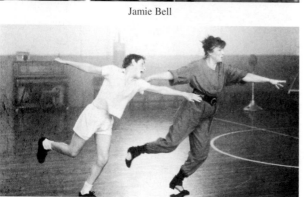

Jamie Bell, Julie Walters

Jamie Bell

BILLY ELLIOT

(UNIVERSAL FOCUS) formerly Dancer; Producers, Greg Brenman, Jon Finn; Executive Producers, Natascha Wharton, Charles Brand, David M. Thompson, Tessa Ross; Director, Stephen Daldry; Screenplay, Lee Hall; Photography, Brian Tufano; Designer, Maria Djurkovic; Editor, John Wilson; Costumes, Stewart Meacham; Music, Stephen Warbeck; Music Supervisor, Nick Angel; Song: *I Believe* by Steve Mac and Wayne Hector/performed by Stephen Gately; Line Producer, Tori Parry; Choreographer, Peter Darling; Casting, Jina Jay; a Working Title Films and BBC Films in association with the Arts Council of England presentation of a Tiger Aspect Pictures production in association with WT2; British; Dolby; Color; Rated R; 111 minutes; American release date: October 13, 2000

Jamie Bell

CAST

Mrs. Wilkinson	Julie Walters
Billy Elliot	Jamie Bell
Tony Elliot	Jamie Draven
Dad	Gary Lewis
Grandma	Jean Heywood
Michael	Stuart Wells
Billy (aged 25)	Adam Cooper
George Watson	Mike Elliot
Mr. Braithwaite	Billy Fane
Debbie	Nicola Blackwell
Librarian	Carol McGuigan
Gary Poulson	Joe Renton
Mr. Wilkinson	Colin MacLachlan
Billy's Mum	Janine Birkett
PC Jeff Peverly	Trevor Fox
Sheila Briggs	Charlie Hardwick
Miner	Denny Ferguson
NCB Official	Dennis Lingard
Simon	Matthew Thomas
Ballet Doctor	Steve Mangan
Tutor in Medical	Paul Ridley
Principal	Patrick Malahide
Vice-Principal	Barbara Leigh-Hunt
Sandra	Zoe Bell
Geography Teacher	Tracey Wilkinson
Michael (aged 25)	Merryn Owen
Tutors	Imogen Claire, Diana Kent, Neil North, Lee Williams
Teacher	Petra Siniawski
Secretary	Merelina Kendall

Jamie Bell, Gary Lewis

Billy Elliot, an eleven-year old living in a dying coal mining town in Northern England, begins taking ballet classes, a fact he keeps from his widowed father and overbearing brother. This film received Oscar nominations for supporting actress (Julie Walters), director, and original screenplay.

© Universal Studios

Jean Heywood, Jamie Bell

Jamie Bell

RATCATCHER

(**FIRST LOOK**) Producer, Gavin Emerson; Executive Producers, Andrea Calderwood, Barbara McKissack, Sarah Radclyffe; Director/Screenplay, Lynne Ramsay; Photography, Alwin Kuchler; Designer, Jane Morton; Costumes, Gill Horn; Editor, Lucia Zucchetti; Music, Rachel Portman; Associate Productions presentation; a Pathé Pictures, BBC Films and the Arts Council of England, Lazennec and Le Studio Canal+, Holy Cow Films production; British, 1999; Dolby; Color; Not rated; 93 minutes; American release date: October, 13, 2000

CAST

Da	Tommy Flanagan
Ma	Mandy Matthews
James	William Eadie
Ellen	Michelle Stewart
Anne Marie	Lynne Ramsay, Jr.
Margaret Anne	Leanne Mullen
Kenny	John Miller
Mrs. Quinn	Jackie Quinn
Mr. Quinn	James Ramsay
Mrs. Fowler	Anne McLean
Matt Monroe	Craig Bonar
Billy	Andrew McKenna
Stef	Mick Maharg
Hammy	James Montgomery
Ryan	Thomas McTaggart
Tommy	Stuart Gordon
Mackie	Stephen Sloan
Miss McDonald	Molly Innes
Mr. Mohan	Stephen King
Insurance Man	John Comerford
Mr. Mullen	Jimmy Grimes
Rita	Anne Marie Lafferty

and Bessie McDonald (Elderly Lady), Leanne Jenkins (Kitten Girl), Ian Cameron, Brian Steel (Soldiers), Dougie Jones, Joe McCrone (Scavengers), James Watson (Bus Driver), Stephen Purdon (Boy on Bike), Marion Connell (Jesse), Robert Farrell (Boy), Donnie McMillan (Artie), Lisa Taylor (Anne Marie's Friend)

A lonely twelve-year-old boy, awaiting news of his family's transfer out of a poor Glasgow neighborhood, creates a separate world from his home life when he befriends a vulnerable fourteen-year-old girl.

William Eadie, Leanne Mullen

William Eadie

William Eadie

Lynne Ramsay, Jr.

Jackie Chan

THE LEGEND DF DRUNKEN MASTER

(DIMENSION) a.k.a. *Drunken Master II* and *Drunken Fist II*; Producers, Eric Tsang, Edward Tang, Barbie Tung; Executive Producer, Leonard Ho; Director, Lau Ka Leung; Screenplay, Edward Tang, Tong Man-Ming, Yuen Chieh Chi; Photography, Cheung Yiu Cho; Associate Producer, Hon Yee Sang; Editor, Cheung Yiu Chung; Martial Arts Choreographers, Lau Ka Leung, Jackie Chan and His Stuntman's Club; Music, Michael Wandmacher; a Raymond Chow/Golden Harvest presentation of a Hong Kong Stuntman Association Ltd. production; Distributed by Miramax; Hong Kong, 1994; Dubbed in English; Dolby; Deluxe color; Rated R; 102 minutes; American release date: October 20, 2000

CAST

Wong Fei-Hung	Jackie Chan
Wong's Father	Ti Lung
Wong's Mother	Anita Mui
Tsang	Felix Wong
Master Fu	Lau Ka Leung
John	Low Houi Kang
Fo Sang	Chin Ka Lok
Henry	Ho Sung Pak
Tso	Tseung Chi Kwong
Hing	Hon Yee Sang
Counter Intelligence Officer	Andy Lau
Fun	Ho Wing Fong
Marlon	Lau Ka Yung
Chiu	Lau Siu Ming
Chiu's Wife	Suki Kwan
Ladies in Coffee Shop	Evonne Yung, Chan Wai Yee
Larry	Wong Shing
Curly	Chan Kwok Kuen
Moe	Tai Bo
Lily	Chan Kui Ying
Cook	Pao Fung

and Ha Chun Chau, Szema Wah Lung (Seniors in Restaurant), Pak Yan (Mrs. Chan), Louis C. Roth (Consul), Therese Renee (Terese), Mark Houghton (Smith), Vincent Tuatanne (Bruno)

When his father's box of ginseng is accidentally mixed up with a box containing an ancient Chinese artifact, kung fu master Wong Fei-Hung finds himself uncovering a plot to smuggle similar valuable treasures.

© Dimension Films

A ROOM FOR ROMEO BRASS

(USA FILMS) Producers, George Faber, Charles Pattinson; Executive Producers, Andras Hamori, David M. Thompson; Director, Shane Meadows; Screenplay, Paul Fraser, Shane Meadows; Line Producer, Ronaldo Vasconcellos; Photography, Ashley Rowe; Designer, Crispian Sallis; Editor, Paul Tothill; Costumes, Robin Fraser Paye; Casting, Abi Cohen; an Alliance Atlantis Communications and BBC Films presentation in association with the Arts Council of England; a Company Pictures/Big Arty production; from October Films; British; Dolby; Color; Rated R; 90 minutes; American release date: October 27, 2000

CAST

Romeo Brass	Andrew Shim
Gavin "Knocks" Woolley	Ben Marshall
Morell	Paddy Considine
Joseph Brass	Frank Harper
Sandra Woolley	Julia Ford
Bill Woolley	James Higgins
Ladine Brass	Vicky McClure
Carol Brass	Ladene Hall
Steven Laws	Bob Hoskins

and Martin Arrowsmith (Dennis Wardrobe), Dave Blunt (School Pianist), Darren Campbell (Darren), Shaun Fields (Male Nurse), Jamahl Peterkin, Nicholas Harvey (Neighbor Lads), Shane Meadows (Fish and Chip Shop Man), Joel Morris, James Tomlinson (Park Lads), Johann Myers (Clifford), Tanya Myers (Headmistress), Sammi Pasha (Ambulance Man)

Two young boys, tough Romeo and sensitive Knocks, form an unlikely friendship until an eccentric stranger comes between them.

© USA Films

Ben Marshall, Bob Hoskins

Paddy Considine, Andrew Shim

VENUS BEAUTY INSTITUTE

(LOT 47) Producer, Gilles Sandoz; Executive Producer, Malek Hamzaoui; Director, Tonie Marshall; Screenplay, Tonie Marshall, Mario Vernoux, Jacques Audiard; Photography, Gerard De Battista, Eric Brun, Stephane Degnieau; Art Director, Michel Vandestien; Costumes, Nathalie Du Roscoat, Claire Gerard-Hirne; Casting, Bruno Levy; an Agat Films & Cie/Arte France Cinema/Tabo Tabo Films production, with the participation of Canal+; French, 1999; Dolby; Color; Not rated; 105 minutes; American release date: October 27, 2000

CAST

Angele	Nathalie Baye
Nadine	Bulle Ogier
Antoine	Samuel Le Bihan
Jacques	Jacques Bonnaffe
Samantha	Mathilde Seigner
Marie	Audrey Tautou
Aviator	Robert Hossein
Evelyne	Elli Medeiros
Aunt Maryse	Micheline Presle
Aunt Lyda	Emmanuelle Riva
Madame Buisse	Claire Nebout
Marianne	Brigitte Rouan

and Edith Scob (Client with Spots), Marie Riviere (Client with Boots) Hélène Fillieres (Antoine's Fiancee), Liliane Rovère (Epilation Client), Claire Denis (Asthmatic Client), Gilbert Melki (Lover at the Station), Patrick Pineau, Philippe Harel (Men in Cafeteria), Chantal Bronner (Angele's Client), Sophie Grimaldi (Marie's Client), Frederic Andrei (Finishing Client), Catherine Hosmalin (Foundation Cream Client), Florence Derive (Zouzou), Eric Petitjean, Rinaldo Rocco (Movers), Martine Audrain (Angele's Neighbor), Laurence Mercier (Mamadem Schmidt), Michel Gauthier, Medhi De Lu (Waiters), Joel Brisse (Poitiers' Friend), Romain Goupil (Doctor), Carole Deroo (Madame Pommerand), Charles-Roger Bour (Pierre), Nicolas Bomsel ("Heure" Type), Michel Vandestien (Warehouse Patron), Olivier Pace (Warehouse Worker), Arnaud Dautzenberg (Cabinet Maker), Vanda Benes (Waitress), Cyril Arvenzag, Cedric Bruzac (Manager's Sons), Alain Peyrollaz (Man on Platform)

A look at the sexual and romantic endeavors of four diverse women all of whom are employed at a Parisian beauty spa.

© Lot 47 Films

Nathalie Baye, Audrey Tautou, Mathilde Seigner

Nathalie Baye, Samuel Le Bihan

A TIME FOR DRUNKEN HORSES

(SHOOTING GALLERY) Producer/Director/Screenplay/Art Director, Bahman Ghobadi; Photography, Sa'ed Nikzat; Editor, Samad Tavazoee; Music, Hossein Alizadeh; Produced with the cooperation of the Farabi Cinema Foundation; a Production of Bahman Ghobadi Films (Iran); a MK2 Diffusion International Release (Paris); Iranian-French; Color; Not rated; 77 minutes; American release date: October 27, 2000

CAST

Ayoub	Ayoub Ahmadi
Rojin	Jouvin Younessi
Amaneh	Amaneh Ekhtiar-Dini
Madi	Madi Ekhtiar-Dini

and Kolsoum Ekhtiar-Dini, Karim Ekhtiar-Dini, Rahman Salehi, Osman Karimi, Nezhad Ekhtiar-Dini

Ayoub and his siblings, living in poverty near the Iran-Iraq border, try to raise money for an operation for their critically ill brother.

© Shooting Gallery

Nezhad Ekhtiar-Dini

Jonathan Lipnicki, Rollo Weeks

Jonathan Lipnicki, Richard E. Grant

Jonathan Lipnicki

THE LITTLE VAMPIRE

(NEW LINE CINEMA) Producer, Richard Claus; Executive Producers, Alexander Buchman, Anthony Waller, Larry Wilson; Director, Uli Edel; Screenplay, Karey Kirkpatrick, Larry Wilson; Based on the novels by Angela Sommer-Bodenburg; Photography, Bernd Heinl; Designer, Joseph Nemec III; Costumes, James Acheson; Editor, Peter R. Adams; Music, Nigel Clarke, Michael Csányi-Wills; Visual Effects Supervisor, John Grower; Co-Producers, Klaus Bauschulte, Carsten Lorenz; Make-Up Artists, Leendert Van Nimwegen, Katja Reinert-Alexis; Casting, Joyce Nettles; a Cometstone Pictures presentation in association with Comet Film, Avrora Media, Stonewood Communications of a Richard Claus production; German-Dutch; Dolby; Color; Rated PG; 97 minutes; American release date: October 27, 2000

CAST

Tony Thompson	Jonathan Lipnicki
Frederick	Richard E. Grant
Freda	Alice Krige
Anna	Anna Popplewell
Rudolph	Rollo Weeks
Rookery	Jim Carter
Lord McAshton	John Wood
Dottie Thompson	Pamela Gidley
Bob Thompson	Tommy Hinkley
Gregory	Dean Cook
Von	Ed Stoppard
Farmer McLaughlin	Jake D'Arcy
Nigel	Ian De Caestecker
Flint	Scott Fletcher
Teacher	Johnny Meres
Babysitter Lorna	Georgie Glen
Elizabeth	Elizabeth Berrington
Caretaker	Harry Jones

After moving with his family to a small Scottish village, 9-year-old Tony Thompson's nightmares about creatures of the night become a reality when he meets a boy his own age, who happens to be a real-life vampire.

© New Line Productions Inc.

Anna Popplewell, Rollo Weeks, Jonathan Lipnicki

Gérard Depardieu

THE BRIDGE

(PHAEDRA) a.k.a. *A Bridge Between Two Shores*; Producer, Gérard Depardieu; Executive Producer, Jacques Bar; Directors, Gérard Depardieu, Frédéric Auburtin; Screenplay, Francois Dupeyon; Based on the novel by Alain Leblanc; Photography, Pascal Ridao; Music, Frédéric Auburtin; Editor, Noelle Boisson; Designer, Michele Abbe-Vannier; Costumes, Tom Rand; a DD Productions, TF1 Films Production, Roissy Films, Compagnie Cinematographique PRIMA, with the participation of Canal+ and the CNC; French, 1999; Dolby; Color; Not rated; 92 minutes; American release date: October 27, 2000

CAST

Georges	Gérard Depardieu
Mina	Carole Bouquet
Matthias	Charles Berling
Tommy	Stanislas Crevillen
Claire Daboval	Dominique Reymond
Lisbeth	Melanie Laurent
Babet	Michelle Goddet
Gaby	Christiane Cohendy
Secretary	Agathe Dronne
Monsieur Daboval	Gerard Dauzat

Mina, eager to expand her limited life, falls in love with engineer Matthias, who is building a bridge across the Seine river, a project on which Mina's husband has found a job.

Carole Bouquet, Gérard Depardieu

Charles Berling, Carole Bouquet

Charles Berling, Carole Bouquet

BOESMAN & LENA

(KINO) Producers, François Ivernel, Pierre Rissient; Director/Screenplay, John Berry; Based on the play by Athol Fugard; Co-Producers, Jeremy Nathan, John Stodel; Associate Producer, Wren Brown; Line Producer, Nina Heyns; Photography, Alain Choquart; Designer, Max Berto; Editor, Claudine Bouché; Music, Wally Badarou; Costumes, Diana Cilliers; a Pathé Image—Primedia Pictures production; French-South African; Dolby; Cinemascope; Color/Black and white; Not rated; 88 minutes; American release date: November 3, 2000

CAST

Boesman ....Danny Glover
Lena..Angela Bassett
Old Man ....Willie Jonah

Boesman and Lena, driven once again from their home by white men, roam the South African Cape Flats, carrying their few possessions and engaging in a bitter dialogue over their circumstances.

© Kino International

Danny Glover, Angela Bassett

Angela Bassett

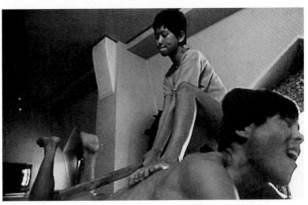

Kim Tae Yeon, Lee Sang Hyun

Lee Sang Hyun, Kim Tae Yeon

LIES

(OFFLINE RELEASING/COWBOY BOOKING) Producer, Shin Chul; Executive Producers, Park Keon Seop, Kim Moo Ryung; Director/Screenplay, Jang Sun Woo; Based on the novel *Tell Me a Lie* by Jang Jung Il; Photography, Kim Woo Hyung; Designer, Kim Myeong Kyeong; Music, Dal Palan; Editor, Park Gok Ji; Digital Video, Kim Yong Gyun; a Shincine Communications production; South Korean; Dolby; Color; Not rated; 111 minutes; U.S. release date: November 17, 2000

CAST

J ....Lee Sang Hyun
Y ....Kim Tae Yeon
Woori ....Jeon Hye Jin
G ....Choi Hyun Joo
Y's Brother...Han Kwon Taek
J's Senior...Kwon Hyuk Poong
Senior's Wife...Jung Myung Keum
Young J ....Shin Min Soo
J's Father..Cho Young Sun
and Ahn Mi Kyung (Noodle Shoop Owner), Yeom Kum Ja (Short Rib Shop Owner), Choi Boo Ho (Motel Owner), Goh Hye Won (Motel Owner's Wife), Kwak Chui Jin, Lee Jin-Ho (Taxi Drivers), Jun Jae Sup, Yim Mi Ran (Noodle Shop Customers)

Y, a high schooler intent on losing her virginity before she graduates, finds herself involved in a relationship with married 38-year-old J, their sexual trysts gradually turning more sadomasochistic.

© Offline Releasing

Dennis Farina, Vinnie Jones

Brad Pitt

SNATCH

(SCREEN GEMS) Producer, Matthew Vaughn; Executive Producers, Peter Morton, Steve Tisch, Stephen Marks, Angad Paul, Trudie Styler; Director/Screenplay, Guy Ritchie; Photography, Tim Maurice-Jones; Designer, Hugo Luczyc-Wyhowski; Editor, Jon Harris; Music, John Murphy; Costumes, Verity Hawkes; Co-Producer, Michael Dreyer; Casting, Lucinda Syson; a Matthew Vaughn production, presented in association with SKA Films; British; Dolby; Deluxe color; Rated R; 102 minutes; American release date: December 6, 2000

CAST

Errol	Andy Beckwith
Mullet	Ewen Bremner
Alex	Nikki Collins
Susi	Teena Collins
Mum O'Neil	Sorcha Cusack
Franky Four Fingers	Benicio del Toro
Rosebud	Sam Douglas
Avi	Dennis Farina
Darren	Jason Flemyng
Gorgeous George	Adam Fogerty
Brick Top	Alan Ford
Vinny	Robbie Gee
Bad Boy Lincoln	Goldie
Tommy	Stephen Graham
Tyrone	Ade
Sol	Lennie James
Bullet Tooth Tony	Vinnie Jones
Mickey "One Punch" O'Neil	Brad Pitt
Doug the Head	Mike Reid
Boris the Blade	Rade Sherbedgia
Turkish	Jason Statham
Neil	William Beck
Gary	Jason Buckham
Liam	Mickey Cantwell
MC	Charles Cork
Horrible Man	James Cunningham
Jack the All Seeing Eye	Mickey Dee
Reuben	Sid Hoare
Referee	Ronald Isaac
Michael	Chuck Julian
John	Dave Legeno
Avi's Colleague	Eric Meyers
Charlie	Jason Ninh Cao
Patrick	Paul O'Boyle
Paulie	Jimmy Roussounis
Pauline	Sidney Sedin
Bomber Harris	Trevor Steedman
Himy	Yuri Stepanov
Sausage Charlie	Peter Szakacs
Salt Peter	John Taheny
Mad Fist Willy	Mick Theo
John the Gun	Andy Till
The Russian	Velibor Topic
Horace "Good Night" Anderson	Scott Welch

and Michael Hughes, Liam McMahon, Jim Warren (Gypsy Men), Austin Drage, Liam Donaghy, Joe Williams (Gypsy Kids), John Farnell, Shaun Pearson, Dean Smith, Roy Snell (Brick Top's Henchmen), Tim Faraday, Andrew Shield (Policemen)

Franky Four Fingers arrives in London to deliver a stolen diamond to Avi, little realizing that he is set up to be robbed at the bookies where he plans to bet on an illegal boxing match, at which boxing promoters Turkish and Tommy have convinced Irish gypsy Mickey O'Neil to fight.

© Screen Gems

Brad Pitt (2nd from left), Jason Flemyng

Benicio del Toro

Dennis Farina

Ade, Lennie James, Robbie Gee

Jason Statham, Stephen Graham, Brad Pitt

THE HOUSE OF MIRTH

Eric Stoltz, Gillian Anderson

(SONY PICTURES CLASSICS) Producer, Olivia Stewart; Executive Producers, Bob Last, Pippa Cross; Director/Screenplay, Terence Davies; Based on the novel by Edith Wharton; Co-Producer, Alan J. Wands; Photography, Remi Adefarasin; Designer, Don Taylor; Costumes, Monica Howe; Editor, Michael Parker; Music Director, Adrian Johnston; Casting, Billy Hopkins, Suzanne Smith, Kerry Barden; a Showtime and Granada presentation in association with the Arts Council of England, Film Four, the Scottish Arts Council and Glasgow Film Fund; British-Scottish-U.S.; Dolby; Super 35 Widescreen; Deluxe color; Rated PG; 141 minutes; American release date: December 22, 2000.

CAST

Lily Bart	Gillian Anderson
Gus Trenor	Dan Aykroyd
Mrs. Peniston	Eleanor Bron
George Dorset	Terry Kinney
Sim Rosedale	Anthony LaPaglia
Bertha Dorset	Laura Linney
Carry Fisher	Elizabeth McGovern
Grace Stepney	Jodhi May
Lawrence Seldon	Eric Stoltz
Judy Trenor	Penny Downie
Percy Gryce	Pearce Quigley
Evie Van Osburgh	Helen Coker
Mrs. Haffen	Mary MacLeod
Jack Stepney	Paul Venables
Gwen Stepney	Serena Gordon
Mrs. Hatch	Lorelei King
Madame Regina	Linda Marlowe
Miss Haines	Anne Marie Timoney
Mrs. Bry	Claire Higgins
Lord Hubert Dacy	Ralph Riach

and Brian Pettifer (Mr. Bry), Philippe De Grossourvre (Ned Silverton), Trevor Martin (Jennings, the Butler), David Ashton (Lawyer), Lesley Harcourt (Mattie Gormer), Mark Dymond (Paul Morpeth), Pamel Dwyer (Edith Fisher), Kate Wooldridge (Parlour Maid), Graham Crammond (Clerk), Roy Sampson (Dorset Butler), Alyxis Daly (Landlady), Joanne Bett, Mary Goonan, Gowan Calder, Morag Siller (Millinery Girls)

Laura Linney, Terry Kinney

In 1905 New York City, Lily Bart, having suffered a terrible financial setback due to gambling debts, searches for a husband to help her regain a position in society, rejecting the true love of suitor Lawrence Seldon.

Elizabeth McGovern

Dan Aykroyd, Gillian Anderson, Anthony LaPaglia

Uma Thurman

Uma Thurman, Gérard Depardieu

VATEL

(MIRAMAX) Producers, Alain Goldman, Roland Joffé; Director, Roland Joffé; Screenplay, Jeanne Labrune; English Adaptation, Tom Stoppard; Photography, Robert Fraisse; Designer, Jean Rabasse; Costumes, Yvonne Lassinot De Nesle; Music, Ennio Morricone; Editor, Noelle Boisson; Line Producer, Patrick Bordier; Choreographer, Corinne Devaux; Casting, Gerard Moulevrier, Karen Lindsay-Stewart; a Gaumont-Legende Enterprises (Paris)/Timothy Burrill Prods. (London), co-production, in association with Nomad, TF1 Films, Canal+; French-British; Dolby; Panavision; Color; Rated PG-13; 102 minutes; American release date: December 25, 2000

CAST

Francois Vatel ....Gérard Depardieu
Anne de Montausier..Uma Thurman
Marquis de Lauzun ....Tim Roth
Gourville ....Timothy Spall
Prince de Conde..Julian Glover
Louis XIV ....Julian Sands
Philippe d'Orleans "Monsieur" ....Murray Lachlan Young
Colbert ....Hywel Bennett
Docter Bourdelot..Richard Griffiths
Princess de Conde..Arielle Dombasle
Athenais de Montespan..Marine Delterme
Duchess de Longueville ....Philippine Leroy-Bealieu
Marquis d'Effiat ....Jerome Pradon
Alcalet ....Feodor Atkine
The Queen Marie Therese..Nathalie Cerda
Louise de la Valliere..Emilie Ohana
Demaury ....Sebastien Davis
and Natacha Koutchoumov (Louis de la Valliere's Maid), Nick Robinson (Colin), Patrick Saverioni (Rochefort), Julie-Anne Roth (Maidservant), Alain Stern (Sharp Equerry), James Thierree (Duc de Longueville), Geoffrey Bateman (Balmour), Nicholas Hawtrey (Lauzun's Secretary), Paul Brandey (Comte de Mirail), David Gablson (Creditor Guillaume), Louise Vincent (Creditor), Andre Chaumeau (The Monkey Handler), Jay Benedict (King's Commode Valet), Dominique Frot (Hysterical Woman), Leslie Clack (Whipping Courtier), David Houri (Vicomte d'Amboise), Christophe Prevost (Lantern Deliveryman), Ron Forfar (Melon Deliveryman), Albert Goldberg (The Leviathan Worker), Vincent Grass (Martin's Father), Patty Hannock (Duchesse at the Banquet), Fiona Curzon (Woman at the Banquet), Adrian Pochna (Foot Servant), Jerome Duranteau (Cavalry Officer), Patrick Albenque (Soldier at Chateau Gate), Vincent Nemeth (Emissary), Edwin Apps (Fish Deliveryman), Helen Later (Servant with Flowers), Remi Roubakha (The Cook), Kevin Greenlaw (The Baritone), Joachim Serreau (The Young Servant), Pia Lagrange (Duc d'Ambroise's Sister), Lionel Vitrant (Large Cook), Alexandre Chaussat (Cook's Apprentice), Louis Bustin (Martin), James Ney, William Hough, Jesse Gage (Colin's Friends)

Prince de Conde, on the verge of bankruptcy, hires Francois Vatel to help him plan a sumptuous weekend of food and merriment in order to impress King Louis XIV and possibly reap a rich financial reward. This film received an Oscar nomination for art direction.

Uma Thurman, Tim Roth

Tim Roth (standing), Julian Glover,
Julian Sands, Murray Lachlan Young

Monica Bellucci

Giuseppe Sulfaro

Monica Bellucci

Monica Bellucci

MALENA

(MIRAMAX) Producers, Harvey Weinstein, Carlo Bernasconi; Executive Producers, Bob Weinstein, Teresa Moneo, Fabrizio Lombardo, Mario Spedaletti; Director/Screenplay, Giuseppe Tornatore; Based on a story by Luciano Vincenzoni; Photography, Lajos Koltai; Designer, Francesco Frigeri; Costumes, Maurizio Millenotti; Editor, Massimo Quaglia; Music, Ennio Morricone; Line Producer, Mario Cotone (Pacific Pictures); Casting, Adolfo Onorati; a Medusa Film presentation; Italian; Dolby; Panavision; Cinecitta color; Rated R; 92 minutes; American release date: December 25, 2000

CAST

Malena Scordia	Monica Bellucci
Renato Amoroso	Giuseppe Sulfaro
Renato's Father	Luciano Federico
Renato's Mother	Matilde Piana
Professor Bonsignore	Pietro Notarianni
Nino Scordia	Gaetano Aronica
Lawyer Centorbi	Gilberto Idone
Political Secretary	Angelo Pellegrino
Baron's Mistress	Pippo Provvidenti
Dr. Cusimano's Wife	Maria Terranova
Lieutenant Cadei	Marcello Catalono
Lupetta	Elisa Morucci
Pharmacist	Domenico Gennaro
Pharmacist's Wife	Vitalba Andrea
Magistrate	Pippo Pattavina
Storekeeper	Franco Catalano
Agostino	Daniele Arena
Piné	Giovanni Litrico
Nicola	Gianluca Guarrera
Sasá	Michel Daniel Bramanti
Tanino	Giuseppe Zizzo

and Toto Borgese (Fascist Soldier), Emanuele Gullotto (Record Store Owner), Rori Quattrocchi (Brothel Owner), Claudia Muzii, Ornella Giusto, Conchita Puglisi (Prostitutes), Noemi Giarratana (Sister Renato), Paola Pace, Lucia Sardo (Lynching Women)

In a small Sicilian village, ravishingly beautiful Malena Scordia, whose husband is away serving in the war, captures the fancy of 13-year-old Renato Amoroso. This film received Oscar nominations for cinematography and original score.

© Miramax Films

THE CLAIM

(UNITED ARTISTS) Producer, Andrew Eaton; Executive Producer, Martin Katz, Andrea Calderwood, Alexis Lloyd; Director, Michael Winterbottom; Screenplay, Frank Cottrell Boyce; Inspired by the novel *The Mayor of Casterbridge* by Thomas Hardy; Photography, Alwin Kuchler; Designers, Mark Tildesley, Ken Rempel; Editor, Trevor Waite; Music, Michael Nyman; Costumes, Joanne Hansen; Line Producer, Anita Overland; Co-Producer, Douglas Berquist; Casting, Wendy Brazington, Billy Hopkins, Suzanne Smith, Kerry Barden; a United Artists Films presentation in association with Pathé Pictures, the Arts Council of England, Le Studio Canal+, BBC Films and Alliance Atlantis, of a Revolution Films/DB Entertainment and Grosvenor Park Production; Distributed by MGM; British-Canadian; Dolby; Super 35 Widescreen; Deluxe color; Rated R; 120 minutes; U.S. release date: December 29, 2000

CAST

Dalglish	Wes Bentley
Lucia	Milla Jovovich
Elena Dillon	Nastassja Kinski
Daniel Dillon	Peter Mullan
Hope Dillon	Sarah Polley
Bellanger	Julian Richings
Sweetley	Sean McGinley
Stagecoach Driver	Ron Anderson
German	Marty Antonini
Priest	Randy Birch
French Sue	Marie Brassard
Mr. Timpson	Bill Chesterman
Delaney	Artur Ciastkowski

and Fernando Davalos (Barman), Duncan Fraser (Crocker), Shirley Henderson (Annie), Kate Hennig (Vauneen), Tim Koetting (Hotel Clerk), Lydia Lau (Li), David LeReaney (Saloon Actor), Janelle Loughlin (Beggar Girl), Tom McCamus (Burn), Matthew Johnson, Billy Morton, Grant Linneberg, Jimmy Herman (Miners), Landon Hicks (Young Miner), Valerie Planche, Linda Miller (Chippies), Karen Minish (Opera Singer), Karolina Muller (Young Elena), Phillipa Peak (Sarah), Royal Sproule (Grimes), Barry Ward (Young Dillon), Frank Zotter (Photographer), Marc Hollogne (Dr. Benoit), Trevor Allan Davies, John Goulart (Saloon Band)

Mr. Dalglish arrives in the thriving mining town of Kingdom Come, surveying the landscape with the intention of expanding the Central Pacific Railroad, a proposal that threatens the power Daniel Dillon holds on the town.

© United Artists

Milla Jovovich, Wes Bentley

Sarah Polley, Nastassja Kinski

Lee Hyo Jung, Cho Seung Woo

CHUNHYANG

(LOT 47) Producer, Lee Tae Won; Executive Producers, Kim Dong Joo, Seok Dong Jun, Park Do Jun; Director, Im Kwon Taek; Screenplay, Kim Myoung Kon; Photography, Jung II Sung; Music, Kim Jung Gil; Editor, Park Soon Duk; Korean; Color; Not rated; 122 minutes; American release date: December 29, 2000

CAST

Chunhyang	Lee Hyo Jung
Mongryong	Cho Seung Woo
Wolmae	Kim Sung Nyu
Governor Byun	Lee Jung Hun
Pangja	Kim Hak Yong
Hyangdan	Lee Hae Eun
Governor Lee	Choi Jin Young
Kisaeng Leader	Hong Kyung Yeun

In 18th Century Korea, Mongryong, a privileged governor's son, secretly marries Chunhyang who is imprisoned and sentenced to death by the succeeding governor after Mongryong has gone off to finish his schooling.

© Lot 47 Films

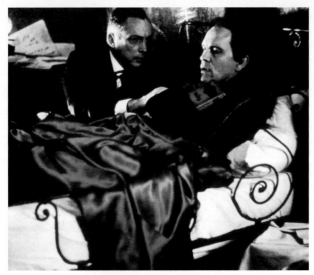

Udo Kier, John Malkovich

SHADOW OF THE VAMPIRE

(LIONS GATE) Producers, Nicolas Cage, Jeff Levine; Executive Producers, Paul Brooks, Alan Howden; Director, E. Elias Merhige; Screenplay, Steven Katz; Co-Producers, Jimmy De Brabant, Richard Johns; Photography, Lou Bogue; Designer, Assheton Gorton; Editor, Chris Wyatt; Costumes, Caroline De Vivaise; Associate Producers, Orian Williams, Norm Golightly; Special Makeup Designers, Julian Murray, Pauline Fowler, Amber Sibley; Casting, Carl Proctor; a Saturn Films presentation of a Long Shot Films production in association with BBC Films and Delux Productions with the Luxembourg Film Fund; British-Luxembourg-U.S.; Dolby; Super 35 Widescreen; Deluxe color; Rated R; 91 minutes; American release date: December 29, 2000

CAST

F.W. Murnau	John Malkovich
Max Schreck ("Count Orlok")	Willem Dafoe
Albin Grau	Udo Kier
Fritz Wagner	Cary Elwes
Greta Schroeder ("Ellen")	Catherine McCormack
Gustav von Wangenheim ("Hutter")	Eddie Izzard
Henrick Galeen	John Aden Gillett
Wolfgang Müller	Ronan Vibert
Paul	Nicholas Elliot
Innkeeper	Milos Hlavak
Innkeeper's Wife	Marja-Leena Junker
Drunken Woman	Sascha Ley
Old Woman	Marie Paule von Roesgen

and Jean Claude Croes, Christophe Chrompin, Graham Johnston , Brian Williams (Murnau's Crew), Derek Kueter, Norman Golightly, Patrick Hastert (Reporters)

Hoping to make the most authentic vampire movie of them all, German director F.W. Murnau hires the mysterious Max Schreck to play Count Orlok in his production of Nosferatu without bothering to inform the other members of the cast that Schreck is, in fact, an actual vampire. This film received Oscar nominations for supporting actor (Willem Dafoe) and makeup design.

Eddie Izzard, Willem Dafoe

Willem Dafoe

Catherine McCormack, Cary Elwes

Isabel Santos, Luis Alberto García in *Life Is To Whistle*
© New Yorker Films

Kestrel's Eye © First Run features

IF YOU ONLY UNDERSTOOD (First Run/Icarus) Executive Producers, Rolando Diaz, Ileana Garcia; Director/Screenplay, Rolando Diaz; Photography, Jose Manuel Riera; Editors, Jorge Abello, David Baute; a Luna Llena Producciones production; Cuban-Spanish, 1999; Color; Not rated; 87 minutes; U.S. release: January 7, 2000. Documentary looks at a diverse group of black Cuban women who have been summoned by director Rolando Diaz to audition for a fictitious musical.

LIFE IS TO WHISTLE (New Yorker) Director, Fernando Pérez; Screenplay, Fernando Pérez, Humberto Jiménez, Eduardo Del Llano; Photography, Raúl Pérez Ureta; Music, Edesio Alejandro; Editor, Julia Yip; Art Director, Raúl Olivia; Costumes, Miriam Duenas; an ICAIC/Wanda Distribution S.A. production; Cuban-Spanish, 1999; Dolby; Color; Not rated; 106 minutes; U.S. release: January 7, 2000. CAST: Luis Alberto García (Elpidio Valdés), Coralia Veloz (Julia), Claudia Rojas (Mariana), Bebé Pérez (Bebé), Isabel Santos (Chrissy), Rolando Brito (Dr. Fernando), Joan Manuel Reyes (Ismael), Mónica Guffanti (Mme. Garces), Luis Ubaldo Benítez (Settimio), Jorge Molina (Bicitaxista), Miguel A. Daranas (Director Asilo)

THE QUARRY (First Run Features) Producer/Director/Screenplay, Marion Hansel; Based on the novel by Damon Galgut; Photography, Bernard Lutic; Art Director, Thierry Leproust; Music, Takashi Kako; Costumes, Yan Tax; Editor, Michele Hubinon; from Catalyst Films; British-South African, 1998; Color; Not rated; 112 minutes; U.S. release: January 21, 2000. CAST: John Lynch (The Man), Jonny Phillips (Captain Mong), Serge-Henri Valcke (The Reverend), Oscar Petersen (Valentine), Jody Abrahams (Small), Sylvia Esau (The Woman)

John Lynch in *The Quarry* © First Run Features

PAN TADEUSZ: THE LAST FORAY IN LITHUANIA (FilmArt) Director, Andrzej Wajda; Screenplay, Andrzej Wajda, Jan Nowina-Zarzycki, Piotr Weresniak; French Adaptation, Marie-Christine d'Aragon; Photography, Pawel Edelman; Designer, Allan Starski; Editors, Wanda Zeman, Anita Wandzel; Costumes, Magdalena Teslawska-Biernawska, Malgorzata Stefaniak; Music, Wojciech Kilar; from Heritage Films, Les Films du Losange in association with Canal+ Polska, Le Studio Canal+; Polish, 1999; Dolby; Color; 120 minutes; U.S. release: January 21, 2000. CAST: Boguslaw Linda (The Bernardin Robak), Daniel Olbrychski (Gervais), Michal Zebrowski (Tadeusz), Grazyna Szapolowska (Télimène), Andrzej Seweryn (The Judge), Marek Kondrat (The Comte), Krzysztof Kolberger (Mickiewicz), Alicja Bachleda-Curus (Sophie), Jerzy Trela (The President), Jerzy Gralek (The Seneschal), Marian Kociniak (Protais), Piotr Gasowski (The Notary), Andrzej Hudziak (The Assessor), Wladyslaw Kowalski (Jankiel), Krzysztof Globisz (Ploute), Siergiej Szakurow (Rikov), Jerzy Binczycki (Mathieu), Cezary Kosinski (The Boring Man), Marek Perepeczko (The Baptist), Piotr Cyrwus (The Watering Can), Wojciech Alaborski (Buchman), Stefan Szmidt (The Prussian)

SOUTH (Milestone) Producer, Xavier Carniaux; Director/Screenplay, Chantal Akerman; Photography, Raymond Fromont; Editor, Claire Atherton; an AMIP/Paradise Films/Chemah I.S. production in association with Carre Noir, RTBF Liege, La Sept Arte, INA, YLE; French-Belgian, 1999; Color; Not rated; 71 minutes; U.S. release: January 21, 2000. Documentary on the effects the racical murder of James Byrd Jr. on the town of Jasper, Texas.

KESTREL'S EYE (First Run Features) Producer/Director/Screenplay/Photography/Editor, Mikael Kristersson; a Picafilms picture; Swedish, 1999; Dolby; Color; Not rated; 86 minutes; U.S. release: January 26, 2000. The world as seen through the eyes of two European falcons.

NOT LOVE, JUST FRENZY (Jour de Fete) Produces, Fernando Colomo, Beatriz de la Gandara; Directors/Screenplay, Alfonso Albacete, Miguel Bardem, David Menkes; Photography, Nestor Calvo; Editor, Miguel Angel Santamaria; Designer, Alain Bainee; Costumes, Paloma Lopez, Angel Schlesser, Vito; Casting, Amelia Ochandiano; Music, Juan Bardem; Canal+Espana, Fernando Colomo Producciones Cinematograficas, SL, Peliculas Freneticas, Televisión Española; Spanish, 1996; Dolby; Color; Not rated; 125 minutes; U.S. release: January 28, 2000. CAST: Nancho Novo (Max), Cayetana Guillen Cuervo (Monica), Ingrid Rubio (Yeye), Beatriz Santiago (Maria), Gustavo Salmeron (Alberto), Javier Manrique (Luis), Javier Albala (Alex), Liberto Rabal (David), Bibi Andersen (Cristina), Juan Diego Botto (Carlos), Daniel Mirabal (Divva), Juanfra Becerra (Doly), Paloma Tabasco (Jacky), Nuria Gallardo (Clara), Carlos Bardem (Miguel), Amanda (Mujer Madura), Ernesto Alterio (Marcos), Maite Pastor (Raquel), Cesar Vea (Julio), Blanca Sanroman (Elsa), Carlos Olivares (Portero), Maria Esteve, Monica Bardem (Girls), Fernando Colomo (Fernando)

Kelly Macdonald, Hans Mathieson in *Stella Does Tricks*
© Strand Releasing

Annie Sprinkle in *Gendernauts* © First Run Features

STELLA DOES TRICKS (Strand) Producer, Adam Barker; Executive Producer, Ben Gibson; Director, Coky Giedroyc; Screenplay, A.L. Kennedy; Photography, Barry Ackroyd; Designers, Tim Ellis, Lynne Whiteread; Costumes, Annie Symmons; Editor, Budge Tremlett; Music, Nick Bicât; from Compulsive Films, Sidewalk Productions; Scottish, 1997; Color; Not rated; 97 minutes; U.S. release: January 28, 2000. CAST: Kelly Macdonald (Stella), James Bolam (Mr. Peters), Hans Mathieson (Eddie), Ewan Stewart (McGuire), Andy Serkis (Fitz), Paul Chahidi (Chris), Lindsay Henderson (Young Stella), Shaun Williamson (Mr. Peters' Driver), Lisa Adam, Jennifer Todd (Young Stella's Friends), Dimitri Andreas (Greek Hotelier), Andrzej Borkowski (Polish Cafe Owner), Emma Faulkner (Belle), Joyce Henderson (Auntie Aileen), Molly Innes (Cake Shop Owner), Suzanne Maddock (Carol), Nick Stringer (Edward), Richard Syms (Donald)

SANTITOS (Latin Universe/New Yorker) Producer/Director, Alejandro Springall; Executive Producers, Thomas Garvin, John Sayles; Screenplay, Maria Amparo Escandon; Photography, Xavier Peréz Grobet; Designers, Eugenio Caballero, Salvador Parra; Costumes, Monica Neumaier; Editor, Carol Dysinger; Casting, Claudia Becker; Mexican-French-Spanish-Canadian; Dolby; Color; Rated R; 105 minutes; U.S. release: January 28, 2000. CAST: Dolores Heredia (Esperanza), Demian Bichir (Cacomixtle), Alberto Estrella (Angel), Pedro Altamirano (Ministerio Publico), Roberto Cobo (Doña Trini), Monica Dionne (La Morena), Juan Duarte (Fidencio), Josefina Echánove (Professor), Felipe Ehrenberg (Alto), Maria Amparo Escandon (La Adicional), Ana Bertha Espin (Soledad), Flor Eduarda Gurrola (Paloma), Pilar Ixquic Mata (La Flaca), Paco Morayta (Don Arlindo), Olimpico (Angel's Manager), Regina Orozco (Vicenta Cortes), Dario T. Pie (Cesar), Jose Sefami (Dr. Ortiz), Fernando Torre Laphame (Padre Salvador), Luis Felipe Tovar (Doroteo), Georgina Tabora (Receptionist), Claudio Valdes (San Judas Tadeo), Maya Zapata (Blanca)

THE GIRAFFE (German Independents/Bavaria Film International) Producer, Stefan Arndt; Director, Dani Levy; Screenplay, Maria Schrader, Dani Levy; Photography, Carl F. Koschnick; Designers, Teresa Mastropierro, Volker Schaefer; Costumes, Ingrida Bendzuk; Music, Niki Reiser; Editor, Sabine Hoffmann; Produced by X-Filme Creative Pool, Condor Films (Zurich) and Extrafilm (Berlin); German-Swiss, 1999; Dolby; Color; Cinemascope; Not rated; 107 minutes; U.S. release: February 2, 2000. CAST: Maria Schrader (Lena Katz), Dani Levy (David Fish), David Strathairn (Charles Kaminski), Nicole Heesters (Lena's Mother), Jeffrey Wright (Win), Lynn Cohen (David's Mother), Lukas Ammann (Eliah Goldberg), Erin Rakow (Slavie Fish), Stephanie Roth (Rahel Fish), R.J. Cutler (Rahel's Husband), Daniel Mastroianni (Menachem Fish), Paul Butler (Lt. Lynch), Mario Giacalone (Det. Pucci), Mark Zimmerman (Bregman), Marcia Jean Kurtz (Rita Teichmann), Francine Beers (Martha Galinski), Sylvia Kauders (Sarah Singer)

BELOVED/FRIEND (Cowboy Booking) Producer/Director, Ventura Pons; Screenplay, Josep M. Benet i Jornet; Based on his play *Testament;* Photography, Jesús Escosa; Music, Carles Cases; Editor, Pere Abadal; Art Director, Bello Torras; an Els Films de la Rambla, S.A. production with the collaboration of Televisión Española, Televisió de Catalunya and Canal+ (Spain); Spanish, 1999; Dolby; Color; Not rated; 90 minutes; U.S. release: Feb. 4, 2000. CAST: Josep Maria Pou (Jaume Clarà), Rosa Maria Sardà (Fanny), Mario Gas (Pere Roure), David Selvas (David Vila), Irene Montalà (Alba)

GENDERNAUTS (First Run Features) Producer/Director/Screenplay, Monika Treut; Photography, Elfi Mikesch; Editor, Eric Schefter; Music, Georg Kajanus; a Hyena Films production, in association with WDR/Arte; German, 1999; Dolby; Color; Not rated; 86 minutes; U.S. release: Feb. 4, 2000. Documentary on gender fluidity and people who alter their bodies and minds using technology and chemistry, featuring Sandy Stone, Texas Tomboy, Susan Stryker, Max Wolf Valerio, Jordy Jones, Stafford, Tornado, Hilda Viloria, Annie Sprinkle.

LIGHTHOUSE (Unapix) a.k.a. *Dead of Night;* Producers, Mark Leake, Tim Dennison; Director/Screenplay, Simon Hunter; Executive Producers, Gary Smith, Chris Craib; Photography, Tony Imi; Designer, Simon Bowles; Editor, Paul Green; Music, Debbie Wiseman; Visual Effects, Roy Field; Co-Producer, Peta Inglesent; British; Dolby; Fuji color; Rated R; 95 minutes; U.S. release: February 4, 2000. CAST: James Purefoy (Richard Spader), Rachel Shelley (Dr. Kirsty McCloud), Chris Adamson (Leo Rook), Paul Brooke (Capt. Campbell), Don Warrington (Prison Officer Ian Goslet), Chris Dunne (Chief Prison Officer O'Neil), Bob Goody (Weevil), Pat Kelman (Spoons), Pete McCabe (Prison Officer Hopkins), Norman Mitchell (Brownlow), Jason Round (Spitfield), Howard Attfield, Stuart Callaghan, Yolande Davis, Sarah Kattridge, Elizabeth Homewood, Neil Johnson, Kenny Ingram, John Kearns

THE ICE RINK (Interama) Producers, Anne-Dominique Toussaint,

Dani Levy, Maria Schrader in *The Giraffe* © Spectra

James Purefoy, Rachel Shelley in *Lighthouse* © A-Pix Entertainment

Kirikou and The Sorceress © ArtMattan Prods.

Pascal Judelewicz; Director/Screenplay, Jean-Philippe Toussaint; Photography, Jean-François Robin; Editors, Ludo Torch, Anne Argouse; from Les Films des Tournelles, Le Studio Canal+, Les Films de l'Étang, RTL/TV1 and Fandango; French, 1999; Color; Not rated; 87 minutes; U.S. release: February 11, 2000. CAST: Tom Novembre (The Director), Mireille Perrier (Assistant), Marie-France Pisier (Producer), Bruce Campbell (Actor), Dolores Chaplin (Actress), Jean-Pierre Cassel (Director of the Ice Rink), Dominique Deruddere (Chief Operator), Gilbert Melki (Stand In of the Actress), Eva Ionesco (Editor), Dominic Gould (Chief Grip), Jean Loup Horwitz (Sound Engineer), Rasa Urbonaite (Interpreter), Alexandre von Sivers (Prop Person), Viktor Senin (Lithuanian Coach), Valerie Lecomte (Continuity Girl), Olivier Dessalles (Journalist), Paolo De Vita (Assistant of the Director of the Italian Festival)

KIRIKOU AND THE SORCERESS (ArtMattan Prods.) Producers, Didier Brunner, Jacques Vercruyssen, Paul Thiltges; Director/Screenplay, Michel Ocelot; Photography, Daniel Borenstein; Music, Youssou N'Dour; Designer, Thierry Million; Head Animator, Inga Riba; Animation, Rija Studio and Exist Studio (Budapest); French-Belgian-Luxembourg, 1998; Dolby; Color; Not rated; 74 minutes; U.S. release: February 18, 2000. VOICE CAST: Theo Sebeko (Kirikou), Antoinette Kellermann (Karaba), Kombisile Sangweni (The Mother), Mabuto Sithole (The Old Man/Viellard), Fezele Mpeka (Uncle)

SINBAD: BEYOND THE VEIL OF MISTS (Phaedra) Producers, Sriram Sundar Rajan, Usha Ganesharajah; Directors, Alan Jacobs, Evan Ricks; Screenplay, Jeff Wolverton; Editor, Scott Conrad; Designers, Joe Alves, Peter Rubin; Casting, Kris Zimmermen; produced by Improvision Corporation; Indian-U.S.; Color; Rated PG; 85 minutes; U.S. release: February 18, 2000. VOICE CAST: Brendan Fraser (Sinbad), Jennifer Hale (Princess Serena), Mark Hamill (Captain of the Guard), Leonard Nimoy (Baraka), John Rhys-Davies (Chandra)

NOT OF THIS WORLD (Entertech Releasing Corp.) Producer, Lionello Cerri; Director, Giuseppe Piccioni; Screenplay, Giuseppe Piccioni, Gualtiero Rosella, Lucia Zei; Photography, Luca Bigazzi; Editor, Esmeralda Calabria; Music, Ludovico Einaudi; Presented in collaboration with RAI-Radiotelevisione Italiana with the contribution of Presidenzia del Consiglio dei Ministri; Italian, 1999; Dolby; Super 35 Widescreen; Color; Not rated; 100 minutes; U.S. release: February 25, 2000. CAST: Margherita Buy (Caterina), Silvio Orlando (Ernesto), Carolina Freschi (Teresa), Maria Cristina Minerva (Esmeralda), Sonia Gessner (Mother Superior), Giuliana Lojodice (Caterina's Mother), Marina Massironi (Girl in Bar), Fabio Sartor (Ernesto's Friend), Alessandro di Natale (Gabriele), Riccardo di Torrebruna (Gianfranco), Stefano Abbati (Jogger), Silvano Piccardi (Man at Nursery School), Carlina Torta (Nurse at Nursery School), Gabriele Garofalo (Fausto, the Child), Daniela Cristofori (Kindergarten Nurse), Tania Casartelli (General Mother), Chantal Ughi (Simona), Andrea Tognasca (Marco), Alessandro Quasimodo (Theology Professor), Gaia Catullo (Bride), Gianni Quilico (Restaurant Owner), Adriana Libretti (Sister Margherita), Tiziana Della Porta (Sister Gaetana), Pierpaolo Nizzola, Renato Sarti (Doctors), Consuelo Maggini (Adoptive Mother), Alessandra Comerio (Teresa's Mother), Francesco Foti (Young Policeman), Olivia Manescalchi, Paola Negri, Valeria Ferrario, Cristina Golotta, Vesna Pavan (Laundry Women)

HOMO SAPIENS 1900 (First Run Features) Producer/Director/Screenplay/Editor, Peter Cohen; Photography, Peter Östlund, Mats Lund; Music, Matti Bye; Narrator, Jan Holmquist; from Arte Factum/Swedish Television; Swedish, 1999; Black and white; Not rated; 88 minutes; U.S. release: March 3, 2000. Documentary on 19th Century racial hygiene and eugenics, using selective breeding for the science of "improving the human species."

Dolores Chaplin in *The Ice Rink* © Interama Inc.

Margherita Buy, Silvio Orlando in *Not of This World*
© Entertech Releasing Corp.

Fernanda Torres in *Midnight* © WinStar Cinema

Caroline Chikezie, Anjela Lauren Smith, Jocelyn Esien in *Babymother*
© Independent Pictures

TWO WOMEN (Iranian Film Society) Director/Screenplay, Tahmineh Milani; Photography, Hossein Djafarian; Designer, Malek Jahan Khazai; Music, Babak Bayat; Editor, Mustafa Kherqepush; Arman Film, Arta Film; Iranian, 1999; Color; Not rated; 95 minutes; U.S. release: March 3, 2000. CAST: Mohammad Reza Forutan (Hassan), Niki Karimi (Fereshteh), Reza Khandan (Fereshteh's Father), Atila Pesiani (Ahmad), Marila Zare'i (Roya)

BE THERE OR BE SQUARE (Independent) Producers, Yang Hong-Guang, Liu Xiaodian; Executive Producers, Zhou Puxiong, Liu Xiaodong, Li Xiaogeng, Yan Yujing; Director, Feng Xiaogang; Screenplay, Gu Xiaoyang, Feng Xiaogang; Photography, Zhao Fei; Editor, Zhou Ying; Music, San Bao; a Beijing Forbidden City/Beijing Film Studio production; Chinese, 1998; Dolby; Color; Not rated; 103 minutes; U.S. release: March 10, 2000. CAST: Ge You (Liu Yuan), Xu Fan (Li Qing)

MIDNIGHT (WinStar) Directors, Daniela Thomas, Walter Salles; Screenplay, Daniela Thomas, Walter Salles, João Emanuel Carneiro; Photography, Walter Carvalho; Editor, Felipe Lacerda; Art Director, Carla Caffé; Music, Antônio Pinto, Eduardo Bid, Naná Vasconcellos; a co-production of La Sept ARTE, Haut et Court, VideoFilmes, RioFilme; Brazilian, 1998; Dolby; Color; Not rated; 72 minutes; U.S. release: March 10, 2000. CAST: Fernanda Torres (Maria), Luiz Carlos Vasconcelos (João), Matheus Nachtergaele (Francisco, Chico), Nelson Sargento (Vovò), Carlos Vereza (Pedro), Tonico Pereira (Carceiro), Áulio Ribeiro (José), Luciana Bezerra (Rosa), Antônio Gomes (Antonio)

Benoît Poelvoorde, Morgane Simon in *The Carriers Are Waiting*
© Samuel Goldwyn

THE CARRIERS ARE WAITING (Samuel Goldwyn) Director, Benoît Mariage; Screenplay, Benoît Mariage, Emmanuelle Bada, Jean-Luc Seigle; Photography, Philippe Guilbert; Editor, Phillippe Bourguell; Costumes, Anne Fournier; Music, Stéphane Huguenin, Yves Sanna; Produced by K-STAR with the participation of Canal+ and the Centre National de la Cinématographie, K2, RTBF, CAB Productions; Belgian-French-Swiss, 1999; Color; Not rated; 94 minutes; U.S. release: March 15, 2000. CAST: Benoît Poelvoorde (Father), Margane Simon (Luise), Bouli Lanners (Coach), Dominique Baeyens (Mother), Philippe Grand d'Henry (Felix), Jean-François Devigne (Michel), Lisa Lacroix (Jocelyne), Phillippe Nahon (Overseer), Edith Le Merdy (Jocelyne's Mother), Patrick Audin (Jocelyne's Father), Claude Caudron (Schoolteacher)

BABYMOTHER (Independent Pictures) Producer, Parminder Vir; Executive Producer, Margaret Matheson; Director, Julian Henriques; Screenplay, Julian Henriques, Vivienne Howard; Co-Producer, Tracey Seaward; Photography, Peter Middleton; Designer, Choi Ho Man; Costumes, Annie Curtis Jones; Editor, Jason Canovas; Music, John Lunn; Choreographer, L'Antoinette "Osun Ide" Stines; Casting, Carol Dudley; a FilmFour in association with the Arts Council of England presentation of a Formation Films Production; British, 1999; Dolby; Technicolor; Rated R; 80 minutes; U.S. release: March 17, 2000. CAST: Anjela Lauren Smith (Anita), Wil Johnson (Byron), Caroline Chikezie (Sharon), Jocelyn Esien (Yvette), Don Warrington (Luther), Tameka Empson (Dionne), Diane Bailey (Bee), Vas Blackwood (Caesar), Andrea Francis (Yvette's Sister), Anton Rice (Anton), Saffron Lashley (Saffron), Corrine Skinner Carter (Mistress Edith), Suzette Llewellyn (Rose), Clive Buckley (Matt), Bushman (DJ on Radio), Badi Uzzaman (Shopkeeper), Tippa Irie (MC), Governor Tiggy (Bee's Act), Peter Hunnigale (Matt's Act), Barbara Lawrence, Stella Pilaya, Tanitia (Dionne's Posse), Dujhan Dennis Planter (Blues Party Performer)

THE DISAPPEARANCE OF FINBAR (Film 4 International/Cowboy Booking) Producers, Bertil Ohlsson, Martin Bruce-Clayton; Executive Producers, Jonathan Olsberg, Ole Sondberg; Director, Sue Clayton; Screenplay, Dermot Bolger, Sue Clayton; Photography, Eduardo Serra; Editor, J. Patrick Duffner; Music, Davy Spillane; Casting, Nuala Moiselle; from Ian Rattray in association with Channel 4; British, 1997; Color; Not rated; 103 minutes; U.S. release: March 17, 2000. CAST: Luke Griffin (Danny Quinn), Jonathan Rhys Meyers (Finbar Flynn), Sean Lawlor (Michael Flynn), Chris Meehan, Toner Quinn, Phil Callery, Fran McPhail, Pete Cummins, Pat Henry, Gerard Cullen (Roscommon Cowboys), Jake Williams (Young Finbar), Robert Hickey (Young Danny), Eleanor Methven (Pat Flynn), Marie Mullen (Ellen Quinn), Don Foley (Grandpa Quinn), Conor Fitzgerald (Fergal Flynn), Aoife Doyle (Jodie Flynn), Lorraine Pilkington (Katie), Laura Brennan (Sinead), Tina Kelleher (Ms. Byrne), Sean McGinley (Det. Byrne), Barry McGovern (Action Committee Chairman), Ciara Wong (Girl in Chip Shop), Derry Power (Barman), Larry Murphy (Bouncer), Joe Savino (Talent Scout), Rob Brown (Pop Singer), Louise Loughman, Pamela Flood (Pop Video Dancers), Jan Mybrand (Immigration Officer), Linda Englund (Girl in

Bar), Per Mattison (Karl), Li Wen (Chinese Man), Zheng Wei (Chinese Woman), Juhani Haapala (Man in Store), Lille-Mor Falk (Woman in Store), Mikael Toyra (Big Finnish Driver), Kent Sturk (Man in Kiosk), Kurt Johansson, Olof Mukka (Singing Miners), Sten Ljunggren (Finn Bar Barman), Antti Reini (Antti), Thomas Hedengran (Matti), Lennart Johansson (Pauli), Thomas Laustiola (Jukka), Fanny Risberg (Abbi), Sif Ruud (Johanna)

SOFT FRUIT (Fox Searchlight) Producer, Helen Bowden; Director/Screenplay, Christina Andreef; Executive Producer, Jane Campion; Photography, Laszlo Baranyai; Designer, Sarah Stollman; Editor, Jane Moran; Costumes, Jane Holland; Music, Antony Partos; Casting, Alison Barrett, Nikki Barrett; The Australian Film Finance Corporation presentation in association with the New South Wales Film and Television Office; Australian, 1999; Dolby; Color; Rated R; 101 minutes; U.S. release: March 17, 2000. CAST: Jeanie Drynan (Patsy), Linal Haft (Vic), Russell Dykstra (Bo), Genevieve Lemon (Josie), Sacha Horler (Nadia), Alicia Talbot (Vera), Jordan Frankland (Thomas), Terry Weaver (Podge), Trevor Mills (Smudge), Cheyenne Dobbs (Gertie), Dion Bilios (Bud), Andrew Hunter, Barry Evans (Bikies), Pat Bishop (Nursing Sister), Marin Mimica (Swifty), Walter Grkovic (Janitor)

X (Manga) Producers, Kazuo Yokoyama, Masanori Maruyama, Kazuhiko Ikeguchi; Director, Rintaro; Executive Producer, Tsunehiko Kadokawa; Screenplay, Asami Watanabe, Nanase Ohkawa, Rintaro; Story, Clamp, Satsuki Igarashi, Mokonaapapa, Nanase Ohkawa, Mikku "Mick" Nekoi; Photography, Jin Yamaguchi; Character Design/Director of Original Drawings, Nobuteru Yuhki; Art Director, Shuh-ichi Hirata; Music, Harumitsu Shimizu; Editors, Harutoshi Ogata, Yukiko Itoh, Satoshi Terauchi; an X Committee Clamp presentation; Japanese, 1996; Dubbed in English; Color; Not rated; 98 minutes; U.S. release: March 24, 2000. VOICE CAST: Tomokazu Seki (Kamui Shiro), Junko Iwao (Kotori Mono), Ken Narita (Fuma Mono)

SUCH A LONG JOURNEY (Shooting Gallery) Producers, Paul Stephens, Simon MacCorkindale; Director, Sturla Gunnarsson; Executive Producer, Victor Solnicki; Screenplay, Sooni Taraporevala, based on the novel by Rohinton Mistry; Photography, Jan Kiesser; Music, Jonathan Goldsmith; Editor, Jeff Warren; Designer, Nitin Desai; Costumes, Lovleen Bains; Line Producers, Stephen J. Turnbull, Don McLean; The Film Works and Amy International Artists presentation with the participation of Telefilm Canada, British Screen, and the Harold Greenberg Fund; Canadian-British, 1999; Dolby; Deallion color; Not rated; 112 minutes; U.S. release: March 24, 2000. CAST: Roshan Seth (Gustad Noble), Soni Razdan (Dilnavaz Noble), Om Puri (Ghulam), Naseeruddin Shah (Jimmy Bilimoria), Ranjit Chowdhry (Pavement Artist), Sam Dastor (Dinshawji), Kurush Deboo (Tehmul), Pearl Padamsee (Mrs. Kutpitia), Vrajesh Hirjee (Sohrab Noble), Shazneen Damania (Roshan Noble), Kurush Dastur

Kamui in *X* © CLAMP/Kadokawa Shoten

(Darius Noble), Noshirwan Jehangir (Inspector Bamji), Dinyar Contractor (Mr. Rabadi), Souad Faress (Mrs. Rabadi), Shivani Jha (Jasmine Rabaldi), Meher Jehangir (Freny Pastikia), Aileen Gonsalves (Laurie Coutinho), Sohrab Ardeshir (Mr. Madon), Rashid Karapiet (Joshi), Chatru L. Gurnani (Bhimsen), Madhav Sharma (Peerbhoy), Pratima Kazmi (Hydraulic Hema), Sunny Bharti (Prostitute), Antony Zaki (Morcha Director), Irfan Khan (Gustad's Father), Anahita Oberoi (Gustad's Mother), Rajesh Tendon (Gustad—20 yrs.), Meral Durlabji (Gustad—10 yrs.), Meet Nandu (Sohrab—8 yrs.), Aloo Heerjibehedin (Gustad's Grandmother), Anupam Shyam (Milkman), Anirudh Agarwal (Street Butcher), Nina Wadia (Sister Constance), Renu Setna (Dr. Paymaster)

PAPA'S SONG (Anthology/Independent) Producer/Story, Norman de Palm; Director, Sander Francken; Screenplay, Norman de Palm, Sander Francken; Photography, Rogier Stoffers; Music, Rob Hauser; Editor, Herman P. Koerts; Casting, Hans Kemna; an Aves-Luna Blou-N.P.S. production; from Shooting Star Film Distribution; Dutch; Dolby; Color; Not rated; 95 minutes; U.S. release: March 30, 2000. CAST: Rene van Asten (Nico), Romana Vrede (Shirley), Lisette Merenciana (Magda), Victor Bottenbley (Hugo), Tyronne Meerzorg (Juan), Vergill Ford (Roy)

CRANE WORLD (Cowboy Booking) Producer/Director/Screenplay, Pablo Trapero; Photography, Cobi Migliora; Editor, Nicolás Goldbart; Art Director, Andrés Tambornino; Produced by Stantic-Univ. del Cine; Argentine, 1999; Color; Not rated; 90 minutes; U.S. release: April 3, 2000. CAST: Luis Margani (Rulo), Adriana Aizemberg (Adriana), Daniel Valenzuela (Torres), Roly Serrano (Walter), Federico Esquerro (Claudio), Graciana Chironi (Rulo's Mother), Alfonso Rememteria (Sartori)

Jeanie Drynan, Russell Dykstra in *Soft Fruit* © Fox Searchlight Pictures

Roshan Seth, Soni Razdan, Vrajesh Hirjee in *Such a Long Journey*
© Shooting Gallery

Francis Barrett in *Southpaw* © Shooting Gallery

Paul Campbell in *Third World Cop* © Palm Pictures

SOUTHPAW (Shooting Gallery) Producers, Robert Walpole, Paddy Breathnach; Director, Liam McGrath; Photography, Cian De Buitlear; Editor, James E. Dalton; Music, Dario Marianelli; a Bord Scannan na hÉireann presentation in association with the Irish Film Board, Radio Telefis Eireann and Channel 4 of a Treasure Films production; Irish, 1999; Color; Not rated; 77 minutes; U.S. release: April 7, 2000. Documentary on light-welterweight boxer Francis Barrett who represented Ireland in the 1996 Olympics.

THE SPECIALIST (Kino Intl.) Producer/Director, Eyal Sivan; Executive Producer, Armelle Laborie; Screenplay, Rony Brauman, Eyal Sivan; Editor, Audrey Maurion; Music, Yves Robert, Krishna Levy, Béatrice Thiriet, Jean-Michel Levy, Tom Waits; Co-Produced by Momento! and France 2 Cinéma, Bremer Institut Film and WDR, Image Création and RTBF, Lotus Film, Amythos and Noga Communication-Channel 8; French-German-Belgian-Austrian-Israeli, 1999; Dolby; Black and white; Not rated; 128 minutes; U.S. release: April 12, 2000. Documentary on the 1961 trial of Nazi war criminal Adolf Eichmann.

THIRD WORLD COP (Palm Pictures) Producer, Carolyn Pfeiffer Bradshaw; Executive Producers, Chris Blackwell, Dan Genetti; Director, Chris Browne; Screenplay, Suzanne Fenn, Chris Browne, Chris Salewicz; Photography, Richard Lannaman; Editor, Suzanne Fenn; Music, Wally Badarou, Sly & Robbie; Costumes, Michelle Haynes; Casting, Sheila Lowe Graham, Suzanne Fenn, Sharon Burke; Presented in association with Hawkes Nest Productions; Jamaican; Color; Not rated; 98 minutes;

U.S. release: April 14, 2000. CAST: Paul Campbell (Capone), Mark Danvers (Ratty), Carl Bradshaw (Oney), Audrey Reid (Rita), Winston "Bello" Bell (Floyd), Lenford Salmon (Not Nice), Desmond Ballentine (Deportee), O'Neil "Elephant Man" Bryan (Tek-9), Andrew "Nittie Kutchie" Reid (Crime), Devon "Angel Doolas" Douglas (Razor), Winsome Wilson (Carla), Ronald "Too Small" Small (Bodyguard), John Jones (Superintendent Lewis), Lillian Foster (Mama), Clive Anderson (Jacko), Lloyd Reckord (Reverend), Kathy Owen (TV Announcer), Natalie Thompson (Port Antonio Superintendent), Robbie Shakespear (Don Next Door), Onandi Lowe (Pool Player), Buccaneer (MC), Junior Frazer, Owen Williams (Detectives); Ricardo Barrett (Teen with Finger), Natasha Budhai, Angela Hunigan, Tesah Linton (Go-Go Dancers), Calvin Mitchell (Accused), Glenville Murphy (Drunk Man), Howard "Muggy" Williams (Crying Convict), Amelia Sewell (Woman), Andre Thompson (Red Stripe Vendor), Daniel Ellis (Marble Kid), Winston Rowe (Spoonhead), Dean Khouri (Stall Vendor)

THE RIVER (Independent) Producers, Hsu Li-kong, Chiu Shunching; Executive Producer, Chung Hu-ping; Director, Tsai Ming-liang; Screenplay Tsai Ming-liang, Yang Pi-ying, Tsai Yi-chun; Photography, Liao Peng-jung; Designer, Lee Paolin; Editor, Chen Sheng-chang; a Central Motion Picture Corp. production; Taiwanese, 1997; Color; Not rated; 115 minutes; U.S. release: April 14, 2000. CAST: Lee Kang-sheng (Xiao-Kang), Miao Tien (Father), Lu Hsiao-ling (Mother), Chen Chao-jung (Young Man at Sauna), Chen Shiang-chyi (Xiao-kang's Girlfriend), Lu Shiao-lin (Mother's Lover), Ann Hui (Film Director)

Adolf Eichmann in *The Specialist* © Kino International

Rufino Echegoyen, Zaide Silvia Gutiérrez, Damián Delgado in *The Other Conquest* © Carrasco & Domingo Films

Stathis Papadopoulos in *From the Edge of the City* © Cowboy Booking

Jean-Marc Barr, Élodie Bouchez, Patrick Catalifo
in *Don't Let Me Die on a Sunday* © First Run Features

THE OTHER CONQUEST (Carrasco & Domingo Films) Producer, Alvaro Domingo; Director/Screenplay/Editor, Salvador Carrasco; Executive Producer, Plácido Domingo; Associate Producer, Enrique González Torres; Line Producer, Rosalia Salazar; Photography, Arturo De La Rosa; Designer, Andrea Sanderson; Music, Samuel Zyman, Jorge Reyes; an Alvaro Domingo production; Mexican; Color; Rated R; 105 minutes; U.S. release: April 19, 2000. CAST: Damián Delgado (Topiltzin/Tomás), José Carlos Rodriguez (Fray Diego de La Coruña), Elpidia Carrillo (Tecuichpo/Doña Isabel), Iñaki Áierra (Hernando Cortés), Honorato Magaloni (Captain Cristóbal Quijano), Zaide Silvia Gutiérrez (Indian Nun), Guillermo Rios (Alanpoyatzin—Brother), Josefina Echánove (Nanahuatzin—Grandmother), Lourdes Villarreal (Cihuacoatl—Aztec Priest), Luisa Avila (Xilonen—Aztec Princess), Ramón Barragán (Ramón Quevedo—Scribe), Rufino Echegoyen (Fray Sebastián), Alvaro Guerrero (Rolando), Diana Bracho (Doña Juana—Cortés' Wife)

FROM THE EDGE OF THE CITY (Picture This!) Producers, Dionysis Samiotis, Anastasios Vasiliou; Director/Screenplay, Constantinos Giannaris; Executive Producer, Maria Powell; Photography, George Argiroilipoulos; Designer, Roula Nicolaou; Costumes, Sanny Alberti; Music, Akis Daoutis; Editor, Ioanna Spiliopoulo; a Mythos Production in association with Rosebud, Hot Shot Productions and the Greek Film Centre; Greek, 1998; Dolby; Color; Not rated; 90 minutes; U.S. release: April 21, 2000. CAST: Stathis Papadopoulos (Sasha), Costas Cotsianidis (Cotsian), Panagiotis Chartomtsidis (Panagiotis), Anestis Polychronidis (Anestis), Dimitri Papoulidis (Giorgos), Nico Camondos (Phillips), Stelios Tsemboglidis (Stelios), George Mavridis (Chrony), Panagiota Vlachosotirou (Elenista), Theodora Tzimou (Natasia)

DON'T LET ME DIE ON A SUNDAY (First Run Features) Producer, Fabrice Coat; Director/Screenplay, Didier le Pêcheur; Photography, Denis Rouden; Editor, Sylvie Landra; Music, Philippe Cohen-Solal; a Program 33 production, with participation of Canal Plus; French, 1999; Dolby; Color; Not rated; 86 minutes; U.S. release: April 21, 1999. CAST: Élodie Bouchez (Teresa), Jean-Marc Barr (Ben), Martin Petitguyot (Ducon), Patrick Catalifo (Boris), Gérard Loussine (Abel), Jean Michel Fête (Nico), Zazie (Jeanne/Helene), Jeanne Casilas (Marie)

THRONE OF DEATH (Flying Elephant Films) Producer, Preeya Nair; Director/Story, Murali Nair; Screenplay, Bharathan Narakkal; Photography, M.J. Radhakrishnan; Editor, Lalitha Krishna; Music, Madhu Apsara; Indian, 1999; Color; Not rated; 60 minutes; U.S. release date: April 26, 2000. CAST: Viswas Narakkal (Krishnan), Lakshmi Raman (His Wife), Suhas Thayat (The Politician), Jeevan Mitva (The Boy), Paul Manadan, Pauly Wilson

HEART OF LIGHT (Phaedra) Producer, Henrik Møller-Sørensen; Director, Jacob Grønlykke; Screenplay, Jacob Grønlykke, Hans Anthon Lynge; Photography, Dan Laustsen; Designer, Anders Engelbrecht; Music, Joachim Holbek; Editor, Wadt Thomsen; Greenland-Danish, 1998; Color;

Not rated; 90 minutes; U.S. release: April 28, 2000. CAST: Rasmus Lyberth (Rasmus), Vivi Nielsen (Marie), Niels Platow (Mikael Bertilsen), Kenneth Rasmussen (Simon), Laila Rasmussen (Karina), Anda Kristensen, Knud Petersen

THE IDIOTS (USA Films) Producer, Vibeke Windeløv; Executive Producer, Peter Aalbæk Jensen; Director/Screenplay/Photography, Lars von Trier; Editor, Molly Malene Stengaard; Co-Producers, Marianne Slot, Peter van Vogelpoel, Eric Schut; Casting, Rie Hedegaard; a Zentropa Entertainments2 presentation; from October Films; Danish, 1998; Dolby; Color; Rated R; 115 minutes; U.S. release: April 28, 2000. CAST: Bodil Jorgensen (Karen), Jens Albinus (Stoffer), Louise Hassing (Susanne), Troels Lyby (Henrik), Nikolaj Lie Kaas (Jeppe), Henrik Prip (Ped), Luis Mesonero (Miguel), Louise Mieritz (Josephine), Knud Romer Jorgensen (Axel), Trine Michelsen (Nana), Anne-Grethe Bjarup Riis (Katrine), Paprika Steen (High-Class Lady), Erik Wedersoe (Stoffer's Uncle), Michael Moritzen (Man from Municipality), Anders Hove (Josephine's Father), Jan Elle (Waiter), Claus Standberg (Guide at Factory), Hans Henrik Clemensen (Anders), Lone Lindorff (Karen's Mother), Erno Muller (Karen's Grandfather), Regitze Estrup (Louise), Lotte Munk (Britta), Marina Bouras (Axel's Wife), Jens Jorn Spottag (Boss at Advertising Agency), John Martinus (Man in Morning-Jacket), Lars Bjarke, Ewald Larsen, Christian Friis, Louise B. Clausen (Rockers), Julie Wierth (Woman with Two Kids), Kirsten Vaupel, Lillian Tillegreen, Birgit Conradi (Art Class Ladies), Albert Wickmann (High Class Man), Peter Froge (Man in the Swimming Pool), Beat Sorensen (Taxi Driver)

Nikolaj Lie Kaas, Louise Mieritz in *The Idiots* © USA Films

Antonio Lopez Garcia in *Dream of Light* © Facets Multimedia

Karin Viard in *The New Eve* © Sceneries Distribution

SKIN FLICK (Cazzo Film) Executive Producer, Jürgen Anger; Director, Bruce LaBruce; Photography, James Carman; Costumes, Edgar Langer; Editors, Manfred Mancini, Jörg Andreas; German, 1999; Not rated; 70 minutes; U.S. release: April 28, 2000. CAST: Steve Master (Dieter), Eden Miller (Dirk), Tom International (Reinhold), Ralph Steel (Wolfgang), Tim Vincent (Manfred), Nikki Richardson (Cameltoe), Jens Hammer (Karl), Bastian (Leroy), Darren James (Plumber), Terry Richardson (Photographer), Patricia Villa (Lady on Bench), Rebecca (Falling Woman), Luis (Fruit Market Vendor), Bruce LaBruce, Eric, Pierrot (Bashing Victims)

DREAM OF LIGHT (Facets Multimedia) Producer, Maria Moreno; Director, Victor Erice; Based on a work by painter Antonio López Garcia; Photography, Javier Aguirresarobe, Angel Luis Fernández; Music, Pascal Gaigne; Editor, Juan Ignacio San Mateo; Spanish, 1992; Color; Not rated; 139 minutes; U.S. release: May 3, 2000. Documentary on Spanish painter Antonio Lopez Garcia.

ADRENALINE DRIVE (Shooting Gallery) Producers, Kiyoshi Mizokami, Kenichi Itaya, Tomohiro Kobayashi; Director/Screenplay/Editor, Shinobu Yaguchi; Photography, Takashi Hamada; Music, Seiichi Yamamoto; an Adrenaline Drive Committee/Kindai Eiga Kyokai Co./Gaga Communications/There's Enterprise/Nippon Suppan Hanbai production; Japanese, 1999; Color; Not rated; 112 minutes; U.S. release: May 5, 2000. CAST: Hikari Ishida (Shizuko Sato), Masanobu Ando

Masanobu Ando, Hikari Ishida in *Adrenaline Drive* © Shooting Gallery

(Satoru Suzuki), Jovi Jova (Chinpira—Yakuza), Maggy (Yamada), Satoru Sakata (Tanaka), Meisui Kinoshita (Nakagawa), Asaharu Hasegawa (Kawakami), Shinji Rokkaku (Ueno), Chikara Ishikura (Nojima), Kazue Tsunogae (Head Nurse), Yutaka Matushige (Kuroiwa), Kouichi Ueda (Kumicho—Arakawa Leader), Yu Tokui (Yamamoto), Kirina Mano (Tomoko), Taro Suwa (Shimada), Mithu Yamamoto (Shimoda Cop), Youji Tanaka (Bus Driver), Kazuhiro Nakahara (Kuroda), Takuji Suzuki (Hosoya), Suzuka Kusunoki (Yoshie), Masumi Kiuchi (Shimizu), Nao Nekota (Sakai)

THE NEW EVE (Sceneries Distribution) Producer, Paulo Branco; Director, Catherine Corsini; Screenplay, Catherine Corsini, Marc Syrigas; Photography, Agnés Godard; Editor, Sabine Mamou; Designer, Solange Zeitoun; Casting, Brigitte Moidon, Richard Rousseau; a co-production of Gemini Films, ARTE France Cinema, with the participation of Canal+, Sofica Sofinergie 4, CNC; French; Color; Not rated; 94 minutes; U.S. release: May 5, 2000. CAST: Karin Viard (Camille), Pierre-Loup Rajot (Alexis), Catherine Frot (Isabelle), Sergi López (Ben), Mireille Roussel (Louise), Nozha Khouadra (Solveig), Laurent Lucas (Emile), Valentine Vidal (Sophie), François Caron (Psychologist), Frédéric Gelard (Octave), Jean-François Galotte (Sophie's Father), Giséle Joly (Sophie's Mother), Nora Armani (Laurence), Alain Baudy, Emmanuel Quatra (Curlies), Philippe Lehembre (Old Man), Vincent Winterhalter (Gilles), Morgane Lombard (Fabienne), Pierre Baux (Denis), Simon Bakhouche (Doctor), François Forêt (Cafe Waiter), Françoise Sakalauskaite (Françoise), Christophe Loisillon (Man with Costume), Hèléne Alexandridis (Socialist Party Woman), Olivier Jahan (Shy Man), Aurélia Petit (Blonde Girl), Dominique Charpentier (Girl in Pullover), Michel Janjan (Supermarket Employee), Louise Penven, Jeanne Moureau (Alexis & Isbaelle's Daughters), Benoit Penven, Tibault Penven (Twins), Thibault Boitier (Puny Child), Charly Sital (Brother), Vanessa Sital (Sister), Isabelle Hetier (Florence), Rene Hernandez (Toady), David Léotard (Alexis' Colleague), Olivier Bouthillier (Barrois), Emmanuel Doucet (Man in Sex Shop)

YOUNG DR. FREUD (Kino) Director, Axel Corti; Screenplay, Georg Stefan Troller; Photography, Wolfgang Treu; Art Director, Ernst Wurzer; Costumes, Barbara Langbein; Austrian-German, 1977; Color; Not rated; 99 minutes; U.S. release: May 17, 2000. CAST: Karlheinz Hackl (Dr. Sigmund Freud), Silvia Haider (Martha Freud-Bernays), Brigitte Swoboda (Amalie Freud), Guido Weiland (Jakob Freud), Maria Urban (Mathilde Fee Breuer), Karl Merkatz (Dr. Josef Breuer), Jacques Alric (Prof. Dr. Charcot), Norbert Kappen (Prof. Dr. Meynert), Peter Luhr (Prof. Dr. Brucke), Marianne Nentwich (Bertha Pappenheim), Eugen Stark (Asst. Dr. Fleisch), Ursula Schult (Frau Bernays), Michael Toost (Family Doctor), Georg Stephen Troller (Offscreen Interviewer)

THE WELL (Cowboy Booking) Producer, Sandra Levy; Executive Producers, Maureen Barron, Noel Ferrier, Errol Sullivan; Director, Samantha Lang; Screenplay, Laura Jones; Based on the novel by Elizabeth Jolley; Photography, Mandy Walker; Designer, Michael Philips;

Karlheinz Hackl in *Young Dr. Freud* © Kino International

Grass © Unapix

Costumes, Anna Borghesi; Editor, Dany Cooper; Music, Stephen Rae; Casting, Ann Robinson, Liz Mullinar Casting; an Australian Film Finance Corp. presentation of a Southern Star Xanadu production, in association with the N.S.W. Film and TV Office; Australian, 1997; Dolby; Color; Not rated; 102 minutes; U.S. release: May 19, 2000. CAST: Pamela Rabe (Hester Harper), Miranda Otto (Katherine), Paul Chubb (Harry Bird), Frank Wilson (Francis Harper), Steve Jacobs (Rod Borden), Genevieve Lemon (Jen Borden)

GRASS (Unapix) Producer/Director, Ron Mann; Screenplay, Solomon Vesta; Music, Guido Luciani; Art Director, Paul Mavrides; Editor, Robert Kennedy; Co-Producer, Sue Len Quon; Graphics Co-Ordinator, Maury Whyte; Narrator, Woody Harrelson; Canadian; Color; Not rated; 80 minutes; U.S. release: May 31, 2000. Documentary on the history of marijuana prohibition in the United States

LIVE VIRGIN (Granite Releasing) Producers, Aissa Djabri, Farid Lahouassa, Manuel Munz; Executive Producer/Director, Jean-Pierre Marois; Screenplay, Jean-Pierre Marois, Ira Israel; Photography, Eagle Egilsson; Editor, Georges Klotz; Music, Gregori Czerkinsky; Designer, Christiaan Wagener; Costumes, Deborah Everton; a Vertigo Prods./M6 Films production with the participation of TPS Cinema; French; Dolby; Color; Rated R; 88 minutes; U.S. release: June 2, 2000. CAST: Bob Hoskins (Joey Quinn), Mena Suvari (Katrina Bartoloti), Robert Loggia (Ronny Bartoloti), Sally Kellerman (Quaint McPherson), Lamont Johnson

(Nick), Gabriel Mann (Brian), Bobbie Phillips (Raquel), Rick Peters (Tommy), O-Lan Jones (Kim), Michael Milhoan (Larry), Freda Foh Shen (Marge), Kristin Norton (Nancy), Alexandra Wentworth (Mitzi), Cynthia LaMontagne (Gloria), Michael Cudlitz (Bob), Kristin Minter (Susie), Jane Morris (Buela Snarp), Octavia Spencer (Agnes Large), Ron Jeremy (Desk Sergeant), Brian Bloom (Brad), Vincent Schiavelli (Cab Driver), John Roarke (George Bush/Jerry Springer/Maury Povitch/Tom Snyder), Thomas G. Waites (Grip), Esai Morales (Jim the Director), Carrie Ann Inaba (Hiromi), Mark Adair-Rios, Mary Jo Smith (Security Guards), Lori New (Tina), Ashlee Turner (Laurie), Jed Rhein (Paul), James Czarnecki (Teacher), Curt Kaplan (George), Billy "Sly" Williams (Blood), Life Garland (Crip), Jason Bercy (Messenger), Elizabeth Guber (Operator), Kim Robillard (Jail Officer), Ira Israel (Ira), Penny Griego (Anchorwoman), Ken Taylor (Anchorman), Kira Reed (Naked Actress), Fernando Sulichin (Hispanic Driver)

THE CHILDREN OF CHABANNES (Castle Hill) Producer, Lisa Gossels; Directors/Editors, Lisa Gossels, Dean Wetherell; Photography, Mustapha Barat, Philippe Bonnier; Co-Producer, Dean Wetherell; Music, Joel Goodman; Narrator, Lisa Gossels; from HBO Signature Double Exposure, Perrenial Pictures; French; Not rated; 91 minutes; U.S. release: June 9, 2000. Documentary on how 400 Jewish refugee children were protected from the Nazis during World War II, by the people of the French village of Chabannes.

Miranda Otto, Pamela Rabe in *The Well* © Cowboy Booking

Mena Suvari in *Live Virgin* © Granite Releasing

Hugo Weaving (center) in *The Interview* © Cinema Guild

Burlesk King © Strand Releasing

CINÉMA VÉRITÉ: DEFINING THE MOMENT (National Film Board of Canada) Producers, Adam Symansky, Éric Michel; Executive Producer, Sally Bochner; Director, Peter Wintonick; Researcher/Screenplay, Kirwan Cox; Photography, Francis Miquet; Editors, Marlo Miazga, Peter Wintonick; Music, Jimmy James; Canadian, 1999; Dolby; Color; Not rated; 105 minutes; U.S. release: June 9, 2000. A documentary about documentaries, featuring a look at some notable non-fiction films, featuring Jean-Pierre Beauviala, Michel Brault, Gillian Caldwell, Marcel Carrière, Robin Cowie, Robert Drew, Jennifer Fox, William Greaves, Gregg Hale, Wolf Koenig, Roman Kroitor, Barbara Kopple, Richard Leacock, Doug Leiterman, Terry Macartney-Filgate, Albert Maysles, D.A. Pennebaker, Pierre Perrault, Karel Reisz, Jean Rouch, Hope Ryden, Floria Sigismondi, Frederick Wiseman.

THE INTERVIEW (Cinema Guild) Producer, Bill Hughes; Director, Craig Monahan; Screenplay, Craig Monahan, Gordon Davie; Photography, Simon Duggan; Art Director, Richard Bell; Costumes, Jeanie Cameron; Editor, Suresh Ayyar; Music, David Hirschfelder; from Pointblank Pictures P/L; Australian, 1998; Dolby; Color; Not rated; 103 minutes; U.S. release: June 16, 2000. CAST: Hugo Weaving (Eddie Rodney Fleming), Tony Martin (John Steele), Aaron Jeffery (Wayne Prior), Paul Sonkkila (Jackson), Michael Caton (Barry Walls), Peter McCauley (Hudson), Glynis Angel (Robran), Leverne McDonnell (Solicitor), Libby Stone (Mrs. Beecroft), Andrew Bayly (Prowse), Doug Dew (Beecroft)

100% ARABICA (ArtMattan) Producer/Director, Mahmoud Zemmouri; Screenplay, Mahmoud Zemmouri, Marie-Laurence Attias; Photography, Noël Very; Costumes, Mahadevi Apavou; Editor, Youcef Tobni; Produced by Fennec Productions (France), Les Film de la Toison d'Or (Belgium) and Incoprom (Switzerland); French-Belgian-Swiss, 1997; Dolby; Color; Not rated; 86 minutes; U.S. release date: June 23, 2000. CAST: Khaled (Rachid), Cheb Mami (Krimo), Mouss (Slimane), Majim Laouriga (Madjid), Farid Fedjer (Kamel), Youssef Diawara (Sylla), Patrice Thibaud (Bernard Lemercier), Mohamed Camara (Salem), Nedjma (Zoubida)

PRAISE (Strand) Producer, Martha Coleman; Director, John Curran; Screenplay, Andrew McGahan, based on his novel; Photography, Dion Beebe; Designer, Michael Philips; Costumes, Emily Seresin; Editor, Alexandre de Franceschi; Music, Dirty Three; Casting, Nikki Barrett; Australian, 1998; Dolby; Color; Not rated; 98 minutes; U.S. release: June 30, 2000. CAST: Peter Fenton (Gordon), Sacha Horler (Cynthia), Marta Dusseldorp (Rachel), Joel Edgerton (Leo), Yvette Duncan (Molly), Ray Bull (Vass), Gregory Perkins (Raymond), Loene Carmen (Cathy), Skye Wansey (Helen), Richard Green (Dave), Lynette Curran (Sexual Health Worker), Susan Prior (Sophie), Paul Lum (Darren), Fiona Mahl (Darren's Girlfriend), Damon Herriman (Skinhead), Mick Innes (Taxi Driver), Jamie Jackson (James), Stephen Shanahan (Steve), Karen Colsten (Mary), Jason Clarke (Frank), Basil Clarke (Footless Old Man), Ken Shorter (Male Nurse), Joy Hruby (Old Woman)

Sacha Horler in *Praise* © Strand Releasing

Malik Zidi, Anna Thomson in *Water Drops on Burning Rocks*
© Zeitgeist Films

Jude Law in *The Wisdom of Crocodiles* © Miramax Films

Natacha Reginier, Salim Kechiouche
in *Criminal Lovers* © Fidelite Prods.

BURLESK KING (Strand) Producer, Robbie Tan; Director, Mel Chionglo; Screenplay, Ricardo Lee; Photography, George Tutanes; Designer, Edgar Martin Littaua; Music, Nonong Buencamino; from Seiko Films; Philippines, 1999; Color; Not rated; 109 minutes; U.S. release: June 30, 2000. CAST: Rodel Velayo (Harry), Nini Jacinto (Brenda), Leonardo Litton (James), Raymond Bagatsing (Mario), Elizabeth Oropesa (Betty), Cherrie Pie Picache (Aileen), Gino Ilustre (Michael), Joonee Gamboa (Miong), Tonio Ortigas (Leo), Joel Lamangan (Odette)

WATER DROPS ON BURNING ROCKS (Zeitgeist) Producers, Olivier Delbosc, Marc Missonnier, Alain Sarde, Christine Gozlan; Director/Screenplay, François Ozon; Based on the play *Troppen auf Heisse Steine* by Rainer Werner Fassbinder; Photography, Jeanne Lapoirie; Sets, Arnaud De Moleron; Costumes, Pascaline Chavanne; Editor, Laurence Bawedin; a Fidélité Production, Les Films Alain Sarde coproduction with Euro Space (Japan) with the participation of Studio Images 6 (France); French-Japanese; Dolby; Color; Not rated; 86 minutes; U.S. release: July 12, 2000. CAST: Bernard Giraudeau (Leopold), Malik Zidi (Franz), Ludivine Sagnier (Anna), Anna Thomson (Vera)

THE WISDOM OF CROCODILES (Miramax) Producers, David Lascelles, Carolyn Choa; Executive Producers, Scott Meek, Dorothy Berwin; Director, Po Chih Leong; Screenplay, Paul Hoffman; Photography, Oliver Curtis; Designer, Andy Harris; Costumes, Anna Sheppard; Line Producer, Laura Julian; Music, John Lunn, Orlando Gough; Editor, Robin Sales; Casting, Michelle Guish; a Zenith Productions, Goldwyn Films, Film Foundry Partners & Entertainment Film Distributors in association with the Arts Council of England presentation of a Zenith Film; British, 1999; Dolby; Deluxe color; Rated R; 98 minutes; U.S. release: July 14, 2000. CAST: Jude Law (Steven Grlscz), Elina Löwensohn (Anne Levels), Timothy Spall (Inspector Healey), Kerry Fox (Maria Vaughn), Jack Davenport (Sgt. Roche), Colin Salmon (Martin), Stuart Bowman, C.J. December (Car Crash Mechanics), Nick Lamont (Toll Bridge Attendant), Joseph O'Conor (Mr. Nancarrow), Hitler Wong (Noodles Chan), Anastasia Hille (Karen), Ashley Artus (Gang Leader), Tom Wu, Hon Ping Tang, Anthony Cotton, Richard Mylan, Carlton Headley, Neran Persaud (Gang Members), Julia Davies (Girl in Operating Theatre), Rupert Farley (Priest), Diane Howse (Mrs. Healey), Cliff Parisi (Labourer), Vincent Keane (Injured Workman)

THE GIRL IN SNEAKERS (Art Bureau of the Organization for the Propaganda of Islamic Thought) Director, Rasul Sadrameli; Screenplay, Fereydoun Farhudi, Peyman Qasemkhani; Photography, Dariush Ayari; Editor, Mustafa Kherqepush; Music, Iraj Panahi; Iranian, 1999; Color; Not rated; 110 minutes; U.S. release: July 14, 2000. CAST: Pegah Ahangarani (Tadai), Majid Hajizadeh (Aideen), Akram Mohammadi (Mahpareh), Abdolreza Akbari, Mahmoud Jafari

CRIMINAL LOVERS (Strand) Producers, Marc Missonnier, Olivier Delbosc; Director/Screenplay, François Ozon; Photography, Pierre Stoeber; Designer, Arnaud de Moleron; Costumes, Pascaline Guillaume;

Editor, Dominique Petrot; Music, Philippe Rombi; from Fidélité Productions, Studio Canal+, La Sept/ARTE, and Euro Space (Japan); French-Japanese, 1999; Dolby; Color; Not rated; 90 minutes; U.S. release: July 21, 2000. CAST: Natacha Reginier (Alice), Jeremie Renier (Luc), Miki Manojlovic (The Woodsman), Salim Kechiouche (Said), Yasmine Belmadi (Karim)

POKÉMON THE MOVIE 2000: THE POWER OF ONE (Warner Bros.) Producers, Norman J. Grossfield, Choji Yoshikawa, Yukako Matsusako, Takemoto Mori; Executive Producers, Masakazu Kubo, Takashi Kawaguchi, Alfred R. Kahn; Director, Kunihiko Yuyama; English Adaptation Director, Michael Haigney; Screenplay, Takeshi Shudo; Based on characters created by Satoshi Tajiri; English Adaptation, Norman J. Grossfield, Michael Haigney; Translation, Paul Taylor; Photography, Hisao Shirai; Animation Producers, Toshiaki Okuno, Shukichi Kanda; Editor, Jay Film; Music, Ralph Schuckett, John Loeffler; Chief Animator, Sayuri Ichiishi; Animation Supervisor, Yoichi Kotabe; Casting, Jim Malone; a Warner Bros. Family Entertainment release of a Kids WB! presentation of a Pikachu Project '99-Shogakukan Inc. production in association with 4Kids Entertainment; Japanese; Dolby; Deluxe color; Rated G; 81 minutes; U.S. release: July 21, 2000. VOICE CAST: Veronica Taylor (Ash Ketchum/Mrs. Ketchum), Rachael Lillis (Misty/Jessie), Ted Lewis (Tracey Sketcher), Eric Stuart (James/Charizard), Addie Blaustein (Meowth), Ikue Ootani (Pikachu), Stan Hart (Professor Oak), Kayzie Rogers (Professor Ivy/Mr. Mime), Megan Hollingshead (Computer Voice)

Pikachu, Ash, Squirtle, Balbasaur in *Pokémon the Movie* 2000
© Pikachu Projects '98

Behzad Dourani in *The Wind Will Carry Carry Us* © New Yorker Films

Orga, Godzilla in *Godzilla 2000* © Toho Co. Ltd./TriStar Pictures

THE WIND WILL CARRY US (New Yorker) Producers, Marin Karmitz, Abbas Kiarostami; Director/Screenplay/Editor, Abbas Kiarostami; based on an idea by Mahmoud Aydein; Photography, Mahmoud Kalari; Music, Payman Yazdanian; from MK2 Production; French-Iranian, 1999; Color; Not rated; 118 minutes; U.S. release: July 28, 2000. CAST: Behzad Dourani (The Engineer), The Inhabitants of the Village of Siah Dareh

MAD ABOUT MAMBO (USA Films) Producer, David P. Kelly; Executive Producers, Gabriel Byrne, Martin Bruce-Clayton; Director/Screenplay, John Forte; Photography, Ashley Rowe; Designer, Fiona Daly; Editor, David Martin; Music, Richard Hartley; Costumes, Eimer Ni Mhaoldomhnaigh; Casting, John and Ros Hubbard; a Gramercy Pictures presentation in association with Phoenix Pictures of a First City production in association with Plurabelle Films; Canadian-British-U.S.;Dolby; Color; Rated PG-13; 92 minutes; U.S. release: August 4, 2000. CAST: William Ash (Danny Mitchell), Keri Russell (Lucy McLoughlin), Brian Cox (Sidney McLoughlin), Theo Fraser Steele (Oliver Parr), Maclean Stewart (Mickey), Tim Loane (Brother McBride), Russell Smith (Gary), Joe Rea (Spike), Brendan Morrissey, Richard Orr (Referees), Inge Dorman (Hockey Goalie), Julian Littman (Rudi Morelli), Daniel Caltagirone (Carlos Rega), Alan McKee (Frank Mallin), Terry Byrne (Gaelic Teacher), Aingeal Grehan (Mrs. Mitchell), Gavin O'Connor (Seamus Mitchell), Rosaleen Linehan (Mrs. Burns), Kelan Lowry O'Reilly (Graham), Jim Norton (Brother Xavier), Pauline Hutton (Winnie), Caroline Kerr

William Ash, Keri Russell in *Mad About Mambo* © USA Films

(Sophie), Jonathan Forbes (George), Jaz Pollock (Mrs. Coulter), Olivia Nash (Mrs. Hannah), Eleanor Methven (Mrs. Parr), Chris Kelly (British Army Soldier), Dominic Wright (Checkpoint Soldier), Mark McCann, Neil Rooney (Boys), Declan Gorman (Shop Assistant), Steve Blount (Beefy Player), Jerry Lavelle (Master of Ceremonies), Jackie Fullerton (Himself), Patrick Fitzsymons (TV Commentator), Abbie Spallen (Receptionist)

GODZILLA 2000 (TriStar) Executive Producer, Shogo Tomiyama; Director, Takao Okawara; Screenplay, Hiroshi Kashiwabara, Wataru Mimura; Photography, Katsuhiro Kato; Art Director, Takeshi Shimizu; Editor, Yoshiyuki Okuhara; Director of Special Effects, Kenji Suzuki; Music, Takayuki Hattori; U.S. Post-Production Editor, Darren Paskal; Voice Casting, Glen Chin; Japanese (dubbed in English); Dolby; Color; Rated PG; 97 minutes; U.S. release: August 18, 2000. CAST: Takehiro Murata (GPN Director Yuji Shinoda), Shiro Sano (CCI Scientist Shiro Miyasaka), Hiroshi Abe (CCI Chief Mitsuo Katagiri), Naomi Nishida (Yuki Ichinose), Mayu Suzuki (Io), Tsutomu Kitagawa (Godzilla), Takeo Nakahara, Takeshi Obayashi, Shiro Namiki, Sakae Kimura

THE MOST TERRIBLE TIME IN MY LIFE (Viz Films/Tidepoint) Producers, Shunsuke Koga, Kaizo Hayashi, Yu Wei Yen; Executive Producer, Yutaka Goto; Director, Kaizo Hayashi; Screenplay, Kaizo Hayashi, Daisuke Tengan; Photography, Yuichi Nagata; Designer, Takeo Kimura; Music, Meina Co.; Editor, Nobuko Tomita; Costumes, Masae Miyamoto; a Shutter Pictures/For Life Records Inc./Film Detective Office co-production; Japanese-Taiwanese, 1993; CinemaScope; Black and white; Not rated; 92 minutes; U.S. release: August 25, 2000. CAST: Masatoshi Nagase (Hama Maiku), Kiyotaka Namba (Hoshino), Shiro Sano (Kanno), Yang Haitin (Yang Haitin), Hou de Jian (Hou de Jian), Kaho Minami (Bai Lan), Shinya Tsukamoto (Yamaguchi), Akaji Maro (Detective Nakayama), Shishido Jo (Shishido Jo)

ORFEU (New Yorker) Producers, Renata Almeida Magalhães, Paula Lavigne; Director, Carlos Diegues; Screenplay, Carlos Diegues, Hermano Vianna, Hamilton Vaz Pereira, Paulo Lins, João Emanuel Carneiro; Based on the play by Vinicius de Moraes; Photography, Affonso Beato; Music, Caetano Veloso; Designer, Clovis Bueno; Editor, Sergio Mekler; Costumes, Emília Duncan; a Rio Vermelho Films production, co-produced by Globo Films; Brazilian; Dolby; Color; Not rated; 110 minutes; U.S. release: August 25, 2000. CAST: Tony Garrido (Orfeu), Patricia França (Euridice), Murilo Benício (Lucinho), Zezé Motta (Conceição), Milton Gonçalves (Nacio), Isabel Fillardis (Mira), Maria Ceiça (Carmen), Stepan Nercessian (Pacheco)

ANATOMY (Columbia) Producers, Jakob Claussen, Thomas Wöbke; Director/Screenplay, Stefan Ruzowitzky; Photography, Peter Von Haller; Designer, Ingrid Henn; Editor, Ueli Christen; Music, Marius Ruhland; Costumes, Nicole Fischnaller; Models and SFX/Makeup Supervisors, Joachim Grüninger, Birger Laube; Anatomy Theatre Designers, Andreas Donhauser, Renate Martin; Casting, Nessie Nesslauer; a Deutsche

Masatoshi Nagase in *The Most Terrible Time in My Life* © Viz Films

Famke Janssen, John Hannah in *Circus*
© Columbia Pictures Industries, Inc.

Columbia Pictures Film Production presentation of a Claussen + Wöbke Film production; German; Dolby; Color; Rated R; 99 minutes; U.S. release: September 8, 2000. CAST: Franka Potente (Paula), Benno Fürmann (Hein), Anna Loos (Gretchen), Sebastian Blomberg (Caspar), Holger Speckhahn (Phil), Traugott Buhre (Prof. Grombek), Oliver K. Wnuk (Ludwig), Arndt Schwering-Sohnrey (David), Andreas Günther (Franz), Antonia Cäcilia Holfelder (Gabi), Rüdiger Vogler (Dr. Henning), Barbara Magdalena Ahren (Mrs. Henning), Werner Dissel (Grandfather), Gennadi Vengerov (Lab Technician), Thomas Meinhardt (Munich Professor), Simon Schwarz (Young Man on Dissecting Table), Alexander Liegl, Martin Pölcher (Lab Assistants), Christoph Hagen Dittmann (Bernie), Berrin Alganer-Lenz (Cleaning Lady), Angelika Sedlmeier (Mrs. Freisinger), Ulrich Matschoss (Judge), Gerald Alexander Held (Policeman), Karl Friedrich (Detective), Susanne Gräbe (Heidelberg Waitress), Johann Nikolussi, Anna Brüggemann (Drug Addicts), Axel Weusten (Alexander)

CIRCUS (Columbia) Producers, Alan Latham, James Gibb; Director, Rob Walker; Screenplay, David Logan; Photography, Ben Seresin; Designer, James Merifield; Editor, Oral Norrie Ottey; Music, Simon Boswell; Costumes, Anna Sheppard; Casting, Michelle Guish; a Film Development Corporation production; British-U.S.; Dolby; Deluxe color; Rated R; 94 minutes; U.S. release: September 15, 2000. CAST: John Hannah (Leo Garfield), Famke Janssen (Lily), Peter Stormare (Julius), Eddie Izzard (Troy), Fred Ward (Elmo), Brian Conley (Bruno), Tiny Lister (Moose), Amanda Donohoe (Gloria), Ian Burfield (Caspar), Neil Stuke (Roscoe), Michael Attwell (Magnus), Jason Watkins (Dom), Christopher Biggins (Arnie), Lucy Akhurst (Helen), Louise Rolfe (Julie), Hinda Hicks (Beautiful Singer), Rob Walker (Old Tramp), Marcus Heath (Paul), Christopher Tune (Boy Racer), Louis Hammond (Jeweller), Evelyn Duah (Jeweller's Assistant), Steve Toussaint (Black), Julie Saunders (Hotel Receptionist), Che Walker (Nightclub Worker)

TABOO (GOHATTO) (New Yorker) Director/Screenplay, Nagisa Oshima; Based on the novellas *Maegami no Sozaburo* and *Sanjogawara Ranjin* from *Shinsengumi Keppuroku* by Ryotaro Shiba; Photography, Toyomichi Kurita; Designer, Yoshinobu Nishioka; Costumes, Emi Wada; Music, Ryuichi Sakamoto; Produced by Shochiku Co. Ltd., Kadokawa Shoten Publishing Company, Imagica Corp., BS Asahi, Eisei Gekijo Co.Ltd., Bac Films, Le Studio Canal+, Recorded Picture Co. Ltd.; Japanese; Color; Not rated; 100 minutes; U.S. release: October 6, 2000. CAST: Takeshi Kitano (Capt. Toshizo Hijikata), Ryuhei Matsuda (Samurai Sozaburo Kano), Shinji Takeda (Lt. Soji Okita), Tadanobu Asano (Samurai Hyozo Tashiro), Koji Matoba (Samurai Heibei Sugano), Tommys Masa (Inspector Jo Yamazaki), Masatoh Eve (Officer Koshitaro Ito), Uno Kanda (The Geisha Nishikigi-dayu), Kazuko Yoshiyuki (The Servant Omatsu), Tomorowo Taguchi (Samurari Tojiro Yuzawa), Yoichi Sai (Commander Isami Kondo), Jiro Sakagami (Lt. Genzaburo Inoue), Zakoba Katsura (Wachigaiya), Kei Sato (The Narrator)

Tony Garrido, Patricia França in *Orfeu* © New Yorker Films

Ryuhei Matsuda, Tadanobu Asano in *Taboo* © New Yorker Films

Gumimon, Veemon, Tai, Wallace in *Digimon: The Movie* © Toei, FFP

James Layton, Lee Williams in *The Wolves of Kromer*
© First Run Features

DIGIMON: THE MOVIE (20th Century Fox) Producers, Terry-Lei O'Malley, Hiromi Seki; Executive Producers, Tan Takaiwa, Teruo Tamamura, Tsutomu Tomari, Yasushi Mitsui, Makoto Shibazki, Makoto Yamashina, Makoto Toriyama; Directors, Mamoru Hosoda, Shigeyasu Yamauchi; English Voice Directors/English Adaptation, Jeff Nimoy, Bob Buchholz; Screenplay, Reiko Yoshida; Original Concept/Character Designer, Akiyoshi Hongo; Photography, Shigeru Ando; Editors, Douglas Purgason, Gary A. Friedman; Music, Udi Harpaz, Amotz Plessner; Animation Directors, Takaaki Yamashita, Hisashi Nakayama, Masahiro Aizawa; Computer Graphics Producer, Toyokazu Hattori; a Fox Kids presentation of a Saban Entertainment/Toei Animation Co. production; Japanese; Dolby; Deluxe color; Rated PG; 82 minutes; U.S. release: October 6, 2000. VOICE CAST: Lara Jill Miller, Joshua Seth, Colleen O'Shaughnessy, Philece Sampler, Bob Glouberman, Mona Marshall, Michael Lindsay, Michael Reisz, Wendee Lee, Dorothy Elias-Fahn, Doug Ehrholtz, Michael Sorich

THE RED STUFF (Independent/Film Forum) Producer, Masja Novikova; Director, Leo de Boer; Photography, Peter Brugman; Editor, Berenike Rozgonyi; produced in cooperation with VPRO, Pieter van Huystee Film & TV; Dutch, 1999; Color/Black and white; Not rated; 78 minutes; U.S. release: October 11, 2000. Documentary on Russia's cosmonauts.

CALLE 54 (Miramax) Producers, Cristina Huete, Fabienne Servan Schreiber; Executive Producer, Laurence Miller; Director, Fernando Trueba; Photography, Jose Luis López-Linares; Editor, Carmen Frías; Line Producer, Jessica Huppert Berman; Spanish-French; Dolby; Color; Rated G; 105 minutes; U.S. release: October 20, 2000. Documentary on Latin jazz, featuring Tito Puente, Jerry Gonzalez and the Fort Apache Band, Chano Dominguez, Eliane Elias, Chico O'Farrill, Gato Barbieri, Paquito D'Rivera, Michel Camilo, Chucho Valdes, Bebo Valdes, Dave Valentin, Orlando "Puntilla" Rios, Carlos Valdes "Patato," Israel Lopez "Cacho."

THE WOLVES OF KROMER (First Run) Producer, Charles Lambert; Director, Will Gould; Screenplay, Charles Lambert, Matthew Read; Based on the play by Charles Lambert; Photography, Laura Remacha; Music, Basil Moore-Asfouri; Editor, Carol Salter; Costumes, Shanti Freed; Casting, Teresa Green, Matthew Read; a Discodog presentation of a Charles Lambert production; British, 1999; Color; Not rated; 82 minutes; U.S. release date: October 20, 2000. CAST: Lee Williams (Seth), James Layton (Gabriel), Rita Davies (Fanny), Kevin Moore (The Priest), Angharad Rees (Mary), Leila Lloyd-Evelyn (Polly), Margaret Towner (Doreen), Rosemarie Dunham (Mrs. Drax), David Prescott (Mark), Matthew Dean (Kester), Alastair Cumming (Michael), Lord Biffen (Mr. Powell), Boy George (Narrator)

Jerry González in *Calle 54* © Miramax Films

Jessica Paré, Thomas Gibson in *Stardom* © Lions Gate Films

Uri Ran Klausner, Guy Amir, Liron Levo, Tomer Ruso in *Kippur*
© Kino International

Zhou Xun in *Suzhou River* © Strand Releasing

STARDOM (Lions Gate) a.k.a. *15 Moments*; Producers, Denise Robert, Robert Lantos; Director, Denys Arcand; Screenplay, Denys Arcand, Jacob Potashnik; Photography, Guy Dufaux; Art Director, Zoe Sakellaropoulo; Costumes, Michel Robidas; Music, François Dompierre; Casting, Deirdre Bowen, Lucie Robitaille; an Alliance Atlantis Communications/Serendipity Point Films/Cinemaginaire/Cine B production; Canadian; Color/Black and white; Rated R; 100 minutes; U.S. release: October 27, 2000. CAST: Jessica Paré (Tina Menzhal), Dan Aykroyd (Barry Levine), Charles Berling (Philippe Gascon), Thomas Gibson (Renny Ohayon), Frank Langella (Blaine de Castillon), Robert Lepage (Bruce Taylor), Patrick Huard (Talk Show Host), Camilla Rutherford (Toni), Tony Calabretta (Bernie Placek), Alain Goulem (Bobby Veau), Larry Day (Brian O'Connell), Danielle Desormeaux (Sheila Rinaldy), Domenic Di Rosa (Principal), Claudia Ferri (Ruth Levine), Susan Glover (Claire Crosby), Jayne Heitmeyer (Penelope Vargas), Lisa Bronwyn Moore (Susie Tucker), Charles Powell (Terry Pfizer), Norm Rebadow (Det. Sam Donahue), Janine Theriault (Irina), François Berléand (French Accountant), Patrick Poivre D'Arvor (French TV Presenter), Rachelle Lefevre (Leslie Bloor), Joel McNichol (Gaby Stern), Jonathan Robert Rondeau (Justin), Eric Civanyan , Bernard Dhéran, Daniel Martin, Thibault de Montalembert (French Intellectual at TV Debate)

KIPPUR (Kino) Producers, Michel Propper, Amos Gitai, Laurent Truchot; Director, Amos Gitai; Screenplay, Amos Gitai, Marie-José Sanselme; Photography, Renato Berta; Designer, Miguel Markin; Music, Jan Garbarek; Costumes, Laura Dinulesco; Editors, Monica Coleman, Kobi Netanel; an MP Productions, Agav Hafakot, Le Studio Canal+, Arte France Cinema, and R&C Produzioni co-production; Israeli-French; Dolby; Color; Not rated; 123 minutes; U.S. release: November 3, 2000. CAST: Liron Levo (Weinraub), Tomer Russo (Ruso), Uri Ran Klausner (Klauzner, the Doctor), Yoram Hattab (Yoram), Guy Amir (Gadassi), Juliano Merr (The Captain)

SUZHOU RIVER (Strand) Producers, Nai An, Philippe Bober; Director/Screenplay, Lou Ye; Photography, Wang Yu; Designer, Li Zhuoyi; Music, Jorg Lemberg; Editor, Karl Riedl; a Coproduction Office presentation of an Essential Film (Berlin)/Dream Factory (Beijing) production; Chinese-German-Italian; Dolby; Color; Not rated; 83 minutes; U.S. release: November 6, 2000. CAST: Zhou Xun (Moudan/Meimei), Jia Hongsheng (Mardar), Hua Zhongkai (Lao B.), Yao Anlian (Boss), Nai An (Mada)

RESTLESS (Arrow) Producer, Peter Shiao; Executive Producers, Lulu, Wang Yang Jun; Director/Screenplay, Jule Gilfillan; Story, Jule Gilfillan,

Peter Shiao; Photography, Yang Shu; Editor, Folmer Wiesinger; Music, Laura Karpman; Designer, Cao Jiu Ping; a Scitech Culture Company presentation (China) of a Celestial Pictures production (US); Chinese-U.S.; Dolby; Color; Not rated; 98 minutes; U.S. release: November 6, 2000. CAST: Catherine Kellner (Leah Quinn), David Wu (Richardo Kao), Sarita Choudhury (Jane Talwani), Geng Le (Master Sun Zhan), Josh Lucas (Jeff Hollingsworth), Chen Shiang-chyi (Lin Qing Qing), Matthew Faber (Ben Gold)

NON-STOP (Shooting Gallery) Producer, Tomoyuki Akaishi; Executive Producer, Masaya Nakamura; Director/Screenplay, Sabu; Photography, Shuji Kuriyama; Art Director, Mutsumi Nasu; Editor, Shinji Tanaka; Music, Diamond Yukai; Casting, Naoto Kano; a Nikkatsu Corporation presentation; Japanese; Color; Not rated; 82 minutes; U.S. release: November 10, 2000. CAST: Tomoro Taguchi (Yasuda), Diamond Yukai (Aizawa), Shinichi Tsutsumi (Takeda), Akaji Maro, Ren Osugi, Hiroshi Simizu, Ikkou Suzuki, Yuji Sawayama, Sabu, Takanori Kikuchi, Masahi Hirakubo, Keisuke Horibe, Ryoko Takizawa, Yuka Torashima, Wataru Shihodo, Tetsuo Yamashita, Satoshi Watanabe, Takashi Matsuyama, Yanagi Yurei, Hitomi Shiraishi, Masaharu Matsuda

Catherine Kellner, Geng Le in *Restless* © Arrow Releasing

Emmanuelle Béart in *La Bûche* © Empire Pictures

Tam Williams in *The Trench* © Blue Sky PM/Skyline

LA BÛCHE (Empire) a.k.a. *Season's Beatings* ; Producer, Alain Sarde; Executive Producer, Christine Gozlan; Director, Danièle ThompsonScreenplay, Danièle Thompson, Christopher Thompson; Photography, Robert Fraisse; Costumes, Elisabeth Tavernier; Editor, Emmanuelle Castro; Music, Michel Legrand; Casting, Francoise Combadiere-Stern; French; Color; Not rated; 107 minutes; U.S. release: November 17, 2000. CAST: Sabine Azema (Louba), Emmanuelle Béart (Sonia), Charlotte Gainsbourg (Milla), Francoise Fabian (Yvette), Claude Rich (Stanislas), Christopher Thompson (Joseph), Jean-Pierre Darroussin (Gilbert), Samuel Labarthe (Pierre), Francoise Brion (Janine), Isabelle Carre (Annabelle), Thierry Hancisse (The Florist), Hélène Fillieres (Véronique)

SASAYAKI (MOONLIGHT WHISPERS) (Viz Films/Tidepoint Pictures) Producers, Hiroyuki Negishi, Satoshi Nakamura; Executive Producer, Masaya Nakamura; Director, Akihiko Shiota; Screenplay, Akihiko Shiota, Yoichi Nishiyama; Based on *Gekko no Sasayaki* by Masahiko Kikuni; Photography, Shigeru Komatsubara; Designer, Norifumi Ataka; Music, Shinsuke Honda; Editor, Yoshio Sugano; a Nikkatsu Corporation production; Japanese, 1999; Dolby; Color; Not rated; 100 minutes; U.S. release: November 22, 2000. CAST: Kenji Mizuhashi (Takaya Hidaka), Tsugumi (Satsuki Kitahara), Kota Kusano (Tadashi Uematsu), Harumi Inoue (Shizuka Kitahara), Chika Fujimura (Satsuki's Friend), Yoshiki Sekino (Maruken)

THE TRENCH (Blue Sky PM/Skyline) Producer, Steve Clark Hall; Director/Screenplay, William Boyd; Photography, Tony Pierce-Roberts; Editors, Jim Clark, Laurence Mery-Clark; Music, Evelyn Glennie, Greg Malcangi; Line Producer, Mairi Bett; Casting, Mary Selway; a Blue Sky PM/Skyline Films/Galatee Films production made with the participation of British Screen in association with the Arts Council of England and Bonaparte Films Ltd.; British-French, 1999; Color; Not rated; 98 minutes; U.S. release: November 22, 2000. CAST: Paul Nicholls (Billy Macfarlane), Daniel Craig (Telford Winter), Julian Rhind-Tutt (Ellis Harte), Danny Dyer (Victor Dell), James D'Arcy (Colin Daventry), Tam Williams (Eddie Macfarlane), Anthony Strachan (Horace Beckwith), Ciaran McMenamin (Charlie Ambrose), Michael Moreland (George Hogg), Adrian Lukis (Colonel Villiers), Cillian Murphy (Rag Rockwood), John Higgins (Cornwallis), Ben Whishaw (James Deamis), Tim Murphy (Bone), Danny Nutt (Dieter), Charles Cartmell (Harold Faithfull), Tom Mullion (Nelson), Jenny Pickering (Maria Corrigan), Tom Silburn, Dahren Davey, Jamie Newell, Liam King, Stan Charity, Luke Duckett, Chris Bridgeman, Guy Barrett (Platoon Members)

MOON SHADOW (PromoFest) Producers, Roberta Manfredi, Alessandro Olivieri; Executive Producers, Conchita Airoldi, Dino Di Dionisio; Director/Screenplay, Alberto Simone; Photography, Roberto Benvenuti; Designer, Andrea Crisanti; Costumes, Beatrice Bordone; Music, Vittorio Cosma; Editor, Enzo Meniconi; from Les Films du

Tsugumi, Kenji Mizuhashi in *Sasayaki* © Viz Films

Tchéky Karyo, Johan Leyson in *Moon Shadow* © Promo Fest

Vusi in *Hillbrow Kids* © Media Line

Amália Rodrigues in *The Art of Amália* © Avatar Films

Dauphine, Odusseia Films, Sidereal Productions; Italian-Dutch-French, 1995; Color; Not rated; 82 minutes; U.S. release: December 1, 2000. CAST: Tchéky Karyo (Lorenzo), Nino Manfredi (Salvatore), Isabelle Pasco (Luisa), Jim Van der Woude (Agostino), Johan Leyson (Titto), Mimmo Mancini (Filippo), Paolo Sassanelli (Michele)

HILLBROW KIDS (Media Line) Producer, Mirjam Quinte; Directors, Michael Hammon, Jacqueline Görgen; Photography, Michael Hammon; Editors, Michael Hammon, Yvonne Loquens; Music, Harald Bernhard, Matthias Kratzenstein; Storyteller, Regina Ndlovu; German-French, 1999; Color; Not rated; 94 minutes; U.S. release: December 8, 2000. Documentary on the street children of the Hillbrow neighborhood in Johannesburg, South Africa.

THE DAY SILENCE DIED (First Run Features) Producer, Martin Proctor; Executive Producer, Ute Gumz; Director, Paolo Agazzi; Screenplay, Guillermo Aguirre, Paolo Agazzi; Photography, Livio Delgado; Art Director, Martha Mendez; Music, Cergio Prudencio; Editor, Nelson Rodriguez; Bolivian, 1998; Color; Not rated; 108 minutes; U.S. release: December 8, 2000. CAST: Dario Grandinetti (Abelardo), Gustavo Angarita (Oscar), Elias Serrano (Ruperto), Norma Merlo (Amelia), Jorge Ortiz (Padro Isidoro), Guillermo Granda (Jose), Maria Laura Garcia (Celeste), Blanca Morisson (Celina), Edgar Vargas (Gumercindo), David Mondaca (Gaston)

THE ART OF AMÁLIA (Avatar Films) Producer, Manuel Falcao; Director, Bruno de Almeida; Screenplay, Bruno de Almeida, Frank Coelho; Photography, Mustapha Barat; Editor, Joao Asensio; Introduction, David Byrne; Narrator, John Ventimiglia; a Valentim de Carvalho Televisão production in association with Arco Films; Portuguese; Color; Not rated; 90 minutes; U.S. release: December 8, 2000. Documentary on legendary Portuguese singer Amália Rodrigues.

VOYAGES (New Yorker) Producer, Yaël Fogiel; Director/Screenplay, Emmanuel Finkiel; Photography, Hans Meier, Jean Claude Larrieu; Editor, Emmanuelle Castro; Casting, Stéphane Touitou, Nathanièle Esther, Rodika Alcalay; a co-production of Les Films du Poisson, Studio Canal+, Arte France Cinema, Héritage Films, Paradise Films, Canal+Polska, FCC, YMC; French-Polish, 1999; Dolby; Color; Not rated; 115 minutes; U.S. release date: December 15, 2000. CAST: Shulamit Adar (Rivka), Liliane Rovère (Régine), Esther Gorintin (Vera), Nathan Cogan (Graneck), Moscu Alcalay (Shimon), Maurice Chevit (Mendelbaum); *In Poland:* Michaël Shillo (Mr. Katz), Abraham Leber (Mr. Zalcberg), Alain Zylbering (Max), Patrick Lizana (Henri), Magdelena Czartoryjska (Tour Guide); *In Paris:* Freddy Earle (Jo Bernstein), Leopold Kozlowski (Pianist), Albert Grinberg (Drummer), Claude Mouton (Double Bass); *In Israel:* Vladimir Fridman (Félix), Natalia Voitulevitch-Manor (Léa), Dan Manor (Félix's Son), Guita Gruzina (Vera's Cousin), Alma Fogiel (Israeli Guide), Shouki Fogiel (Neighbor), Doron Avrahami (Taxi Driver), Sasha Chernichovsky (Hotel Employee)

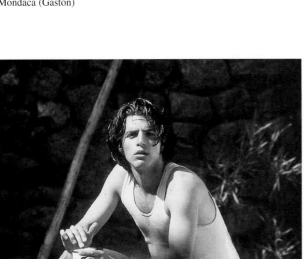

Guillermo Granda in *The Day Silence Died* © First Run Pictures

Esther Gorintin in *Voyages* © New Yorker Films

Giuseppe Sanfelice di Monteforte, Silvio Muccino
in *But Forever in My Mind* © Intra Films

Bill Switzer, David Bowie in *Mr. Rice's Secret* © Panorama Entertainment

BUT FOREVER IN MY MIND (Intra Films) Producer, Domenico Procacci; Executive Producer, Gianluca Arcopinto; Director, Gabriele Muccino; Screenplay, Gabriele Muccino, Silvio Muccino, Adele Tulli; Story, Gabriele Muccino, Silvio Muccino; From an idea of Marco Valerio Fusco; Photography, Arnaldo Catinari; Designer, Eugenia F. di Napoli; Costumes, Roberta Bocca; Editor, Claudio Di Mauro; Music, Paolo Buonvino; a Domenico Procacci presentation of a Fandango and Mikado production in association with RAI–Radiotelevisione Italiana, RAI Cinema; Italian, 1999; Color; Not rated; 88 minutes; U.S. release: December 20, 2000. CAST: Silvio Muccino (Silvio Ristuccia), Giuseppe Sanfelice di Monteforte (Ponzi), Giulia Steigerwalt (Claudia), Giulia Carmignani (Valentina), Luca De Filippo (Silvio's Father), Anna Galiena (Silvio's Mother), Enrico Silvestrin (Allberto Ristuccia), Giulia Ciccone (Chiara Ristuccia), Simone Pagani (Martino), Caterina Silva (Giulia), Sara Pelagalli (Marta), Saverio Micheli (Filippo), Cristiano Iuliano (Lorenzo), Nicola Campiotti (Gustavo), Alessandro Palombo (Leon), Adele Tulli (Veronica), Valeria D'Obici (Giulia's Mother), Mauro Marino (Leon's Father), Luis Molteni (School Headmaster), Antonello Grimaldi (Head of Police)

NOWHERE TO HIDE (Lions Gate) Producer, Chung Tae-Won; Executive Producer, Kang Woo-Suk; Director/Screenplay/Designer, Lee Myung-Se; Photography, Jeong Kwang-Seok, Song Haeng-Ki; Editor, Go Im Pyo; Music, Cho Sung-Woo; a Cinema Service presentation of a Taewon Entertainment production, in association with Kookmin Venture Capital, Samboo Finance Entertainment and Fox Video Korea; South Korean, 1999; Dolby; Color; Not rated; 112 minutes; U.S. release date: December 22, 2000. CAST: Park Joong-Hoon (Detective Woo), Ahn Sung-Ki (Chang Sungmin), Jang Dong-Kun (Detective Kim), Choi Ji-Woo (Juyon)

MR. RICE'S SECRET (Panorama Entertainment) Producer, Colleen Nystedt; Executive Producers, Beau Rogers, David Forrest; Director, Nicholas Kendall; Screenplay, J.H. Wyman; Associate Producer, Sally Dixon; Line Producer, Mary Anne McCarthy; Supervising Producer, Christopher Courtney; Photography, Gregory Middleton; Designer, Jillian Scott; Costumes, Gregory B. Mah; Editor, Ron E. Yoshida; Music, Simon Kendall, Al Rodger; Casting, Carol Kelsay; a New City Productions presentation, with the participation of the Province of British Columbia Film Incentive BC Canada; Canadian; Dolby; Color; Not rated; 113 minutes; U.S. release date: December 22, 2000. CAST: David Bowie (Mr. Rice), Bill Switzer (Owen Walters), Teryl Rothery (Marilyn Walters), Garwin Sanford (Stan Walters), Zachary Lipovsky (Funnel Head), Jason Anderson (Veg), Tyler Thompson (Gilbert), Campbell Lane (Mr. Death), Richard De Klerk (Simon), Tyler Labine (Percy), Eric Keenleyside (Ray), Colleen Rennison (Molly), Lyle Labine (Jonathan), Tim Dixon (Priest), Juno Ruddell (Cindy), Frank C. Turner (Thin Man), Shawn Solberg, Shayne Zwickel (Baseball Kids), D. Neil Mark (Coach), Peter Bryant (Umpire), P. Lynn Johnson (Dr. Vogel), Terry David Mulligan (Potential Buyer), Merrilyn Gann (Veg's Mom), Kevin Blatch (Mr. Death's Assistant)

Joey Lauren Adams

Ben Affleck

Casey Affleck

Gillian Anderson

BIOGRAPHICAL DATA
(Name, real name, place and date of birth, school attended)

AAMES, WILLIE (William Upton): Los Angeles, CA, July 15, 1960.

AARON, CAROLINE: Richmond, VA, Aug. 7, 1954. Catholic U.

ABBOTT, DIAHNNE: NYC, 1945.

ABBOTT, JOHN: London, June 5, 1905.

ABRAHAM, F. MURRAY: Pittsburgh, PA, Oct. 24, 1939. UTx.

ACKLAND, JOSS: London, Feb. 29, 1928.

ADAMS, BROOKE: NYC, Feb. 8, 1949. Dalton.

ADAMS, CATLIN: Los Angeles, Oct. 11, 1950.

ADAMS, DON: NYC, Apr. 13, 1926.

ADAMS, EDIE (Elizabeth Edith Enke): Kingston, PA, Apr. 16, 1927. Juilliard, Columbia.

ADAMS, JOEY LAUREN: Little Rock, AR, Jan. 6, 1971.

ADAMS, JULIE (Betty May): Waterloo, IA, Oct. 17, 1926. Little Rock, Jr. College.

ADAMS, MASON: NYC, Feb. 26, 1919. UWi.

ADAMS, MAUD (Maud Wikstrom): Lulea, Sweden, Feb. 12, 1945.

ADJANI, ISABELLE: Germany, June 27, 1955.

AFFLECK, BEN: Berkeley, CA, Aug. 15, 1972.

AFFLECK, CASEY: Falmouth, MA, Aug. 12, 1975.

AGAR, JOHN: Chicago, IL, Jan. 31, 1921.

AGUTTER, JENNY: Taunton, England, Dec. 20, 1952.

AIELLO, DANNY: NYC, June 20, 1933.

AIMEE, ANOUK (Dreyfus): Paris, France, Apr. 27, 1934. Bauer-Therond.

AKERS, KAREN: NYC, Oct. 13, 1945, Hunter College.

ALBERGHETTI, ANNA MARIA: Pesaro, Italy, May 15, 1936.

ALBERT, EDDIE (Eddie Albert Heimberger): Rock Island, IL, Apr. 22, 1908. U of Minn.

ALBERT, EDWARD: Los Angeles, Feb. 20. 1951. UCLA.

ALBRIGHT, LOLA: Akron, OH, July 20, 1925.

ALDA, ALAN: NYC, Jan. 28, 1936. Fordham.

ALEANDRO, NORMA: Buenos Aires, Dec. 6, 1936.

ALEJANDRO, MIGUEL: NYC, Feb. 21, 1958.

ALEXANDER, JANE (Quigley): Boston, MA, Oct. 28, 1939. Sarah Lawrence.

ALEXANDER, JASON (Jay Greenspan): Newark, NJ, Sept. 23, 1959. Boston U.

ALICE, MARY: Indianola, MS, Dec. 3, 1941.

ALLEN, DEBBIE (Deborah): Houston, TX, Jan. 16, 1950. Howard U.

ALLEN, JOAN: Rochelle, IL, Aug. 20, 1956. EastIllU.

ALLEN, KAREN: Carrollton, IL, Oct. 5, 1951. UMd.

ALLEN, NANCY: NYC, June 24, 1950.

ALLEN, TIM: Denver, CO, June 13, 1953. W. MI. Univ.

ALLEN, WOODY (Allan Stewart Konigsberg): Brooklyn, Dec. 1, 1935.

ALLEY, KIRSTIE: Wichita, KS, Jan. 12, 1955.

ALLYSON, JUNE (Ella Geisman): Westchester, NY, Oct. 7, 1917.

ALONSO, MARIA CONCHITA: Cuba, June 29, 1957.

ALT, CAROL: Queens, NY, Dec. 1, 1960. HofstraU.

ALVARADO, TRINI: NYC, Jan. 10, 1967.

AMIS, SUZY: Oklahoma City, OK, Jan. 5, 1958. Actors Studio.

AMOS, JOHN: Newark, NJ, Dec. 27, 1940. Colo. U.

ANDERSON, GILLIAN: Chicago, IL, Aug. 9, 1968. DePaul U.

ANDERSON, KEVIN: Waukeegan, IL, Jan. 13, 1960.

ANDERSON, LONI: St. Paul, MN, Aug. 5, 1946.

ANDERSON, MELISSA SUE: Berkeley, CA, Sept. 26, 1962.

ANDERSON, MELODY: Edmonton, Canada, 1955. Carlton U.

ANDERSON, MICHAEL, JR.: London, England, Aug. 6, 1943.

ANDERSON, RICHARD DEAN: Minneapolis, MN, Jan. 23, 1950.

ANDERSSON, BIBI: Stockholm, Sweden, Nov. 11, 1935. Royal Dramatic Sch.

ANDES, KEITH: Ocean City, NJ, July 12, 1920. Temple U., Oxford.

ANDRESS, URSULA: Bern, Switzerland, Mar. 19, 1936.

ANDREWS, ANTHONY: London, Dec. 1, 1948.

ANDREWS, JULIE (Julia Elizabeth Wells): Surrey, England, Oct. 1, 1935.

ANGLIM, PHILIP: San Francisco, CA, Feb. 11, 1953.

ANISTON, JENNIFER: Sherman Oaks, CA, Feb. 11, 1969.

ANN-MARGRET (Olsson): Valsjobyn, Sweden, Apr. 28, 1941. Northwestern U.

ANSARA, MICHAEL: Lowell, MA, Apr. 15, 1922. Pasadena Playhouse.

ANSPACH, SUSAN: NYC, Nov. 23, 1945.

ANTHONY, LYSETTE: London, 1963.

ANTHONY, TONY: Clarksburg, WV, Oct. 16, 1937. Carnegie Tech.

ANTON, SUSAN: Yucaipa, CA, Oct. 12, 1950. Bemardino College.

ANTONELLI, LAURA: Pola, Italy, Nov. 28, 1941.

ANWAR, GABRIELLE: Lalehaam, England, Feb. 4, 1970

APPLEGATE, CHRISTINA: Hollywood CA, Nov. 25, 1972.

ARCHER, ANNE: Los Angeles, Aug. 25, 1947.

ARCHER, JOHN (Ralph Bowman): Osceola, NB, May 8, 1915. USC.

ARDANT, FANNY: Monte Carlo, Mar 22, 1949

Anne Archer

ARKIN, ADAM: Brooklyn, NY, Aug. 19, 1956.
ARKIN, ALAN: NYC, Mar. 26, 1934. LACC.
ARMSTRONG, BESS: Baltimore, MD, Dec. 11, 1953.
ARNAZ, DESI, JR.: Los Angeles, Jan. 19, 1953.
ARNAZ, LUCIE: Hollywood, July 17, 1951.
ARNESS, JAMES (Aurness): Minneapolis, MN, May 26, 1923. Beloit College.
ARQUETTE, DAVID: Winchester, VA, Sept. 8, 1971.
ARQUETTE, PATRICIA: NYC, Apr. 8, 1968.
ARQUETTE, ROSANNA: NYC, Aug. 10, 1959.
ARTHUR, BEATRICE (Frankel): NYC, May 13, 1924. New School.
ASHER, JANE: London, Apr. 5, 1946.
ASHLEY, ELIZABETH (Elizabeth Ann Cole): Ocala, FL, Aug. 30, 1939.
ASHTON, JOHN: Springfield, MA, Feb. 22, 1948. USC.
ASNER, EDWARD: Kansas City, KS, Nov. 15, 1929.
ASSANTE, ARMAND: NYC, Oct. 4, 1949. AADA.
ASTIN, JOHN: Baltimore, MD, Mar. 30, 1930. U Minn.
ASTIN, MacKENZIE: Los Angeles, May 12, 1973.
ASTIN, SEAN: Santa Monica, Feb. 25, 1971.

ATHERTON, WILLIAM: Orange, CT, July 30, 1947. Carnegie Tech.
ATKINS, CHRISTOPHER: Rye, NY, Feb. 21, 1961.
ATKINS, EILEEN: London, June 16, 1934.
ATKINSON, ROWAN: England, Jan. 6, 1955. Oxford.
ATTENBOROUGH, RICHARD: Cambridge, England, Aug. 29, 1923. RADA.
AUBERJONOIS, RENE: NYC, June 1, 1940. Carnegie Tech.
AUDRAN, STEPHANE: Versailles, France, Nov. 8, 1932.
AUGER, CLAUDINE: Paris, France, Apr. 26, 1942. Dramatic Cons.
AULIN, EWA: Stockholm, Sweden, Feb. 14, 1950.
AUMONT, JEAN PIERRE: Paris, France, Jan. 5, 1909. French Nat'l School of Drama.
AVALON, FRANKIE (Francis Thomas Avallone): Philadelphia, PA, Sept. 18, 1939.
AYKROYD, DAN: Ottawa, Canada, July 1, 1952.
AZARIA, HANK: Forest Hills, NY, Apr. 25, 1964. AADA, Tufts Univ.
AZNAVOUR, CHARLES (Varenagh Aznourian): Paris, France, May 22, 1924.
AZZARA, CANDICE: Brooklyn, NY, May 18, 1947.
BACALL, LAUREN (Betty Perske): NYC, Sept. 16, 1924. AADA.
BACH, BARBARA: Queens, NY, Aug. 27, 1946.
BACH, CATHERINE: Warren, OH, Mar. 1, 1954.
BACKER, BRIAN: NYC, Dec. 5, 1956. Neighborhood Playhouse.
BACON, KEVIN: Philadelphia, PA, July 8, 1958.
BAIN, BARBARA: Chicago, IL, Sept. 13, 1934. U Ill.
BAIO, SCOTT: Brooklyn, NY, Sept. 22, 1961.
BAKER, BLANCHE: NYC, Dec. 20, 1956.
BAKER, CARROLL: Johnstown, PA, May 28, 1931. St. Petersburg, Jr. College.
BAKER, DIANE: Hollywood, CA, Feb. 25, 1938. USC.
BAKER, JOE DON: Groesbeck, TX, Feb.12, 1936.
BAKER, KATHY: Midland, TX, June 8, 1950. UC Berkley.
BAKULA, SCOTT: St. Louis, MO, Oct. 9, 1955. KansasU.
BALABAN, BOB: Chicago, IL, Aug. 16, 1945. Colgate.
BALDWIN, ADAM: Chicago, IL, Feb. 27, 1962.
BALDWIN, ALEC: Massapequa, NY, Apr. 3, 1958. NYU.
BADLWIN, DANIEL: Massapequa, NY, Oct. 5, 1960.
BALDWIN, STEPHEN: Massapequa, NY, 1966.
BALDWIN, WILLIAM: Massapequa, NY, Feb. 21, 1963.
BALE, CHRISTIAN: Pembrokeshire, West Wales, Jan. 30, 1974.
BALK, FAIRUZA: Point Reyes, CA, May 21, 1974.
BALLARD, KAYE: Cleveland, OH, Nov. 20, 1926.
BANCROFT, ANNE (Anna Maria Italiano): Bronx, NY, Sept. 17, 1931. AADA.
BANDERAS, ANTONIO: Malaga, Spain, Aug. 10, 1960.

Patricia Arquette

BANERJEE, VICTOR: Calcutta, India, Oct. 15, 1946.
BANES, LISA: Chagrin Falls, OH, July 9, 1955. Juilliard.
BARANSKI, CHRISTINE: Buffalo, NY, May 2, 1952. Juilliard.
BARBEAU, ADRIENNE: Sacramento, CA, June 11, 1945. Foothill College.
BARDEM, JAVIER: Gran Canaria, Spain, May 1, 1969.
BARDOT, BRIGITTE: Paris, France, Sept. 28, 1934.
BARKIN, ELLEN: Bronx, NY, Apr. 16, 1954. Hunter College.
BARNES, CHRISTOPHER DANIEL: Portland, ME, Nov. 7, 1972.
BARR, JEAN-MARC: San Diego, CA, Sept. 1960.
BARRAULT, JEAN-LOUIS: Vesinet, France, Sept. 8, 1910.
BARRAULT, MARIE-CHRISTINE: Paris, France, Mar. 21, 1944.
BARREN, KEITH: Mexborough, England, Aug. 8, 1936. Sheffield Playhouse.
BARRETT, MAJEL (Hudec): Columbus, OH, Feb. 23, 1939. Western Reserve U.
BARRIE, BARBARA: Chicago, IL, May 23, 1931.
BARRY, GENE (Eugene Klass): NYC, June 14, 1919.
BARRY, NEILL: NYC, Nov. 29, 1965.
BARRYMORE, DREW: Los Angeles, Feb. 22, 1975.

David Arquette

Rosanna Arquette

BARRYMORE, JOHN DREW: Beverly Hills, CA, June 4, 1932. St. John's Military Academy.

BARYSHNIKOV, MIKHAIL: Riga, Latvia, Jan. 27, 1948.

BASINGER, KIM: Athens, GA, Dec. 8, 1953. Neighborhood Playhouse.

BASSETT, ANGELA: NYC, Aug. 16, 1958.

BATEMAN, JASON: Rye, NY, Jan. 14, 1969.

BATEMAN, JUSTINE: Rye, NY, Feb. 19, 1966.

BATES, ALAN: Allestree, Derbyshire, England, Feb. 17, 1934. RADA.

BATES, JEANNE: San Francisco, CA, May 21, 1918. RADA.

BATES, KATHY: Memphis, TN, June 28, 1948. S. Methodist U.

BAUER, STEVEN (Steven Rocky Echevarria): Havana, Cuba, Dec. 2, 1956. U Miami.

BAXTER, KEITH: South Wales, England, Apr. 29, 1933. RADA.

BAXTER, MEREDITH: Los Angeles, June 21, 1947. Intelochen Acad.

BAYE, NATHALIE: Maineville, France, July 6, 1948

BEACHAM, STEPHANIE: Casablanca, Morocco, Feb. 28, 1947.

BEALS, JENNIFER: Chicago, IL, Dec. 19, 1963.

BEAN, ORSON (Dallas Burrows): Burlington, VT, July 22, 1928.

BEAN, SEAN: Sheffield, Yorkshire, England, Apr. 17, 1958.

BÉART, EMMANUELLE: Gassin, France, Aug. 14, 1965.

BEATTY, NED: Louisville, KY, July 6, 1937.

BEATTY, WARREN: Richmond, VA, Mar. 30, 1937.

BECK, JOHN: Chicago, IL, Jan. 28, 1943.

BECK, MICHAEL: Memphis, TN, Feb. 4, 1949. Millsap College.

BECKINSALE, KATE: England, July 26, 1974.

BEDELIA, BONNIE: NYC, Mar. 25, 1946. Hunter College.

BEGLEY, ED, JR.: NYC, Sept. 16, 1949.

BELAFONTE, HARRY: NYC, Mar. 1, 1927.

BEL GEDDES, BARBARA: NYC, Oct. 31, 1922.

BELL, TOM: Liverpool, England, 1932.

BELLER, KATHLEEN: NYC, Feb. 10, 1957.

BELLWOOD, PAMELA (King): Scarsdale, NY, June 26, 1951.

BELMONDO, JEAN PAUL: Paris, France, Apr. 9, 1933.

BELUSHI, JAMES: Chicago, IL, June 15, 1954.

BELZER, RICHARD: Bridgeport, CT, Aug. 4, 1944.

BENEDICT, DIRK (Niewoehner): White Sulphur Springs, MT, March 1, 1945. Whitman College.

BENEDICT, PAUL: Silver City, NM, Sept. 17, 1938.

BENIGNI, ROBERTO: Tuscany, Italy, Oct. 27, 1952.

BENING, ANNETTE: Topeka, KS, May 29, 1958. SFSt. U.

BENJAMIN, RICHARD: NYC, May 22, 1938. Northwestern U.

BENNENT, DAVID: Lausanne, Sept. 9, 1966.

BENNETT, ALAN: Leeds, England, May 9, 1934. Oxford.

Armand Assante

Lauren Bacall

Kathy Baker

BENNETT, BRUCE (Herman Brix): Tacoma, WA, May 19, 1909. U Wash.

BENNETT, HYWEL: Garnant, So. Wales, Apr. 8, 1944.

BENSON, ROBBY: Dallas, TX, Jan. 21, 1957.

BENTLEY, WES: Jonesboro, AR, Sept. 4, 1978.

BERENGER, TOM: Chicago, IL, May 31, 1950, U Mo.

BERENSON, MARISA: NYC, Feb. 15, 1947.

BERG, PETER: NYC, March 11, 1964. Malcalester College.

BERGEN, CANDICE: Los Angeles, May 9, 1946. U PA.

BERGEN, POLLY: Knoxville, TN, July 14, 1930. Compton, Jr. College.

BERGER, HELMUT: Salzburg, Austria, May 29, 1942.

BERGER, SENTA: Vienna, Austria, May 13, 1941. Vienna Sch. of Acting.

BERGER, WILLIAM: Austria, Jan. 20, 1928. Columbia.

BERGERAC, JACQUES: Biarritz, France, May 26, 1927. Paris U.

BERGIN, PATRICK: Dublin, Feb. 4, 1951.

BERKLEY, ELIZABETH: Detroit, MI, July 28, 1972.

BERKOFF, STEVEN: London, England, Aug. 3, 1937.

BERLE, MILTON (Berlinger): NYC, July 12, 1908.

BERLIN, JEANNIE: Los Angeles, Nov. 1, 1949.

BERLINGER, WARREN: Brooklyn, Aug. 31, 1937. Columbia.

BERNHARD, SANDRA: Flint, MI, June 6, 1955.

BERNSEN, CORBIN: Los Angeles, Sept. 7, 1954. UCLA.

BERRI, CLAUDE (Langmann): Paris, France, July 1, 1934.

BERRIDGE, ELIZABETH: Westchester, NY, May 2, 1962. Strasberg Inst.

BERRY, HALLE: Cleveland, OH, Aug. 14, 1968.

BERRY, KEN: Moline, IL, Nov. 3, 1933.

BERTINELLI, VALERIE: Wilmington, DE, Apr. 23, 1960.

BEST, JAMES: Corydon, IN, July 26, 1926.

BETTGER, LYLE: Philadelphia, PA, Feb. 13, 1915. AADA.

BEY, TURHAN: Vienna, Austria, Mar. 30, 1921.

BEYMER, RICHARD: Avoca, IA, Feb. 21, 1939.

BIALIK, MAYIM: San Diego, CA, Dec. 12, 1975.

BIEHN, MICHAEL: Anniston, AL, July 31, 1956.

BIGGS, JASON: Pompton Plains, NJ, May 12, 1978.

BIKEL, THEODORE: Vienna, May 2, 1924. RADA.

BILLINGSLEY, PETER: NYC, Apr. 16, 1972.

BINOCHE, JULIETTE: Paris, France, Mar. 9, 1964.

BIRCH, THORA: Los Angeles, Mar. 11, 1982.

BIRKIN, JANE: London, Dec. 14, 1947

BIRNEY, DAVID: Washington, DC, Apr. 23, 1939. Dartmouth, UCLA.

BIRNEY, REED: Alexandria, VA, Sept. 11, 1954. Boston U.

Christian Bale

Angela Bassett

Emmanuelle Béart

Warren Beatty

BISHOP, JOEY (Joseph Abraham Gotllieb): Bronx, NY, Feb. 3, 1918.
BISHOP, JULIE (Jacqueline Wells): Denver, CO, Aug. 30, 1917. Westlake School.
BISSET, JACQUELINE: Waybridge, England, Sept. 13, 1944.
BLACK, KAREN (Ziegler): Park Ridge, IL, July 1, 1942. Northwestern.
BLACK, JACK: Edmonton, Alberta, Canada, Apr. 7, 1969.
BLACK, LUCAS: Danville, AL, Nov. 29, 1982.
BLACKMAN, HONOR: London, Aug. 22, 1926.
BLADES, RUBEN: Panama City, July 16, 1948. Harvard.
BLAIR, BETSY (Betsy Boger): NYC, Dec. 11, 1923.
BLAIR, JANET (Martha Jane Lafferty): Blair, PA, Apr. 23, 1921.
BLAIR, LINDA: Westport, CT, Jan. 22, 1959.
BLAKE, ROBERT (Michael Gubitosi): Nutley, NJ, Sept. 18, 1933.
BLAKELY, SUSAN: Frankfurt, Germany, Sept. 7, 1950. U TX.
BLAKLEY, RONEE: Stanley, ID, 1946. Stanford U.
BLANCHETT, CATE: Melbourne, Australia, May 14, 1969.
BLETHYN, BRENDA: Ramsgate, Kent, Eng., Feb. 20, 1946.
BLOOM, CLAIRE: London, Feb. 15, 1931. Badminton School.
BLOOM, VERNA: Lynn, MA, Aug. 7, 1939. Boston U.
BLOUNT, LISA: Fayettville, AK, July 1, 1957. UAk.
BLUM, MARK: Newark, NJ, May 14, 1950. UMinn.
BLYTH, ANN: Mt. Kisco, NY, Aug. 16, 1928. New Waybum Dramatic School.
BOCHNER, HART: Toronto, Canada, Oct. 3, 1956. U San Diego.
BOCHNER, LLOYD: Toronto, Canada, July 29, 1924.
BOGOSIAN, ERIC: Woburn, MA, Apr. 24, 1953. Oberlin College.
BOHRINGER, RICHARD: Paris, France, Jan. 16, 1941.

BOLKAN, FLORINDA (Florinda Soares Bulcao): Ceara, Brazil, Feb. 15, 1941.
BOLOGNA, JOSEPH: Brooklyn, NY, Dec. 30, 1938. Brown U.
BOND, DEREK: Glasgow, Scotland, Jan. 26, 1920. Askes School.
BONET, LISA: San Francisco, CA, Nov. 16, 1967.
BONHAM-CARTER, HELENA: London, England, May 26, 1966.
BOONE, PAT: Jacksonville, FL, June 1, 1934. Columbia U.
BOOTHE, JAMES: Croydon, England, Dec.19, 1930
BOOTHE, POWERS: Snyder, TX, June 1, 1949. So. Methodist U.
BORGNINE, ERNEST (Borgnino): Hamden, CT, Jan. 24, 1917. Randall School.
BOSCO, PHILIP: Jersey City, NJ, Sept. 26, 1930. CatholicU.
BOSLEY, TOM: Chicago, IL, Oct. 1, 1927. DePaul U.
BOSTWICK, BARRY: San Mateo, CA, Feb. 24, 1945. NYU.
BOTTOMS, JOSEPH: Santa Barbara, CA, Aug. 30, 1954.
BOTTOMS, SAM: Santa Barbara, CA, Oct. 17, 1955.
BOTTOMS, TIMOTHY: Santa Barbara, CA, Aug. 30, 1951.
BOULTING, INGRID: Transvaal, So. Africa, 1947.
BOUTSIKARIS, DENNIS: Newark, NJ, Dec. 21, 1952. CatholicU.
BOWIE, DAVID (David Robert Jones): Brixton, South London, England, Jan. 8, 1947.
BOWKER, JUDI: Shawford, England, Apr. 6, 1954.
BOXLEITNER, BRUCE: Elgin, IL, May 12, 1950.
BOYLE, LARA FLYNN: Davenport, IA, Mar. 24, 1970.
BOYLE, PETER: Philadelphia, PA, Oct. 18, 1933. LaSalle College.
BRACCO, LORRAINE: Brooklyn, NY, 1955.
BRACKEN, EDDIE: NYC, Feb. 7, 1920. Professional Children's School.
BRAEDEN, ERIC (Hans Gudegast): Kiel, Germany, Apr. 3, 1942.

BRAGA, SONIA: Maringa, Brazil, June 8, 1950.
BRANAGH, KENNETH: Belfast, No. Ireland, Dec. 10, 1960.
BRANDAUER, KLAUS MARIA: Altaussee, Austria, June 22, 1944.
BRANDIS, JONATHAN: CT, Apr. 13, 1976.
BRANDO, JOCELYN: San Francisco, Nov. 18, 1919. Lake Forest College, AADA.
BRANDO, MARLON: Omaha, NB, Apr. 3, 1924. New School.
BRANDON, CLARK: NYC, Dec. 13, 1958.
BRANDON, MICHAEL (Feldman): Brooklyn, NY, Apr. 20, 1945.
BRANTLEY, BETSY: Rutherfordton, NC, Sept. 20, 1955. London Central Sch. of Drama.
BRATT, BENJAMIN: San Francisco, Dec. 16, 1963.
BRENNAN, EILEEN: Los Angeles, CA, Sept. 3, 1935. AADA.
BRENNEMAN, AMY: Glastonbury, CT, June 22, 1964.
BRIALY, JEAN-CLAUDE: Aumale, Algeria, 1933. Strasbourg Cons.
BRIDGES, BEAU: Los Angeles, Dec. 9, 1941. UCLA.
BRIDGES, JEFF: Los Angeles, Dec. 4, 1949.
BRIMLEY, WILFORD: Salt Lake City, UT, Sept. 27, 1934.
BRINKLEY, CHRISTIE: Malibu, CA, Feb. 2, 1954.
BRITT, MAY (Maybritt Wilkins): Sweden, Mar. 22, 1936.
BRITTANY, MORGAN (Suzanne Cupito): Los Angeles, Dec. 5, 1950.
BRITTON, TONY: Birmingham, England, June 9, 1924.
BRODERICK, MATTHEW: NYC, Mar. 21, 1962.
BRODY, ADRIEN: NYC, Dec. 23, 1976,
BROLIN, JAMES: Los Angeles, July 18, 1940. UCLA.
BROLIN, JOSH: Los Angeles, Feb. 12, 1968.
BROMFIELD, JOHN (Farron Bromfield): South Bend, IN, June 11, 1922. St. Mary's College.
BRON, ELEANOR: Stanmore, England, Mar. 14, 1934.
BRONSON, CHARLES (Buchinsky): Ehrenfield, PA, Nov. 3, 1920.

312

Kate Beckinsale

Harry Belafonte

James Belushi

Roberto Benigni

BROOKES, JACQUELINE: Montclair, NJ, July 24, 1930. RADA.

BROOKS, ALBERT (Einstein): Los Angeles, July 22, 1947.

BROOKS, MEL (Melvyn Kaminski): Brooklyn, NY, June 28, 1926.

BROSNAN, PIERCE: County Meath, Ireland. May 16, 1952.

BROWN, BLAIR: Washington, DC, Apr. 23, 1947. Pine Manor.

BROWN, BRYAN: Panania, Australia, June 23, 1947.

BROWN, GARY (Christian Brando): Hollywood, CA, 1958.

BROWN, GEORG STANFORD: Havana, Cuba, June 24, 1943. AMDA.

BROWN, JAMES: Desdemona, TX, Mar. 22, 1920. Baylor U.

BROWN, JIM: St. Simons Island, NY, Feb. 17, 1935. Syracuse U.

BROWNE, LESLIE: NYC, 1958.

BROWNE, ROSCOE LEE: Woodbury, NJ, May 2, 1925.

BUCHHOLZ, HORST: Berlin, Germany, Dec. 4, 1933. Ludwig Dramatic School.

BUCKLEY, BETTY: Big Spring, TX, July 3, 1947. TxCU.

BUJOLD, GENEVIEVE: Montreal, Canada, July 1, 1942.

BULLOCK, SANDRA: Arlington, VA, July 26, 1964.

BURGHOFF, GARY: Bristol, CT, May 24, 1943.

BURGI, RICHARD: Montclair, NJ, July 30, 1958.

BURKE, PAUL: New Orleans, July 21, 1926. Pasadena Playhouse.

BURNETT, CAROL: San Antonio, TX, Apr. 26, 1933. UCLA.

BURNS, CATHERINE: NYC, Sept. 25, 1945. AADA.

BURNS, EDWARD: Valley Stream, NY, Jan. 28, 1969.

BURROWS, DARREN E.: Winfield, KS, Sept. 12, 1966

BURROWS, SAFFRON: London, 1973.

BURSTYN, ELLEN (Edna Rae Gillhooly): Detroit, MI, Dec. 7, 1932.

BURTON, LeVAR: Los Angeles, CA, Feb. 16, 1958. UCLA.

BUSCEMI, STEVE: Brooklyn, NY, Dec. 13, 1957.

BUSEY, GARY: Goose Creek, TX, June 29, 1944.

BUSFIELD, TIMOTHY: Lansing, MI, June 12, 1957. E. Tenn. St. U.

BUTTONS, RED (Aaron Chwatt): NYC, Feb. 5, 1919.

BUZZI, RUTH: Westerly, RI, July 24, 1936. Pasadena Playhouse.

BYGRAVES, MAX: London, Oct. 16, 1922. St. Joseph's School.

BYRNE, DAVID: Dumbarton, Scotland, May 14, 1952.

BYRNE, GABRIEL: Dublin, Ireland, May 12, 1950.

BYRNES, EDD: NYC, July 30, 1933.

CAAN, JAMES: Bronx, NY, Mar. 26,1939.

CAESAR, SID: Yonkers, NY, Sept. 8, 1922.

CAGE, NICOLAS (Coppola): Long Beach, CA, Jan.7, 1964.

CAIN, DEAN (Dean Tanaka): Mt. Clemens, MI, July 31, 1966.

CAINÉ, MICHAEL (Maurice Micklewhite): London, Mar. 14, 1933.

CAINE, SHAKIRA (Baksh): Guyana, Feb. 23, 1947. Indian Trust College.

CALLAN, MICHAEL (Martin Calinieff): Philadelphia, Nov. 22, 1935.

CALLOW, SIMON: London, June 15, 1949. Queens U.

CALVERT, PHYLLIS: London, Feb. 18, 1917. Margaret Morris School.

CALVET, CORRINE (Corinne Dibos): Paris, France, Apr. 30, 1925. U Paris.

CAMERON, KIRK: Panorama City, CA, Oct. 12, 1970.

CAMP, COLLEEN: San Francisco, CA, 1953.

CAMPBELL, BILL: Chicago, IL, July 7, 1959.

CAMPBELL, GLEN: Delight, AR, Apr. 22, 1935.

CAMPBELL, NEVE: Guelph, Ontario, Canada, Oct. 3, 1973.

CAMPBELL, TISHA: Oklahoma City, OK, Oct. 13, 1968.

CANALE, GIANNA MARIA: Reggio Calabria, Italy, Sept. 12, 1927.

CANNON, DYAN (Samille Diane Friesen): Tacoma, WA, Jan. 4, 1937.

CAPERS, VIRGINIA: Sumter, SC, Sept. 25, 1925. Juilliard.

CAPSHAW, KATE: Ft. Worth, TX, Nov. 3, 1953. UMo.

CARA, IRENE: NYC, Mar. 18, 1958.

CARDINALE, CLAUDIA: Tunis, N. Africa. Apr. 15, 1939. College Paul Cambon.

CAREY, HARRY, JR.: Saugus, CA, May 16, 1921. Black Fox Military Academy.

CAREY, PHILIP: Hackensack, NJ, July 15, 1925. U Miami.

CARIOU, LEN: Winnipeg, Canada, Sept. 30, 1939.

CARLIN, GEORGE: NYC, May 12, 1938.

CARLYLE, ROBERT: Glasgow, Scotland, Apr. 14, 1961.

CARMEN, JULIE: Mt. Vernon, NY, Apr. 4, 1954.

CARMICHAEL, IAN: Hull, England, June 18, 1920. Scarborough College.

CARNE, JUDY (Joyce Botterill): Northampton, England, 1939. Bush-Davis Theatre School.

CARNEY, ART: Mt. Vernon, NY, Nov. 4, 1918.

CARON, LESLIE: Paris, France, July 1, 1931. Nat'l Conservatory, Paris.

CARPENTER, CARLETON: Bennington, VT, July 10, 1926. Northwestern.

CARRADINE, DAVID: Hollywood, Dec. 8, 1936. San Francisco State.

CARRADINE, KEITH: San Mateo, CA, Aug. 8, 1950. Colo. State U.

CARRADINE, ROBERT: San Mateo, CA, Mar. 24, 1954.

CARREL, DANY: Tourane, Indochina, Sept. 20, 1936. Marseilles Cons.

CARRERA, BARBARA: Managua, Nicaragua, Dec. 31, 1945.

CARRERE, TIA (Althea Janairo): Honolulu, HI, Jan. 2, 1965.

CARREY, JIM: Jacksons Point, Ontario, Canada, Jan. 17, 1962.

CARRIERE, MATHIEU: Hannover, West Germany, Aug. 2, 1950.

CARROLL, DIAHANN (Johnson): NYC, July 17, 1935. NYU.

Elizabeth Berkley

Thora Birch

Peter Boyle

CARROLL, PAT: Shreveport, LA, May 5, 1927. Catholic U.

CARSON, JOHN DAVID: California, Mar. 6, 1952. Valley College.

CARSON, JOHNNY: Corning, IA, Oct. 23, 1925. U of Neb.

CARSTEN, PETER (Ransenthaler): Weissenberg, Bavaria, Apr. 30, 1929. Munich Akademie.

CARTER, NELL: Birmingham, AL, Sept. 13, 1948.

CARTLIDGE, KATRIN: London, 1961.

CARTWRIGHT, VERONICA: Bristol, England, Apr 20, 1949.

CARUSO, DAVID: Forest Hills, NY, Jan. 7, 1956.

CARVEY, DANA: Missoula, MT, Apr. 2, 1955. SFST.CoI.

CASELLA, MAX: Washington D.C, June 6, 1967

CASEY, BERNIE: Wyco, WV, June 8, 1939.

CASSAVETES, NICK: NYC, 1959, Syracuse U, AADA.

CASSEL, JEAN-PIERRE: Paris, France, Oct. 27, 1932.

CASSEL, SEYMOUR: Detroit, MI, Jan. 22, 1935.

CASSIDY, DAVID: NYC, Apr. 12, 1950.

CASSIDY, JOANNA: Camden, NJ, Aug. 2, 1944. Syracuse U.

CASSIDY, PATRICK: Los Angeles, CA, Jan. 4, 1961.

CATES, PHOEBE: NYC, July 16, 1962.

CATTRALL, KIM: Liverpool, England, Aug. 21, 1956. AADA.

CAULFIELD, MAXWELL: Glasgow, Scotland, Nov. 23, 1959.

CAVANI, LILIANA: Bologna, Italy, Jan. 12, 1937. U Bologna.

CAVETT, DICK: Gibbon, NE, Nov. 19, 1936.

CHAKIRIS, GEORGE: Norwood, OH, Sept. 16, 1933.

CHAMBERLAIN, RICHARD: Beverly Hills, CA, March 31, 1935. Pomona.

CHAMPION, MARGE (Marjorie Belcher): Los Angeles, Sept. 2, 1923.

CHAN, JACKIE: Hong Kong, Apr. 7, 1954

CHANNING, CAROL: Seattle, WA, Jan. 31, 1921. Bennington.

CHANNING, STOCKARD (Susan Stockard): NYC, Feb. 13, 1944. Radcliffe.

CHAPIN, MILES: NYC, Dec. 6, 1954. HB Studio.

CHAPLIN, GERALDINE: Santa Monica, CA, July 31, 1944. Royal Ballet.

CHAPLIN, SYDNEY: Los Angeles, Mar. 31, 1926. Lawrenceville.

CHARISSE, CYD (Tula Ellice Finklea): Amarillo, TX, Mar. 3, 1922. Hollywood Professional School.

CHARLES, JOSH: Baltimore, MD, Sept. 15, 1971.

CHARLES, WALTER: East Strousburg, PA, Apr. 4, 1945. Boston U.

CHASE, CHEVY (Cornelius Crane Chase): NYC, Oct. 8, 1943.

CHAVES, RICHARD: Jacksonville, FL, Oct. 9, 1951. Occidental College.

CHAYKIN, MAURY: Canada, July 27, 1954

CHEN, JOAN (Chen Chung): Shanghai, Apr. 26, 1961. CalState.

CHER (Cherilyn Sarkisian): El Centro, CA, May 20, 1946.

CHILES, LOIS: Alice, TX, Apr. 15, 1947.

CHONG, RAE DAWN: Vancouver, Canada, Feb. 28, 1962.

CHONG, THOMAS: Edmonton, Alberta, Canada, May 24, 1938.

CHRISTIAN, LINDA (Blanca Rosa Welter): Tampico, Mexico, Nov. 13, 1923.

CHRISTIE, JULIE: Chukua, Assam, India, Apr. 14, 1941.

CHRISTOPHER, DENNIS (Carrelli): Philadelphia, PA, Dec. 2, 1955. Temple U.

CHRISTOPHER, JORDAN: Youngstown, OH, Oct. 23, 1940. Kent State.

CILENTO, DIANE: Queensland, Australia, Oct. 5, 1933. AADA.

CLAPTON, ERIC: London, Mar. 30, 1945.

CLARK, CANDY: Norman, OK, June 20, 1947.

CLARK, DICK: Mt. Vernon, NY, Nov. 30, 1929. Syracuse U.

CLARK, MATT: Washington, DC, Nov. 25, 1936.

CLARK, PETULA: Epsom, England, Nov. 15, 1932.

CLARK, SUSAN: Sarnid, Ont., Canada, Mar. 8, 1943. RADA.

CLAY, ANDREW DICE (Andrew Silverstein): Brooklyn, NY, Sept. 29, 1957. Kingsborough College.

CLAYBURGH, JILL: NYC, Apr. 30, 1944. Sarah Lawrence.

CLEESE, JOHN: Weston-Super-Mare, England, Oct. 27, 1939, Cambridge.

CLOONEY, ROSEMARY: Maysville, KY, May 23, 1928.

CLOSE, GLENN: Greenwich, CT, Mar. 19, 1947. William & Mary College.

COBURN, JAMES: Laurel, NB, Aug. 31, 1928. LACC.

COCA, IMOGENE: Philadelphia, Nov. 18, 1908.

CODY, KATHLEEN: Bronx, NY, Oct. 30, 1953.

COFFEY, SCOTT: HI, May 1, 1967.

COLE, GEORGE: London, Apr. 22, 1925.

COLEMAN, GARY: Zion, IL, Feb. 8, 1968.

COLEMAN, DABNEY: Austin, TX, Jan. 3, 1932.

COLEMAN, JACK: Easton, PA, Feb. 21, 1958. Duke U.

COLIN, MARGARET: NYC, May 26, 1957.

COLLET, CHRISTOPHER: NYC, Mar. 13, 1968. Strasberg Inst.

COLLETTE, TONI: Sydney, Australia, Nov. 1, 1972.

COLLINS, JOAN: London, May 21, 1933. Francis Holland School.

COLLINS, PAULINE: Devon, England, Sept. 3, 1940.

COLLINS, STEPHEN: Des Moines, IA, Oct. 1, 1947. Amherst.

COLON, MIRIAM: Ponce, PR., 1945. UPR.

COLTRANE, ROBBIE: Ruthergien, Scotland, Mar. 30, 1950.

COMER, ANJANETTE: Dawson, TX, Aug. 7, 1942. Baylor, Tex. U.

CONANT, OLIVER: NYC, Nov. 15, 1955. Dalton.

CONAWAY, JEFF: NYC, Oct. 5, 1950. NYU.

CONNELLY, JENNIFER: NYC, Dec. 12, 1970

CONNERY, SEAN: Edinburgh, Scotland, Aug. 25, 1930.

CONNERY, JASON: London, Jan. 11, 1963.

CONNICK, HARRY, JR.: New Orleans, LA, Sept. 11, 1967.

CONNOLLY, BILLY: Glasgow, Scotland, Nov. 24, 1942.

Jeff Bridges

Matthew Broderick

Albert Brooks

Saffron Burrows

CONNORS, MIKE (Krekor Ohanian): Fresno, CA, Aug. 15, 1925. UCLA.
CONRAD, ROBERT (Conrad Robert Falk): Chicago, IL, Mar. 1, 1935. Northwestern U.
CONSTANTINE, MICHAEL: Reading, PA, May 22, 1927.
CONTI, TOM: Paisley, Scotland, Nov. 22, 1941.
CONVERSE, FRANK: St. Louis, MO, May 22, 1938. Carnegie Tech.
CONWAY, GARY: Boston, Feb. 4, 1936.
CONWAY, KEVIN: NYC, May 29, 1942.
CONWAY, TIM (Thomas Daniel): Willoughby, OH, Dec. 15, 1933. Bowling Green State.
COOGAN, KEITH (Keith Mitchell Franklin): Palm Springs, CA, Jan. 13, 1970.
COOK, RACHAEL LEIGH: Minneapolis, MN, Oct. 4, 1979.
COOPER, BEN: Hartford, CT, Sept. 30, 1930. Columbia U.
COOPER, CHRIS: Kansas City, MO, July 9, 1951. UMo.
COOPER, JACKIE: Los Angeles, Sept. 15, 1921.
COPELAND, JOAN: NYC, June 1, 1922. Brooklyn College, RADA.
CORBETT, GRETCHEN: Portland, OR, Aug. 13, 1947. Carnegie Tech.
CORBIN, BARRY: Dawson County, TX, Oct. 16, 1940. Texas Tech. U.
CORCORAN, DONNA: Quincy, MA, Sept. 29, 1942.
CORD, ALEX (Viespi): Floral Park, NY, Aug. 3, 1931. NYU, Actors Studio.
CORDAY, MARA (Marilyn Watts): Santa Monica, CA, Jan. 3, 1932.
COREY, JEFF: NYC, Aug. 10, 1914. Fagin School.
CORNTHWAITE, ROBERT: St. Helens, OR, Apr. 28, 1917. USC.
CORRI, ADRIENNE: Glasgow, Scot., Nov. 13, 1933. RADA.
CORT, BUD (Walter Edward Cox): New Rochelle, NY, Mar. 29, 1950. NYU.
CORTESA, VALENTINA: Milan, Italy, Jan. 1, 1924.
COSBY, BILL: Philadelphia, PA, July 12, 1937. Temple U.

COSTER, NICOLAS: London, Dec. 3, 1934. Neighborhood Playhouse.
COSTNER, KEVIN: Lynwood, CA, Jan. 18, 1955. CalStaU.
COURTENAY, TOM: Hull, England, Feb. 25, 1937. RADA.
COURTLAND, JEROME: Knoxville, TN, Dec. 27, 1926.
COX, BRIAN: Dundee, Scotland, June 1, 1946. LAMDA.
COX, COURTENEY: Birmingham, AL, June 15, 1964.
COX, RONNY: Cloudcroft, NM, Aug. 23, 1938.
COYOTE, PETER (Cohon): NYC, Oct. 10, 1941.
CRAIG, MICHAEL: Poona, India, Jan. 27, 1929.
CRAIN, JEANNE: Barstow, CA, May 25, 1925.
CRAVEN, GEMMA: Dublin, Ireland, June 1, 1950.
CRAWFORD, MICHAEL (Dumbel-Smith): Salisbury, England, Jan. 19, 1942.
CREMER, BRUNO: Paris, France, 1929.
CRENNA, RICHARD: Los Angeles, Nov. 30, 1926. USC.
CRISTAL, LINDA (Victoria Moya): Buenos Aires, Feb. 25, 1934.
CROMWELL, JAMES: Los Angeles, CA, Jan. 27, 1940.
CRONYN, HUME (Blake): Ontario, Canada, July 18, 1911.
CROSBY, DENISE: Hollywood, CA, Nov. 24, 1957.
CROSBY, HARRY: Los Angeles, CA, Aug. 8, 1958.
CROSBY, MARY FRANCES: Los Angeles, CA, Sept. 14, 1959.
CROSS, BEN: London, Dec. 16, 1947. RADA.
CROSS, MURPHY (Mary Jane): Laurelton, MD, June 22, 1950.
CROUSE, LINDSAY: NYC, May 12, 1948. Radcliffe.
CROWE, RUSSELL: New Zealand, Apr. 7, 1964.

CROWLEY, PAT: Olyphant, PA, Sept. 17, 1932.
CRUDUP, BILLY: Manhasset, NY, July 8, 1968. UNC/Chapel Hill.
CRUISE, TOM (T. C. Mapother, IV): July 3, 1962, Syracuse, NY.
CRUZ, PENÉLOPE (P.C. Sanchez): Madrid, Spain, Apr. 28, 1974.
CRYER, JON: NYC, Apr. 16, 1965, RADA.
CRYSTAL, BILLY: Long Beach, NY, Mar. 14, 1947. Marshall U.
CULKIN, KIERAN: NYC, Sept. 30, 1982.
CULKIN, MACAULAY: NYC, Aug. 26, 1980.
CULLUM, JOHN: Knoxville, TN, Mar. 2, 1930. U Tenn.
CULLUM, JOHN DAVID: NYC, Mar. 1, 1966.
CULP, ROBERT: Oakland, CA, Aug. 16, 1930. U Wash.
CUMMING, ALAN: Perthshire, Scotland, 1964.
CUMMINGS, CONSTANCE: Seattle, WA, May 15, 1910.
CUMMINGS, QUINN: Hollywood, Aug. 13, 1967.
CUMMINS, PEGGY: Prestatyn, N. Wales, Dec. 18, 1926. Alexandra School.
CURRY, TIM: Cheshire, England, Apr. 19, 1946. Birmingham U.
CURTIN, JANE: Cambridge, MA, Sept. 6, 1947.
CURTIS, JAMIE LEE: Los Angeles, CA, Nov. 22, 1958.
CURTIS, KEENE: Salt Lake City, UT, Feb. 15, 1925. U Utah.
CURTIS, TONY (Bernard Schwartz): NYC, June 3, 1924.
CUSACK, JOAN: Evanston, IL, Oct. 11, 1962.
CUSACK, JOHN: Chicago, IL, June 28, 1966.
CUSACK, SINEAD: Dalkey, Ireland, Feb. 18, 1948.
DAFOE, WILLEM: Appleton, WI, July 22, 1955.
DAHL, ARLENE: Minneapolis, Aug. 11, 1928. U Minn.

Neve Campbell   Kate Capshaw   Kim Cattrall   Stockard Channing

DALE, JIM: Rothwell, England, Aug. 15, 1935.

DALLESANDRO, JOE: Pensacola, FL, Dec. 31, 1948.

DALTON, TIMOTHY: Colwyn Bay, Wales, Mar. 21, 1946. RADA.

DALTREY, ROGER: London, Mar. 1, 1944.

DALY, TIM: NYC, Mar. 1, 1956. Bennington College.

DALY, TYNE: Madison, WI, Feb. 21, 1947. AMDA.

DAMON, MATT: Cambridge, MA, Oct. 8, 1970.

DAMONE, VIC (Vito Farinola): Brooklyn, NY, June 12, 1928.

DANCE, CHARLES: Plymouth, England, Oct. 10, 1946.

DANES, CLAIRE: New York, NY, Apr. 12, 1979.

D'ANGELO, BEVERLY: Columbus, OH, Nov. 15, 1953.

DANGERFIELD, RODNEY (Jacob Cohen): Babylon, NY, Nov. 22, 1921.

DANIELS, JEFF: Athens, GA, Feb. 19, 1955. EMichSt.

DANIELS, WILLIAM: Brooklyn, NY, Mar. 31, 1927. Northwestern.

DANNER, BLYTHE: Philadelphia, PA, Feb. 3, 1944. Bard College.

DANNING, SYBIL (Sybille Johanna Danninger): Vienna, Austria, May 4, 1949.

DANSON, TED: San Diego, CA, Dec. 29, 1947. Stanford, Carnegie Tech.

DANTE, MICHAEL (Ralph Vitti): Stamford, CT, 1935. U Miami.

DANZA, TONY: Brooklyn, NY, Apr. 21, 1951. UDubuque.

D'ARBANVILLE-QUINN, PATTI: NYC, 1951.

DARBY, KIM (Deborah Zerby): North Hollywood, CA, July 8, 1948.

DARCEL, DENISE (Denise Billecard): Paris, France, Sept. 8, 1925. U Dijon.

DARREN, JAMES: Philadelphia, PA, June 8, 1936. Stella Adler School.

DARRIEUX, DANIELLE: Bordeaux, France, May 1, 1917. Lycee LaTour.

DAVENPORT, NIGEL: Cambridge, England, May 23, 1928. Trinity College.

DAVID, KEITH: NYC, June 4, 1954. Juilliard.

DAVIDOVICH, LOLITA: Toronto, Ontario, Canada, July 15, 1961.

DAVIDSON, JAYE: Riverside, CA, 1968.

DAVIDSON, JOHN: Pittsburgh, Dec. 13, 1941. Denison U.

DAVIES, JEREMY (Boring): Rockford, IA, Oct. 28, 1969.

DAVIS, CLIFTON: Chicago, IL, Oct. 4, 1945. Oakwood College.

DAVIS, GEENA: Wareham, MA, Jan. 21, 1957.

DAVIS, HOPE: Tenafly, NJ, 1967.

DAVIS, JUDY: Perth, Australia, Apr. 23, 1955.

DAVIS, MAC: Lubbock, TX, Jan. 21,1942.

DAVIS, NANCY (Anne Frances Robbins): NYC, July 6, 1921. Smith College.

DAVIS, OSSIE: Cogdell, GA, Dec. 18, 1917. Howard U.

DAVIS, SAMMI: Kidderminster, Worcestershire, England, June 21, 1964.

DAVISON, BRUCE: Philadelphia, PA, June 28, 1946.

DAWBER, PAM: Detroit, MI, Oct. 18, 1954.

DAY, DORIS (Doris Kappelhoff): Cincinnati, Apr. 3, 1924.

DAY, LARAINE (Johnson): Roosevelt, UT, Oct. 13, 1917.

DAY–LEWIS, DANIEL: London, Apr. 29, 1957. Bristol Old Vic.

DAYAN, ASSI: Israel, Nov. 23, 1945. U Jerusalem.

DEAKINS, LUCY: NYC, 1971.

DEAN, JIMMY: Plainview, TX, Aug. 10, 1928.

DEAN, LOREN: Las Vegas, NV, July 31, 1969.

DeCAMP, ROSEMARY: Prescott, AZ, Nov. 14, 1913.

DeCARLO, YVONNE (Peggy Yvonne Middleton): Vancouver, B.C., Canada, Sept. 1, 1922. Vancouver School of Drama.

DEE, FRANCES: Los Angeles, Nov. 26, 1907. Chicago U.

DEE, JOEY (Joseph Di Nicola): Passaic, NJ, June 11, 1940. Patterson State College.

DEE, RUBY: Cleveland, OH, Oct. 27, 1924. Hunter College.

DEE, SANDRA (Alexandra Zuck): Bayonne, NJ, Apr. 23, 1942.

DeGENERES, ELLEN: New Orleans, LA, Jan. 26, 1958.

DeHAVEN, GLORIA: Los Angeles, July 23, 1923.

DeHAVILLAND, OLIVIA: Tokyo, Japan, July 1, 1916. Notre Dame Convent School.

DELAIR, SUZY (Suzanne Delaire): Paris, France, Dec. 31, 1916.

DELANY, DANA: NYC, March 13, 1956. Wesleyan U.

DELPY, JULIE: Paris. Dec, 21, 1969.

DELON, ALAIN: Sceaux, France, Nov. 8, 1935.

DELORME, DANIELE: Paris, France, Oct. 9, 1926. Sorbonne.

DEL TORO, BENICIO: Santurce, Puerto Rico, Feb. 19, 1967.

DeLUISE, DOM: Brooklyn, NY, Aug. 1, 1933. Tufts College.

DeLUISE, PETER: NYC, Nov. 6, 1966.

DEMONGEOT, MYLENE: Nice, France, Sept. 29, 1938.

DeMORNAY, REBECCA: Los Angeles, Aug. 29, 1962. Strasberg Inst.

DEMPSEY, PATRICK: Lewiston, ME, Jan. 13, 1966.

DeMUNN, JEFFREY: Buffalo, NY, Apr. 25, 1947. Union College.

DENCH, JUDI: York, England, Dec. 9, 1934.

DENEUVE, CATHERINE: Paris, France, Oct. 22, 1943.

DeNIRO, ROBERT: NYC, Aug. 17, 1943. Stella Adler.

DENNEHY, BRIAN: Bridgeport, CT, Jul. 9, 1938. Columbia.

DENVER, BOB: New Rochelle, NY, Jan. 9, 1935.

DEPARDIEU, GERARD: Chateauroux, France, Dec. 27, 1948.

DEPP, JOHNNY: Owensboro, KY, June 9, 1963.

DEREK, BO (Mary Cathleen Collins): Long Beach, CA, Nov. 20, 1956.

DERN, BRUCE: Chicago, IL, June 4, 1936. UPA.

DERN, LAURA: Los Angeles, Feb. 10, 1967.

DeSALVO, ANNE: Philadelphia, Apr. 3.

DEVANE, WILLIAM: Albany, NY, Sept. 5, 1939.

DeVITO, DANNY: Asbury Park, NJ, Nov. 17, 1944.

DEXTER, ANTHONY (Walter Reinhold Alfred Fleischmann): Talmadge, NB, Jan. 19, 1919. U Iowa.

DEY, SUSAN: Pekin, IL, Dec. 10, 1953.

DeYOUNG, CLIFF: Los Angeles, CA, Feb. 12, 1945. Cal State.

DIAMOND, NEIL: NYC, Jan. 24, 1941. NYU.

DIAZ, CAMERON: Long Beach, CA, Aug. 30, 1972.

DiCAPRIO, LEONARDO: Hollywood, CA, Nov.11, 1974.

DICKINSON, ANGIE (Angeline Brown): Kulm, ND, Sept. 30, 1932. Glendale College.

DIGGS, TAYE (Scott Diggs): Rochester, NY, 1972.

DILLER, PHYLLIS (Driver): Lima, OH, July 17, 1917. Bluffton College.

DILLMAN, BRADFORD: San Francisco, Apr. 14, 1930. Yale.

DILLON, KEVIN: Mamaroneck, NY, Aug. 19, 1965.

DILLON, MATT: Larchmont, NY, Feb. 18, 1964. AADA.

DILLON, MELINDA: Hope, AR, Oct. 13, 1939. Goodman Theatre School.

DIXON, DONNA: Alexandria, VA, July 20, 1957.

DOBSON, KEVIN: NYC, Mar. 18, 1944.

DOBSON, TAMARA: Baltimore, MD, May 14, 1947. MD Inst. of Art.

DOHERTY, SHANNEN: Memphis, TN, Apr. 12, 1971.

DOLAN, MICHAEL: Oklahoma City, OK, June 21, 1965.

DONAHUE, TROY (Merle Johnson): NYC, Jan. 27, 1937. Columbia U.

DONAT, PETER: Nova Scotia, Jan. 20, 1928. Yale.

DONNELLY, DONAL: Bradford, England, July 6, 1931.

D'ONOFRIO, VINCENT: Brooklyn, NY, June 30, 1959.

DONOHOE, AMANDA: London, June 29 1962.

DONOVAN, MARTIN: Reseda, CA, Aug. 19, 1957.

DONOVAN, TATE: NYC, Sept. 25, 1963.

DOOHAN, JAMES: Vancouver, BC, Mar. 3, 1920. Neighborhood Playhouse.

DOOLEY, PAUL: Parkersburg WV, Feb. 22, 1928. U WV.

DORFF, STEPHEN: CA, July 29, 1973.

DOUG, DOUG E. (Douglas Bourne): Brooklyn, NY, Jan. 7, 1970.

DOUGLAS, DONNA (Dorothy Bourgeois): Baywood, LA, Sept. 26, 1935.

DOUGLAS, ILLEANA: MA, July 25, 1965.

DOUGLAS, KIRK (Issur Danielovitch): Amsterdam, NY, Dec. 9, 1916. St. Lawrence U.

DOUGLAS, MICHAEL: New Brunswick, NJ, Sept. 25, 1944. U Cal.

DOUGLASS, ROBYN: Sendai, Japan, June 21, 1953. UCDavis.

DOURIF, BRAD: Huntington, WV, Mar. 18, 1950. Marshall U.

DOWN, LESLEY-ANN: London, Mar. 17, 1954.

DOWNEY, ROBERT, JR.: NYC, Apr. 4, 1965.

DRAKE, BETSY: Paris, France, Sept. 11, 1923.

DRESCHER, FRAN: Queens, NY, Sept. 30, 1957.

DREW, ELLEN (formerly Terry Ray): Kansas City, MO, Nov. 23, 1915.

Cher

Julie Christie

John Cleese

DREYFUSS, RICHARD: Brooklyn, NY, Oct. 19, 1947.

DRILLINGER, BRIAN: Brooklyn, NY, June 27, 1960. SUNY/Purchase.

DRIVER, MINNIE (Amelia Driver): London, Jan. 31, 1971.

DUCHOVNY, DAVID: NYC, Aug. 7, 1960. Yale.

DUDIKOFF, MICHAEL: Torrance, CA, Oct. 8, 1954.

DUGAN, DENNIS: Wheaton, IL, Sept. 5, 1946.

DUKAKIS, OLYMPIA: Lowell, MA, June 20, 1931.

DUKE, BILL: Poughkeepsie, NY, Feb. 26, 1943. NYU.

DUKE, PATTY (Anna Marie): NYC, Dec. 14, 1946.

DULLEA, KEIR: Cleveland, NJ, May 30, 1936. SF State College.

DUNAWAY, FAYE: Bascom, FL, Jan. 14, 1941. Fla. U.

DUNCAN, SANDY: Henderson, TX, Feb. 20, 1946. Len Morris College.

DUNNE, GRIFFIN: NYC, June 8, 1955. Neighborhood Playhouse.

DUNST, KIRSTEN: Point Pleasant, NJ, Apr. 30, 1982.

DUPEREY, ANNY: Paris, France, 1947.

DURBIN, DEANNA (Edna): Winnipeg, Canada, Dec. 4, 1921.

DURNING, CHARLES: Highland Falls, NY, Feb. 28, 1923. NYU.

DUSSOLLIER, ANDRE: Annecy, France, Feb. 17, 1946.

DUTTON, CHARLES: Baltimore, MD, Jan. 30, 1951. Yale.

DUVALL, ROBERT: San Diego, CA, Jan. 5, 1931. Principia College.

DUVALL, SHELLEY: Houston, TX, July 7, 1949.

DYSART, RICHARD: Brighton, ME, Mar. 30, 1929.

DZUNDZA, GEORGE: Rosenheim, Germ., July 19, 1945.

EASTON, ROBERT: Milwaukee, WI, Nov. 23, 1930. U Texas.

EASTWOOD, CLINT: San Francisco, May 31, 1931. LACC.

EATON, SHIRLEY: London, 1937. Aida Foster School.

EBSEN, BUDDY (Christian, Jr.): Belleville, IL, Apr. 2, 1910. U Fla.

ECKEMYR, AGNETA: Karlsborg, Sweden, July 2. Actors Studio.

EDELMAN, GREGG: Chicago, IL, Sept. 12, 1958. Northwestern U.

EDEN, BARBARA (Huffman): Tucson, AZ, Aug. 23, 1934.

EDWARDS, ANTHONY: Santa Barbara, CA, July 19, 1962. RADA.

EDWARDS, LUKE: Nevada City, CA, Mar. 24, 1980.

EGGAR, SAMANTHA: London, Mar. 5, 1939.

EICHHORN, LISA: Reading, PA, Feb. 4, 1952. Queens Ont. U RADA.

EIKENBERRY, JILL: New Haven, CT, Jan. 21, 1947.

EILBER, JANET: Detroit, MI, July 27, 1951. Juilliard.

EKBERG, ANITA: Malmo, Sweden, Sept. 29, 1931.

EKLAND, BRITT: Stockholm, Sweden, Oct. 6, 1942.

ELDARD, RON: Long Island, NY, Feb. 20, 1965.

ELFMAN, JENNA (Jennifer Mary Batula): Los Angeles, Sept. 30, 1971.
ELIZONDO, HECTOR: NYC, Dec. 22, 1936.
ELLIOTT, ALISON: San Francisco, CA, 1969.
ELLIOTT, CHRIS: NYC, May 31, 1960.
ELLIOTT, PATRICIA: Gunnison, CO, July 21, 1942. UCol.
ELLIOTT, SAM: Sacramento, CA, Aug. 9, 1944. U Ore.
ELWES, CARY: London, Oct. 26, 1962.
ELY, RON (Ronald Pierce): Hereford, TX, June 21, 1938.
EMBRY, ETHAN (Ethan Randall): Huntington Beach, CA, June 13, 1978.
ENGLUND, ROBERT: Glendale, CA, June 6, 1949.
ERBE, KATHRYN: Newton, MA, July 2, 1966.
ERDMAN, RICHARD: Enid, OK, June 1, 1925.
ERICSON, JOHN: Dusseldorf, Ger., Sept. 25, 1926. AADA.
ERMEY, R. LEE (Ronald): Emporia, KS, Mar. 24, 1944
ESMOND, CARL (Willy Eichberger): Vienna, June 14, 1906. U Vienna.
ESPOSITO, GIANCARLO: Copenhagen, Denmark, Apr. 26, 1958.
ESTEVEZ, EMILIO: NYC, May 12, 1962.
ESTRADA, ERIK: NYC, Mar. 16, 1949.
EVANS, DALE (Francis Smith): Uvalde, TX, Oct. 31, 1912.
EVANS, JOSH: NYC, Jan. 16, 1971.
EVANS, LINDA (Evanstad): Hartford, CT, Nov. 18, 1942.
EVERETT, CHAD (Ray Cramton): South Bend, IN, June 11, 1936.
EVERETT, RUPERT: Norfolk, England, 1959.
EVIGAN, GREG: South Amboy, NJ, Oct. 14, 1953.
FABARES, SHELLEY: Los Angeles, Jan. 19, 1944.
FABIAN (Fabian Forte): Philadelphia, Feb. 6, 1943.
FABRAY, NANETTE (Ruby Nanette Fabares): San Diego, Oct. 27, 1920.
FAHEY, JEFF: Olean, NY, Nov. 29, 1956.

FAIRCHILD, MORGAN (Patsy McClenny): Dallas, TX, Feb. 3, 1950. UCLA.
FALK, PETER: NYC, Sept. 16, 1927. New School.
FARENTINO, JAMES: Brooklyn, NY, Feb. 24, 1938. AADA.
FARGAS, ANTONIO: Bronx, NY, Aug. 14, 1946.
FARINA, DENNIS: Chicago, IL, Feb. 29, 1944.
FARINA, SANDY (Sandra Feldman): Newark, NJ, 1955.
FARR, FELICIA: Westchester, NY, Oct. 4. 1932. Penn State College.
FARROW, MIA (Maria): Los Angeles, Feb. 9, 1945.
FAULKNER, GRAHAM: London, Sept. 26, 1947. Webber-Douglas.
FAVREAU, JON: Queens, NY, Oct. 16, 1966.
FAWCETT, FARRAH: Corpus Christie, TX, Feb. 2, 1947. TexU.
FEINSTEIN, ALAN: NYC, Sept. 8, 1941.
FELDMAN, COREY: Encino, CA, July 16, 1971.
FELDON, BARBARA (Hall): Pittsburgh, Mar. 12, 1941. Carnegie Tech.
FELDSHUH, TOVAH: NYC, Dec. 27, 1953, Sarah Lawrence College.
FELLOWS, EDITH: Boston, May 20, 1923.
FENN, SHERILYN: Detroit, MI, Feb. 1, 1965.
FERRELL, CONCHATA: Charleston, WV, Mar. 28, 1943. Marshall U.
FERRELL, WILL: Irvine, CA, July 16, 1968.
FERRER, MEL: Elbeton, NJ, Aug. 25, 1912. Princeton U.
FERRER, MIGUEL: Santa Monica, CA, Feb. 7, 1954.
FERRIS, BARBARA: London, 1943.
FIEDLER, JOHN: Plateville, WI, Feb. 3, 1925.
FIELD, SALLY: Pasadena, CA, Nov. 6, 1946.
FIELD, SHIRLEY-ANNE: London, June 27, 1938.
FIELD, TODD (William Todd Field): Pomona, CA, Feb. 24, 1964.
FIENNES, JOSEPH: Salisbury, Wiltshire, England, May 27, 1970.
FIENNES, RALPH: Suffolk, England, Dec. 22, 1962. RADA.

FIERSTEIN, HARVEY: Brooklyn, NY, June 6, 1954. Pratt Inst.
FINCH, JON: Caterham, England, Mar. 2, 1941.
FINLAY, FRANK: Farnworth, England, Aug. 6, 1926.
FINNEY, ALBERT: Salford, Lancashire, England, May 9, 1936. RADA.
FIORENTINO, LINDA: Philadelphia, PA, Mar. 9, 1960.
FIRTH, COLIN: Grayshott, Hampshire, England, Sept. 10, 1960.
FIRTH, PETER: Bradford, England, Oct. 27, 1953.
FISHBURNE, LAURENCE: Augusta, GA, July 30, 1961.
FISHER, CARRIE: Los Angeles, CA, Oct. 21, 1956. London Central School of Drama.
FISHER, EDDIE: Philadelphia, PA, Aug. 10, 1928.
FISHER, FRANCES: Orange, TX, 1952.
FITZGERALD, GERALDINE: Dublin, Ireland, Nov. 24, 1914. Dublin Art School.
FITZGERALD, TARA: London, Sept. 17, 1968.
FLAGG, FANNIE: Birmingham, AL, Sept. 21, 1944. UAl.
FLANAGAN, FIONNULA: Dublin, Dec. 10, 1941.
FLANNERY, SUSAN: Jersey City, NJ, July 31, 1943.
FLEMING, RHONDA (Marilyn Louis): Los Angeles, Aug. 10, 1922.
FLEMYNG, ROBERT: Liverpool, England, Jan. 3, 1912. Haileybury College.
FLETCHER, LOUISE: Birmingham, AL, July 22 1934.
FLOCKHART, CALISTA: Stockton, IL, Nov. 11, Rutgers U.
FOCH, NINA: Leyden, Holland, Apr. 20, 1924.
FOLEY, DAVE: Toronto, Canada, Jan. 4, 1963.
FOLLOWS, MEGAN: Toronto, Canada, Mar. 14, 1968.
FONDA, BRIDGET: Los Angeles, Jan. 27, 1964.
FONDA, JANE: NYC, Dec. 21, 1937. Vassar.
FONDA, PETER: NYC, Feb. 23, 1939. U Omaha.

Billy Crudup

Penélope Cruz

Claire Danes

Ossie Davis

Catherine Deneuve

Gerard Depardieu

Martin Donovan

Minnie Driver

FONTAINE, JOAN: Tokyo, Japan, Oct. 22, 1917.

FOOTE, HALLIE: NYC, 1953. UNH.

FORD, GLENN (Gwyllyn Samuel Newton Ford): Quebec, Canada, May 1, 1916.

FORD, HARRISON: Chicago, IL, July 13, 1942. Ripon College.

FOREST, MARK (Lou Degni): Brooklyn, NY, Jan. 1933.

FORLANI, CLAIRE: London, July 1, 1972.

FORREST, FREDERIC: Waxahachie, TX, Dec. 23, 1936.

FORREST, STEVE: Huntsville, TX, Sept. 29, 1924. UCLA.

FORSLUND, CONNIE: San Diego, CA, June 19, 1950. NYU.

FORSTER, ROBERT (Foster, Jr.): Rochester, NY, July 13, 1941. Rochester U.

FORSYTHE, JOHN (Freund): Penn's Grove, NJ, Jan. 29, 1918.

FORSYTHE, WILLIAM: Brooklyn, NY, June 7, 1955

FOSSEY, BRIGITTE: Tourcoing, France, Mar. 11, 1947.

FOSTER, BEN: Boston, MA, Oct. 29, 1980.

FOSTER, JODIE (Ariane Munker): Bronx, NY, Nov. 19, 1962. Yale.

FOSTER, MEG: Reading, PA, May 14, 1948.

FOX, EDWARD: London, Apr. 13, 1937. RADA.

FOX, JAMES: London, May 19, 1939.

FOX, MICHAEL J.: Vancouver, BC, June 9, 1961.

FOXWORTH, ROBERT: Houston, TX, Nov. 1, 1941. Carnegie Tech.

FRAKES, JONATHAN: Bethlehem, PA, Aug. 19, 1952. Harvard.

FRANCIOSA, ANTHONY (Papaleo): NYC, Oct. 25, 1928.

FRANCIS, ANNE: Ossining, NY, Sept. 16, 1932.

FRANCIS, ARLENE (Arlene Kazanjian): Boston, Oct. 20, 1908. Finch School.

FRANCIS, CONNIE (Constance Franconero): Newark, NJ, Dec. 12, 1938.

FRANCKS, DON: Vancouver, Canada, Feb. 28, 1932.

FRANKLIN, PAMELA: Tokyo, Feb. 4, 1950.

FRANZ, ARTHUR: Perth Amboy, NJ, Feb. 29, 1920. Blue Ridge College.

FRANZ, DENNIS: Chicago, IL, Oct. 28, 1944.

FRASER, BRENDAN: Indianapolis, IN, Dec. 3, 1968.

FRAZIER, SHEILA: NYC, Nov. 13, 1948.

FRECHETTE, PETER: Warwick, RI, Oct. 1956. URI.

FREEMAN, AL, JR.: San Antonio, TX, Mar. 21, 1934. CCLA.

FREEMAN, KATHLEEN: Chicago, IL, Feb. 17, 1919.

FREEMAN, MONA: Baltimore, MD, June 9, 1926.

FREEMAN, MORGAN: Memphis, TN, June 1, 1937. LACC.

FREWER, MATT: Washington, DC, Jan. 4, 1958, Old Vic.

FRICKER, BRENDA: Dublin, Ireland, Feb. 17, 1945.

FRIELS, COLIN: Glasgow, Sept. 25, 1952.

FRY, STEPHEN: Hampstead, London, Eng., Aug. 24, 1957.

FULLER, PENNY: Durham, NC, 1940. Northwestern U.

FUNICELLO, ANNETTE: Utica, NY, Oct. 22, 1942.

FURLONG, EDWARD: Glendale, CA, Aug. 2, 1977.

FURNEAUX, YVONNE: Lille, France, 1928. Oxford U.

GABLE, JOHN CLARK: Los Angeles, Mar. 20, 1961. Santa Monica College.

GABOR, ZSA ZSA (Sari Gabor): Budapest, Hungary, Feb. 6, 1918.

GAIL, MAX: Derfoil, MI, Apr. 5, 1943.

GAINES, BOYD: Atlanta, GA, May 11, 1953. Juilliard.

GALECKI, JOHNNY: Bree, Belgium, Apr. 30, 1975.

GALLAGHER, PETER: NYC, Aug. 19, 1955. Tufts U.

GALLIGAN, ZACH: NYC, Feb. 14, 1963. ColumbiaU.

GALLO, VINCENT: Buffalo, NY, Apr. 11, 1961.

GAM, RITA: Pittsburgh, PA, Apr. 2, 1928.

GAMBLE, MASON: Chicago, IL, Jan. 16, 1986.

GAMBON, MICHAEL: Dublin, Ireland, Oct. 19, 1940.

GANDOLFINI, JAMES: Westwood, NJ, Sept. 18, 1961.

GANZ, BRUNO: Zurich, Switzerland, Mar. 22, 1941.

GARBER, VICTOR: Montreal, Canada, Mar. 16, 1949.

GARCIA, ADAM: Wahroonga, New So. Wales, Australia, June 1, 1973.

GARCIA, ANDY: Havana, Cuba, Apr. 12, 1956. FlaInt.

GARFIELD, ALLEN (Allen Goorwitz): Newark, NJ, Nov. 22, 1939. Actors Studio.

GARFUNKEL, ART: NYC, Nov. 5, 1941.

GARLAND, BEVERLY: Santa Cruz, CA, Oct. 17, 1926. Glendale College.

GARNER, JAMES (James Baumgarner): Norman, OK, Apr. 7, 1928. Okla. U.

GAROFALO, JANEANE: Newton, NJ, Sept. 28, 1964.

GARR, TERI: Lakewood, OH, Dec. 11, 1949.

GARRETT, BETTY: St. Joseph, MO, May 23, 1919. Annie Wright Seminary.

GARRISON, SEAN: NYC, Oct. 19, 1937.

GARY, LORRAINE: NYC, Aug. 16, 1937.

GAVIN, JOHN: Los Angeles, Apr. 8, 1935. Stanford U.

GAYLORD, MITCH: Van Nuys, CA, Mar. 10, 1961. UCLA.

GAYNOR, MITZI (Francesca Marlene Von Gerber): Chicago, IL, Sept. 4, 1930.

GAZZARA, BEN: NYC, Aug. 28, 1930. Actors Studio.

GEARY, ANTHONY: Coalsville, UT, May 29, 1947. UUt.

GEDRICK, JASON: Chicago, IL, Feb. 7, 1965. Drake U.

GEESON, JUDY: Arundel, England, Sept. 10, 1948. Corona.

GELLAR, SARAH MICHELLE: NYC, Apr. 14, 1977.

GEOFFREYS, STEPHEN: Cincinnati, OH, Nov. 22, 1964. NYU.

GEORGE, SUSAN: West London, England, July 26, 1950.

GERARD, GIL: Little Rock, AR, Jan. 23, 1940.

GERE, RICHARD: Philadelphia, PA, Aug. 29, 1949. U Mass.

GERROLL, DANIEL: London, Oct. 16, 1951. Central.

David Duchovny

Kirsten Dunst

GERSHON, GINA: Los Angeles, June 10, 1962.

GERTZ, JAMI: Chicago, IL, Oct. 28, 1965.

GETTY, BALTHAZAR: Los Angeles, CA, Jan. 22, 1975.

GETTY, ESTELLE: NYC, July 25, 1923. New School.

GHOLSON, JULIE: Birmingham, AL, June 4, 1958.

GHOSTLEY, ALICE: Eve, MO, Aug. 14, 1926. Okla U.

GIANNINI, GIANCARLO: Spezia, Italy, Aug. 1, 1942. Rome Acad. of Drama.

GIBB, CYNTHIA: Bennington, VT, Dec. 14, 1963.

GIBSON, HENRY: Germantown, PA, Sept. 21, 1935.

GIBSON, MEL: Peekskill, NY, Jan. 3, 1956. NIDA.

GIBSON, THOMAS: Charleston, SC, July 3, 1962.

GIFT, ROLAND: Birmingham, England, May 28 1962.

GILBERT, MELISSA: Los Angeles, CA, May 8, 1964.

GILES, NANCY: NYC, July 17, 1960, Oberlin College.

GILLETTE, ANITA: Baltimore, MD, Aug. 16, 1938.

GILLIAM, TERRY: Minneapolis, MN, Nov. 22, 1940.

GILLIS, ANN (Alma O'Connor): Little Rock, AR, Feb. 12, 1927.

GINTY, ROBERT: NYC, Nov. 14, 1948. Yale.

GIRARDOT, ANNIE: Paris, France, Oct. 25, 1931.

GISH, ANNABETH: Albuquerque, NM, Mar. 13, 1971. DukeU.

GIVENS, ROBIN: NYC, Nov. 27, 1964.

GLASER, PAUL MICHAEL: Boston, MA, Mar. 25, 1943. Boston U.

GLASS, RON: Evansville, IN, July 10, 1945.

GLEASON, JOANNA: Winnipeg, Canada, June 2, 1950. UCLA.

GLEASON, PAUL: Jersey City, NJ, May 4, 1944.

GLENN, SCOTT: Pittsburgh, PA, Jan. 26, 1942. William and Mary College.

GLOVER, CRISPIN: NYC, Sept 20, 1964.

GLOVER, DANNY: San Francisco, CA, July 22, 1947. SFStateCol.

GLOVER, JOHN: Kingston, NY, Aug. 7, 1944.

GLYNN,CARLIN: Cleveland, Oh, Feb. 19, 1940. Actors Studio.

GOLDBERG, WHOOPI (Caryn Johnson): NYC, Nov. 13, 1949.

GOLDBLUM, JEFF: Pittsburgh, PA, Oct. 22, 1952. Neighborhood Playhouse.

GOLDEN, ANNIE: Brooklyn, NY, Oct. 19, 1951.

GOLDSTEIN, JENETTE: Beverly Hills, CA, 1960.

GOLDTHWAIT, BOB: Syracuse, NY, May 1, 1962.

GOLDWYN, TONY: Los Angeles, May 20, 1960. LAMDA.

GOLINO, VALERIA: Naples, Italy, Oct. 22, 1966.

GONZALEZ, CORDELIA: Aug. 11, 1958, San Juan, PR. UPR.

GONZALES-GONZALEZ, PEDRO: Aguilares, TX, Dec. 21, 1926.

GOODALL, CAROLINE: London, Nov. 13, 1959. BristolU.

GOODING, CUBA, JR.: Bronx, N.Y., Jan. 2, 1968.

GOODMAN, DODY: Columbus, OH, Oct. 28, 1915.

GOODMAN, JOHN: St. Louis, MO, June 20, 1952.

GORDON, KEITH: NYC, Feb. 3, 1961.

GORDON-LEVITT, JOSEPH: Los Angeles, Feb. 17, 1981.

GORMAN, CLIFF: Jamaica, NY, Oct. 13, 1936. NYU.

GORSHIN, FRANK: Pittsburgh, PA, Apr. 5, 1933.

GORTNER, MARJOE: Long Beach, CA, Jan. 14, 1944.

GOSSETT, LOUIS, JR.: Brooklyn, NY, May 27, 1936. NYU.

GOULD, ELLIOTT (Goldstein): Brooklyn, NY, Aug. 29, 1938. Columbia U.

GOULD, HAROLD: Schenectady, NY, Dec. 10, 1923. Cornell.

GOULD, JASON: NYC, Dec. 29, 1966.

GOULET, ROBERT: Lawrence, MA, Nov. 26, 1933. Edmonton.

GRAF, DAVID: Lancaster, OH, Apr. 16, 1950. OhStateU.

GRAFF, TODD: NYC, Oct. 22, 1959. SUNY/Purchase.

GRAHAM, HEATHER: Milwauke, WI, Jan. 29, 1970.

GRANGER, FARLEY: San Jose, CA, July 1, 1925.

GRANT, DAVID MARSHALL: Westport, CT, June 21, 1955. Yale.

GRANT, HUGH: London, Sept. 9, 1960. Oxford.

GRANT, KATHRYN (Olive Grandstaff): Houston, TX, Nov. 25, 1933. UCLA.

GRANT, LEE: NYC, Oct. 31, 1927. Juilliard.

GRANT, RICHARD E: Mbabane, Swaziland, May 5, 1957. Cape Town U.

GRAVES, PETER (Aurness): Minneapolis, Mar. 18, 1926. U Minn.

GRAVES, RUPERT: Weston-Super-Mare, England, June 30, 1963.

GRAY, COLEEN (Doris Jensen): Staplehurst, NB, Oct. 23, 1922. Hamline.

GRAY, LINDA: Santa Monica, CA, Sept. 12, 1940.

GRAY, SPALDING: Barrington, RI, June 5, 1941.

GRAYSON, KATHRYN (Zelma Hedrick): Winston-Salem, NC, Feb. 9, 1922.

GREEN, KERRI: Fort Lee, NJ, Jan. 14, 1967. Vassar.

GREEN, SETH: Philadelphia, PA, Feb. 8, 1974.

Faye Dunaway

Giancarlo Esposito

Ralph Fiennes

GREENE, ELLEN: NYC, Feb. 22, 1950. Ryder College.

GREENE, GRAHAM: Six Nations Reserve, Ontario, June 22, 1952

GREENWOOD, BRUCE: Quebec, Canada, Aug. 12, 1956.

GREER, JANE: Washington, DC, Sept. 9, 1924.

GREER, MICHAEL: Galesburg, IL, Apr. 20, 1943.

GREIST, KIM: Stamford, CT, May 12, 1958.

GREY, JENNIFER: NYC, Mar. 26, 1960.

GREY, JOEL (Katz): Cleveland, OH, Apr. 11, 1932.

GREY, VIRGINIA: Los Angeles, Mar. 22, 1917.

GRIECO, RICHARD: Watertown, NY, Mar. 23, 1965.

GRIEM, HELMUT: Hamburg, Germany, Apr. 6, 1932. HamburgU.

GRIER, DAVID ALAN: Detroit, MI, June 30, 1955. Yale.

GRIER, PAM: Winston-Salem, NC, May 26, 1949.

GRIFFITH, ANDY: Mt. Airy, NC, June 1, 1926. UNC.

GRIFFITH, MELANIE: NYC, Aug. 9, 1957. Pierce Col.

GRIFFITH, THOMAS IAN: Hartford, CT, Mar. 18, 1962.

GRIFFITHS, RACHEL: Melbourne, Australia, 1968.

GRIMES, GARY: San Francisco, June 2, 1955.

GRIMES, SCOTT: Lowell, MA, July 9, 1971.

GRIMES, TAMMY: Lynn, MA, Jan. 30, 1934. Stephens College.

GRIZZARD, GEORGE: Roanoke Rapids, NC, Apr. 1, 1928. UNC.

GRODIN, CHARLES: Pittsburgh, PA, Apr. 21, 1935.

GROH, DAVID: NYC, May 21, 1939. Brown U, LAMDA.

GROSS, MARY: Chicago, IL, Mar. 25, 1953.

GROSS, MICHAEL: Chicago, IL, June 21, 1947.

GRUFFUD, IOAN: Cardiff, Wales, Oct. 6, 1973.

GUEST, CHRISTOPHER: NYC, Feb. 5, 1948.

GUEST, LANCE: Saratoga, CA, July 21, 1960. UCLA.

GUILLAUME, ROBERT (Williams): St. Louis, MO, Nov. 30, 1937.

GULAGER, CLU: Holdenville, OK, Nov. 16 1928.

GUTTENBERG, STEVE: Massapequa, NY, Aug. 24, 1958. UCLA.

GUY, JASMINE: Boston, Mar. 10, 1964.

HAAS, LUKAS: West Hollywood, CA, Apr. 16, 1976.

HACK, SHELLEY: Greenwich, CT, July 6, 1952.

HACKETT, BUDDY (Leonard Hacker): Brooklyn, NY, Aug. 31, 1924.

HACKMAN, GENE: San Bernardino, CA, Jan. 30, 1930.

HAGERTY, JULIE: Cincinnati, OH, June 15, 1955. Juilliard.

HAGMAN, LARRY (Hageman): Weatherford, TX, Sept. 21, 1931. Bard.

HAID, CHARLES: San Francisco, June 2, 1943. CarnegieTech.

HAIM, COREY: Toronto, Canada, Dec. 23, 1972.

HALE, BARBARA: DeKalb, IL, Apr. 18, 1922. Chicago Academy of Fine Arts.

HALEY, JACKIE EARLE: Northridge, CA, July 14, 1961.

HALL, ALBERT: Boothton, AL, Nov. 10, 1937. Columbia.

HALL, ANTHONY MICHAEL: Boston, MA, Apr. 14, 1968.

HALL, ARSENIO: Cleveland, OH, Feb. 12, 1959.

HAMEL, VERONICA: Philadelphia, PA, Nov. 20, 1943.

HAMILL, MARK: Oakland, CA, Sept. 25, 1952. LACC.

HAMILTON, CARRIE: NYC, Dec. 5, 1963.

HAMILTON, GEORGE: Memphis, TN, Aug. 12, 1939. Hackley.

HAMILTON, LINDA: Salisbury, MD, Sept. 26, 1956.

HAMLIN, HARRY: Pasadena, CA, Oct. 30, 1951.

HAMPSHIRE, SUSAN: London, May 12, 1941.

HAMPTON, JAMES: Oklahoma City, OK, July 9, 1936. NTexasStU.

HAN, MAGGIE: Providence, RI, 1959.

HANDLER, EVAN: NYC, Jan. 10, 1961. Juilliard.

Teri Garr

HANKS, TOM: Concord, CA, Jul. 9, 1956. CalStateU.

HANNAH, DARYL: Chicago, IL, Dec. 3, 1960. UCLA.

HANNAH, PAGE: Chicago, IL, Apr. 13, 1964.

HARDEN, MARCIA GAY: LaJolla, CA, Aug. 14, 1959.

HARDIN, TY (Orison Whipple Hungerford, II): NYC, June 1, 1930.

HAREWOOD, DORIAN: Dayton, OH, Aug. 6, 1950. U Cinn.

HARMON, MARK: Los Angeles, CA, Sept. 2, 1951. UCLA.

HARPER, JESSICA: Chicago, IL, Oct. 10, 1949.

HARPER, TESS: Mammoth Spring, AK, 1952. SWMoState.

HARPER, VALERIE: Suffern, NY, Aug. 22, 1940.

HARRELSON, WOODY: Midland, TX, July 23, 1961. Hanover College.

HARRINGTON, PAT: NYC, Aug. 13, 1929. Fordham U.

HARRIS, BARBARA (Sandra Markowitz): Evanston, IL, July 25, 1935.

HARRIS, ED: Tenafly, NJ, Nov. 28, 1950. Columbia.

Edward Furlong

Ben Gazzara

Richard Gere

Gina Gershon

Caroline Goodall

Heather Graham

HARRIS, JULIE: Grosse Point, MI, Dec. 2, 1925. Yale Drama School.

HARRIS, MEL (Mary Ellen): Bethlehem, PA, 1957. Columbia.

HARRIS, RICHARD: Limerick, Ireland, Oct. 1, 1930. London Acad.

HARRIS, ROSEMARY: Ashby, England, Sept. 19, 1930. RADA.

HARRISON, GEORGE: Liverpool, England, Feb. 25, 1943.

HARRISON, GREGORY: Catalina Island, CA, May 31, 1950. Actors Studio.

HARRISON, NOEL: London, Jan. 29, 1936.

HARROLD, KATHRYN: Tazewell, VA, Aug. 2, 1950. Mills College.

HARRY, DEBORAH: Miami, IL, July 1, 1945.

HART, ROXANNE: Trenton, NJ, 1952, Princeton.

HARTLEY, MARIETTE: NYC, June 21, 1941.

HARTMAN, DAVID: Pawtucket, RI, May 19, 1935. Duke U.

HASSETT, MARILYN: Los Angeles, CA, Dec. 17, 1947.

HATCHER, TERI: Sunnyvale, CA, Dec. 8, 1964.

HATOSY, SHAWN: Fredrick, MD, Dec. 29, 1975.

HAUER, RUTGER: Amsterdam, Holland, Jan. 23, 1944.

HAVER, JUNE: Rock Island, IL, June 10, 1926.

HAVOC, JUNE (Hovick): Seattle, WA, Nov. 8, 1916.

HAWKE, ETHAN: Austin, TX, Nov. 6, 1970.

HAWN, GOLDIE: Washington, DC, Nov. 21, 1945.

HAWTHORNE, NIGEL: Coventry, Eng., Apr. 5, 1929.

HAYEK, SALMA: Coatzacoalcos, Veracruz, Mexico, Sept. 2, 1968.

HAYES, ISAAC: Covington, TN, Aug. 20, 1942.

HAYS, ROBERT: Bethesda, MD, July 24, 1947, SD State College.

HEADLY, GLENNE: New London, CT, Mar. 13, 1955. AmCollege.

HEALD, ANTHONY: New Rochelle, NY, Aug. 25, 1944. MIStateU.

HEARD, JOHN: Washington, DC, Mar. 7, 1946. Clark U.

HEATHERTON, JOEY: NYC, Sept. 14, 1944.

HECHE, ANNE: Aurora, OH, May 25, 1969.

HECKART, EILEEN: Columbus, OH, Mar. 29, 1919. Ohio State U.

HEDAYA, DAN: Brooklyn, NY, July 24, 1940.

HEDISON, DAVID: Providence, RI, May 20, 1929. Brown U.

HEDREN, TIPPI (Natalie): Lafayette, MN, Jan. 19, 1931.

HEGYES, ROBERT: Metuchen, NJ, May 7, 1951.

HELMOND, KATHERINE: Galveston, TX, July 5, 1934.

HEMINGWAY, MARIEL: Ketchum, ID, Nov. 22, 1961.

HEMMINGS, DAVID: Guilford, England, Nov. 18, 1941.

HEMSLEY, SHERMAN: Philadelphia, PA, Feb. 1, 1938.

HENDERSON, FLORENCE: Dale, IN, Feb. 14, 1934.

HENDRY, GLORIA: Jacksonville, FL, 1949.

HENNER, MARILU: Chicago, IL, Apr. 6, 1952.

HENRIKSEN, LANCE: NYC, May 5, 1940.

HENRY, BUCK (Henry Zuckerman): NYC, Dec. 9, 1930. Dartmouth.

HENRY, JUSTIN: Rye, NY, May 25, 1971.

HEPBURN, KATHARINE: Hartford, CT, May 12, 1907. Bryn Mawr.

HERRMANN, EDWARD: Washington, DC, July 21, 1943. Bucknell, LAMDA.

HERSHEY, BARBARA (Herzstein): Hollywood, CA, Feb. 5, 1948.

HESSEMAN, HOWARD: Lebanon, OR, Feb. 27, 1940.

HESTON, CHARLTON: Evanston, IL, Oct. 4, 1922. Northwestern U.

HEWITT, JENNIFER LOVE: Waco, TX, Feb. 21, 1979.

HEWITT, MARTIN: Claremont, CA, Feb. 19, 1958. AADA.

HEYWOOD, ANNE (Violet Pretty): Birmingham, England, Dec. 11, 1932.

HICKMAN, DARRYL: Hollywood, CA, July 28, 1933. Loyola U.

HICKMAN, DWAYNE: Los Angeles, May 18, 1934. Loyola U.

HICKS, CATHERINE: NYC, Aug. 6, 1951. Notre Dame.

HIGGINS, ANTHONY (Corlan): Cork City, Ireland, May 9, 1947. Birmingham Sch. of Dramatic Arts.

HIGGINS, MICHAEL: Brooklyn, NY, Jan. 20, 1926. AmThWing.

HILL, ARTHUR: Saskatchewan, Canada, Aug. 1, 1922. U Brit. College.

HILL, BERNARD: Manchester, England, Dec. 17, 1944.

HILL, STEVEN: Seattle, WA, Feb. 24, 1922. U Wash.

HILL, TERRENCE (Mario Girotti): Venice, Italy, Mar. 29, 1941. U Rome.

HILLER, WENDY: Bramhall, Cheshire, England, Aug. 15, 1912. Winceby House School.

HILLERMAN, JOHN: Denison, TX, Dec. 20, 1932.

HINES, GREGORY: NYC, Feb.14, 1946.

HINGLE, PAT: Denver, CO, July 19, 1923. Tex. U.

HIRSCH, JUDD: NYC, Mar. 15, 1935. AADA.

HOBEL, MARA: NYC, June 18, 1971.

HODGE, PATRICIA: Lincolnshire, England, Sept. 29, 1946. LAMDA.

HOFFMAN, DUSTIN: Los Angeles, Aug. 8, 1937. Pasadena Playhouse.

HOFFMAN, PHILIP SEYMOUR: Fairport, NY, July 23, 1967.

HOGAN, JONATHAN: Chicago, IL, June 13, 1951.

HOGAN, PAUL: Lightning Ridge, Australia, Oct. 8, 1939.

HOLBROOK, HAL (Harold): Cleveland, OH, Feb. 17, 1925. Denison.

HOLLIMAN, EARL: Tennesas Swamp, Delhi, LA, Sept. 11, 1928. UCLA.

HOLM, CELESTE: NYC, Apr. 29, 1919.

HOLM, IAN: Ilford, Essex, England, Sept. 12, 1931. RADA.

HOLMES, KATIE: Toledo, OH, Dec. 18, 1978.

HOMEIER, SKIP (George Vincent Homeier): Chicago, IL, Oct. 5, 1930. UCLA.

HOOKS, ROBERT: Washington, DC, Apr. 18, 1937. Temple.

HOPE, BOB (Leslie Townes Hope): London, May 26, 1903.

HOPKINS, ANTHONY: Port Talbot, So. Wales, Dec. 31, 1937. RADA.

HOPPER, DENNIS: Dodge City, KS, May 17, 1936.

HORNE, LENA: Brooklyn, NY, June 30, 1917.

HORSLEY, LEE: Muleshoe, TX, May 15, 1955.

HORTON, ROBERT: Los Angeles, July 29, 1924. UCLA.

HOSKINS, BOB: Bury St. Edmunds, England, Oct. 26, 1942.

HOUGHTON, KATHARINE: Hartford, CT, Mar. 10, 1945. Sarah Lawrence.

HOUSER, JERRY: Los Angeles, July 14, 1952. Valley, Jr. College.

HOWARD, ARLISS: Independence, MO, 1955. Columbia College.

HOWARD, KEN: El Centro, CA, Mar. 28, 1944. Yale.

HOWARD, RON: Duncan, OK, Mar. 1, 1954. USC.

HOWARD, RONALD: Norwood, England, Apr. 7, 1918. Jesus College.

HOWELL, C. THOMAS: Los Angeles, Dec. 7, 1966.

HOWELLS, URSULA: London, Sept. 17, 1922.

HOWES, SALLY ANN: London, July 20, 1930.

HOWLAND, BETH: Boston, MA, May 28, 1941.

HUBLEY, SEASON: NYC, May 14, 1951.

HUDDLESTON, DAVID: Vinton, VA, Sept. 17, 1930.

HUDSON, ERNIE: Benton Harbor, MI, Dec. 17, 1945.

HUDSON, KATE: Los Angeles, Apr. 19, 1979.

HUGHES, BARNARD: Bedford Hills, NY, July 16, 1915. Manhattan College.

HUGHES, KATHLEEN (Betty von Gerkan): Hollywood, CA, Nov. 14, 1928. UCLA.

HULCE, TOM: Plymouth, MI, Dec. 6, 1953. N.C. Sch. of Arts.

HUNNICUT, GAYLE: Ft. Worth, TX, Feb. 6, 1943. UCLA.

HUNT, HELEN: Los Angeles, June 15, 1963.

HUNT, LINDA: Morristown, NJ, Apr. 1945. Goodman Theatre.

HUNT, MARSHA: Chicago, IL, Oct. 17, 1917.

HUNTER, HOLLY: Atlanta, GA, Mar. 20, 1958. Carnegie-Mellon.

HUNTER, KIM (Janet Cole): Detroit, Nov. 12, 1922.

HUNTER, TAB (Arthur Gelien): NYC, July 11, 1931.

HUPPERT, ISABELLE: Paris, France, Mar. 16, 1955.

HURLEY, ELIZABETH: Hampshire, Eng., June 10, 1965.

HURT, JOHN: Lincolnshire, England, Jan. 22, 1940.

HURT, MARY BETH (Supinger): Marshalltown, IA, Sept. 26, 1948. NYU.

HURT, WILLIAM: Washington, DC, Mar. 20, 1950. Tufts, Juilliard.

HUSSEY, RUTH: Providence, RI, Oct. 30, 1917. U Mich.

HUSTON, ANJELICA: Santa Monica, CA, July 9, 1951.

HUTTON, BETTY (Betty Thornberg): Battle Creek, MI, Feb. 26, 1921.

HUTTON, LAUREN (Mary): Charleston, SC, Nov. 17, 1943. Newcomb College.

HUTTON, TIMOTHY: Malibu, CA, Aug. 16, 1960.

HYER, MARTHA: Fort Worth, TX, Aug. 10, 1924. Northwestern U.

ICE CUBE (O'Shea Jackson): Los Angeles, June 15, 1969.

IDLE, ERIC: South Shields, Durham, England, Mar. 29, 1943. Cambridge.

INGELS, MARTY: Brooklyn, NY, Mar. 9, 1936.

IRELAND, KATHY: Santa Barbara, CA, Mar. 8, 1963.

IRONS, JEREMY: Cowes, England, Sept. 19, 1948. Old Vic.

IRONSIDE, MICHAEL: Toronto, Canada, Feb. 12, 1950.

IRVING, AMY: Palo Alto, CA, Sept. 10, 1953. LADA.

IRWIN, BILL: Santa Monica, CA, Apr. 11, 1950.

ISAAK, CHRIS: Stockton, CA, June 26, 1956. UofPacific.

IVANEK, ZELJKO: Lujubljana, Yugo., Aug. 15, 1957. Yale, LAMDA.

IVEY, JUDITH: El Paso, TX, Sept. 4, 1951.

IZZARD, EDDIE: Yemen, Feb. 7, 1962.

JACKSON, ANNE: Alleghany, PA, Sept. 3, 1926. Neighborhood Playhouse.

JACKSON, GLENDA: Hoylake, Cheshire, England, May 9, 1936. RADA.

JACKSON, JANET: Gary, IN, May 16, 1966.

JACKSON, KATE: Birmingham, AL, Oct. 29, 1948. AADA.

JACKSON, MICHAEL: Gary, IN, Aug. 29, 1958.

JACKSON, SAMUEL L.: Atlanta, Dec. 21, 1948.

JACKSON, VICTORIA: Miami, FL, Aug. 2, 1958.

JACOBI, DEREK: Leytonstone, London, Oct. 22, 1938. Cambridge.

JACOBI, LOU: Toronto, Canada, Dec. 28, 1913.

JACOBS, LAWRENCE-HILTON: Virgin Islands, Sept. 14, 1953.

JACOBY, SCOTT: Chicago, IL, Nov. 19, 1956.

JAGGER, MICK: Dartford, Kent, England, July 26, 1943.

JAMES, CLIFTON: NYC, May 29, 1921. Ore. U.

JANNEY, ALLISON: Dayton, OH, Nov. 20, 1960. RADA.

JARMAN, CLAUDE, JR.: Nashville, TN, Sept. 27, 1934.

JEAN, GLORIA (Gloria Jean Schoonover): Buffalo, NY, Apr. 14, 1927.

JEFFREYS, ANNE (Carmichael): Goldsboro, NC, Jan. 26, 1923. Anderson College.

JEFFRIES, LIONEL: London, June 10, 1926. RADA.

JERGENS, ADELE: Brooklyn, NY, Nov. 26, 1922.

Rupert Graves

Pam Grier

Gene Hackman

Neil Patrick Harris

JETER, MICHAEL: Lawrenceburg, TN, Aug. 26, 1952. Memphis St.U.
JILLIAN, ANN (Nauseda): Cambridge, MA, Jan. 29, 1951.
JOHANSEN, DAVID: Staten Island, NY, Jan. 9, 1950.
JOHN, ELTON (Reginald Dwight): Middlesex, England, Mar. 25, 1947. RAM.
JOHNS, GLYNIS: Durban, S. Africa, Oct. 5, 1923.
JOHNSON, DON: Galena, MO, Dec. 15, 1950. UKan.
JOHNSON, PAGE: Welch, WV, Aug. 25, 1930. Ithaca.
JOHNSON, RAFER: Hillsboro, TX, Aug. 18, 1935. UCLA.
JOHNSON, RICHARD: Essex, England, July 30, 1927. RADA.
JOHNSON, ROBIN: Brooklyn, NY, May 29, 1964.
JOHNSON, VAN: Newport, RI, Aug. 28, 1916.
JOLIE, ANGELINA (Angelina Jolie Voight): Los Angeles, June 4, 1975.
JONES, CHRISTOPHER: Jackson, TN, Aug. 18, 1941. Actors Studio.
JONES, DEAN: Decatur, AL, Jan. 25, 1931. Actors Studio.
JONES, GRACE: Spanishtown, Jamaica, May 19, 1952.
JONES, JACK: Bel-Air, CA, Jan. 14, 1938.
JONES, JAMES EARL: Arkabutla, MS, Jan. 17, 1931. U Mich.
JONES, JEFFREY: Buffalo, NY, Sept. 28, 1947. LAMDA.
JONES, JENNIFER (Phyllis Isley): Tulsa, OK, Mar. 2, 1919. AADA.
JONES, L.Q. (Justice Ellis McQueen): Aug 19, 1927.
JONES, ORLANDO: Mobile, AL, Apr. 10, 1968.
JONES, SAM J.: Chicago, IL, Aug. 12, 1954.
JONES, SHIRLEY: Smithton, PA, March 31, 1934.
JONES, TERRY: Colwyn Bay, Wales, Feb. 1, 1942.
JONES, TOMMY LEE: San Saba, TX, Sept. 15, 1946. Harvard.
JOURDAN, LOUIS: Marseilles, France, June 19, 1920.
JOVOVICH, MILLA: Kiev, Ukraine, Dec. 17, 1975.
JOY, ROBERT: Montreal, Canada, Aug. 17, 1951. Oxford.
JUDD, ASHLEY: Los Angeles, CA, Apr. 19, 1968.
JURADO, KATY (Maria Christina Jurado Garcia): Guadalajara, Mex., Jan. 16, 1927.
KACZMAREK, JANE: Milwaukee, WI, Dec. 21, 1955.
KANE, CAROL: Cleveland, OH, June 18, 1952.
KAPLAN, MARVIN: Brooklyn, NY, Jan. 24, 1924.
KAPOOR, SHASHI: Calcutta, India, Mar. 18, 1938.
KAPRISKY, VALERIE (Cheres): Paris, France, Aug. 19, 1962.
KARRAS, ALEX: Gary, IN, July 15, 1935.
KARTHEISER, VINCENT: Minneapolis, MN, May 5, 1979.
KATT, WILLIAM: Los Angeles, CA, Feb. 16, 1955.
KAUFMANN, CHRISTINE: Lansdorf, Graz, Austria, Jan. 11, 1945.

Dan Hedaya

Charlton Heston

Katie Holmes

KAVNER, JULIE: Burbank, CA, Sept. 7, 1951. UCLA.
KAZAN, LAINIE (Levine): Brooklyn, NY, May 15, 1942.
KAZURINSKY, TIM: Johnstown, PA, March 3, 1950.
KEACH, STACY: Savannah, GA, June 2, 1941. U Cal., Yale.
KEATON, DIANE (Hall): Los Angeles, CA, Jan. 5, 1946. Neighborhood Playhouse.
KEATON, MICHAEL: Coraopolis, PA, Sept. 9, 1951. KentStateU.
KEEGAN, ANDREW: Los Angeles, Jan. 29, 1979.
KEEL, HOWARD (Harold Leek): Gillespie, IL, Apr. 13, 1919.
KEENER, CATHERINE: Miami, FL, 1960.
KEESLAR, MATT: Grand Rapids, MI, 1972.
KEITEL, HARVEY: Brooklyn, NY, May 13, 1939.
KEITH, DAVID: Knoxville, TN, May 8, 1954. UTN.
KELLER, MARTHE: Basel, Switzerland, 1945. Munich Stanislavsky Sch.
KELLERMAN, SALLY: Long Beach, CA, June 2, 1936. Actors Studio West.
KELLY, MOIRA: Queens, NY, Mar. 6, 1968.
KEMP, JEREMY (Wacker): Chesterfield, England, Feb. 3, 1935. Central Sch.
KENNEDY, GEORGE: NYC, Feb. 18, 1925.
KENNEDY, LEON ISAAC: Cleveland, OH, 1949.
KENSIT, PATSY: London, Mar. 4, 1968.
KERR, DEBORAH: Helensburg, Scotland, Sept. 30, 1921. Smale Ballet School.
KERR, JOHN: NYC, Nov. 15, 1931. Harvard, Columbia.
KERWIN, BRIAN: Chicago, IL, Oct. 25, 1949.
KEYES, EVELYN: Port Arthur, TX, Nov. 20, 1919.
KIDDER, MARGOT: Yellow Knife, Canada, Oct. 17, 1948. UBC.
KIDMAN, NICOLE: Hawaii, June 20, 1967.
KIEL, RICHARD: Detroit, MI, Sept. 13, 1939.
KIER, UDO: Koeln, Germany, Oct. 14, 1944.
KILMER, VAL: Los Angeles, Dec. 31, 1959. Juilliard.
KINCAID, ARON (Norman Neale Williams, III): Los Angeles, June 15, 1943. UCLA.
KING, ALAN (Irwin Kniberg): Brooklyn, NY, Dec. 26, 1927.
KING, PERRY: Alliance, OH, Apr. 30, 1948. Yale.
KINGSLEY, BEN (Krishna Bhanji): Snaiton, Yorkshire, England, Dec. 31, 1943.
KINNEAR, GREG: Logansport, IN, June 17, 1963.
KINSKI, NASTASSJA: Berlin, Ger., Jan. 24, 1960.
KIRBY, BRUNO: NYC, Apr. 28, 1949.
KIRK, TOMMY: Louisville, KY, Dec.10 1941.
KIRKLAND, SALLY: NYC, Oct. 31, 1944. Actors Studio.
KITT, EARTHA: North, SC, Jan. 26, 1928.
KLEIN, CHRIS: Hinsdale, IL, March 14, 1979.
KLEIN, ROBERT: NYC, Feb. 8, 1942. Alfred U.
KLINE, KEVIN: St. Louis, MO, Oct. 24, 1947. Juilliard.
KLUGMAN, JACK: Philadelphia, PA, Apr. 27, 1922. Carnegie Tech.

Holly Hunter

KNIGHT, MICHAEL E.: Princeton, NJ, May 7, 1959.
KNIGHT, SHIRLEY: Goessel, KS, July 5, 1937. Wichita U.
KNOX, ELYSE: Hartford, CT, Dec. 14, 1917. Traphagen School.
KOENIG, WALTER: Chicago, IL, Sept. 14, 1936. UCLA.
KOHNER, SUSAN: Los Angeles, Nov. 11, 1936. U Calif.
KORMAN, HARVEY: Chicago, IL, Feb. 15, 1927. Goodman.
KORSMO, CHARLIE: Minneapolis, MN, July, 1978.
KOTEAS, ELIAS: Montreal, Quebec, Canada, 1961. AADA.
KOTTO, YAPHET: NYC, Nov. 15, 1937.
KOZAK, HARLEY JANE: Wilkes-Barre, PA, Jan. 28, 1957. NYU.
KRABBÉ, JEROEN: Amsterdam, The Netherlands, Dec. 5, 1944.
KREUGER, KURT: St. Moritz, Switzerland, July 23, 1917. U London.
KRIGE, ALICE: Upington, So. Africa, June 28, 1955.
KRISTEL, SYLVIA: Amsterdam, The Netherlands, Sept. 28, 1952.
KRISTOFFERSON, KRIS: Brownsville, TX, June 22, 1936, Pomona College.
KRUGER, HARDY: Berlin, Germany, April 12, 1928.

KRUMHOLTZ, DAVID: NYC, May 15, 1978.
KUDROW, LISA: Encino, CA, July 30, 1963.
KURTZ, SWOOSIE: Omaha, NE, Sept. 6, 1944.
KUTCHER, ASHTON (Christopher A. K.): Cedar Rapids, IA, Feb. 7, 1978.
KWAN, NANCY: Hong Kong, May 19, 1939. Royal Ballet.
LaBELLE, PATTI: Philadelphia, PA, May 24, 1944.
LACY, JERRY: Sioux City, IA, Mar. 27, 1936. LACC.
LADD, CHERYL (Stoppelmoor): Huron, SD. July 12, 1951.
LADD, DIANE (Ladner): Meridian, MS, Nov. 29, 1932. Tulane U.
LAHTI, CHRISTINE: Detroit, MI, Apr. 4, 1950. U Mich.
LAKE, RICKI: NYC, Sept. 21, 1968.
LAMAS, LORENZO: Los Angeles, Jan. 28, 1958.
LAMBERT, CHRISTOPHER: NYC, Mar. 29, 1958.
LANDAU, MARTIN: Brooklyn, NY, June 20, 1931. Actors Studio.
LANDRUM, TERI: Enid, OK, 1960.
LANE, ABBE: Brooklyn, NY, Dec. 14, 1935.
LANE, DIANE: NYC, Jan. 22, 1963.
LANE, NATHAN: Jersey City, NJ, Feb. 3, 1956.
LANG, STEPHEN: NYC, July 11, 1952. Swarthmore College.
LANGE, HOPE: Redding Ridge, CT, Nov. 28, 1931. Reed College.
LANGE, JESSICA: Cloquet, MN, Apr. 20, 1949. U Minn.
LANGELLA, FRANK: Bayonne, NJ, Jan. 1, 1940. SyracuseU.
LANSBURY, ANGELA: London, Oct. 16, 1925. London Academy of Music.
LaPAGLIA, ANTHONY: Adelaide, Australia. Jan 31, 1959.
LARROQUETTE, JOHN: New Orleans, LA, Nov. 25, 1947.
LASSER, LOUISE: NYC, Apr. 11, 1939. Brandeis U.
LATIFAH, QUEEN (Dana Owens): East Orange, NJ, 1970.
LAUGHLIN, JOHN: Memphis, TN, Apr. 3.
LAUGHLIN, TOM: Minneapolis, MN, 1938.
LAUPER, CYNDI: Astoria, Queens, NYC, June 20, 1953.
LAURE, CAROLE: Montreal, Canada, Aug. 5, 1951.
LAURIE, HUGH: Oxford, Eng., June 11, 1959.
LAURIE, PIPER (Rosetta Jacobs): Detroit, MI, Jan. 22, 1932.
LAUTER, ED: Long Beach, NY, Oct. 30, 1940.
LAVIN, LINDA: Portland, ME, Oct. 15 1939.
LAW, JOHN PHILLIP: Hollywood, CA, Sept. 7, 1937. Neighborhood Playhouse, U Hawaii.
LAW, JUDE: Lewisham, Eng., Dec. 29, 1972.
LAWRENCE, BARBARA: Carnegie, OK, Feb. 24, 1930. UCLA.
LAWRENCE, CAROL (Laraia): Melrose Park, IL, Sept. 5, 1935.
LAWRENCE, MARTIN: Frankfurt, Germany, Apr. 16, 1965.
LAWRENCE, VICKI: Inglewood, CA, Mar. 26, 1949.

William Hurt

Anjelica Huston

LAWSON, LEIGH: Atherston, England, July 21, 1945. RADA.
LEACHMAN, CLORIS: Des Moines, IA, Apr. 30, 1930. Northwestern U.
LEARY, DENIS: Boston, MA, Aug. 18, 1957.
LEAUD, JEAN-PIERRE: Paris, France, May 5, 1944.
LeBLANC, MATT: Newton, MA, July 25, 1967.
LEE, CHRISTOPHER: London, May 27, 1922. Wellington College.
LEE, MARK: Sydney, Australia, 1958.
LEE, MICHELE (Dusiak): Los Angeles, June 24, 1942. LACC.
LEE, PEGGY (Norma Delores Egstrom): Jamestown, ND, May 26, 1920.
LEE, SHERYL: Augsburg, Germany, Arp. 22, 1967.
LEE, SPIKE (Shelton Lee): Atlanta, GA, Mar. 20, 1957.
LEGROS, JAMES: Minneapolis, MN, Apr. 27, 1962.
LEGUIZAMO, JOHN: Columbia, July 22, 1965. NYU.
LEIBMAN, RON: NYC, Oct. 11, 1937. Ohio Wesleyan.
LEIGH, JANET (Jeanette Helen Morrison): Merced, CA, July 6, 1926. ColofPacific.
LEIGH, JENNIFER JASON: Los Angeles, Feb. 5, 1962.
LeMAT, PAUL: Rahway, NJ, Sept. 22, 1945.

Lauren Hutton

LEMMON, CHRIS: Los Angeles, Jan. 22, 1954.

LEMMON, JACK: Boston, Feb. 8, 1925. Harvard.

LENO, JAY: New Rochelle, NY, Apr. 28, 1950. Emerson College.

LENZ, KAY: Los Angeles, Mar. 4, 1953.

LENZ, RICK: Springfield, IL, Nov. 21, 1939. U Mich.

LEONARD, ROBERT SEAN: Westwood, NJ, Feb. 28, 1969.

LEONI, TÉA (Elizabeth Tea Pantaleoni): NYC, Feb. 25, 1966.

LERNER, MICHAEL: Brooklyn, NY, June 22, 1941.

LESLIE, JOAN (Joan Brodell): Detroit, Jan. 26, 1925. St. Benedict's.

LESTER, MARK: Oxford, England, July 11, 1958.

LETO, JARED: Bossier City, LA, Dec. 26, 1971.

LEVELS, CALVIN: Cleveland. OH, Sept. 30, 1954. CCC.

LEVIN, RACHEL: NYC, 1954. Goddard College.

LEVINE, JERRY: New Brunswick, NJ, Mar. 12, 1957. Boston U.

LEVY, EUGENE: Hamilton, Canada, Dec. 17, 1946. McMasterU.

LEWIS, CHARLOTTE: London, Aug.7, 1967.

LEWIS, GEOFFREY: San Diego, CA, Jan. 1, 1935.

LEWIS, JERRY (Joseph Levitch): Newark, NJ, Mar. 16, 1926.

LEWIS, JULIETTE: Los Angeles CA, June 21, 1973.

LIGON, TOM: New Orleans, LA, Sept. 10, 1945.

LILLARD, MATTHEW: Lansing, MI, Jan. 24, 1970.

LINCOLN, ABBEY (Anna Marie Woolridge): Chicago, IL, Aug. 6, 1930.

LINDEN, HAL: Bronx, NY, Mar. 20, 1931. City College of NY.

LINDO, DELROY: London, Nov. 18, 1952.

LINDSAY, ROBERT: Ilketson, Derbyshire, England, Dec. 13, 1951, RADA.

LINN-BAKER, MARK: St. Louis, MO, June 17, 1954, Yale.

LINNEY, LAURA: New York, NY, Feb. 5, 1964.

LIOTTA, RAY: Newark, NJ, Dec. 18, 1955. UMiami.

LISI, VIRNA: Rome, Nov. 8, 1937.

LITHGOW, JOHN: Rochester, NY, Oct. 19, 1945. Harvard.

LIU, LUCY: Queens, NY, Dec. 2, 1967.

LL COOL J (James Todd Smith): Queens, NY, Jan. 14, 1968.

LLOYD, CHRISTOPHER: Stamford, CT, Oct. 22, 1938.

LLOYD, EMILY: London, Sept. 29, 1970.

LOCKE, SONDRA: Shelbyville, TN, May, 28, 1947.

LOCKHART, JUNE: NYC, June 25, 1925. Westlake School.

LOCKWOOD, GARY: Van Nuys, CA, Feb. 21, 1937.

LOGGIA, ROBERT: Staten Island, NY, Jan. 3, 1930. UMo.

LOLLOBRIGIDA, GINA: Subiaco, Italy, July 4, 1927. Rome Academy of Fine Arts.

LOM, HERBERT: Prague, Czechoslovakia, Jan. 9, 1917. Prague U.

LOMEZ, CELINE: Montreal, Canada, May 11, 1953.

LONE, JOHN: Hong Kong, Oct 13, 1952. AADA.

LONG, NIA: Brooklyn, NY, Oct. 30, 1970.

LONG, SHELLEY: Ft. Wayne, IN, Aug. 23, 1949. Northwestern U.

LOPEZ, JENNIFER: Bronx, NY, July 24, 1970.

LOPEZ, PERRY: NYC, July 22, 1931. NYU.

LORDS, TRACY (Nora Louise Kuzma): Steubenville, OH, May 7, 1968.

LOREN, SOPHIA (Sophia Scicolone): Rome, Italy, Sept. 20, 1934.

LOUIS-DREYFUS, JULIA: NYC, Jan. 13, 1961.

LOUISE, TINA (Blacker): NYC, Feb. 11, 1934, Miami U.

LOVE, COURTNEY (Love Michelle Harrison): San Francisco, July 9, 1965.

LOVETT, LYLE: Klein, TX, Nov. 1, 1957.

LOVITZ, JON: Tarzana, CA, July 21, 1957.

LOWE, CHAD: Dayton, OH, Jan. 15, 1968.

LOWE, ROB: Charlottesville, VA, Mar. 17, 1964.

LOWITSCH, KLAUS: Berlin, Apr. 8, 1936, Vienna Academy.

LUCAS, LISA: Arizona, 1961.

LUCKINBILL, LAURENCE: Fort Smith, AK, Nov. 21, 1934.

LUFT, LORNA: Los Angeles, Nov. 21, 1952.

LULU (Marie Lawrie): Glasgow, Scotland, Nov. 3, 1948.

LUNA, BARBARA: NYC, Mar. 2, 1939.

LUNDGREN, DOLPH: Stockolm, Sweden, Nov. 3, 1959. Royal Inst.

LuPONE, PATTI: Northport, NY, Apr. 21, 1949, Juilliard.

LYDON, JAMES: Harrington Park, NJ, May 30, 1923.

LYNCH, KELLY: Minneapolis, MN, Jan. 31, 1959.

LYNLEY, CAROL (Jones): NYC, Feb. 13, 1942.

LYON, SUE: Davenport, IA, July 10, 1946.

LYONNE, NATASHA: NYC, 1978.

MacARTHUR, JAMES: Los Angeles, Dec. 8, 1937. Harvard.

MACCHIO, RALPH: Huntington, NY, Nov. 4, 1961.

MacCORKINDALE, SIMON: Cambridge, England, Feb. 12, 1953.

MacDOWELL, ANDIE (Rose Anderson MacDowell): Gaffney, SC, Apr. 21, 1958.

MacGINNIS, NIALL: Dublin, Ireland, Mar. 29, 1913. Dublin U.

MacGRAW, ALI: NYC, Apr. 1, 1938. Wellesley.

MacLACHLAN, KYLE: Yakima, WA, Feb. 22, 1959. UWa.

MacLAINE, SHIRLEY (Beaty): Richmond, VA, Apr. 24, 1934.

MacLEOD, GAVIN: Mt. Kisco, NY, Feb. 28, 1931.

MacNAUGHTON, ROBERT: NYC, Dec. 19, 1966.

MACNEE, PATRICK: London, Feb. 1922.

MacNICOL, PETER: Dallas, TX, Apr. 10, 1954. UMN.

MacPHERSON, ELLE: Sydney, Australia, 1965.

MacVITTIE, BRUCE: Providence, RI, Oct. 14, 1956. BostonU.

MACY, W. H. (William): Miami, FL, Mar. 13, 1950. Goddard College.

MADIGAN, AMY: Chicago, IL, Sept. 11, 1950. Marquette U.

MADONNA (Madonna Louise Veronica Cicone): Bay City, MI, Aug. 16, 1958. UMi.

MADSEN, MICHAEL: Chicago, IL, Sept. 25, 1958.

MADSEN, VIRGINIA: Winnetka, IL, Sept. 11, 1963.

MAGNUSON, ANN: Charleston, WV, Jan. 4, 1956.

MAGUIRE, TOBEY: Santa Monica, CA, June 27, 1975.

MAHARIS, GEORGE: Astoria, NY, Sept. 1, 1928. Actors Studio.

MAHONEY, JOHN: Manchester, England, June 20, 1940, WUIll.

MAILER, STEPHEN: NYC, Mar. 10, 1966. NYU.

MAJORS, LEE: Wyandotte, MI, Apr. 23, 1940. E. Ky. State College.

MAKEPEACE, CHRIS: Toronto, Canada, Apr. 22, 1964.

MAKO (Mako Iwamatsu): Kobe, Japan, Dec. 10, 1933. Pratt.

MALDEN, KARL (Mladen Sekulovich): Gary, IN, Mar. 22, 1914.

MALKOVICH, JOHN: Christopher, IL, Dec. 9, 1953, IllStateU.

MALONE, DOROTHY: Chicago, IL, Jan. 30, 1925.

MANN, TERRENCE: KY, 1945. NCSchl Arts.

MANOFF, DINAH: NYC, Jan. 25, 1958. CalArts.

MANTEGNA, JOE: Chicago, IL, Nov. 13, 1947. Goodman Theatre.

MANZ, LINDA: NYC, 1961.

MARAIS, JEAN: Cherbourg, France, Dec. 11, 1913, St. Germain.

MARCEAU, SOPHIE (Maupu): Paris, Nov. 17, 1966.

MARCOVICCI, ANDREA: NYC, Nov. 18, 1948.

MARGULIES, JULIANNA: Spring Valley, NY, June 8, 1966.

MARIN, CHEECH (Richard): Los Angeles, July 13, 1946.

MARIN, JACQUES: Paris, France, Sept. 9, 1919. Conservatoire National.

MARINARO, ED: NYC, Mar. 31, 1950. Cornell.

MARS, KENNETH: Chicago, IL, 1936.

MARSDEN, JAMES: Stillwater, OK, Sept. 18, 1973.

MARSH, JEAN: London, England, July 1, 1934.

MARSHALL, KEN: NYC, 1953. Juilliard.

MARSHALL, PENNY: Bronx, NY, Oct. 15, 1942. UN. Mex.

MARSHALL, WILLIAM: Gary, IN, Aug. 19, 1924. NYU.

MARTIN, ANDREA: Portland, ME, Jan. 15, 1947.

MARTIN, DICK: Battle Creek, MI Jan. 30, 1923.

MARTIN, GEORGE N.: NYC, Aug. 15, 1929.

MARTIN, MILLICENT: Romford, England, June 8, 1934.

MARTIN, PAMELA SUE: Westport, CT, Jan. 15, 1953.

MARTIN, STEVE: Waco, TX, Aug. 14, 1945. UCLA.

MARTIN, TONY (Alfred Norris): Oakland, CA, Dec. 25, 1913. St. Mary's College.

MASON, MARSHA: St. Louis, MO, Apr. 3, 1942. Webster College.

Amy Irving

Samuel L. Jackson

Ashley Judd

Diane Keaton

MASSEN, OSA: Copenhagen, Denmark, Jan. 13, 1916.

MASTERS, BEN: Corvallis, OR, May 6, 1947. UOr.

MASTERSON, MARY STUART: Los Angeles, June 28, 1966, NYU.

MASTERSON, PETER: Angleton, TX, June 1, 1934. Rice U.

MASTRANTONIO, MARY ELIZABETH: Chicago, IL, Nov. 17, 1958. UIll.

MASUR, RICHARD: NYC, Nov. 20, 1948.

MATHESON, TIM: Glendale, CA, Dec. 31, 1947. CalState.

MATHIS, SAMANTHA: NYC, May 12, 1970.

MATLIN, MARLEE: Morton Grove, IL, Aug. 24, 1965.

MATTHEWS, BRIAN: Philadelphia, Jan. 24. 1953. St. Olaf.

MAY, ELAINE (Berlin): Philadelphia, Apr. 21, 1932.

MAYO, VIRGINIA (Virginia Clara Jones): St. Louis, MO, Nov. 30, 1920.

MAYRON, MELANIE: Philadelphia, PA, Oct. 20, 1952. AADA.

MAZURSKY, PAUL: Brooklyn, NY, Apr. 25, 1930. Bklyn College.

MAZZELLO, JOSEPH: Rhinebeck, NY, Sept. 21, 1983.

McCALLUM, DAVID: Scotland, Sept. 19, 1933. Chapman College.

McCAMBRIDGE, MERCEDES: Jolliet, IL, Mar. 17, 1918. Mundelein College.

McCARTHY, ANDREW: NYC, Nov. 29, 1962, NYU.

McCARTHY, KEVIN: Seattle, WA, Feb. 15, 1914. Minn. U.

McCARTNEY, PAUL: Liverpool, Eng- land, June 18, 1942.

McCLANAHAN, RUE: Healdton, OK, Feb. 21, 1934.

McCLORY, SEAN: Dublin, Ireland, Mar. 8, 1924. U Galway.

McCLURE, MARC: San Mateo, CA, Mar. 31, 1957.

McCLURG, EDIE: Kansas City, MO, July 23, 1950.

McCOWEN, ALEC: Tunbridge Wells, England, May 26, 1925. RADA.

McCRANE, PAUL: Philadelphia, PA, Jan. 19. 1961.

McCRARY, DARIUS: Walnut, CA, May 1, 1976.

McDERMOTT, DYLAN: Waterbury, CT, Oct. 26, 1962. Neighborhood Playhouse.

McDONALD, CHRISTOPHER: NYC, 1955.

McDONNELL, MARY: Wilkes Barre, PA, Apr. 28, 1952.

McDORMAND, FRANCES: Illinois, June 23, 1957.

McDOWELL, MALCOLM (Taylor): Leeds, England, June 19, 1943. LAMDA.

McELHONE, NATASCHA (Natasha Taylor): London, Mar. 23, 1971.

McENERY, PETER: Walsall, England, Feb. 21, 1940.

McENTIRE, REBA: McAlester, OK, Mar. 28, 1955. SoutheasternStU.

McGAVIN, DARREN: Spokane, WA, May 7, 1922. College of Pacific.

McGILL, EVERETT: Miami Beach, FL, Oct. 21, 1945.

McGILLIS, KELLY: Newport Beach, CA, July 9, 1957. Juilliard.

McGINLEY, JOHN C.: NYC, Aug. 3, 1959. NYU.

McGOOHAN, PATRICK: NYC, Mar. 19, 1928.

McGOVERN, ELIZABETH: Evanston, IL. July 18, 1961. Juilliard.

McGOVERN, MAUREEN: Youngstown, OH, July 27, 1949.

McGREGOR, EWAN: Perth, Scotland, March 31, 1971

McGUIRE, BIFF: New Haven, CT, Oct. 25. 1926. Mass. Stale College.

McGUIRE, DOROTHY: Omaha, NE, June 14, 1918.

McHATTIE, STEPHEN: Antigonish, NS, Feb. 3. Acadia U AADA.

McKAY, GARDNER: NYC, June 10, 1932. Comell.

McKEAN, MICHAEL: NYC, Oct. 17, 1947.

McKEE, LONETTE: Detroit, MI, July 22, 1955.

McKELLEN, IAN: Burnley, England, May 25, 1939.

McKENNA, VIRGINIA: London, June 7, 1931.

McKEON, DOUG: Pompton Plains, NJ, June 10, 1966.

McKERN, LEO: Sydney, Australia, Mar. 16, 1920.

McKUEN, ROD: Oakland, CA, Apr. 29, 1933.

McLERIE, ALLYN ANN: Grand Mere, Canada, Dec. 1, 1926.

McMAHON, ED: Detroit, MI, Mar. 6, 1923.

McNAIR, BARBARA: Chicago, IL, Mar. 4, 1939. UCLA.

McNAMARA, WILLIAM: Dallas, TX, Mar. 31, 1965.

McNICHOL, KRISTY: Los Angeles. CA, Sept. 11, 1962.

McQUEEN, ARMELIA: North Carolina, Jan. 6, 1952. Bklyn Consv.

McQUEEN, CHAD: Los Angeles, CA, Dec. 28, 1960. Actors Studio.

McRANEY, GERALD: Collins, MS, Aug. 19, 1948.

McSHANE, IAN: Blackburn, England, Sept. 29, 1942. RADA.

McTEER, JANET: York, England, 1961.

MEADOWS, JAYNE (formerly Jayne Cotter): Wuchang, China, Sept. 27, 1924. St. Margaret's.

MEANEY, COLM: Dublin, May 30, 1953.

MEARA, ANNE: Brooklyn, NY, Sept. 20, 1929.

MEAT LOAF (Marvin Lee Aday): Dallas, TX, Sept. 27, 1947.

MEDWIN, MICHAEL: London, 1925. Instut Fischer.

MEKKA, EDDIE: Worcester, MA, June 14, 1952. Boston Cons.

MELATO, MARIANGELA: Milan, Italy, 1941. Milan Theatre Acad.

MEREDITH, LEE (Judi Lee Sauls): Oct. 22, 1947. AADA.

MERKERSON, S. EPATHA: Saganaw, MI, Nov. 28, 1952. Wayne St. Univ.

MERRILL, DINA (Nedinia Hutton): NYC, Dec. 29, 1925. AADA.

MESSING, DEBRA: Brooklyn, NY, Aug. 15, 1968.

METCALF, LAURIE: Edwardsville, IL, June 16, 1955., IIIStU.

Sally Kellerman

Val Kilmer

Ben Kingsley

Greg Kinnear

METZLER, JIM: Oneonda, NY, June 23. Dartmouth.

MICHELL, KEITH: Adelaide, Australia, Dec. 1, 1926.

MIDLER, BETTE: Honolulu, HI, Dec. 1, 1945.

MILANO, ALYSSA: Brooklyn, NY, Dec. 19, 1972.

MILES, JOANNA: Nice, France, Mar. 6, 1940.

MILES, SARAH: Ingatestone, England, Dec. 31, 1941. RADA.

MILES, SYLVIA: NYC, Sept. 9, 1934. Actors Studio.

MILES, VERA (Ralston)**:** Boise City, OK, Aug. 23, 1929. UCLA.

MILLER, ANN (Lucille Ann Collier): Chireno, TX, Apr. 12, 1919. Lawler Professional School.

MILLER, BARRY: Los Angeles, CA, Feb. 6, 1958.

MILLER, DICK: NYC, Dec. 25, 1928.

MILLER, JASON: Long Island City, NY, Apr. 22, 1939. Catholic U.

MILLER, JONNY LEE: Surrey, England, Nov. 15, 1972.

MILLER, LINDA: NYC, Sept. 16, 1942. Catholic U.

MILLER, PENELOPE ANN: Santa Monica, CA, Jan. 13, 1964.

MILLER, REBECCA: Roxbury, CT, 1962. Yale.

MILLS, DONNA: Chicago, IL, Dec. 11, 1945. UII.

MILLS, HAYLEY: London, Apr. 18, 1946. Elmhurst School.

MILLS, JOHN: Suffolk, England, Feb. 22, 1908.

MILLS, JULIET: London, Nov. 21, 1941.

MILNER, MARTIN: Detroit, MI, Dec. 28, 1931.

MIMIEUX, YVETTE: Los Angeles, Jan. 8, 1941. Hollywood High.

MINNELLI, LIZA: Los Angeles, Mar. 19, 1946.

MIOU-MIOU (Sylvette Henry): Paris, France, Feb. 22, 1950.

MIRREN, HELEN (Ilynea Mironoff)**:** London, July 26, 1946.

MITCHELL, JAMES: Sacramento, CA, Feb. 29, 1920. LACC.

MITCHELL, JOHN CAMERON: El Paso, TX, Apr. 21, 1963. NorthwesternU.

MITCHUM, JAMES: Los Angeles, CA, May 8, 1941.

MODINE, MATTHEW: Loma Linda, CA, Mar. 22, 1959.

MOFFAT, DONALD: Plymouth, England, Dec. 26, 1930. RADA.

MOFFETT, D. W.: Highland Park, IL, Oct. 26, 1954. Stanford U.

MOHR, JAY: New Jersey, Aug. 23, 1971.

MOKAE, ZAKES: Johannesburg, So. Africa, Aug. 5, 1935. RADA.

MOLINA, ALFRED: London, May 24, 1953. Guildhall.

MOLL, RICHARD: Pasadena, CA, Jan. 13, 1943.

MONK, DEBRA: Middletown, OH, Feb. 27, 1949.

MONTALBAN, RICARDO: Mexico City, Nov. 25, 1920.

MONTENEGRO, FERNADA (Arlete Pinheiro): Rio de Janiero, Brazil, 1929.

MONTGOMERY, BELINDA: Winnipeg, Canada, July 23, 1950.

MOODY, RON: London, Jan. 8, 1924. London U.

MOOR, BILL: Toledo, OH, July 13, 1931. Northwestern.

MOORE, CONSTANCE: Sioux City, IA, Jan. 18, 1919.

MOORE, DEMI (Guines): Roswell, NM, Nov. 11, 1962.

MOORE, DICK: Los Angeles, Sept. 12, 1925.

MOORE, DUDLEY: Dagenham, Essex, England, Apr. 19, 1935.

MOORE, JULIANNE (Julie Anne Smith): Fayetteville, NC, Dec. 30, 1960.

MOORE, KIERON: County Cork, Ireland, 1925. St. Mary's College.

MOORE, MARY TYLER: Brooklyn, NY, Dec. 29, 1936.

MOORE, ROGER: London, Oct. 14, 1927. RADA.

MOORE, TERRY (Helen Koford): Los Angeles, Jan. 7, 1929.

MORALES, ESAI: Brooklyn, NY, Oct. 1, 1962.

MORANIS, RICK: Toronto, Canada, Apr. 18, 1954.

MOREAU, JEANNE: Paris, France, Jan. 23, 1928.

MORENO, RITA (Rosita Alverio): Humacao, P.R., Dec. 11, 1931.

MORGAN, HARRY (HENRY) (Harry Bratsburg): Detroit, Apr. 10, 1915. U Chicago.

MORGAN, MICHELE (Simone Roussel): Paris, France, Feb. 29, 1920. Paris Dramatic School.

MORIARTY, CATHY: Bronx, NY, Nov. 29, 1960.

MORIARTY, MICHAEL: Detroit, MI, Apr. 5, 1941. Dartmouth.

MORISON, PATRICIA: NYC, Mar. 19, 1915.

MORITA, NORIYUKI "PAT": Isleton, CA, June 28, 1932.

MORRIS, GARRETT: New Orleans, LA, Feb. 1, 1937.

MORRIS, HOWARD: NYC, Sept. 4, 1919. NYU.

MORROW, ROB: New Rochelle, NY, Sept. 21, 1962.

MORSE, DAVID: Hamilton, MA, Oct. 11, 1953.

MORSE, ROBERT: Newton, MA, May 18, 1931.

MORTENSEN, VIGGO: New York, NY, 1958.

MORTON, JOE: NYC, Oct. 18, 1947. Hofstra U.

MORTON, SAMANTHA: Nottingham, England, 1977.

MOSES, WILLIAM: Los Angeles, Nov. 17, 1959.

MOSS, CARRIE-ANNE: Vancouver, BC, Canada, Aug. 21, 1967.

MOSTEL, JOSH: NYC, Dec. 21, 1946. Brandeis U.

MOUCHET, CATHERINE: Paris, France, 1959. Ntl. Consv.

MUELLER-STAHL, ARMIN: Tilsit, East Prussia, Dec. 17, 1930.

MULDAUR, DIANA: NYC, Aug. 19, 1938. Sweet Briar College.

MULGREW, KATE: Dubuque, IA, Apr. 29, 1955. NYU.

MULHERN, MATT: Philadelphia, PA, July 21, 1960. Rutgers Univ.

MULL, MARTIN: N. Ridgefield, OH, Aug. 18, 1941. RISch. of Design.

MULRONEY, DERMOT: Alexandria, VA, Oct. 31, 1963. Northwestern.

MUMY, BILL (Charles William Mumy, Jr.): San Gabriel, CA, Feb. 1, 1954.

MURPHY, DONNA: Queens, NY, March 7, 1958.

Robert Klein

Jude Law

Denis Leary

Téa Leoni

MURPHY, EDDIE: Brooklyn, NY, Apr. 3, 1961.

MURPHY, MICHAEL: Los Angeles, CA, May 5, 1938. UAz.

MURRAY, BILL: Wilmette, IL, Sept. 21, 1950. Regis College.

MURRAY, DON: Hollywood, CA, July 31, 1929.

MUSANTE, TONY: Bridgeport, CT, June 30, 1936. Oberlin College.

MYERS, MIKE: Scarborough, Canada, May 25, 1963.

NABORS, JIM: Sylacauga, GA, June 12, 1932.

NADER, GEORGE: Pasadena, CA, Oct. 19, 1921. Occidental College.

NADER, MICHAEL: Los Angeles, CA, 1945.

NAMATH, JOE: Beaver Falls, PA, May 31, 1943. UAla.

NAUGHTON, DAVID: Hartford, CT, Feb. 13, 1951.

NAUGHTON, JAMES: Middletown, CT, Dec. 6, 1945.

NEAL, PATRICIA: Packard, KY, Jan. 20, 1926. Northwestern U.

NEESON, LIAM: Ballymena, Northern Ireland, June 7, 1952.

NEFF, HILDEGARDE (Hildegard Knef): Ulm, Germany, Dec. 28, 1925. Berlin Art Acad.

NEILL, SAM: No. Ireland, Sept. 14, 1947. U Canterbury.

NELL, NATHALIE: Paris, France, Oct. 1950.

NELLIGAN, KATE: London, Ont., Canada, Mar. 16, 1951. U Toronto.

NELSON, BARRY (Robert Nielsen): Oakland, CA, Apr. 16, 1920.

NELSON, CRAIG T.: Spokane, WA, Apr. 4, 1946.

NELSON, DAVID: NYC, Oct. 24, 1936. USC.

NELSON, JUDD: Portland, ME, Nov. 28, 1959, Haverford College.

NELSON, LORI (Dixie Kay Nelson): Santa Fe, NM, Aug. 15, 1933.

NELSON, TRACY: Santa Monica, CA, Oct. 25, 1963.

NELSON, WILLIE: Abbott, TX, Apr. 30, 1933.

NEMEC, CORIN: Little Rock, AK, Nov. 5, 1971.

NERO, FRANCO (Francisco Spartanero): Parma, Italy, Nov. 23, 1941.

NESMITH, MICHAEL: Houston, TX, Dec. 30, 1942.

NETTLETON, LOIS: Oak Park, IL, 1931. Actors Studio.

NEUWIRTH, BEBE: Dec. 31, 1958.

NEWHART, BOB: Chicago, IL, Sept. 5, 1929. Loyola U.

NEWMAN, BARRY: Boston, MA, Nov. 7, 1938. Brandeis U.

NEWMAN, LARAINE: Los Angeles, Mar. 2, 1952.

NEWMAN, NANETTE: Northampton, England, 1934.

NEWMAN, PAUL: Cleveland, OH, Jan. 26, 1925. Yale.

NEWMAR, JULIE (Newmeyer): Los Angeles, Aug. 16, 1933.

NEWTON, THANDIE: Zambia, 1972.

NEWTON-JOHN, OLIVIA: Cambridge, England, Sept. 26, 1948.

NGUYEN, DUSTIN: Saigon, Vietnam, Sept. 17, 1962.

NICHOLAS, DENISE: Detroit, MI, July 12, 1945.

NICHOLAS, PAUL: London, 1945.

NICHOLS, NICHELLE: Robbins, IL, Dec. 28, 1933.

NICHOLSON, JACK: Neptune, NJ, Apr. 22, 1937.

NICKERSON, DENISE: NYC, 1959.

NICOL, ALEX: Ossining, NY, Jan. 20, 1919. Actors Studio.

NIELSEN, BRIGITTE: Denmark, July 15, 1963.

NIELSEN, LESLIE: Regina, Saskatchewan. Canada, Feb. 11, 1926. Neighborhood Playhouse.

NIMOY, LEONARD: Boston, MA, Mar. 26, 1931. Boston College, Antioch College.

NIXON, CYNTHIA: NYC, Apr. 9, 1966. Columbia U.

NOBLE, JAMES: Dallas, TX, Mar. 5, 1922, SMU.

NOIRET, PHILIPPE: Lille, France, Oct. 1, 1930.

NOLAN, KATHLEEN: St. Louis, MO, Sept. 27, 1933. Neighborhood Playhouse.

NOLTE, NICK: Omaha, NE, Feb. 8, 1940. Pasadena City College.

NORRIS, BRUCE: Houston, TX, May 16, 1960. Northwestern.

NORRIS, CHRISTOPHER: NYC, Oct. 7, 1943. Lincoln Square Acad.

NORRIS, CHUCK (Carlos Ray): Ryan, OK, Mar. 10, 1940.

NORTH, HEATHER: Pasadena, CA, Dec. 13, 1950. Actors Workshop.

NORTH, SHEREE (Dawn Bethel): Los Angeles. Jan. 17, 1933. Hollywood High.

NORTHAM, JEREMY: Cambridge, Eng., Dec. 1, 1961.

NORTON, EDWARD: Boston, MA, Aug. 18, 1969.

NORTON, KEN: Jacksonville, Il, Aug. 9, 1945.

NOSEWORTHY, JACK: Lynn, MA, Dec. 21, 1969.

NOURI, MICHAEL: Washington, DC, Dec. 9, 1945.

NOVAK, KIM (Marilyn Novak): Chicago, IL, Feb. 13, 1933. LACC.

NOVELLO, DON: Ashtabula, OH, Jan. 1, 1943. UDayton.

NUYEN, FRANCE (Vannga): Marseilles, France, July 31, 1939. Beaux Arts School.

O'BRIAN, HUGH (Hugh J. Krampe): Rochester, N,. Apr. 19, 1928. Cincinnati U.

O'BRIEN, CLAY: Ray, AZ, May 6, 1961.

O'BRIEN, MARGARET (Angela Maxine O'Brien): Los Angeles, Jan. 15, 1937.

O'BRIEN, VIRGINIA: Los Angeles, Apr. 18, 1919.

O'CONNELL, JERRY (Jeremiah O'Connell): New York, NY, Feb. 17, 1974.

O'CONNOR, CARROLL: Bronx, NY, Aug. 2, 1924. Dublin National Univ.

O'CONNOR, DONALD: Chicago, IL, Aug. 28, 1925.

O'CONNOR, GLYNNIS: NYC, Nov. 19, 1955. NYSU.

O'DONNELL, CHRIS: Winetka, IL, June 27, 1970.

O'DONNELL, ROSIE: Commack, NY, March 21, 1961.

O'HARA, CATHERINE: Toronto, Canada, Mar. 4, 1954.

O'HARA, MAUREEN (Maureen Fitz-Simons): Dublin, Ireland, Aug. 17, 1920.

O'HERLIHY, DAN: Wexford, Ireland, May 1, 1919. National U.

O'KEEFE, MICHAEL: Larchmont, NY, Apr. 24, 1955. NYU, AADA.

OLDMAN, GARY: New Cross, South London, England, Mar. 21, 1958.

OLIN, KEN: Chicago, IL, July 30, 1954. UPa.

OLIN, LENA: Stockholm, Sweden, Mar. 22, 1955.

OLMOS, EDWARD JAMES: Los Angeles, Feb. 24, 1947. CSLA.

O'LOUGHLIN, GERALD S.: NYC, Dec. 23, 1921. U Rochester.

OLSON, JAMES: Evanston, IL, Oct. 8, 1930.

OLSON, NANCY: Milwaukee, WI, July 14, 1928. UCLA.

OLYPHANT, TIMOTHY: HI, May 20, 1968.

O'NEAL, GRIFFIN: Los Angeles, 1965.

O'NEAL, RON: Utica, NY, Sept. 1, 1937. Ohio State.

O'NEAL, RYAN: Los Angeles, Apr. 20, 1941.

O'NEAL, TATUM: Los Angeles, Nov. 5, 1963.

O'NEIL, TRICIA: Shreveport, LA, Mar. 11, 1945. Baylor U.

O'NEILL, ED: Youngstown, OH, Apr. 12, 1946.

O'NEILL, JENNIFER: Rio de Janeiro, Feb. 20, 1949. Neighborhood Playhouse.

ONTKEAN, MICHAEL: Vancouver, B.C., Canada, Jan. 24, 1946.

O'QUINN, TERRY: Newbury, MI, July 15, 1952.

ORBACH, JERRY: Bronx, NY, Oct. 20, 1935.

O'SHEA, MILO: Dublin, Ireland, June 2, 1926.

OSMENT, HALEY JOEL: Los Angeles, Apr. 10, 1988.

O'TOOLE, ANNETTE (Toole): Houston, TX, Apr. 1, 1953. UCLA.

O'TOOLE, PETER: Connemara, Ireland, Aug. 2, 1932. RADA.

OVERALL, PARK: Nashville, TN, Mar. 15, 1957. Tusculum College.

OWEN, CLIVE: Coventry, Eng., 1965.

OZ, FRANK (Oznowicz): Hereford, England, May 25, 1944.

PACINO, AL: NYC, Apr. 25, 1940.

PACULA, JOANNA: Tamaszow Lubelski, Poland, Jan. 2, 1957. Polish Natl. Theatre Sch.

PAGET, DEBRA (Debralee Griffin): Denver, Aug. 19, 1933.

PAIGE, JANIS (Donna Mae Jaden): Tacoma, WA, Sept. 16, 1922.

PALANCE, JACK (Walter Palanuik): Lattimer, PA, Feb. 18, 1920. UNC.

PALIN, MICHAEL: Sheffield, Yorkshire, England, May 5, 1943. Oxford.

PALMER, BETSY: East Chicago, IN, Nov. 1, 1926. DePaul U.

PALMER, GREGG (Palmer Lee): San Francisco, Jan. 25, 1927. U Utah.

PALMINTERI, CHAZZ (Calogero Lorenzo Palminteri): New York, NY, May 15, 1952.

PALTROW, GWYNETH: Los Angeles, Sept. 28, 1972

PANEBIANCO, RICHARD: NYC, 1971.

PANKIN, STUART: Philadelphia, Apr. 8, 1946.

PANTOLIANO, JOE: Jersey City, NJ, Sept. 12, 1954.

PAPAS, IRENE: Chiliomodion, Greece, Mar. 9, 1929.

PAQUIN, ANNA: Winnipeg, Manitoba, Canada, July, 24, 1982.

PARÉ, MICHAEL: Brooklyn, NY, Oct. 9, 1959.

PARKER, COREY: NYC, July 8, 1965. NYU.

PARKER, ELEANOR: Cedarville, OH, June 26, 1922. Pasadena Playhouse.

John Leguizamo

Jared Leto

Nia Long

PARKER, FESS: Fort Worth, TX, Aug. 16, 1925. USC.

PARKER, JAMESON: Baltimore, MD, Nov. 18, 1947. Beloit College.

PARKER, JEAN (Mae Green): Deer Lodge, MT, Aug. 11, 1912.

PARKER, MARY-LOUISE: Ft. Jackson, SC, Aug. 2, 1964. Bard College.

PARKER, NATHANIEL: London, 1963.

PARKER, SARAH JESSICA: Nelsonville, OH, Mar. 25, 1965.

PARKER, SUZY (Cecelia Parker): San Antonio, TX, Oct. 28, 1933.

PARKER, TREY: Auburn, AL, May 30, 1972.

PARKINS, BARBARA: Vancouver, Canada, May 22, 1943.

PARKS, MICHAEL: Corona, CA, Apr. 4, 1938.

PARSONS, ESTELLE: Lynn, MA, Nov. 20, 1927. Boston U.

PARTON, DOLLY: Sevierville, TN, Jan. 19, 1946.

PATINKIN, MANDY: Chicago, IL, Nov. 30, 1952. Juilliard.

PATRIC, JASON: NYC, June 17, 1966.

PATRICK, DENNIS: Philadelphia, Mar. 14, 1918.

PATTERSON, LEE: Vancouver, Canada, Mar. 31, 1929. Ontario College.

PATTON, WILL: Charleston, SC, June 14, 1954.

PAULIK, JOHAN: Prague, Czech., 1975.

PAVAN, MARISA (Marisa Pierangeli): Cagliari, Sardinia, June 19, 1932. Torquado Tasso College.

PAXTON, BILL: Fort Worth, TX, May. 17, 1955.

PAYMER, DAVID: Long Island, NY, Aug. 30, 1954.

PAYS, AMANDA: Berkshire, England, June 6, 1959.

PEACH, MARY: Durban, S. Africa, 1934.

PEARCE, GUY: Ely, England, Oct. 5, 1967.

PEARSON, BEATRICE: Dennison, TX, July 27, 1920.

PECK, GREGORY: La Jolla, CA, Apr. 5, 1916. U Calif.

PEET, AMANDA: NYC, Jan. 11, 1972.

PEÑA, ELIZABETH: Cuba, Sept. 23, 1961.

PENDLETON, AUSTIN: Warren, OH, Mar. 27, 1940. Yale U.

PENHALL, BRUCE: Balboa, CA, Aug. 17, 1960.

PENN, SEAN: Burbank, CA, Aug. 17, 1960.

PEREZ, JOSE: NYC, 1940.

PEREZ, ROSIE: Brooklyn, NY, Sept. 6, 1964.

PERKINS, ELIZABETH: Queens, NY, Nov. 18, 1960. Goodman School.

PERKINS, MILLIE: Passaic, NJ, May 12, 1938.

PERLMAN, RHEA: Brooklyn, NY, Mar. 31, 1948.

PERLMAN, RON: NYC, Apr. 13, 1950. UMn.

PERREAU, GIGI (Ghislaine): Los Angeles, Feb. 6, 1941.

PERRINE, VALERIE: Galveston, TX, Sept. 3, 1943. U Ariz.

PERRY, LUKE (Coy Luther Perry, III): Fredricktown, OH, Oct. 11, 1966.

PESCI, JOE: Newark, NJ. Feb. 9, 1943.

PESCOW, DONNA: Brooklyn, NY, Mar. 24, 1954.

PETERS, BERNADETTE (Lazzara): Jamaica, NY, Feb. 28, 1948.

PETERS, BROCK: NYC, July 2, 1927. CCNY.

PETERSEN, PAUL: Glendale, CA, Sept. 23, 1945. Valley College.

PETERSEN, WILLIAM: Chicago, IL, Feb. 21, 1953.

PETERSON, CASSANDRA: Colorado Springs, CO, Sept. 17, 1951.

PETTET, JOANNA: London, Nov. 16, 1944. Neighborhood Playhouse.

PETTY, LORI: Chattanooga, TN, 1964.

PFEIFFER, MICHELLE: Santa Ana, CA, Apr. 29, 1958.

PHILLIPPE, RYAN (Matthew Phillippe): New Castle, DE, Sept. 10, 1975.

PHILLIPS, LOU DIAMOND: Phillipines, Feb. 17, 1962, UTx.

PHILLIPS, MacKENZIE: Alexandria, VA, Nov. 10, 1959.

PHILLIPS, MICHELLE (Holly Gilliam): Long Beach, CA, June 4, 1944.

PHILLIPS, SIAN: Bettws, Wales, May 14, 1934. UWales.

PHOENIX, JOAQUIN: Puerto Rico, Oct. 28, 1974.

PICARDO, ROBERT: Philadelphia, PA, Oct. 27, 1953. Yale.

PICERNI, PAUL: NYC, Dec. 1, 1922. Loyola U.

PIDGEON, REBECCA: Cambridge, MA, 1963.

PIERCE, DAVID HYDE: Saratoga Springs, NY, Apr. 3, 1959.

PIGOTT-SMITH, TIM: Rugby, England, May 13, 1946.

PINCHOT, BRONSON: NYC, May 20, 1959. Yale.

PINE, PHILLIP: Hanford, CA, July 16, 1920. Actors' Lab.

PISCOPO, JOE: Passaic. NJ, June 17, 1951.

PISIER, MARIE-FRANCE: Vietnam, May 10, 1944. U Paris.

PITILLO, MARIA: Mahwah, NJ, 1965.

PITT, BRAD (William Bradley Pitt): Shawnee, OK, Dec. 18, 1963.

PIVEN, JEREMY: NYC, July 26, 1965.

PLACE, MARY KAY: Tulsa OK, Sept. 23, 1947. U Tulsa.

PLATT, OLIVER: Oct. 10, 1960.

PLAYTEN, ALICE: NYC, Aug. 28, 1947. NYU.

PLESHETTE, SUZANNE: NYC, Jan. 31, 1937. Syracuse U.

PLIMPTON, MARTHA: NYC, Nov. 16, 1970.

PLOWRIGHT, JOAN: Scunthorpe, Brigg, Lincolnshire, England, Oct. 28, 1929. Old Vic.

PLUMB, EVE: Burbank, CA, Apr. 29, 1958.

PLUMMER, AMANDA: NYC, Mar. 23, 1957. Middlebury College.

PLUMMER, CHRISTOPHER: Toronto, Canada, Dec. 13, 1927.

PODESTA, ROSSANA: Tripoli, June 20, 1934.

POITIER, SIDNEY: Miami, FL, Feb. 27, 1927.

POLANSKI, ROMAN: Paris, France, Aug. 18, 1933.

POLITO, JON: Philadelphia, PA, Dec. 29, 1950. Villanova U.

POLITO, LINA: Naples, Italy, Aug. 11, 1954.

POLLACK, SYDNEY: South Bend, IN, July 1, 1934.

Courtney Love

Shirley MacLaine

Michael Madsen

POLLAK, KEVIN: San Francisco, Oct. 30, 1958.

POLLAN, TRACY: NYC, June 22, 1960.

POLLARD, MICHAEL J.: Passaic, NJ, May 30, 1939.

POLLEY, SARAH: Jan. 8, 1979.

PORTMAN, NATALIE; Jerusalem, June 9, 1981.

POSEY, PARKER: Baltimore, MD, Nov. 8, 1968.

POSTLETHWAITE, PETE: London, Feb. 7, 1945.

POTTER, MONICA: Cleveland, OH, June 30, 1971.

POTTS, ANNIE: Nashville, TN, Oct. 28, 1952. Stephens College.

POWELL, JANE (Suzanne Burce): Port-land, OR, Apr. 1, 1928.

POWELL, ROBERT: Salford, England, June 1, 1944. Manchester U.

POWER, TARYN: Los Angeles, CA, Sept. 13, 1953.

POWER, TYRONE, IV: Los Angeles, CA, Jan. 22, 1959.

POWERS, MALA (Mary Ellen): San Francisco, CA, Dec. 29, 1921. UCLA.

POWERS, STEFANIE (Federkiewicz): Hollywood, CA, Oct. 12, 1942.

PRENTISS, PAULA (Paula Ragusa): San Antonio, TX, Mar. 4, 1939. Northwestern U.

PRESLE, MICHELINE (Micheline Chassagne): Paris, France, Aug. 22, 1922. Rouleau Drama School.

PRESLEY, PRISCILLA: Brooklyn, NY, May 24, 1945.

PRESNELL, HARVE: Modesto, CA, Sept. 14, 1933. USC.

PRESTON, KELLY: Honolulu, HI, Oct. 13, 1962. USC.

PRESTON, WILLIAM: Columbia, PA, Aug. 26, 1921. PaStateU.

PRICE, LONNY: NYC, Mar. 9, 1959. Juilliard.

PRIESTLEY, JASON: Vancouver, Canada, Aug, 28, 1969.

PRIMUS, BARRY: NYC, Feb. 16, 1938. CCNY.

PRINCE (P. Rogers Nelson): Minneapolis, MN, June 7, 1958.

PRINCIPAL, VICTORIA: Fukuoka, Japan, Jan. 3, 1945. Dade, Jr. College.

PRINZE, FREDDIE, JR.: Los Angeles, March 8, 1976.

PROCHNOW, JURGEN: Berlin, June 10, 1941.

PROSKY, ROBERT: Philadelphia, PA, Dec. 13, 1930.

PROVAL, DAVID: Brooklyn, NY, May 20, 1942.

PROVINE, DOROTHY: Deadwood, SD, Jan. 20, 1937. U Wash.

PRYCE, JONATHAN: Wales, UK, June 1, 1947, RADA.

PRYOR, RICHARD: Peoria, IL, Dec. 1, 1940.

PULLMAN, BILL: Delphi, NY, Dec. 17, 1954. SUNY/Oneonta, UMass.

PURCELL, LEE: Cherry Point, NC, June 15, 1947. Stephens.

PURDOM, EDMUND: Welwyn Garden City, England, Dec. 19, 1924. St. Ignatius College.

QUAID, DENNIS: Houston, TX, Apr. 9, 1954.

QUAID, RANDY: Houston, TX, Oct. 1, 1950. UHouston.

QUINLAN, KATHLEEN: Mill Valley, CA, Nov. 19, 1954.

Dylan McDermott

Meat Loaf

Jay Mohr

Jeanne Moreau

QUINN, AIDAN: Chicago, IL, Mar. 8, 1959.
QUINN, ANTHONY: Chihuahua, Mex., Apr. 21, 1915.
RAFFERTY, FRANCES: Sioux City, IA, June 16, 1922. UCLA.
RAFFIN, DEBORAH: Los Angeles, Mar. 13, 1953. Valley College.
RAGSDALE, WILLIAM: El Dorado, AK, Jan. 19, 1961. Hendrix College.
RAILSBACK, STEVE: Dallas, TX, 1948.
RAINER, LUISE: Vienna, Austria, Jan. 12, 1910.
RALSTON, VERA (Vera Helena Hruba): Prague, Czech., July 12, 1919.
RAMIS, HAROLD: Chicago, IL, Nov. 21, 1944. WashingtonU.
RAMPLING, CHARLOTTE: Surmer, England, Feb. 5, 1946. U Madrid.
RAMSEY, LOGAN: Long Beach, CA, Mar. 21, 1921. St. Joseph.
RANDALL, TONY (Leonard Rosenberg): Tulsa, OK, Feb. 26, 1920. Northwestern U.
RANDELL, RON: Sydney, Australia, Oct. 8, 1920. St. Mary's College.
RAPAPORT, MICHAEL: March 20, 1970.
RAPP, ANTHONY: Chicago, Oct. 26, 1971.
RASCHE, DAVID: St. Louis, MO, Aug. 7, 1944.
REA, STEPHEN: Belfast, No. Ireland, Oct. 31, 1949.
REAGAN, RONALD: Tampico, IL, Feb. 6, 1911. Eureka College.
REASON, REX: Berlin, Ger., Nov. 30, 1928. Pasadena Playhouse.
REDDY, HELEN: Melbourne, Australia, Oct. 25, 1942.
REDFORD, ROBERT: Santa Monica, CA, Aug. 18, 1937. AADA.
REDGRAVE, CORIN: London, July 16, 1939.
REDGRAVE, LYNN: London, Mar. 8, 1943.
REDGRAVE, VANESSA: London, Jan. 30, 1937.
REDMAN, JOYCE: County Mayo, Ireland, 1919. RADA.
REED, PAMELA: Tacoma, WA, Apr. 2, 1949.

REEMS, HARRY (Herbert Streicher): Bronx, NY, 1947. U Pittsburgh.
REES, ROGER: Aberystwyth, Wales, May 5, 1944.
REESE, DELLA: Detroit, MI, July 6, 1932.
REEVE, CHRISTOPHER: NYC, Sept. 25, 1952. Cornell, Juilliard.
REEVES, KEANU: Beiruit, Lebanon, Sept. 2, 1964.
REGEHR, DUNCAN: Lethbridge, Canada, Oct. 5, 1952.
REID, ELLIOTT: NYC, Jan. 16, 1920.
REID, TIM: Norfolk, VA, Dec, 19, 1944.
REILLY, CHARLES NELSON: NYC, Jan. 13, 1931. UCt.
REILLY, JOHN C.: Chicago, IL, May 24, 1965.
REINER, CARL: NYC, Mar. 20, 1922. Georgetown.
REINER, ROB: NYC, Mar. 6, 1947. UCLA.
REINHOLD, JUDGE (Edward Ernest, Jr.): Wilmington, DE, May 21, 1957. NCSchool of Arts.
REINKING, ANN: Seattle, WA, Nov. 10, 1949.
REISER, PAUL: NYC, Mar. 30, 1957.
REMAR, JAMES: Boston, MA, Dec. 31, 1953. Neighborhood Playhouse.
RENFRO, BRAD: Knoxville, TN, July 25, 1982.
RENO, JEAN (Juan Moreno): Casablanca, Morocco, July 30, 1948.
REUBENS, PAUL (Paul Reubenfeld): Peekskill, NY, Aug. 27, 1952.
REVILL, CLIVE: Wellington, NZ, Apr. 18, 1930.
REY, ANTONIA: Havana, Cuba, Oct. 12, 1927.
REYNOLDS, BURT: Waycross, GA, Feb. 11, 1935. Fla. State U.
REYNOLDS, DEBBIE (Mary Frances Reynolds): El Paso, TX, Apr. 1, 1932.
RHOADES, BARBARA: Poughkeepsie, NY, Mar. 23, 1947.
RHODES, CYNTHIA: Nashville, TN, Nov. 21, 1956.

RHYS-DAVIES, JOHN: Salisbury, England, May 5, 1944.
RHYS-MEYERS, JONATHAN: Cork, Ireland, July 27, 1977.
RIBISI, GIOVANNI: Los Angeles, CA, Dec. 17, 1974.
RICCI, CHRISTINA: Santa Monica, CA, Feb. 12, 1980.
RICHARD, CLIFF (Harry Webb)**:** India, Oct. 14, 1940.
RICHARDS, DENISE: Downers Grove, IL, Feb. 17, 1972.
RICHARDS, MICHAEL: Culver City, CA, July 14, 1949.
RICHARDSON, JOELY: London, Jan. 9, 1965.
RICHARDSON, MIRANDA: Southport, England, Mar. 3, 1958.
RICHARDSON, NATASHA: London, May 11, 1963.
RICKLES, DON: NYC, May 8, 1926. AADA.
RICKMAN, ALAN: Hammersmith, England, Feb. 21, 1946.
RIEGERT, PETER: NYC, Apr. 11, 1947. U Buffalo.
RIFKIN, RON: NYC, Oct. 31, 1939.
RIGG, DIANA: Doncaster, England, July 20, 1938. RADA.
RILEY, JOHN C.: Chicago, May 24, 1965.
RINGWALD, MOLLY: Rosewood, CA, Feb. 16, 1968.
RITTER, JOHN: Burbank, CA, Sept. 17, 1948. US. Cal.
RIVERS, JOAN (Molinsky): Brooklyn, NY, NY, June 8, 1933.
ROACHE, LINUS: Manchester, England, 1964.
ROBARDS, SAM: NYC, Dec. 16, 1963.
ROBBINS, TIM: NYC, Oct. 16, 1958. UCLA.
ROBERTS, ERIC: Biloxi, MS, Apr. 18, 1956. RADA.
ROBERTS, JULIA: Atlanta, GA, Oct. 28, 1967.
ROBERTS, RALPH: Salisbury, NC, Aug. 17, 1922. UNC.

ROBERTS, TANYA (Leigh): Bronx, NY, Oct. 15, 1954.

ROBERTS, TONY: NYC, Oct. 22, 1939. Northwestern U.

ROBERTSON, CLIFF: La Jolla, CA, Sept. 9, 1925. Antioch College.

ROBERTSON, DALE: Oklahoma City, July 14, 1923.

ROBINSON, CHRIS: West Palm Beach, FL, Nov. 5, 1938. LACC.

ROBINSON, JAY: NYC, Apr. 14, 1930.

ROBINSON, ROGER: Seattle, WA, May 2, 1940. USC.

ROCHEFORT, JEAN: Paris, France, 1930.

ROCK, CHRIS: Brooklyn, NY, Feb. 7, 1966.

ROCKWELL, SAM: Daly City, CA, Nov. 5, 1968.

ROGERS, MIMI: Coral Gables, FL, Jan. 27, 1956.

ROGERS, WAYNE: Birmingham, AL, Apr. 7, 1933. Princeton.

RONSTADT, LINDA: Tucson, AZ, July 15, 1946.

ROOKER, MICHAEL: Jasper, AL, Apr. 6, 1955.

ROONEY, MICKEY (Joe Yule, Jr.): Brooklyn, NY, Sept. 23, 1920.

ROSE, REVA: Chicago, IL, July 30, 1940. Goodman.

ROSEANNE (Barr): Salt Lake City, UT, Nov. 3, 1952.

ROSS, DIANA: Detroit, MI, Mar. 26, 1944.

ROSS, JUSTIN: Brooklyn, NY, Dec. 15, 1954.

ROSS, KATHARINE: Hollywood, Jan. 29, 1943. Santa Rosa College.

ROSSELLINI, ISABELLA: Rome, June 18, 1952.

ROSSOVICH, RICK: Palo Alto, CA, Aug. 28, 1957.

ROTH, TIM: London, May 14, 1961.

ROUNDTREE, RICHARD: New Rochelle, NY, Sept. 7, 1942. Southern Ill.

ROURKE, MICKEY (Philip Andre Rourke, Jr.): Schenectady, NY, Sept. 16, 1956.

ROWE, NICHOLAS: London, Nov. 22, 1966, Eton.

ROWLANDS, GENA: Cambria, WI, June 19, 1934.

RUBIN, ANDREW: New Bedford, MA, June 22, 1946. AADA.

RUBINEK, SAUL: Fohrenwold, Germany, July 2, 1948.

RUBINSTEIN, JOHN: Los Angeles, CA, Dec. 8, 1946. UCLA.

RUCK, ALAN: Cleveland, OH, July 1, 1960.

RUCKER, BO: Tampa, FL, Aug. 17, 1948.

RUDD, PAUL: Boston, MA, May 15, 1940.

RUDD, PAUL: Passaic, NJ, Apr. 6, 1969.

RUDNER, RITA: Miami, FL, Sept. 17, 1955.

RUEHL, MERCEDES: Queens, NY, Feb. 28, 1948.

RULE, JANICE: Cincinnati, OH, Aug. 15, 1931.

RUPERT, MICHAEL: Denver, CO, Oct. 23, 1951. Pasadena Playhouse.

RUSH, BARBARA: Denver, CO, Jan. 4, 1927. U Calif.

RUSH, GEOFFREY: Toowoomba, Queensland, Australia, July 6, 1951. Univ. of Queensland.

RUSSELL, JANE: Bemidji, MI, June 21, 1921. Max Reinhardt School.

RUSSELL, KURT: Springfield, MA, Mar. 17, 1951.

RUSSELL, THERESA (Paup): San Diego, CA, Mar. 20, 1957.

RUSSO, JAMES: NYC, Apr. 23, 1953.

RUTHERFORD, ANN: Toronto, Canada, Nov. 2, 1920.

RYAN, JOHN P.: NYC, July 30, 1936. CCNY.

RYAN, MEG: Fairfield, CT, Nov. 19, 1961. NYU.

RYAN, TIM (Meineslschmidt): Staten Island, NY, 1958. Rutgers U.

RYDER, WINONA (Horowitz): Winona, MN, Oct. 29, 1971.

SACCHI, ROBERT: Bronx, NY, 1941. NYU.

SÄGEBRECHT, MARIANNE: Starnberg, Bavaria, Aug. 27, 1945.

SAINT, EVA MARIE: Newark, NJ, July 4, 1924. Bowling Green State U.

SAINT JAMES, SUSAN (Suzie Jane Miller): Los Angeles, Aug. 14, 1946. Conn. College.

ST. JOHN, BETTA: Hawthorne, CA, Nov. 26, 1929.

ST. JOHN, JILL (Jill Oppenheim): Los Angeles, Aug. 19, 1940.

SALA, JOHN: Los Angeles, CA, Oct. 5, 1962.

SALDANA, THERESA: Brooklyn, NY, Aug. 20, 1954.

SALINGER, MATT: Windsor, VT, Feb. 13, 1960. Princeton, Columbia.

SALT, JENNIFER: Los Angeles, Sept. 4, 1944. Sarah Lawrence College.

SAMMS, EMMA: London, Aug. 28, 1960.

SAN GIACOMO, LAURA: Orange, NJ, Nov. 14, 1961.

SANDERS, JAY O.: Austin, TX, Apr. 16, 1953.

SANDLER, ADAM: Bronx, NY, Sept. 9, 1966. NYU.

SANDS, JULIAN: Yorkshire, England, Jan 15, 1958.

SANDS, TOMMY: Chicago, IL, Aug. 27, 1937.

SAN JUAN, OLGA: NYC, Mar. 16, 1927.

SARA, MIA (Sarapocciello): Brooklyn, NY, June 19, 1967.

SARANDON, CHRIS: Beckley, WV, July 24, 1942. U WVa., Catholic U.

SARANDON, SUSAN (Tomalin): NYC, Oct. 4, 1946. Catholic U.

SARRAZIN, MICHAEL: Quebec City, Canada, May 22, 1940.

SAVAGE, FRED: Highland Park, IL, July 9, 1976.

SAVAGE, JOHN (Youngs): Long Island, NY, Aug. 25, 1949. AADA.

SAVIOLA, CAMILLE: Bronx, NY, July 16, 1950.

SAVOY, TERESA ANN: London, July 18, 1955.

SAXON, JOHN (Carmen Orrico): Brooklyn, NY, Aug. 5, 1935.

SBARGE, RAPHAEL: NYC, Feb. 12, 1964.

SCACCHI, GRETA: Milan, Italy, Feb. 18, 1960.

SCALIA, JACK: Brooklyn, NY, Nov. 10, 1951.

SCARWID, DIANA: Savannah, GA, Aug. 27, 1955, AADA. Pace U.

SCHEIDER, ROY: Orange, NJ, Nov. 10, 1932. Franklin-Marshall.

SCHEINE, RAYNOR: Emporia, VA, Nov. 10. VaCommonwealthU.

SCHELL, MARIA: Vienna, Jan. 15, 1926.

SCHELL, MAXIMILIAN: Vienna, Dec. 8, 1930.

SCHLATTER, CHARLIE: Englewood, NJ, May 1, 1966. Ithaca College.

Samantha Morton

Armin Mueller-Stahl

Gwyneth Paltrow

SCHNEIDER, JOHN: Mt. Kisco, NY, Apr. 8, 1960.

SCHNEIDER, MARIA: Paris, France, Mar. 27, 1952.

SCHREIBER, LIEV: San Francisco, CA, Oct. 4, 1967.

SCHRODER, RICK: Staten Island, NY, Apr. 13, 1970.

SCHUCK, JOHN: Boston, MA, Feb. 4, 1940.

SCHULTZ, DWIGHT: Milwaukee, WI, Nov. 10, 1938. MarquetteU.

SCHWARZENEGGER, ARNOLD: Austria, July 30, 1947.

SCHWARTZMAN, JASON: Los Angeles, June 26, 1980.

SCHWIMMER, DAVID: Queens, NY, Nov. 12, 1966.

SCHYGULLA, HANNA: Katlowitz, Germany, Dec. 25, 1943.

SCIORRA, ANNABELLA: NYC, Mar. 24, 1964.

SCOFIELD, PAUL: Hurstpierpoint, England, Jan. 21, 1922. London Mask Theatre School.

SCOGGINS, TRACY: Galveston, TX, Nov. 13, 1959.

SCOLARI, PETER: Scarsdale, NY, Sept. 12, 1956. NYCC.

SCOTT, CAMPBELL: South Salem, NY, July 19, 1962. Lawrence.

SCOTT, DEBRALEE: Elizabeth, NJ, Apr. 2, 1953

SCOTT, GORDON (Gordon M. Werschkul): Portland, OR, Aug. 3, 1927. Oregon U.

SCOTT, LIZABETH (Emma Matso): Scranton, PA, Sept. 29, 1922.

SCOTT, MARTHA: Jamesport, MO, Sept. 22, 1914. U Mich.

SCOTT THOMAS, KRISTIN: Redruth, Cornwall, Eng., May 24, 1960.

SEAGAL, STEVEN: Detroit, MI, Apr. 10, 1951.

SEARS, HEATHER: London, Sept. 28, 1935.

SECOMBE, HARRY: Swansea, Wales, Sept. 8, 1921.

SEDGWICK, KYRA: NYC, Aug. 19, 1965. USC.

SEGAL, GEORGE: NYC, Feb. 13, 1934. Columbia.

SELBY, DAVID: Morganstown, WV, Feb. 5, 1941. UWV.

SELLARS, ELIZABETH: Glasgow, Scotland, May 6, 1923.

SELLECK, TOM: Detroit, MI, Jan. 29, 1945. USCal.

SERBEDZIJA, RADE: Bunic, Yugoslavia, July 27, 1946.

SERNAS, JACQUES: Lithuania, July 30, 1925.

SERRAULT, MICHEL: Brunoy, France. Jan. 24, 1928. Paris Consv.

SETH, ROSHAN: New Delhi, India. 1942.

SEWELL, RUFUS: Twickenham, Eng., Oct. 29, 1967.

SEYMOUR, JANE (Joyce Frankenberg): Hillingdon, England, Feb. 15, 1952.

SHALHOUB, TONY: Oct. 7, 1953.

SHARIF, OMAR (Michel Shalhoub): Alexandria, Egypt, Apr. 10, 1932. Victoria College.

SHANDLING, GARRY: Chicago, IL, Nov. 29, 1949.

SHATNER, WILLIAM: Montreal, Canada, Mar. 22, 1931. McGill U.

SHAVER, HELEN: St. Thomas, Ontario, Canada, Feb. 24, 1951.

SHAW, FIONA: Cork, Ireland, July 10, 1955. RADA.

SHAW, STAN: Chicago, IL, 1952.

SHAWN, WALLACE: NYC, Nov. 12, 1943. Harvard.

SHEA, JOHN: North Conway, NH, Apr. 14, 1949. Bates, Yale.

SHEARER, HARRY: Los Angeles, Dec. 23, 1943. UCLA.

SHEARER, MOIRA: Dunfermline, Scotland, Jan. 17, 1926. London Theatre School.

SHEEDY, ALLY: NYC, June 13, 1962. USC.

SHEEN, CHARLIE (Carlos Irwin Estevez): Santa Monica, CA, Sept. 3, 1965.

SHEEN, MARTIN (Ramon Estevez): Dayton, OH, Aug. 3, 1940.

SHEFFER, CRAIG: York, PA, Apr. 23, 1960. E. StroudsbergU.

SHEFFIELD, JOHN: Pasadena, CA, Apr. 11, 1931. UCLA.

SHELLEY, CAROL: London, England, Aug. 16, 1939.

SHEPARD, SAM (Rogers): Ft. Sheridan, IL, Nov. 5, 1943.

SHEPHERD, CYBILL: Memphis, TN, Feb. 18, 1950. Hunter, NYU.

SHER, ANTONY: England, June 14, 1949.

SHERIDAN, JAMEY: Pasadena, CA, July 12, 1951.

SHIELDS, BROOKE: NYC, May 31, 1965.

SHIRE, TALIA: Lake Success, NY, Apr. 25, 1946. Yale.

SHORT, MARTIN: Toronto, Canada, Mar. 26, 1950. McMasterU.

SHUE, ELISABETH: S. Orange, NJ, Oct. 6, 1963. Harvard.

SIEMASZKO, CASEY: Chicago, IL, March 17, 1961.

SIKKING, JAMES B.: Los Angeles, Mar. 5, 1934.

SILVA, HENRY: Brooklyn, NY, 1928.

SILVER, RON: NYC, July 2, 1946. SUNY.

SILVERMAN, JONATHAN: Los Angeles, CA, Aug. 5, 1966. USC.

SILVERSTONE, ALICIA: San Francisco, CA, Oct. 4, 1976.

SILVERSTONE, BEN: London, Eng, Apr. 9, 1979.

SIMMONS, JEAN: London, Jan. 31, 1929. Aida Foster School.

SIMON, PAUL: Newark. NJ, Nov. 5, 1942.

SIMON, SIMONE: Bethune, France, Apr. 23, 1910.

SIMPSON, O. J. (Orenthal James): San Francisco, CA, July 9, 1947. UCLA.

SINBAD (David Adkins): Benton Harbor, MI, Nov. 10, 1956.

SINCLAIR, JOHN (Gianluigi Loffredo): Rome, Italy, 1946.

SINDEN, DONALD: Plymouth, England, Oct. 9, 1923. Webber-Douglas.

SINGER, LORI: Corpus Christi, TX, May 6, 1962. Juilliard.

SINISE, GARY: Chicago, Mar. 17. 1955.

SIZEMORE, TOM: Detroit, MI, Sept. 29, 1964.

SKARSGÅRD, STELLAN: Gothenburg, Vastergotland, Sweden, June 13, 1951.

SKERRITT, TOM: Detroit, MI, Aug. 25, 1933. Wayne State U.

SKYE, IONE (Leitch): London, England, Sept. 4, 1971.

SLATER, CHRISTIAN: NYC, Aug. 18, 1969.

SLATER, HELEN: NYC, Dec. 15, 1965.

SMITH, CHARLES MARTIN: Los Angeles, CA, Oct. 30, 1953. CalState U.

SMITH, JACLYN: Houston, TX, Oct. 26, 1947.

SMITH, JADA PINKETT: Baltimore, MD, Sept. 18, 1971.

Natalie Portman

Brad Renfro

Joely Richardson

Mimi Rogers

Paul Rudd

Susan Sarandon

Greta Scacchi

David Schwimmer

SMITH, KERR: Exton, PA, Mar. 9, 1972.

SMITH, KEVIN: Red Bank, NJ, Aug. 2, 1970.

SMITH, KURTWOOD: New Lisbon, WI, Jul. 3, 1942.

SMITH, LANE: Memphis, TN, Apr. 29, 1936.

SMITH, LEWIS: Chattanooga, TN, 1958. Actors Studio.

SMITH, LOIS: Topeka, KS, Nov. 3, 1930. U Wash.

SMITH, MAGGIE: Ilford, England, Dec. 28, 1934.

SMITH, ROGER: South Gate, CA, Dec. 18, 1932. U Ariz.

SMITH, WILL: Philadelphia, PA, Sept. 25, 1968.

SMITHERS, WILLIAM: Richmond, VA, July 10, 1927. Catholic U.

SMITS, JIMMY: Brooklyn, NY, July 9, 1955. Cornell U.

SNIPES, WESLEY: NYC, July 31, 1963. SUNY/Purchase.

SNODGRESS, CARRIE: Chicago, IL, Oct. 27, 1946. UNI.

SOBIEKSI, LEELEE (Liliane Sobieski): NYC, June 10, 1982.

SOLOMON, BRUCE: NYC, 1944. U Miami, Wayne State U.

SOMERS, SUZANNE (Mahoney): San Bruno, CA, Oct. 16, 1946. Lone Mt. College.

SOMMER, ELKE (Schletz): Berlin, Germany, Nov. 5, 1940.

SOMMER, JOSEF: Greifswald, Germany, June 26, 1934.

SORDI, ALBERTO: Rome, Italy, June 15, 1920.

SORVINO, MIRA: Tenafly, NJ, Sept. 28, 1967.

SORVINO, PAUL: NYC, Apr. 13, 1939. AMDA.

SOTHERN, ANN (Harriet Lake): Valley City, ND, Jan. 22, 1909.

SOTO, TALISA (Miriam Soto): Brooklyn, NY, Mar. 27, 1967.

SOUL, DAVID: Chicago, IL, Aug. 28, 1943.

SPACEK, SISSY: Quitman, TX, Dec. 25, 1949. Actors Studio.

SPACEY, KEVIN: So. Orange, NJ, July 26, 1959. Juilliard.

SPADE, DAVID: Birmingham, MS, July 22, 1964.

SPADER, JAMES: Buzzards Bay, MA, Feb. 7, 1960.

SPANO, VINCENT: Brooklyn, NY, Oct. 18, 1962.

SPENSER, JEREMY: Ceylon, 1937.

SPINELLA, STEPHEN: Naples, Italy, Oct. 11, 1956. NYU.

SPRINGFIELD, RICK (Richard Spring Thorpe): Sydney, Australia, Aug. 23, 1949.

STACK, ROBERT: Los Angeles, Jan. 13, 1919. USC.

STADLEN, LEWIS J.: Brooklyn, NY, Mar. 7, 1947. Neighborhood Playhouse.

STAHL, NICK: Dallas, TX, Dec. 5, 1979.

STALLONE, FRANK: NYC, July 30, 1950.

STALLONE, SYLVESTER: NYC, July 6, 1946. U Miami.

STAMP, TERENCE: London, July 23, 1939.

STANG, ARNOLD: Chelsea, MA, Sept. 28, 1925.

STANLEY, KIM (Patricia Reid): Tularosa, NM, Feb. 11, 1925. U Tex.

STANTON, HARRY DEAN: Lexington, KY, July 14, 1926.

STAPLETON, JEAN: NYC, Jan. 19, 1923.

STAPLETON, MAUREEN: Troy, NY, June 21, 1925.

STARR, RINGO (Richard Starkey): Liverpool, England, July 7, 1940.

STEEL, ANTHONY: London, May 21, 1920. Cambridge.

STEELE, BARBARA: England, Dec. 29, 1937.

STEELE, TOMMY: London, Dec. 17, 1936.

STEENBURGEN, MARY: Newport, AR, 1953. Neighborhood Playhouse.

STEIGER, ROD: Westhampton, NY, Apr. 14, 1925.

STERLING, JAN (Jane Sterling Adriance): NYC, Apr. 3, 1923. Fay Compton School.

STERLING, ROBERT (William Sterling Hart): Newcastle, PA, Nov. 13, 1917. UPittsburgh.

STERN, DANIEL: Bethesda, MD, Aug. 28, 1957.

STERNHAGEN, FRANCES: Washington, DC, Jan. 13, 1932.

STEVENS, ANDREW: Memphis, TN, June 10, 1955.

STEVENS, CONNIE (Concetta Ann Ingolia): Brooklyn, NY, Aug. 8, 1938. Hollywood Professional School.

STEVENS, FISHER: Chicago, IL, Nov. 27, 1963. NYU.

STEVENS, STELLA (Estelle Eggleston): Hot Coffee, MS, Oct. 1, 1936.

STEVENSON, PARKER: Philadelphia, PA, June 4, 1953. Princeton.

STEWART, ALEXANDRA: Montreal, Canada, June 10, 1939. Louvre.

STEWART, ELAINE (Elsy Steinberg): Montclair, NJ, May 31, 1929.

STEWART, FRENCH (Milton French Stewart): Albuquerque, NM, Feb. 20, 1964.

STEWART, JON (Jonathan Stewart Liebowitz): Trenton, NJ, Nov. 28, 1962.

STEWART, MARTHA (Martha Haworth): Bardwell, KY, Oct. 7, 1922.

STEWART, PATRICK: Mirfield, England, July 13, 1940.

STIERS, DAVID OGDEN: Peoria, IL, Oct. 31, 1942.

STILES, JULIA: NYC, Mar. 28, 1981.

STILLER, BEN: NYC, Nov. 30, 1965.

STILLER, JERRY: NYC, June 8, 1931.

STING (Gordon Matthew Sumner): Wallsend, England, Oct. 2, 1951.

STOCKWELL, DEAN: Hollywood, Mar. 5, 1935.

STOCKWELL, JOHN (John Samuels, IV): Galveston, TX, Mar. 25, 1961. Harvard.

STOLTZ, ERIC: Whittier, CA, Sept. 30, 1961. USC.

STONE, DEE WALLACE (Deanna Bowers): Kansas City, MO, Dec. 14, 1948. UKS.

STONE, SHARON: Meadville, PA, Mar. 10 1958

STORM, GALE (Josephine Cottle): Bloomington, TX, Apr. 5, 1922.

STOWE, MADELEINE: Eagle Rock, CA, Aug. 18, 1958.

STRAIGHT, BEATRICE: Old Westbury, NY, Aug. 2, 1916. Dartington Hall.

STRASSMAN, MARCIA: New Jersey, Apr. 28, 1948.

STRATHAIRN, DAVID: San Francisco, Jan. 26, 1949.

STRAUSS, PETER: NYC, Feb. 20, 1947.

STREEP, MERYL (Mary Louise): Summit, NJ, June 22, 1949. Vassar, Yale.

STREISAND, BARBRA: Brooklyn, NY, Apr. 24, 1942.

Michel Serrault

Wallace Shawn

Tom Sizemore

Stellan Skarsgård

STRITCH, ELAINE: Detroit, MI, Feb. 2, 1925. Drama Workshop.

STROUD, DON: Honolulu, HI, Sept. 1, 1937.

STRUTHERS, SALLY: Portland, OR, July 28, 1948. Pasadena Playhouse.

STUDI, WES (Wesley Studie): Nofire Hollow, OK, Dec. 17, 1947.

SUMMER, DONNA (LaDonna Gaines): Boston, MA, Dec. 31, 1948.

SUTHERLAND, DONALD: St. John, New Brunswick, Canada, July 17, 1935. U Toronto.

SUTHERLAND, KIEFER: Los Angeles, CA, Dec. 18, 1966.

SUVARI, MENA: Newport, RI, Feb. 9, 1979.

SVENSON, BO: Goreborg, Sweden, Feb. 13, 1941. UCLA.

SWANK, HILARY: Bellingham, WA, July 30, 1974.

SWAYZE, PATRICK: Houston, TX, Aug. 18, 1952.

SWEENEY, D. B. (Daniel Bernard Sweeney): Shoreham, NY, Nov. 14, 1961.

SWINBURNE, NORA (Elinore Johnson): Bath, England, July 24, 1902. RADA.

SWIT, LORETTA: Passaic, NJ, Nov. 4, 1937. AADA.

SYLVESTER, WILLIAM: Oakland, CA, Jan. 31, 1922. RADA.

SYMONDS, ROBERT: Bistow, AK, Dec. 1, 1926. TexU.

SYMS, SYLVIA: London, June 1, 1934. Convent School.

SZARABAJKA, KEITH: Oak Park, IL, Dec. 2, 1952. UChicago.

T, MR. (Lawrence Tero): Chicago, IL, May 21, 1952.

TABORI, KRISTOFFER (Siegel): Los Angeles, Aug. 4, 1952.

TAKEI, GEORGE: Los Angeles, CA, Apr. 20, 1939. UCLA.

TALBOT, NITA: NYC, Aug. 8, 1930. Irvine Studio School.

TAMBLYN, RUSS: Los Angeles, Dec. 30, 1934.

TARANTINO, QUENTIN: Knoxville, TN, Mar. 27, 1963.

TATE, LARENZ: Chicago, IL, Sept. 8, 1975.

TAYLOR, ELIZABETH: London, Feb. 27, 1932. Byron House School.

TAYLOR, LILI: Glencoe, IL, Feb. 20, 1967.

TAYLOR, RENEE: NYC, Mar. 19, 1935.

TAYLOR, ROD (Robert): Sydney, Aust., Jan. 11, 1929.

TAYLOR-YOUNG, LEIGH: Washington, DC, Jan. 25, 1945. Northwestern.

TEEFY, MAUREEN: Minneapolis, MN, 1954, Juilliard.

TEMPLE, SHIRLEY: Santa Monica, CA, Apr. 23, 1927.

TENNANT, VICTORIA: London, England, Sept. 30, 1950.

TERZIEFF, LAURENT: Paris, France, June 25, 1935.

TEWES, LAUREN: Braddock, PA, Oct. 26, 1954.

THACKER, RUSS: Washington, DC, June 23, 1946. Montgomery College.

THAXTER, PHYLLIS: Portland, ME, Nov. 20, 1921. St. Genevieve.

THELEN, JODI: St. Cloud, MN, 1963.

THERON, CHARLIZE: Benoni, So. Africa, Aug. 7, 1975.

THEWLIS, DAVID: Blackpool, Eng., 1963.

THOMAS, HENRY: San Antonio, TX, Sept. 8, 1971.

THOMAS, JAY: New Orleans, July 12, 1948.

THOMAS, JONATHAN TAYLOR (Weiss): Bethlehem, PA, Sept. 8, 1981.

THOMAS, MARLO (Margaret): Detroit, Nov. 21, 1938. USC.

THOMAS, PHILIP MICHAEL: Columbus, OH, May 26, 1949. Oakwood College.

THOMAS, RICHARD: NYC, June 13, 1951. Columbia.

THOMPSON, EMMA: London, England, Apr.15, 1959. Cambridge.

THOMPSON, FRED DALTON: Sheffield, AL, Aug. 19, 1942

THOMPSON, JACK (John Payne): Sydney, Australia, Aug. 31, 1940.

THOMPSON, LEA: Rochester, MN, May 31, 1961.

THOMPSON, REX: NYC, Dec. 14, 1942.

THOMPSON, SADA: Des Moines, IA, Sept. 27, 1929. Carnegie Tech.

THORNTON, BILLY BOB: Hot Spring, AR, Aug. 4, 1955.

THORSON, LINDA: Toronto, Canada, June 18, 1947. RADA.

THULIN, INGRID: Solleftea, Sweden, Jan. 27, 1929. Royal Drama Theatre.

THURMAN, UMA: Boston, MA, Apr. 29, 1970.

TICOTIN, RACHEL: Bronx, NY, Nov. 1, 1958.

TIERNEY, LAWRENCE: Brooklyn, NY, Mar. 15, 1919. Manhattan College.

TIFFIN, PAMELA (Wonso): Oklahoma City, OK, Oct. 13, 1942.

TIGHE, KEVIN: Los Angeles, Aug. 13, 1944.

TILLY, JENNIFER: Los Angeles, CA, Sept. 16, 1958.

TILLY, MEG: Texada, Canada, Feb. 14, 1960.

TOBOLOWSKY, STEPHEN: Dallas, Tx, May 30, 1951. So. Methodist U.

TODD, BEVERLY: Chicago, IL, July 1, 1946.

TODD, RICHARD: Dublin, Ireland, June 11, 1919. Shrewsbury School.

TOLKAN, JAMES: Calumet, MI, June 20, 1931.

TOMEI, MARISA: Brooklyn, NY, Dec. 4, 1964. NYU.

TOMLIN, LILY: Detroit, MI, Sept. 1, 1939. Wayne State U.

TOPOL (Chaim Topol): Tel-Aviv, Israel, Sept. 9, 1935.

TORN, RIP: Temple, TX, Feb. 6, 1931. UTex.

TORRES, LIZ: NYC, Sept. 27, 1947. NYU.

TOTTER, AUDREY: Joliet, IL, Dec. 20, 1918.

TOWNSEND, ROBERT: Chicago, IL, Feb. 6, 1957.

TRAMMELL, SAM: Los Angeles, CA, May 15, 1971.

TRAVANTI, DANIEL J.: Kenosha, WI, Mar. 7, 1940.

TRAVIS, NANCY: Astoria, NY, Sept. 21, 1961.

TRAVOLTA, JOHN: Englewood, NJ, Feb. 18, 1954.

TREMAYNE, LES: London, Apr. 16, 1913. Northwestern, Columbia, UCLA.

TRINTIGNANT, JEAN-LOUIS: Pont-St. Esprit, France, Dec. 11, 1930. DullinBalachova Drama School.

TRIPPLEHORN, JEANNE: Tulsa, OK, 1963.

TSOPEI, CORINNA: Athens, Greece, June 21, 1944.

TUBB, BARRY: Snyder, TX, 1963. AmConsv Th.

TUCCI, STANLEY: Katonah, NY, Jan. 11, 1960.

TUCKER, CHRIS: Atlanta, GA, 1972.

TUCKER, MICHAEL: Baltimore, MD, Feb. 6, 1944.

TUNE, TOMMY: Wichita Falls, TX, Feb. 28, 1939.

Wesley Snipes

Leelee Sobieski

Sylvester Stallone

Rod Steiger

TURNER, JANINE (Gauntt): Lincoln, NE, Dec. 6, 1963.
TURNER, KATHLEEN: Springfield, MO, June 19, 1954. UMd.
TURNER, TINA (Anna Mae Bullock): Nutbush, TN, Nov. 26, 1938.
TURTURRO, JOHN: Brooklyn, NY, Feb. 28, 1957. Yale.
TUSHINGHAM, RITA: Liverpool, England, Mar. 14, 1940.
TUTIN, DOROTHY: London, Apr. 8, 1930.
TWIGGY (Lesley Hornby): London, Sept. 19, 1949.
TWOMEY, ANNE: Boston, MA, June 7, 1951. Temple U.
TYLER, BEVERLY (Beverly Jean Saul): Scranton, PA, July 5, 1928.
TYLER, LIV: Portland, ME, July 1, 1977.
TYRRELL, SUSAN: San Francisco, 1946.
TYSON, CATHY: Liverpool, England, June 12, 1965. Royal Shake. Co.
TYSON, CICELY: NYC, Dec. 19, 1933. NYU.
UGGAMS, LESLIE: NYC, May 25, 1943. Juilliard.

ULLMAN, TRACEY: Slough, England, Dec. 30, 1959.
ULLMANN, LIV: Tokyo, Dec. 10, 1938. Webber-Douglas Acad.
ULRICH, SKEET (Bryan Ray Ulrich): North Carolina, Jan. 20, 1969.
UMEKI, MIYOSHI: Otaru, Hokaido, Japan, Apr. 3, 1929.
UNDERWOOD, BLAIR: Tacoma, WA, Aug. 25, 1964. Carnegie-Mellon U.
UNGER, DEBORAH KARA: Victoria, British Columbia, 1966.
URICH, ROBERT: Toronto, Canada, Dec. 19, 1946.
USTINOV, PETER: London, Apr. 16, 1921. Westminster School.
VACCARO, BRENDA: Brooklyn, NY, Nov. 18, 1939. Neighborhood Playhouse.
VALANDREY, CHARLOTTE (Anne Charlone Pascal): Paris, France, 1968.
VALLI, ALIDA: Pola, Italy, May 31, 1921. Academy of Drama.
VALLONE, RAF: Riogio, Italy, Feb. 17, 1916. Turin U.
VAN ARK, JOAN: NYC, June 16, 1943. Yale.
VAN DAMME, JEAN-CLAUDE (J-C Vorenberg): Brussels, Belgium, Apr. 1, 1960.
VAN DE VEN, MONIQUE: Netherlands, 1952.
VAN DER BEEK, JAMES: Chesire, CT, March 8, 1977.
VAN DEVERE, TRISH (Patricia Dressel): Englewood Cliffs, NJ, Mar. 9, 1945. Ohio Wesleyan.
VAN DIEN, CASPER: Ridgefield, NJ, Dec. 18, 1968.
VAN DOREN, MAMIE (Joan Lucile Olander): Rowena SD, Feb. 6, 1933.
VAN DYKE, DICK: West Plains, MO, Dec. 13, 1925.
VANITY (Denise Katrina Smith): Niagara, Ont., Can, Jan. 4, 1959.
VAN PALLANDT, NINA: Copenhagen, Denmark, July 15, 1932.
VAN PATTEN, DICK: NYC, Dec. 9, 1928.
VAN PATTEN, JOYCE: NYC, Mar. 9, 1934.
VAN PEEBLES, MARIO: NYC, Jan. 15, 1958. Columbia U.
VAN PEEBLES, MELVIN: Chicago, IL, Aug. 21, 1932.
VANCE, COURTNEY B.: Detroit, MI, Mar. 12, 1960.

VAUGHN, ROBERT: NYC, Nov. 22, 1932. USC.
VAUGHN, VINCE: Minneapolis, MN, Mar. 28, 1970.
VEGA, ISELA: Mexico, 1940.
VELJOHNSON, REGINALD: NYC, Aug. 16, 1952.
VENNERA, CHICK: Herkimer, NY, Mar. 27, 1952. Pasadena Playhouse.
VENORA, DIANE: Hartford, CT, 1952. Juilliard.
VERNON, JOHN: Montreal, Canada, Feb. 24, 1932.
VEREEN, BEN: Miami, FL, Oct. 10, 1946.
VICTOR, JAMES (Lincoln Rafael Peralta Diaz): Santiago, D.R., July 27, 1939. Haaren HS/NYC.
VINCENT, JAN-MICHAEL: Denver, CO, July 15, 1944. Ventura.
VIOLET, ULTRA (Isabelle Collin-Dufresne): Grenoble, France, 1935.
VITALE, MILLY: Rome, Italy, July 16, 1928. Lycee Chateaubriand.
VOHS, JOAN: St. Albans, NY, July 30, 1931.

Kiefer Sutherland

Wes Studi

Sam Trammell

John Turturro

VOIGHT, JON: Yonkers, NY, Dec. 29, 1938. Catholic U.

VON BARGEN, DANIEL: Cincinnati, OH, June 5, 1950. Purdue.

VON DOHLEN, LENNY: Augusta, GA, Dec. 22, 1958. UTex.

VON SYDOW, MAX: Lund, Sweden, July 10, 1929. Royal Drama Theatre.

WAGNER, LINDSAY: Los Angeles, June 22, 1949.

WAGNER, NATASHA GREGSON: Los Angeles, CA, Sept. 29, 1970.

WAGNER, ROBERT: Detroit, Feb. 10, 1930.

WAHL, KEN: Chicago, IL, Feb. 14, 1953.

WAITE, GENEVIEVE: South Africa, 1949.

WAITE, RALPH: White Plains, NY, June 22, 1929. Yale.

WAITS, TOM: Pomona, CA, Dec. 7, 1949.

WALKEN, CHRISTOPHER: Astoria, NY, Mar. 31, 1943. Hofstra.

WALKER, CLINT: Hartfold, IL, May 30, 1927. USC.

WALLACH, ELI: Brooklyn, NY, Dec. 7, 1915. CCNY, U Tex.

WALLACH, ROBERTA: NYC, Aug. 2, 1955.

WALLIS, SHANI: London, Apr. 5, 1941.

WALSH, M. EMMET: Ogdensburg, NY, Mar. 22, 1935. Clarkson College, AADA.

WALSTON, RAY: New Orleans, Nov. 22, 1917. Cleveland Playhouse.

WALTER, JESSICA: Brooklyn, NY, Jan. 31, 1944 Neighborhood Playhouse.

WALTER, TRACEY: Jersey City, NJ, Nov. 25, 1942.

WALTERS, JULIE: London, Feb. 22, 1950.

WALTON, EMMA: London, Nov. 1962. Brown U.

WARD, BURT (Gervis): Los Angeles, July 6, 1945.

WARD, FRED: San Diego, CA, Dec. 30, 1942.

WARD, RACHEL: London, Sept. 12, 1957.

WARD, SELA: Meridian, MS, July 11, 1956.

WARD, SIMON: London, Oct. 19, 1941.

WARDEN, JACK (Lebzelter): Newark, NJ, Sept. 18, 1920.

WARNER, DAVID: Manchester, England, July 29, 1941. RADA.

WARNER, MALCOLM-JAMAL: Jersey City, NJ, Aug. 18, 1970.

WARREN, JENNIFER: NYC, Aug. 12, 1941. U Wisc.

WARREN, LESLEY ANN: NYC, Aug. 16, 1946.

WARREN, MICHAEL: South Bend, IN, Mar. 5, 1946. UCLA.

WARRICK, RUTH: St. Joseph, MO, June 29, 1915. U Mo.

WASHINGTON, DENZEL: Mt. Vernon, NY, Dec. 28, 1954. Fordham.

WASSON, CRAIG: Ontario, OR, Mar. 15, 1954. UOre.

WATERSTON, SAM: Cambridge, MA, Nov. 15, 1940. Yale.

WATLING, JACK: London, Jan. 13, 1923. Italia Conti School.

WATSON, EMILY: London, Jan. 14, 1967.

WAYANS, DAMON: NYC, Sept. 4, 1960.

WAYANS, KEENEN IVORY: NYC, June 8, 1958. Tuskegee Inst.

WAYNE, PATRICK: Los Angeles, July 15, 1939. Loyola.

WEATHERS, CARL: New Orleans, LA, Jan. 14, 1948. Long Beach CC.

WEAVER, DENNIS: Joplin, MO, June 4, 1924. U Okla.

WEAVER, FRITZ: Pittsburgh, PA, Jan. 19, 1926.

WEAVER, SIGOURNEY (Susan): NYC, Oct. 8, 1949. Stanford, Yale.

WEBER, STEVEN: Queens, NY, March 4, 1961.

WEDGEWORTH, ANN: Abilene, TX, Jan. 21, 1935. U Tex.

WEISZ, RACHEL: London, Mar. 7, 1971.

WELCH, RAQUEL (Tejada): Chicago, IL, Sept. 5, 1940.

WELD, TUESDAY (Susan): NYC, Aug. 27, 1943. Hollywood Professional School.

WELDON, JOAN: San Francisco, Aug. 5, 1933. San Francisco Conservatory.

WELLER, PETER: Stevens Point, WI, June 24, 1947. AmThWing.

WENDT, GEORGE: Chicago, IL, Oct. 17, 1948.

WEST, ADAM (William Anderson): Walla Walla, WA, Sept. 19, 1929.

WETTIG, PATRICIA: Cincinatti, OH, Dec. 4, 1951. TempleU.

WHALEY, FRANK: Syracuse, NY, July 20, 1963. SUNY/Albany.

WHALLEY-KILMER, JOANNE: Manchester, England, Aug. 25, 1964.

WHEATON, WIL: Burbank, CA, July 29, 1972.

WHITAKER, FOREST: Longview, TX, July 15, 1961.

WHITAKER, JOHNNY: Van Nuys, CA, Dec. 13, 1959.

WHITE, BETTY: Oak Park, IL, Jan. 17, 1922.

WHITE, CHARLES: Perth Amboy, NJ, Aug. 29, 1920. Rutgers U.

WHITELAW, BILLIE: Coventry, England, June 6, 1932.

WHITMAN, STUART: San Francisco, Feb. 1, 1929. CCLA.

WHITMORE, JAMES: White Plains, NY, Oct. 1, 1921. Yale.

WHITNEY, GRACE LEE: Detroit, MI, Apr. 1, 1930.

WHITTON, MARGARET: Philadelphia, PA, Nov. 30, 1950.

WIDDOES, KATHLEEN: Wilmington, DE, Mar. 21, 1939.

WIDMARK, RICHARD: Sunrise, MN, Dec. 26, 1914. Lake Forest.

WIEST, DIANNE: Kansas City, MO, Mar. 28, 1948. UMd.

WILBY, JAMES: Burma, Feb. 20, 1958.

WILCOX, COLIN: Highlands, NC, Feb. 4, 1937. U Tenn.

WILDER, GENE (Jerome Silberman): Milwaukee, WI, June 11, 1935. UIowa.

WILLIAMS, BILLY DEE: NYC, Apr. 6, 1937.

WILLIAMS, CARA (Bernice Kamiat): Brooklyn, NY, June 29, 1925.

WILLIAMS, CINDY: Van Nuys, CA, Aug. 22, 1947. KACC.

WILLIAMS, CLARENCE, III: NYC, Aug. 21, 1939.

WILLIAMS, ESTHER: Los Angeles, Aug. 8, 1921.

WILLIAMS, JOBETH: Houston, TX, Dec 6, 1948. Brown U.

WILLIAMS, MICHELLE: Kalispell, MT, Sept. 9, 1980.

WILLIAMS, PAUL: Omaha, NE, Sept. 19, 1940.

WILLIAMS, ROBIN: Chicago, IL, July 21, 1951. Juilliard.

WILLIAMS, TREAT (Richard): Rowayton, CT, Dec. 1, 1951.

WILLIAMS, VANESSA L.: Tarrytown, NY, Mar. 18, 1963.

WILLIAMSON, FRED: Gary, IN, Mar. 5, 1938. Northwestern.

WILLIAMSON, NICOL: Hamilton, Scotland, Sept. 14, 1938.

WILLIS, BRUCE: Penns Grove, NJ, Mar. 19, 1955.

Courtney B. Vance   Damon Wayans   Keenen Ivory Wayans   James Woods

WILLISON, WALTER: Monterey Park, CA, June 24, 1947.

WILSON, DEMOND: NYC, Oct. 13, 1946. Hunter College.

WILSON, ELIZABETH: Grand Rapids, MI, Apr. 4, 1925.

WILSON, LAMBERT: Paris, France, 1959.

WILSON, LUKE: Dallas, TX, Sept. 21, 1971.

WILSON, SCOTT: Atlanta, GA, 1942.

WINCOTT, JEFF: Toronto, Canada, May 8, 1957.

WINCOTT, MICHAEL: Toronto, Canada, Jan. 6, 1959. Juilliard.

WINDE, BEATRICE: Chicago, IL, Jan. 6.

WINDOM, WILLIAM: NYC, Sept. 28, 1923. Williams College.

WINFIELD, PAUL: Los Angeles, May 22, 1940. UCLA.

WINFREY, OPRAH: Kosciusko, MS, Jan. 29, 1954. TnStateU.

WINGER, DEBRA: Cleveland, OH, May 17, 1955. Cal State.

WINKLER, HENRY: NYC, Oct. 30, 1945. Yale.

WINN, KITTY: Washington, D.C., Feb, 21, 1944. Boston U.

WINNINGHAM, MARE: Phoenix, AZ, May 6, 1959.

WINSLET, KATE: Reading, Eng., Oct. 5, 1975.

WINSLOW, MICHAEL: Spokane, WA, Sept. 6, 1960.

WINTER, ALEX: London, July 17, 1965. NYU.

WINTERS, JONATHAN: Dayton, OH, Nov. 11, 1925. Kenyon College.

WINTERS, SHELLEY (Shirley Schrift): St. Louis, Aug. 18, 1922. Wayne U.

WITHERS, GOOGIE: Karachi, India, Mar. 12, 1917. Italia Conti.

WITHERS, JANE: Atlanta, GA, Apr. 12, 1926.

WITHERSPOON, REESE (Laura Jean Reese Witherspoon): Nashville, TN, Mar. 22, 1976.

WOLF, SCOTT: Newton, MA, June 4, 1968.

WONG, B.D.: San Francisco, Oct. 24,1962.

WONG, RUSSELL: Troy, NY, 1963. SantaMonica College.

WOOD, ELIJAH: Cedar Rapids, IA, Jan 28, 1981.

WOODARD, ALFRE: Tulsa, OK, Nov. 2, 1953. Boston U.

WOODLAWN, HOLLY (Harold Ajzen-berg): Juana Diaz, PR, 1947.

WOODS, JAMES: Vernal, UT, Apr. 18, 1947. MIT.

WOODWARD, EDWARD: Croyden, Surrey, England, June 1, 1930.

WOODWARD, JOANNE: Thomasville, GA, Feb. 27, 1930. Neighborhood Playhouse.

WORONOV, MARY: Brooklyn, NY, Dec. 8, 1946. Cornell.

WORTH, IRENE (Hattie Abrams): Nebraska, June 23, 1916. UCLA.

WRAY, FAY: Alberta, Canada, Sept. 15, 1907.

WRIGHT, AMY: Chicago, IL, Apr. 15, 1950.

WRIGHT, MAX: Detroit, MI, Aug. 2, 1943. WayneStateU.

WRIGHT, ROBIN: Dallas, TX, Apr. 8, 1966.

WRIGHT, TERESA: NYC, Oct. 27, 1918.

WUHL, ROBERT: Union City, NJ, Oct. 9, 1951. UHouston.

WYATT, JANE: NYC, Aug. 10, 1910. Barnard College.

WYLE, NOAH: Los Angeles, June 2, 1971.

WYMAN, JANE (Sarah Jane Fulks): St. Joseph, MO, Jan. 4, 1914.

WYMORE, PATRICE: Miltonvale, KS, Dec. 17, 1926.

WYNN, MAY (Donna Lee Hickey): NYC, Jan. 8, 1930.

WYNTER, DANA (Dagmar): London, June 8. 1927. Rhodes U.

YORK, MICHAEL: Fulmer, England, Mar. 27, 1942. Oxford.

YORK, SUSANNAH: London, Jan. 9, 1941. RADA.

YOUNG, ALAN (Angus): North Shield, England, Nov. 19, 1919.

YOUNG, BURT: Queens, NY, Apr. 30, 1940.

YOUNG, CHRIS: Chambersburg, PA, Apr. 28, 1971.

YOUNG, SEAN: Louisville, KY, Nov. 20, 1959. Interlochen.

YULIN, HARRIS: Los Angeles, Nov. 5, 1937.

CHOW YUN-FAT: Lamma Island, Hong Kong, May 18, 1955.

ZACHARIAS, ANN: Stockholm, Sweden, Sweden, 1956.

ZADORA, PIA: Hoboken, NJ, 1954.

ZELLWEGER, RENÉE: Katy, TX, Apr. 25, 1969.

ZERBE, ANTHONY: Long Beach, CA, May 20, 1939.

ZETA-JONES, CATHERINE: Swansea, Wales, Sept. 25, 1969.

ZIMBALIST, EFREM, JR.: NYC, Nov.30, 1918. Yale.

ZUNIGA, DAPHNE: Berkeley, CA, Oct. 28, 1963. UCLA.

OBITUARIES — 2000

LEWIS ALLEN (Alfred Lewis Allen), 94, British-born motion picture and television director, best known for the 1944 supernatural thriller *The Uninvited,* died on May 3, 2000 in Santa Monica, CA. Among his other credits are *Our Hearts Were Young and Gay, The Unseen, Desert Fury, So Evil My Love, The Sealed Verdict, A Bullet for Joey,* and *Another Time Another Place.* Survived by his second wife, a son, three brothers, two grandchildren, and five great-grandchildren.

STEVE ALLEN, 78, New York City-born motion picture and television actor-comedian-host-songwriter, best known for hosting the original "The Tonight Show" and his own series "The Steve Allen Show," died of a heart attack at his home in Los Angeles on Oct. 30, 2000. On screen he was seen in such movies as *I'll Get By, The Benny Goodman Story* (in the title role), *The Big Circus, College Confidential, Warning Shot, Where Were You When the Lights Went Out?, The Comic, Amazon Women on the Moon, Great Balls of Fire!,* and *The Player.* Among his many credits as songwriter, the best known was "This Could Be the Start of Something Big." He is survived by his second wife (of 46-years), actress Jayne Meadows; four sons; eleven grandchildren; and three great-grandchildren.

Steve Allen

Paul Bartel

EDWARD ANHALT, 86, New York-born screenwriter, who won Academy Awards for the scripts for *Panic in the Streets* and *Becket,* died at his home in Pacific Palisades, CA, on Sept. 3, 2000. Among his other credits were *The Sniper* (Oscar nomination), *The Member of the Wedding, Not as a Stranger, The Young Lions, Girls! Girls! Girls!, The Madwoman of Chaillot, Jeremiah Johnson,* and *The Right Stuff.* He is survived by his fifth wife, and a daughter.

PAUL BARTEL, 61, Brooklyn-born actor, director, and writer, best known for his black comedy *Eating Raoul,* died in his sleep on May 13, 2000 at his Manhattan home. Two weeks earlier he had undergone surgery for cancer of the liver ducts. As an actor he was seen in such movies as *Hi Mom!, Private Parts* (also director), *Hollywood Boulevard, Cannonball* (also director and writer), *Grand Theft Auto, Heart Like a Wheel, Not for Publication* (also director and writer), *Into the Night, National Lampoon's European Vacation, Shakedown, Amazon Women on the Moon, Out of the Dark, Scenes from the Class Struggle in Beverly Hills* (also director and writer), *The Pope Must Die, Posse, Grief, The Usual Suspects, Escape from L.A., Basquiat,* and *Hamlet* (2000, as Osric). He is survived by his father, two sisters, and a brother.

BILLY BARTY (William John Bertanzetti), 76, Pennsylvania-born motion picture and television actor, and founder of Little People of America, died of heart failure on Dec. 23, 2000 in Glendale, CA. As Hollywood's best known dwarf actor he appeared in such movies as *Gold Diggers of 1933, Footlight Parade, Alice in Wonderland* (1933), *Gift of Gab, Bride of Frankenstein, A Midsummer Night's Dream* (1935), *Nothing Sacred, The Clown, Billy Rose's Jumbo, Pufnstuf, The Day of the Locust, W.C. Fields and Me, Won Ton Ton the Dog Who Saved Hollywood, The Amazing Dobermans, Rabbit Test, Foul Play, Skatetown USA, Hardly Working, Under the Rainbow, Legend, Tough Guys, Master of the Universe, Rumplestiltskin, Willow, UHF, Life Stinks,* and *Radioland Murders.* He is survived by his wife, a son, a daughter, and a granddaughter.

Billy Barty

Eric Christmas

EDWARD L. BERNDS, 94, motion picture director who helmed several short subjects for the Three Stooges, died of natural causes on May 20, 2000 in Van Nuys, CA. Among his feature credits were *The Bowery Boys Meet the Monsters, World Without End, Dig That Uranium, Space Master X-7, Queen of Outer Space, Quantrill's Raiders, High School Hellcats, Return of the Fly, The Three Stooges Meet Hercules,* and *The Three Stooges in Orbit.* Survived by a son, two grandchildren, and three great-grandchildren.

DORI BRENNER, 54, Manhattan-born screen and television actress, died of cancer on September 16, 2000 in Los Angeles, Following her motion picture debut in *Summer Wishes Winter Dreams,* she appeared in such movies as *The Other Side of the Mountain, Next Stop Greenwich Village, Altered States, Baby Boom, For the Boys,* and *Infinity.*

ERIC CHRISTMAS, 84, London-born screen and television character actor, died of unspecified causes on July 22, 2000 in Camarillo, CA. He made his motion picture debut in *Monte Walsh* and was thereafter seen in such movies as *The Andromeda Strain, Johnny Got His Gun, Harold and Maude, The Last Tycoon, Attack of the Killer Tomatoes, The Changeling, Porky's, The Philadelphia Experiment, All of Me, Bugsy, Air Bud,* and *Mouse Hunt.*

MARGUERITE CHURCHILL, 90, Kansas City-born movie actress, who co-starred with John Wayne in his first major film, *The Big Trail,* died in Broken Arrow, OK, on January 9, 2000. Her other films include *The Valiant, They Had to See Paris, Harmony at Home, Born Reckless, Quick Millions, Riders of the Purple Sage, Ambassador Bill, Forgotten Commandments, The Walking Dead, Legion of Terror,* and *Dracula's Daughter.* She is survived by her daughter from her marriage to actor George O'Brien.

NICHOLAS CLAY, 53, London-born actor died of cancer in London on May 25, 2000. His movie credits include *The Night Digger, Zulu Dawn, Excalibur* (as Lancelot), *Evil Under the Sun,* and *Lionheart.*

Nicholas Clay

John Colicos

JOHN COLICOS, 71, Toronto-born movie and television character actor, died in Toronto after a series of heart attacks on March 6, 2000. Among his movie credits are *Anne of the Thousand Days, Raid on Rommel, Red Sky at Morning, Doctors' Wives, The Wrath of God, Drum, The Changeling,* and *The Postman Always Rings Twice* (1981). Survived by his wife and two sons.

FRANCES DRAKE (Frances Dean), 91, New York City-born actress, best remembered for starring in the cult horror film *Mad Love,* died of natural causes on January 17, 2000 in Irvine, CA. Her other movies include *Bolero* (1934), *Forsaking All Others, Les Miserables* (1935; as Eponine), *The Invisible Ray, Midnight Taxi, I Take This Woman,* and *The Affairs of Martha,* in 1942, after which she retired from acting.

DAVID DUKES, 55, San Francisco-born screen, stage and television actor died of a heart attack while on location for a mini-series in Spanaway, WA, on October 9, 2000. He was seen in such motion pictures as *The Wild Party* (1975), *A Little Romance, The First Deadly Sin, Only When I Laugh, Rawhead Rex, The Men's Club, Date With an Angel, See You in the Morning, Me and the Kid, Fled,* and *Gods and Monsters.* He is survived by his wife, a daughter, and a son from a previous marriage.

GEORGE DUNING, 92, Indiana-born film composer died in Los Angeles on February 27, 2000. He received Oscar nominations for his work on *Jolson Sings Again, No Sad Songs for Me, From Here to Eternity, Picnic,* and *The Eddy Duchin Story.* His other scores include *My Sister Eileen* (1955), *Bell Book and Candle,* and *That Touch of Mink.* Survived by his wife, two daughters, a brother, two stepchildren, and five grandchildren.

JULIUS J. EPSTEIN, 91, New York City-born screenwriter who, along with his late twin brother Philip (who died in 1952), won an Academy Award for writing the classic film *Casablanca,* died in Los Angeles on Dec. 30, 2000. His other screenplay credits include *In Caliente, Four Daughters* (Oscar nomination), *Saturday's Children, The Bride Came C.O.D., The Strawberry Blonde, The Man Who Came to Dinner, The Male Animal, Mr. Skeffington, Arsenic and Old Lace, Romance on the High Seas, Forever Female, The Tender Trap, The Reluctant Debutante, Take a Giant Step, Fanny, Send Me No Flowers, Pete 'n' Tillie* (Oscar nomination), *Once is Not Enough,* and *Reuben Reuben* (Oscar nomination).

REX EVERHART, 79, Illinois-born screen, stage and television character actor died of lung cancer on March 13, 2000 in Branford, CT. Among his film credits are *The Seven-Ups, Superman, Friday the 13th,* and *Family Business.* Survived by his wife, his daughter, and a granddaughter.

DOUGLAS FAIRBANKS, JR., 90, New York City-born screen actor who followed in his famous father's footsteps to become a star in such adventure films as *The Prisoner of Zenda* (1937) and *Gunga Din* died in Manhattan on May 7, 2000. Following his 1925 debut in *Stephen Steps Out* he was seen in such movies as *Wild Horse Mesa, Is Zat So?, The Power of the Press, A Woman of Affairs, Our Modern Maidens, The Show of Shows, The Dawn Patrol* (1930), *Outward Bound, Little Caesar, I Like Your Nerve, It's Tough to Be Famous, Love is a Racket, Scarlet Dawn, Parachute Jumper, Morning Glory, The Life of Jimmy Dolan, Catherine the Great, The Amateur Gentleman, Joy of Living, Having Wonderful Time, The Young in Heart, Rulers of the Sea, Green Hell, Safari, Angels Over Broadway* (which he also associate produced), *The Corsican Brothers, Sinbad the Sailor, The Fighting O'Flynn* (also co-producer and co-writer), *That Lady in Ermine, State Secret, Mr. Drake's Duck,* and *Ghost Story.* He is survived by his third wife, his three daughters from his second marriage, eight grandchildren, and six great-grandchildren. His first marriage, to actress Joan Crawford, produced no offspring.

David Dukes

Rex Everhart

RICHARD FARNSWORTH, 80, Los Angeles-born stuntman-turned-actor died of a self-inflicted gunshot wound at his home in Lincoln, NM, on Oct. 6, 2000. He'd been battling cancer for many years and had been left partially paralyzed. Earlier in the year he had received his second Oscar nomination, for *The Straight Story.* In 1978 he was in the running for the award for *Comes a Horseman.* After doing stuntwork and bit parts for years he segued into larger roles in the 1960s and eventually became a noted character player. Among his films are *Texas Across the River, The Life and Times of Judge Roy Bean, The Duchess and the Dirtwater Fox, Tom Horn, Resurrection, The Legend of the Lone Ranger, The Grey Fox, The Natural, Rhinestone, Into the Night, Sylvester, Misery, Havana,* and *Lassie.* Survived by his daughter and his son, Richard "Diamond" Farnsworth, who was also a stuntman.

Douglas Fairbanks, Jr.

Midnight, The Loved One, Sebastian, The Shoes of the Fisherman, The Charge of the Light Brigade (1968), *Oh! What a Lovely War, Julius Caesar* (1971; as Caesar), *Lost Horizon* (1973), *Luther, Murder on the Orient Express, Galileo, Providence, Murder by Decree, The Human Factor, The Elephant Man, Chariots of Fire, Gandhi, Scandalous, Plenty,*

Richard Farnsworth   Vittorio Gassman

Getting It Right, Prospero's Books, Shining Through, The Power of One, First Knight, Shine, The Portrait of a Lady, Hamlet (1996; as Priam), and *Elizabeth.* There were no immediate survivors; his companion of many years, Martin Hensler, had died the year before. He was knighted in 1953.

SHEILAGH FRASER, 77, British actress died in London on September 13, 2000. Her films include *Esther Waters, Son of Robin Hood, Staircase, Thank You All Very Much, Star Wars,* and *Hope and Glory.*

VITTORIO GASSMAN, 77, one of Italy's leading film actors died of a heart attack on June 29, 2000 at his home in Rome. After becoming an international star with the 1950 release *Bitter Rice,* he was seen in such motion pictures as *The Glass Wall, Sombrero, Cry of the Hunted, Rhapsody, Mambo, Beautiful But Dangerous, War and Peace* (1956), *Kean* (which he also co-directed and co-wrote), *Tempest* (1959), *Big Deal on Madonna Street, The Miracle, Barabbas, The Easy Life, Il Successo/The Success, Let's Talk About Women, The Dirty Game, The Devil in Love, Woman Times Seven, The Tiger and the Pussycat, Ghosts Italian Style, L'Alibi* (also co-writer), *Senza Famiglia* (also director), *Scent of a Woman* (1975), *And We All Loved Each Other So Much, A Wedding, Quintet, The Nude Bomb, Sharky's Machine, Tempest* (1982), *Life is a Bed of Roses, The Family, To Forget Palermo,* and *Sleepers.* Survived by his third wife and four children.

JOHN GIELGUD (Arthur John Gielgud), 96, one of the greatest performers of the British theatre, who also enjoyed his share of success in films, winning an Academy Award for playing Dudley Moore's acerbic butler, Hobson, in *Arthur,* died at his home near Aylesbury, England, on May 21, 2000. He made his motion picture debut in 1925 in *Who is the Man?,* and would only appear on screen sporadically for the first part of his career. In time, however, he would amass a considerable number of screen credits including *The Good Companions, The Secret Agent* (1936), *The Prime Minister* (as Benjamin Disraeli), *Julius Caesar* (1953; as Cassius), *Richard III* (as Clarence), *Around the World in 80 Days, The Barretts of Wimpole Street* (1957), *Saint Joan* (as Warwick), *Becket* (as King Louis VII, for which he received an Oscar nomination), *Chimes at*

John Gielgud

Alec Guinness

LEO GORDON, 78, New York City-born character actor and writer died on Dec. 26, 2000 in Los Angeles after a brief illness. He was seen in such movies as *Hondo, China Venture, All the Brothers Were Valiant, Soldier of Fortune, The Conqueror, Johnny Concho, Baby Face Nelson* (as John Dillinger), *Quantrill's Raiders, The Jayhawkers, The Big Operator, McLintock!, The Haunted Palace, The St. Valentine's Day Massacre,* and *Big Top Pee-wee*. He received script credit on such pictures as *Hot Car Girl, Tower of London* (1962), *Tobruk,* and *You Can't Win 'em All*.

Leo Gordon   Charles Gray

CHARLES GRAY (Donald Marshall Gray), 71, British screen, stage and television actor, best known for playing the Criminologist in the cult film *The Rocky Horror Picture Show,* died on March 7, 2000 in London of unspecified causes. He could be seen in such other films as *I Accuse, The Entertainer, Masquerade* (1965), *The Night of the Generals, You Only Live Twice, The Secret War of Harry Frigg, Cromwell, Diamonds Are Forever* (as the villain, Ernst Stavro Blofeld), *The Seven Percent Solution, The Legacy,* and *The Mirror Crack'd*. No reported survivors.

JOSÉ GRECO, 82, world famous flamenco dancer who helped popularize the art in the U.S. and Europe in the 1940s and 50s, died at his home in Lancaster, PA, on Dec. 31, 2000. He was seen performing in such films as *Sombrero, Around the World in 80 Days, Holiday for Lovers,* and *Ship of Fools*. Survived by his fifth wife, a sister, and five children.

ALEC GUINNESS (Alec Guinness de Cuffe), 86, one of England's most versatile and popular actors, who won the Academy Award for playing the stubborn Colonel Nicholson in the classic 1957 film *The Bridge on the River Kwai,* died of liver cancer on Aug. 5, 2000 in Sussex, England. The London-born actor became world famous through his chameleon-like performances in such notable films as *Oliver Twist* (as Fagin), *The Lavender Hill Mob* (for which he received an Oscar nomination), *The Ladykillers, Lawrence of Arabia* (as Prince Feisal), and *Star Wars* (Oscar nominated for playing the Jedi Knight Obi-Wan Kenobi). His many other motion pictures include *Great Expectations* (1946; as Herbert Pocket), *Kind Hearts and Coronets* (playing eight roles in his first film for Ealing Studios, with which his name would become synonymous), *Last Holiday, The Mudlark, The Man in the White Suit, The Card/The Promoter, The Captain's Paradise, Father Brown/The Detective, The Prisoner, The Swan, All at Sea/Barnacle Bill, The Scapegoat* (which he also produced), *The Horse's Mouth* (which he also wrote, earning an Oscar nomination for his script), *Our Man in Havana, Tunes of Glory, A Majority of One, Damn the Defiant!/H.M.S. Defiant, The Fall of the Roman Empire, Situation Hopeless But Not Serious, Doctor Zhivago, Hotel Paradiso, The Comedians, Cromwell, Scrooge* (as Marley's Ghost), *Hitler: The Last Ten Days, Murder by Death, The Empire Strikes Back, Raise the Titanic!, Return of the Jedi, A Passage to India, A Handful of Dust, Little Dorrit* (Oscar nomination), and *Kafka*. He is survived by his wife of 62 years, and his son. He was knighted in 1959.

DAVID HASKELL, 52, California-born screen and televison actor, who played Judas in the 1973 film of *Godspell,* died of brain cancer on August 30, 2000 in Woodland Hills, CA. His other movies include *Seems Like Old Times, Deal of the Century, Body Double,* and *The Boost*.

ROSE HOBART (Rose Kefer), 94, New York City-born actress died of natural causes on August 29, 2000 in Woodland Hills, CA. After her 1930 debut in *Liliom* she was seen in such movies as *Dr. Jekyll & Mr. Hyde, Scandal for Sale, Tower of London* (1939), *Susan and God, Ziegfeld Girl, No Hands on the Clock, Mr. & Mrs. North, Nothing But the Truth, The Mad Ghoul, Song of the Open Road, Brighton Strangler, Canyon Passage, The Farmer's Daughter* (1947), *Cass Timberlane,* and *Bride of Vengeance*. Survived by her son.

JEAN HOWARD (Ernestine Hill), 89, Texas-born actress who found greater fame when she left acting and became a noted Hollywood photographer, died at her home in Beverly Hills, CA, on March 20, 2000. As a startlet she was seen in such movies as *Dancing Lady, Break of Hearts,* and *The Final Hour*. Survived by her husband.

RICK JASON, 74, New York City-born screen and television actor, best known for starring on the 1960s series "Combat," died in Moorpark, CA, on Oct. 16, 2000 of a self-inflicted gunshot wound. His motion picture credits included *The Saracen Blade, The Lieutenant Wore Skirts, RX Murder, Sierra Baron, Color Me Dead, The Witch Who Came from the Sea,* and *Unfaithfully Yours* (1984). Survivors include his wife.

Rose Hobart   Rick Jason

TODD KARNS, 79, Hollywood-born actor, best known for playing James Stewart's younger brother, Harry Bailey, in the 1946 classic *It's a Wonderful Life,* died of cancer at his home in Ajijic, Mexico on Feb. 5, 2000. Among his other movie credits are *Andy Hardy's Private Secretary, Eagle Squadron, The Courtship of Andy Hardy, Good Sam, My Foolish Heart, China Venture, Invaders from Mars* (1953), and *The Caine Mutiny*. The son of actor Roscoe Karns (who died in 1970), he is survived by his wife, a son, and two daughters.

LILA KEDROVA, 82, Russian-born actress, who won the Academy Award for playing the aging courtesan Madame Hortense in *Zorba the Greek,* died of heart failure in Sault Ste. Marie, Ontario, on Feb. 16, 2000. Her other films include *A High Wind in Jamaica, Torn Curtain, Penelope, The Girl Who Couldn't Say No, The Kremlin Letter, Undercovers Hero, The Tenant, Tell Me a Riddle, Testament,* and *Some Girls.* Survived by her second husband, director Richard Howard.

FRED KELLY, 83, Pittsburgh-born dancer-choreographer-director died of cancer on Mar. 15, 2000 in Tucson, AZ. He was seen dancing on screen with his brother, Gene Kelly, in the number "I Love to Go Swimmin' With Wimmen" in the 1955 film *Deep in My Heart.* Survived by his son, two sisters, a daughter, and eight grandchildren.

WERNER KLEMPERER, 80, German screen, stage, and television performer, who won two Emmy Awards for playing the comical Nazi Colonel Klink on the series "Hogan's Heroes," died of cancer at his New York home on Dec. 6, 2000. On screen he was seen in such movies as *Death of a Scoundrel, The Wrong Man, Kiss Them for Me, Houseboat, The High Cost of Loving, Youngblood Hawke, Operation Eichmann* (as Adolf Eichmann), *Judgment at Nuremberg, Ship of Fools,* and *The Wicked Dreams of Paula Schultz.* Survived by two children and a sister.

Lila Kedrova   Werner Klemperer

HEDY LAMARR (Hedwig Eva Maria Kiesler), 86, Vienneese actress who was hailed as one of the most glamorous Hollywood stars of the 1930s and 40s, was found dead in her Orlando, FL, home on January 19, 2000. After causing a sensation with her nude scene in the 1933 Czech film *Ecstasy,* she came to America to co-star in *Algiers,* opposite Charles Boyer. She went on to appear in such movies as *I Take This Woman, Lady of the Tropics, Boom Town, Comrade X, Come Live With Me, Ziegfeld Girl, H.M. Pulham Esq., Tortilla Flat, White Cargo, The Heavenly Body, Her Highness and the Bellboy, Dishonored Lady* (opposite her then-husband, actor John Loder), *Samson and Delilah, Lady Without a Passport, Copper Canyon, My Favorite Spy, The Story of Mankind,* and *The Female Animal.* Survived by an adopted son and her two children from her marriage to Loder.

RING LARDNER, JR. (Ringgold Wilmer Lardner, Jr.), 85, screenwriter who won Academy Awards for *Woman of the Year* (written with Michael Kanin), and *M*A*S*H,* but was blacklisted in between, died of cancer at his Manhattan home on Oct. 31, 2000. He was credited with writing such scripts as *Meet Dr. Christian, The Cross of Lorraine, Tomorrow the World, Cloak and Dagger,* and *Forever Amber,* before becoming one of the Hollywood Ten after refusing to name names before the House

Un-American Activities Committee. Using pseudonymns he wrote movies like *The Forbidden Street, Four Days Leave, Virgin Island,* and *The Cardinal,* and later resumed writing under his own name on such movies as *The Cincinnati Kid* and *The Greatest.* Survived by his second wife, three sons, two daughters, seven grandchildren, and five great-grandchildren.

Hedy Lamarr   Francis Lederer

FRANCIS LEDERER, 100, Prague-born screen and stage actor, perhaps best known for his starring role in the 1939 film *Confessions of a Nazi Spy,* died of natural causes on May 25, 2000 at his home in Palm Springs, CA. Following some German films (including *Pandora's Box*) he came to Hollywood where he would appear in such movies as *The Pursuit of Happiness, Romance in Manhattan, Lone Wolf in Paris, One Rainy Afternoon, The Man I Married, The Bridge of San Luis Rey, Diary of a Chambermaid* (1946), *Captain Carey USA, A Woman of Distinction, The Ambassador's Daughter, Lisbon, The Return of Dracula,* and *Terror is a Man.* Survived by his third wife.

Nancy Marchand   Joan Marsh

Walter Matthau

JOSEPH H. LEWIS, 93, Brooklyn born low-budget film director, best known for the 1949 cult film *Gun Crazy*, died on August 30, 2000 in Marina Del Rey, CA. Among his other films are *Singing Outlaw, The Invisible Ghost, Bombs Over Burma, The Falcon in San Francisco, The Return of October, Retreat Hell!, The Big Combo, The Seventh Cavalry, The Halliday Brand,* and *Terror in a Texas Town.* He is survived by his wife, a daughter, and two grandchildren.

LARRY LINVILLE, 60, California-born screen, stage, and television actor, best known for playing Major Frank Burns on the television series adaptation of "M*A*S*H," died of complications from pneumonia on April 10, 2000 in Manhattan. He was seen in such movies as *Kotch, Earth Girls Are Easy,* and *A Million to Juan.* Survived by his wife.

JULIE LONDON (Julie Peck), 74, California-born actress-singer died on Oct. 18, 2000 in Encino, CA. She suffered a stroke five years earlier and had been in declining health. In addition to selling such hit records as "Cry Me a River," she acted in such films as *Nabonga, The Red House, Tap Roots, Task Force, The Fat Man, The Great Man, The Girl Can't Help It, Crime Against Joe, Drango, Voice in the Mirror, Saddle the Wind, Man of the West, The Wonderful Country, Night of the Quarter Moon, The Third Voice,* and *The George Raft Story.* From 1972 to 1977 she played Nurse Dixie McCall in the series "Emergency." It was executive produced by her first husband (1947-52) Jack Webb and co-starred her second husband, musician-actor Bobby Troupe, whom she married in 1959 (he died in 1999). She is survived by a daughter from her marriage to Webb, and a daughter and twin sons from her marriage to Troupe.

George Montgomery   Richard Mulligan

NANCY MARCHAND, 71, Buffalo-born screen, stage, and television actress, who won four Emmy Awards for playing publisher Margaret Pynchon on the series "Lou Grant," died at her home in Stratford, CT, on June 18, 2000, one day short of her 72nd birthday. Among her film credits were *The Bachelor Party* (1957), *Ladybug Ladybug, Me Natalie, Tell Me That You Love Me Junie Moon, The Hospital, The Bostonians, From the Hip, The Naked Gun: From the Files of Police Squad!, Brain Donors, Jefferson in Paris, Reckless, Sabrina* (1995), and *Dear God.* At the time of her death she was playing Livia Soprano on the series "The Sopranos." Her husband, actor Paul Sparer, had died in November of 1999. She is survived by a son, two daughters, and seven grandchildren.

CHRISTIAN MARQUAND, 73, Marseilles-born actor and director died near Paris of complications from Alzheimer's disease on Nov. 22, 2000. He acted in such movies as *Atilla, Lady Chatterly's Lover, And God Created Woman* (1956), *End of Desire, The Corrupt Ones,* and *The Other*

Side of Midnight, and directed *Of Flesh and Blood* and *Candy.* Survived by his son from actress Dominique Sanda.

JOAN MARSH (Dorothy Rosher), 85, California-born screen actress who started in films as a child, died on Aug. 10, 2000 in Ojai, CA. Among her movies were *Daddy Long Legs* (1919), *Pollyana* (1920), *The King of Jazz, Dance Fools Dance, All Quiet on the Western Front, You're Telling Me, Charlie Chan on Broadway, Road to Zanzibar,* and *Follow the Leader.* No reported survivors.

Harold Nicholas   Patricia Owens

HELEN MARTIN, 90, St. Louis-born screen, stage, and television character actress died of a heart attack at her home in Monterey, CA, on Mar. 25, 2000. She appeared in such movies as *Cotton Comes to Harlem, Death Wish, Deal of the Century, Repo Man, Hollywood Shuffle, A Rage in Harlem, Doc Hollywood, Beverly Hills Cop III, Kiss the Girls,* and *Bulworth.* No reported survivors.

WALTER MATTHAU (Walter Matuschanskayasky), 79, Manhattan-born screen, stage and television actor, who became one of Hollywood's most adept comic actors in such movies as *The Fortune Cookie* (for which he won an Academy Award for playing scheming lawyer Willie Gingrich), *The Odd Couple, Hello Dolly!, Kotch* (Oscar nomination), *The Sunshine Boys* (Oscar nomination), and *The Bad News Bears,* died of a heart attack on July 1, 2000 in Santa Monica, CA. Following his film debut in 1955 in *The Ketuckian,* he went on to appear in such motion pictures as *The Indian Fighter, Bigger Than Life, A Face in the Crowd, Voice in the Mirror, King Creole, Onionhead, The Gangster Story* (which he also directed), *Lonely Are the Brave, Who's Got the Action?, Island of Love, Charade, Ensign Pulver, Fail-Safe, Mirage, A Guide for the Married Man, The Secret Life of an American Wife, Cactus Flower, A New Leaf, Plaza Suite, Pete 'n' Tillie, Charley Varrick, The Laughing Policeman, The Taking of Pelham One Two Three, The Front Page* (1974), *Casey's Shadow, House Calls, California Suite, Little Miss Marker* (1980), *Hopscotch, First Monday in October, Buddy Buddy, I Ought To Be in Pictures, The Survivors, Pirates, The Couch Trip, JFK, Dennis the Menace, Grumpy Old Men, I.Q., Grumpier Old Men, The Grass Harp, Out to Sea,* and *Hanging Up.* Survived by his wife, a son, director Charles Matthau, two children from a previous marriage, another son, and a daughter.

FRANCIS MERCER, 85, New Rochelle-born actress died on Nov. 12, 2000 in Los Angeles. She was seen in such movies as *Vivacious Lady, The Story of Vernon and Irene Castle, The Mad Miss Manton,* and *Society Lawyer.* No immediate survivors.

DAVID MERRICK, 88, famous Broadway showman who produced such hits as *Hello Dolly!* and *42nd Street,* died in his sleep in London on Apr. 26, 2000. He also produced four motion pictures: *Child's Play, The Great Gatsby* (1974), *Semi-Tough,* and *Rough Cut.* His five marriages ended in divorce; he is survived by two daughters.

GEORGE MONTGOMERY (George Montgomery Letz), 84, Montana-born screen actor, best known for his Western roles, died of heart failure at his home in Rancho Mirage, CA, on Dec. 12, 2000. He debuted under his real name in 1936 in *Singing Vagabond* and continued under this billing for such movies as *Conquest, Come on Rangers, Shine on Harvest Moon,* and *Wall Street Cowboy,* until changing his name to George Montgomery, which is how he appeared in such films as *Young People, Riders of the Purple Sage, Orchestra Wives, Ten Gentlemen from West Point, China Girl, Roxie Hart, Bombers' Moon, Coney Island, Three Little Girls in Blue, Lulu Belle, Belle Starr's Daughter, Dakota Lil, Iroquois Trail, The Texas Rangers, Indian Uprising, The Pathfinder, Fort Ti, Gun Belt, The Lone Gun, Robber's Roost, Huk, Gun Duel at Durango, Pawnee, Badman's Country, Toughest Gun in Tombstone, Battle of the Bulge, Watusi, Hostile Guns,* and *Hallucination Generation.* He directed as well as appeared in *The Steel Claw, Samar!, From Hell to Borneo, Guerillas in Pink Lace,* and *Ride the Tiger.* Survived by a son and a daughter, from his marriage (1943-60) to singer Dinah Shore.

RICHARD MULLIGAN, 67, Bronx-born actor, who won Emmy Awards for his comedic roles in the series "Soap" and "Empty Nest," died of cancer at his Los Angeles home on Sept. 28, 2000. He was seen in such films as *One Potato Two Potato, Love With the Proper Stranger, The Group, The Undefeated, Little Big Man* (as General George Armstrong Custer), *From the Mixed-Up Files of Mrs. Basil E. Frankweiler, The Big Bus, Scavenger Hunt, S.O.B., Teachers, Micki + Maude,* and *A Fine Mess.* He is survived by a son and two brothers, one of whom is director Robert Mulligan.

N. RICHARD NASH (Nathan Richard Nasbaum), 87, Philadelphia-born writer, best known for the Broadway play *The Rainmaker,* which he also adapted into a 1956 film, died on Dec. 11, 2000 in Manhattan. He was credited on such screenplays as *Welcome Stranger, Nora Prentiss, Dear Wife, Molly, Mara Maru,* and *Porgy and Bess.* Survived by two daughters and a son.

HAROLD NICHOLAS, 79, North Carolina-born performer, who, along with his older brother Fayard, became one of the most dazzling of all dancers, died of heart failure following surgery, in Manhattan, on July 3, 2000. After making a splash at the Cotton Club the brothers were invited to Hollywood and they appeared in speciality numbers in such movies as *Kid Millions, The Big Broadcast of 1936, Down Argentine Way, Tin Pan Alley, Sun Valley Serenade* (performing "Chattanooga Choo-Choo" alongside Dorothy Dandridge, to whom Harold was later married), *Stormy Weather* (performing their classic "Jumpin' Jive" staircase number), and *The Pirate.* Solo, Harold was later seen in the films *Uptown Saturday Night, Tap,* and *The Five Heartbeats.* In addition to his brother, he is survived by his third wife, his sister, a daughter, a son, and two stepchildren.

JACK NITZSCHE (Bernard Alfred Nitzsche), 63, Chicago-born composer, who won an Academy Award for co-writing the song "Up Where We Belong" from the film *An Officer and a Gentleman,* died in Hollywood on Aug. 25, 2000, of cardiac arrest, brought on by a recurring bronchial infection. He was credited with scoring such movies as *Performance, Greaser's Palace, One Flew Over the Cuckoo's Nest* (for which he received an Oscar nomination), *Personal Best, Starman, Stand by Me,* and *The Crossing Guard.* Survived by his son.

ALAN NORTH, 79, character actor died of kidney and lung cancer on January 19, 2000 in Port Jefferson, NY. In addition to co-starring on the cult series "Police Squad!" he was seen in such movies as *Plaza Suite, Serpico, And Justice for All, The Formula, Highlander, The Fourth Protocol, Lean on Me, See No Evil Hear No Evil, Glory, Twenty Bucks,* and *I'm Not Rappaport.*

SAM O'STEEN, 76, film editor, who received Oscar nominations for his work on *Who's Afraid of Virginia Woolf?, Chinatown,* and *Silkwood,* died

of a heart attack in Atlantic City, NJ, on Oct. 11, 2000. His other films include *Robin and the 7 Hoods, The Graduate, Catch-22,* and *Carnal Knowledge.* He directed the film *Sparkle.* Survived by his wife, and four daughters.

PATRICIA OWENS, 75, Canadian-born actress, best remembered for playing the heroine of the 1958 sci-fi classic *The Fly,* died in Lancaster, CA, on Aug. 31, 2000. Among her other films were *The Happiest Days of Your Life, Colonel March Investigates, Island in the Sun, Sayonara, No Down Payment, The Law and Jake Wade, Five Gates to Hell, Hell to Eternity, X-15, Black Spurs,* and *The Destructors.*

JEAN PETERS (Elizabeth Jean Peters), 73, Ohio-born actress who appeared in such 20th Century Fox productions as *Viva Zapata!* and *Three Coins in the Fountain,* died of leukemia on Oct. 13, 2000 in Carlsbad, CA. Among her other movies were *Captain from Castile* (her debut, in 1947), *Deep Waters, It Happens Every Spring, Love That Brute, As Young as You Feel, Wait Till the Sun Shines Nellie!, O. Henry's Full House, Niagara, Pickup on South Street, Vicki, Apache, Broken Lance,* and *A Man Called Peter.* She retired from acting to marry millionaire Howard Hughes in 1957 (they divorced in 1971). She later returned to acting in some television films. Survivors include a sister.

Jean Peters   Logan Ramsey

CHRISTOPHER PETTIET, 24, Dallas-born screen and television actor died of an accidental drug overdose on April 12, 2000 in Los Angeles. He was seen in such films as *Don't Tell Mom the Babysitter's Dead, Point Break, Carried Away,* and *Boys.*

JUSTIN PIERCE, 25, London-born actor, best known for playing Casper in the 1995 film *Kids,* hanged himself in his hotel room in Las Vegas, NV, on July 10, 2000. His other films include *A Brother's Kiss, Next Friday,* and *The Big Tease.* Survived by his wife, his mother and his father.

TITO PUENTE, 77, beloved New York City-born bandleader and percussionist, died of complications after open heart surgery in Manhattan on May 31, 2000. He appeared as himself in such films as *Radio Days, Salsa, The Mambo Kings,* and *Calle 54.* Survivors include his three sons and his daughter.

LOGAN RAMSEY, 79, screen, stage, and television character actor died of a heart attack on June 26, 2000 in Los Angeles. His film credits include *The Hoodlum Priest, Head, The Rievers, The Travelling Executioner, What's the Matter With Helen?, Walking Tall, Farewell My Lovely, Cornbread Earl and Me, Any Which Way You Can, Scrooged,* and *Fat Man and Little Boy.* He was married to actress Anne Ramsey, who died in 1988. Survived by his sister.

STEVE REEVES, 74, Montana-born bodybuilder-turned-actor, best remembered for playing the title role in the Italian-import *Hercules,* died of complications from lymphoma in Escondido, CA, on May 1, 2000. Afer winning the bodybuilding titles of Mr. America and Mr. Universe he came to Hollywood where he was seen in such films as *Athena* and *The Hidden Face.* After the success of *Hercules* he was seen in such further adventures as *Hercules Unchained, The Giant of Marathon, The Thief of Baghdad, Morgan the Pirate, Duel of the Titans (Romulus and Remus), The Last Days of Pompeii,* and *Son of Spartacus.* He retired in 1969 to become a rancher. No reported survivors.

BEAH RICHARDS, 79, Mississippi-born character actress, who received an Oscar nomination for playing Sidney Poitier's mother in *Guess Who's Coming to Dinner,* died of emphysema on Sept. 14, 2000 in Vicksburg, MI. Four days earlier she had won her second Emmy Award, for guesting on "The Practice." She was seen in such other films as *Take a Giant Step, Gone Are the Days, Hurry Sundown, In the Heat of the Night, The Great White Hope, The Biscuit Eater* (1972), *Mahogany, Drugstore Cowboy,* and *Beloved.* Survived by several nieces and nephews.

Steve Reeves

Beah Richards

JASON ROBARDS, 78, Chicago-born screen, stage, and television actor, who became one of the most acclaimed stage actors of the post-war generation and went on to win Academy Awards for his roles in *All the President's Men* (as *Washington Post* editor Ben Bradlee) and *Julia* (as writer Dashiell Hammett), died in Bridgeport, CT, on Dec. 26, 2000, after a long battle with cancer. On stage he was proclaimed the chief interpreter of the works of Eugene O'Neill (in such plays as *Long Day's Journey Into Night* and *The Iceman Cometh*). Following his 1959 motion picture debut in *The Journey,* he was seen in such films as *By Love Possessed, Tender is the Night, Long Day's Journey Into Night* (repeating his stage role, as James Tyrone, Jr.), *Act One* (as George S. Kaufman), *A Thousand Clowns, Any Wednesday, A Big Hand for the Little Lady, Divorce American Style, The St. Valentine's Day Massacre* (as Al Capone), *The Night They Raided Minsky's, Isadora, Once Upon a Time in the West, Tora! Tora! Tora!, The Ballad of Cable Hogue, Fools, Murders in the Rue Morgue, The War Between Men and Women, A Boy and His Dog, Comes a Horseman, Hurricane, Melvin and Howard* (Oscar nomination, for playing Howard Hughes), *The Legend of the Lone Ranger, Something Wicked This Way Comes, Max Dugan Returns, Square Dance, Bright Lights Big City, The Good Mother, Dream a Little Dream, Parenthood, Quick Change, The Adventures of Huck Finn, Philadephia, The Paper, Enemy of the State,* and *Magnolia.* He is survived by his fourth wife, and six children, including actor Sam Robards from his marriage (1961-73) to actress Lauren Bacall.

RAUL ROULIEN (Raul Pepe Acolti Gil), 94, Brazilian singer-actor died on pneumonia on Sept. 8, 2000 in Sao Paulo. In addition to making movies in his native country he appeared in such American releases as *Delicious, The Painted Woman, Flying Down to Rio, The World Moves On,* and *Road to Rio.*

Jason Robards

FRAN RYAN, 83, Los Angeles-born screen and television character actress died of natural causes on January 15, 2000 in Burbank, CA. She was seen in such movies as *Scandalous John, The Apple Dumpling Gang, Straight Time, The Long Riders, Pale Rider, The Sure Thing,* and *Out Cold.*

CLAUDE SAUTET, 76, French film director-writer whose film *A Simple Story* was nominated for a Foreign Film Oscar, died of liver cancer on July 22, 2000 in Paris. His other films include *The Things of Life, Cesar and Rosalie, Vincent Francois Paul and the Others, Mado, A Few Day With Me,* and *A Heart in Winter.* No reported survivors.

CHARLES SCHULZ, 77, Minneapolis-born cartoonist, whose *Peanuts* became one of the best loved comic strips of all time, died of colon cancer at his home in Santa Rosa, CA, on Feb. 12, 2000, hours before his last comic strip ran in the Sunday newspapers. In addition to countless television specials, animated versions of such memorable Schulz characters as Charlie Brown, Snoopy, Lucy and Linus Van Pelt were seen in four full-length motion pictures which he wrote, *A Boy Named Charlie Brown, Snoopy Come Home, Race for Your Life Charlie Brown,* and *Bon Voyage Charlie Brown.* He is survived by his wife, three daughters, two sons, two stepchildren, and eighteen grandchildren.

WALTER SHENSON, 81, San Francisco-born motion picture producer, whose best known productions were the Beatles films *A Hard Day's Night* and *Help!,* died on Oct. 17, 2000 in Woodland Hills, CA. Among his other films are *The Mouse That Roared, A Matter of Who, The Mouse on the Moon, Don't Raise the Bridge Lower the River, 30 is a Dangerous Age Cynthia, Reuben Reuben,* and *Echo Park.* Survived by two sons, a sister, and four grandchildren.

MAX SHOWALTER, 83, Kansas-born screen, stage, and television actor died in Middletown, CT, on July 30, 2000. Using both the names "Casey Adams" and "Max Showalter" he was seen in such movies as *Always Leave Them Laughing, With a Song in My Heart, Niagara, Down Three Dark Streets, Night People, The Indestructible Man, Bus Stop, The Monster That Challenged the World, The Naked and the Dead, Elmer Gantry, Summer and Smoke, Bon Voyage, The Music Man, Sex and the Single Girl, How to Murder Your Wife, Lord Love a Duck, 10, Racing With the Moon,* and *Sixteen Candles.* Survived by a sister.

Max Showalter   Craig Stevens

CURT SIODMAK, 98, German-born screenwriter and director, best known for writing such horror scripts as *The Wolf Man* and *I Walked With a Zombie,* died at his home in Three Rivers, CA, on Sept. 2, 2000. His other writing credits include *Her Jungle Love, Black Friday, The Invisible Man Returns, The Ape, Aloma of the South Seas, Invisible Agent, Frankenstein Meets the Wolf Man, House of Frankenstein, Lady and the Monster, The Climax, The Beast with Five Fingers, Riders to the Stars,* and *Earth vs. the Flying Saucers.* He directed as well as wrote *Bride of the Gorilla, Magnetic Monsters,* and *Curucu Beast of the Amazon.* He is survived by his wife, and a son. His brother, director Robert Siodmak, died in 1973.

CRAIG STEVENS (Gail Shikles, Jr.), 81, Missouri-born screen, stage, and television actor, best known for starring in the detective series "Peter Gunn," died May 10, 2000 in Los Angeles. His movie credits include *Dive Bomber, Hollywood Canteen, God is My Co-Pilot, Roughly Speaking, Humoresque, That Way with Women, Night Unto Night, Where the Sidewalk Ends, Phone Call from a Stranger, Abbott and Costello Meet Dr. Jekyll and Mr. Hyde, The Deadly Mantis, Buchanan Rides Alone, Gunn,* and *S.O.B.* He was married to actress Alexis Smith from 1944 to her death in 1993. No survivors.

ANDREW L. STONE, 96, Oakland-born film director-producer-writer of such movies as *Stormy Weather* and *The Last Voyage* died in June of 1999. His death went unreported for more than a year until the sale of his house brought attention to his passing. His other films included *The Great Victor Herbert, There's Magic in Music, Hi Diddle Diddle, Sensations of 1945, Confidence Girl, The Night Holds Terror, Julie, Cry Terror!, The Decks Ran Red, The Password is Courage, Song of Norway,* and *The Great Waltz* (1972). His ex-wife Virginia Stone collaborated with him on several of his films as editor and producer. Survived by his second wife and two children.

GLORIA TALBOT, 69, California-born star of the 1958 cult sci-fi film *I Married a Monster from Outer Space,* died on Sept. 19, 2000 in Glendale, CA. She was seen in such other films as *We're No Angels, Lucy Gallant, All That Heaven Allows, Daughter of Dr. Jekyll, Cyclops, The Oregon Trail, The Leech Woman,* and *An Eye for an Eye* (1966).

SAMUEL TAYLOR, 87, Chicago-born writer, best known for his play *Sabrina Fair,* which he helped adapt into the classic film *Sabrina,* died at his home in Blue Hill, ME, on May 26, 2000. His other screenplay credits include *The Eddy Duchin Story, Vertigo, Goodbye Again, The Pleasure of His Company* (from his play), *Rosie!,* and *Topaz.* Survived by his wife, two sons, a stepdaughter, and nine grandchildren.

BILL THOMAS (William Thomas Petersen), 79, Chicago-born costume designer, who received an Academy Award for his work on the film *Spartacus,* died at his Beverly Hills, CA, home on May 30, 2000. His many other films include *You Never Can Tell, Meet Danny Wilson, The Mississippi Gambler, The Purple Mask, The Benny Goodman Story, Tammy and the Bachelor, Touch of Evil, Operation Petticoat, Babes in Toyland, Summer Magic, It's a Mad Mad Mad Mad World, Ship of Fools, That Darn Cat!, The Happiest Millionaire, The Love Bug, Bedknobs and Broomsticks,* and *Pete's Dragon.* No reported survivors.

David Tomlinson   Claire Trevor

DAVID TOMLINSON, 83, British character actor, best known for playing Mr. Banks in the classic 1964 Disney film *Mary Poppins,* died in Buckinghamshire, England, on June 24, 2000. He appeared in such other movies as *Pimpernel Smith, The Way to the Stars, I See a Dark Stranger* (*The Adventuress*), *School for Secrets* (*Secret Flight*), *Miranda, So Long at the Fair, Hotel Sahara, Calling Bulldog Drummond, Three Men in a Boat, Up the Creek* (1958), *Tom Jones, The Truth About Spring, The Love Bug, Bedknobs and Broomsticks,* and *The Fiendish Plot of Dr. Fu Manchu.* Surived by his wife and four sons.

CLAIRE TREVOR (Claire Wemlinger), 91, Brooklyn-born screen, stage, and television actress, who won an Academy Award for playing Edward G. Robinson's alcoholic mistress in *Key Largo,* died in Newport Beach, CA, April 8, 2000. She had been suffering from respiratory ailments. Following her 1933 debut in *Life in the Raw,* she was seen in such movies as *The Mad Game, Hold That Girl, Baby Take a Bow, Elinor Norton, Dante's Inferno, To Mary With Love, Career Woman, King of Gamblers, Dead End* (Oscar nomination), *Big Town Girl, Walking Down Broadway, The Amazing Dr. Clitterhouse, Valley of the Giants, Five of a Kind, Stagecoach* (1939), *Allegheny Uprising, Honky Tonk, Texas, The*

Woman of the Town, Murder My Sweet, Johnny Angel, Born to Kill, Raw Deal (1948), *The Babe Ruth Story, The Velvet Touch, Best of the Badmen, Stop You're Killing Me, The Stranger Wore a Gun, The High and the Mighty* (Oscar nomination), *Man Without a Star, The Mountain, Marjorie Morningstar, Two Weeks in Another Town, The Stripper, How to Murder Your Wife,* and *Kiss Me Goodbye.* Survived by two stepsons.

ROGER VADIM (Roger Vladimir Plemiannikov), 72, French director-writer, best known for the 1956 film *And God Created Woman,* which made an international star of Brigitte Bardot (to whom he was married, from 1952 to 1957), died of cancer in Paris on Feb. 11, 2000. His other films include *The Night Heaven Fell, Les Liaisons Dangereuses, Blood and Roses, Love on a Pillow, Nutty Naughty Chateau, Circle of Love, The Game is Over, Barbarella, Pretty Maids All in Row, Charlotte, Night Games,* and the 1988 remake of *And God Created Woman.* He is survived by his fifth wife, actress Marie-Christine Barrault; a daughter from his second marriage, to actress Annette Stroyberg; a son, actor Christian Vadim, from his relationship with actress Catherine Deneuve; a daughter from his third marriage, to actress Jane Fonda; and a daughter from his fourth marriage.

Roger Vadim   Gwen Verdon

JIM VARNEY, 50, Kentucky-born comedian, who created the character of the clumsy, know-it-all yokel Ernest P. Worrell for a series of commercials, that were spun off into several feature films, died of lung cancer on Feb. 10, 2000 at his home in White House, TN. In addition to the "Ernest" films *Ernest Goes to Camp, Ernest Saves Christmas, Ernest Goes to Jail,* and *Ernest Rides Again,* and supplying the voice of "Slinky Dog" in *Toy Story* and its sequel, he was seen in such movies as *The Beverly Hillbillies,* and *100 Proof.* No reported survivors.

GWEN VERDON, 75, California-born dancer-actress, who became one of Broadway's most beloved performers, winning Tony Awards for *Can-Can, Damn Yankees, New Girl in Town,* and *Redhead,* died of natural causes in Woodstock, VT, on Oct. 18, 2000. In addition to repeating her role of the temptress Lola in the 1958 film version of *Damn Yankees,* she was seen in such movies as *On the Riviera, Meet Me After the Show, The I Don't Care Girl, The Cotton Club, Cocoon, Alice,* and *Marvin's Room.* She is survived by her daughter from her marriage to choreographer-director and frequent collaborator Bob Fosse.

SY WEINTRAUB, 76, New York-born movie producer responsible for re-vitalizing the Tarzan franchise in the late 1950s, died of pancreatic cancer on Apr. 4, 2000 in Beverly Hills, CA. His films include *Tarzan's Greatest Adventure, Tarzan the Magnificent, Tarzan's Three Challenges,* and *Tarzan Goes to India.* Survived by two daughters, and four grandchildren.

Marie Windsor   G. Wood

DON WEIS, 78, Milwaukee-born movie and television director died on July 26, 2000 in Santa Fe, NM. His films include *Half a Hero, The Affairs of Dobie Gillis, The Gene Krupa Story, Critic's Choice,* and *Billie.* Survived by his fourth wife, two daughters, a stepdaughter, and two grandchildren.

GEORGE WELLS, 91, New York City-born film writer died at his home in Newport Beach, CA, on Nov. 29, 2000. Under contract to MGM he contributed to such scripts as *Till the Clouds Roll By, The Hucksters, Take Me Out to the Ballgame, Three Little Worlds, Summer Stock, Excuse My Dust, Angels in the Outfield* (1951), *Lovely to Look At, I Love Melvin, Don't Go Near the Water, Party Girl* (1958), *The Gazebo, Where the Boys Are* (1960), *The Horizontal Lieutenant,* and *The Impossible Years.* He is survived by his second wife, two children, and three grandchildren.

BERNHARD WICKI, 80, German actor-director died on Jan. 5, 2000 at his home in Munich. As an actor he was seen in such movies as *Escape from Sahara, Despair,* and *Paris Texas,* while his directorial credits included *The Bridge, The Longest Day* (sharing credit with Ken Annakin and Andrew Marton), *The Visit* (1964), and *Morituri.* Survived by his wife.

MARIE WINDSOR (Emily Marie Bertelsen), 80, Utah-born screen and television actress, best remembered for playing hard-boiled women in such movies as *The Narrow Margin* and *The Killing,* died at her Beverly Hills home on Dec. 10, 2000 of unspecified causes. She made her motion picture debut in 1941 in *All American Co-Ed,* and was later seen in such movies as *The Hucksters, Song of the Thin Man, Force of Evil, The Fighting Kentuckian, Dakota Lil, Frenchie, Little Big Horn, The Sniper, Outlaw Woman, The Tall Texan, Trouble Along the Way, The City That Never Sleeps, The Eddie Cantor Story, Cat Women of the Moon, Hell's Half Acre, Silver Star, Abbott and Costello Meet the Mummy, No Man's Woman, Swamp Women, The Girl in Black Stockings, The Story of Mankind, The Day of the Bad Man, Mail Order Bride, Bedtime Story* (1964), *Cahill: U.S. Marshal, The Apple Dumpling Gang,* and *Freaky Friday.* She is survived by her husband, her son, a brother, and a sister.

G. WOOD (George Wood), 80, screen, stage, and television actor, who played General Hammond in the 1970 film *M*A*S*H,* died of congestive heart failure on July 24, 2000 in Macon, Ga. He was also seen in the films *Brewster McCloud, Harold and Maude,* and *Bank Shot.* Survived by his sister.

LORETTA YOUNG (Gretchen Michaela Young), 87, Salt Lake City-born actress, who became one of the top stars of the 1930s and 40s, winning an Academy Award for her performance as the Swedish housemaid who runs for congress in *The Farmer's Daughter,* died in Los Angeles of ovarian cancer on Aug. 12, 2000. Starting as an extra in the 1926 film *The Only Way,* she went on to star in such movies as *Laugh Clown Laugh, The Man from Blankley's, The Devil to Pay, Too Yuong to Marry* (opposite Grant Withers, to whom she was briefly married), *Platinum Blonde, Taxi!, The Hatchet Man, Life Begins, Employees' Entrance, Zoo in Budapest, The Life of Jimmy Dolan, Midnight Mary, A Man's Castle, House of Rothschild, Bulldog Drummond Strikes Back, Born to Be Bad, The White Parade, Clive of India, Call of the Wild* (1935), *The Crusades, The Unguarded Hour, Ramona, Ladies in Love, Love is News, Cafe Metropole, Four Men and a Prayer, Suez, Kentucky, The Story of Alexander Graham Bell, The Doctor Takes a Wife, The Lady from Cheyenne, Bedtime Story* (1942), *A Night to Remember* (1942), *China, And Now Tomorrow, Along Came Jones, The Stranger, The Perfect Marriage, The Bishop's Wife, Rachel and the Stranger, The Accused* (1949), *Come to the Stable* (Oscar nomination), *Key to the City, Cause for Alarm, Paula,* and *It Happens Every Thursday.* After her film career she starred in the highly popular television series "The Loretta Young Show." She is survived by her sister and three children.

Loretta Young

Bilios, Dion, 295
Billings, Joshua, 96
Billingsley, Peter, 311
Billy Budd, Sailor, 244
Billy Elliot, 216, 229, 234, 276–277
Billy Hector Trio, 180
Bilous, Edward, 209
Bilzerian, Lana, 174
Binczycki, Jerzy, 291
Binder, John, 77
Binder, Mike, 132–133
Binder, Ron N., 182
Binev, Nikolai, 245
Bing, Steve, 130
Biniak, Holly, 43
Binkley, Gregg, 188
Binkley, James, 101, 181
Binoche, Juliette, 158–159, 227, 261, 311
Birch, Randy, 67, 289
Birch, Thora, 214, 311, 314
Birch, Yan, 97
Bird, Timothy, 201
Birkell, Lauren, 170
Birkett, Janine, 277
Birkett, Thaddeus, 40
Birkin, Jane, 249, 311
Birman, Matt, 97
Birnbaum, Lillian, 150
Birnbaum, Roger, 45, 67, 151
Birney, David, 311
Birney, Reed, 311
Birtwell, Ralph, 247
Bisbee, Sam, 201
Biscoe, Donna, 182
Bishop, Dan, 99, 214
Bishop, Joey, 312
Bishop, Julie, 312
Bishop, Kelly, 23
Bishop, Leilani, 199
Bishop, Paige, 167
Bishop, Pat, 295
Bishopric, Kirsten, 54
Bissell, James, 146
Bisset, Jacqueline, 312
Bissmeier, Joachim, 255
Bisson, Chris, 247
Bittersweet Films, 201
Bittersweet Motel, 201
Bivens, J.B., 110
Bizos, George, 186
Bjarke, Lars, 297
Bjerke, Birgitta, 95
Björk, 273
Black and White, 40
Black, Catherine, 44, 87
Black, Charles, 78
Black, Claudia, 20
Black, David, 85
Black, Don, 198
Black Hawk Entertainment, 192
Black, Ian, 190
Black, Jack, 36–37, 257, 312
Black, James, 99
Black, Jim, 208
Black, Karen, 312
Black, Kevin, 77

Black, Lucas, 176, 312
Black, Robert, 182
Black, Shauna, 205
Black, Teri, 64
Black, Varen, 105
Blackburn, Richard, 87
Blackburn, Sarah, 250
Blackman, Honor, 312
Blackson, Michael, 10
Blackthorne, Paul, 187
Blackwell, Chris, 296
Blackwell, Nicola, 277
Blackwood, Sharon, 117
Blackwood, Vas, 294
Blades, Ruben, 176, 312
Blaikie, Peter, 14
Blaine, Phillip, 191
Blainey, Sue, 235
Blair, Betsy, 312
Blair, Janet, 312
Blair, Linda, 312
Blair, Selma, 12, 183
Blaisdell, Nesbitt, 54
Blake, Andre, 211
Blake, Dalias, 77
Blake, Deryck, 85
Blake, Geoffrey, 170
Blake, Kelly, 180
Blake, Perry Andelin, 141
Blake, Robert, 312
Blakely, Susan, 312
Blakemore, Margaret, 247
Blakeney, Eric, 15
Blakley, Ronee, 312
Blamont, Delphine, 266
Blanc, Mel, 52
Blanchard, Carlos, 155
Blanchard, Rachel, 65
Blanchard, Terence, 10, 50, 123
Blanche, Robert, 142
Blanchett, Cate, 166, 312
Blanco, Uxia, 258
Blanco-Hall, Danny, 268
Bland, John Harrington, 95
Blankenship, Joann, 11
Blanquefort, Antoine, 266
Blasband, Philippe, 266
Blasi, Vera, 114
Blatch, Kevin, 203, 308
Blatt, Stuart, 149
Blau, Andrew, 215
Blaustein, Addie, 301
Blaustein, Barry W., 89
Blazer, Jonathan, 252
Blechman, Jonah, 185
Blechman, Jonathan Ethan, 198
Bleck, Memphis, 202
Bleeth, Yasmine, 190
Blendell, Troy, 200
Blessing, Jack, 177
Bless the Child, 97, 234
Blethyn, Brenda, 264, 312
Bleu, Corbin, 188
Blincoe, Peter, 186
Blinding Edge Pictures, 151

Bliss, Ian, 83
Bliss, Thomas A., 102, 173, 177
Bliss, Tom, 196
Bloch, David, 78
Bloch, Débora, 249
Bloch, Jonas, 114
Bloch, Scotty, 64
Block, Bruce A., 162
Block, Larry, 14, 112
Block, Philip, 199
Block, Rory, 180
Block, Susan, 156
Blohm, Jennifer, 17
Blom, Jani, 123
Blomberg, Sebastian, 303
Blommaert, Susan J., 12
Blomquist, Alan C., 148, 158
Blondrage, Adam, 25
Bloodworth, Baker, 63
Bloody Syndicate, 181
Bloom, Akivah, 195
Bloom, Brian, 299
Bloom, Charlene, 71
Bloom, Claire, 312
Bloom, John, 72
Bloom, Paul, 102
Bloom, Verna, 312
Bloomstein, Henry, 209
Blount, Lisa, 312
Blount, Steve, 302
Blow Up Pictures, 86
Blu Cinematografica, 259
Bluebell, Bobbie, 13
Blue Moon, 212
Blue Moon, 212
Blue Moon Productions, 137
Blue Rider Pictures, 202
Blue Sky Entertainment Inc. Film, 209
Blue Sky PM, 306
Bluestone, Rene, 28
Blum, Bill, 209
Blum, Jason, 59
Blum, Lisa Suzanne, 83
Blum, Mark, 12, 77, 312
Blumberg, Rena, 45
Blumberg, Stuart, 45
Blumberg, Ted, 41
Blumenberg, H.C., 265
Blumenthal, George, 179
Blunden, Christopher, 201
Blunt, Dave, 279
Blunt, Ed, 123
Bluteau, Lothaire, 111
Bluth, Don, 194
Bluth, Toby, 17
Bluto, Tony, 150
Blye, Margaret, 184
Blyth, Ann, 312
Bo Zenga, 83
Boardman, Paul Harris, 205
Bob, Sam, 24
Bobb, Anika, 23
Bobbitt, Jimmy, 165
Bobbitt, Sean, 262
Bober, Philippe, 305
Bocanegra, Elisa, 118

Bocca, Roberta, 308
Boccia, Joseph, 112
Bochner, Hart, 205, 312
Bochner, Lloyd, 312
Bochner, Sally, 300
Bock, Larry, 102
Bocquet, Gavin, 80
Boddicker, Edie Lehmann, 63
Bode, Ralf, 194
Boden, Christina, 195
Boden, Kristina, 183
Bodnar, Eden, 35
Bodrov, Sergei, 70
Bodrov, Serguei, 245
Bodrov, Serguei, Jr., 245
Boehle, Michelle, 134
Boehler, Ted, 207
Boen, Earl, 89
Boer, Leo de, 304
Boesman & Lena, 283
Bogaert, Stephen, 44
Bogart, Timothy Scott, 200
Bogdanovich, Peter, 190
Bognár, Dr. Zoltán, 255
Bognar, Steven, 203
Bogonova, Carmen, 199
Bogosian, Eric, 188, 312
Bogue, Lou, 290
Bogush, Elizabeth, 194
Bohan, Jessica, 95
Bohringer, Richard, 312
Boidin, Theophile, 256
Boiler Room, 21
Boisson, Noelle, 282, 287
Boitier, Thibault, 298
Bokaba, Patrick, 57
Bolam, James, 292
Boland, Mary Clay, 189
Bolden, Philip D., 141
Bolger, Dermot, 294
Bolger, John, 40, 208
Bolkan, Florinda, 312
Bolling, Angie, 131
Bologna, Joseph, 312
Bolt, Ian, 154
Bolton, Michael, 33
Bomba, David J., 11
Bombardier, Leticia, 179
Bomsel, Nicolas, 280
Bonaparte Films Ltd., 306
Bonar, Craig, 278
Bonati, Giancarlo, 105
Bond, Derek, 312
Bondam, Klaus, 239
Bondoc, Ryan, 205
Bonds, De'Aundre, 183
Bonelli, Jamie, 60
Bones, Frankie, 191
Bonet, Lisa, 36–37, 312
Bongfeldt, Katherine, 131
Bongiorno, Frank, 204
Bongiorno, Joseph, 40
Bonham-Carter, Helena, 312
Boniface, Greg, 179
Bonilla, Michelle, 38
Bonilla, Tera, 94
Bon Jovi, Jon, 49, 136

Bonnaffe, Jacques, 280
Bonnaire, Sandrine, 245
Bonner, Gary, 212
Bonnie, 25
Bonnier, Philippe, 299
Bonnot, François, 266
Bookbinder, Ben, 144
Booker, Benjamin, 65
Booker, Landra, 211
Booker T., 187
Book of Shadows: Blair Witch 2, 210–211, 234
Bookspan, Adam, 206
Bookwars, 194
Boon, Jak, 16
Boondock Saints, The, 181
Boone, Blair, 262
Boone, Pat, 197, 312
Boorem, Mika, 78
Boorem, Mike, 79
Boortz, Jeff, 209
Booth, Kristin, 188
Booth, Matthew, 188
Booth, Tony, 133
Boothby, Andrew, 133
Boothe, James, 312
Boothe, Powers, 142, 312
Bootmen, 217, 274
Booz, Emmanuel, 240
Boraine, Nick, 57
Borayo, Olga, 168
Borden, Rainbow, 71, 199
Borden, Steve "Sting," 186
Border, W.K., 175, 196
Bordier, Patrick, 287
Bordone, Beatrice, 306
Bord Scannan na hÉireann, 249, 296
Boren, Lisette, 15
Borenstein, Daniel, 293
Borges, Alexandre, 249
Borgese, Toto, 288
Borghesi, Anna, 20, 299
Borgnine, Ernest, 215, 312
Boriuca's Bond, 194–195
Borkowski, Andrzej, 292
Borlenghi, Matt, 104
Borman, Moritz, 47, 107
Born, Victoria, 60
Borstelmann, Jim, 60
Bortolotti, Ann, 20
Bosch, Andrew, 67
Bosco, Philip, 23, 72, 312
Bosley, Tom, 312
Bosmajian, Harlan, 189
Bossa Nova, 249
Bossdorf, Pamela, 25
Bossert, David A., 8
Bossi, Caroline, 212
Bostrom, Zachary, 63
Bostwick, Barry, 312
Boswell, Anthony, 71
Boswell, Simon, 303
Bosworth, Kate, 116–117
Botha, Albert, 130
Bottenbley, Victor, 295
Botto, Juan Diego, 291
Bottoms, Joseph, 312

Gibbs, Richard, 46, 69
Gibbs, Tony, 24
Gibby, Ross, 44
Giblin, Phillipe, 266
Gibson, Ben, 238, 292
Gibson, Chic, 33
Gibson, Dean Paul, 203
Gibson, Deionne, 182
Gibson, Henry, 320
Gibson, Katrina, 38
Gibson, Lance, 33
Gibson, Mark, 197
Gibson, Mel, 6, 75,
  78–79, 162–163, 320
Gibson, Scott, 35
Gibson, Thomas, 52, 94,
  304–305, 320
Gibson, William, 42
Gidley, Pamela, 281
Gieb, Joe, 186
Gieco, Giovanni, 86
Giedroyc, Coky, 292
Gielgud, John, 342
Gifaldi, Sam, 190
Gift, Roland, 320
Gift, The, 166
Giguere, Edi, 11, 19,
  196, 213
Gil, Annie, 168
Gil, Arturo, 113
Gilbert, Chris Payne, 120
Gilbert, Melissa, 320
Gilbert, Peter, 196
Gilbert, Sara, 13, 37, 215
Gilbert, Tim, 139
Gilborn, Steven, 107
Gilchriest, Gail, 11
Gildea, Sean P., 76
Giles, Jennifer, 13
Giles, Nancy, 320
Giles, Richard, 105
Gilfillan, Jule, 305
Gilker, Garth, 235
Gill, Allan, 143
Gill, Jack, 30, 167
Gill, Pierre, 268
Gill, Ted, 83
Gillard, Nick, 72
Gillen, Aidan, 185
Gillen, Anne Marie, 113
Gillen, Brett, 14
Gillen, Juliandra, 162
Gillett, John Aden, 290
Gillette, Anita, 320
Gilliam, Mike, 209
Gilliam, Terry, 320
Gilliard, Larry, Jr., 96,
  211
Gillies, Andrew, 51
Gillis, Alec, 91, 146
Gillis, Ann, 320
Gillis, Stephen Troy, 262
Gilman, Larry, 32
Gil-Martinez, Antonio,
  158
Gilmour, Alexa, 97
Gil, Peter, 96
Gilpin, Peri, 156
Gilroy, Grace, 18
Gilroy, Natalie, 246
Gilroy, Tim, 204
Gilroy, Tom, 77, 156, 183
Gilroy, Tony, 112, 155

Gilroy, William, 156
Gingerich, Tanya, 59
Ginsberg, Stuart, 208
Ginsburg, Allen, 185
Ginsburg, David R., 209,
  261
Ginther, Greg, 90
Ginther, Mark, 196
Ginty, Robert, 320
Giobbe, Annie, 195
Giordano, Martine, 261
Giordano, Nick, 13
Giordano, Vince, 165
Giorgiewa, Walentine,
  238
Giraffe, The, 292
Girardeau, Frank, 65, 210
Girardet, Stefan, 187
Girardot, Annie, 320
Giraudeau, Bernard, 301
Girlfight, 118, 218
Girl in Sneakers, The,
  301
Girl Next Door, The, 187
Girl on the Bridge, The,
  263
Giroudon, Gérard, 269
Girvan, Neil, 51, 97
Gish, Annabeth, 320
Gish, Sheila, 201
Gitai, Amos, 237, 305
Gitlin, Todd, 213
Giusto, Ornella, 288
Giv'en Films, 13, 199
Given, Gretchen, 56
Givens, Robin, 320
Glackin, Artie, 192
Glade, Martin, 49
Gladiator, 219–222, 228,
  233
Glanz, Ben, 272
Glaser, Paul Michael,
  320
Glasgow, Diana, 181
Glasgow Film Fund, 241,
  286
Glass Eye Pix, 204
Glass, Jason, 67
Glass, Ron, 320
Glassing, Ken, 184
Glassman, Carol, 213
Glattes, Wolfgang, 240
Glaudini, Lola, 12, 70
Glave, Karen, 54
Glawson, John, 67
Glazer, Abe, 149
Glazer, Russ, 196
Gleason, Joanna, 320
Gleason, Mary Pat, 179
Gleason, Paul, 320
Glebas, Francis, 8
Gleeson, Brendan, 66
Gleeson, John, 262
Gleizer, Michele, 158
Glen, Eddie, 198
Glen, Georgie, 281
Glenn, Allison, 214
Glenn, Christen, 214
Glenn, Scott, 51, 154,
  320
Glennie, Evelyn, 306
Glennie-Smith, Nick, 201
Glennon, James, 215
Glick, Marc H., 151

Glick, Michael S., 104
Glickman, Jonathan, 45,
  67
Glickman, Rana Joy, 198
Glienna, Greg, 124
Glinwood, Terry, 251
Globisz, Krzysztof, 291
Globo Filmes, 249
Globo Films, 302
Gloor, Fred, 203
Glouberman, Bob, 304
G. Love and Special
  Sauce, 180
Glover, Crispin, 107,
  139, 320
Glover, Danny, 283, 320
Glover, John, 320
Glover, Julian, 287
Glover, Savion, 122–123
Glover, Susan, 305
Glynn, Carlin, 25, 320
GND Productions, 187
Goana, Jessica, 185
Goar, Johnny, 19
*Goat on Fire & Smiling
  Fish,* 200
Goavec, Patrick, 261
Gobodo-Madikizela,
  Pumla, 186
Godard, Agnès, 244, 298
Goddet, Michelle, 269,
  282
Godineaux, Edgar, 15
Godin, Nicolas, 51
God's Army, 184–185
*Gods of Times Square,
  The,* 204
Godwin, Alicia, 55
Godzilla 2000, 302
Goebel, Raimond, 270
Goemaere, Amanda, 256
Goff, Carolyn, 87, 101
Goff, Ivan, 139
Goffette, Kevin, 261
Goggins, Walton, 67
Gohary, Magdi, 150
Goh Hye Won, 283
Go Im Pyo, 308
Goines, Siena, 13
Gold, Ari, 70
Gold, Elon, 13
Gold, Eric L., 83
Gold, Gary, 19
Gold, L. Harvey, 203
Gold, Nina, 252
Goldbart, Nicolás, 295
Goldberg, Adam, 199
Goldberg, Albert, 266,
  287
Goldberg, Bill, 186
Goldberg, Daniel, 65
Goldberg, Dr. Erwin, 235
Goldberg, Elyse, 191
Goldberg, Eric, 8
Goldberg, Eric Ian, 167
Goldberg, Gail, 82
Goldberg, Leonard, 139
Goldberg, Mirjam, 182
Goldberg, Nicole, 25
Goldberg, Sam, 45
Goldberg, Stephanie, 25
Goldberg, Steve, 8

Goldberg, Susan
  McKinsey, 8
Goldberg, Whoopi, 80,
  320
Goldberger, Julian L.,
  180
Goldblatt, Mark, 91
Goldblum, Jeff, 320
Golden, Annie, 320
Golden Harvest, 279
Golden, Jim, 184
Golden, Kit, 158
Golden, Lee, 257
Golden Lion, 211
Golden, Marita, 23
Golden, Stephanie, 111
Goldenberg, Jeffrey, 212
Goldenberg, William, 90
Goldenhersh, Heather,
  189
Goldfine, Philip B., 204
Goldheart Pictures, 198
Goldie, 207, 284
Goldie, W. Scott, 209
Goldman, Alain, 287
Goldman, Gary, 194
Goldman, Jill, 207
Goldman, Nina, 60
Goldman, Sheliah, 200
Gold-Miller, 83
Goldpaugh, Kathleen, 98
Goldsmith, Jerry, 91
Goldsmith, Jonathan, 295
Goldsmith, Josh, 162
Goldsmith, Merwin, 41
Goldstein, Al, 182
Goldstein, Edward B., 14
Goldstein, Jenette, 320
Goldstein, Rich, 194
Goldstone, John, 130
Goldthwait, Bob, 320
Goldwyn, 270
Goldwyn Films, 301
Goldwyn, Tony, 146,
  148, 320
Golfo, 258
Golightly, Norm, 290
Golightly, Norman, 290
Golino, Valeria, 320
Golin, Steve, 107, 148
Golotta, Cristina, 293
Golubeva, Katerina, 270
Golzarandi, Michail, 248
Gomes, Antônio, 294
Gómez, Andrés Vincent,
  271
Gomez, Audrey, 50
Gomez, Carlos, 104
Gómez, Eduardo, 258
Goméz, Fernando
  Fernán, 258
Gomez, Fidel, 189
Gomez, Georgiana, 203
Gomez, Leticia, 180
Gomez, Mike, 113, 189
Gomez, Nick, 25
Gomez, Rita, 179
Gomez, Veronica, 164
Gomez-Rejon, Alfonso,
  138
Gomoll, Heather, 209
Gonçalves, Alfonso, 180
Goncalves, Edison, 194

Gonçalves, Milton, 302
Gone in Sixty Seconds,
  71, 233
Goniwe, Nyameka, 186
Gonnsen, Kirk, 51
Gonsalves, Aileen, 295
Gonzaga, Neil, 140
Gonzales, Israel, 182
Gonzales, Marina
  Palmier, 189
Gonzales, Steven, 137
Gonzalez, Angel, 118
Gonzalez, Ariel Gabino
  Martinez, 199
Gonzalez, Cordelia, 320
Gonzalez, Irene, 131
Gonzalez, Jamie, 198
Gonzalez, Joseph Julian,
  38
Gonzalez, Juan, 213
González, Manuel, 168
González, Martin, 181
Gonzalez, Pietro, 195
Gonzalez, Ramiro, 179
Gonzalez, Rick, 205
Gonzalez-Gonzalez,
  Pedro, 320
Gonzalo, Alvaro, 190
Good Baby, A, 214
Good, Greg, 78
Good Machine, 95, 191
Good Machine
  International, 230
Good, Meagan, 183
Good Medicine, 180
Good Work, 244
Goodall, Caroline, 320,
  322
Goodall, Jim, 137
Goode, Christopher, 135
Goode, Conrad, 76
Goodhand, Donna, 85
Goodhaert, Ami, 128
Goodheart, Carol, 210
Gooding, Cuba, Jr., 142,
  320
Gooding, Ian S., 63
Goodman, Dana, 95
Goodman, Dody, 320
Goodman, Elisa, 214
Goodman, Greer, 95
Goodman, Gregory, 166
Goodman, Jenniphr, 95
Goodman, Joel, 299
Goodman, John, 27, 80,
  90, 157, 172, 320
Goodman, Patrice, 202
Goodman, Samantha, 43
Goodrich, John, 262
Goodridge, Thomas, 238
Goodwin, Aaron, 182
Goodwin, Eric, 182
Goodwin, Michael, 133
Goodwin, Randy J., 211
Goodwin, Walter, 202
Goody, Bob, 292
Goonan, Mary, 286
Goor, Gabriella A., 184
Goossen, Gregory B., 99
Gop, 235
Gopal, 235
Gordon, Bette, 191
Gordon, Bradley H., 101

Grkovic, Walter, 295
Grobet, Xavier Pérez, 168, 292
Grodenchik, Max, 80
Grodin, Charles, 321
Groener, Harry, 185
Grogan, Jane, 215
Groh, David, 321
Gromoff, Brian, 67
Grønlykke, Jacob, 297
Grønvall, Christian, 239
Groom, Winston, 11
Groove, 70
Gropman, David, 60, 158
Gropman, Sonya, 182
Gropper, Allan, 118
Gross, Arye, 71
Gross, Davena, 60
Gross, Gill, 200
Gross, H. Daniel, 201
Gross, Larry, 112
Gross, Mary, 321
Gross, Michael, 321
Grossfield, Norman J., 301
Grossman, Marc, 185
Grossman, Scott, 167
Grossourvre, Philippe De, 286
Grosvenor Park Production, 289
Grote, Andy, 85
Groupé, Larry, 133
Groupé, Lawrence Nash, 28
Grove, Gordon, 189
Grove, Gregory, 211
Grover, Gulshan, 194
Grower, John, 281
Growney, Michael, 208
Gruben, Adrienne, 185
Gruber, Michael, 10
Gruffudd, Ioan, 150, 267
Gruffud, Ioan, 321
Grunberg, Greg, 91
Grundvig, Marjorie, 113
Grüninger, Joachim, 302
Gruzina, Guita, 307
Gryff, Stefan, 155
Gu Xiaoyang, 294
Guangxi Film, 238
Guari, Taimak, 193
Guarrera, Gianluca, 288
Guastaferro, Vincent, 174
Guay, Kenny, 28
Guay, Richard, 28
Guber, Elizabeth, 188, 299
Guccini, Francesco, 237
Guegamian, Lilite, 261
Guenoden, Rodolphe, 39
Guerig, Marc-Philippe, 256
Guerrasio, Stephanie, 247
Guerrero, Alvaro, 297
Guerrero, Juventud, 187
Guerrero, Mando, 106
Guerrero, Philip, 130
Guertler, Dave, 133
Guess, Maxine, 34
Guest, Christopher, 115, 321

Guest, Lance, 321
Guest, Renee, 25
Guez, Gerard, 52
Guffanti, Mónica, 291
Guggenheim, Charles, 188
Guggenheim, David, 188
Guggenheim, Marion, 188
Gugliemi, Noel, 38
Guichet, Christophe, 269
Guidera, John, 98
Guido, Michael, 105
Guidry, Cynthia, 50
Guiho, Benedicte, 261
Guilbert, Philippe, 294
Guiliani, Jesse, 181
Guillaume, Pascaline, 301
Guillaume, Robert, 321
Guillermo, Jeanette, 182
Guillo, Alain, 259
Guillory, Bennet, 183
Guillot, Bruno, 259
Guinness, Alec, 343–344
Guinness, Kristi Lee, 98
Guiry, Thomas, 49, 126
Guish, Michelle, 201, 301, 303
Guittier, Marief, 269
Guizar, Luis, 184
Gulager, Clu, 321
Gulino, John P., 204
Gullane Pictures, 198
Gullette, Sean, 128
Gullotto, Emanuele, 288
Gulnac, Michael, 180
Gumz, Ute, 307
Gun for Hire Films, 199
Gun Shy, 15
Gund, Jeffrey R., 184
Gundersen, Erik, 37
Gunlocke, Gretchen, 199
Gunn, Anna, 207
Gunn, Brian, 204
Gunn, James, 204
Gunn, Jon, 211
Gunn, Sean, 204
Gunn, Vincenetta, 141
Gunnarsson, Sturla, 295
Günther, Andreas, 303
Gunton, Bob, 81
Gupta, Neena, 241
Gurnani, Chatru L., 295
Gurnik, Ica, 255
Gurrola, Flor Eduarda, 292
Gurwitch, Annabelle, 161
Guss, Louis, 104, 118, 127, 165
Gustoitis, Christian, 137
Gutheinz, Steven, 182
Guthrie, Arlo, 200
Guthrie, Michelle, 142
Guthrie, Nora, 200
Gutiérrez, Zaide Silvia, 296–297
Gutrecht, Paul, 185
Guttenberg, Steve, 321
Gutterman, Jamie, 162
Guttman, Eliana, 114
Guttman, Ronald, 210
Guy, Jasmine, 321

Guy, Joyce, 185
Guyett, Roger, 80
Guyot, Marion, 117
Guyot, Pascaline, 256
Guzda, Laurie, 167
Guzelian, Eddie, 17
Guzman, Gabby, 118
Guzman, Lisa, 173
Guzman, Luis, 178–179
Guzman, Yiyo, 118
Gwathmey, Ann, 33
Gwynn, Cora, 202
Gyamtso, Dundrup, 236
Gyatso, Palden, 236
Gyllenhaal, Maggie, 96

H

Ha, Benita, 146
Ha Nguyen, 199
Haaland, Heidi, 191
Haapala, Juhani, 295
Haas, Barbara, 45, 127
Haas, Belinda, 56
Haas, Lukas, 70, 321
Haas, Philip, 56
Haas, Robert, 201
Haase, Karin, 207
Habakus, Ron, 213
Haber, Alan, 213
Haber, Alessandro, 237
Haberny, Greg, 180
Hache, Corinne, 261
Hache, Joellë, 263
Hack, Shelley, 321
Hacker, Rüdiger, 265
Hackett, Buddy, 321
Hackford, Rio, 185
Hackford, Taylor, 155
Hackin, Dennis, 215
Hackl, Karlheinz, 298–299
Hackman, Gene, 99, 113, 321, 323
Hacohen, Gil, 162
Hadary, Jonathan, 112
Haffner, Craig, 272
Hafitz, Andrew, 185
Hafizka, Nayeem, 241
Haft Entertainment, 126
Haft, Linal, 295
Haft, Steven, 126
Hagan, Anna, 24
Hagen, Kelwin, 107
Hager, Dave, 179
Hagerty, Julie, 190, 321
Hagman, Larry, 321
Hagopian, Dean, 34
Hahn, Don, 8, 157
Hahn, Jody, 186
Hahn, Rob, 87
Hai, Longo, 262
Hai Yan, 230
Haid, Charles, 321
Haider, Silvia, 298
Haigler, Natalia, 60
Haigney, Michael, 301
Haim, Corey, 321
Haim, Soly, 193
Hainsworth, John, 32
Hairston, Ronald E., 30
Hajee, Zahf, 203
Hajizadeh, Majid, 301

Hakuhodo Inc., 275
Halász, Péter, 255
Hald, Birgitte, 239
Hale, Barbara, 321
Hale, Chris, 51
Hale, Gregg, 300
Hale, Jennifer, 293
Hale, Jessica, 167
Haley, Jackie Earle, 321
Haley, R.M., 134
Halfon, Lianne, 214
Halicki, Denice Shakarian, 71
Halicki, Toby, 71
Halkin, Vered, 187
Hall, Albert, 321
Hall, Allen, 49
Hall, Anthony Michael, 321
Hall, Arsenio, 321
Hall, Barbara A., 52
Hall, Corwin, 87
Hall, Craig, 60, 193
Hall, Daisy, 185
Hall, Demene E., 142
Hall, Dolly, 180
Hall, Doug, 176
Hall, Ellis, 69
Hall, Hanna, 51
Hall, John, 94
Hall, Ladene, 279
Hall, Lee, 277
Hall, Lois, 71
Hall, Paul, 72
Hall, Philip Baker, 42, 133, 207
Hall, Regina, 50, 83
Hall, Steve Clark, 306
Hall, Tim, 51, 165
Hall, Troy, 173
Hall, Vondie Curtis, 202
Hallet, Bill, 264
Hallett, Mark, 63
Halliday, Ayun, 59
Hallier, Lori, 198
Halligan, Tim, 92
Hallinan, Candace, 201
Halloran, Brian, 197
Halloran, Gordon, 202
Halloran, Jaz, 202
Halloran, Lori, 202
Hallowell, Todd, 144
Hallström, Lasse, 158
Hallynck, Lucien, 256
Halprin, Philip, 197
Halsey, Michael, 185
Halsted, Dan, 51, 268
Halston, Julie, 41, 64
Hamada, Takashi, 298
Hamashige, Shane, 95
Hamburg, John, 124
Hamel, Michèle, 246
Hamel, Veronica, 321
Hamill, Cara, 40
Hamill, Katie, 40
Hamill, Mark, 293, 321
Hamilton, Billy, 188
Hamilton, Carrie, 321
Hamilton, David, 248
Hamilton, George, 321
Hamilton, Josh, 111
Hamilton, Linda, 321
Hamilton, Paula, 268

Hamilton, Sandy, 60
Hamilton, Tim, 250
Hamilton, Trip, 140
Hamlet, 59
Hamlett, Robert, 172
Hamlin, Harry, 321
Hamm, Jon, 92
Hammar, Louise, 53
Hammel, Tom, 214
Hammer, Jack, 182
Hammer, Jens, 298
Hammer, Mark, 124
Hammer, Van, 187
Hammerschmitt, Leland, 206
Hammon, Michael, 307
Hammond, Alexander, 133
Hammond, Josh, 193
Hammond, Lisa, 153
Hammond, Louis, 303
Hammond, Roger, 56, 134
Hammonds, Shannon, 60
Hamori, Andras, 255, 279
Hampshire, Susan, 321
Hampton, James, 321
Hampton, Janice, 149
Hampton, Mel, 193
Hampton, Peter J., 67
Hampton, Wade Randolph, 70
Hamza, 241
Hamzaoui, Malek, 280
Han Kwon Taek, 283
Han, Maggie, 321
Han Zhenhu, 268
Hanbury-Tenison, Merlin, 155
Hancisse, Thierry, 306
Hancock, Ian, 187
Hancock, John D., 181
Hancock, John Lee, 11
Handler, Evan, 321
Handler, Paige, 98
Handy, James, 28, 151
Handy, Rachael, 137
Haneke, Tom, 210
Hanes, Connie, 205
Hanging Up, 20, 234
Hanisch, Uli, 265
Hankerson, Barry, 33
Hankerson, Jomo, 33
Hanks, Colin, 186
Hanks, Tom, 6, 170–171, 226, 321
Hanley, Chris, 44, 51
Hanley, Dan, 144
Hanley, Roberta, 51
Hanlon, James, 41
Hanlon, Mark, 185
Hanlon, Peter, 83, 203
Hanna, John, 191
Hanna, Stephen, 60
Hanna, Sylvia, 191
Hanna, William, 321
Hanna-Barbera, 52
Hanna-Barbera Productions, Inc., 52
Hannah, Daryl, 201, 321
Hannah, John, 303
Hannah, Page, 321

Pegg, Ann Warn, 110, 190, 209
Pelagalli, Sara, 308
Peliculas Freneticas, 291
Pellarini, Lorena, 271
Pellegrino, Angelo, 288
Pellegrino, Mark, 25
Pellham-Davis, Holly, 131
Pellington, Mark, 109
Peloso, Glen, 261
Pemberton, Robert, 181
Pemelton, Hailey, 211
Pemelton, Rachel, 211
Peña, Alexis, 211
Peña, Elizabeth, 330
Pena, Lucas, 202
Pena, Michael A., 71
Pena, Natalie, 55
Penacoli, Jerry, 114
Penberthy, Kirk, 133
Pender, Paul, 92
Pendleton, Austin, 330
Pendleton, Sha'ri, 181
Peng Kaili, 275
Penhall, Bruce, 330
Penn & Teller, 8
Penn, Robin Wright, 151
Penn, Sean, 56, 168, 330
Penn, Zak, 86
Pennebaker, D.A., 300
Pennello, Tony, 187
Penner, Jonathan, 207
Penny, Bob, 140
Pentecost, Del, 90, 172
Pentecost, John, 184
Pentz, Robert, Jr., 42
Penven, Benoit, 298
Penven, Louise, 298
Penven, Tibault, 298
Pepin, Megan, 60
Peplowski, Andrew, 268
Peppe, Chris, 13, 21
Pepper, Barry, 58
Pequero, Jorge, 212
Perabo, Piper, 80, 90, 208
Peraino, Vince, 186
Peralta, Oscar, 181
Peranio, Vincent, 96
Pereira, René, 168
Pereira, Tonico, 294
Perel, Sylvie, 256
Perell, Tim, 97
Perella, Marco, 167
Perepeczko, Marek, 291
Perera, Brian, 191
Peretz, Clara, 139
Pereyra, Rena, 179
Pérez, Antonio, 258
Pérez, Antonio P., 270
Pérez, Bebé, 291
Perez, Fawn, 184
Pérez, Fernando, 291
Perez, Gary, 190, 204, 210
Perez, Jose, 106, 330
Perez, Judy Schiffer, 213
Perez, Rosie, 39, 330
Perez, Salvador, 142
Perez, Sandra, 50
Perez, Vincent, 57, 259

Pérez-Reverte, Arturo, 240
Perfect Storm, The, 81, 233
Pergament, Annika, 135
Périer, Annie, 263
Periera, Hamilton Vaz, 302
Perillo, Joey, 97
Perkins, Elizabeth, 46, 330
Perkins, Gregory, 300
Perkins, Millie, 330
Perkins, William, 8, 97
Perl, Frank, 28
Perler, Gregory, 150
Perlin, Rachel, 211
Perlman, Itzhak, 8
Perlman, Philip, 25
Perlman, Rhea, 330
Perlman, Ron, 38, 194, 330
Perna, Tommy, 112
Pero, John, 210
Peroni, Geraldine, 131
Perrault, Pierre, 300
Perreau, Gigi, 330
Perrenial Pictures, 299
Perrette, Pauley, 109
Perrier, Mireille, 293
Perrin, Bryce, 214
Perrin, Jean-Claude, 266
Perrine, Valerie, 162–163, 183, 330
Perrineau, Harold, Jr., 114
Perritt, Jessica, 57
Perron, Michel, 47, 58, 235
Perry, Craig, 32
Perry, Dein, 274
Perry, Freda, 29
Perry, Jaime, 156
Perry, Karen, 199, 208
Perry, Keith, 45
Perry, Lisa, 274
Perry, Luke, 330
Perry, Manny, 15
Perry, Matthew, 19, 82
Perry, Reid, 274
Perry, Theo, 202
Perryson, Jeff, 96
Persaud, Kavita, 87
Persaud, Neran, 301
Pervakov, Alexander, 130, 203
Pervis, Adam, 46
Pesce, Frank, 40, 211
Pesci, Joe, 330
Pescow, Donna, 330
Pescucci, Gabriella, 259
Pesery, Bruno, 270
Pesiani, Atila, 294
Pessin, Malu, 114
Petardi, Pascal, 34
Petcka, Joe, 162
Peterkin, Jamahl, 279
Peterman, Don, 144
Peters, Bernadette, 331
Peters, Brock, 331
Peters, Jean, 348
Peters, John, 188
Peters, Oliver, 215

Peters, Paul, 55
Peters, Rachel, 143
Peters, Rick, 15, 299
Peters, Robert, 120, 196
Peters, Tony, 238
Petersen, Ann, 272
Petersen, Curtis J., 202
Petersen, Katelin, 26
Petersen, Knud, 297
Petersen, Mark, 205
Petersen, Oscar, 291
Petersen, Paul, 331
Petersen, Sally, 203
Petersen, William, 35, 133, 331
Petersen, Wolfgang, 81
Peterson, Alan C., 67
Peterson, Avilla, 210
Peterson, Brian Wayne, 83
Peterson, Brittany, 25
Peterson, Cassandra, 331
Peterson, Floyd, 138
Peterson, H. Lee, 63
Peterson, Jill, 36–37
Peterson, Jillian, 105
Peterson, Kirk, 60
Peterson, Liza Jessie, 123
Peterson, Mark, 202
Peterson, Richard, 65
Peterson, Robyn, 99
Pethig, Hazel, 268
Pétillon, Daniel, 256
Petit, Aurélia, 298
Petitguyot, Martin, 297
Petit-Jacques, Isabelle, 263
Petitjean, Eric, 280
Petrie, Daniel, Jr., 146
Petrie, Donald, 167
Petrocelli, Antonio, 237
Petrocelli, Richard, 210
Petrot, Dominique, 301
Petruccelli, Kirk M., 78
Pettersson, Dan, 196
Pettet, Joanna, 331
Pettiet, Christopher, 348
Pettifer, Brian, 286
Petty, Lori, 331
Pevner, Stephen, 107
Peyrollaz, Alain, 280
Peyton, Tom, 65
Pezza, Francis J., 196
Pfarrer, Chuck, 212
Pfeifercorn, Martin, 207
Pfeiffer, Michelle, 88, 331
Pfingsten, Darrell, 139
Pfluegel, Edelgard, 101
Pflüger, Frédéric, 263
Phaedra, 196, 203–204, 209, 211, 215, 282, 293, 297
Phaedra Cinema, 184, 235
Phali, Zacharia, 57
Pham, Jimmy, 149
Phaneuf, Mark, 165
Pharmboys Partners, 195
Phelps, Robert, 119
Phifer, Mekhi, 72, 205
Phil, 114
Philbin, Regis, 141

Philippi, Charles, 8
Philips, Dan, 39
Philips, Michael, 298, 300
Philips, Sara, 211
Philipson, Jacques, 263
Phillippe, Ryan, 106, 331
Phillips, Alex, 189
Phillips, Andrew, 76
Phillips, Angelina, 110
Phillips, Bijou, 40, 109
Phillips, Bobbie, 299
Phillips, Cary, 208
Phillips, Cecil, 85
Phillips, Don, 199
Phillips, Dorothea, 150
Phillips, Emo, 124
Phillips, Erica Edell, 81
Phillips, Gersha, 261
Phillips, Jason, 188
Phillips, Jeniene, 268
Phillips, Jonny, 238, 291
Phillips, Katrina, 83
Phillips, Lara, 181
Phillips, Leslie, 264
Phillips, Lloyd, 70, 154
Phillips, Lou Diamond, 12, 331
Phillips, Mackenzie, 331
Phillips, Maurice, 195
Phillips, Michelle, 207, 331
Phillips, Neville, 248
Phillips, Sian, 331
Phillips, Todd, 65, 201
Phillips, Tracy, 15, 138
Phillips-Palo, Linda, 51, 215
Phish, 201
Phlong, Rada, 65
Phoenician Entertainment, 137
Phoenix, Joaquin, 135, 152–153, 220–221, 228, 331
Phoenix Pictures, 146, 186, 205, 302
Phoenix, Rain, 198
Phoenix, Summer, 188
Phutaroth, Somboon, 16
Piana, Matilde, 288
Piaskowska, Eva, 168
Picache, Cherrie Pie, 301
Picafilms, 291
Picardo, Robert, 331
Picasso, Bernard, 185
Piccardi, Silvano, 293
Piccinni, Angela, 60
Piccioli, Gianfranco, 237
Piccioni, Giuseppe, 293
Picerni, Chuck, Jr., 71
Picerni, C.J., 71
Picerni, Paul, 331
Picho, Aristoteles, 155
Pick, Victoria, 25
Pickens, David, 11
Pickens, James, Jr., 179
Picker, Si, 173
Pickering, Jenny, 306
Pickett, Wiley, 81
Picknett, Murray, 246, 274
Picoy, Kane, 209

Picture Farm, 105
Picture Me Rollin' Productions, 205
Picture This!, 297
Piddock, Jim, 115
Pidgeon, Matthew, 174
Pidgeon, Rebecca, 174, 331
Pie, Dario T., 292
Piece of Eden, A, 181
Piech, Lauren, 181
Piedade, Ana Paul, 24
Piedrahita, Juan, 45
Pieller, Jacques, 259
Pierce, David Hyde, 14, 331
Pierce, Justin, 10, 13, 348
Pierce-Roberts, Tony, 306
Pieri, Gilbert, 240
Pierre or the Ambiguities, 270
Pierrot, 298
Pierson, John, 186
Pieter van Huystee Film & TV, 304
Pietropinto, Angela, 72
Piggee, Timothy McCuen, 142
Pignataro, Josephine, 118
Pigott-Smith, Tim, 331
Pikachu Project '99, 301
Pike, Nicholas, 43
Pike, Tamsin, 187
Pike, Vicky, 156
Pilavin, Barbara, 196
Pilaya, Stella, 294
Pilcher, Lydia Dean, 257
Pilcher, Richard, 99
Pilchie, Rudy, 262
Pileggi, Mitch, 15
Pilkington, Lorraine, 250, 294
Pimental, Ashley, 30
Pimental, Brittany, 30
Pina, Juan, 71
Pinchot, Bronson, 331
Pincus, Saul, 202
Pineau, Patrick, 280
Pineda, Geovanny, 195
Pineda, Roberto Enrique, 176
Pine, Frankie, 114
Pine, Larry, 64
Pine, Phillip, 331
Pine, Robert, 83
Pinero, Dadi, 118
Pinette, John, 110, 202
Pingue, Joe, 112, 181
Piñiero, Manuel, 258
Pink, Steve, 37
Pinker, Steven, 213
Pinkett-Smith, Jada, 123
Pinkney, Contrelle, 13
"Pinky," 202
Pinnock, Arnold, 97, 112, 130
Pinot, Natalie, 271
Pinsent, Leah, 34
Pinto, Antônio, 294
Pinto, Joaquim, 114
Pionilla, Nadja, 144
Pioreck, Ralph, 211